C000318871

SHAKESPEARE'S BINDING LANGUAGE

SHAKESPEARE'S BINDING LANGUAGE

JOHN KERRIGAN

Great Clarendon Street, Oxford, OX2 6DP
United Kingdom

Oxford University Press is a department of the University of Oxford. It furthers the University's objective of excellence in research, scholarship, and education by publishing worldwide. Oxford is a registered trade mark of Oxford University Press in the UK and in certain other countries

First Edition published in 2016

Impression: 1

Published in the United States of America by Oxford University Press
198 Madison Avenue, New York, NY 10016, United States of America

British Library Cataloguing in Publication Data
Data available

Library of Congress Control Number: 2015944872

ISBN 978–0–19–875758–0

Printed in Great Britain by
Clays Ltd, St Ives plc

For Niamh, again

Contents

Preface

This is a book about binding language: oaths, vows, promises, asseverations, legal bonds, gages, contracts; the whole array of utterances and acts by which people in early modern England committed themselves to the truth of things past, present, and to come. As we shall see, these engagements were thought about from several perspectives: religious, legal, casuistical, customary. Just as important to this book is the dramaturgical potential of such language. When a character in Shakespeare swears to the truth of something, is he committing himself under the eye of God or trying to convince someone of that something? Or trying to convince himself? Would he be more persuasive if he just *said* x, or swore 'by Jove' rather than 'by the moon, th'inconstant moon'? It is clearly, dramatically effective to have vows taken or bonds signed in Act 1 of a play. An audience will want to see whether characters deliver in Act 5, or substitute something else, or find good excuses for not keeping their word.

The Introduction to this study establishes the field of enquiry. After noticing some critical problems raised by binding language in *Troilus and Cressida*, and sketching out related issues across the works of Shakespeare, it establishes historical contexts by looking at the contentious yet relatively stable set of beliefs that people held about oaths, vows, bonds, and the rest between the 1530s and the 1660s. A brief survey of existing scholarship leads into a summary account of the perplexities that made binding language so attractive to Shakespeare as a dramatist. Some of these points return in the Epilogue (Chapter 18), where a new angle is opened up on the plays by looking at what Shakespeare does with oaths, vows, and lies in the Sonnets.

Each of Chapters 2–17 addresses a different facet of the subject: revenge oaths in half a dozen plays; group oaths (how different from individual ones?); fealty in the history plays; Jewish oaths and financial bonds in *The Merchant of Venice*; profanity, oaths, and the law in *Measure for Measure*; bans and spells in *Macbeth*; Roman *fides* in *Coriolanus*; and so on. By the end of the book, the reader should have acquired a deeper understanding of some of the most important systems, institutions, and controversies in early modern England, and of the wiring of Shakespearean dramaturgy. What I offer are linked case studies, with a chronological movement. At a few points, such as Chapter 5, discussion has to draw on plays from more than one period of Shakespeare's writing life. For similar reasons, the chapters on the Reformation (14 and 15) loop back to the Henrician and late Elizabethan periods before getting to *Henry VIII*. Although the chapters are focused by topics, I have sought to reflect in my discussion the unfolding of plays in performance time, as in the theatre. This approach, whatever its constraints, allows one to show how problems with binding language mesh, develop, and counterpoint one another in onstage situations.

Except in the case of *Pericles*, which I quote from the 1609 quarto, and that of *Sir Thomas More*, where I follow John Jowett's Arden edition (2011), I cite the first edition of *The Norton Shakespeare*, gen. ed. Stephen Greenblatt (New York: Norton, 1997). The Norton absorbs most of the textual advances made by the Oxford *Complete Works* of 1986, but moderates some of its features. I have rejected a number of Norton readings, briefly giving reasons, and at a few points revert to traditional names and titles (Henry V not King Harry, Imogen not Innogen, *Henry VIII* not *All is True*). Where words are italicized for emphasis in Shakespeare quotations, those italics are my own. Unless otherwise indicated, citations from scripture are taken from the Geneva Bible (1560), which we know Shakespeare read, though he will have heard the Bishops' Bible (1568; rev. 1572) in church. Where I quote from early modern books, I have corrected evident misprints and expanded a few abbreviations and contractions ('&' becomes 'and', 'ye' as an article becomes 'the'). Titles have been lightly regularized. Greek has been transliterated. In the notes and brief references, the *Oxford English Dictionary* becomes *OED*, while *Records of Early English Drama* is reduced to REED. The dates of plays and other works are given in the body of the text with what is meant to be helpful frequency rather than mechanical regularity. With plays my policy has been, in general, to provide the consensus date for composition/first performance, plus the date of print publication where relevant, though sometimes date of print publication is close enough to composition/first performance to suffice. With non-dramatic works, I give date of print publication, with indications of likely date of composition or manuscript circulation if that is significant.

The *Oxford English Dictionary* has often been my recourse, though it is a work in progress, and slanted unrepresentatively towards Shakespeare. By the time this book settles onto the library shelves, some of the *OED* entries that it cites and challenges—e.g. that on vow, *n.*—will no doubt have been updated. I have also, needless to say, read extensively in Shakespeare criticism. Specific debts and overlaps are recorded in my notes, where I additionally, from time to time, refer the reader to works that contextualize the matter in hand. Apart from the brief, necessary review of secondary literature in section (vi) of the Introduction, however, I have exercised restraint. Online bibliographies are the best guide to the state of criticism.

Work on this topic began when I was invited to give the 2009 British Academy Shakespeare Lecture. It was advanced by the opportunity to lecture on *Henry V* at a conference on 'Performing Shakespeare in Ireland, 1660–1922' at the Moore Institute, National University of Ireland, Galway, in 2010. Research would have stopped at that point had I not been awarded a Research Fellowship by the Leverhulme Trust in 2012–13. I am grateful to these institutions for giving me the chance to develop my thoughts, and to audiences at the following universities for responding to sections of the book as lectures and seminar papers: Liverpool; St Andrews; National University of Singapore; University of Western Australia; Sydney; UCLA; Caltech; University of California, Berkeley; Aberystwyth; Cardiff; Auckland; Otago; Glasgow; UEA; Oxford; Cambridge. Elements of the Introduction and Chapter 17 appeared in *Proceedings of the British Academy*, 167 (2009); versions of Chapters 9 and 16 were published in *The Review of English Studies*, 63 (2012) and *Essays in Criticism*, 62 (2012).

A number of people have advised and encouraged me. Specific thanks are given here and there in the notes. Others who should be mentioned are David Fox, Jane Heal, David Hillman, Lorna Hutson, David Ibbetson, Michael and Peter Kerrigan, Subha Mukherji, Malcolm Schofield, and Jörg Rüpke. My nearest and dearest know how intrusive the writing of this book became. I have benefited from the resources of the Cambridge English Faculty and St John's College, Cambridge. At a late stage, Michael Neill commented on several chapters with his customary generosity. Five other people read the entire typescript, and to them I owe a special debt: an anonymous OUP reader, Colin Burrow, Nick de Somogyi (who also made the index), Helen Small, and John Spurr.

I

Introduction

(i) Enter Hector and Andromache

The action of *Troilus and Cressida* is moving towards its broken catastrophe. Enter the Trojan warrior Hector and his devoted wife Andromache. He is armed for battle; she, troubled by dreams, urges him not to fight. 'You train me to offend you,' he declares, then swears a mighty oath: 'By all the everlasting gods, I'll go' (5.3.4–5). Oaths, according to early modern commentators, resolve disputed matter.[1] For Shakespeare, however, their decisiveness is frequently deceptive; sworn over points of doubt, they are hedged, conflicted, and unravel. Certainly, when Cassandra, his sister, enters, she is not satisfied with Hector's insistence that 'The gods have heard me swear'. 'The gods are deaf', she replies, 'to hot and peevish vows' (15–16). Seeking to persuade her husband not to 'hurt by being just' (20), Andromache offers an elaborate, tangential analogy between Hector's sworn commitment and robbery with violence for the sake of charity; to which Cassandra adds: 'It is the purpose that makes strong the vow, | But vows to every purpose must not hold' (23–4).

Re-reading this passage a few years ago, I realized that, as so often, the familiarity of the dialogue was hiding my ignorance from me. Is Andromache's ingenuity desperate, or is she justifiably reminding Hector that oaths are not free-standing commitments but caught up in moral reasoning? And how convincing is Cassandra, with her subtle, loaded shift between 'purpose' as intention and 'purpose' as plan of action? For a late Elizabethan audience, was Hector's oath binding? When I turned to recent editions, the only guidance I could find was a quotation from Dr Johnson, in the commentary of the Arden edition: 'The mad Prophetess speaks here with all the coolness and judgment of a skilful casuist.'[2] It is easy to see why Arden has preserved this. Johnson's magisterial disparagement, both of Cassandra's character and of Shakespeare's ability to present it consistently, is obtuse but thought-provoking, and he is also historically perceptive, because he identifies the context of Andromache's ingenuity and concedes that what an eighteenth-century reader will deprecate as casuistry in Cassandra exhibits skill and judgement. Though he is alive to the issues,[3] however, Johnson barely scratches the surface of a topic that turns out to be dramaturgically vital right across the plays of Shakespeare.

From an Elizabethan point of view, Cassandra's position is orthodox. The homily 'Against Swearyng and Periury', read out regularly in churches during Shakespeare's lifetime, insists, against radical Protestants, on the legitimacy of oaths and vows.[4] Through marriage, oaths of office, and sworn testimony in court, binding language knits together the commonwealth. 'Thou shalte dreade thy Lorde God', the homily quotes from Deuteronomy (6: 13), 'and shalt sweare by hys name.' Abraham, David, and other Godly men swore, as did Christ himself, though mildly, saying 'verely, verely' (L4r). Oaths, however, are sacred and should not be sworn either casually or 'rasshely and vnaduisedly' (L4v). This is where Cassandra comes in. Shakespeare's audience would know from the homily, and from the widely acknowledged points of difficulty that were sifted in the casuistical literature, that to keep 'a rash oath, adds sin vnto sin'.[5]

It would be wrong to import too much sixteenth-century Protestantism. Unlike *Julius Caesar*, *Coriolanus*, and other classical plays of the period, *Troilus and Cressida* does not attempt a rigorous re-creation of antiquity. Written *c.*1601–2, it has a relatively immediate, often satirical, bearing on late Elizabethan society. What Cassandra says about Hector's 'hot and peevish vows' is, nevertheless, classical in form. 'They are polluted off'rings,' she declares, 'more abhorred | Than spotted livers in the sacrifice' (17–18). When he calls the gods to witness ('By all the everlasting gods'), Hector formally swears an oath. By describing what he says as vowing, that is, as a *votive* utterance (from *votum*, 'prayer, promise, offering'), his sister makes it analogous to animal sacrifice. She invokes the ancient practice (widely reported in Latin sources) of inspecting the innards of offerings, and, where a diseased heart or liver is found, judging the beast polluted and of ill omen. Hector's oath/vow, Cassandra says, is faulty and unacceptable to the gods, so he need not keep it. He should cast it aside as ominous. Shakespeare could have found what he needed for these lines in the lurid description of the diseased offering in Seneca's *Oedipus*, in the Trojan sacrifices of Virgil's Aeneas, and in the sacrifice of a bull to Jupiter in Book II of the *Iliad*, translated in 1598 by Chapman.[6]

Just how 'peevish' Hector is being when he swears by all the gods is ultimately up to the actor, but he is resisting a troublesome wife, not exercising deliberation. Does the element of rashness discharge him from an obligation to keep his word? Not straightforwardly, it seems, in classical or Elizabethan terms, for although his oath is 'rash' it is hardly to be set aside as a culpable 'bonde of iniquity'.[7] Once uttered, his oath is not disabled by the conditions set out in the homily, any more than by the Homeric warrior code, because what he swears to do is neither 'against the lawe of almightie God' nor beyond 'his power to performe'. He will not 'double' his 'offence' (in the words of the homily) if he keeps his word and goes out to fight, though he does risk weakening Troy.[8]

All, however, is not lost for Cassandra and Andromache. Most members of Shakespeare's audience would agree with the moderate Royalist divine, Robert Sanderson, whose treatise *De Juramento* (1655) is a digest of mainstream casuistry on oaths, that binding words need only be kept if they are not overruled by a higher power—such as a father overruling a son, or a king a subject—and 'if things remain in the same state'.[9] I shall get to the latter condition, often crucial in Shakespeare, in a moment. But it should already be clear why, once Cassandra has been rebuffed, she leaves Hector to be harassed by Troilus (who wants his brother to go out and kill Greeks) and re-enters with his king and father. As the Trojan royal family gather and group against him on stage, it becomes even harder for Hector to draw back from his oath.[10] In deference to Priam's authority, however, he does justify his inflexibility by telling him, what the audience already knows, that he 'stand[s] engaged to many Greeks, | Even in the faith of valour, to appear | This morning to them' (70–2).

Were the faiths exchanged on Hector's visit to the Greek camp, when he fought with Ajax (4.7), anything more than pleasantries? Oaths and vows can be problematic because they are uttered in one context but still make claims on fidelity when the setting changes. Once fired off, like rockets, they cannot be recalled. They can, of course, be 'unsworn' (that is, 'denied'), which everyone agreed to be contemptible, or they can be more boldly 'forsworn', but the contradictoriness of that word, which could mean 'sworn against' as well as 'broken', and sometimes, as in *Love's Labour's Lost* (4.3.293), both at once, is telling. The potential for moral confusion is pointed up by Worcester, when he says of Henry IV: 'I told him... Of his oath-breaking, which he mended thus: | By now forswearing that he is forsworn' (*1 Henry IV*, 5.2.36–8). The readiest way to adapt an oath or vow was—improperly, according to the scrupulous—to counter it with another ('confounding oath on oath', in Puck's mischievous muddle),[11] which is one reason why, once admitted, they become so plentiful and layered in Shakespeare. Behind his oath to Andromache, Hector chose not to tell Cassandra, was his light-sounding engagement to many Greeks. What lies behind what he tells Priam? Audiences will not forget the exchange with his greatest rival Achilles when they plighted their troth like lovers:

ACHILLES Dost thou entreat me, Hector?
Tomorrow do I meet thee, fell as death;
Tonight, all friends.
HECTOR Thy hand upon that match. (4.7.152–4)

This is the tryst that matters. Hector's subsequent faiths and oaths start to look like a pretext for ensuring that this fight will happen.

Because scholars have not explored the binding language in this play they have had no reason to explicate what is arguably the biggest change made by Shakespeare to the story of Troy as he found it. In Caxton and Lydgate, Achilles does not see and fall in love with Polyxena until the anniversary of Hector's death. To win her, he then takes a vow that he will not fight alongside the Greeks. In Shakespeare, by contrast—although Ulysses chooses to conceal this, for resentful reasons of his own—he is lurking in his tent from the outset because of that vow. Conceivably he forgets it in the intensity of his tryst with Hector. Even before he goes into his tent to drink with his enemy, however, he announces to Patroclus:

Here is a letter from Queen Hecuba,
A token from her daughter, my fair love,
Both taxing me, and gaging me to keep
An oath that I have sworn. I will not break it.
Fall, Greeks; fail, fame; honour, or go or stay.
My major vow lies here; this I'll obey. (5.1.34–9)

This is the language of casuistry filtered through chivalric romance. And it casts an ironic light on Hector's exchange with Cassandra, because he insists on keeping a faith which Achilles has already dismissed as bendable and expendable.

This is not the full chain of Achilles' oaths and vows. The prologue says of the Greek generals, 'their vow is made | To ransack Troy' (7–8). Again, this is not in Caxton and it marks a promise made before the expedition that Achilles breaks when he lolls in his tent. The play goes on as it begins, shot through with verbal bonds, formal, slackly profane, confrontational, or peculiarly displaced—as when Pandarus says to Troilus, the tongue-tied wooer of Cressida, 'Swear the oaths now to her that you have sworn to me' (3.2.39–40). It is a drama of high-flown vows, but also of what Thersites calls 'crafty swearing rascals' (5.4.8). Is Achilles above such shifts? Having resolved to keep his major vow, he later abandons it to revenge the death of Patroclus. Does he finally step aside and leave the Myrmidons to kill the unarmed Hector because he is cowardly or unfit for combat, as critics usually argue, or determined to degrade his enemy? Or is he casuistically keeping that major vow after all?

Somewhere near the heart of the play is the uncertain scene of troth-plighting between Troilus and Cressida. Here, as blocking can bring out, is a parallel with the sequence in which Hector and Achilles eye each other up and clasp hands to seal their faith. But it is also, by virtue of Shakespeare's bold treatment of his sources, counterpointed by the attenuated love plot that ties Achilles to Polyxena. Three word-bound relationships cut across by war, and tied into action with pledges—letters, tokens, fingers. Perhaps we should say four. Because when Cressida submits to Diomedes, she is caught up with a man who is, according to Thersites, a notorious vow-breaker (5.1.80–6). Is Cressida just as bad? Troilus assumes so, but her binding words and gestures are inextricable from her predicament. We should remember at this point the principle of defeasibility. Cressida has been forced into an unprotected position by Troilus' choice or inability to look after her. Once she goes to the Greek camp, things do not (in Sanderson's words) 'remain in the same state'. As we shall see in Chapter 10, a late Elizabethan audience would have taken a view of this situation rather different from that to be found in modern commentary, whether misogynistic or feminist.

(ii) Works

It should be clear from this summary analysis of just one strand of a single play that *Shakespeare's Binding Language* addresses a significant topic. Across the Shakespeare canon, oaths are sworn and bonds dissolved at points of decision and uncertainty that produce what we now call 'character'. Vows, engagements, and the like are speech acts that precipitate action. They structure multiple plot-lines and the relationships between them. One of the denser passages in the homily 'Against Swearyng and Periury' reminds Elizabethan churchgoers how binding language regulates the most diverse areas of life: covenants, peace treaties, marriage vows, undertakings to obey the law, oaths of allegiance and office (sworn by 'Iudges, Magistrates, and officers'), the promises given by clergymen (L3v–4r). The passage encourages us to notice how, in such multi-centred plays as *Troilus*, binding language can function in distinct spheres which have things to say about one another.

Once the topic is opened up, it will be seen to be important in most parts of Shakespeare's output. Certainly, the issues that I started with go back to the earliest plays. 'Unheedful vows may heedfully be broken,' says Proteus in *The Two Gentlemen of Verona*, often dated to 1590–1 (2.6.11). Whether it is Salisbury declaring 'It is great sin to swear unto a sin, | But greater sin to keep a sinful oath,' or Clarence citing Jephthah, as a warning against keeping bad vows, when he returns to the Yorkist faction, the flexibility of the orthodoxy set out in the homily is exploited in the first tetralogy (*c.* 1591).[12] As we shall see in Chapters 2 and 8, the *Henry VI* plays and *Richard II* are riven with revenge oaths that conflict with the oaths of fealty and allegiance that were sworn to medieval monarchs—as a section of Shakespeare's audience would know from reading the legal texts of Britton[13] and Henry de Bracton[14] as well as the chronicles. From *The Comedy of Errors* (1592?) to *A Midsummer Night's Dream* (1594–6), oaths and vows mark changes in motive and attachment—vertiginously so in the green wood, where love-in-idleness wreaks havoc, Lysander swearing 'Hermia's' vows to Helena, and Demetrius the other way round, until it all comes right enough.[15] Oaths can be offensive weapons—Petruccio uses them to browbeat Kate, in *The Taming of the Shrew*—or trip-wire indicators of confidence, as when Gremio offers, then refuses, to swear that Vincentio is the right Vincentio.[16]

The picture that I want to paint is not a simple one of authorial development. The binding language in the playscripts owes more to genre than date: lovers' vows in the comedies; oaths of Church and State—including a coronation oath—in *King John*; perjury in the problem plays; oaths turning into spells and curses in *Lear*, *Macbeth*, and *Timon of Athens*; faith and counsel in the late romances. In the Sonnets and *A Lover's Complaint*, as we shall see in the Epilogue, poems of uncertain date, both in composition and revision (though reaching beyond 1603), become peculiarly intense about oaths, vows, and perjury. Nonetheless, we can safely say that, by the middle of the 1590s, Shakespeare was doubly engaged by the ethical weight and airiness of verbal bonds. *Love's Labour's Lost* (1594–5) is about little else, starting, as it does, from Navarre and his lords' oath to study for three years, a promise which, with typical unstraightforwardness, is shedding its conditions even before it is fully subscribed. Pandolf in *King John* (*c.*1596) is the sort of equivocating papist whose slippery handling of vows gives casuistry a bad name.[17] And Bolingbroke's oath at Doncaster not to unthrone Richard II is repeatedly invoked by the rebels in *1* and *2 Henry IV* (1596–8). They are finally, ironically, defeated when Prince John sticks so precisely to the terms of the oath that he shares with them that he can send them to execution.[18] This is one of many points where binding words prove to be not the opposite of lying but a means of deception.

Most oaths in Shakespeare are not self-consciously framed. They are casual, incidental profanities, circulating in conversation, more interpersonal than individual. Robert Boyle, in the mid-seventeenth century, compared swearing to yawning.[19] We pick up and echo oaths without noticing what we are doing. In such late 1590s plays as *Much Ado About Nothing*, fashionable, light profanity sets a social tone; yet these oaths can suddenly escalate, convincing Don Pedro and Claudio that Hero is unfaithful, and binding Benedick to kill his friend. At this date Shakespeare develops what was already felt in the first tetralogy: the element of threat in promise. Whether it is Shylock's bond hanging over Antonio, or Henry V's warnings to the citizens of Harfleur, binding language proposes a violence that is barely wrapped up in legality. *Othello* (1604?), *All's Well That Ends Well* (1605–7), and other plays about sexual betrayal from the same middle period as *Troilus*, similarly show oaths and vows shifting from casual interjection to intensity. This is one of the ways in which female characters are disadvantaged. As we shall see in section (v) of this Introduction, full-strength oaths were usually disapproved of in women. Desdemona would bewhore herself if she swore her truth with Othello's vehemence.

Macbeth, staged at the Globe by the summer of 1606, is often regarded as the play in which equivocation destabilizes language, making the unthinkable thought and conjuring with damnation. A fascination with casuistry, however, and a delight in how seemingly impossible conditions can be met to fulfil assurances, goes back to the earlier plays—Hero, in *Much Ado*, for example, brought back from the dead to marry Claudio—and it adds to what is problematic in the middle-period comedies. Among the circumstances of *Measure for Measure* (1604) are the religious vows which Isabella aspires to take, and the pre-empted or suspended spousal and marriage vows of Claudio, Juliet, Mariana, and Angelo. In a twist of ingenuity that would delight a casuist, Bertram, in *All's Well*, fulfils his marriage vows to Helena precisely by (as he thinks) breaking them, when he sleeps with her under the misapprehension that he is sleeping with Diana.

In 1606, Godly opposition to profanity, already evident in the homily 'Against Swearyng and Periury', issued in an Act of Parliament which made it a fineable offence 'in any Stage-play, Interlude, Shew, Maygame, or Pageant, iestingly, and prophanely [to] speake, or vse the holy Name of God, or of Christ Iesus, or of the holy Ghost, or of the Trinitie'.[20] The Act to Restrain Abuses of Players led to the excision or softening of oaths in a number of the earlier plays published in the 1623 Shakespeare Folio, damage which cannot (in F-only texts) be put right with any confidence.[21] It may be that the Act played a part in moving Shakespeare away from contemporary subject matter into classical plays and romances where characters could swear by Jupiter or Apollo. That it prompted deeper soul-searching is unlikely, though there may have been unease on his part—as has been proposed in the case of Ben Jonson—about the scale of profanity of some of the oaths in his earlier plays.[22]

Reflecting on as well as reflecting the change in theatrical culture that was brought about by the Act, Shakespeare's use of binding language was to some extent redirected. The avoidance of oaths itself became a dramatic issue. There had been refusers before 1606, but they tend, like Richard III, to be more villainous than those who swear, or, like Brutus in *Julius Caesar,* to be too complacent about honour to believe that oaths add any security to the word of a noble Roman. Pericles and Marina not only refuse to swear but, in the shadow of the Act, draw on lines of argument that go back to the Tudor homily. 'Ile take thy word, for faith,' Pericles tells Helicanus, in the 1609 quarto, 'not aske thine oath, | Who shuns not to breake one, will cracke both' (B2v). In this play, those who swear are likely not just to be bad but to use oaths to spur their badness. Thus Thaliard, who has sworn to kill Pericles, shuffles off any blame: 'for if a king bidde a man bee a villaine, he's bound by the indenture of his oath to bee one' (B3r). Pericles does vow 'by bright *Diana*' (E4v). But Marina is impeccable, almost an exemplar of the reaction against profanity that would lead, in 1623—the very year in which the Folio was published—to a law imposing fines on those who swore offstage as well as on. 'Faith', says Boult, mildly, 'I must rauish her, or shee'le . . . make our swearers priests' (G3v).

After 1606, Shakespeare was not less interested in oaths. In Chapter 17 I show, through a discussion of *The Winter's Tale*, how he thought creatively about the outlawed practices. Gender differences in usage are re-negotiated, and the contrast between saying and swearing shifts. As *The Two Noble Kinsmen*—discussed in the Epilogue—indicates, binding language remained, to the end of his career (1613–14), a device for coupling and dividing characters, and piling up irresolvable dilemmas. But late Shakespeare also went back to an earlier, Elizabethan concern—first developed in *King John*—about oaths sworn to king or Pope regarding authority in matters of religion. Stimulated by the imposition of an Oath of Allegiance on Catholics after the Gunpowder Plot of 1605, he co-wrote with John Fletcher, probably in 1613, a play about conspiracy—*Henry VIII*—that is set in a phase of the English Reformation when this oath was often said to originate.

(iii) Judaeo-Christian and classical traditions

All utterances sworn to or vowed involve a binding of the agent to the truth of what is said. This is so even in cases of frank profanity, where the purpose of the oath lies in shocking with what is sworn by rather than securing what is sworn. In the early modern period, this sort of binding is spoken of in relation to assertory oaths, which testify to matters past and present: 'I dare be bound he's true,' a lord insists of Shakespeare's Pisanio;[23] 'an *Oath of Conscience*... bindes before God vpon paine of periurie', says a treatise *Of Oathes*.[24] Binding even more often describes promissory oaths, vows, and contracts, i.e. truths about the future.[25] 'Whosoeuer maketh any promise, bindyng hymself thereunto by an othe,' declares the homily 'Against Swearyng and Periury', 'let him forese, that the thyng whiche he promiseth, bee good' (M3r). It was a commonplace that assertion and promise were ethically of a piece. As Sanderson summarily puts it, an 'oath is binding' because 'the party swearing is bound for the present to say truth', whether this be of 'some fact past or present' or of 'the present' and 'future'.[26]

In asseveration or promise, a word merely given could bind without oath or vow. Your word was then your bond. More often, the given word was explicitly framed as a speech act ('I swear, by Heaven, *x* is true,' 'I vow to give you *y*'). The 'by' construction of an oath was often correctly regarded as a calling of God—or one of His creatures—to witness the truth to which the speaker was bound. Even the pious acknowledged, however, that such an utterance could have the more worldly characteristics of a pledge. John Downame, for instance, notes that 'God is my witnes' (Romans 1: 9) is a pure form of oath, but that 'also in our oathes we sometimes pawne and pledge vnto God those things which are deere to vs, as it were suerties of our truth; as, *By my soule, by my faith*, &c., that is, I pawne my soule and faith vnto God, for the confirmation of this truth.'[27] The words that pledge faith or honour—common enough in Shakespeare—acquire a degree of substantiality, while invocations of the Divine have their own theatrical aura. When characters bind themselves, there is often a note of self-dramatization, even of melodrama or bathos.

Binding language does not just bind the speaker to what is said or subscribed. Because assertory oaths are made to satisfy or convince others of the truth of something, and because sworn promises or vows are calculated to generate faith (i.e. to persuade people about the shape of the future), there is a social, lateral binding between those who speak or write bindingly and those who accept the given words with whatever degree of trust. The definitions and citations of *bind*, *bond*, and *binding* in the *Oxford English Dictionary*, and the searchable databases of early modern texts, confirm what is evident from plays, that the semantics of these words take users, readers, and audiences along both axes. You are bound to what you say, but also bound to those whose acceptance of your word might be thought to leave them with an obligation to trust that meshes with your responsibility to speak the truth.

One point should be underlined. Bound up with binding exchanges, as Shakespeare often brings out, is the drive to bring round and persuade. Early modern commentators do not just write about oaths and vows in relation to Divine witness and sanction; they are interested, up to a point, in the interactive and communicative. They pursue the question, for example, of how far an oath should be understood to have the meaning that it has for the person who proposes it (e.g. a magistrate) and how far it should bear the meaning attributed to it by the swearer; and they ask, especially later in the period, whether attaching a profanity to a statement really makes it more convincing. For all that, the moralists and rhetoricians are less exercised than Shakespeare is about performatives that are acts of persuasion. We should remember the tacit contribution of the addressee of an oath ('I swear to *you*, by God') or the promisee of a vow. Like the contracts and covenants with which they have so much in common, oaths and vows are usually 'joint actions'.[28]

During Shakespeare's lifetime the cluster of words around *bind*, *bound*, and *bond* was used of so many kinds of connection—bonds of kin, allegiance to a monarch, material threads and cords, being bound by good will or service, not to mention the power of the clergy (for some) to bind and loose from sin—that usage was coloured with implications that allow binding as act and description to draw fields of meaning together. The results are sometimes playful, and sometimes seriously so. Here, for example, is the beginning of a sermon commemorating King James's deliverance from the Gowrie Plot: 'Religious Reader; I am bold to call thee by a binding word, because I suppose thee to be no loose companion. This Sermon is bound for thee, and may bee much bound to thee.'[29] There are even more bonds and binds in this than meet the modern eye because the word 'religious' was usually derived from *religio*, 'I bind'.[30]

That religious readers—bound to God and his commandments, bound by the rites of the Church—would share in the general view that oaths and vows bound speakers not just to what they said (with God as witness) but to their addressees and auditors in the community of credit, is beyond question. The moderate Calvinist William Perkins, for instance, digging into Judaeo-Christian tradition, declares:

> In euery lawfull oath, there is a double bond; First, it bindes one man to another, for the performing of the thing hee sweareth to doe. Secondly, it bindes a man vnto God, for he that sweareth, inuocates God as a witnesse, and a Iudge of the truth of his assertion; and hee stands bound vnto God, till the thing sworne vnto, bee performed, if it bee lawfull and possible. And herein the Pharises are good Teachers, . . .[31]

As we shall see in Chapter 7, it was more common than we might expect for commentators on oaths to go back to the Jewish teachers. Even if you did not, the lessons of the Old Testament were clear. First, as the homily 'Against Swearyng and Periury' stresses, you are allowed to swear by the name of God—'Thou shalt feare the Lord thy God, and serue him, and shalt sweare by his Name' (Deuteronomy 6: 13; cf. Psalms 63: 11)—but you must do so with truth and purpose. In the words of the third commandment, 'Thou shalt not take the Name of the Lord thy God in vaine' (Exodus 20: 7). Second, leaning into the promissory, when you swear you must keep your word: 'Whosoeuer voweth a vow vnto the Lord, or sweareth an othe to binde him selfe by a bonde, he shal not breake his promes, *but* shal do according to all that proceadeth out of his mouth' (Numbers 30: 3).

The extent to which these injunctions had been qualified by the Gospel was a subject much discussed. The Anabaptists who refused all swearing could point to the Sermon on the Mount, where Christ denied that the Pharisees were good teachers and imposed a ban:

> Againe, ye haue heard that it was said to them of olde time, Thou shalt not forsweare thy self, but shalt performe thine othes to the Lord.
>
> But I say vnto you, Sweare not at all, nether by heauen, for it is the throne of God:
>
> Nor yet by the earth: for it is his fote stole: nether by Ierusalem: for it is the citie of the great King.
>
> Nether shalt thou sweare by thine head, because thou canst not make one heere white or blacke.
>
> But let your communication be, Yea, yea: Nay, nay. For whatsoeuer *is* more then these, commeth of euil. (Matthew 5: 33–7)

Over the course of this book, I shall return to this passage a number of times, unpacking its implications. For now, it is enough to notice that it marks a break in Judaeo-Christian tradition that could not be entirely resolved by such texts as 'Against Swearyng and Periury'. To argue that lawful oaths are justified but that vain, everyday ones are not is to turn the shift in teaching into a polarity. On the one hand the Bible encouraged solemn, even terrible invocations of God's name; on the other it forbade them. Sometimes the plays capitalize on the former; sometimes they draw on the language of Christ's prohibition. In *The Merchant of Venice*, Shakespeare sets an Old Testament view of swearing, in Shylock, against the flexible oaths and vows of Christian Venice and Belmont. No other early modern play comes closer than this one to dealing with the Hebraic roots of binding language.

While Christianity had its rules about when and how people should swear (if they should swear at all), it also transmitted the belief that God Himself is a swearer. Scripture tells us plainly that He swore to His covenant with Abraham (Genesis 12–17). For those who wanted to allow lawful oaths (to the magistrate, in peace treaties, and so on) this set an important precedent. In swearing with truth and purpose we follow the example of God. After the Reformation, this defence of oaths took its place as one aspect of a 'covenant theology' according to which God's promises, given to Adam, Noah, Abraham, and others, guaranteed the salvation of mankind through Christ's blood, in the Atonement, the sacrifice on the cross. A passage in Paul's Epistle to the Hebrews was often cited: 'be not slothful', the Apostle urged,

> but followers of them, which through faith and patience, inherite the promises.

> For when God made the promes to Abraham, because he had no greater to sweare by, he sware by him self,
>
> Saying, Surely I wil abundantly blesse thee and multiplie thee marueilously....
>
> So God willing more abundantly to shewe vnto the heires of promes the stablenes of his counsel, bound him self by an othe...(6: 12–17)

That Englishmen and women were the heirs of God's sworn promise to Abraham was a fundamental point of doctrine inculcated daily through the Book of Common Prayer.[32]

How far this shaped culture and conduct is a fascinating question. In *The Economy of Obligation* (1998), Craig Muldrew argues that the belief deeply affected the collective understanding of credit, neighbourliness, and commerce. God's promise to Abraham was more than a model for the lawful oath, it set a pattern for fidelity and trust:

> The covenant became for Tyndale the guarantee of God's reliability, and justification by faith meant justification by trust, which not only guaranteed God's fidelity, but enabled man's responsive faithfulness.... Although the nature of the covenant has most often been described in terms of the harsh Old Testament authority of legally binding contracts,... it is more realistic to describe it as a relation of mutual commitment. The emphasis was on interpersonal trust more than authority, just as it was in an equitable bargain between believing Christian neighbours, in which benefit, profit and mutual sociability were meant to be the result if trust was kept.[33]

You might wonder how far this summary can be reconciled with *The Merchant of Venice*. If the play shows the limits and dangers of a 'harsh Old Testament...legally binding contract' (in Shylock's obsession with his bond), it pitches against it not Christian mercy—we can hardly take Portia's great speech about mercy as a guide to her conduct—but something like an ethos of entitlement. In Venice, the Atonement has sunk into an assumption of privilege, a notion (most developed in Bassanio) that someone else will pay the bill. Muldrew qualifies his account by noting how the rising tide of legal cases involving debts and broken contracts—to which we might add the changing basis of litigation, which allowed the given word to become a focus of argument in cases of *assumpsit* (see p. 33)—made covenant theology itself more Mosaic in tone (141–2).

There is no doubt that Muldrew identifies a truth and a trend, but he still leaves difficulties to resolve. Many of these difficulties feed into the machinations of city comedy, where trust and grace are largely ineffectual and legal authority does not fare much better. Behind it all are deeper ambivalences in Judaeo-Christian tradition. Search the English Bible for *trust* and you will not find it commended as a social virtue. On the contrary, we are enjoined *not* to trust in this world but only (the Psalmist tells us) in God who is our buckler, our horn of salvation and high tower. Christian apologetics strike the same note in a different key. *Contemptus mundi* is the default. The fallen world is unreliable, and although we may strive to follow God's example in faith and trust we should beware of the snares set for the unwary and not decline into credulity.

The varieties of classical humanism that blended with these Christian beliefs in Tudor educational practice identified a bindingness in language that owed more to rhetoric, reason, and ethics than it did to the example of God's promise. Cicero, whose insistence in the *De Officiis* on our obligation to keep our oaths, to maintain, 'that is to say, a constancy and truth of words and couenants',[34] will be mentioned several times in this book, was a potent source. Writing of 'the connection subsisting between all the members of the human race', he declares, 'that bond of connection is reason and speech, which ... associate men together and unite them in a sort of natural fraternity'.[35] Symptomatically, Cicero's word for 'bond', *vinculum*, was often used to mean 'oath' or 'binding word'. When rhetoricians like Thomas Wilson, in a passage that Shakespeare will have read, describe the figure of Hercules Gallicus with chains of eloquence coming out of his mouth, drawing and leading men from barbarism into civility, they encouraged the belief that language is a bond of order and progress, and binding words a subset.[36] 'Nothing makes vs men,' wrote Montaigne, 'and no other meanes, keepes vs bound one to another, but the word.'[37] When Florio's 1603 translation was published again, in 1613, 'the word' had become 'our word'.[38] 'Speach makes vs men', agrees Marston's Sophonisba, 'and thers no other bond | Twixt man and man, but words: O equall Gods | Make vs once know the consequences of vowes—.'[39]

If the power of language to bind was in many such accounts the origin of civilization, others of a classical bent liked to measure the moral decline of society by its lapses in fidelity. In *The Boke Named the Gouernour* (1531), Sir Thomas Elyot returns to Cicero: 'to speke in what estimacion this vertue was of olde tyme amonge gentiles, whiche nowe ... is so neglected throughout christendome, that neither regarde of religion or honour, solemne othes or terrible cursis can cause hit to be obserued.... O what publike weale shulde we hope to haue there, where lacketh fidelitie? whiche as Tulli saieth, is the fundation of iustyce.'[40] Elyot goes on at length. Turks and Saracens regard us with contempt because they keep their word—usually without even taking a bond or an oath—while Christians do not (fol. 191v). Instead of supporting truth and faith, the law creates loopholes. All the learned legal men in England 'can nat with all their study deuise so sufficient an instrument, to bynde a man to his promyse or couenaunt'. Bad for individuals, this weakens the fabric of the commonwealth (fol. 195v). Complaints of moral decline are routine in most periods. What makes so many early modern complaints distinctive is their focus on oaths and vows. Sometimes the stress is on profanity, but perjury is rarely far behind. 'Was euer any age so outragious in Othes? So blasphemous in railing? So rooted in periurie?', asked Edmond Bicknoll in 1579.[41] 'Mens hearts, are growne so false, that most are loath | To trust each others *Words*, or *Bands*, or *Oath*,' wrote George Wither in 1635.[42] Between such moralizing and the plays of Shakespeare there is a gulf, yet both follow the same course in the sense that the plays are far less often about truthful, assertory oaths and fulfilled promises than about broken vows, lying asseverations, and a bond for a pound of flesh.

(iv) Words

At the top of the scale of stringency is the *oath*, a word with Germanic roots[43] that has been part of the English language since the Anglo-Saxon period. We have noted some variant constructions already (pp. 9–10), but, during Shakespeare's lifetime, assertory and promissory oaths were typically sworn '*by* God' or one of His creatures. Because they invoke the Divine, oaths have an affinity with prayer, and they can imply the sort of conditional self-curse that is often explicit in the Old Testament[44] as in Greek antiquity.[45] If what I say is false, by Heaven, may *x* descend upon me. In the early modern period, *oath* could also denote everyday effing and blinding. This is appropriate enough. Such forceful oaths as ''Sfoot' and ''Slid' ['by God's foot/eyelid'] did overlap in use with expletives, obscenities, and curses—'Pish', 'Tush', 'Foh, a fico' ['a fig/female genitals'], 'Beshrew thee', 'A murrain [pestilence] on't', 'A pox on't', and the rest (all of the above in Shakespeare). What you casually swear or profanely invoke can rebound on you, as an abuse of God and language. Solemn oaths are caught up in a blasphemous counter-life, the surging, phatic noise of the collectively profane. As when the priest asks Petruccio 'if Katherine should be his wife, | "Ay, by Gog's woun's", quoth he, and swore so loud | That all amazed the priest let fall the book' (*Shrew*, 3.3.32–4).

In response to this question, a tractable groom would have taken his marriage vows. *Vow* comes into English, out of French, in the late thirteenth century.[46] We vow not *by* but *to* God, or, during Shakespeare's lifetime (and the *Oxford English Dictionary* credits him, suggestively though not plausibly, with initiating this change), we make a vow to another person promising fidelity in love.[47] Classically, vowing is involved with presenting votive gifts and doing a deal with the Divine. Hence Cassandra's comparison of 'hot and peevish vows', in the exchange with which this Introduction began, to 'polluted off'rings . . . in the sacrifice'. In medieval thought and practice, the sacred was never far from vows.[48] These religious associations persisted: think of the vows taken by the nuns in *Measure for Measure*, and of the Duke's deceptive oath 'By the vow of mine order' (1.4.7–13, 4.2.156).

Vow was attractive to Shakespeare because, unlike *oath*, it was lexically well connected (*devotion*, *devout*, and so on) and quick to coin new forms—terms like *votary* and *votaress*.[49] *Oath* was almost always a noun, but *vow* could be a verb. It was close, moreover, to 'avow' (which became ''vow', in its aphetic form), and thus to 'avouch' and 'vouch'—words that must have encouraged Shakespeare's use (again, according to the *OED*, for the first time) of *vow* to mean 'A solemn . . . asseveration'.[50] *Vow* in this sense is almost an assertory oath, rather as a promissory oath can do the work of a vow. When Hector swears 'By all the everlasting gods', that is an oath, yet Cassandra calls it a 'vow' (5.3.5, 16, 23–4); Achilles initially calls his 'major vow' an 'oath' (5.1.37–9). Shakespeare often uses the terms interchangeably, alert to the hooks and eyes that can link situations and plots.

Flexible in usage, these words bled into other words. When you vowed to marry someone, you could be—in early modern spelling—'betr-oath-ed' as well as 'betrothed'.[51] When Prospero says, 'The strongest oaths are straw,' or Pistol warns that 'oaths are straws, men's faiths are wafer-cakes', there is a gratuitous, knowing play between 'oats' and 'straw'[52] (the *-th* would sound close to *-t*). Pistol's wafer-cakes, rather neatly, are the flimsy eucharistic wafers *on* which medieval and Roman Catholic oaths were taken, and *by* which (e.g. in the form 'God's bodykins',[53] meaning 'by God's dear body') other oaths again were sworn. Beyond this fringe of slippage, other categories of binding language were waiting to be unbound. To *protest*, for example, can mean to speak against[54] something that is also asserted or vowed;[55] Diana seizes this ambiguity when she tells Bertram (to discredit his oaths), 'This has no holding, | To swear by him whom I protest to love | That I will work against him.'[56] For Regan to *profess* love to Lear is for her both to 'avow' or 'vow' it and—as now—merely to say it, i.e. to dissimulate (see p. 349).

Shakespeare is always attuned to derivation and resonance. In *Hamlet*, we become aware of the common roots of *pledge* and *play* (p. 224). Such words as *engagement* and *compromise* have semantics that will be unpacked in Chapters 7 and 8 (*gage*, *wager*, *promise*). The sound of *vow* in *vouch*—despite their different etymologies[57]—is sharpened by *safe* ('secure') in the complications of *vouchsafe* (p. 110). *Binding* (from Old English *bindan*) can be shadowed by or slide into *bondage*, both the shackling up of a prisoner (*bond* as fetter) and the condition of serf, bondman, or slave (from Anglo-Norman *bonde*). Sometimes the keywords of this book carry a biblical charge: *covenant*, only used thrice in Shakespeare, is an obvious example,[58] *assurance*, used almost thirty times, is sometimes another. Both terms, however, have legal associations, as do *testify* and *attest*. There are words for giving things up: *abjure* (four times in Shakespeare), *revoke*, *revoked*, and *revokement*. There are also words for giving up given words: to *defy*, in some contexts, can mean 'to renounce faith, allegiance, or affiance';[59] to *adjure*, by contrast,[60] is not found in the plays and poems, though the practice of extorting or exhorting testimony from someone under oath was such a live topic in the 1590s thanks to controversy about torture and the imposition of *ex officio* oaths in the ecclesiastical courts that one wonders how Shakespeare did without it.

There was argument about which of these practices were acceptable, and what the limits were. Some were guided by Christ's commandment not to swear at all, though to judge by the comments of moralists people were often not persuaded when a man barely asseverated. Credibility in such a case required a record of verity, even if there was a Christian obligation (or almost) upon others to believe, based on a New Testament generosity of spirit towards our neighbours and a responsibility to make it unnecessary for them to swear. We 'ought to... speake so truly', Bale declares, 'that yf he sayd / yea / then his neighbour shulde beleue him to saye truth / yf he sayd / naye / lykewyse to beleue it not to be truth'.[61] Since a proper oath, according to Deuteronomy, was one sworn by God, 'yea' and 'naye' could be regarded as an inadequate commitment. But what of swearing 'by the creature', where something in the created world either stood in for God or stood between the swearer and God? Did Christ have this in mind when he forbade swearing by Jerusalem, or by the hairs on your head? When Joseph swore '*by* the life of Pharaoh' (Genesis 42: 15), was he swearing by the creature (since God made the Pharaoh), or, as Sanderson concluded with relief, giving 'an asseveration rather confirmed by a vehement obtestation'.[62]

The dissolution of bonds was a particularly thorny issue. Everyone agreed that assurances given contrary to the ten commandments did not bind, though it was especially wrong to swear them. A person promised something could release you from your promise, though, for many commentators, if a promise was sworn, to be released from your promise was not the end of the matter because the oath (to which God was witness) remained. Could the Pope dispense with oaths, marriage vows, leagues between kings, and other inconvenient engagements? In a Protestant country, did an archbishop or the sovereign inherit any of these powers? These were points of dispute. Then there was equivocation and mental reservation, those Jesuitical practices where the speaker worked with ambiguities to evade the apparent meaning of a given word, or swore something while qualifying or correcting it silently on the grounds that God would accept the truth of what was thought not what was said.

All these forms of dissolution matter to such plays as *King John*, *Macbeth*, and *All's Well*, but there are prior uncertainties in *Hamlet*. It was agreed that children, fools, and madmen were not bound by their words. Is the mad prince to be tied to his oath and vow, whether to the ghost or to Ophelia? How far was a promise extorted under fear binding—a Catholic priest in the hands of interrogators? a prince enjoined by a ghost?—and what degree of fear brought in the limitation?[63] Moralists drew the line at swearing to a lie (to bear false witness breaks the ninth commandment), but it was a serious question for some whether you were allowed to mislead (call it perjury) for the commonweal or for your prince.[64] Was it legitimate to break oaths made to heretics? Catholics were said to believe so.[65] Must we keep our word with enemies? Some contended that Hector and the Trojans were at a disadvantage when fighting the Greeks because they were 'troubled in conscience... for breaking their oaths and Covenants'.[66]

It should not be imagined that the finer points of argument were trivial. Large cultural differences could hang on them; alternative scales of value, Catholic and reformed, Protestant and more strictly Protestant, converged on the sticking points. Nor should it be assumed that the disputation was arid. Among the hundreds of treatises on oaths, vows, and casuistry are many that can still be read with admiration if not pleasure. How could this be otherwise when the intricacies attracted such writers as Donne, not just in his love poetry but in the prose tract *Pseudo-martyr* (1610)? Take the question of whether it was legitimate to swear on the Bible. Many Protestants believed that it was, because the Bible contained the Word of God. It was the truth of the Gospels on which you were swearing, not the paper and string of the book. Others, of a warmer sort, argued that such an oath made the book an idol, and was equivalent to swearing on creatures. This was not a new quarrel. It went back to the Lollards, but it put out more branches during the Elizabethan period and it could be animated rather than staled by rehearsal.

There is a striking treatment of the question in James Morice's *Briefe Treatise of Oathes* (1590), a puritan-sympathizing critique of the *ex officio* oaths imposed on those called to testify on matters of doctrine and church discipline in front of the ecclesiastical courts. Morice waxes satirical:

> For the deponent forsooth, must laye his three middle fingers stretched out right vppon the booke, in signification of the holie trinitie and Catholique faith, and his thumbe and little finger hee must put downe-wardes vnder the booke, in token of damnation, both of bodie and soule, if hee say not the trueth: the thumbe belike, as the greater, representing the heauie masse of the bodie, and the little finger, the light and incorporeall substaunce of the soule.[67]

A counter-suggestible modern reader might find in this body language a certain symbolic appeal. The comedy is ramped up, however, when Morice introduces Bishop Bonner. Conventionally, oaths were sealed by kissing a copy of the New Testament. Bonner was so committed to hierarchy that he held that 'a Bishop may sweare (such is his priuiledge) *inspectis Euangelijs et non tactis,* bare sight of the booke without touche or kisse'.[68] With a surge of physical revulsion at the rags of superstition, Morice links swearing on the book with the other 'corporal oaths' taken by medieval Catholics with their hands on sacred objects.[69] 'The imposing of oathes vpon the rotten bones, ragges and reliques of their canonized and counterfeit saints', he declares, 'and vpon the Image of the Crucifige, is both foolishe and idolatrous' (57). From a secular perspective, this line looks hard to answer. It is not, however, itself secular, and cogent arguments are brought against it, from theology, tradition, and the Church Fathers in Richard Cosin's *Apologie for Svndrie Proceedings by Iurisdiction Ecclesiasticall* (1593).[70]

Rituals and distinctions of this kind could be translated straight into drama. In Thomas Randolph's *Aristippus: Or, The Ioviall Philosopher* (1630), a student called Simplicius attends an initiation in the Dolphin tavern. 'Giue him the oath,' Aristippus commands, after which a scholar instructs him to 'Lay your hand on the booke.' The book, naturally, is a bottle (Aristippus of Cyrene was a hedonist). Simplicius asks, in the spirit of Bonner, 'Will *tactus virtualis* serue the turne Sir?' and is told, 'No it must be *reale quid, et extra intellectum*.' After swearing 'to defend the honour of *Aristippus,* to the disgrace of Brewers, Alewiues, and Tapsters', he is invited to seal his oath: 'Kisse the booke. | *He Drinkes.*'[71] Those taking an oath of allegiance were probably required to kiss the book, because the ritual went back, wherever else, to medieval oaths of fealty—all of which makes it appropriate to this rite of initiation and submission. The same joke is found in *The Tempest*, where Caliban kisses the book (drinks from a leather bottle, as a book would be bound in leather)[72] when he is sworn in as Stefano's servant.

Morice's resistance to superstitious oaths is typical of hotter Protestants. Puritans had the reputation of disliking oaths of all sorts; even those imposed by the magistrate would be searched for a bruise to the conscience. The literary record mocks them for it. The 'Shee-Precise. Hypocrite' in John Earle's *Micro-cosmographie* 'accounts nothing Vices but Superstition, and an Oath, and thinkes Adultery a lesse sinne, then to sweare by my Truely'.[73] This sounds too absurd to be likely, but sometimes the puritans went beyond satire in their precision. Perkins does not allow commitments to be made 'by yea' or 'by no' because 'by' makes them oaths (compare 'by my Truely').[74] All you are allowed to give is your bare 'yea', 'nay'. Among various objections to puritanical pickiness and insubordination, it was held that this was a sort of formalism, paying more attention to the words of the oath than the truth it was designed to define. As Overbury says of 'A Precisian' in his *Characters*: 'He can better afford you tenne lies, then one oath, and dare commit any sinne gilded with a pretence of sanctitie.'[75] It was not until the Ranters, a generation or two later, that the Godly began to revel in their antinomian licence to swear.[76]

What instances of binding language did warm Protestants object to? On the whole, they are too decorous to explain. An unusually rich sampler of profanity is provided, however, by William Vaughan in his *Arraignment of Slander Periury Blasphemy* (1630):

> When they sweare by his head, as our swaggering swil-bowles will sweare by any part, they plaite another Crowne of thornes vpon his hallowed head. When they sweare by his foote, they naile his innocent feete to the Crosse anew.... When they sweare by senseles blocks and stocks, by the *Masse,* by *Gog* or *magog,* they detract from *Gods* honour, in attributing his due to dumbe and deafe Idols. But when they wilfully sweare betwixt party and partie in iudiciall proceedings, by *Gods* Sacraments, or forsweare themselues vpon his louely Legates, the Testament eyther olde or new, they blasphemously detract from *the Father, the Word, and the holy Ghost,* ...[77]

Vaughan does not give the impression of actually spending much time in the alehouse. The passage must constitute in part a Godly fantasy about what oaths were like among the irreverent. Yet we can take seriously the claim that medieval, Catholic survivals were widespread. Oaths, vows, and other phatics easily become fossilized. *Hamlet* alone gives us 'by the mass', 'by'r Lady', 'By Gis, and by Saint Charity'.[78] Presenting oaths of this sort was tactical on Vaughan's part. He could demonize swearing more effectively by showing profanities to be not just contrary to the commandments but doctrinally objectionable as well, so that swearing by God's sacraments, for example, detracts from the Father, the Word, and the Holy Ghost. Given the force of his Protestantism, it is ironic that the effects of swearing by the body of Christ *on* the body of Christ are represented with a corporeal immediacy that would not be out of place in a late medieval tract against swearing.[79]

There is a historical truth to be extracted from that faintly paradoxical conclusion, which has a bearing on Catholic oaths in Shakespeare. It should not be assumed, on the basis of the bulk and vehemence of Protestant writing against swearing, that the Romanists were indulgent. This claim is sometimes made for polemical purposes, but serious commentators such as Perkins are respectful of Catholic discussions, however misguided, of contentious practices and locutions. Divines of both a Roman and an English Protestant persuasion were engaged in parallel campaigns to clean up profanity. The Jesuit controversialist Robert Parsons, for instance, might be a puritan preacher when he laments that 'He shal heare at euerie mans mouth almost; vanitie, pride, detraction, enuie, deceit, dissimulation, wantonnesse, dissolution, lying, swearing, periurie, and blaspheming.'[80] Gillian Woods has reviewed the range of reactions that were current around the time of Shakespeare to the oath 'by the Mass'.[81] She reminds us that, for strenuous Protestants, such as Arthur Dent, author of the several-times reprinted *Plaine Mans Path-Way to Heauen* (1601), 'it is an hainous thing to sweare by idols: as S. *Mary*, Our Lady, by the Masse, by the Rood, &c.' Others regarded the formula as outworn and harmless. John Earle, for instance, a future bishop in the Church of England, wrote that 'by the Masse' and 'by our Ladie' were 'old out of date innocent othes'. There was not one view but several, depending on the zeal of those involved and in what context they encountered the phrase. The main thing that is missing from Woods's discussion is an acknowledgement that devoted Catholics would have been as firmly against the oath as puritans. If anything, they would have been firmer, because of their commitment to the mass.

We have evidence of this in a treatise by the Irish Jesuit Henry Fitzsimon, *The Iustification and Exposition of the Diuine Sacrifice of the Masse* (1611). 'For one thing I am very thankeful to our Reformers', he writes, with barely a flicker of irony, 'that they imitat lesse euerie day the corrupt custome of our louse Catholikes, who vsually sweare at euery occasion, by the *Masse*. Yet I ame sorie, that they are proceeded to a greater inconuenience, by what succeedeth.' What they have moved on to he explains by printing a poem by Sir John Harington later included in his *Epigrams* (1618). This is Fitzsimon's (slightly inferior) text:

> In Elder times an ancient custume t'was,
> to sweare in weightie maters by the Masse.
> But when Masse was put down, as Ould men note,
> They swore then by the Crosse of this graye grote.
> And when the Crosse was held like wise in scorne
> Then Faith, and trowth, for common oathes weare sworne.
> But now men banisht haue both faith and trouth,
> So that God damne me, is the common oath.
> So custome keeps Decorum, by gradation,
> Loosing masse, Crosse, Faith, trouth, followth damnation.[82]

Harington gives us a witty version of the story of cultural decline lamented almost a century earlier by Elyot, except that he is focused on the specific words used to bind. 'By the Masse' now typically survives in the mouths of old men like Polonius. 'By the Crosse', which is here pecuniary, found on the back of a groat, then gives way to the more Godly 'in Faith' and 'in trowth'. But now the swaggering captains with their lovelocks and scarves are afoot—Paroles and his friends from *All's Well*—and with them comes 'God damne me'. In its basics entirely traditional, the bare root of a self-curse ('May I be damned if I do not do *x*, or lie in saying *x*'), this mounts and twists into a newfangled, libertine defiance of God.

Rather than be guided by the likes of Vaughan, Fitzsimon, or even Harington, here is a sampler of my own: 'God's wounds!' (James I);[83] 'by my sword—' (Shakespeare's Antony) 'And target' (Cleopatra); 'Ile warrant thee by mine honour' (in Greene), 'by the white hand of Rosalind' (*As You Like It*), 'By the foot of Pharaoh' (Jonson's Bobadill), ''Od's pitykins' and 'Uds'death' (Shakespeare's Imogen, Webster's Flamineo), and—a joke from Middleton's *Puritan Widow*—'By gold'.[84] Actually, that last might count as a 'minced' oath, the sort of blasphemy-avoiding fudge that we still have in 'Gosh' (God) or 'by Golly' (by God) or 'by heck' (hell). Middleton's comedy makes much of the oath-allergic piety of London citizens, who threaten to 'fall down in a swoon' in the face of such profanities as Corporal Oath's 'by Vulcan's leather codpiece point' (1.3.35–9). The Corporal is the epitome of soldierly bad language, but his name is also a quibble on the 'corporal oath' sworn by the benighted on relics and crosses. As for Pieboard, he displays exactly the cupidity and hypocrisy of his kind when he discreetly swears 'By gold'. Minced oaths can be commonplace or playful ('Gogs blood'), but they can also speak of more than they say. When Ophelia sings of the men who seduce and abandon women, 'By Cock, they are to blame', there is a troubling double entendre (4.5.60). Aiming to avoid the sinfulness of oaths, while harnessing some of their force, and getting credit for being fastidious, minced oaths were so current that commentators were proportionately scathing: 'Be not decieved, God is not mocked; since... He taketh the wise in their own craftiness.'[85]

All these oaths are formulaic—even Corporal Oath's, and certainly those in Vaughan. For binding language to convince, it has to be conventional, a ledge of received wordage lodged in the flow of dialogue, never more than varying a formula. Minced oaths that follow the contours of a real oath are a minimal example of such variation. Almost all the oaths and vows in Shakespeare are not *his* but have a life and history beyond the plays. When Hector swears 'By all the everlasting gods' (at the start of this Introduction) it is the established nature of the formula that gives his promise weight. The 'untraded oath' that he swears to Menelaus, taunting him 'By Mars his gauntlet', is, by contrast, a mockery (4.7.61–2). When an oath or vow is fresh it is as likely to sound more suspect than sincere. That Romeo swears to Juliet 'by yonder blessèd moon... | That tips with silver all these fruit-tree tops' is inventive and exquisite (2.1.149–50). In performance it is charged with his yearning up to her balcony, his stretching finger-tips. But she is also right to doubt him.[86] His tongue is tipped with silver, and false to Rosaline. The oath, though efficiently articulated,[87] still acts as a species of lie-detector, drawn to an emblem of inconstancy which says more about the truth than Romeo would admit.

And yet, by Vulcan's codpiece, this is always a matter of degree. The familiarity of a formula can generate mistrust as well. When the derivative wording of an oath is put into a parodic context, the results can be devastating as well as entertaining. This is what Hermia says to Lysander when asked to meet him outside the city gates in *A Midsummer Night's Dream*:

> My good Lysander.
> I swear to thee by Cupid's strongest bow,
> By his best arrow with the golden head,
> By the simplicity of Venus' doves,
> By that which knitteth souls and prospers loves,
> And by that fire which burned the Carthage queen
> When the false Trojan under sail was seen;
> By all the vows that ever men have broke—
> In number more than ever women spoke—
> In that same place thou hast appointed me
> Tomorrow truly I will meet with thee. (1.1.168–78)

The brilliance of this partly lies in the use it makes of the catalogue—oaths are never enough to prove what is said, and the more of them you swear the less effective they seem—but partly in the deft movement from tacky divine imperfection to downright human falsity called in as a witness to truth. Everything that is sworn by is as predictable and unreliable as Aeneas, who in turn exemplifies the typical brokenness of men's vows. Yet the riff is dramatically alive because excitement builds as Hermia slips in so many cautions about love and faith that we wonder whether she will agree to meet Lysander, and, if so, in what convincing terms. The speech creates authority for the speaker in the asymmetry which it notes, that although women are allowed to vow they do not do so often, and do not, by implication, break their word. Hermia deals with the lack of female entitlement by insinuating, Who would want the right to vow, it is so absurd? All you need to say is 'truly'.

So Shakespeare's early audiences would not have regarded oaths, promises, protestations, and the rest as just one thing. Even if, like Elyot, they ran 'faythe', 'credence', 'truste', and 'loyaltie' all together into fidelity,[88] they would have distinguished between the speech acts, an asseveration (at least in principle) counting for less than an oath, a promise less than a vow. Even when oaths are exclamatory, percussive rather than deliberative, semantics make themselves felt. In a society more face to face than our own, where your honour, credit, and even survival depended on your ability to give your word and have it taken, people would have been responsive to the histories, associations, and (as the philosophers say) institutions represented by each kind of speech act. They would have been attuned to what such utterances as 'God damn me' and 'verily' tell you about the speakers. They would have known, as we still know, that Pistol's oaths are in an entirely different register from those of Hermia. Finally, and importantly for this book, without being experts like Parsons or Perkins, they would have recognized that there were disagreements about what constituted binding language, how it worked, and when it should be used.

The interest of early audiences in such language can be inferred not just from Shakespeare but from the drama of his contemporaries: Middleton, Jonson, Webster, Ford. The armature of oaths and vows in each case is different, reflecting choices of subject matter as well as authorial outlook. In city comedy, many of the decisive bonds are literal rather than oral. We see and hear more about legal instruments in such plays as *Volpone* or *Michaelmas Term* than we do in Shakespeare, with the exception of *The Merchant of Venice*. His is not a theatre of deeds, mortgages, and wills. The reason for the unusually high incidence of verbal bonds lies elsewhere. His attraction to the oral, vowing world of romance and to the matter of English history, with its fealty, coronation, and revenge oaths, was driven by several factors, but it has consequences for what he makes of binding language and for its developed profile in his output as compared with, for instance, Lyly.

The specific responsiveness of audiences is harder to calibrate, but not always impossible. Thus the seventeenth-century reader of the copy of the First Folio now held at Meisei University picked out vows, oaths, and accounts of swearing with special assiduity. He notes and underlines morals ('Mens Vowes are womens Traitors'), flags up points of advice ('oathes confirmers of false recknings'), and marks the verbal bonds that articulate plot, especially in the histories.[89] He is attracted to the sorts of dilemma that preoccupy early modern casuists, such as whether we should trust the word of someone who swears by a god that he knows we do not believe in (Aaron trusting Lucius at the end of *Titus*).[90] Of the Hector, Cassandra, and Andromache exchange, from which this Introduction began, he diligently notes: 'In what sort vowes are laufull and bind honor more deere to man then life'. What needs to be addressed next is whether 'man' in that note is gendered.

(v) Gender, status, and cultural difference

The evidence of the plays, as of social history, is that, while women were allowed to asseverate and promise, they were limited in the bargains or covenants they could make not just because of the inequitable ownership of property but because they were constrained in their capacity to swear. Hermia's 'By all the vows that ever men have broke— | In number more than ever women spoke' both registers a lack of entitlement and makes a virtue of it by jesting that the only profit that comes to men from their ability so freely to vow is that they are often perjured. Juliet's rebuke to Romeo, 'O swear not by the moon, th'inconstant moon' (2.1.151), shows a similar scepticism. She is willing to vow but not swear (169–70), and would rather he just told her he loved her than have their constancy subject to a speech act so often betrayed by men.

There is nothing new in these differences and inequalities. In ancient Greece, women swore by Artemis while the men invoked Zeus or Heracles; Roman women swore by Castor, the men by his twin brother Pollux, or, like the soldier in *Antony and Cleopatra*, by Hercules (3.7.67). To judge from Plautus, Tibullus, Juvenal, and Ovid, the goddesses Juno and Venus were mostly called upon by women though also by lovers and feminized men. In the corpus of ancient Greek drama, there is a lack of female oath-taking. As Judith Fletcher observes, 'the oath is both explicitly and implicitly congruent with masculine potency.... By analogy it becomes the parent of action, ... most of the oaths in Greek drama are sworn by men, a phenomenon that reflects the historical evidence.'[91] *Most*, but not all, which gives such female oaths as there are a peculiar, even transgressive force. The same is true of early modern drama, though the inhibitions on female swearing also encourage subtle reflections on the asymmetry.

It is characteristic of Shakespeare's impulse to engage critically with the socially given, that, in the best-known passage about women's oaths, we do not see a male character preventing a woman from swearing but encouraging her to let rip. When Lady Percy, at the court of Glendower, in *1 Henry IV*, insists that she will not sing, 'in good sooth', Hotspur replies

> Heart, you swear like a comfit-maker's wife: 'Not you, in good sooth!' and 'As true as I live!' and
> 'As God shall mend me!' and 'As sure as day!';
> And giv'st such sarcenet surety for thy oaths
> As if thou never walk'st further than Finsbury.
> Swear me, Kate, like a lady as thou art,
> A good mouth-filling oath, and leave 'in sooth'
> And such protest of pepper gingerbread
> To velvet-guards and Sunday citizens.
> Come, sing.
> LADY PERCY I will not sing. (3.1.242–54)

Far from stepping up to a profanity, Lady Percy resists her husband's railing by notching down to a bare statement. As so often in male–female dialogue around oaths, the mere declaration of a truth is shown to have greater power than Mars his gauntlet and Vulcan's codpiece.

Equally striking is the stress placed by Hotspur on rank. From Elizabeth I—whose wonted oath was 'God's death'[92]—to Margaret Cavendish, Duchess of Newcastle, noble women had a reputation for mouth-filling oaths. With the queen one might suspect an element of kingly role-play were the pattern of elite practice not so clear. While modest citizens' wives, like their male companions, Pieboard and his friends, would *troth* and *sooth* for emphasis, noble women would cry *zounds* with the boldest—though the fact that this was remarked on indicates a stretching of the boundaries and a degree of tension about what was acceptable. When gentle or noble women are disguised as boys in Shakespeare, they avoid or skirt profanity when binding themselves to sooths. 'By my troth, and in good earnest, and so God mend me, and by all pretty oaths that are not dangerous,' swears Rosalind (as Ganymede) to Orlando, mocking the decorum she observes. 'By innocence I swear, and by my youth,' says Viola as Cesario.[93]

One widely promulgated belief was that noblemen and gentlemen were of all social groups the most likely to be truth-tellers. They were so oath-worthy that, in some cases, it was not necessary for them to swear. As Steven Shapin notes in his *Social History of Truth*:

> Peacham reported it as routinely accepted that 'we ought to give credit to a noble or gentleman before any of the inferior sort.' Modern historians note that 'one of the traditional privileges of the aristocrat had been his right to testify in court without bond and without witnesses.' His word might be taken as sufficient in itself, requiring no voucher and no external support.[94]

Many said that the well born were truth-tellers by nature. They were ethically as well as physiologically superior. Others stressed nurture, arguing that those of high status were brought up to value *fides* ('faith', for the classically tutored). Social factors did play a part, however prejudicially the point was made. Noblemen and gentlemen had honour at stake in their word. To accuse someone of lying, to 'give the lie', was, as we shall see in Chapter 8, enough to provoke a duel.

Tradesmen, servants, and the like were not members of the community of truth—as far as the elites were concerned—because they had so little honour to lose but also because they were subject to pressure from their masters or economic need. They lacked the unconstraint that bound a gentleman to tell the truth. Dromio of Ephesus in *The Comedy of Errors* is joking about his status as a slave, a 'bondman', who should not go surety for Antipholus of Ephesus' debts (be a 'bondman' in another sense), when he tells his master, as they are bound with ropes, 'I am here entered in bond for you' (4.4.120). Though he is bound in several ways his word is not his bond but a jest. 'There was wide agreement', Shapin notes, 'that the servant's word was *not* his bond, and that the reason for this distinction between masters and servants was the latter's dependence and compromised integrity of action.... As one early seventeenth-century guide cautioned, "to take a man [servant] of his own word, is the worst of all."'[95] The oath which a man took to swear himself into service reduced the credit of his oaths. In court, the word of a subordinate would count for less than that of a master.

Yet the condescension of the conduct books will have passed ordinary people by as they gave testimony or struck bargains or became betrothed by exchanging rings and vows. Literature aimed at the middling sort could be sceptical about the honour code of the nobility, finding honesty among the modest. In Shakespeare there is plenty of truth in servants, and a lot of 'i'faith', 'By my soul', and 'By my troth' to go with it. There is also—though not always—scruple among those who have taken oaths of service when required to do intolerable things.[96] Sometimes clowns parody the more high-flown formulations of the honourable: 'Lance, by mine honesty, welcome to Milan,' cries Speed, in *The Two Gentlemen of Verona*. 'Forswear not thyself, sweet youth,' Lance replies, 'for I am not welcome' (2.5.1–2). More often, low-life characters observe their own decorum. The murderers of Clarence urge themselves and each other on with a defiantly blasphemous ''Swounds' (*Richard III*, 1.4.119, 136). 'O Lord, sir, I'll be sworn upon all the books in England,' cries the honest tapster Francis (*1 Henry IV*, 2.5.45–6).

Because women, with a few exceptions—Queen Elizabeth among them—were dependent on fathers and husbands for their social and legal status, they were disadvantaged as word-givers. They resembled, in this respect, the inferiors who were bound to their masters or who relied economically on others. Usually their exclusion from the circle of trust was tacit, but some conduct literature explicitly questioned women's truthfulness, and there was a long philosophical tradition—going back to Aristotle—that regarded women as 'more false of speech, more deceptive' than men.[97] The casual misogyny of the period was drawn to, and legitimized by, this supposed failing. To the question 'What are womens vowes?', the obvious answer was 'Words written in the wind.' 'What are their promisses?',

'Carracters figured in the ayre, and figures grauen in the snow.'[98] In the *Rich Cabinet* of 1616, 'Oathes are monstrous in a woman, in whom impudency ioyned with prophanation makes them the more odious and loathsome.'[99]

The pressure of this assumption can certainly be felt in Shakespeare. Timon says that Alcibiades' whores will 'swear' to do what he wants in exchange for gold (destroy Athens, or anything), but they are not, as he puts it, 'oathable'.[100] They cannot be trusted on oath. Their willingness to swear is an index of their unreliability (see p. 359). Yet the plays are often nuanced. Doll Tearsheet's and Mistress Quickly's asseverations are mild ('By my troth', 'i' good truth', 'O' my word', 'I'faith'),[101] and the kind-hearted Hostess is patently truthful when, pursuing an action of debt against Falstaff, she reminds him, in front of the Lord Chief Justice (no less), how 'Thou didst swear to me upon a parcel-gilt goblet, sitting in my Dolphin chamber, at the round table, by a sea-coal fire, upon Wednesday in Wheeson week, when the Prince broke thy head for liking his father to a singing-man of Windsor—thou didst swear to me then, as I was washing thy wound, to marry me, and make me my lady thy wife' (*2 Henry IV*, 2.1.79–84). What she says, and adds, does not show her to be hopeless at relating history[102] but rather the giver of testimony that circumstantiates an unprovable promise and consequently follows, not unusually for Shakespeare, though in scrambled form, the received, classical rules for arguments of proof: 'causes, time, place, occasion, instruments, means'.[103]

If the standard Elizabethan procedures were followed, Mistress Quickly's testimony would be taken down, put into legal form by a clerk, sworn, subscribed to, and presented in court—a process which, it has been argued, both resembles and informs the representation of events onstage by actors.[104] Whether or not that large claim about early modern theatre holds, it is worth noticing that, in workaday legal experience, sworn testimony did not always reproduce the actual words of a plainant or witness. Though the point was controversial, binding language could be attached to the gist or essentials of a case.[105] The Lord Chief Justice has no difficulty in concluding that Sir John has 'practised upon the easy-yielding spirit of this woman' (105). The judgement is dramatically compelling because it finds an old whore to be oathable. Whether Mistress Quickly would have won her action, had it come to trial, is, however, to be doubted. It is common in the period to find sworn testimony by women undermined, not least in court, where younger women would be asked whether they knew what an oath meant in its solemnity and legal force.[106] Again this is a structure of distrust that Shakespeare provocatively represents, in the attempt of Isabella and Mariana to have their deposition against Angelo accepted in the final scene of *Measure for Measure*.

Women can say that they will or would swear, and then not actually swear, in Shakespeare, earning by the undertaking something of the seriousness of an oath. After the Act to Restrain Abuses, there is a levelling of the genders which creates a new dynamic. As we shall see in Chapter 17, it is enabling for Hermione to be able to say 'A lady's "verily"'s | As potent as a lord's.'[107] Even before that, Shakespeare excels in scripting exchanges where the male ability and impulse to swear is tempered by, for instance, embarrassment or uncertainty and there is a mutual twining of bonds which catches the way relationships start:

BEATRICE As strange as the thing I know not. It were as possible for me to say I loved nothing so well as you, but believe me not, and yet I lie not. I confess nothing nor I deny nothing. I am sorry for my cousin.

BENEDICK By my sword, Beatrice, thou lovest me.

BEATRICE Do not swear and eat it.

BENEDICK I will swear by it that you love me, and I will make him eat it that says I love not you.

BEATRICE Will you not eat your word?[108]

Beatrice's riddling around asseveration entices Benedick's attention, and prompts him to swear an oath which itself creates flirtatious wordplay. The bonds of language entangle them more engagingly than Benedick's binding exclamation 'By my sword'.

So much for gender and status. What of cultural difference? When Elyot says that Turks and Saracens are better at keeping their promises and covenants than Christians, he is engaging in denunciation rather than comparative anthropology. But argument about what constituted legitimate binding language—large-scale, substantive argument, thrashed out in practice as well as theory, to which, in general terms, Shakespeare's plays contributed—did encourage writers to think comparatively, and this gave drive and purpose to accounts of other cultures. In his compilation of the reports of travellers and antiquarians, *Purchas his Pilgrimage* (1613), for instance, Samuel Purchas reflects on English practice when listing Islamic oaths: 'by the order of Angels, by the Alcoran, by the blowing windes, by the watery clouds, . . . '. He scarcely dare mention them, he says, lest they encourage extravagant swearing in 'our *Gull-gallants* of these times'.[109] With corporal oaths, he is equally engaged. On Goa, 'When they take their oathes, they are set within a circle of ashes, on the pauement, and laying a few ashes on their head, the other on their breasts, sweare by their *Pagodes* to tell the truth' (415). Among the kings of Malabar, he finds a coronation oath involving a ring and candle that any reader would compare with those in England (422). Sworn rituals of trial by ordeal resemble practices that antiquarians found in early medieval Europe.[110]

Travellers and overseas traders often found themselves a long way from the systems of trust and law that could be taken for granted in England. They encountered other nations at the limits of supply and military support, where giving and taking pledges could be a crucial aid to survival. It is consequently not surprising that, in Hakluyt's *Principal Nauigations* (1599–1600), peoples are so often characterized as true or false in word. In Japan they 'keepe their promises'.[111] Despite an exchange of hostages, the Africans near Cape Verde do not (II, Eee6r). Neither do the Moors of Barbary, even after 'casting vp their eyes to heauen, and after looking downe vpon the ground, as though they had sworne by heauen and earth, promising peace' (III, Rrr1r).[112] Closer to home, English authors warned, the flattering, Machiavellian Italians, the hot-blooded, papistical Spaniards, the Greeks of Constantinople ('*Chi fida in Grego, sara intrigo*'),[113] and the unreliable French, were negative exemplars. 'It hath bene an old tricke of the French', Robert Dallington declares, 'to obserue neither promise, nor oath.'[114]

Fidelity and truth-telling were acknowledged to be culturally variable. But was the dishonesty of other peoples a matter of innate wickedness or were social factors in play? Hakluyt, for instance, says that the Japanese keep their promises because they live simple lives, limited by poverty. How should the differences be negotiated? Jean Hotman, a French diplomat who lived for a time in England and served Leicester in the Low Countries, declared in 1603 that an ambassador should be 'sparing in promising and religious in obseruing that once he hath promised'. He noted that it was not easy for him to take his own advice, because he was acculturated by expectations not far from Dallington's description of the French:

> The Germans and other Nations of that Climate make more account of a promise made, then wee doe, who most commonly serue our turnes therewith to ridde our handes of such as are importunate.... the Swissers... do note downe, the place, day and houre, that they were spoken with, yea euery word of an Ambassador, still seeking to engage him in his promise: and do carefully keepe the letters which hee writeth vnto them: and take hold of the very hopes that are giuen vnto them: and would make the same to stand insteed of a bill or obligation: how much more a promise written, or his word giuen?[115]

The comparative element in these compilations and treatises resembles what we find in Shakespeare. His classical plays have their oath-sacrifices and rituals, alien to Christian sensibility. Portia's appeal to be of Brutus' counsel on the grounds of their 'great vow' (i.e. the 'bond of marriage') invokes a Roman constancy that she has proved by giving herself, and keeping secret, a voluntary wound on her thigh.[116] As we shall see in Chapter 16, Coriolanus is driven to disaster by the tragic potential of Roman *fides*. When the oath-breaking lords in *Love's Labour's Lost* disguise themselves as Russians, the supposed mendacity of that people might be part of the joke (pp. 108–9). Like Purchas, Shakespeare makes something of the distinctiveness of Jewish oaths (Chapter 7). Elizabethan observers were interested—and military men had to be—in Irish customs of oath-swearing, notably by the hand. The Irish were believed to be faithful to one another and perjurious with their enemies. All this leaves traces in *Henry V* (Chapter 9). In *Hamlet*, pledges are given not just by the word but by quaffing alcohol (Chapter 8). The notorious drinking culture of the Danes is integrated into the play's other means by which promises are given and forgotten. There are hot-blooded honour-oaths in such African/Mediterranean plays as *Othello*, while more temperate, even self-mocking routines are deployed in Arden and Eastcheap. A shift of only a few miles can have a remarkable effect. When Falstaff moves to Windsor, in *The Merry Wives*, he sheds his profanities and becomes almost respectable, castigating Pistol for 'your red-lattice phrases, and your bold-beating oaths' (2.2.25).

(vi) Scholarship

Surprisingly little work has been done on Shakespeare's binding language. Frances A. Shirley's *Swearing and Perjury in Shakespeare's Plays* (1979) gives a useful account of early modern attitudes. Critically, however, she has a true-or-false mindset that best fits the early plays. The approach can lead her astray, as when she says of the Cressida–Diomed scene, 'There is no doubt about the reaction we are supposed to have as Cressida's lust overcomes any prior commitments.'[117] That we now know more about Cressida's commitment to Troilus is in large part due to the excellent work done over the last couple of decades on marriage contracts and drama.[118] The troth-plight between the lovers, with Pandarus acting as a witness, never mentions marriage, but it deliberately, confusingly resembles an Elizabethan hand-fasting.

Research into spousals, however, has underinvestigated the role played by binding language[119] in these rituals.

The growing body of scholarship about early modern drama and law is at one remove from this book but it sheds important side-lights.[120] Much can be learned from the work of Lorna Hutson and others on late Elizabethan hostility to expurgation (swearing your innocence) in the ecclesiastical courts and the common law belief that promises were secured not by oaths or vows but by consideration: by cash, goods, or services.[121] Any serious Shakespearean can expect, these days, to read about the action of *assumpsit*[122] and *fidei laesio* in the ecclesiastical courts,[123] though it remains an open question how far changes in legal culture went into Shakespeare's plays—affecting, it may be, the encouragement given to audiences to infer obligations from actions and exchanges.[124] When thinking about the problem raised at the start of this Introduction, it is clearly worth knowing about legal contexts as we try to gauge the reaction of what was most likely an Inns of Court theatre audience[125] to Hector's vow to fight the Greek leaders. For Elizabethan common lawyers, as for Hobbes, and the legal philosopher P. S. Atiyah more recently, Hector's obligation would be minimal, given that the Greeks' only loss if he unarmed would be a disappointed expectation.[126]

One other book-length study that I must single out is by my namesake, William Kerrigan. *Shakespeare's Promises* (1999) gives a bold, under-historicized account of vows in *Othello* and bonds in *The Merchant of Venice*. Its readings are distorted by the unsustainable thesis that the plays are drawn back to the Christian belief that those who break their word will be punished.[127] Such plays as *All's Well* do show, at what can be for modern audiences excessive and obvious length, the social price paid by characters like Paroles who abuse the oaths and vows that were so important in binding together early modern society. But to look for metaphysical payback is to find Falstaff sighing, in *The Merry Wives of Windsor*, 'I never prospered since I forswore myself at primero' (4.5.82–3). Hector keeps his oath and is slaughtered; Achilles breaks one vow to keep another, then goes back on his word, and triumphs.

This is not to say that the religious aspect of oaths had no effect. As Brian Cummings has shown, in a fine essay on More and Shakespeare, connections can be made between the trial and burning of heretics in the early sixteenth century and the heated, improperly conducted processes of inquisition in *Othello*, where boundaries between private conscience and public oath-taking are violated.[128] Larger theses can be advanced. In *Shakespeare and the Grammar of Forgiveness* (2011), Sarah Beckwith argues that, after the English Reformation, it was hard to see how 'Confessing, forgiving, absolving, initiating, swearing' could count as 'performative utterances'. Because authority was no longer located 'in the speech acts of the sacramental priesthood', there was a quest for community in the theatre. Shakespeare 'takes up this terrible burden and gift of human relating when nothing but language secures or grounds human relations'.[129] It leaves out a great deal of religious belief and material culture to claim that, during Shakespeare's lifetime, language alone secured human relations.

The neglect of a big topic is a sufficient justification for addressing it. There are reasons, however, for thinking that this is a good time to take up my theme. First, new work by historians has probed swearing as a social practice.[130] Previously, too much reliance was placed on the line of treatises that runs from Becon's *Inuectyue agenst Swearing* (1543) to Edmund Calamy's *Practical Discourse Concerning Vows* (1697). Armed with this material, and limited data from social history, Christopher Hill and others argued for a declining belief in the power of oaths due to their over-imposition by kings and parliaments, desacralization, and a new emphasis on interest and contract.[131] It is likely that such changes occurred. But when Defoe argued against the use of oaths on grounds of reason and politeness, he was responding to deeper shifts in conduct and morality, caught up in evolving attitudes to virtuous respectability. He develops an objection to swearing heard increasingly in the later seventeenth century: that it is *unreasonable*. Why would you expect to be more firmly believed for invoking God?[132] Blasphemy was not the only way of giving utterance an edge. Scatology and sexuality were becoming the primary locus of 'bad language'.[133]

There are contexts to consider, because oaths and vows can be frivolous in one setting yet solemn in another. Thanks to David Martin Jones and Edward Vallance, we now know a great deal more about oaths of allegiance and supremacy, bonds of association, and national covenants—relevant to *Sir Thomas More* and *Henry VIII*, but also to *Titus Andronicus*.[134] Oaths of office have been analysed by Conal Condren.[135] Historians of print culture have shown how liberally copies of the oaths taken by constables like Dogberry and those made freemen of the city were distributed in London.[136] Laura Gowing has given us insights into the gendered aspects of oath-taking.[137] Victoria Kahn uses both historical and literary material to investigate 'the social and linguistic mechanisms of obligation' in the mid-seventeenth century.[138] And John Spurr has shown, in a series of rich essays, how willingly or reluctantly people took oaths, and how context-dependent swearing was. Marriage vows were one thing, dicers' oaths another.[139] Any attempt to trace a decline or desacralization must acknowledge the potency of oaths and vows in specific situations right through the seventeenth century.

The second reason for feeling timely is that moral philosophy has reacted against Kantian, deontological thinking when it comes to verbal commitments, and it now connects more clarifyingly with a period in which face-to-face relationships and defeasibility were key. God is far more important in the casuistical literature than in J. L. Austin's *How to Do Things with Words* (1962). But Shakespeare's use of binding language still has points of contact with Austin and with the arguments between John Searle, Jacques Derrida, and Judith Butler on speech acts and social performance. When Sanderson starts *De Juramento* by declaring that an oath is 'a religious act', he is explicitly modifying Cicero's 'An Oath... is a religious affirmation' (5). Like Austin, he is wary of imputing intention[140] and believes, almost always, that the speech act binds, regardless.[141] Both are ordinary language philosophers who give the benefit of the doubt to usage. Sanderson acutely considers whether '*In faith*' is an oath, since it should formally be '*By my faith*', and asks why '*In faith*' should be customarily so taken when '*In truth*' is regarded as an asseveration. In each case, he concludes, how formulae are understood in use is decisive (167–9, 174–5).

A third reason for feeling timely has to do with our willingness to acknowledge the inextricability of real-life performatives and speech acts scripted for performance. It is a token of this that Sanderson's doubts about '*In faith*' applied equally in the theatre. When Charles I overruled the Master of the Revels, Sir Henry Herbert's expurgation of Davenant's *The Wits* (1634), Sir Henry put it on record that 'The king is pleasd to take *faith*, *death*, *slight* for asseverations, ... but, under favour, [I] conceive them to be oaths.'[142] With some loss as well as gain, theatre studies have shifted attention away from what happens in the playhouse into performativity more largely.[143] Oaths, vows, and the like are performatives that are also performed, onstage and off. The desire to keep these phenomena separate may be understandable in philosophers. It is there in Austin's insistence that performatives uttered on stage are '*parasitic* upon... normal use'.[144] This was a false dichotomy ripe for Derrida to deconstruct, and for Judith Butler and Eve Sedgwick to think with and against in their performative accounts of identity.[145]

Where did Shakespeare learn about the binding language that punctuates and propels his plays? Here biographical scholarship can help us. The earliest life record we have concerns his baptism (in 1564), when, as required by the Book of Common Prayer, his godparents took vows on his behalf. One of the latest, in 1612, finds him giving sworn, duly cautious, evidence in a breach of promise case.[146] Shakespeare learned from the church and the law courts, from the street, the market-place, and the tavern, but also from the classics. Cicero, Seneca, Plutarch, and Ovid all figure in this book. From Quintilian, if not from Aristotle, he would have learned about the tactical advantages of taking an oath in court.[147] Aristotelian tradition is greatly interested in the relative value of the oath, as 'inartificial proof'.[148] The Tudor rhetoricians are, by comparison, disinclined to discuss oaths and their uses. That they are on a spectrum with profanity, and more immediately a topic for moralists, must be one reason for this. Even so, Henry Peacham gives a full account of the make-up of oaths, vows, and imprecations in the 1593 *Garden of Eloquence*.[149] When reading *The Boke Named the Gouernour*, Shakespeare must have encountered Elyot's influential discussion of *fides*, and how foul-mouthed 'Children . . . do playe with the armes and bones of Christe, as they were chery stones', while witnesses and juries perjure themselves.[150] Holinshed and Montaigne will have informed him. But he must also have learned about oaths and vows, perhaps supremely, in the theatre.

The anti-theatrical writers, from Gosson to Prynne, encourage us to recognize, whatever we make of their antipathy, that the playhouse was not just a place where young gentlemen, card players, and drinkers went to mill about: on stage, swearing by the heathen gods and taking the Lord's name in vain set a bad example.[151] In his *Anatomie of Abuses* (1583), Stubbes says you should go to the theatre 'if you will learn to playe the vice, to swear, teare, and blaspheme, both Heauen and Earth'.[152] Even the non-puritan John Earle thought of the playhouse as a hotbed of oaths. 'His Parts find him oathes and good words', he wrote in his character of 'A Player', 'which he keeps for his vse and Discourse, . . . He is tragicall on the Stage, but rampant in the Tyring-house, and sweares oathes there which he neuer con'd.'[153] Friends of the playhouse reversed this libel. Plays, according to John Taylor, the Water Poet, show 'stabbing, drabbing, dicing, drinking' and, at the end of the line, 'swearing' in their true, instructive horror.[154] He could point to the tipsy Cassio in *Othello*, quarrelsome and 'high in oath', then bitterly rebuking himself (2.3.218, 243–90). But no one will seriously believe that Shakespeare was drawn to swearing because he wanted to be didactic. More relevant is Nashe's defence of the stage, where he celebrates a sequence in

The Famous Victories of Henry the Fifth, a play from the 1580s well known to Shakespeare, in which the King of France and the Dauphin take an oath on Henry's sword: 'what a glorious thing it is to haue *Henrie* the fifth represented on the Stage, leading the French King prisoner, and forcing both him and the Dolphin to sweare fealty.'[155] It is a vivid reminder of the theatrical, even the histrionic power of oaths, which this book aims to unlock.

(vii) Perplexities

Shakespeare was not often drawn to the oath as primary utterance, to the moment, so important to moralists, when an isolated character gives his word under the eye of God. He was more interested in 'joint actions', where speech act and doubt go together. Admittedly, there is Hamlet, alone after seeing the ghost, declaring, 'Now to my word: | It is "Adieu, adieu, remember me". | I have sworn't' (1.5.111–13). It is typical of Shakespeare, however, to destabilize the situation by having Hamlet rebut while echoing the ghost, who wants to be revenged. And the prince's words are further confounded because this initiates a long, stagey sequence that parodies the sort of swearing presented by *The Famous Victories*, as Horatio and Marcellus are required to swear on Hamlet's sword that they will keep the secret of the ghost.

The connection between Hamlet's swearing and the repeated injunctions by prince and ghost which push the scene into fearful comedy are often reinforced in performance by having him swear on his own sword. This impulse to externalize and take hold of something solid goes with the performativity of oaths and vows even outside the theatre. Early modern commentators were struck by the scriptural, classical, and more far-flung evidence of swearers touching Abraham's thigh, holding up their hands, or casting away a stone.[156] In origin these gestures are mnemonic. They made the speech acts easier to recall, in primarily oral societies.[157] But they readily elided with the sacred as people swore on missals or altars. Traditionally, Hamlet swears not just on his sword but the cross of its hilt. He is giddily beside himself and needs to grip his weapon because his distrust of Claudius has been vindicated but also, more obscurely, because we are not quite ourselves when we asseverate or promise. We are trying to manifest a truth, or lean into the future self that will deliver on the vow. We utter 'by heaven' differently from saying 'by' and 'heaven', as though making it citational.

There is an impulse to phatic density which makes the voice a material projection and gives the sworn word the weight of a pledge.[158] But whatever the aspiration, the voice cannot itself be a bond. The speech act, so complete for Austin, is dramatically potent because insufficient. Even in plays less sophisticated than *Hamlet*, there is an invitation to audiences to gauge the voice against word, hand, and eye, and impute degrees of purpose.[159]

An oath is framed by a formula which gives the language of the speech act something of the firmness of the God or the honour which is called upon to secure it. The mnemonic, ritual context is brought into the utterance. That the form of an oath or vow is given makes it already external enough to be uttered as a thing. This is why I can give you my word—even without subscribing to a bond. At the end of *Measure* and *All's Well*, when Isabella, Mariana, Diana, and Helena utter binding, opaque truths, Shakespeare brings out the quasi-magical aspects of such formulae,[160] which stem not just from an affinity with incantation but because they jump the gap between doubt and truth and promise to deliver the future. Yet the quality of the performance affects the quality of the performative. I can say 'by heaven' with a frivolous as well as a solemn air, or impetuously like Hamlet to his friends (1.4.62). This makes oaths and vows an acutely sensitive resource for judgements of intention by audiences, and a subtle opportunity for the actor, who can qualify the absoluteness of asseveration or promise enshrined in the speech act.

So when Hamlet calls upon Horatio and the soldier to swear, the situation oscillates unstably. They do swear, by custom at least, 'in faith', to keep what they have seen secret, but are then asked to swear on his sword. As men of honour, they are mildly insulted. Does Hamlet, like Sanderson, doubt that 'in faith' is binding? The prince quickly discovers that repetition and emphasis will not secure an oath. As it happens, in all three early texts of the play, Horatio and Marcellus are not given 'I swear', or anything like it, to say. Every time the ghost bellows 'Swear', there is a flurry of bewildered reaction, yet no word, it seems, is uttered. Casuists did allow that, when you could not speak to swear, you could nod or raise your hand.[161] Perhaps we might take, then, the laying of their hands on the sword as an oath. There are word and deed quibbles in Hamlet's instruction, 'Indeed, upon my sword, indeed'[162]—*sword*, *word*, and *sworn* were close in pronunciation,[163] and *sword* was often spelt *sweard*.[164] But if the actors do opt for the gesture, the rest of their body language can hardly be affirmative. Their posture is going to qualify any utterance in word or deed. Austin regards the body as effectively a cipher, included in or cohering with the speech act rather than seething away around it in an interpretatively dissonant, theatrically involving, way. Judith Butler more accurately observes that 'the body rhetorically exceeds the speech act it also performs'.[165]

The mobility of this scene, as the actors range about, makes palpable for the audience how uncontaining oaths can be. The prince is playing catch-up with a speech act while his friends run away from the ghost. It is not just the taking but the keeping. As the action spins about, Hamlet—who will soon enough break his vows to Ophelia, and probably his word to the ghost—anticipates the temptations. He starts to sound like Polonius as he spells out all the ways in which his associates should not betray their word. They must swear not even to hint at what drives his antic disposition, he says, putting on a mad little pageant,

> With arms encumbered thus, or this headshake,
> Or by pronouncing of some doubtful phrase
> As 'Well, we know' or 'We could an if we would',
> Or 'If we list to speak', or 'There be, an if they might',
> Or such ambiguous giving out, . . . (175–9)

The sworn word is meant to be brief and sufficient. As Sanderson puts it, '*Simplicity above all things becometh an Oath*' (37). In practice—better say 'in performance'—it summons up a mass of supplementary glossing to cover the eventualities. We could be historical and notice how oaths imposed by the state became increasingly elaborate, to guard against equivocation and mental reservation.[166] But the drive to qualification goes deeper. Because of psychological and communicative ambiguities, the binding word generates verbiage.

Love's Labour's Lost is a classic case. Charged with courting Jaquenetta, in the King of Navarre's park, when 'It was proclaimed a year's imprisonment to be taken with a wench' (1.1.270–1), the clever yokel Costard says he was taken with a damsel (also proclaimed), virgin (ditto), and maid (who will not serve his turn). The proclamation of the oath, extrapolating it as law, must have been a copious document.[167] Meanwhile, the sworn word dissolves back into the ordinary language that gives it grammar and function. If we did not say 'by' and 'heaven' we could not swear 'by heaven'. That binding speech is grounded in the lexis and syntax of usage is one source of its semantic authority, but it also exposes it to the risk of being reduced to empty signs. When Armado tells the page boy Mote that he has sworn to study with the King for three years, the tender juvenile can reply: 'how easy it is to put "years" to the word "three" and study "three years" in two words, the dancing horse will tell you' (1.2.48–50). The lords go further down the same path, once they have fallen in love with the ladies. 'Vows are but breath, and breath a vapour is,' Longueville declares in his sonnet (4.3.63).

We are getting into a nest of paradoxes congenial to a dramatist who was drawn to plurality and interpenetrating ambiguities. The word that cannot be fixed is subverted by its performance and needs massive supplements to explicate. It is a forceful commitment of the self couched in markedly derivative language. Oaths and vows can reinforce the very doubt they are meant to allay. They gain you credit, but put you into debt. They are sociable, joint actions which it can be narcissistic to follow through (as with Hector). Expletives that ease pain,[168] and that release whatever chemistry goes with making a commitment,[169] they can be surprisingly indecisive. The act of asseveration can make people and characters aware that they only think they know what they know. When the speech acts are promissory, they can be substitutes for action, even substitutes for a decision to act.

To rely too much on vowing is, we might say, *young*. It represents a development which, for the psychoanalytically minded, is regressive because it undoes the hard-earned distinction between word and deed. It falls back on 'magical thinking', and substitutes a binding word for the moral judgements of maturity.[170] Oaths make claims on truth which expose you to being false, or claims on a future which 'reckoning time, whose millioned accidents | Creep in 'twixt vows and change decrees of kings' is likely to prove hubristic.[171] When, as in *Troilus*, what's past and what's to come are strewn with husks and ruin, and faith and troth are only of the moment (4.7.50–2), vows and oaths have no purchase. Time does not connect. The play unfolds in what is virtually a space of interruption,[172] where binding language contributes to the sense of events suspended, hung up between declaration and act.

Engagements and promises broken bring more than the loss of the expected. Like Troilus betrayed, as he believes, by Cressida, they can put the whole cosmos in doubt by breaking the 'bonds' of heaven (5.2.156). Because 'we become promising through the promises made to us',[173] the prospect of things not yet had can help us bring them about, but also more. Are solicited promises promises, or acts of ventriloquism? Does a promise generate an obligation, or should the word merely be taken as evidence of an intention? Grand promises are brave or delusional, and may carry a charge of violence, because they have to control so many circumstances to deliver what is undertaken.[174] One legitimate response to them is complacently to anticipate their failure. We promise things in order to remember them but also to shelve and forget them, leaving ourselves room to flourish beyond the strictures of a bond, or just (as Bacon observed) to carry on doing what we usually do: 'a Man would wonder, to heare Men Professe, Protest, Engage, Give Great Words, and then Doe iust as they haue Done before: As if they were Dead Images, and Engines moued onely by the wheeles of *Custome*.'[175]

For all that they can be evasive, vows, assurances, and promises are close to creativity because they conjure into language matters not yet known or done. Yet there is dead weight in there too. When we promise we put the present, as it becomes the past, onto the neck of the future. What, however, in Shakespeare, is static? The meaning of what we vow is mutable because relative. When I promise you *x* it is not *x* but the prospect of what *x* will be. Then when I perform *x* (if I do) it will have absorbed the value of my fidelity and it will also have shifted in meaning because much else in life will have changed. Swearing is the honourable man's privilege and mark of status. He lives a life of risk and purpose in which the stake is himself, his standing. Yet not if he vows by proxy, or fulfils his oath by proxy, as Henry V does to Williams through Fluellen. Then vowing gets interestingly problematic because it displays in acute form the always discernible fact that an oath or vow is independent of those involved in the joint action. As Nerissa says to Graziano, though not for her, yet for his oaths, he should not have given away her ring.[176] This does not mean, of course, that there is no way out of oaths and engagements; they can be ways out in themselves, ways of avoiding responsibility, of saying that you are bound by a promise to God or your past self to act in a certain way. The binding word simplifies life by removing deliberation. Othello's oaths to punish Desdemona are only the most conspicuous case.

Those are impassioned utterances. Oaths and vows can be outbursts, excesses of agitation, as Thomas Wright and Robert Burton notice in their lively accounts of gamesters,[177] yet they spring from our need for security, the drive to know and plan. Along with prophecies and curses, they consequently feed into Shakespeare's characteristic preference (as Coleridge put it) for expectation over surprise.[178] It would be a mistake to imagine, however, that time under a vow is the same as time without one. Promised things are more exciting than gifts because anticipation is a nervous pleasure.

Then postponement stales and the arrival of what was promised or engaged will be an anticlimax. This is very Troilus. By the same token, though not quite, a truth sworn does not have the same weight as one inferred. It might well weigh less. Yet sworn assertions, like promises, are not just a matter of what is said, but the tying of people into bonds. Which is what this book is about.

2

Early Revenge

3 Henry VI to *Titus Andronicus*

Shakespeare's first, full-blown revenge tragedy is *Titus Andronicus* (1593–4?). You can find the beginnings of *Titus*, however, and even elements of *Hamlet*, in the collaborative *Henry VI* plays (*c.*1591), where feudalism is crossed with feuding, revenge and ambition rip through England, and binding language proliferates. Oaths of allegiance sworn to Henry[1] are undone within the action, thwarted, or compounded by vengeance. Salisbury shakes off his fealty and joins the Yorkists by arguing, in orthodox terms, 'It is great sin to swear unto a sin, | But greater sin to keep a sinful oath.'[2] Richard of Gloucester, the future Richard III, likewise tells his father that 'An oath is of no moment, being not took | Before a true and lawful magistrate.' Since Henry is not a legitimate king, the oath that York took before him to live quietly during his reign was 'vain and frivolous'.[3] Faction and revenge cut through fealty and order. Yet they also sustain loyalty to the crown.

Take the example of the Cliffords. In *2 Henry VI*, 5.1, Old Clifford stands with Henry as the Yorkists defy him at court. He is killed in battle by York, and when his son finds the body he promises a revenge as unrelenting as the violence of Medea when she dismembered and scattered the corpse of her brother:

> Henceforth I will not have to do with pity.
> Meet I an infant of the house of York,
> Into as many gobbets will I cut it
> As wild Medea young Absyrtus did.
> In cruelty will I seek out my fame.
> Come, thou new ruin of old Clifford's house,
> *He takes [his father's body] up on his back*
> As did Aeneas old Anchises bear,
> So bear I thee upon my manly shoulders. (5.3.56–63)

Shakespearean in authorship or not,[4] this draws on grammar-school passages in Ovid, Seneca, and Virgil that inform the language of his revengers from Titus through to the First Player's speech about the fall of Troy in *Hamlet*. More strikingly, it displays a quality that is common to many early modern stage revengers, in the metadramatic impulse to escalate what is promised into allusion and emulation.

As I showed in *Revenge Tragedy: Aeschylus to Armageddon*, the revenger's histrionic reflexivity owes a great deal to the fact that his (or, more rarely, her) task is imposed, by a ghost calling for vengeance, the appeal of an injured loved one, or the shape of the violence that has already been perpetrated.[5] To become a revenger the character must adopt a role to fulfil a pre-formed action, like an actor playing his part. Yet reflexivity is also generated by the promise or oath of revenge, which escalates so readily into a promise made to the audience. The revenger tells us what he will do, and insists that he will stick to his plan. To his potential as a *re*-actor,[6] the revenger adds the capacity—latent in any actor who comes onstage[7]—to initiate action through the promise of action. This is how the play will turn out, whatever intrigues disrupt it, if it becomes a revenge tragedy. Only by the standards of psychological naturalism is it dramaturgically inept that Young Clifford already seems to know that, in *Part 3*, he will encounter York's child, Rutland, and kill him. The speech act projects the play's action as well as its own performance. That Clifford scans the future into his binding utterance would have made it, for an Elizabethan audience, a fuller representation of his commitment to his word, reflecting the integrity of his promise.

Before the killing of Rutland, the audience of *3 Henry VI* is presented with another scenario that is typical of the interplay between revenge and binding language: the volatile relationship between an individuating, even isolating revenge task, and the group formation that comes with revenge as a sworn, common objective. This topic will be explored extensively in Chapter 5, but, in the opening scene of *3 Henry VI*, the audience is shown the rudiments. York sits presumptuously in the throne, a de facto king, but also a mockery king who will soon be murdered. Henry enters with his supporters, and declares:

> My lords, look where the sturdy rebel sits—
> Even in the chair of state! Belike he means,
> Backed by the power of Warwick, that false peer,
> To aspire unto the crown and reign as king.
> Earl of Northumberland, he slew thy father—

> And thine, Lord Clifford—and you both have vowed revenge
> On him, his sons, his favourites, and his friends. (1.1.50–6)

Clifford is spurred into action by the yoking of his vow with Northumberland's. Henry incites the bitterness of the revengers in the interests of the Lancastrian faction, pitched against the Yorkists. The scene might not be by Shakespeare, but it sets out the group psychology that links vengeance with politics in the tetralogy.

As the action advances, language and event become undeniably Shakespearean. First, we get earnest of revenge, when Clifford and his soldiers find York's youngest son, Rutland, isolated and adrift on stage, accompanied by only his tutor, a priest, who is carried off, pleading for the boy's life. In Hall's *Chronicle* (1548), Rutland is a youth; Shakespeare makes him a child, hopelessly asking for pity. He argues that he should not die for what his father did, and justly says that by killing him Clifford might be passing death sentence on his own son. It is to no avail:

> Thy father slew my father, therefore die.
> [*He stabs him*]
> RUTLAND *Di faciant laudis summa sit ista tuae.* [*He dies*]
> CLIFFORD Plantagenet—I come, Plantagenet!
> And this thy son's blood cleaving to my blade
> Shall rust upon my weapon till the blood,
> Congealed with this, do make me wipe off both. (1.3.47–52)

The votive line of Latin[8] makes Rutland seem like a sacrifice, impiously torn from the arms of his chaplain. His death is an early revenge, not just in the sense of coming early in the development of Shakespearean stagecraft but in anticipating the killing of York. Clifford stamps out part of the lineage, a piece of the future of the house. The blood of both stabbings will congeal into one on his blade. Blood will have blood, as the saying goes, for Old Clifford yet out of Rutland.

When the revenge is brought to York, Shakespeare gives it a Kydian twist. The rebel is made to sit or stand upon a molehill, and he is taunted with a napkin dipped into Rutland's blood. Audiences would remember how, in the popular *Spanish Tragedy* (*c.* 1587), Horatio brings back from battle a napkin stained with his friend Andrea's blood, and how this is passed on in turn to become a revenge-inciting token for Hieronimo when his son is murdered. In *3 Henry VI*, the dejected father is punished by his inability to revenge his son and by Queen Margaret (Henry VI's wife) putting a paper crown on his head. He is mocked not just for failing to get his hands on the real crown but for breaking his 'solemn oath' to stand back from power for as long as Henry reigned (1.4.100–3). Margaret harps on this 'holy oath', and York is goaded into a response. 'O tiger's heart wrapped in a woman's hide!' he cries, in a line that evidently lodged in the minds of contemporaries.[9] York threatens revenge for Rutland in the only way that he can, with his tears: 'every drop cries vengeance for his death | 'Gainst thee, fell Clifford, and thee, false Frenchwoman' (149–50). But he does not have much time left for poetical conceits. Clifford stabs him on the gestural line, 'Here's for my oath, here's for my father's death' (176). This elides the vow to revenge described by Henry in 1.1 with its action, but it also fuses Clifford's motive into factional loyalty, reminding us of his fealty, his oath of allegiance, to the king. There is a double, or treble, realization of design, which would be banal if Clifford were committed through statements rather than speech acts. His vows and oaths play out in the killing of York. Binding language has a physical force, like that of the bloody sword, stained with early revenge, that is thrust into York's body.

* * *

Let me return to Young Clifford's promise, over his father's corpse. To cry 'In cruelty will I seek out my fame' is to push beyond the future indicative: 'I will' becoming 'will I' is charged with 'I engage my will'. The escalation of intention is more than a matter of pitch. Illocutionary energy turns the words into action. The speech act articulates, like the flexing of a muscle, or the picking off of an intermediate target (a Rutland), the payoff (the destruction of York). Meanwhile, the utterance both propels forward a plot and sets a baseline for events. A wrong has been committed, but action starts *now*. What is carried into the future is the form of the wrong. Even if this could be come to terms with by the subject, the revenge oath sticks within or to him. Responsibility goes with the swearer. The very inadequacy of the speech act—compared with the wrong it responds to—can act as a goad to action. It is itself, like the corpse of Old Clifford, or the napkin soaked in Rutland's blood, a mnemonic, a small, charged piece of language that sets out the data of resentment and is steeped in implications of violence. Not that the bloody oath always leads straight to blood. The violence of the performative can give substitutional satisfactions.

When a promise becomes an oath, as most revengers' promises in tragedy do, it invokes the Divine forces that are supposed to punish wrong in the world, so the act of calling on God as a witness is also an awakening of metaphysical powers to aid the revenger. In that sense—to revert to plurality—the revenger is never alone, even if the dead abandon him. In another sense again, bracing himself, putting himself into an action, he must always be other to himself in the plot, never quite singular. Yet the obduracy of the revenge action, trangressively pitched as it may be not just against the powers of this world but the biblical injunction to leave revenge to God,[10] can carry with it an aura of sacrilegious, even devilish power. The protagonist can swear by blood, by villainy, by the ghost that impels revenge. There is a violent and impressive syzygy of the intentional and the metaphysical, mediated through a physical body which is the means of utterance, the medium of the vow—by wagging a tongue, or by swearing on a sword—and a piece of the machinery that delivers revenge by assailing the enemy. As a result, the bodily will loom large in this chapter.

For a conventional template of revenge oath and action, we can turn to John Marston's *Antonio's Revenge*, a play that was written at about the same time as *Hamlet* (*c.*1600) and has much the same outline, as a result of a common debt to the now-lost, probably Kydian, *Ur-Hamlet*.[11] Antonio's father, Andrugio, poisoned by the usurping brother Piero, appears to his son as a ghost and urges him to 'Revenge my blood!'[12] Antonio responds with a triple oath:

> By the astoning terror of swart night,
> By the infectious damps of clammy graves,
> And by the mould that presseth down
> My dead father's skull, I'll be revenged. (3.2.25–8)

With a zeal that shows him to be more 'apt' than Hamlet, he adds the self-excoriating curse that is anciently part of such an oath:[13]

> May I be cursèd by my father's ghost
> And blasted with incensèd breath of heaven
> If my heart beat on ought but vengeance.
> May I be numbed with horror and my veins
> Pucker with singeing torture, if my brain
> Digest a thought but of dire vengeance;
> May I be fettered slave to coward chance,
> If blood, heart, brain, plot ought save vengeance. (34–41)

Hamlet, as we shall see in Chapter 8, is alert to how chance cuts across all the designs of life, including the desire of protagonists to turn their vengeful actions into providence. Such is the vigour of Antonio's oath and the formulaic panache of Marston's plot that his words do drive forward a path to fulfilment.

The audience is shown the potency of a revenge oath almost immediately. The usurper has a young son called Julio. He comes on stage while Antonio is still heated with the provocation to revenge. It is like Clifford seizing on Rutland, except that, this time, the child-killing has even stronger (and classical) overtones of sacrifice. The ritual effect is the more potent because the scene is set among the tombs of a great cathedral. Lest Antonio's purpose slacken, Andrugio's ghost cries 'Revenge' from under the stage, like the ghost of Old Hamlet crying 'Swear' to Marcellus and Horatio. The spirit groans in satisfaction when a libation of Piero's blood is poured out of Julio's veins. 'Thy father's blood', Antonio cries, 'I thus make incense of: to Vengeance.... Blood cries for blood, and murder murder craves' (3.3.61–71). The blood that cries for more blood is not just that of Andrugio, which calls for the blood of his usurping brother, but that of Julio, which whets the appetite for Piero's death, his murder flowing from that of Julio.

As one death anticipates the other, Julio solves the structural problem incident to revenge plots, that the payback necessary for the action risks shutting it down pre-emptively and reducing revenge to retaliation. Intrigue, exile, lack of evidence, madness: these are the conventional ways of holding off closure. By introducing a Rutland or a Julio, as a troubling foretaste of revenge, the dramatist can give us a slice of the payback while holding the rest of it over. A single, bizarrely consistent yet serial action gives us two murders for the price of one. What makes this structural gambit more than mechanical is partly the challenge that it poses to an audience thinking about revenge by virtue of the Rutland or Julio figure being only guilty by association or substitution. What also works on us however is the metonymical use of the victim to demonstrate the revenger's commitment, initiated by his oath. Julio is a pledge of revenge as well as a sacrifice.

* * *

Although the sequence in *Antonio's Revenge* resembles the killing of Rutland, it is more immediately modelled—I believe—on what might be distantly behind the history play: the section of Seneca's *Thyestes* in which the vengeful Atreus sacrifices the sons of Thyestes. This play was, of course, widely read in Elizabethan England. On the death of their father Pelops, Atreus and Thyestes agreed to take turns on the throne, but Thyestes seduced his brother's wife (shades of Piero and Maria, Claudius and Gertrude) and stole, with her help, the golden-fleeced ram that brought with it the right to rule. Now Thyestes has been drawn back by ostensible forgiveness and his boys are given as pledges, hostages, to new, given faith: 'obsides fidei accipe', he says to Atreus, 'hos innocentes, frater',[14] 'for pledges [of my faith] take thou | O brother deere, these gyltles babes', in Jasper Heywood's mid-Tudor translation.[15] Like York, adorned with a paper crown, Thyestes is risibly crowned with the diadem of Pelops that he will not be allowed to keep while Atreus takes his sons away ostensibly to arrange an animal sacrifice. 'This crown, set on thy reverend head, wear thou; but I the destined victims to the gods will pay' (lines 544–5). The crowning is riven with irony because the word Atreus chooses is *vincla*, which can be used of headgear but which also means oaths/bonds, as in *gerere vinc(u)la*, 'to be bound by chains'.[16] By getting Thyestes to accept the diadem he has made him helplessly captive. He has mock-crowned him (again, like York) with an already broken *fides* or oath.

What happens next made a powerful impression on Renaissance readers and dramatists. Ritual dismemberment and the punitive presentation of body parts feature in many neoclassical tragedies from Cinthio's *Orbecche* (1541) onwards. Often the effect is gratuitous, designed to astonish and appal. Shakespeare, even in *Titus*, finds in cruel ingenuity a keener way of creating wonder.[17] He knits sacrifice and bloody banquet into a mordantly logical plot, in which revenge shows its affinity with ritual. He does, however, learn from what is surely the most lurid and blasphemous sequence in all of Seneca's plays. Taking the sons of Thyestes into a dark grove, the Nuntius reports, Atreus fetters and binds them, and observing the rites of sacrifice (incense, wine, knife, salted meal) he takes these *devotos* or votive offerings (line 693), slaughters them, inspects their innards for prophetic marks, like a priest, then dismembers and cooks them. Everything is skewered, roasted, and boiled except their heads, which are reserved for identification and horror, 'the hands that had been given to him in pledge of faith' (line 764)—heads and hoofs were kept back, in animal sacrifices[18]—and the blood, which is mixed into wine. This is the feast of horror served up to Thyestes late in the action.

One of the blacker jokes in this grim play is that the boys are treated as the oath-sacrifices that would commonly in classical Rome accompany the swearing of *fides*. Just as Thyestes, having once broken faith, can only be treated now, as the vicious Atreus sees it, to the travesty of an agreement, so the boys, in a travesty of oath ritual, stand in for the lamb or (more often) pig that was slaughtered in the sanctuary of a god to mark any agreement worth keeping. At the killing of such a sacrifice, the implication was: if I break my agreement, may I be killed (and dismembered) like this animal. The children in the play are not just guests, hostages, and victims; Seneca will have known that children were used in the Greek world of the Atreidae—as they were in Rome—as witnesses to oaths. 'In serious oaths, the swearer invoked destruction on himself and his descendants in case of perjury, and might have present in person the children by whom he swore. This threat to descendants is constantly mentioned in connection with broken oaths.'[19] Atreus saves time by killing Thyestes' sons, who have come to witness their *fides*, as (and in punitive fulfilment of) an oath-sacrifice, inflicting destruction on his brother's descendants, because Thyestes, he believes, cannot be a promise-keeper. Since their league will be broken again, let his brother's flesh and blood be killed and dismembered like the oath-sacrifice that the boys are. In this version of early, anticipatory, revenge, the day of feasting is proposed to consolidate their *fides*: 'With mutual accord, brother, let us keep this festal day; this is the day which shall make strong my sceptre and bind firm the bonds of peace assured.'[20] Instead, the bloody banquet abrogates and destroys the faith. Hence Thyestes' cry, after the nature of his supper is revealed: 'Hoc foedus? haec est gratia, haec fratris fides?'; Heywood: 'Is this thy league? may this thy loue and fayth of brother bee?'[21]

Oath-sacrifices are ancient. They can be found in Homer and the Old Testament, and they go back into prehistory.[22] When an agreement was made, when a faith was given, an animal would be slaughtered and sacrificed. The creature was cut, dismembered, and in some accounts its testicles were trampled.[23] The principle was presumably, 'this oath is irreversible, the beast is now broken up', but also, as we have noted, 'if I break my word, may I (or my lineage, or people) be similarly destroyed'. The Roman account that was best known in the early modern period is in Book I of Livy's History, which describes the oath-sacrifice that preceded the combat of the Horatii (representing the Romans) and the Curiatii (the Albani). After he had 'read out the covenant and oath', the Roman *pater patratus* declared:

> from these articles I say, shall not the people of Rome start backe first, nor make default: If they shall first goe backe and faile therein by publicke consent, and fraudulently; that day, O *Iupiter*, smite thou the citie of Rome, as I to day will strike this swine: yea and smite thou home so much more, as thou art more able and powerfull than my selfe. And after he had thus said, he smote the swine with a flint stone. The Albanes likewise repeated their prescript forme of words, and the oath, by their Dictator and Priests for the purpose.[24]

The oath and the sacrificial victim are so tightly fused that the verb used to describe killing the pig, *ferire* ('to smite, knock dead'), is the same as that for sealing a contract.[25] Which reinforces, at a point of origin,[26] the idea that sacrificing an animal or person is to make an oath physical, to make the dead thing—Julio, 'punched' by Antonio's dagger, Thyestes' sons, stabbed at the altar—earnest of a promised end.

It fuels the inversions of *Thyestes* that what is sacred in this ritual is desecrated, devoted to the gods by being taken apart and devoured. Though the practice was disputed, the meat of a sacrifice was often eaten (it was too valuable to waste) and, in Roman custom, the sacrifice was in any case followed by a banquet. This was a formal procedure; the eating of parts of the animal was socially stratified and allocated with care. The gods received their portion when the innards of the beast were burnt on a fire in the sanctuary.[27] All this helps explain why in *Thyestes* and the English plays under its influence, from *Titus Andronicus* through *Antonio's Revenge* into Middleton and Dekker's *The Bloody Banquet* (*c.*1609?), the more or less ritualized killing of victims leads into a cannibalistic banquet.

Behind it all lies human sacrifice, for which animals were, in classical culture, a substitute (think of Iphigenia, replaced by a deer), but not always. As Walter Burkert writes in *Homo Necans*: 'The closer the bond, the more gruesome the ritual.... It was generally believed that conspiracies practised human sacrifice and cannibalism.'[28] The practice lingered into the Roman period, until at least the reign of Hadrian,[29] and knowledge of it was transmitted by epic and drama. Homer and Virgil depict it at the funerals of Patroclus and Pallas.[30] Polyxena is sacrificed on the tomb of Achilles, in Euripides' *The Trojan Women* and *Hecuba*, and in Seneca's reworking of the same material, *Troades*. As we shall see, the influence of *Troades* runs into *Titus Andronicus*, where the action is initiated by the sacrifice of Alarbus, son of Tamora, Queen of the Goths, at the Andronici tomb. In *Thyestes*, which becomes the dominant classical presence in *Titus*, Seneca lets human sacrifice back into the house of civilization through the window of revenge.

So an oath-sacrifice made to sustain a league modulates into a votive offering to the gods to bring the sacrificer (i.e. Atreus) his wish, which is horribly to revenge the desecration of an agreement. This turning of the oath-sacrifice towards the aim of destroying an enemy is, again, ancient. Think of the Oath of Plataea, sworn by the Athenians and the Spartans as they united against the Persians: 'They swore these oaths, covered the sacrificial victims with their shields and | at the sound of the trumpet made a curse: if they transgressed what was sworn and did not keep true | to what had been written in the oath, a curse was to be upon the very people that had sworn.'[31] This sort of oath found its way into Greek tragedy, as in the prologue to Aeschylus' *Seven against Thebes*, where the Scout tells the audience of the oath sworn by Polynices and his associates: 'Seven men, bold leaders of companies, slaughtered a bull, let its blood run into a black-rimmed shield, and touching the bull's blood with their hands swore an oath by Ares, Enyo, and blood-loving Terror [*Arē t' Enuō kai philaimaton Phobon* | *hōrkōmotēsan*], that they would either bring destruction on the city, sacking the town of the Cadmeans by force, or perish and mix their blood into the soil of this land.'[32]

Ancient Greek sources were mostly inaccessible to Shakespeare and his contemporaries. Many were familiar, however, with the military oaths sworn in Rome,[33] and they read in Livy and elsewhere about the oaths and sacrifices sworn to by groups and factions against the city's internal enemies. Every educated Elizabethan knew the oath sworn by Lucius Junius Brutus and the conspirators against the Tarquins after the rape and suicide of Lucretia: '*Brutus* drew forth the knife out of the wound of *Lucretia*, and holding it out afore him, all embrewed and dropping with bloud, Now I swear (quoth he) by this bloud, by this most chast and pure bloud...'[34] As we shall see in Chapter 5, Shakespeare elaborated this oath at the end of *The Rape of Lucrece*. When he did so, he troubled readers by making Lucrece seem as much an oath-sacrifice securing rebellion as a suicide victim who deserved pity or condemnation for her act. This shift has behind it the power of the oath-sacrifice as a pledge of revenge that is registered in the plays, but it also resonates with an event that Shakespeare could read about in Plutarch, when Brutus and the other conspirators swear upon sacrifices to expel the Tarquins:

> when *Brutus*, who stoode in iealousie of some, would by othe be assured of the Senate, and had appointed them a daye solemnely to take their othes vpon the sacrifices: *Valerius* then with a good cheerefull countenaunce came into the market place, and was the first that tooke his othe he would leaue nothing vndone, that might preiudice the *Tarquines*, but with all his able power he would fight against them, and defend the libertie of the cittie. This othe of his maruelously reioyced the Senate, and gaue great assuraunce also to the Consuls, but specially, bicause his dedes dyd shortly after performe his wordes.[35]

The fascination with the human sacrifices that persisted along the margins of the empire (e.g. in North Africa), and that were still associated with conspiracy, quickly comes into play in Plutarch's account of the Brutus story. He describes how two of the hero's sons were caught up in a counter-plot to readmit the Tarquins. This plot required them to swear an oath upon an oath-sacrifice more shocking than those employed by Valerius and the rest in the market-place:

> After these two young men had geuen their consent to be of the confederacie, and had spoken with the *Aquilians*: they all thought good to be bounde one to another, with a great and horrible othe, drincking the bloude of a man, and shaking hands in his bowells, whom they would sacrifice. This matter agreed vpon betweene them, they met together to put their sacrifice in execution, in the house of the *Aquilians*.[36]

Early modern readers who did not get to this passage in Plutarch would find the same scenario anyway in accounts of Catiline's conspiracy against the republic. This plot was supposedly sealed by the drinking of the blood of a sacrificed child or slave (Sallust, Florus), or by the sacrifice of a slave and eating of his flesh (Plutarch).

Just as Livy got into *Lucrece*, so Catiline became a presence in Renaissance drama. When Ben Jonson wrote *Catiline his Conspiracy* (1611), he made much of the plot. 'Bring the wine and blood | You have prepared there', Catiline calls.

> I've killed a slave,
> And of his blood caused to be mixed with wine.
> Fill every man his bowl. There cannot be
> A fitter drink to make this sanction in.
> Here I begin the sacrament to all.[37]

As we shall see again, 'sacrament' can mean, in early modern English (as in Latin *sacramentum*), 'oath', but it also carries an implication of ritual, and if, as seems likely, the whole sequence echoes the Gunpowder Plot (cf. p. 317), it blasphemously recalls the eucharist (another cannibal feast) which sealed the oath of Guy Fawkes, Catesby, and the rest to blow up the House of Lords in 1605. In Catiline's grotesque oath, drunk to and sworn by the conspirators (491–9), there is a conjunction between the obscurity of a plot—an obscurity which is part of its attraction—and the occult crime of human sacrifice, a sacrifice which is also a pledge of retribution against the republican leaders (499–504).

The mystique of human oath-sacrifice haunts late classical and Renaissance views of Rome, but it penetrates revenge tragedy in particular, with its hypertrophic scenes of swearing and its ineradicable impulse to build its mnemonics on blood and the body. It is a genre which gives the projected-back anger of victims a voice in the oaths of protagonists who carve up more victims in turn as an act of vindictive remembrance. It chimes with Nietzsche: 'When a man decided he had to a make a memory for himself, it never happened without blood, torments and sacrifices: the most horrifying sacrifices and forfeits . . . , the most disgusting mutilations . . . , the cruellest rituals of all religious cults . . . —all this has its origin in that particular instinct which discovered that pain was the most powerful aid to mnemonics.'[38] That is one reason why this chapter moves towards *Titus Andronicus*, a play in which 'disgusting mutilations' are mnemonically re-enacted as sworn revenge.

* * *

To return from the matter of antiquity to the early modern period, take Henry Chettle's *Hoffman*, another play written (*c.*1602–3), like *Antonio's Revenge*, in the shadow of the Hamlet story. Towards the end of the action, Hoffman's side-kick, Lorrique, offers to come over to his master's enemies by giving *himself* as an oath-sacrifice, a pledge of the counter-revenge that they plan:

Let me be Prologue to your scene of wrath,
And as the Romane Cateline resolu'd
His doubtfull followers by exhausting blood
From the liue body, so draw mine, cast mine
Vpon the troubled and offended earth;
Offer blood fit for an infernall sacrifice, . . .
As you hope to thriue in your reuenge, smite me, . . .[39]

Lorrique promises to betray Hoffman and hand him over, but being such a rogue is not sure on what he can swear to convince them that he means to deliver. This is an obvious problem for a villain; Richard III, for instance, tries swearing his good faith to Queen Elizabeth when he is trying to win her daughter, Elizabeth of York, 'by my George, my garter, and my crown', then 'by myself . . . by the world . . . My father's death', then 'by God', by 'The time to come', but as the queen points out, all these witnesses have been discredited or violated by his actions (4.4.297–321). Lorrique ends up swearing, ingeniously, 'by all the gods that shall giue ill men life'. In one of those ritual sequences that make you realize how intimately revenge shares a performativeness with the swearing of oaths—both of them actions that demonstrate commitment and crave witnesses, actions that are communicative—the conspirators join hands, ring Lorrique around, kneel, lay their right hands on his head 'and sweare | Vengeance against *Hoffman*' (K1r).

In the event, the revenge goes beautifully, partly because Lorrique does get his just deserts. After another mini-crisis about what he can convincingly swear by, he gives false faith to his master by taking up the only language that Hoffman can believe—the revenger's oath: 'by villany, by blood, by sleightes, | By all the horrours tortures can present, | By Hell, and by reuenges purple hand' (K2v). Even so, Hoffman sees through his melodramatic duplicity, and Lorrique is stabbed to keep him secret, becoming the oath-sacrifice he proposed. The revenge plotters capture Hoffman and punish him by putting the red-hot crown on his head that was first put on his father's head and then by Hoffman on the head of Otho, son of his enemy, as earnest of his full revenge. The planned campaign of vengeance has fallen short, while running to excess.

This is inherent, in one sense, to revenge, which is rarely exact or extreme enough for the driven revenger. At the end of *Thyestes*, Atreus regrets that he could not make his brother drink the blood of his children straight from their bodies, to make his revenge just that bit worse. In Hoffman's case, more mechanically, there is disappointment in the frustration of oaths. Early on, after killing Otho, in a pledge of revenge against the Duke of Luninberg, Hoffman turned Senecan-Ovidian like Young Clifford over his father's body, and boasted:

> He was the prologue to a Tragedy,
> That if my destinies deny me not,
> Shall passe those of Thyestes, Tereus,
> Iocasta, or Duke Iasons iealous wife; ... (C2v)

Now he has to admit that by falling for Martha, Luninberg's wife—swearing love to her (L1r) and trusting her—he has disrupted the double determination of oath and intended revenge, and the pile-up of victims that he had in mind. The destiny that he should have forged by keeping his promise to the audience has been disrupted by tangential vows:

> A man resolu'd in blood, bound by a vow
> For noe lesse vengeance, then his fathers death,
> Yet become amorous of his foes wife! (L2r)

We get the same pattern of pledge murder through oath to vengeance in *Antonio's Revenge*, where the agonizingly unresolved argument of *Thyestes* is played out in the murder of Piero. In Seneca, Thyestes is punished by not being murdered but left in the torment of knowing he has brought death upon his sons. There is a moment open to such affliction in Marston's play, between the exposure of the bloody banquet (Julio is cooked and fed to his father) and the stabbing of Piero, but the audience is given the closure of oaths and action. This is entirely in line with Renaissance adaptations of Seneca, though Marston, influenced by *Titus*, is unusually keen to resolve all grievances in atrocity. Thus Antonio goes from his sacrifice of Julio to act against Piero by gathering others around him, into a knot of *Omnes*:

They wreath their arms.
PANDULPH Now swear we by this Gordian knot of love,
By the fresh turned up mould that wraps my son,
By the dead brow of triple Hecate,
Ere night shall close the lids of yon bright stars
We'll sit as heavy on Piero's heart,
As Etna doth on groaning Pelorus.
ANTONIO Thanks, good old man. We'll cast at royal chance.
Let's think a plot; then pell-mell vengeance!
Exeunt, their arms wreathed. (4.4.88–95)

They are physically a 'Gordian knot', a tie-up of bodies or vengeful hydra bound by their common purpose. It matters that, in both Latin and early modern English—as we shall see in Chapter 12—*nodus* and knot both meant *oath*. They are oath-bound by their commitment to go after Piero. Like Antonio's initial, spoken oath, the fixedness of the knot is a weapon against 'royal chance'. The bond promises the audience that the future is determined by the activity ('pell-mell') and purpose ('plot') of 'vengeance'. The connectedness of the escalation is signalled in the language. The unusual 'pell-mell' was heard at the sacrifice of Julio. It will come back for the third and last time when Piero is stabbed.

In *Thyestes* the serving and eating of the bloody banquet is reported by a Messenger. Marston puts this on stage, after the conspirators '*bind* PIERO' and tear out his tongue. Binding is not just the obvious way to subdue and control a victim. It translates binding language into action, binds the victim with double determination:

ANTONIO ...
Here lies a dish to feast thy father's gorge.
Here's flesh and blood which I am sure thou lovest.
[*Uncovering the dish that contains* JULIO's *limbs*]
PIERO *seems to condole his son....*
Now, pell-mell! Thus the hand of heaven chokes
The throat of murder. This for my father's blood! *He stabs* PIERO (5.5.48–77)

This would suffice for Antonio's revenge, but one of the joys of group revenge (as we shall see in Chapter 5) is that multiple motives seethe within the knot of the undertaking. And so, the other revengers step forward to have their stab, until they are united in killing:

PANDULPHO This for my son! [*Stabs him.*]
ALBERTO This for them all!
And this, and this; sink to the heart of hell!
They run all at PIERO *with their rapiers.*
PANDULPHO Murder for murder, blood for blood doth yell.
GHOST OF ANDRUGIO 'Tis done, and now my soul shall sleep in rest.
Sons that revenge their father's blood are blest.
The curtains being drawn, exit ANDRUGIO (78–82)

The concluding lines rhyme with what early modern commentators such as Puttenham call a 'band' (or 'bond').[40] Not that any audience would need to know or remember that. The audible links and knots bring the binding words of the conspirators to bear on the miscreant Piero. Denounced as a 'black dog!', a 'snurling cur' (40), he is trussed up like an animal, then subjected to ritual slaughter.

* * *

Marston is brilliantly effective in the staging of ritualized violence, but the most shocking depictions of sacrifice in early modern tragedy can be found in *Titus Andronicus*. Returning to Rome in triumph, with Tamora, Queen of the Goths, and three of her sons captive, Titus, riding in his chariot, with his living and dead sons (in coffins) before him, and '*others as many as may be*' (1.1.69), is so commanding a figure that he is offered rule of the empire (which he refuses) and the privilege of choosing an emperor from the rival brothers Saturninus and Bassianus (he selects the former, which is a mistake). What the writing of the role most strongly projects in the opening scene, however, is his saturation in grief and pride at the loss of so many of his sons in battle down the years and his desire to lay to rest the latest of the dead. To lower their coffins into the Andronici tomb—presumably, in Elizabethan performances, the stage trap—is only part of what needs to be done. Invoking ancient rites, with a dash of grammar-school Latin, Lucius, his eldest son, demands:

Give us the proudest prisoner of the Goths,
That we may hew his limbs and on a pile
Ad manes fratrum[41] sacrifice his flesh
Before this earthy prison of their bones,
That so the shadows be not unappeased,
Nor we disturbed with prodigies on earth. (96–101)

Neither sacrifice nor tomb can be found in the prose chapbook which is as least an analogue of the play and may constitute its major source.[42] If Shakespeare got all this from anywhere, it was from Seneca's *Troades*, where sacrifices and tombs are awesomely central.[43] Certainly, Tamora's plea to Titus not to sacrifice her son Alarbus owes something to Andromache's attempts to persuade Ulysses in the *Troades* to spare the life of Astyanax—that *pignus* or 'pledge' of the Trojans, their 'security' and 'guarantee' of survival if not revenge.[44] The enforced suicide of this boy, who has been hiding in his father Hector's tomb, is indeed virtually sacrificial (lines 1100–3). He leaves a trace in *Titus* and his shadow hangs over *King John*.[45] Yet Tamora's lines owe more, structurally and in general conception, to those of Agamemnon arguing with Pyrrhus near the start of Seneca's tragedy that Polyxena should not be sacrificed on the tomb of Achilles. It is Pyrrhus who prevails, and later we are told that 'The shed blood stayed not...; instantly the savage mound sucked it down and drank the whole draught of gore' (lines 1162–4). A similarly cannibalistic element enters into the sacrifice of Alarbus; it reverberates through the play as far as the final, bloody banquet: 'Alarbus' limbs are lopped | And entrails feed the sacrificing fire' (1.1.143–4).

Among the changes made to Seneca in Jasper Heywood's translation of *Troades* (1559) was the introduction of a 'speche of Achilles spright, rysing from hell to require the sacrifice of Polixena'.[46] In the Latin, Pyrrhus asks whether Achilles will receive no reward ('praemium') for fighting the Trojans (line 292). Is Polyxena not his to claim? Heywood faithfully translates this,[47] but he evidently found the notion of sharing the spoils of war with the dead culturally alien and inadequate to motivate a demand for human sacrifice. In his version, Achilles' spirit calls for revenge and provides a back-story to his rancour. He is the first revenge tragedy ghost in Elizabethan drama, precursor of Don Andrea in *The Spanish Tragedy* and the ghost in *Hamlet*. He was not killed in battle, Achilles complains, but basely ambushed by Paris, when he was tricked into attending a pretended marriage with Polyxena (B4v). Unless Polyxena is sacrificed, the Greek fleet will not be able to sail home; there will be no favourable wind. His language is floridly and repetitively vindictive, making the ghosts in Kyd and *Hamlet* seem laconic by comparison: 'Not yet reuenged hath the depest hell, | Achilles blood on them that did him slay | But now of vengeans comes the yrefull day' (B4v). This spirit is usually regarded as a spin-off from *The Mirror for Magistrates* (1559), where the ghosts of (mostly) great men justify themselves and make their claims on the world. It is better understood as

Heywood's importation from *Thyestes* of a revenge motive (cf. Atreus) that made sense of human sacrifice as a wicked, punitive excess.

Heywood's reworking of *Troades* is consistent with the unease we find about human sacrifice in versions of the *Titus* story written during and after Shakespeare's lifetime. Alarbus does not appear, for instance, in the prose chapbook *The Tragical History*, or the ballad that derives from the play,[48] nor in the 1620 German version of the tragedy;[49] in a Dutch variant, Jan Vos's play *Aran en Titus* (1641), Aaron, rather than Alarbus, is saved from sacrifice.[50] When Edward Ravenscroft adapted *Titus Andronicus* after the Restoration (1687), he matched the drift of Heywood's *Troas* by recasting Alarbus' sacrifice as an act of 'Revenging Piety'. Titus feels obliged to command this death because one of his own sons was sacrificed by the Goths before the action. As Lucius reminds the pleading Tamora:

Deaf like the Gods when Thunder fills the Air,
Were you to all our suppliant *Romans* then;
Unmov'd beheld him made a Sacrifice
T'appease your Angry Gods;...
TITUS Then did his sorrowfull Brethren here,
These other Sons of mine, from me Exact
A Vow, This was the Tenor which it bore,
'If any of the Cruel *Tamora*'s Race
'Should fall in *Roman* hands, him I wou'd give
'To their Revenging Piety.[51]

Titus' aim is only 'a Sons groaning Shadow to appease, | By Priestly Butchers Murder'd on your Altars'. The whole exchange is awkward in its attempt not just to motivate the sacrifice of Alarbus as an act of retribution but as a civilizing rebuke to barbarism. Alarbus dies for piety as well as payback, and certainly not 'to revenge their Bloods we now bring home' (the sons of Titus killed in battle). The general is bound by a vow as well as by a cultural mission to exact a punishment that is designed, according to Quintus, to teach the Goths the opposite of what the sacrifice appears to say, 'That Cruelty is not the Worship of the Gods.'

Initially, *Titus Andronicus* looks different, and bolder than Heywood or Ravenscroft. Revenge is not even mentioned as a motive for Alarbus' sacrifice, and there is no exacted vow. As the action develops, however, vengeance is pulled in backwards, reframing Alarbus' death, while vows, oaths, and other sorts of binding language compel retribution. They do so, with an ingenuity that is psychologically plausible, both in the breach and in the observance; the breaking of bonds inspires revenge, oaths sustain that action. The lopping of Alarbus becomes a proleptic pledge of the vengeance—another early revenge—that is exacted from Tamora's kin. One of the consequences of the serial, linked structure of a revenge plot is that the end is implicit in the beginning, so that pledges along the way (both uttered and enacted) are pre-shocks of the outcome. The cannibalistic, rhyme-bonded rituals that conclude *Titus*—a climax that impressed Marston—are anticipated in the initial sacrifice, which becomes a foretaste of structured mayhem.

It is likely that Act 1 of *Titus* was written by George Peele. This does not preclude the possibility that Shakespeare added the sequence that deals with Alarbus' sacrifice. There is evidence of revision by one hand or another in the survival, in the First Quarto, of lines early in 1.1 that are not found in Q2, Q3, and the Folio. Titus has returned to Rome five times after fighting the Goths, we are told, 'bearing his valiant sons | In coffins from the field'. Q1 then adds (in modernized form): 'and at this day | To the monument of the Andronici | Done sacrifice of expiation, | And slain the noblest prisoner of the Goths' (1.1.35.1–4). The likeliest reason why these lines appear sixty lines ahead of Lucius' request for Alarbus' sacrifice is that they reflect evolving intentions in authorial manuscript. An early reference to the sacrifice was replaced (but in error not erased) by the fuller, onstage depiction of Tamora's pleading, Titus' resistance, and Lucius' account of the killing. Whatever the explanation for lines 35.1–4, the cues set up in the fuller account (lines 95–145) are intricately developed later. The vigorous, memorable verbs in 'Alarbus' limbs are *lopped* | And entrails *feed* the sacrificing fire' prepare the audience for retaliations that run through the rape of Lavinia—who is 'lopped and hewed' by Chiron and Demetrius (Alarbus' brothers), who also cut out her tongue—and their stuffing of her murdered husband Bassianus into the 'ragged entrails' and 'swallowing womb' of a woodland pit (2.4.17; 2.3.230, 239), to the murder of the youths by Titus and his feeding of them to Tamora. They are returned to the 'womb' (which can mean 'stomach') which bred them, while her wicked paramour, the Moor Aaron, is left to starve to death in a hole in the ground in revenge for Bassianus' death in the pit.

Meshed with the drama made out of sacrifice and revenge is the correlation or interactivity between binding language and payback. As the action of *Titus* advances, this takes the form familiar from *3 Henry VI* and *Antonio's Revenge* and many another revenge play of retributive violence sworn to. Yet the plots are also hinged and impelled by broken agreements, vows, and plights. Titus, for example, agrees to give his daughter Lavinia to Saturninus in marriage, an honour to the Andronici (1.1.238–52). Inconveniently, it emerges that she is already vowed to his brother. When Lucius and his brothers join Bassianus in snatching Lavinia away, they stress the bindingness of her commitment:

[TITUS] Traitor, restore Lavinia to the Emperor.
LUCIUS Dead, if you will, but not to be his wife
That is another's lawful promised love. (292–4)

In the mêlée around this stand-off, Titus kills his own son, Mutius. As a piece of patriarchal destructiveness, it is matched only by his eventual killing of the violated Lavinia, as he expunges the dishonour done to the Andronici by Tamora and her faction. Lucius already shows, however, in his insistence on Lavinia's betrothal, how much more important is the honour of the family than is his sister's life ('Dead, if you will'). As the body of Mutius is lowered into the trap, the tomb of the Andronici claims a second sacrificial victim. Julie Taymor included in Act 3 of her stage production a flashback image of Mutius as (in the words of the caption) '*Half boy | half sacrificial lamb*'. In her film, there is an allusion to Abraham sacrificing Isaac, while the blade that approaches the body of the boy/lamb is that of the sword that dismembered Alarbus.[52]

It goes without saying, however, that the sequence shows the audience how the sacrifice of Alarbus generates payback through further sacrifices. What it more remarkably explores is how revenge is animated by a violence that is inherent in oaths and vows—the world must be made to fit the word, even if men like Mutius get in the way—and the violence that is bred in turn by conflicting or broken bonds. If the lopping of Lavinia is revenge for the lopping of Alarbus, her 'rape' in the forest (her violation) is payback for her 'rape' (her seizure) by Bassianus, which breaks Titus' agreement with the emperor.[53] Because Bassianus' 'true betrothèd love' becomes his 'wife'—one flesh, his 'own' (1.1.402–3)—his 'rape' of her can be retributed by the sexually emblematic throwing of him into the vagina-like pit[54] in the woods. The twisted logic goes further. If Lavinia gets Alarbus' lopping and Bassianus' rape visited upon her, Bassianus' gets Alarbus' sacrifice, which is a version of Mutius' also. Martius finds him in the pit/tomb 'All on a heap, like to a slaughtered lamb, | In this detested, dark, blood-drinking pit' (2.3.222–4).

Agreements are made, broken, and occasionally kept, from start to finish of *Titus*. After Lavinia is snatched by Bassianus, the audience is shown a troth-plight between Saturninus and Tamora: 'here I swear by all the Roman gods', 'here, in sight of heaven, to Rome I swear' (1.1.319, 326). Tamora's 'in sight of' evades a problem of what a Goth—a non-believer in Jupiter, Venus, and Mars—should swear *by*, which a play less interested in binding language would not pursue. *Titus*, however, prises this open when Lucius avoids making his father's mistake in sacrificing Alarbus by swearing to spare Aaron's child by Tamora if the Moor tells him what he and the queen have been up to in their vicious intrigues (5.1.53–124). Varying a question that was much discussed in early modern Europe—whether you should take the word of a pagan when he swore by gods in whom you did not believe[55]—Lucius asks the Moor, 'Who should I swear by? Thou believest no god' (71). Shakespeare gives Aaron a radical answer, that the plausibility of an oath depends on the observed behaviour of the swearer, rather than the validity of his religious framework, but he also ironizes the assent of the audience by associating this Machiavellian judgement with an anti-papistical bias widely held by ordinary Elizabethans against trusting the words of Catholics who were held to deceive Protestants with oaths:

Yet for I know thou art religious
And hast a thing within thee callèd conscience,
With twenty popish tricks and ceremonies
Which I have seen thee careful to observe,
Therefore I urge thy oath; for that I know
An idiot holds his bauble for a god,
And keeps the oath which by that god he swears,
To that I'll urge him, therefore thou shalt vow
By that same god, what god soe'er it be,
That thou adorest and hast in reverence,
To save my boy, to nurse and bring him up,
Or else I will discover naught to thee.
LUCIUS Even by my god I swear to thee I will. (74–86)

The violence created by broken words and generated by the revenge oaths that follow them is staged most forensically in 3.1. Aaron, nicely parodic of the high Roman commitment to oaths and honour, comes to Lucius to announce that his sons Quintus and Martius, framed by the Moor himself for the murder of Bassianus, will be spared from execution if one of the Andronici gives them a hand:

my lord the Emperor
Sends thee this word: that, if thou love thy sons,
Let Marcus, Lucius or thyself, old Titus,

> Or any one of you, chop off your hand
> And send it to the King. He for the same
> Will send thee hither both thy sons alive,
> And that shall be the ransom for their fault. (3.1.150–6)

The result is an appalling, grotesque scramble by Titus, Marcus, and Lucius to be the one to lose a hand: 'Lend me thy hand,' says Titus to the Moor, 'and I will *give* thee mine.... Good Aaron, *give* his majesty my hand' (186, 192). The hand is both the ransom and a sign of the agreement that secures it. Titus gives his hand to Saturninus in the same way that Tamora gives him his hand in marriage.[56] Except that it is sent back, bloody and derided, with the heads of Quintus and Martius. The body parts become pledges of the capacious revenge that Tamora intends, the Hecuba-like quittance of 'bloody wrongs' that she was incited to by Demetrius after the killing of Alarbus (1.1.135–41). The delay that is typical of revenge tragedy is not imposed by obstacles or scruples but geared to opportunity and sadistic delectation; the almost casual hacking at the Andronici leaves them to suffer the sight of their losses and makes each injury a sign of more to come.

In a theatrically astonishing scene that will be discussed further in Chapter 5, Titus draws the maimed Andronici around him and swears to revenge their injuries among the stumps, severed heads, and bloody mouths that are the product of revenge but also the wreckage of the oaths and vows that in their abrogation bring down violence upon the rhetorical instruments—heads, hands, and (Lavinia's) tongue—that are used to make them. As Thomas P. Anderson puts it, 'Circulating in the blood and gore of bleeding bodies and body parts, Titus' vow is gruesomely entangled with reminders of other promises that have been violated.'[57] Yet 'entangled' is not intense enough. Revenge incorporates the injuries into what is an unspoken vow in the text as we have it (3.1.275–8), turning physical mnemonics into pledges that are caught up in an oath that is, at this point, taken through gesture. Depending on the director—though the prompts are clear enough—*Titus* touches, embraces, or knots with the heads and stumps and bloody mouth, and makes them pledges of a violence that will mutilate Chiron and Demetrius.

* * *

When retaliation comes, it follows the same logic, literally so in depending—in imitation of the *Thyestes*—on the killing of sons who are too trustingly given as hostages. The endgame starts with Saturninus trying to do another deal with the Andronici. He wants to persuade Lucius to agree a truce and call off the Gothic army that he is leading in 'revenge' to Rome (4.4.66). Instructing Aemilius, he says: 'if he stand on hostage for his safety, | Bid him demand what pledge will please him best' (104–5). The offer can hardly surprise Lucius. When he leaves Rome in 3.1. to raise an army of Goths, Lucius acknowledges that the Andronici are now effectively hostages, and says that 'He loves his pledges dearer than his life' (290). Aemilius delivers the emperor's message to him, making the pledges part of the offer:

He craves a parley at your father's house,
Willing you to demand your hostages,
And they shall be immediately delivered.
A GOTH What says our general?
LUCIUS Aemilius, let the Emperor give his pledges
Unto my father and my uncle Marcus,
And we will come. (5.1.159–65)

This passage is neglected by commentators, but it shows Shakespeare working on the template of *Thyestes* towards a killing of Chiron and Demetrius as a vengeful oath-sacrifice not just for agreements already broken by Saturninus and Tamora's faction but on the expectation that this further deal will be betrayed and the Goths turned against Lucius at the parley (4.4.107–11, 5.2.74–80).

Titus is an early play, and the intrigue could be more clearly articulated, but Shakespeare's design is evident. Because they neglect this strand of Senecan influence,[58] commentators are more baffled than they should be by Tamora's coming to Titus' house disguised (in masquerade) as Revenge, bringing her sons with her as Rapine and Murder, then leaving them in Titus' clutches. The youths are left because Titus says that, if they are not, he will prevent Lucius from coming to the parley. Further back, they become the pledges that Lucius has agreed with Aemilius that Saturninus will give. But further back again, where the catastrophe springs from Seneca, the youths are, like Thyestes' sons, pledges put in jeopardy, and, like them, they are 'bound' (and their mouths stopped).[59] Denied the use of hands and tongue they share the plight of Lavinia, who juggles a basin in her stumps to catch the blood from their throats as they are ritually slaughtered like animals in what is not just a revenge action but—like the human sacrifice in *Thyestes*—repayment for broken agreements and also anticipatory payback for an agreement that *would* be broken.

Titus is now ready to give the revenger's metadramatic promise, letting the audience know, in the style of Young Clifford, what his plot will deliver. Like Hoffman announcing that he will outdo Thyestes, Tereus, Jocasta, and jealous Medea, he utters a vow and a boast. He will race up the escalator of excess and out-revenge his exemplars (Progne and Philomel as much as Atreus). Young Clifford and Hoffman, however, share their plans only with the audience. By addressing Chiron and Demetrius, Titus makes the pair suffer through anticipation the part that they will play in the banquet:

Hark, villains, I will grind your bones to dust,
And with your blood and it I'll make a paste,
And of the paste a coffin I will rear,
And make two pasties of your shameful heads,
And bid that strumpet, your unhallowed dam,
Like to the earth swallow her own increase.
This is the feast that I have bid her to,
And this the banquet she shall surfeit on;
For worse than Philomel you used my daughter,
And worse than Progne I will be revenged. (5.2.185–94)

The mnemonics of revenge are sharply etched. The 'two pasties of your shameful heads' recall the heads of Martius and Quintus sent to Titus in Act 3. In emulation of Seneca, they also resemble the heads of Thyestes' sons reserved from chopping and roasting when Atreus sets to work. The comparison of Tamora to the 'earth' that will 'swallow her own increase' does not just tie the banquet back to the stowing of Bassianus' body in the pit but looks forward to the punishment of Aaron, set 'breast-deep in earth' and starved (5.3.178). The point, we can now see, is that, like Tamora, he must die consuming his own flesh and blood.

In the final, Thyestean feast, Titus keeps his word. The sight of Tamora eating the flesh of her children appals audiences by transgressing boundaries, but the chaos of the situation is bound by rhymes and rhyming actions. In Marston, as we saw, Antonio cries, 'This for my father's blood!' and stabs Piero; Pandulpho and Alberto then follow him with 'And this, and this'. The utterances reinforce the acts with basic, physical impulsion. In *Titus*, with finer art, which has learned from the stabbing of York, couplets build sequentially through the denunciation of Chiron and Demetrius and on to the killing of Titus and the emperor, by which stage the ferocity of the action piles up internal as well as end rhymes. The mayhem has a logic, binding actions to the vowed revenge;[60] and fixed into its machinery is Titus' killing of Tamora: ''Tis true, 'tis true'—an absolute asseveration—'witness my knife's sharp point' (62). This has no rhyming line to match it because Titus' thrusting gesture makes up a silent line and delivers a perfect rhyme with the point of his dagger, a point which manifests (in a Shakespearean quibble)[61] his verbal point. It is a speech act *as* action as well as the redemption of a vow.

3

Swearing in Jest

Love's Labour's Lost

The Gray's Inn Christmas revels of 1594–5 were extravagant, creative, and unruly. After a 'space of three or four Years' in which 'such Pass-times' had been suspended because of the plague,[1] there was an appetite for ceremony and mischief. The immediate origins of the festivities published much later as *Gesta Grayorum* (1688) lay in the inventiveness of such law students as the young Francis Bacon, but the conventions that they worked with went back decades. One precedent can be found in the Inner Temple Revels described by Gerard Legh in *The Accedens of Armory* (1562).[2] Ahead lay the entertainments of *Le Prince d'Amour* at the Middle Temple in 1597–8 and the Gray's Inn Revels of 1617–18. The records of these events (others have slipped from history) are fascinating in the insights they offer into the relationship between revelry, oaths, and law. More immediately, they provide contexts for thinking about *Love's Labour's Lost* (1594–5), a play that is usually associated with noble audiences and performances at court,[3] but that is linked to Elizabethan institutions of 'higher education', to the Inns of Court, Oxford, and Cambridge.

Gesta means 'actions, gestures, games' and it runs from Latin through French into the English word 'jests'. The jests at Gray's Inn involved mock legal procedures, including a general pardon with elaborate exceptions, issued by the Prince of Purpoole,[4] lists of officers in the Prince's household, a knightly challenge to combat, and visits by 'Ambassadors' from the Inner Temple and then ostensibly from Russia.[5] As all Shakespeareans know, the second night of the revels fell into 'disordered Tumult', followed by 'Dancing and Revelling with Gentlewomen' and a performance of *The Comedy of Errors*.[6] The joking disrespect with which the players are described in *Gesta Grayorum* shows the high regard in which Shakespeare and his fellow actors were held.[7] More central, however, to the *Gesta*, was a different sort of performance: an elaborate oath ceremony by students initiated into 'the Order of the Helmet'.[8] The King of Arms declared:

> you must every one of you kiss your Helmet, and thereby promise and vow to observe and practise, or otherwise, as the Case shall require, shun and avoid all these Constitutions and Ordinances, which, out of the Records of my Office of Arms, I shall read unto you.
>
> Then the King at Arms took his Book, and turned to the Articles of the Orders, and read them, as followeth.
>
> *Imprimis*, Every Knight of this honourable Order, whether he be a Natural Subject, or Stranger born, shall promise never to bear Arms against His Highness's Sacred Person, nor his State; but to assist him in all his lawful Wars, and maintain all his just Pretences and Titles; especially, His Highness's Title to the Land of the *Amazons*, and the Cape of *Good Hope*....
>
> *Item*, Every Knight of this Order shall endeavour to add Conference and Experience by Reading; and therefore shall not only read and peruse *Guizo*, the *French* Academy, *Galiatto* the Courtier, *Plutarch*, the *Arcadia*, and the Neoterical Writers, from time to time; but also frequent the Theatre,...[9]

There was nothing new in this. In Legh's *Accedens*, we hear of gentlemen in the Inner Temple becoming Pallas' knights by swearing on the cross of a sword.[10] In *Le Prince d'Amour* oaths were sworn on a copy of Ovid's *De Arte Amandi* to initiate members of the Order of the Quiver. Again, the Order was governed by semi-nonsense, licentious statutes, read by a Herald. For example:

> Item, *that every Knight of this Order shall still be well horsed and well armed, and have those things in readiness which Ladies desire, as the Launce for the Ring, and such like; and shall twice a week at the least Tilt and Turne for Ladies, shewing them all their cunning in Arms when they lust or command....*[11]

The students were asked 'Are ye content to swear to all these Articles', then each took his oath, knelt, and withdrew from the royal presence, 'making solemn Congies' (46–7). When the Prince of Purpoole resumed his reign at Gray's Inn in 1617–18, the 'Knights of the most noble Order of the Cressent' were bound by such 'Articles' as this:

> If any of you have vowed service to some great and worthy lady, then doe it honorably, not kissinge her glove when you may kisse her bare hand, nor her bare hand when you may reach her lipp, nor her lipp when you may doe her more knightly service.[12]

Group formation among young people often has a ritualized element. Oaths contribute to such rituals because they bond while they bind, and, in the case of the Inns of Court, because there was something edgy, in a period which took swearing seriously, about swearing oaths in jest. Like the roistering and breaking into chambers[13] that characterized the revels (not to mention the head-bashing and stabbing),[14] swearing was the sort of infraction that brought and kept participants together. Think of old Justice Shallow still remembering his exploits with little John Doit, black George Barnes, and the rest, when they were students at Clement's Inn.[15] Moralists said that swearing in jest was not a forgivable error of youth but rash and blasphemous, a short cut to the sin and common law offence of perjury. Edmond Bicknoll cites the case, recorded by Melanchthon, of 'two wanton young men, makyng but a iest of Gods most glorious name, . . . but their iestyng was so odious in Gods syght, that the one of them was presently stryken with madnesse'.[16]

The rites of disorder encouraged by the revels did not subvert the institutions that allowed them. As Natalie Zemon Davis observes of the youth groups known as 'Abbeys of Misrule', active in sixteenth-century France, 'Misrule always implies the Rule that it parodies.'[17] The oaths sworn by initiates of the Orders were teasing, playful versions of the admittance oaths that were taken when students enrolled.[18] It was one of the 'Ancient Standing Orders' of Gray's Inn, matched elsewhere, 'That every Gentleman *admitted* into the Fellowship of this Society, enter Bond with two Sureties before he come in Commons, to pay and discharge Commons and Duties.'[19] Promotion up the hierarchy was similarly secured: readers, for instance, swore oaths when they took office, and heard their statute recited by the sub-lector.[20] For revellers such as Bacon, the initiation rites of the Orders were rehearsals for the oaths and ceremonies that they would pass through when they became justices or were knighted. Parody was not easily separated from institutional progression, a mix that can be found elsewhere, not least in the university and college oaths and saltings at Oxford and Cambridge.

Because a second, equally striking source for the oaths sworn by the King of Navarre and his three lords that begin *Love's Labour's Lost* lies in these ceremonies of enrolment and initiation. The importance of matriculation oaths was repeatedly stressed, after the incorporation of Oxford and Cambridge by Act of Parliament in 1570; they were favoured as a means of regulating conduct and rooting out recusants. In 1581, the Earl of Leicester, as chancellor, asked 'That no scholar be admitted into any college or hall in the University of Oxford, unless he first before the Chancellor subscribe to the Articles of Religion agreed upon, take the oath of the Queen's Majesty's Supremacy, swear to observe the statutes of the University, and have his name registered in the matriculation-book'.[21] The colleges had their own requirement that scholars and fellows swear to obey the statutes and decrees of what were, at least in theory, austere institutions. For anyone who went through the still-ritualistic Oxbridge system in the days before men's colleges admitted women, this is a starting-point for the comedy so obvious that it is astonishing to find it overlooked in the criticism.[22]

Here is how the play begins, with Navarre addressing his lords:

> Let fame, that all hunt after in their lives,
> Live registered upon our brazen tombs,
> And then grace us in the disgrace of death
> When, spite of cormorant devouring time,
> Th'endeavour of this present breath may buy
> That honour which shall bate his scythe's keen edge
> And make us heirs of all eternity.
> Therefore, brave conquerors—for so you are,
> That war against your own affections
> And the huge army of the world's desires—
> Our late edict shall strongly stand in force.
> Navarre shall be the wonder of the world.
> Our court shall be a little academe,
> Still and contemplative in living art.
> You three—Biron, Dumaine, and Longueville—
> Have sworn for three years' term to live with me
> My fellow scholars, and to keep those statutes
> That are recorded in this schedule here.
> Your oaths are passed; and now subscribe your names,... (1.1.1–19)

This reiterates commonplaces used in the speeches by the counsellors that address the Prince of Purpoole once the Order of the Helmet has been established. In these orations, probably written by Francis Bacon, the counsellors recommend, respectively, military success, becoming a philosopher king, building monuments, governing with virtue, and stocking up with treasure, 'to win Fame, and to eternize your Name'.[23] Particularly striking is the language of the sixth, final counsellor, who rejects austere advice, 'as if a Man should come to some young Prince... and immediately after his Coronation, be in hand with him to make himself a sumptuous and stately Tomb.... What! Nothing but Tasks, nothing but Working-days? No Feasting, no Musick, no Dancing, no Triumphs, no Comedies, no Love, no Ladies?'[24] This is the voice of Biron, when he challenges Navarre's statutes: 'O, these are barren tasks, too hard to keep— | Not to see ladies, study, fast, not sleep' (47–8).

Whatever the influence of *Gesta Grayorum*, the oaths that start *Love's Labour's Lost* are clearly versions of matriculation and college oaths. They are not simply parodic but open up a vein of comedy by showing how unlikely the actual oaths were to guide the conduct of young men. The Elizabethan universities were, in principle, strict.[25] A student's day began between 4 and 5 a.m., with prayer and preaching. Diet could be spartan—beef, pottage, oatmeal, salt—and recreation was limited: 'No sword-playing, fencing, or dancing-school, or gaming-house, shall exist, or be frequented, within the town of Cambridge.... Dice shall at no time be used.'[26] Yet the reiteration of the rules shows how hard it was to impose them, especially on the affluent. Women were a constant temptation. There was hunting, dicing, bull- and bear-baiting, a bowling game called 'nine-Hoals',[27] and the 'lewd example'[28] of plays. To keep such vices at bay, a five-mile exclusion zone was maintained around the Cambridge colleges.[29] Actors were paid not to perform but to keep away.[30] Yet 'the lord chamberlain's players came to Cambridge at least once, in 1594–5, perhaps with Shakespeare among them'.[31] It is entirely possible, in other words, that, around the time *Errors* was staged at *Gesta Grayorum*, and shortly before the composition of *Love's Labour's Lost*, Shakespeare visited Cambridge.

Just as the Gray's Inn admittance oaths lie somewhere behind the Order of the Helmet, so matriculation and college oaths at Oxford and Cambridge were accompanied by mock initiation rites. Saltings can be found among the writings of Thomas Randolph and, less expectedly, Milton, as well as from anonymous hands.[32] A student, acting as the 'father' of a group of freshmen, would make speeches about them, comparing them to parts of the body, for example, or dishes on a table, and invite replies. If their responses pleased, they were given a drink, if not, a salty drink, while their chin was scratched with a thumbnail (to make the salt sting?). Anthony Wood adds, of the saltings at Merton: 'Afterwards when they were to be admitted into the fraternity, the senior cook was to administer to them an oath over an old shoe, part of which runs thus—"Item tu jurabis quod penniless bench non visitabis" &c.... After which spoken with gravity, the Freshman kist the shoe, put on his gowne and band, and took his place among the seniors.'[33]

Would anyone seriously claim that *Love's Labour's Lost* is set on the banks of the Cam or the Isis? Does not its parkland milieu, and mix of *commedia* and rustic types ('The pedant, the braggart, the hedge-priest, the fool, and the boy' (5.2.536)), point to a royal court decamped to a great house? Scholars used to compare this setting with the chateau-based Renaissance academies surveyed by Frances Yates,[34] and it is true that Pierre de La

Primaudaye's *The French Academie* (prescribed reading, as we have seen, for the Order of the Helmet) does seem to be one of the play's 'sources and analogues'.[35] As striking, however, and more symptomatic, is the affinity with Boccaccio's *Decameron*, which starts with a group of young men and women who have escaped from the plague in Florence to play games and tell jokes and stories (gambling, jousting, disguises, music) in Fiesole. The plague of 1593, which claimed 15,000 lives in London, shut down the theatres, and prevented the revels at Gray's Inn, is a fearsome background and overhanging threat in *Love's Labour's Lost*, reaching a climax in the arrival of Mercadé to announce the death of the King of France and the penance given Biron to tend the sick in a hospital.

The colleges of Oxford and Cambridge were, at this date, semi-rural, backing into meadows, ponds, and orchards. And at both universities, bear-baiting, huckling, and play-acting were excluded not just for the sake of student morality but because crowds of people, including strangers, up from London, were a source of contagion. Thus the Cambridge authorities, in 1591–3: 'What perill of sicknes will hereof ensue by the throngeinge together of Companies in this contagious time, the Lord knoweth.'[36] To that extent, you could make a case for the Cambridge colleges providing a suggestive analogue for Navarre and his celibate 'vow-fellows'[37] living a studious life in retreat from the plague. When the queen went to Oxford in 1592, it was partly to escape the capital at a time of infection.[38] But a deeper, rustic retreat was consistent with college life. When the plague did reach Oxford and Cambridge, students withdrew with their tutors to country houses kept for that purpose.[39] Academic routine was maintained, stipends paid.[40] Navarre's academy resembles, among other things, this sort of retreat.

The threat of the plague in *Love's Labour's Lost* evolves, but its influence is felt from the start, in the King's fear of death and anticipation of his tomb. Longueville reveals the men's anxiety in his description of their studies: 'I am resolved. 'Tis but a three years' fast. | The mind shall banquet, though the body pine' (1.1.24–5). In early modern, as in medieval, times, fasting was one of the pieties practised to stave off the plague. It was ordained by the *Fourme to be Vsed in Common Prayer* issued during the great epidemics of 1563 and 1593.[41] Health manuals, in any case, agreed that a spare diet kept the pestilence at bay. The point is brought home by Dumaine:

> My loving lord, Dumaine is mortified. . . .
> To love, to wealth, to pomp I pine and die;
> With all these living in philosophy. (28–32)

The academic oath will have an apotropaic effect: turn me into skin and bone, deny the pleasures of life, and death will pass me by. The signing of the bond which follows Biron's show of resistance has been compared to Faustus's signing of his bond with the devil in Marlowe's play.[42] There are echoes in situation and language, but also, it should be noted, in context. Modern audiences assume that Faustus's bond is merely a bad bargain. We should remember, however, the horrific pestilence in London during the composition of *Dr Faustus*. As Christopher Ricks has pointed out, for Faustus to secure himself twenty-four years free of the plague is more attractive than we might now recognize.[43]

The imminence of plague explains not just the strenuousness of the King's opening lines about the disfiguring disgrace of death but the Cambridge-style exclusion zone that is set up by the *Gesta Grayorum*-like articles[44] attached to the oath: 'Item: that no woman shall come within a mile of my court' (119–20). In the explicit plot of the play, this edict is challenged by the approach of the Princess of France and her ladies, but the more implicit, troubling concern is what they might bring with them. When Navarre falls for the Princess he is said to be 'infected' (2.1.229). The women bring pleasure, life, and hope but also time and death. They do this not just by coupling love with reproduction and mortality but by unleashing revelry, disguise, intrigue, and the sort of play-watching (the Pageant of the Nine Worthies) that was believed to draw down the sickness. Ricks observes that '*Play* tolls with *plague* (guilt by association and infection)'.[45] Going to the theatre was one of the social abuses that moralists believed brought down the plague as punishment.[46] Even if that were doubted, going to the playhouse made contagion more likely.

So the association between playing and the plague was not just a thematic one for audiences of *Love's Labour's Lost*. To be watching this comedy (even in a small, court theatre) was to be conscious of the risk of infection. It was a risk compounded by the fact that the plague was so often seen as Divine retribution for rash, unnecessary oaths, for swearing in jest and the oath-breaking that went with it. Swearing and perjury were put high among the social abuses that brought down pestilence.[47] As Bicknoll warned, out of Ecclesiasticus (23: 11): 'A man that vseth much swearing, shalbe fylled with iniquitie, and the plague shal neuer go from his house.'[48] This has its effect even on the stability of the *Love's Labour's Lost* playtext. Quarto-Folio variation in the use and style of oaths is one symptom of the larger question about how far one can go in profanity without tempting Divine wrath. The play's preoccupation with 'purgation' as a treatment for disease, and as punishment, and as a way of being released from legal charges by means of oaths, is inextricable from the *expurgation* of such profanities as 'by God' and 'in faith', after the passing of the Act to Restrain Abuses (p. 8), in the performance-related Folio.[49]

★ ★ ★

The opening of *Love's Labour's Lost* would have spoken to a larger audience than courtiers, lawyers, and students because oath-bound groups had a significant place in the associational world of Elizabethan England. Apprentices, for instance, 'were required to swear an oath that they would remain obedient throughout their years of training to the regulations of the company and the rule of its governors'.[50] Like Navarre and his lords they undertook to work hard, live a sober life, and not marry for a specified period. 'Each apprentice had to write out an oath . . . or at least to acknowledge his acceptance of its conditions by writing his name or his mark at the foot of the oath.'[51] Nor were the customs of the Inns of Court and the universities confined to those institutions. They had parallels in popular culture and spilled out into taverns, alehouses, and other social spaces. The Order of the Helmet is the elder brother of such societies as the Order of the Bugle, and the turbulent Tityre-tu, where initiates swore oaths on a dagger put into a pottle of wine.[52] At Cambridge, the vice-chancellor had some say in the election of the Lord of Taps, a lord of misrule at Stourbridge Fair, who enrolled followers with a 'mock-solemn nicknaming' ceremony.[53] As we saw in the Introduction, Thomas Randolph, author of a salting, also depicts, in *Aristippus*, an initiation in a tavern, where a student is 'matriculated' by taking swigs out of a bottle and swearing to a number of articles. 'Kisse the booke', is the instruction, after every article is announced.[54] Convivial London must have been full of such rituals, where to drink a 'pledge' meant to salute someone, but also to make a wager or affirm allegiance.[55]

Group oaths have a special dramatic potential because of the possibilities of slippage and obscurity. How far is a man bound by an oath which those who swore it with him have betrayed? This becomes a key question in the second half of *Love's Labour's Lost*. From the outset, though, we face another issue: how far is a man bound by an oath the articles of which he did not know, because they belong to the minor clauses, the 'terms and conditions' that rarely get read when people make agreements? Apprentices must often have subscribed their oaths without knowing all the regulations of their company. It was a phenomenon that gave an opening for conscience to worry at. Biron's first move against the academic oath is consequently to say that he has sworn to something other than the full text of the articles. 'I can but say their protestation over,' he declares—edging 'protestation' as asseveration towards a legally reserved 'denial',[56] as though Longueville and Dumaine were tacitly rejecting what they had subscribed to:

> So much, dear liege, I have already sworn:
> That is, to live and study here three years.
> But there are other strict observances, . . . (33–6)

The articles, he notices with alarm, resemble monastic 'observances'—strictures of the sort that had been swept away by the Reformation (though they still had a grip in the universities). He is expected not to see women, to fast completely one day in seven, eat once a day the rest of the week, and sleep no more than three hours a night (37–48). Though careful to stress his oath-bound allegiance to his King ('dear liege'), Biron has to object:

> KING Your oath is passed to pass away from these.
> BIRON Let me say no, my liege, an if you please.
> I only swore to study with your grace,
> And stay here in your court, for three years' space.
> LONGUEVILLE You swore to that, Biron, and to the rest.
> BIRON By yea and nay, sir, then I swore in jest. (49–54)

The word 'jest' occurs more often in *Love's Labour's Lost* than in any other play by Shakespeare—sometimes to mean verbal witticism, sometimes closer to practical joking, *gesta*. Nowhere, though, is it used as provocatively and wittily as here. 'By yea and nay' is the emphatic of a man who mock-scrupulously follows the guidance of Christ at Matthew 5: 37: 'let your communication be, Yea, yea: Nay, nay' (p. 12). It is a droll way of reminding the King that, according to Christ, we should not swear at all (5: 34–5), so the whole academic bond is dubious. In the witty setting of the line, however, 'By yea and nay' is also an equivocation, a device that was deplored as Jesuitical by a broad range of Protestant opinion, and certainly by those most likely to swear 'By yea and nay', who would not want to hear Christ's asseveration being represented as duplicitous. Biron's oath against swearing is almost blasphemous in its virtue.

Did Biron know about the minor clauses? Probably not, an audience will conclude: the oath, its articles, and edicts seem to have been putting out branches. We will soon be told that a proclamation against women approaching the court went out four days ago, and that Longueville added in a punishment about cutting out the tongue of any lady who disobeys. Shakespeare has given the oath a slippery, halfway character between individually, even competitively, introduced initiatives and jointly subscribed articles. In any case, academic oaths and statutes were notoriously disputable instances of binding language. Some took the view that even the fine print of statutes should be strictly adhered to. Since the spiritual life and death of the swearer were at risk, those imposing statutes had a responsibility to ensure that they were understood before they were subscribed.[57] Others, more realistic or resistant, distinguished between 'principall or fundamentall' statutes, those which, once sworn to, should be kept, and those 'lesse principall, or mixt, that serue for order or decencie' which incurred only a fine. As the firm, thoughtful Calvinist William Perkins put it:

> The breach of the former makes a man guilty of periurie; but it is otherwise in the latter, so be it the delinquent party be content to beare the mulct if it be imposed. Thus, students and others belonging to such societies, may in some sort excuse themselues, from the sinne of periurie, though not from all fault, in breaking some of the lesser locall statutes, els few could liue in any societie without periurie.[58]

These distinctions, evidently crucial to the unfolding of *Love's Labour's Lost*, were entirely mainstream and still viable half a century later. As Robert Sanderson, another, more Anglican divine, noted in *De Juramento* (1655), keeping statutes was a conditional matter:

> where an oath is required of [a] member of any Community, as of a City, University, or Colledge, Society of Merchants, or Handicrafts men, to *observe the Statutes*, Customes and Liberties of that Corporation; If you ask what the obligation is? I answer, *first*, that the party sworn, is obliged simply unto the observation, as far as in him lyeth, of all *fundamentall Statutes*. By *fundamentall*, I understand such as most necessarily and nearly concern the preservation of the publique estate, order, and honour of the whole body or Community.[59]

Even these, he adds—going beyond Perkins—need not be 'alwayes and necessarily' observed, 'to the rigour of the letter, but as they are put in practise, and received by custome, and as they are with approbation observed by others'. The 'lesser Statutes appertaining only unto externall form and decency', he concludes, one may 'pretermit'.[60]

In line with contemporary reasoning, Biron asks what is '*fundamentall*' to the academy and seeks to show that the proper aims can be pursued by another means. 'What is the end of study, let me know?', he asks: 'Why, that to know which else we should not know' (55–6). His inspiring vision of sun-like study trumps the dogged, university-based curriculum:

Small have continual plodders ever won
  Save base authority from others' books....
KING How well he's read, to reason against reading!
DUMAINE Proceeded well, to stop all good proceeding.
LONGUEVILLE He weeds the corn, and still lets grow the weeding.
BIRON The spring is near, when green geese are a-breeding.
DUMAINE How follows that?
BIRON Fit in his place and time.
DUMAINE In reason nothing.
BIRON Something then in rhyme. (86–99)

The men turn to pattern-making, where the fourness of the oaths modulates into the fourness of a jokey rhyme—a structure that will be repeated, from the quatrain riddle about the fox, the ape, the humble-bee, and the goose, played out between the fantastical Spaniard Armado and his page boy Mote (3.1.74–87), through the 'four woodcocks in a dish' (the men who have broken their oaths by falling in love with the visiting women) in Act 4 (3.77), all the way to that odd, unexplained moment in Act 5 when the King assumes that the five lowly actors in the Pageant of the Nine Worthies are four (5.2.532–8), a failure of numeracy that goes deeper into the play than satire on the neglect of mathematics in Elizabethan education.

Biron's 'when green geese are a-breeding' shows the spirit of play jumping up to clinch a consonance. His 'Something then in rhyme' (which is itself a rhyme) displays the power of words to bind and bond men into a band even without the words of an oath. As we have seen, Puttenham writes of 'band' (variant of 'bond') to describe this effect of rhyme and form (p. 57); Milton, less enthusiastic, wrote of the 'modern bondage of Rimeing'.[61] Biron's riposte about the geese is a pre-emptive fulfilment of the word, binding flipped into wit. Yet the numbers also carry a message of time-honoured, time-honouring wisdom. A green goose is silly and sexual, either an emblem of the foolish young men or of the purchasable flesh they might turn to (geese are prostitutes, in Elizabethan demotic). Things should be done appropriately in relation to place and time, in men's lives as in a rhymed quatrain. 'A-breeding' would not be something in rhyme if it were not fitted to its place in a four-line stretch of dialogue which measures out, in miniature, the four-season-like passage of time. 'At Christmas I no more desire a rose', Biron goes on, 'Than wish a snow in May's new-fangled shows.' We should 'like of each thing that in season grows' (1.1.105–7). This is a message that resonates all the way to the closing songs of Ver and Hiems.

You could call what Biron says folk wisdom, but intellectually—in this play about students—it also draws on the natural law tradition that infused English legal thought, and early modern humanism generally, from Fortescue and St Germain in the late fifteenth and early sixteenth centuries.[62] According to this view, positive law (*ius positum*)—the man-made law of decrees and edicts—must be qualified by and reconciled with the claims of reason based in the nature of things. So Biron's argument with Navarre, Dumaine, and Longueville cannot be reduced to common sense v. cultural artificiality because it involves lines of thought (going back to Aquinas and Aristotle) that belong within legal culture. It is 'too late' (108) to study now, he insists, too late to be 'Still and contemplative' (14). The men should be looking for wives. The oath and its three-year schedule share with the games of the park a 'Pass-time' quality, while real time is passing them by.

So the rhyme on the green geese a-breeding is a jest that gives reason in (and through) the audible time-form of rhyme, while it wrong-foots the King and his lords. Like 'I swore in jest' (also a rhyme) it does not just describe the spirit in which oaths are sworn but indicates a connection between jests and oaths. How deep does this connection go? Oaths can, and those in *Love's Labour's Lost* do, set up a frame situation, what Huizinga, in *Homo Ludens*, calls a magic circle.[63] The players have an area of regulated interaction (like a chessboard, arena, or stage), set apart from everyday life, though drawing on its conventions. The oath and its articles constitute an arena for the exercise of wit, but the analogy goes deeper. Huizinga notes that 'play' and 'to play' descend from Anglo-Saxon *plega, plegan*. These and related words have

> an abstract sense which is not that of play. The oldest meaning is 'to vouch or stand guarantee for, to take a risk, to expose oneself to danger for someone or something'. Next comes 'to bind or engage oneself (*sich verpflichten*), to attend to, take care of (*verpflegen*)'.

The truths of social psychology are not enshrined in word derivation; but Huizinga has clearly identified a significant map of practice. 'Play and danger, risk, chance, feat—it is all a single field of action where something is at stake. One is tempted to conclude that the words *play* and *pflegen* together with their derivatives are not only formally but semantically identical.'[64]

Oaths are mixed into games as ribald, dissonant phatics, but they also mark points of structure (shouted out to seal a pledge, greeting victories, gains, and losses). Moralists disapproved of dicing, card-games, and so on partly because they generated oaths. Looking back on the Christmas Revels at the Inns of Court, Sir Simonds D'Ewes wrote: 'When sometimes I turned in thither to behold their sports, and saw the many oaths, execrations, and quarrels that accompanied their design, I began seriously to loathe it, though, at the time, I conceived the sport itself to be lawfull.'[65] In *Love's Labour's Lost*, the academic oath is a pledge, the stake for which the men gamble against their flagging sense of purpose.[66] Whether they will fast, go without sleep, and avoid the company of women is already less the question than whether they will keep their word to do so. An oath can be an attractive device for starting a comedy; swiftly set up, rigid but fragile, rich in concentrations of intention, vulnerable to what happens next. What makes Shakespeare's treatment of it typically resourceful is the way it falls apart internally even before it is put at risk by the arrival of the Princess and her ladies.

When faced with the King's injunction 'Well, sit you out. Go home, Biron. Adieu' (110), Biron cannot bear to be left out, to be the 'spoil-sport' that is so much more negatively regarded than a cheat.[67] To be left out of the group now would invite exclusion once the game is over.[68] He offers to sign the articles. As soon as he gets them, however, he discovers a further reason to object: 'Item: if any man be seen to talk with a woman within the term of three years, he shall endure such public shame as the rest of the court can possible devise' (128–30). The King has broken the rules before the game is properly begun:

This article, my liege, yourself must break;
  For well you know here comes in embassy
The French King's daughter with yourself to speak—
  A maid of grace of complete majesty—
About surrender-up of Aquitaine
  To her decrepit, sick, and bedrid father.
Therefore this article is made in vain,
  Or vainly comes th'admirèd Princess hither.
KING What say you, lords? Why, this was quite forgot. (131–9)

This is a likely excuse. When it comes to the ins and outs of diplomatic agreement around Aquitaine, the King will prove just as forgetful. It is also psychologically probable that narrowing one's focus down to what is pledged by an oath prevents one taking in the bigger picture.

But the King resists 'well you know' not just to avoid appearing stupid but because forgetfulness is an escape clause. Biron is not the only slippery reasoner in the play. How much should be made of the fact that Navarre has the same name as that of the arch-casuist and unraveller of oaths Navarrus (Martín de Azpilcueta), as it appeared in English texts?[69] When he characterizes the Princess's arrival as unlooked for, the King is wriggling towards a loophole. Even strict advocates of the sanctity of oaths, such as the cleric Richard Cosin, defender of oaths imposed *ex officio* in the ecclesiastical courts (p. 19), admitted that oaths need not be kept 'when as some vnlooked for accident is discouered, or falleth out afterwarde; that was not thought vpon before'.[70] Cosin has in mind the sort of unforeseen, serious circumstance in which 'the oath cannot be perfourmed without crime and impietie', and we might wonder how far the Princess really thinks it a 'deadly sin' to deny her hospitality (2.1.104). Underlying Cosin's position, however, is the broadly acknowledged, destabilizing Christian view that a sworn promise need not be kept if circumstantial factors *of necessity* prevent it being fulfilled. As John Bale (or Coverdale), had noted, citing Augustine on the Sermon on the Mount:

> If I shulde chaunce to appoynte with the magistrates to come before them at suche an howre / and in the meane tyme be letted by terrible sycknesse / I shuld thus breake no iuste promesse made with them / if I come not. Neyther shuld I breake conuenaunte (as sayth saynt Austen) If I promysed a payment at a daye / and were robbed of my money by the waye / comynge thyder warde.[71]

The orthodox, summary note beside this passage, 'God holdeth necessyte excusyd', explains the weight given to 'necessity' by the King:

KING We must of force dispense with this decree.
She must lie here, on mere necessity.
BIRON Necessity will make us all forsworn
 Three thousand times within this three years' space;
For every man with his affects is born,
 Not by might mastered, but by special grace.
If I break faith, this word shall speak for me:
I am forsworn on mere necessity.
So to the laws at large I write my name,
 And he that breaks them in the least degree
Stands in attainder of eternal shame.
 [*He signs*]
Suggestions are to other as to me,
But I believe, although I seem so loath,
I am the last that will last keep his oath. (145–58)

If the King is prepared to invoke 'necessity' to excuse entertaining the Princess, Biron observes, why not use the word not of incidental, awkward circumstances but of the 'mere necessity' of the affects, which also and more powerfully point towards seeing the women. It is a trenchant, nimble rebuttal—with the heft of Protestant feeling against constrained, vowed celibacy behind it. Having flourished in argument, however, which is most of what matters to him, Biron subscribes to the oath. He is a natural academic. As with 'By yea and nay', he quibbles even while he signs. He will be the last to break his word but also the last to keep it. He equivocates while committing perjury, not, or not merely, in the commonplace early modern sense of breaking a promissory oath but in swearing to the verity of what he knows to be false. It is the sort of compound infringement that would outrage or amuse a lawyer.[72]

The phrase 'mere necessity' was widely used. Shakespeare will have encountered it in dozens of texts before and after Ascham's *The Scholemaster* (1570). In Heneage Finch's 'Arithmetic Lecture' (Inner Temple, *c.*1605), we hear this about innumeracy: 'Others through the same defect not being able to keepe true accompt of the dayes doe many tymes forfeit bonds vpon meere necessity.'[73] That appeals to 'meere necessity' were routine when breaking 'faithfull promisses'[74] makes Navarre's use of the phrase more pliably superficial. Yet the words carry an undertow, towards keeping not breaking oaths. For it was the mainstream, respectful view that oaths should themselves be sworn 'on mere necessity', to secure truths which could not be otherwise established. Before we conclude, however, that the King's position is weak, susceptible to demolition by Biron, we should consider what an Elizabethan audience would have made of the first half of his couplet: 'We must of force dispense with this decree. | She must lie here, on mere necessity.' Could a king dispense with an oath, at least when reformulated as a decree, and with what kind of force—merely by the force of necessity or by that of royal right?

John Bale (or Coverdale) reports it as a 'saynge... amonge men / that the word / promes or othe / of a kynge shulde stande'.[75] That this belief was so widely current[76] explains why the claim of Machiavelli that the prince need not keep his word was found so shocking.[77] English readers like Shakespeare would have been receptive to La Primaudaye's contention, in *The French Academie*, that kings should uphold faith, truth, and promise as 'the bond of humane societie'.

> For the obligation is double: the one in respect of naturall equitie, which wil haue couenants and promises kept: the other in regard of the Prince his faith, which he must obserue inuiolable, although he receiue losse thereby, bicause he

> is the formall Warrantie vnto all his subiects, of that fidelitie which is amongst themselues: so that no fault is more detestable in a Prince than periurie.[78]

Fortunately for Navarre, there were other, more nuanced positions. Cosin, for example, argues that a king *can* dispense with the articles and edicts associated with oaths, though not the oath itself:

> a *dispensation* of *relaxation* by a *Soueraigne Prince* or other thereunto aucthorized may be graunted; for release of an oathe, made in performance of some *positiue* lawe. But this is onely by way of abrogating such Lawe or Statute; either altogether, or as towardes that person, or for some particular action and time; and not, by way of *releasing* the very *bond of the oathe,* which is not subiect to mans power. For when such Lawe or Statute is disanulled and gone (as locall Statutes of *Colledges* &c. may bee euen heere in *Englande*) then the Oathe made vnto them, as vnto Lawes or Statutes; must needes (withall) so farre cease, and be released.[79]

We are back with academic statutes as prime, debatable instances of binding language. Decades after Cosin, the dispensability of college statutes recurs in Sanderson.[80] It starts to look as though *Love's Labour's Lost* is not just a play about an academy in which oaths figure, or even a play about an academy and therefore one in which oaths figure, but a play about oaths and so one in which an academy figures because of the tricky points about keeping oaths raised by the status of statutes.

Equally relevant is what Cosin goes on to say about the solvent effect of dispensation when what has been sworn to is as unattractive to the Protestant conscience as cloistered celibacy and fasting:

> a *dispensation of true interpretation,* hath place in this very especially... in respect of the very *matter promised by Oathe* to bee perfourmed, being (indeede) no due matter for an oathe. As the oathe for single life, vowed by such, as haue not the speciall gift of *Continencie* [or] as if I sweare and vowe to God, to keepe some certaine spare and so straite a diet; as (through weakenesse and infirmities after happening) I can not possiblie obserue, without apparent daunger of the losse of my life.[81]

One meal a day, one day a week entirely without food, no more than three hours' sleep at night. The very 'abstinence' required by the oath, as Biron later objects, 'engenders maladies' (4.3.291). For some, the Catholic associations of celibacy and hard diet made such undertakings dispensable without any need for dispensation: 'if a man bind himselfe by oath to liue in single life without marriage', writes Perkins, 'and after findes that God hath not giuen him the gift of continencie; in this case, his oath becomes impossible to be kept, and therefore beeing reversed by God, and becomming vnlawful, it may be broken without impiety.'[82] In any case, the imminence of the Princess and her ladies melts the edges of Navarre's rigorous oath. This is the more so because the Princess's visit was forgotten, leaving 'necessity' to solve the problem. 'Sometimes', Cosin goes on, 'this kinde of *dispensation* may haue necessarie place; whereas some thing doth after fall out, or (at least) is discouered; which I neuer forethought, or if I had, by all probabilitie, I woulde neuer have vowed or vndertaken so much.'[83]

At this point the King's attachment to his oath, winged but not destroyed by Biron, is tested by the arrival of Dull, the constable, with Costard, the clown, in his custody, and a letter from Armado announcing that Costard has been found, 'contrary to thy established proclaimed edict and continent canon', consorting with Jaquenetta, the dairymaid, in the King's 'curious-knotted garden'—that emblem of his binding articles (235–47).[84] There is a striking resemblance to the sequence of infraction and punishment found in *Gesta Grayorum* and *Le Prince d'Amour*. In the former, those held responsible for allowing the 'disordered Tumult' before *The Comedy of Errors*—confusions which led the Inner Temple ambassador to withdraw—were put on trial and then into the stocks. In *Le Prince d'Amour*, a grand jury and petty jury are sworn in to try Carolus Asinius Bestia for his miscreancy as a lover. But Shakespeare plots his law comedy more connectedly than do the organizers of the largely episodic revels,[85] putting the King into a hypocritical position if he punishes Costard and Jaquenetta, and tying the infraction back to the initial oaths. For the articles sworn by the men, to govern their conduct—'We can become a law unto our selves, by vows and promises', as Jeremy Taylor later pointed out[86]—become a law unto those who have not subscribed to the King's ambitious, collegiate rules.

The mutation of sworn articles into law is the readier because in this period the word 'statutes' could be used of promises that were contingent on existing 'bands and obligacions',[87] promises that had the force of 'legal instruments ... based on the authority of a statute'.[88] Navarre, it must be said, is less imperious in his swearing and law-making than the Prince of *Gesta Grayorum*.[89] *Love's Labour's Lost* is not a study in Roman law and tyranny. Yet the choices of an advised monarch, taking counsel from his lords, can still become impositions on the people once exclusive, academic statutes turn into legal statutes. The potential for comedy is the greater because—to cite the moderate, Royalist Taylor again—a king's capacity to abrogate the law ('The same power that makes the law, the same can annul it') is qualified if 'the Prince be obliged by oath or promise to preserve this law'.[90] Whatever the terms of his coronation oath, as Navarre's academic oath turns into a law it carries a promise to maintain it. But what if the law does not reach the people, or is too ridiculous to be taken up? Taylor is representative of mainstream, Protestant casuistry when he says of such a law: 'if it be *not publish'd,* it is not born; if it be *generally dislik'd,* it is suppos'd to be uncharitable, and therefore is as good as if it were not born.'[91] Imperfection in dissemination matches gappiness in understanding. When asked 'Did you hear the proclamation?', Costard replies, as plausibly as Biron claiming ignorance of the articles, 'I do confess much of the hearing it, but little of the marking of it' (267–9).

The insistence on continence in the King's proclamation would not have surprised an Elizabethan audience, though it would have struck many as 'uncharitable' (a point to which Biron will return). The situation anticipates that in *Measure for Measure* where Angelo issues a 'proclamation' (1.2.76–7) against sexual immorality. The 'strict statutes and most biting laws' left to fall into disuse by the Duke are reanimated and republished by his deputy (1.3.19). Both plays make an issue of hypocrisy when Navarre and Angelo break the laws they have had proclaimed. In the background are the waves of social reformation that swept across early modern England, punishing fornicators, adulterers, and swearers through the ecclesiastical courts.[92] Just as the exclusion of bull- and bear-baiting around the Cambridge colleges was justified not as a special measure but as the rigorous application of standards that should apply to the whole commonwealth,[93] so Navarre requires of those around his academy the moral improvement that Godly magistrates sought under Elizabeth and James. The waves of reforming zeal became particularly active after outbreaks of the plague.[94]

So the academic oaths are about the making of the law as well as about study and mortality. Like a number of his more philosophical contemporaries, Shakespeare was interested in the extent to which sworn obligations and law were similar, complementary, or conflicting. Both were a species of 'binding language'. Shakespeare's only use of the word 'binding' appears to be in *Measure,* where Angelo describes the 'manacles | Of the all-binding law' that hold the fornicator Claudio (2.4.93–4).[95] Oaths were used in constructing legal institutions, and in legal process (to swear in juries, for compurgation, and so on). But there was a deeper affinity between bonds and sworn obligations, as well as distinctions to do with legal history. As

Sanderson puts it, 'every obligatory Bond... derives it self from some Law, as the *Law* is twofold, the one part divine and naturall, the other civill and humane'. Sometimes you are doubly bound, as in the obligation under both natural and civil law to feed your aged parents. Yet the law is not one thing: 'In the matter of oathes we consider the *Morall*, or *Naturall obligation* only, or at the least especially; the other, the *Civill* we leave to Lawyers.'[96]

Sanderson is simplifying the task he has set himself in *De Juramento*—setting aside a body of material—rather than claiming a duplicity in the law. He does not mean that oaths and related speech acts have no valency in civil law, but he does highlight the point that there are natural law as well as positive law contexts for thinking about them. What happens when moral obligation, as understood by the natural law tradition, conflicts with civil or indeed common law? The promulgation of the statutes in *Love's Labour's Lost* shows the answer to that question to be humanly untidy but dramatically fascinating. The men are what Boyet later calls them, 'competitors in oath' (2.1.82). Through emulative bonding they impose *on themselves* 'strict statutes'—as the laws regulating sexuality are called in *Measure for Measure*—that as individuals they would hardly have chosen. The oaths taken by Navarre, his lords, and their co-swearer Armado are on a coercive spectrum with the laws that fall upon the heads of Costard, Jaquenetta, and the rest.

⋆ ⋆ ⋆

The arrival of the Princess has been referred to specific, historical sources, the one most often cited being 'an actual visit in 1578 to Henry of Navarre at Nérac by Marguerite de Valois and her mother, Catherine of France. The royal visitors were accompanied by *l'escadron volant* of ladies in waiting, and Aquitaine was discussed as part of Marguerite's dowry.'[97] Recent, rehistoricizing approaches have built this into accounts that place the play more generally in the context of the French wars of religion, comparing, for instance, the oath sworn at the start of the play to Henry of Navarre's abandoning of Protestantism in favour of Catholicism in 1593, an apostasy that was sometimes represented as a broken oath.[98] There is evidently some input from recent French history. The names of Navarre, Biron, and the rest are a reminder that France is relevant, if only as a setting to escape from into comic fantasy.[99]

But there are analogues that were more familiar to Elizabethan audiences. The queen's progresses, for instance, were often entertained with open-air encounters in the manner of the masque of Russians and the Pageant of the

Nine Worthies presented to the Princess and her ladies later in the comedy. We might recall the visits made by the young, marriageable queen to Cambridge and Oxford in 1564 and 1566, visits that were back in people's minds around the time of *Love's Labour's Lost* because of her return to Oxford in 1592. In 1564, Elizabeth was met by an academic deputation at Wolvercote, and escorted, with the Spanish ambassador, into the university, where, at Christ Church, she was entertained with plays, including a version of the *Palamon and Arcite* story that Shakespeare would later co-dramatize in *The Two Noble Kinsmen*. With its rivalry between the two kinsmen ('whom the bond of affinity and the swearing of oaths had made brothers')[100] for the hand of Emilia, who prefers virginity, but who ends up marrying the knight chosen by the gods, its relevance to the marriageable queen would have been clear, if not intrusive. As we know from contemporary accounts, the play was, like the Pageant of the Nine Worthies, disrupted by incompetent performers and observers. One actor, 'beinge owte of his p*ar*te & missinge his kewe', offered 'his servise to ye ladyes swearinge by ye masse or Gotes blutt I am owte'. Elizabeth dismissed him with a mild oath: 'God*es* pitty saythe ye Quene what a knave it tis.'[101]

I am not going to argue that *Love's Labour's Lost* is about the young Elizabeth, any more than it is about Marguerite of Valois. That the Princess has come on an embassy makes it the more likely that the source for this part of the play is once again the Inns of Court. Legh's Christmas Prince had been surrounded by visiting ambassadors in 1561–2.[102] This was remembered in *Gesta Grayorum*, with its embassy from the Inner Temple,[103] followed by that supposedly from the tsar, an episode which, by general consent, lies behind the masque of Muscovites in *Love's Labour's Lost*. Ambassadors return in *Le Prince d'Amour*, where the Middle Temple was visited by students from Lincoln's Inn,[104] and there was an 'Embassage from Lubber-land' in the Christmas Revels at St John's College, Oxford, 1607–8.[105] Sending ambassadors between the Inns allowed for a ritualization of difference, much play with fancy dress, and a display of rhetorical skill that showed off the ability of the participants. For such contemporaries as the Jacobean theatre licenser Sir George Buck, 'the Art of *Reuels*' was a distinct subject on the curriculum of the Inns of Court, distinguished enough to have its own coat of arms.[106] Students, practising this art, eloquent and personable young lawyers, may have hoped for a career in diplomacy. But all participants would have been aware of the growing topicality of embassies as a discipline of statecraft. Books were appearing on the subject, stimulated by the importance of diplomacy during the wars of religion.[107] The principles were discussed by such scholars as Jean Hotman and Alberico Gentili (who came to England from France and Italy, won the patronage of the Earl of Leicester, and were entered at Gray's Inn in 1588 and 1600).

What does this have to do with binding language? In *Gesta Grayorum* Templaria replies to the Grayans' request for an ambassador by returning the good will that the 'Bond of our ancient Amity and League requireth and deserveth'; in *Le Prince d'Amour*, an embassy from the Lincolnians is designed to renew their 'League' with the Middle Temple.[108] The making and renewing of bonds and leagues was a central aim of diplomacy—so much so that early modern authors writing about oaths frequently cite the case of Joshua,[109] who gave his word to an embassy of Gibeonites, when they came to the Israelites in the guise of strangers from a far-away country, and who decided to keep his promise despite their deception because he had used the name of God. Diplomacy was an exemplary arena for thinking about oaths and bonds[110] between peoples who had different values and belief-systems. This had medieval roots: 'On the premise that the violation of an oath was a breach of the moral law . . . the canonists had erected a whole theory of the sanctity of treaties.'[111] But the issue was no less testing in the war-torn late sixteenth century, when keeping faith with heretics was in question. Just how large a part swearing and subscription played in diplomatic transactions is shown by the exchanges between Elizabeth and Ivan IV of Russia,[112] which must lie behind the parodic correspondence with the tsar in *Gesta Grayorum* and consequently behind *Love's Labour's Lost*. The major contribution of the civil war in France to the play may not be the names of the lords, but the importance of leagues and diplomacy in the conflict that shows through in, for instance, Jean Hotman's *The Ambassador* (1603).

So the league, or promise, involving Aquitaine is the second big piece of binding language in the play. Shakespeare has introduced it as an international parallel to the academic oath. Both have complicated conditions which those bound by the deal may not have grasped. It is important that, although the Princess has a wit and authority in dialogue that mean she must come across on stage as more than a match for Navarre, she arrives as her father's representative, his 'embassy'. When she enters with her three ladies, the chief courtier Boyet urges:

> Now, madam, summon up your dearest spirits.
> Consider who the King your father sends,
> To whom he sends, and what's his embassy:

> Yourself, held precious in the world's esteem,
> To parley with the sole inheritor
> Of all perfections that a man may owe,
> Matchless Navarre; the plea of no less weight
> Than Aquitaine, a dowry for a queen. (2.1.1–8)

Yet how can a proper embassy be undertaken when Navarre denies the Princess hospitality? The speech of an ambassador on arrival at court was meant to be a major statement. She is not met at the jurisdictional limits and escorted in, as the young Elizabeth was at Oxford and Cambridge, and on country house progresses. The Princess knows why she is to be left kicking her heels: 'Navarre hath made a vow | Till painful study shall outwear three years | No woman may approach his silent court' (22–4). But the men are lucky that she does not leave, affronted, like the ambassador from the Inner Temple in *Gesta Grayorum*.

The Princess, always pragmatic, sends Boyet to announce their 'business, craving quick dispatch' (31). Speed was commendable in embassies.[113] But there is also a need to tie things up before the King of France dies; his sick and bed-ridden mortality hangs over what turns into a royal courtship. Boyet declares that Navarre would rather treat the Princess 'Like one that comes here to besiege his court, | Than seek a dispensation for his oath' (86–7). If we were serious about setting the play in the French civil wars that would make Boyet a Catholic—or a satirical Protestant. As commentators such as Perkins relentlessly pointed out, Romanists believed that 'the Pope and other inferiour Bishops, haue power to giue relaxations and dispensations . . . from a true and lawfull oath'.[114] English Protestants might argue that a prince could suspend a law or dispose of the articles of an oath, but '*the Popes of Rome*' had no authority to dispense 'with Vows and Oathes'.[115] The debate was strident, and had been so since Luther; yet this does not seem to impact on the cultivated wit of the play. Rather than entering the lists as a Catholic or Protestant apologist, Shakespeare points to yet another way in which binding language might be untieable.

When the pair do meet and the King promises to respond promptly to her suit, while not admitting her to his court, the Princess harps on his unreliability: 'You will the sooner that I were away, | For you'll prove perjured if you make me stay' (111–12). We have seen that a premium was put on speed, but dispatch is now being sought, the Princess quips, so that the King will break his vow as minimally as possible. There has to be a suspicion of diplomatic advantage-seeking. This, the first use of the word 'perjury' in the play, stresses that Navarre is a breaker of his word before they even get to the topic of Aquitaine. The King will almost immediately accuse the French king of being economical with the truth. Treatises about diplomacy say that ambassadors should avoid lying and promise-breaking.[116] Gentili says of 'the breaking of oaths and treaties, ... neither friends nor foes have any confidence left in men guilty of such violations'.[117] With Navarre breaking his oath to study even by speaking to the Princess, how can his word be trusted? Even before he comes to her in Act 5 disguised as a Russian, he is as unreliable as a Gibeonite. When the Princess concludes their initial negotation with the phrase 'We arrest your word' (158), it carries a charge, even a rebuke. His word is not secure unless it is bound like a criminal.

So what is the business about Aquitaine?

> Madam, your father here doth intimate
> The payment of a hundred thousand crowns,
> Being but the one-half of an entire sum
> Disbursèd by my father in his wars.
> But say that he or we—as neither have—
> Received that sum, yet there remains unpaid
> A hundred thousand more, in surety of the which
> One part of Aquitaine is bound to us,
> Although not valued to the money's worth.
> If then the King your father will restore
> But one half which is unsatisfied,
> We will give up our right in Aquitaine
> And hold fair friendship with his majesty.
> But that, it seems, he little purposeth,
> For here he doth demand to have repaid
> A hundred thousand crowns, and not demands,
> On payment of a hundred thousand crowns,
> To have his title live in Aquitaine,
> Which we much rather had depart withal,
> And have the money by our father lent,
> Than Aquitaine, so gelded as it is. (127–47)

Editors do not agree on how to interpret the dispute. If Navarre is to be believed, his father spent 200,000 crowns supporting the King of France in his wars[118] on the understanding that the money would be repaid. France now 'intimates' that half that sum *has* been repaid—which Navarre denies, adding that a second hundred thousand crowns are due, secured by his holding a portion of Aquitaine (not worth the second hundred thousand) from France. In any case, France wants back the hundred thousand crowns that he says he has sent, rather than sending a second payment of a hundred thousand and demanding full title in Aquitaine, which he would be entitled to on clearing the debt.

That Shakespeare was manufacturing a financial tangle to give a comic courtship time to develop is indicated for an audience by the elaboration of Navarre's speech as well as by the resolvable awkwardness of the disagreement. Yet the dispute is neither gratuitous nor unlikely. Early modern monarchs often inherited loans and debts that could not be honoured. When Henry of Navarre succeeded Henri III in 1589, the overhang of liabilities was such that repayment had to be selective. His conversion to Catholicism in 1593 was often seen as financially compelled. Through the mid-1590s and beyond, he was notoriously in debt not just to bankers but to foreign powers,[119] including England,[120] whose own insolvency would come on stage in such plays as Heywood's *If You Know Not Me, Part II* (1605).[121] Audiences of *Love's Labour's Lost* would have understood that kings (like other men) had to manage the demands of credit, would get married or marry off their daughters to relieve debt (as Henry IV married Marie de Médicis for her dowry in 1600),[122] would have their contribution to proxy wars interpreted as repayment (as Henry's payments to the Dutch were counted against his debt to England in 1603),[123] and would, above all, keep track of, and if possible manipulate, the bonds that tied debts up. Hence the legal overtones of 'surety', 'bound', and, as we come to realize, 'Aquitaine'.

This is how the exchange ends:

PRINCESS You do the King my father too much wrong,
And wrong the reputation of your name,
In so unseeming to confess receipt
Of that which hath so faithfully been paid.
KING I do protest I never heard of it,
And if you prove it I'll repay it back
Or yield up Aquitaine.
PRINCESS We arrest your word. (152–8)

We have already been alerted to the possibility of an expedient marriage because Boyet has said that Aquitaine is 'a dowry for a queen'. It is likely that the King of France has sent her to Navarre with this in mind.[124] But any province would do for a dowry. Why Aquitaine in particular? The historical Henry of Navarre had possession of and dealings with this south-west corner of modern France. But the names Guyenne and Gascony were more usual in the sixteenth century. More relevantly, Aquitaine—divided and redivided down the centuries—was an English possession until the Hundred Years War. It was part of the story of English involvement in France that figures in *1 Henry VI*, *King John*, and *Henry V*. Shakespeare will have known that the duchy came to the English crown (almost as a dowry) when Eleanor of Aquitaine, after the annulment of her marriage to Louis VII, married the soon-to-be Henry II. In *King John*, where Eleanor, as the king's mother, has a substantial role, John offers to Philip of France, at the prompting of Eleanor, 'Anjou and fair Touraine, Maine, Poitou' (2.1.488) as a dowry for his niece, Blanche, in marrying Louis the Dauphin. The exchange of provinces at marriage was part of Shakespeare's picture of France. Did historical reading ahead of *King John* inform the comedy? Holinshed describes an episode in which 'quéene Elianor, togither with capteine Marchades entred into Anjo[u]'.[125] In Quarto and Folio spelling, 'Marcade' is the name of the messenger who brings news of the French king's death at the end of *Love's Labour's Lost*.

There is a case for seeing in the circumstances of Eleanor's diplomatically swift, youthful marriage to Louis VII, under the shadow of the loss not just of her father but the illness and death (communicated by messenger) of Louis VI, germs of the situation that we find in Shakespeare's play. It would be as limiting, however, to look for a historical explanation for the appearance of Aquitaine in the comedy as it would be for saying that 'capteine Marchades' motivated the appearance of 'Marcade'. Just as the latter evokes 'Mercury' (the messenger) and 'Mar-Arcady', so the main attraction of the duchy was the legal resonance of the name. 'Aquitaine' offers the possibility of 'acquittance', a word which 'commeth from the french (*quicter* or *quitter*. . . .) and signifieth a release or discharge from a dept formerly due'.[126] An acquittance was typically a sealed document stating that money loaned on a bond had been repaid. Hence what the Princess says next:

Boyet, you can produce acquittances
For such a sum from special officers
Of Charles, his father.
KING Satisfy me so.
BOYET So please your grace, the packet is not come
Where that and other specialties are bound.
Tomorrow you shall have a sight of them. (159–64)

A specialty is 'A special contract, obligation, or bond, expressed in an instrument under seal'.[127] So the acquittances are 'bound' not just in the elliptical sense of being bound hitherward, but are sealed and legally regular and also packaged together in a bundle.

⋆ ⋆ ⋆

Aquitaine/acquittance belongs to a train of wordplay that points to the potential looseness of what is bound in language. Its beginnings go back a scene or two, to the sequence in which Armado, alone onstage with Mote, confesses that, having 'promised to study three years with the Duke' (1.2.34), he is now in love with Jaquenetta. The page shows his master how to tear the oath to tatters. The term of Armado's obligation can be reduced to 'one, thrice told' (or, in the innumerate, gambling idiom of the Spaniard, 'the gross sum of deuce-ace'), 'and how easy it is to put "years" to the word "three", and study "three years" in two words, the dancing horse will tell you' (37–50). Mote brilliantly re-presents the pledge as play, as play in words and numbers. We do not stop at three; four, the number of oaths sworn by the King and his lords, is predominant. When Armado and Mote talk about Jaquenetta's visage it is in terms of the four complexions: 'Of all the four, or the three, or the two, or one of the four' (73). And rhyming in the dialogue goes alternately, in fours. The binding of the men is adumbrated in both numbers and the numbers of the verse.[128]

Dull then enters, bringing in Jaquenetta and Costard. According to the articles, the clown was meant to be imprisoned for a year for talking to a woman. The King, variously compromised, said that he must 'fast a week with bran and water' (1.1.279–80). Armado, threatening his rival, cries, 'Thou shalt be heavily punished', to which the clown replies, 'I am more bound to you than your fellows, for they are but lightly rewarded' (1.2.135–7). Mote, or Moth (as he is called in Q and F), scintillates beside his master and the clown, as one would expect from a character whose name with dancing polysemy means *word* (*le mot*, motto, motty), *winged insect*, *speck* (as in mote and beam),[129] and probably *scruple*,[130] all of which undoes the grander, now-lost implication 'fixed utterance', 'oath'.[131] A *mote* or *moat* is also a *moot*: a legal argument, whether in litigation or played out as a mock dispute in one of the Inns of Court.[132] This is the sort of Gray's Inn virtuosity that Mote carries into the play. But he is not the only wit. Being punished by Armado (bound, tied up), Costard says that he is more obliged (bound) to his captor than is Mote, his page, who gets such small tips. He is also bound to Armado in fellowship, since they are both attracted to Jaquenetta. Costard sees a way of loosening the bonds, much as Biron tried to help the King and as Mote reassured Armado: 'Let me not be pent up, sir', he quips, 'I will fast, being loose.' To which Mote smartly replies, 'No, sir. That were fast and loose. Thou shalt to prison' (140–1). He will be loose if bran gives him the runs, and he can fast out of prison as well as in. But 'fast and loose' plays fast and loose with the King's curious-knotted regime. The punishment is slackly woven, untieable like a gypsy's knot.[133] Costard can hope for acquittance.

For, just as these word routines parody the academic oath and articles, so, after the arrival of the Princess, Armado and Mote get into an embassage plot, one which amusingly unravels. In 3.1, Armado tells his page to let Costard out of confinement to 'carry me a letter', to which the boy replies: 'A message well sympathized—a horse to be ambassador for an ass' (41–3). Jokes about bondage are sidelined, but not for long. When Costard is brought in, having tripped over the threshold of his prison, Mote declares, 'A wonder, master—here's a costard broken in a shin' (61). This is a forced joke on 'broken in the shin' meaning 'worsted in love' (because Armado now has the upper hand), with a further jest about an apple, a costard, having a shin in the first place. Armado, not quite getting it, asks for an exposition:

> Some enigma, some riddle; come, thy *l'envoi*. Begin.
> COSTARD No egma, no riddle, no *l'envoi*, no salve in the mail, sir. O sir, plantain, a plain plantain—no *l'envoi*, no *l'envoi*, no salve, sir, but a plantain. (62–5)

There is another stab at diplomacy in this, as the wordplay itself becomes enigmatic. Though an *envoi* is a 'farewell' and a 'salve' an ointment, as the Quarto and Folio spelling '*lenuoy*' brings out an *envoi* is also, *inter alia*, an ambassador (an envoy) and *salve* (in Latin) is the 'welcome' that the Princess complains she has not been given.[134]

Yet this is Inns of Court diplomacy. We are in the sphere of academic humour. The jokes about enigmas, enemas, and being loose come close to surprisingly rude moments in Milton's salting for Christ's College, Cambridge. 'Nolim enim hilari vocis sono obstrepat in hoc coetu posticus gemitus', he writes at one point: 'solvat ista medici qui alvum solvunt!' In English, that goes: 'I don't want any groaning posteriors to obstruct the sound of merry voices here. Let the medics give the enigma an enema'[135]—more literally, 'Let the doctors who know how to loosen (*solvere*) blocked bowels "loosen" the riddle too.' What is being loosed is verbal as much as medical, an incontinence of punning. Inadvertently, Costard mixes up salve as ointment with salve as 'solution of a difficulty'.[136] Compare Huizinga on play and riddles: 'The answer to an enigmatic question is not found by reflection or logical reasoning. It comes quite literally as a sudden *solution*—a loosening of the tie by which the questioner holds you bound.'[137] Armado's and Mote's words are bondage for Costard in the sense that they tyrannize over his ignorance, but they are loosed with remarkable ease, salved by the grace or grease of ignorance.[138]

Armado is amused by Costard's uncouthness and swears a mild oath (he is always affectedly cleanly) in enforcing this: 'By virtue, thou enforcest laughter—thy silly thought my spleen.' Does Costard, he says, 'take salve for *l'envoi*, and the word *l'envoi* for a salve?' (66–9). Actually, he does not. Costard speaks of salve in the mail as ointment in a bag. It is Armado who, ignorant, in turn, of everyday usage, thinks the clown is getting beginnings and ends mixed up.[139] In any case, as Mote sharply asks, as though with Huizinga in view, 'Is not *l'envoi* a salve?' It is, as the *solving* of a riddle. The preposterous idea that a greeting can be an epilogue prompts Armado's rhyme about 'The fox, the ape, and the humble-bee' and Mote's closing of the foursome with a goose that is an *oie* ('A good *l'envoi*, ending in the goose'). Shakespeare may have been led to write this by the snippets of animal fable in Abraham Fraunce's *Lawiers Logike* (1588), lifted from *The Shepheardes Calender*.[140] But he remains in the orbit of academic and lawyerly licence. Compare the Gray's Inn Revels of 1617–18: 'Jeffrye Wisacres claimes a hide of arable land in Cunelania, by teachinge a goose to singe salve, salve, to the Maior of Letherlania, when he rides to take his oath.'[141] This is an enigma, but once you find the *con* in Cunelania and remember that a goose is a prostitute, you are not far from working out what the ride is and why the goose sings.

Costard is not entirely left behind in the flow of wit. Whores were stereotypically called Frances. So when Armado offers to 'enfranchise' Costard, he can be in on the joke:

O, marry me to one Frances! I smell some *l'envoi*, some goose, in this.
ARMADO By my sweet soul, I mean setting thee at liberty, enfreedoming thy person.
Thou wert immured, restrained, captivated, bound.
COSTARD True, true, and now you will be my purgation and let me loose.
(110–16)

Armado frees Costard from durance in the lodge, where he is bound by a reduced version of the punishment required by the articles, as the men are to be freed from the academy and their oaths. As Henry Woudhuysen notes in his Arden edition, there is a play on being freed from constipation. This is probably the most outrageous joke about binding language in the canon. What clinches the jest, however, is 'purgation'. It refers not just (if at all) to purging a crime through punishment (as Woudhuysen claims) but to compurgation in the ecclesiastical courts, oaths sworn by the defendant and by witnesses (at 1*s*. 6*d*. or 9*d*. a go) to release those charged from the accusation of sexual misdemeanours.[142] As John Cowell says of *purgation*: 'the forme whereof is vsuall in the spirituall courte, the man suspected taking his oath that he is cleere, of the fault obiected, and bringing so many of his honest neighbours, being not aboue twelue, as the court shall assigne him, to sweare vpon their consciences and credulitie that he sweareth truly, or hath taken a true oath.'[143]

So this is a way of setting the word against the word, and freeing the bond of an oath by using oaths. Also creeping into earshot, however, are several verses from scripture that will prove to be of importance to such plays as *King John* and *Measure for Measure*. First, the binding and loosing of Matthew 16: 19, where Christ says to Peter: 'I wil giu vnto thee the keyes of the kingdome of heauen, and whatsoeuer thou shalt binde vpon earth, shalbe bound in heauen: and whatsouer thou shalt lose on earth, shalbe losed in heauen.'[144] Catholics argued that the 'power of the keys' gave the Pope (following Peter) authority to govern the Church, to determine questions of faith, and to dispense with oaths and vows. The verse had also for centuries been taken as giving priests the absolving power to bind and loose sins (i.e. to provide *purgation*, in another use of that word). Protestant commentators objected: 'did ever any of the Apostles or Apostolical men suppose that S. *Peter* could in any case dispense with vow-breach, or the violation of a lawful oath? Was not all that power which was then promis'd to him wholly relative to the matter of Fraternal correption?'[145] This line of rebuttal runs together, as *Love's Labour's Lost* also lightly does, the big Reformation questions of whether binding oaths and vows can be loosed (dispensed with, by the Pope) and whether sin can be purged by absolution, or merely reproved.

Costard's quip is not doctrinally committed, but it draws some of its comic energy from the cavilling disputation that went on around Matthew 16: 19. The clown sets purgation in the ecclesiastical courts—a tribunal that shared the penitential structure of pre-Reformation modes of confession—against the legal force of the academic oaths as they regulate conduct in the park. A spirit as nimble as his is not going to be bound for long. Once he is given liberty, he is also given licence (as reformers complained about absolution) to go off and sin again, with Frances or Jaquenetta. In the background is a scriptural contrast between the Old Law of Moses (here, the academic oath) and the liberty brought by Christ (Armado), as represented by Paul—who was himself 'losed... from *his* bondes' after detention by the Romans (Acts 22: 30). For the Apostle, we were 'children,... in bondage vnder the rudiments of the worlde' until Christ came to 'redeme them which were vnder the Law' (Galatians 4: 3–5). It is a droll, half-blasphemous contrast that Biron will exploit later in the play. For the King and his lords will soon, if they do not already, want to wriggle out of their oath. They want acquittance in turn. To be *acquitted* of an *oath* was a standard formula, expressing release.[146] How they achieve it—for one another, and with the hindrance and help of the women—is the subject of Chapter 4.

4

A World-Without-End Bargain

Love's Labour's Lost

Love's Labour's Lost seems to rewind at the start of Act 4, when the Princess, out hunting with her ladies, reflects on the hunt for fame which preoccupied Navarre at the start of the play:

> Glory grows guilty of detested crimes
> When for fame's sake, for praise, an outward part,
> We bend to that the working of the heart,
> As I for praise alone now seek to spill
> The poor deer's blood that my heart means no ill. (4.1.31–5)

He swore to bend the working of his heart—all his affective, appetitive energies—to the academic oath, ostensibly in order to study and subliminally to avoid mortality, but actually to excel in the enactment of what the philosopher R. M. Hare, a touch disparagingly, calls 'the Promising Game'.[1] His academy is a virtual institution, which, as it fails to become a real one, increasingly enshrines what John R. Searle (Hare's opponent in arguments about promising) calls the 'institution of promising', the set of linguistic conventions and conditions within which promissory speech acts have meaning.[2] We shall return to linguistic philosophy, but why, for now, does he wish to excel? For the sake of fame, less resonantly known as praise. Like Huizinga, the Princess knows that games are not just about rules and systems put into play to create pattern, form, and aesthetic effect. 'We play or compete "for" something. The object for which we play and compete is first and foremost victory, but victory is associated with ... honour, esteem, prestige.' We may compete for a *pledge* or a *gage* or a *prize*, but 'prize' is cognate with 'praise'.[3] The fame won by the victor, the Princess might say out of Huizinga, is the ultimate, idealized victory.

This helps us develop the analysis of the men's oaths as wagers in a game (pp. 78–9). They are 'competitors in oath' (2.1.82) because they compete for fame in the world in and beyond the play, and this edges into rivalry with each other in pursuit of their common aim. Sometimes they play as a team, but they are also like members of a gang daring one another by making the articles and punishments more severe. To return to 1.1 from the angle of the Princess's lines in 4.1 is to see that the distress experienced by the men at forswearing the academic oath has less to do than it might with remorse for oath-breaking and more with having performed badly in 'the Promising Game' and lost the prize. This is why we find them, later in Act 4, producing so many *arguments* about why they are not really forsworn, rather than venting regret. 'Shame' is the word they keep using, an aspect of public identity, of fame, rather than anything more inward. The only consolation, and it is a huge one, is that they have all lost the game together. Even then, the competitive spirit will not be kept in check. Once they have discovered with relief that they are equally forsworn, they start to compete about which has the fairest and which the least attractive mistress.

The Princess is wisely aware that the women are not free of this impulse. Engaged in the game of hunting, one of the ancient games discussed by Huizinga,[4] she shoots a harmless deer, punning emblem of love, as the King bends the working of his heart (dear/hart). She is herself, as Boyet puts it, 'held precious in the world's esteem' (2.1.4). If the men quarrel about which has the most beautiful mistress, the women spar about their looks and pick on Catherine for her smallpox scars (5.2.41–6). And they collectively compete with the men. When Navarre and his lords come to woo them, disguised as Muscovites, in Act 5, the masked women's deflection of their suits is not purely, virtuously driven by a wish to expose the folly of rash oaths, but designed to frustrate and fool them, and to relish the praise that they take from the other women when wooed by the 'wrong' men. They acutely but remorselessly press their advantage once the men return as themselves. The drama devolves into binary contests, supporting Huizinga's contention that play tends to antithetical competition between teams or pairs of opponents.[5] It rises to one such confrontation when the Pageant of the Nine Worthies breaks into disorder and Costard and Armado square up for a fight. Not until the songs of Ver and Hiems, at the very end of the play, will contest and debate be brought into a sort of balance, though the lovely morphing of antagonism into an acceptance of things set in their proper seasons (there is a time for study, a time for wooing, and a time for dying) is not without residual difficulties left by the breakability of oaths and vows.

⋆ ⋆ ⋆

The Princess's lines at the start of Act 4 are thematically active, but they also show us, in character terms, much that criticism of the play, increasingly feminist in style, has come to admire in the role. She is thoughtful, self-aware, generous. In the to-and-fro of performance, however, there is also plenty of scope for the actor to bring out the more combative, decisive traits that she shares with her ladies. Even as she reflects on her pastime, she is alive to the pace of diplomacy: 'Well, lords, to-day we shall have our dispatch' (5). This means both that the legal bonds which have been dispatched to them from France will come into their hands, and that they will end their diplomatic mission and go home.[6] Given the emphasis on celerity, the question arises why the sureties have been delayed. It might be a sign of the efficiency with which the Princess has mustered her train: she has got ahead of the paperwork. It might equally be a tactic calculated to let Navarre see something of a potential bride before the papers about Aquitaine arrive. One thing, however, is clear. This is one of a series of documents that goes astray on embassies in the play. Another is about to turn up. Shakespeare has introduced the mission from France not just to parallel the academic oaths (pp. 87, 96), but dramatically to explore how written missives, like the men's written oaths, can miss their target.

The first scene of the play takes a turn against the King's hunt for fame when Dull enters with Costard, carrying Armado's letter, which reveals that the proclamation against seeing women has been disobeyed by the clown and the dairymaid. Costard also enters 4.1, again with a letter, this time purportedly from Biron to Rosaline, but actually, by mistake, another of Armado's. He has misdelivered the letter he was given in 3.1, when, in the playful terms of Mote, he became 'ambassador for an ass' (43). Displaying her decisive streak, the Princess is unscrupulously eager to open this missive, and Boyet is 'bound' to unloose it.

BOYET I am bound to serve.
This letter is mistook. It importeth none here.
It is writ to Jaquenetta.
PRINCESS We will read it, I swear.
Break the neck of the wax, and everyone give ear. (56–9)

'I swear' is enablingly vehement, and surprising. For audiences, this is the first hint of something that will matter greatly to this chapter: that the King and his circle are not the only swearers in the play.

BOYET [*reads*] 'By heaven, that thou art fair is most infallible, true that thou art beauteous, truth itself that thou art lovely. More fairer than fair, beautiful than beauteous, truer than truth itself,...' (60–3)

This hyperbolizing asseveration varies what Costard said in 1.1, after he has tried to wriggle out of the proclamation against seeing a wench, a damsel, a maid: that 'Jaquenetta is a true girl' (290). Indeed, we have just heard him say to the Princess, 'truth is truth' (4.1.48). As early modern commentators keep saying, oaths are sworn to confirm the verity of something; that is why they are useful. But what if the truth is self-evident and given by nature? Why bother then with oaths, which become empty exclamations (like Armado's 'By heaven')? It may sound Shakespearean to say that nature suffices, that words merely supplement, but this is only one among several, more sophisticated views of language in the play. Eventually, oaths will prove their worth by securing relationships and bridging time.

The next missive to go astray is this poem, read by the parson, Nathaniel, after it is brought to him and the schoolmaster, Holofernes, by Costard and Jaquenetta.

'If love make me forsworn, how shall I swear to love?
  Ah, never faith could hold, if not to beauty vowed.
Though to myself forsworn, to thee I'll faithful prove.
  Those thoughts to me were oaks, to thee like osiers bowed.
Study his bias leaves, and makes his book thine eyes,
  Where all those pleasures live that art would comprehend.
If knowledge be the mark, to know thee shall suffice.
  Well learnèd is that tongue that well can thee commend;...'

(4.2.97–105)

The audience knows that this is the missive that the Princess hoped to break into because we have seen Biron hand it to Costard and because its arguments resemble some of the sophistries he has already used. But Holofernes has to look at what Armado and Mote in their riddling scene (3.1) call the 'salve' and '*l'envoi*'—'To the snow-white hand of the most beauteous Lady Rosaline... Your ladyship's... Biron' (121–5)—to work out what this missive is. His uncertainty is not surprising. The poem could have been penned by the King or any of his lords since they all face the same problem of loosening the binding oath, or loosening it yet further.

There are the beginnings here of a comedy of interchangeability that will intensify in Act 5 where the masked women are wooed by the 'wrong' men. In the Antipholus and Dromio plots of *The Comedy of Errors*, confusion between the twins had given rise to searching reflections on the nature of identity. In *Love's Labour's Lost*, by contrast, the energies of confusion spill out into misplaced language, vows, casuistical regrouping, and limits are set to depth. The academic oath gives a powerful impetus, but much that follows is defined in relation to keeping or finessing it. You can see why W. H. Auden and Chester Kallman reduced Dumaine and Longueville to one in their libretto based on the play. Doing so is both a dramatic economy and a continuation of the comic logic. Yet it detracts from the elaborate pattern-making which is the essence of play in the play. When the men observe each other fall into perjury through their poems, an imbalance is set up (without which there would be stasis, the opposite of play), then resolved into an order. What they say along the way could often be redistributed. In one sense, this is what love is like; it makes everyone the same sort of fool. But from a dramaturgical point of view, the plot makes the men counters in a game in which their oaths are pledges. This curbs what could be psychological plenitude, the emotional unpredictability we expect with Shakespeare, making composition in that sense too easy. If you can see why a dramatist so interested in binding language would write *Love's Labour's Lost*, you can also see why he never again let a play be so dominated by oaths.

* * *

In 4.3 this interchangeability develops as the men are drawn into a Chinese box of multiple eavesdropping. They feel less isolated as oath-breaking reconciles them. But there are still problems to address:

LONGUEVILLE Ay me! I am forsworn.
BIRON [*aside*] Why, he comes in like a perjure, wearing papers....
LONGUEVILLE Am I the first that have been perjured so?
BIRON [*aside*] I could put thee in comfort, not by two that I know. (42–7)

Longueville uses 'perjured' in the everyday sense of oath-breaking, not the technical sense of swearing to a known untruth that had been made (or, more accurately, regularized as)[7] a common law offence by the Perjury Act of 1563. But the rites of public shaming also associated with punishment for *fidei laesio* in the ecclesiastical courts hang over the description. As Judith Hudson has brought out in her valuable essay, 'Punishing Perjury in *Love's Labour's Lost*',[8] the whole field of retribution and penance for false oaths and broken, binding promises was fraught in the late sixteenth century not just because of overlapping jurisdictions between common and ecclesiastical law but because perjury was seen as an offence against God as well as man. The play is variously, idiomatically interested in both statutes and the sorts of infamy that went to the church courts. But perjury, as Biron and Longueville conceive it, is not in principle a minor offence.

Yet it cannot be said that any of the men displays much remorse. The parts are not scripted that way. Biron conveys a sense of relief as the infractions of the other men reduce his shame; and Longueville treats the audience to a surprisingly resourceful poem designed to evade humiliation as far as possible by showing that he has not really lost in 'the Promising Game', or that, if he has, it is not his fault. With a mocking glance at the frivolities of love poetry, he argues that, since his mistress is a goddess, not a woman, he did not swear against seeing her. In any case,

> '...Vows are but breath, and breath a vapour is.
> Then thou, fair sun, which on my earth dost shine,
> Exhal'st this vapour-vow; in thee it is....' (63–5)

Early modern life was no doubt full of evaporating vows. But sworn, devoted speech acts were supposed to bind, whatever their intention. For moralists they carried a religious burden. It is a weakness, however, of 'the institution of promising', that, as Hare shows, if its rules are construed only linguistically, vows become as empty as breath: 'Unless a sufficient number of people were prepared to assent to the moral principles which are the constitutive rules of the institution of promising, ... the word "promise" would become mere noise.'[9]

Longueville, aware of his shallowness, has a strengthening argument to add:

> '...If broken then, it is no fault of mine.
> If by me broke, what fool is not so wise
> To lose an oath to win a paradise?' (66–8)

'If broken then' has a lawyerly captiousness in its reluctance to concede, and the final line is equally ruthless in addressing the root of the matter, which is that, while breaking a vow is bad, it is sometimes worth cheating in one game to win the big prize in another. What props this up, and enriches it for an audience, is the play on binding and loosing that, as we saw in Chapter 3, runs back to the opening scenes. The Q/F reading is 'loose', which implies unbinding, but with a quibble in Elizabethan pronunciation on 'lose', educed by 'win'. The version of this sonnet that appears with non-Shakespearean material in *The Passionate Pilgrim* (1599), along with the poems by the King, Dumaine, and Biron, reads 'breake', and that is the only substantive variant. 'Lose' is the stronger reading, but the poem may owe it to its position in the play.

Dumaine's slender poem rehearses what are by now routine casuistries. His vow was unmeet for youth.'Do not call it sin in me', he urges Catherine (a plea masked as an imperative),'That I am forsworn for thee' (I am breaking my oath for you, so you must bear the responsibility). 'This will I send, and something else more plain,' he adds, worried that his verses will not be understood (and performance will always leave some doubt as to the wilfulness of the women's misconstruction), 'That shall express my true love's fasting pain' (love is starting to provide the conditions of intensity and deprivation that the academy had offered in 1.1):

> O, would the King, Biron, and Longueville
> Were lovers too! Ill, to example ill
> Would from my forehead wipe a perjured note,[10]
> For none offend where all alike do dote. (109–22)

This is entirely about the results of 'the Promising Game', not truth. Longueville and the King and then Biron step forward to accuse the others of forswearing:

> BIRON Not you to me, but I betrayed by you.
> I that am honest, I that hold it sin
> To break the vow I am engagèd in. (172–4)

Mutual discovery ups the chances of comedy, by letting the real motives of the sequence (competitiveness and solidarity) turn 'sin' into a point-scoring, hypocritical word, taking some of the sting out of what part of every Elizabethan auditor would believe to be troublingly true.

Sin or treachery? Enter Costard and Jaquenetta with Biron's letter to Rosaline, misdirected by Holofernes to the King.'Some certain treason', cries Costard, initiating a laborious exchange with Navarre. What he says is comically disproportionate, but it reflects a half-baked awareness that by breaking the King's edict, and their academic oath, the men have betrayed their allegiance (university and Inns of Court oaths usually included a declaration of allegiance to the monarch). La Primaudaye, in his discussion of oath-breaking in *The French Academie*, argues that tolerating perjury is a short cut to letting in treachery.[11] But here, absurdly enough, the King is one of the traitors, and, in any case, it would now betray the group to be faithful to the oath. Biron feels safe enough to 'confess' his guilt. The oddness of the three becomes the evenness of four. Whether as 'traitors' (Costard) or 'pickpurses in love' (Biron), the men 'deserve to die' (185–209). What drives this joke about capital punishment is the testing thought in the play that love brings in mortality.

The remainder of the scene is dominated by Biron's attempt to justify their oath-breaking.

Sweet lords, sweet lovers!—O, let us embrace.
As true we are as flesh and blood can be.
The sea will ebb and flow, heaven show his face.
Young blood doth not obey an old decree. (210–13)

Mutability, the skies, youth, none can be curbed by an outmoded law, the sort of statute fallen into disuse that Sanderson has in mind when he says that college statutes can be neglected (see p. 76). 'And the like is to be understood', he adds, 'of the publique *Laws* of a *Kingdome*.'[12] So what sounds specious in Biron does have early modern foundations, especially since a 'decree' sounds arbitrary. 'We cannot cross the cause why we were born', he goes on, 'Therefore of all hands must we be forsworn' (214–15). This is another familiar justification for oath-breaking, where obligations are in conflict with the bonds of nature. 'Therefore' accordingly sounds hasty, even fallacious, but unanswerable. 'Of all hands' means 'in any case', but there has to be some play on swearing 'by this hand' (a common gesture) and on 'all' the 'hands' that signed the oath.

The inclusiveness of 'all' is important. It shares the liberating sweep of 'let us embrace'. Oath-breaking has separated the men, but it now brings them together the more firmly because by sharing their shame they are the less ashamed, or shame-proof; it consolidates their bond by unbinding them. Yet their being free to woo does not prevent them remaining 'competitors'. They are soon busy ranking their mistresses, each protesting he has the best. This is the stuff of the Sonnets (e.g. 21, 130), especially when Biron cries up the unconventional beauty of his own dark lady, Rosaline. Yet their assertions hit a problem. What can they swear or swear to that will not be discredited?

KING By heaven, thy love is black as ebony.
BIRON Is ebony like her? O word divine! A wife of such wood were felicity.
O, who can give an oath? Where is a book...? (243–6)

Swearing gravely on a Bible or New Testament: that might trump their broken oaths. But 'Who can give an oath?' remains a question now they are all publicly forsworn, like the false swearers on the book who were prevented from swearing again in court by the 1563 Perjury Act.[13]

That I may swear beauty doth beauty lack
If that she learn not of her eye to look?
No face is fair that is not full so black. (247–9)

This is not just about male rivalry. Biron continues to put oaths in doubt, by saying that he will swear the opposite of what is true for everyone else but still be true. When verity is reversible, what is the use of an oath? In this flux of difficulty, the men are unsure how to proceed. Longueville calls for 'Some tricks, some quillets how to cheat the devil' (because they are marked for damnation by their swearing). Dumaine adds 'Some salve for perjury' (284–5). We are back with the salve and *l'envoi* riddles between Armado, Mote, and Costard.[14]

It does not seem to have been noted that Dumaine employs a once common but now obsolete meaning of *salve*: 'a sophistical excuse or evasion'.[15] Up to a point, such a salve would ease, like ointment; the *Oxford English Dictionary* gives a further, now rare sense, 'A remedy (esp. for spiritual disease, sorrow, and the like).'[16] Biron takes up the invitation to ease or exculpate:

> O, 'tis more than need.
> Have at you, then, affection's men-at-arms.
> Consider what you first did swear unto:
> To fast, to study, and to see no woman—
> Flat treason 'gainst the kingly state of youth. (285–9)

This salve harks back to Costard, Jaquenetta, and their entry with the letter. No, the lords were not traitors when they fell in love, Biron argues. They were not treasonous against their oaths of allegiance to the King. It was their initial oaths that were treasonous against the kingly state of youth. This has behind it the oft-heard early modern excuse that you need not keep an unlawful oath. As casuistry it is underwhelming.

At this point both the Quarto and Folio duplicate lines in such a way that we can see one attempt at writing a big speech for Biron (4.3.291.1–23) giving way in authorial manuscript to a second, rather different version without the false-start being deleted. The first version is too close to the dilemma of an oath-breaking student to be fully interesting for a public-theatre audience. When the speech restarts, Biron quickly advances into an exalted description of Love. Nonetheless, he does glance back at the academic oath, and what he says is significant, not just because he seeks to remain within reach of orthodoxy by repeating from 1.1 the argument that the fundamental purpose of the oath can be upheld by shifting the object of study from books to women's eyes, but because, for the first time in dialogue, he calls the oath a *vow*—a change of tack worth discussing in a moment:

> O, we have made a vow to study, lords,
> And in that vow we have forsworn our books;

For when would you, my liege, or you, or you
In leaden contemplation have found out
Such fiery numbers as the prompting eyes
Of beauty's tutors have enriched you with? (292–7)

This has a familiar, unconvincing logic, but the account of Love that follows almost transcends the problems: 'when love speaks, the voice of all the gods | Make heaven drowsy with the harmony' (318–19).

Almost, and not for long. Drowsiness is not a lasting fix. The promotion of love into Love fails to dispose of perjury, and so, with a twist of wordplay that is the more adroit for being so obvious, Biron says that the initial oath was not just treachery, it was a forswearing. When you forswore the women in the sense of renouncing them,[17] you were, as it were, breaking an oath (i.e. forswearing),[18] and that can only be put right by giving way to wisdom, love, and nature:

Then fools you were these women to forswear,
Or keeping what is sworn, you will prove fools....
Let us once lose our oaths to find ourselves,
Or else we lose ourselves to keep our oaths.
It is religion to be thus forsworn,
For charity itself fulfils the law,
And who can sever love from charity? (329–39)

The loose/lose gambit continues its easing work (Q and F again read 'loose'). But Biron goes further by invoking one of the best-known declarations of Paul, at Galatians 5: 14 and Romans 13: 10, 'For all the Law is fulfilled in one worde, which is this, Thou shalt loue thy neighbour as thy self,' 'therefore is loue the fulfilling of the Law'. The men's oaths and articles, the laws that apply in Navarre's park, are like the Old Law of the Pentateuch, which can be fulfilled, according to the Apostle, by obeying Christ's injunction to love our neighbours—which here means loving the women, love as 'charity' (*caritas*) slipping into love as *eros*. 'Fulfilled' not only secures the allusion but quips that, by showing charity, fulfilling the broken law (the statutes of the park) in a Pauline sense, the men are also fulfilling their forsworn promises, their subscribed oaths.

As usual, Biron is alert to the more ingenious considerations aired in the period. It was a commonplace that oaths and vows sworn to do unlawful things should be broken. 'Void therfore must we proclaime that Oath', Christopher White declares, 'which cannot be, vnlesse vnlawfully performed.' But White goes on to contend, and many agreed with him, that oaths 'against charitie' were also untenable. Vows, John Mabb observed, should be 'Charitable and glorious: tending to the honor of almightie God, and good of man'. White gives the example of an oath-taker who 'swear[s] neuer to lend money, not to goe to such a mans house, neuer to bee friends with another, and the like: Of which Oathes I may safely say, *they are not to be kept*.' In words that chime with Biron's, he quotes St Bernard: 'For... *What is intended for the aduancement of charitie, may not beare armes against charitie.* The solemnitie of an Oath was ordained for the benefit of humane societie, and therefore may not be employed for the ruine of it.' It stands high among universal principles that '*Thou shalt loue thy neighbour as thy selfe:* and... an Oath made against the fulfilling of them, directly tends to the violation of Gods Lawes.'[19]

Embracing love transforms the men's circumstances by eliding *eros* with *caritas* and consequently easing their oaths but also by changing the landscape of the promise. It is one thing to forswear women indifferently, another to slight the future mother of your children. There is a ripple of excitement among the men, as they start to hope that the women can validate the commutation of their oath. This was controversial territory, and Biron prepares the ground with as much care as ardour. Protestant commentators resisted the claim made by Roman Catholic casuists 'that a private man of his own authority... may commute a vow, or oath, into that which is evidently better', notwithstanding the authority of St Gregory, who declared, 'He infringeth not his promise or purpose, who changeth it for the better.' Sanderson bluntly concludes 'that the bond of an oath cannot be remitted or losed... by Commutation, without consent of all the parties; But the consent of him unto whom the oath is made, is more especially required, because such right is acquired unto him, as without his own consent ought not to be taken away.'[20]

Though Shakespeare often uses 'oath' and 'vow' interchangeably, there are differences in tone and address that can affect how the word is employed. In the first three acts of *Love's Labour's Lost*, the men (unlike the Princess) call their promise to study an 'oath'. The elevated pitch of the sonnets that they write to the women brings 'vow' into play, as the purer, more poetical term, but Biron's redescription of the oath as a 'vow' becomes lodged in his speeches in 4.3 because it points the given words towards heaven and shades out obligation *to others*. The beneficiaries of the promise to study would be the students (if the academy is indeed beneficial). They may owe each other a degree of mutual support in their studies, but no one else loses a right if the *vow* is quietly shelved. As Sanderson goes on to argue:

> Neither is the case of a *Vow*, and of an *Oath* altogether alike in respect of Commutation; for in a vow seeing it is made to God alone, some liberty may perhaps be granted unto the person vowing of changing the same into another

> which may be evidently better, and more acceptable unto God, there being nothing in this alteration injurious unto a third person: but in an *oath* which is made unto man, *injury* might be done him, if it should without his consent, and against his will be commuted into any other thing.[21]

This was not the only way of construing the difference. Catholic commentators could invoke Aquinas[22] and see vows as more binding than oaths precisely because they are devoted to God. Sanderson's point of view is securely in the English mainstream. The notion that the women could help the men commute their oath/vow as the only incidental but relevant party left unconsulted would be readily absorbed if not assumed by an audience familiar with the common law. In worldly terms at least, beyond an erosion of trust, they would suffer no injury from commutation, only a refusable opportunity.

There is another, rather simpler explanation for the buoyancy that is loosed as the band becomes unbound but discovers itself to be re-bonded around the task of wooing: the sense that others' transgression salves you. The men can break their oaths collectively because others have abrogated them individually. Oaths sworn to obey 'the Statutes of any College or Society' lose their power to bind, Sanderson argues, when they are not 'put in practise . . . by others' and are 'abrogated'.[23] But the energetic mustering onstage does not remove all doubts. Lingering for a moment, Biron worries that payback is coming: 'Sowed cockle reaped no corn, | And justice always whirls in equal measure. | Light wenches may prove plagues to men forsworn' (357–9). The women might scorn the men and prove 'Light', inconstant, in turn, when the men come to them perjured. Ominously, there is also a reminder of the plague.

★ ★ ★

The disguising of Navarre and his lords as Muscovites can be a joyous thing in production. The men burst out in fancy dress, ready to party. Yet why do they go to the women in this way? Huizinga, again:

> The 'differentness' and secrecy of play are most vividly expressed in 'dressing up'. Here the 'extra-ordinary' nature of play reaches perfection. The disguised or masked individual 'plays' another part, another being. He *is* another being.[24]

The men are embarrassed to appear to the women as themselves since that would make evident their oath-breaking. The disguise that they choose, while not unknown in courtly entertainments,[25] is not ideal for the task in hand, because Russians were notorious for promise-breaking.[26] But there is a more immediate stimulus, which comes, as we have noted (pp. 86–7), from the success of the comedy in *Gesta Grayorum* where the Prince of Purpoole receives an embassy from the Emperor of Russia and Muscovy. Boyet puts the visiting Russians into the play's preoccupation with embassies when he tells the women how their herald, Mote, has 'conned his embassage' (5.2.98).

The problem is that the disguise, though enabling for the men, reinforces the women's sense that they are unreliable. Evidently now oath-breakers, they are also role-players. Are the Princess and her ladies right to believe that the men want to be both themselves and, as Huizinga would put it, other beings? Robert Tofte's celebrated lines about an early performance of *Love's Labour's Lost* offer some insight into the conundrum of duplicity. 'This *Play* no *Play*, but Plague was vnto me, | For there I lost the Loue I liked most,' he writes,

> Each Actor plaid in cunning wise his part,
> But chiefly Those entrapt in *Cupids* snare:
> Yet All was fained, twas not from the hart,
> They seemde to grieue, but yet they felt no care:
> Twas I that Griefe (indeed) did beare in brest,
> The others did but make a show in Iest.[27]

The women are wise to be wary of what might be merely 'show', and to meet the men on equal terms. They exchange the 'favours' that the men have sent them—bejewelled portraits, pearls, gloves[28]—and put on masks to conceal the most identifiable of their bodily favours.[29] This does not, however, pre-empt the troubling drama of speech acts that the wooing men unleash. For they mount a 'show in Iest' that turns on binding words. When they swear undying love (and to the 'wrong' women) their recapitulation of the initial oaths is calculated to breed mistrust. How are the ladies to know whether the men are swearing in jest?

If it were simply a question of listening, this would not matter so much. But the men are looking for an assurance. They want to make bonds out of question and answer, wit and combative mock, rhyme and pun. Their aim is shown by the sudden, heavy use of 'vouchsafe', as in Biron to 'Rosaline' (the Princess): 'Vouchsafe to show the sunshine of your face | That we, like savages, may worship it' (5.2.200–1). The King says to 'the Princess' (Rosaline), 'Vouchsafe, bright moon, and these thy stars, to shine' (204). Her repartee does not dash him entirely. 'Then in our measure do but vouchsafe one change,' he requests. He gets only one snatch of dance out of her, then must ask again, 'The music plays, vouchsafe some motion to it', to which she pertly replies, 'Our ears vouchsafe it' (208–17). This is shuttling between doing something to evidence willingness and merely hearing graciously. The ladies are refusing to enter into even an approximation of vouching-as-vowing, not offering surety or giving warrant for anything yet.

Love's Labour's Lost has a dozen uses of 'vouchsafe', far more than usual in a Shakespeare play, and most of them appear in this visit by the Russians. The commonest meaning of the word in the early modern period is 'give, grant, bestow' or 'notice, respond to, reply'. But 'vouchsafe' is *vouch* plus *safe* and the word can mean 'vouch safely' (and securely) as 'vouch' can itself mean 'vouchsafe'. The audible overlap between vouch and vow, reinforced by *safe*, edges vouchsafing into binding. To grant a word in response to a request, or give ears and favour to an approach, is halfway to making a bargain. There are also legal overtones. A person would come to court to *vouch* for the truth of something or someone, to offer testimony or witness or warrant, a process that involved oath-taking.[30] A lady asked to vouchsafe is invited to respond by giving an attention which warrants or affirms the approach. *Vouchsafe* is the more nearly *vowing* because dialogue, a prescripted response, especially when in binding rhyme, is a form of security in speech.

So the women refuse to vouchsafe. They rebuff the men by using puns and rhymes to counter, rather than meet, join, and bond, and split them up into four individuals all conversing apart. 'Will you vouchsafe with me to change a word?', Dumaine asks 'Catherine' (Maria), but she takes 'change' to mean alter rather than exchange and sends 'Fair lady—' back as 'Fair lord' (238–9). The ludic becomes ludicrous. When Biron asks 'Rosaline' (the Princess) for 'one sweet word', she gives him 'Honey and milk and sugar'. He offers to make up the 'two treys' of a dicing game by saying 'Metheglin, wort, and malmsey—well run, dice!' (230–3). He holds his own in the wit combat, but at the cost of seeing his suit turned into the sort of number routine that the play is so often reduced to. How deep the connection goes, philosophically and theologically, is a hard question, but *lots* were associated with *oaths* in early modern controversy, not just because swearing went along with the intensity of gaming but because throwing dice or dealing cards and invoking God as your witness in minor matters tempts providence and demeans the Divine.[31] In *Love's Labour's Lost*, the ludic toys with blasphemy in the men's oath-taking as a sort of pledging or betting against their own natures; it constructs an order which inevitably generates odds and disorder. The witty wooing of the women by the men is designed, not entirely effectively, to crystallize a new order. Seeking to raise and resolve their game, Navarre, Biron, and presumably the other lords make the mistake of swearing again. The audience does not hear the oaths directly (that would pre-empt the impact of the bargains made at the end of the play), but they are convincingly reported. 'Biron did swear himself out of all suit,' announces the Princess. 'The King is my love sworn,' Rosaline declares, to which the Princess adds, 'quick Biron hath plighted faith to me' (275–83).

For audiences, the verbally orchestrated quadrille is delightful to behold, as the couples spin away in turn to the edge of the playing area, before the men retreat in confusion. There is an interchange of oaths and identities in an organized sequence of errors. But this is more than design: it is aimed at specific cruces in early modern binding language. If you plighted your troth to *x* thinking you were plighting it to *y*, the commitment was not easily evaded. Sanderson, for instance, takes an oath to be so potent that he holds 'the party deliberately swearing to be bound, whether he intend to oblige himself or not'.[32] In his *Treatise of Spousals*, Henry Swinburne argues that 'since it is the very Consent of Mind only which maketh Matrimony, we are to regard not [people's] Words, but their Intents, not the formality of the Phrase, but the drift of their Determination', yet he goes on to develop the question: 'how can we *know* a Man's meaning but by his words?'[33] What the men swear may be more binding than their intentions, which may in turn, as the women know and show, be less honourable than they believe.

Towards the end of his treatise Swinburne observes that 'if the Man do err in the Person of the Woman, as did *Jacob* when he was married to *Leah*, instead of *Rachel*... the Marriage [is] void and of none effect, by reason of the said Error' (176). Navarre and his lords swear in favour of those who they think bear their favours, but if the 'wrong' women receive the oaths, surely they are off the hook? Before we conclude that they are, we should notice that Biron praises the white hand of the lady he woos—not Rosaline but the Princess, even though she is Leah to his Rachel. In performance it can be deliciously clear that the men are drawn by the physical allure of the women as well as the redistributed favours. This is one reason why the Princess and her ladies are so gleeful on the men's departure. They take their oaths as compliments. This is not quite *A Midsummer Night's Dream*, where Lysander pursues Helena despite his oaths and vows to Hermia, because of the love juice,[34] but the men are attracted by and swear to the 'wrong' women's comely favours,[35] not just the favours that they wear, and that must colour their plights.

Yet the men, confounded, return:

KING We came to visit you, and purpose now
To lead you to our court. Vouchsafe it, then.
PRINCESS This field shall hold me, and so hold your vow.
Nor God nor I delights in perjured men. (343–6)

'Vouchsafe' fails again. The ladies do have it in their power to release the men from their oaths as Muscovites because, as Sanderson put it in *De Juramento*, in widely though not universally accepted terms, 'if an oath be sworn in favour of another, . . . it is not binding, except he in whose favour it is made, accept, and ratifie the same'.[36] That still leaves, however, as the Princess goes on to remind the King, the group oath or vow to study. By this stage, it seems an old decree. How is an audience to take the apparent seriousness of the Princess? And how are we to reconcile this with something new and on the face of it surprising, that she does not just say 'I swear' but fulsomely swears a pledge?

Now by my maiden honour, yet as pure
As the unsullied lily, I protest,
A world of torments though I should endure,
I would not yield to be your house's guest,
So much I hate a breaking cause to be
Of heavenly oaths, vowed with integrity. (351–6)

The mockery in 'vowed with integrity' may soften her severity towards Navarre. Her oath can even be played as sympathetically upholding what has been shown as weak in his vow. But the formula that she uses, 'by my maiden honour', is by any measure strong.

* * *

Swearing was a male prerogative in many areas of early modern life, so it is easy uncritically to assume that the same goes for *Love's Labour's Lost*. As we have begun to see, however, Irene G. Dash is wrong to argue, in the only substantial discussion of oaths in the play, that

> Women constitute the subject of the men's vows, although the men swear first to reject women, then pledge to pursue them, and finally to marry them. The ironic progression suggests that since the oath-takers are men, Shakespeare is mocking the male tradition of oath-taking, insisting that it be linked with honesty. In contrast, the Princess of France and the women of her court reject

> the offers of marriage of the King and his courtiers, refusing to be bound by this timeless oath. One of the men objects that this is no way to end a comedy. Thus Shakespeare presents a woman's point of view on honesty and truth, endowing the play with a significance that goes beyond the limits of the comic world.[37]

On the contrary, *Love's Labour's Lost* is unusual in the outspokenness it encourages among royal and noble women, who were able, as Hotspur reminds Kate in *1 Henry IV*, to swear good, mouth-filling oaths when they chose. We have seen that they sometimes did (p. 27). The 'God*es* pitty' sworn by the young Elizabeth at the Oxford performance of *Palamon and Arcite* (p. 86) was mild by her standards. More importantly, Dash overlooks how the women seize the initiative and use oaths to secure bonds with the men.

In *Love's Labour's Lost*, the women not only swear, they also swear in jest. When the King says, 'O, you have lived in desolation here, | Unseen, unvisited, much to our shame', the Princess replies,

Not so, my lord. It is not so, I swear.
  We have had pastimes here, and pleasant game.
A mess of Russians left us but of late.
KING How, madam? Russians?
PRINCESS Ay, in truth, my lord.
Trim gallants, full of courtship and of state. (357–63)

Rosaline makes it clear that the women have not been deceived ('Madam, speak true'), and calls the men fools. To which Biron replies 'This jest is dry to me' (364–73). The Princess's swearing in jest greatly enhances the comedy because it is her swearing that the men were Russians that makes it so invidious for the men to admit that they were not. They have made her swear falsely, and have done so after she made it clear how serious she takes swearing to be.

Biron adds, 'Thus pour the stars down plagues for perjury' (394). The payback that he feared at the end of 4.3 is coming. Rash oaths and forswearing breed a linguistic version of the plague that Bicknoll warned against (p. 73). It is a particularly grim sort of payback for Biron because it involves being at a disadvantage in wit combats, losing the mocking contest. So he resolves to give up 'Taffeta phrases, silken terms precise', and other forms of rhetorical showing-off:

I do forswear them, and I here protest,
  By this white glove—how white the hand, God knows!—
Henceforth my wooing mind shall be expressed
  In russet yeas, and honest kersey noes. (406–13)

Biron swears ('*By* this white glove') against verbal folly, the chief of which has been swearing. He forswears swearing, then, not to 'forswear' in breaking his word (this time) but in giving up certain kinds of word, rhetorical and/or binding, which is why he deftly alludes in 'yeas, and... noes' to Christ's prohibition in Matthew: 'let your communication be, Yea, yea: Nay, nay.'[38] A lady's hand can itself be an instrument of engagement, of binding. Biron's dialogue cues the actor to take Rosaline's white-gloved hand at this point. He must knowingly protest by a mere appearance that he mistrusts superficiality. Perversely enough, his recantation requires another protestation, another vow-like appeal, marked by an empty phatic: 'And to begin, wench, so God help me, law! | My love to thee is sound, sans crack or flaw' (414–15).

When Rosaline takes him to task, for the affectation of 'sans', Biron replies with the play's fullest statement of the link between perjurable words and the plague:

Yet I have a trick
Of the old rage. Bear with me, I am sick.
I'll leave it by degrees. Soft, let us see.
Write 'Lord have mercy on us' on those three.
They are infected, in their hearts it lies.
They have the plague, and caught it of your eyes.
These lords are visited, you are not free;
For the Lord's tokens on you do I see.
PRINCESS No, they are free that gave these tokens to us.
BIRON Our states are forfeit. Seek not to undo us.
ROSALINE It is not so, for how can this be true,
That you stand forfeit, being those that sue? (416–27)

Behind the pleasantry and wit is an attempt to shift responsibility for the systemic abuse of language of which the oath-breaking is part. Love is a plague, Biron drolly if unoriginally proposes, caught by the men from the women. Both sexes are now equally infected: surely, he insinuates, the ladies are now falling for the lords. The women turn the tables with unrelenting alacrity. The Princess had been a suitor to the King in the matter of Aquitaine, but now the men are suitors to the women, yet powerless because forfeit.[39] The audience is likely to remember Biron's 'Light wenches may prove plagues to men forsworn' (4.3.359). But there is a deeper fear than scorn, that the visitation of the ladies has brought in the perils of the world beyond the park, above all the plague, with its sores, its houses full of the dying, and 'Lord have mercy on us' written over the door. A correlation between swearing, perjury, and plague was widely believed in, and feared (pp. 73–4). We have seen why a dramatist interested in binding language would write a play about academic oaths and statutes (p. 82). It may be, more formatively still, that Shakespeare made swearing and perjury the prime matter of a play that had pestilence behind and over it because he could create a plot in which oaths sworn to avoid the plague threaten to bring it down.

Biron cannot argue or apologize his way out of the men's collective folly. When the King assures the Princess that he was 'well advised' when he gave his word (therefore qualified to utter a binding promise), and will not betray what he swore ('Upon mine honour, no'), she expresses the doubt one could justly have of a man already forsworn ('Your oath once broke, you force not to forswear'). This gives the compromised King little alternative but to insist, and to have to deal with Rosaline recapitulating what he said to her: 'he swore that he did hold me dear | As precious eyesight.' (Eyesight is satirically relevant because, if the King was using his eyes, it was to admire the 'wrong' woman.) On cue, if a little slow-wittedly, he swears, 'By my life, my troth, | I never swore this lady such an oath', to which Rosaline responds with an oath of her own: 'By heaven, you did, and to confirm it plain, | You gave me this. But take it, sir, again.' By handing over the token, the King has put himself into the sphere of troth-plighting, risking engagement to the 'wrong' woman.[40] Yet there is a saving wordplay. He gave her the token to confirm his word, but to confirm that he wrongly gave her the token she gives him it back again (434–53).

When the King tries to justify his mistake by saying that he knew the Princess 'by this jewel' (almost an oath) 'on her sleeve' (455), his mistress spells out the trick that fooled the men. By now the wheels of comedy are turning rather predictably. It would be handy to have, as in *Le Prince d'Amour*, an archflamen among the King's officers, able 'to give absolution or dissolution for false Protestations, affectionate Oathes, &c.'[41] But Shakespeare lets the machinery run on because there is a radical potential in all this piling of oath upon oath: contrary to the moralists, the more often the men are forsworn the easier it seems to become to let them off and to judge them by other measures. The role of Biron is not situated, nor (it may be) historically equipped, to exploit that potential. Instead his anger is displaced as he rounds on Boyet for betraying to the Princess what the women would instantly have worked out for themselves, that the embassage was the men in disguise. It is a stand-off only stopped by the entry of Costard to announce the pageant planned by the commoners for the nobility.

⋆ ⋆ ⋆

The Pageant of the Nine Worthies finds an appropriate audience in the King and his lords, who have committed themselves to study for the sake of 'fame', but who now, when they mock the show, to deflect shame from themselves, disrespect or defame Pompey, Samson, Hector, and the rest.[42] As the scene becomes dissonant and darkens, audiences would be recalled to Christian themes. For Catholics and Calvinists alike, the world's 'promises of renoune' were 'false', and reputation was debased by the sinfulness of speech.[43] It is not just Hector who is fleered at, but the character who plays his part, once Costard accuses Armado of getting Jaquenetta pregnant. 'Dost thou infamonize me among potentates?' the Spaniard cries, 'Thou shalt die' (658–65). The show put on for the Princess and her ladies becomes a pageant of infamy not fame, of moral judgement not just renown. To be of 'ill fame', implying fornication or adultery, could be the grounds of a charge in the ecclesiastical courts. Punishment is in the air, for the same surge of sexual appetite that afflicts the King and his lords: 'Then shall Hector be whipped for Jaquenetta that is quick by him, and hanged for Pompey that is dead by him' (666–7). The King's plan for reformation (p. 84) is rising to a noisy climax.

Act 5 advances from team games through agonistic confrontation to a species of trial by combat. This, as Huizinga points out, is one of the origins and the apogee of play.[44] It is certainly the sort of *agon* that found its way into the Inns of Court revels—to go back to the start of Chapter 3—hedged about with threats and oaths.[45] The challenge in *Love's Labour's Lost* is more abrupt, but the magic circle of the game is still marked out with a lofty oath:

ARMADO By the North Pole, I do challenge thee.
COSTARD I will not fight with a pole, like a northern man. I'll slash, I'll do it by the sword. I bepray you, let me borrow my arms again. (678–81)

Costard is verbally alert. He has weighed up his 'remuneration' (from Armado) and found it eleven pence and a farthing lighter than the 'guerdon' of a shilling given him by Biron (3.1.156–8). Naturally his interest extends to an appreciation of swearing. After Boyet has been defeated in an obscene wit combat with Maria, Costard praises his courtly accomplishments: 'how most sweetly a will swear' (4.1.142). This time, though, he is baffled, taking

'By the North Pole' to be not a star renowned for its fixed position but a weapon used in the north country.

What breaks the deadlock and prevents the play from descending into ribald farce is another oath entirely, much plainer though still enigmatic. It comes with the entry of Mercadé when he brings news of the French King's death. In the big, generic picture, this turn of events is not surprising. A movement towards death was familiar in seasonally preoccupied entertainments put on in big houses and colleges. Compare the ending of *Summers Last Will and Testament*, where Summer is borne on a bier by satyrs and wood-nymphs singing 'Autumne hath all the Summers fruitefull treasure;... From winter, plague, & pestilence, good Lord, deliuer vs.'[46] Or the St John's College, Oxford, revels of Christmas, 1607–8, supposed to conclude with the Prince as 'cheife mourner' in his own funeral procession.[47] In its particulars and atmospherics, too, the play has been waiting for Mercadé from the opening talk of brazen tombs, through Biron's lines about the 'decrepit, sick, and bedrid' King of France, the death of Catherine's sister, to Hector, now 'dead and rotten'.[48] For all that, the entry is a shock, and Mercadé's news is emotionally intense, requiring tact:

Enter a messenger, Monsieur MERCADÉ
MERCADÉ God save you, madam.
PRINCESS Welcome, Mercadé,
But that thou interrupt'st our merriment.
MERCADÉ I am sorry, madam, for the news I bring
Is heavy in my tongue. The King your father—
PRINCESS Dead, for my life. (699–703)

'God save you, madam' is a prayer, wish, or charm, against illness and mortality. In that it distantly resembles another greeting, *salve*, 'be healthy'. It also evokes 'God save the queen', which helps the Princess anticipate what she will be told. Her 'Welcome' is typically courteous, despite her misgivings; she is better at greeting than the men. But the most striking thing about the exchange is that she anticipates the news with an oath. 'For my life', 'in asseverative phrases, exclamations, and oaths', is the same as 'by my life'.[49] 'By my life' is what the King swore to the Princess when he denied swearing love to Rosaline. Compared with such choice conjurations as 'By the North Pole', 'for my life' is spontaneous, unstudied but sombre. One should not overinterpret an oath used by Shakespeare elsewhere half a dozen times, but 'Dead' educes here a burden of time and inheritance, the idea of a father dying to make way for the child. The King of France's death is part of the same mortal nature that gave the Princess life. Come to that, 'for my life' sounds like a stake in a bet: 'I bet my life that he is dead.' This is grotesquely consistent with other wagers and calculations in the play, except that death is now as always a certainty.

⋆ ⋆ ⋆

There is a dissolution of disorder in performance, as Mercadé's news scatters the broken Pageant. Yet he leaves the play with the larger problem of finding its way to an ending. The King seeks, with concern, but rather feebly, to attract the Princess's attention, 'How fares your majesty?', but the focus of this now-regal character is impressively on affairs of state: 'Boyet, prepare. I will away tonight' (708–9). Her apologies for mockery and banter are gracious but brief. There is hardly time for us to hear of a bond being resolved, the diplomatic one: 'Excuse me so coming too short of thanks, | For my great suit so easily obtained' (720–1). The audience might wonder in that moment how the suit was won. Did the King give Aquitaine away too readily because he dotes on the Princess or did the arrival of the sureties sort things out? The matter passes 'easily' through the scene. But it provides a telling precedent for the acquittance that the men want from the women—permission to leave behind the academic oaths and to commit themselves to marriage.

The pressure of time is now felt, not least for a theatre audience conscious that the play has almost used up its hours. From the lassitude of a three years' retreat in which pastimes are the only hope we are thrown into a crisis requiring speed. Men who proposed to be 'Still and contemplative in living art' (1.1.14) must learn to chase Time's foot. This is the reality of the suddenness of death and the chaotic ripples it can set up, even when anticipated. Navarre tries to seize the moment:

> The extreme parts of time extremely forms
> All causes to the purpose of his speed,
> And often at his very loose decides
> That which long process could not arbitrate.... (5.2.722–5)

But this attempt to win scope for wooing is awkward and unconvincing, to the point where an audience will side with the Princess's elegantly apologetic resistance: 'I understand you not. My griefs are double' (734). She may understand what he is driving at, but still not understand how he thinks the pressing of his suit appropriate at a time of loss. The action has reached a stalemate, unbreakable by Biron's attempts to recycle the arguments of 4.3, shufflings off of blame which sound shabby when addressed to the women (735–58). 'We have received your letters full of love,' the Princess concedes, 'Your favours the ambassadors of love', but they took these emissaries to be 'courtship, pleasant jest, and courtesy' (759–62). 'Jest' in the sense of *gesta*, more like japes than anything substantive.

But Shakespeare has another coup in store. When Navarre pleads for a love-deal at 'the latest minute of the hour' (769), the Princess responds with a speech that draws on the powers of binding language entirely to alter the outlook.

> A time, methinks, too short
> To make a world-without-end bargain in.
> No, no, my lord, your grace is perjured much,
> Full of dear guiltiness, and therefore this:
> If for my love—as there is no such cause—
> You will do aught, this shall you do for me:
> Your oath I will not trust, but go with speed
> To some forlorn and naked hermitage
> Remote from all the pleasures of the world.
> There stay until the twelve celestial signs
> Have brought about the annual reckoning.
> If this austere, insociable life
> Change not your offer made in heat of blood;
> If frosts and fasts, hard lodging and thin weeds
> Nip not the gaudy blossoms of your love,
> But that it bear this trial and last love,
> Then at the expiration of the year
> Come challenge me, challenge me by these deserts,
> And, by this virgin palm now kissing thine,
> I will be thine, and till that instance shut
> My woeful self up in a mourning house,
> Raining the tears of lamentation
> For the remembrance of my father's death.
> If this thou do deny, let our hands part,
> Neither entitled in the other's heart. (770–94)

Ignorance of early modern betrothal has encouraged scholars to take 'A time, methinks, too short' and 'No, no' as refusal.[50] It is nothing like as simple as that. The King of France has himself tried to sort out a league or bond at the latest minute of the hour (while on his death bed), and the Princess is adroit at extracting an appropriate outcome from a similar moment of pressure. Youth was known as 'the *choosing time*', because life decisions were made then,[51] and to be decisive, like the Princess, is always the work of a moment, however prudently prepared and reviewed. Aquitaine, 'so gelded as it is' (2.1.147), can be ungelded, made a potent bridge, and their two realms be joined, if the right order of courtship and mourning is observed. The play's competitive challenges can become the more positive 'challenge' in which her word will be tested.

How can this be done? In *Love's Labour's Lost*, where the punishment for oath-breaking is not the sort of Divine wrath that is threatened by such pamphleteers as Bicknoll—though fear of that is once again to be heightened—but involves sanctions and acts of penance that reflect a failure of mutuality, the Princess says that she will not 'trust' the King's oath. She will not 'trust' a protestation of love or the marriage vow that he has not yet been allowed to take. The word 'trust' is only used twice in the play, but that does not prevent it carrying, at this point, weight from the experience of eroded faith that we have seen in the break-up of oaths and vows. The Princess needs a proof or vouch more substantial than a word. So she sets him a test or trial by ordeal that will show and temper his love, and swears corporally, 'by this virgin palm'—taking his hand in a *de futuro* spousal, a pre-contract—that she will marry him, if, at the end of this year of penance, he comes to find her.

I use the word 'penance' with caution but 'the forlorn and naked hermitage' does point up a religious dimension. Elizabethan audiences inherited from medieval Christianity the belief that an illicit, forsworn oath to do something not inherently bad ('such as swearing to marry after having vowed chastity') could legitimately be kept, but 'penance had to be done for making it'.[52] As for 'test' and 'trial', the year of austerity requires perseverance of the King, but it is not an extraordinary demand, given that so many early modern marriages—not just princely ones,[53] but often those—involved a long period of negotation and delay. Although the practice of taking spousal vows ahead of a church wedding was falling out of use in late Elizabethan England, as pressure grew for people merely and definitively to marry in church, it was a custom which persisted.[54] 'Some sixteenth- and early seventeenth-century moralists' positively commended delay because it was sanctioned by the Bible and because the gap between vowing and marriage provided—as Navarre's time at the hermitage should—'an opportunity for spiritual preparation between contract and solemnisation'.[55] In any case, as *Hamlet* reminds us, the death of a monarch required an extended period of mourning, not the cold recycling of funeral baked meats at the marriage table.[56]

Among the precise articulations of the Princess's words to the King, there are legal indicators. The sentence of a year, 'a twelvemonth an' a day' (854), is not so much a delay as a terminable period, a legal span, the time of an audit. Judith Hudson comments:

> The King will, in effect, un-break his oath, keeping the terms of the original vow to retire from the world, albeit with a somewhat reduced 'sentence'. As if in mitigation of her clemency, the Princess will take upon herself the same term of retirement... So, as in their first meeting at the gates of the court, the Princess will 'salve' the King's perjury far more effectively than could Berowne's 'tricks' and 'quillets'.[57]

This is worth thinking over, but it is not clear that the Princess does 'salve' the King's perjury when they first meet—if anything, she draws attention to it, for diplomatic or competitive advantage—and I would interpret the trial of a year and a day rather differently. 'It was proclaimed a year's imprisonment', the King tells Costard, 'to be taken with a wench' (1.2.270–1). He then reduces the sentence to a week with bran and water. The Princess reinstates the penalty and imposes it on the King, not his put-upon subjects. There is not a reduction from three to one, but the sentence of a year does become a test of love, penance mitigated by hope. It is less about having broken an oath and more about fulfilling a faith. It is the warmer because it parallels the year that she will spend mourning the death of her father. The betrothed couple will be together in their deprivations although they live apart.

In Elizabethan English, as now, 'bargain' is an everyday word suggesting not just bargaining to an agreement but value for money. The modesty of the term is if anything brought out by 'world-without-end', which leaves us in no doubt as to the seriousness of the contract for the Princess. There is something paradoxical about this, because early modern commentators would regard the 'oaths' and 'vows' that start the play as being more exalted (since they involve a Divine witness or promisee) than a bargain. In the play, however, the initial oaths, whether or not 'vowed with integrity', seem, or come to seem, narcissistic and foreshortened, not carrying real conviction. The Princess's position resembles that of modern philosophers convinced that 'the Promising Game' is a set of verbal conventions inherently unable to turn an 'is' into an 'ought'.[58] One influential, alternative tack looks at the role of commitment, notably in the work of Michael H. Robins, who conceives of the promise as belonging with agreements on the third, top level of a structure which has intention as the necessary, primitive first storey, and vowing as the second storey. 'The ascent from vows to promises is very critical', he writes in *Promising, Intending, and Moral Autonomy*, 'because I see it as an ascent from private acts to acts that are genuinely social.'[59] 'Vows', he argues, forgetting God, as Sanderson (see pp. 107–8) could not quite, 'are not obligations to anybody; there is no "vowee" as there is a promisee' (85). Yet without intention and commitment, he maintains, neither vow nor promise could be solid.

There are limits to any suggestion that the workings of drama catapulted Shakespeare out of the assumptions of his period into relatively modern ideas about intention and autonomy. Yet, just as the pile-up of broken oaths and vows from the men in Act 5 must have suggested to early audiences that multiple perjury does not necessarily deepen into sin but can resolve itself in absurdity, so the Princess's emphasis not on the sanctity of oaths and vows but on the importance of *meaning* your promises must have been thought-provoking. This is not to deny that her 'world-without-end bargain', her momentous pre-contract, is clinched by social conventions that are perforce historical. To an extent, the rituals of betrothal draw their power to bind precisely from being historical—inherited, widely understood, and properly observed. They include, and in the Princess's case incorporate, the sort of emphatic speech act that one would expect at a time of *choosing*. Another way into grasping what is emotionally literate rather than procedural about the view of binding language that informs her gesture would come from the point that is made by Robins about vows in his sense not having a vowee. The Princess makes Navarre a promise which is generous because he need not take up the offer, but it can be a bargain if he matches it by showing her his commitment. We can no doubt accept Robins's own promise, when he writes, of contracts in general, 'let the reader take my word that [one] cannot give an account of the binding character of such agreements without smuggling into its motivational structure the primitive concept of commitment' (107).

The agreements between Dumaine and Longueville and their ladies are less elaborate. But the terms imposed on Biron not only enforce a social dimension but bring in penance and plague. Rosaline's offer survives, instructively, in two forms. In the first, evidently draft lines she requires Biron to 'be purgèd, too ... You are attaint with faults and perjury.' Matching the condition set by the Princess she says, 'Therefore if you my favour mean to get | A twelvemonth shall you spend, and never rest | But seek the weary beds of people sick.' The second version of the speech insists on the proper use of language to encourage not mock, while heightening the horror of sickness as a deprivation of speech. Rosaline tells Biron that he must entertain 'the speechless sick', 'groaning wretches', and he replies: 'To move wild laughter in the throat of death?...Mirth cannot move a soul in agony' (798.2–6, 827–34). These are the victims of the plague kept out at the start of the play. They are what men 'attaint with faults and perjury' deserve to become. Biron has not just to face the reality of the pining mortification that the academic oath was supposed to bring on, but risk infection. This was a period in which the plague-stricken were left to die, with their houses shut up.[60] You were supposed to care for them out of charity,[61] but few did. To jest for a twelvemonth in a hospital is far more than the symbolic ordeal modern audiences take it to be. Biron must re-enter the world at its most dangerous and face the imminence of every man's death.

We do not see the King and his lords living out their year and a day. 'That's too long for a play' (855). Perhaps the audience of *Love's Labour's Won* did see this, or heard tell of it.[62] But there is time enough for an extra playlet, and one that carries quite a lot of weight because it transports the onstage characters through a year and a day (and they remain together). Since it consists of songs by Spring and Winter, it also has something of a 'world-without-end' quality to it, an annual return of the seasons. 'This side is Hiems, winter,' announces Armado, 'This Ver, the spring, the one maintained by the owl, | The other by the cuckoo' (866–8). If we remember the background of the play in Christmas, institutional revels, the seasonal, calendrical basis of the dialogue is not surprising. Compare the twelve days of Christmas in the St John's College, Oxford, revels,[63] or Winter and Spring invited to entertain the bridal couple in the Gray's Inn *Maske of Flowers* (1614).[64] The songs in *Love's Labour's Lost* are not incidental, however, but integrated into the play's combative ethos. To 'maintain', which has legal and chivalric, agonistic overtones, is 'To support or uphold in speech or argument'.[65] So this is a return to disputation of the sort that was intellectually central to the Inns of Court, in moots as well as revels (the law, as Huizinga points out, is one of the great arenas of play).[66] We can return to issues and *gesta* discussed in Chapter 3 because the songs recapitulate and modulate all the challenges and wit combats of the play.

They are, though, paradoxical. Winter, the second song, is more lively and vital than Spring. Its owl has 'a merry note', one that puns ingeniously on the jests and wooings of the play ('Tu-whit, tu-whoo!'). In Spring, there are delightful, artificial displays of flowers, but also a warning about binding vows:

When daisies pied and violets blue,
  And lady-smocks, all silver-white,
And cuckoo-buds of yellow hue

Do paint the meadows with delight,
The cuckoo then on every tree
Mocks married men, for thus sings he:
Cuckoo!
Cuckoo, cuckoo—O word of fear,
Unpleasing to a married ear. (869–77)

The buried pun in 'lady-smocks' ('ladies' mocks') becomes explicit in the mockery of the cuckoo, who reminds us that marriage vows are not the end of the matter, that the weddings projected at the end of the action are only a step in life's tribulations where oath-breaking and infidelity are rife. This is pressed home in the second stanza, 'When turtles tread, and rooks and daws', which starts with sex between a faithful pair of birds, but then slides into sex between deceivers and fools.[67]

'And send you many lovers' is Biron's bold wish for Rosaline, when they parley in Act 2 (1.124). By the end of Act 5, she has been wooed by at least two. When the 'Light wenches' are married they will have plenty of time in which to 'prove plagues'. As Moth, in the Auden and Kallman libretto, amusingly sings: 'Who cheat for love will hear *Cuckoo!* | Once they have won it. Fie! | I know what men and women do, | But can't imagine why.'[68] From this perspective, Armado's decision to wed Jaquenetta, announced just before these songs ('I have vowed... To hold the plough for her sweet love three year' (5.2.860–1)), is touching but distinctly gullible. In most productions, Costard is more her type, and her being 'two months gone' might put Armado out of the frame for paternity.[69] As a gentleman, we remember, he believes that adding up 'fitteth the spirit of a tapster' (1.2.38). Heneage Finch, joking about such innumeracy to an Inns of Court audience, wrote: 'And (which is not much to be envied) some for want of numbring the weeks aright have had their new maried wives brought to bed before eyther Cradle provided or godfathers once thought on.'[70] The ludicrous, engaging Spaniard is likely to be mocked by the cuckoo as a cuckold. It is a sad, merry assumption in Shakespeare that lovers' vows will be broken. What is different about *Love's Labour's Lost* is that it focuses on how vows are broken to bring love about. But this does not exclude an apprehensive scepticism about the likeliness of them being kept. The songs of Ver and Hiems are alive to the ongoing risk that binding language will prove loose.

5

Group Revenge

Titus Andronicus to *Othello*

At the start of his career, Shakespeare was fascinated by the visually articulate tableau created by a group revenge oath. When Young Clifford is killed for the murder of York, in *3 Henry VI* (*c.*1591), it is as a result of just such an undertaking. Richard of Gloucester comes to Warwick and says that Warwick's brother has been slaughtered in battle by Clifford:

> Thy brother's blood the thirsty earth hath drunk,
> Broached with the steely point of Clifford's lance.
> And in the very pangs of death he cried,
> Like to a dismal clangour heard from far,
> 'Warwick, revenge—brother, revenge my death!' (2.3.15–19)

The dead brother, still audible by report, will become one in a chorus, or knot, of revengers, committed to Clifford's death. He is a ghost participant, like Andrugio in *Antonio's Revenge*, whose part in Antonio's campaign was discussed in Chapter 2. Warwick takes up the call. Bending his body to the task, but also to the speech act, he kneels and devotes himself to revenge, with a 'vow to God above' (29), while Edward (a son of York), spurred by his example, joins in, followed by Richard himself:

EDWARD [*kneeling*] O, Warwick, I do bend my knee with thine,
And in this vow do chain my soul to thine.
And, ere my knee rise from the earth's cold face,
I throw my hands, mine eyes, my heart to Thee,
Thou setter up and plucker down of kings, . . .
RICHARD Brother, give me thy hand; and, gentle Warwick,
Let me embrace thee in my weary arms. (33–45)

The individual vow is not just tied into words. A structure of shared kneelings and thrown, articulate bodyparts (hands, eyes, heart) consolidates a faction, and is another step towards regime change. Acted out in this way, the vows begin to define new lines of allegiance, making the group more than the sum of its parts. To foreground swearing in this way enhances the motive to revenge, for the characters as well as the audience, even while enforcing it. Predictably, when they catch up with Clifford and vaunt over him, the revengers return, as Clifford and Margaret had done over York, to a mockery of binding language that can only add to its significance:

WARWICK They mock thee, Clifford—swear as thou wast wont.
RICHARD What, not an oath? Nay, then, the world goes hard
When Clifford cannot spare his friends an oath.
I know by that he's dead— (2.6.76–9)

The Rape of Lucrece (1594), similarly, ends with a collective vow, sworn over the corpse of the heroine, to punish the Tarquins. For the body that is implicated in an oath—as when Warwick kneels—need not only be that of the swearer. It can be the corpse of Andrugio left in its sepulchre as his spirit takes flight, or the body of Warwick's brother broadcasting a message of revenge from the battlefield. Both can be turned by words into pledges of retribution as lethal as Rutland's blood on a napkin. Calling upon Lucrece's husband Collatinus to kneel with him, Brutus swears a sextuple oath—probably the longest and grandest in Shakespeare—swears it twice, in fact, and so draws together a plot:

'Now by the Capitol that we adore,
And by this chaste blood so unjustly stained,
By heaven's fair sun that breeds the fat earth's store,
By all our country rights in Rome maintained,
And by chaste Lucrece' soul that late complained
  Her wrongs to us, and by this bloody knife,
  We will revenge the death of this true wife.'

This said, he struck his hand upon his breast,
And kissed the fatal knife to end his vow,
And to his protestation urged the rest,
Who, wond'ring at him, did his words allow.
Then jointly to the ground their knees they bow,
  And that deep vow which Brutus made before
  He doth again repeat, and that they swore. (lines 1835–48)

The passage deftly points up the sacramental and bodily aspects of swearing. Brutus' oath in Livy—*iuro*, 'I swear', is his verb, as he calls the gods to witness[1]—is twice here called a 'vow', even though the form of his utterance ('*by* the Capitol... *By* heaven's fair sun') is most definitely that of an oath. The kneeling utterances sworn by Warwick, Edward, and Richard, like those, as we shall see, by Titus and his family, slide into the category of *vowing* for the same ritualistic reason. 'Vow' can mean 'prayer' (*votum*) in Shakespeare, as in early modern English generally. The rites of revenge elicit an appeal to God or the gods, which genuflection reinforces. When Brutus and the conspirators bow 'jointly', they bend their joints to their word, kneeling reverently or even religiously[2] as well as in obedience. 'Bow', already enriched by 'allow', in the rhyme royal rhyme-scheme, has an internal rhyme with 'vow', putting the action into the word.

* * *

After these early tableaux, Shakespeare denied himself the easy contrivance of group revenge and subjected the scenario to startling reinvention. There are signs of what was afoot in *King John* (*c.*1596), which is at various points an adaptation of *The Troublesome Raigne of Iohn* (composed about 1589). In the anonymous play, King Louis of France and the English barons who revolt against John swear fidelity to each other, but, when Louis is left alone with Melun, he swears that he will dispose of 'the English traitors' once he conquers England. 'This is an excellent scene', Geoffrey Bullough observes, 'and by omitting most of it Shakespeare lost a dramatic opportunity.'[3] There are reasons internal to *King John* why Shakespeare rewrote as he did, giving us these events by report; but there must also have been a sense that he had already exhausted the potential of the head-on, onstage oath.

In *Julius Caesar* (1599), the conspirators visit Brutus by night to persuade him to join their plot against Caesar, who is showing signs of wanting to take the imperial crown. The audience, and apparently the characters, including Cassius, who proposes an oath (2.1.112), expect a scene along the lines of Lucius Junius Brutus and the conspirators after the suicide of Lucrece. What Brutus calls 'The sufferance of our souls, the time's abuse' points to such a scenario (114). As the essayist Cornwallis noted, gatherings of the disaffected tend to oaths and revenge:

> Sufferances of some kinde are holesomer then reuenge. Now the last are like horses that rub one another by consent,... he calls him wise, the other him valiant, he sweares, the other sweares, and so ouercome with the opinion of their plot, they passe assemblies, increasing the number of their follies, not praises.[4]

The conspirators flatter Brutus, whetting his sufferance into revenge. The surprise (though it is in Plutarch) is that they do *not* swear, because, as Brutus asks, 'What other bond' do they need, beyond being

secret Romans, that have spoke the word
And will not palter? And what other oath
Than honesty to honesty engaged
That this shall be or we will fall for it?
Swear priests and cowards... (123–8)

There is no need for an 'oath', he repeats, when every Roman would prove himself not Roman if he broke 'the smallest particle | Of any promise' (138–9). To this fine, too noble distinction the hard-headed Cassius does not respond. It is a group revenge oath without the occasion for revenge and without an oath.

As we began to see in the Introduction, and will see more fully at the end of this chapter, all this goes further in *Hamlet* (1600). There the audience is shown deflection and fragmentation in what in more conventional plays would be a vengeful group oath sworn by the prince, Horatio, and Marcellus, with the ghost adding his voice from under the stage. In *Othello* (1604?), at least as potently, the kneeling of Edward with Warwick, or Lucius Junius Brutus with Collatine and the rest, is recast as mocking parody, when the Moor commits himself to a misplaced revenge against Desdemona: 'In the due reverence of a sacred vow | I here engage my words' (3.3.464–5). Picking up on his intensity and turning it towards melodrama, Iago binds himself to Othello; 'Do not rise yet', he says, and joins him, kneeling, in a double conjuration:

Witness you ever-burning lights above,
You elements that clip us round about,
Witness that here Iago doth give up
The execution of his wit, hands, heart
To wronged Othello's service. (465–70)

It is a clever, cynical imitation of 'the Othello music', degrading the general in Iago's eyes and splitting the sympathy of the audience.

The material just quoted is in both the 1622 Quarto text of *Othello* and the 1623 Folio. Editors differ on whether Q is a later, cut-down version of the text behind F or represents an earlier version amplified in revision[5] (the older view, that they derive from a single, lost original, carries less conviction). Either way, this sequence shows significant variation. For in F, Othello's vow is compellingly larger in scope as well as length, including the words between square brackets below:

> Never, [Iago. Like to the Pontic Sea,
> Whose icy current and compulsive course
> Ne'er knows retiring ebb, but keeps due on
> To the Propontic and the Hellespont,
> Even so my bloody thoughts with violent pace
> Shall ne'er look back, ne'er ebb to humble love,
> Till that a capable and wide revenge
> Swallow them up.
> [*He kneels*]
> Now, by yon marble heaven,]
> In the due reverence of a sacred vow... (456–63)

The epic or Senecan, driven syntax[6] gives an idea of what the plot will be like: unrelenting, overrunning, culminating with the abruptness of a caesura, with Desdemona smothered trying to pray. Othello's language is marked as impulsively self-generating ('icy *c*urrent and *c*ompulsive *c*ourse'), while heaven is obdurate and sepulchral. It is visually striking too: grey, opaque, streaked with cloud, made of the 'elements that clip us round', bracketing general and ensign together. For all Othello's 'reverence', his 'sacred vow' has nothing to do with the God so often invoked in 'by Heaven'. It has been pointed out by a number of critics that his name contains 'hell'. When he cracks up and swears this oath, his name breaks up also and says more: Oath/hell/o. *Oth*, it should be noted, was a common spelling-variant of *oath*.

That the recasting of this passage was purposeful, and probably directed towards expansion, is suggested by a related change a few scenes later, where Othello's F-only oath, 'by yon marble heaven', combines with Iago's kneeling and 'ever-burning lights above' to inform an F-only speech given to Desdemona. Painfully aware that her marriage is unravelling, she turns to Emilia and Iago for support, and swears to the ensign, in both texts, 'by this light of heaven, | I know not how I lost him' (4.2.154–5). In the Folio she then kneels and utters a solemn asseveration, bound with an oath's conditional self-curse—as near to a full-blown oath as her gender and breeding allow:

> Here I kneel.
> If e'er my will did trespass 'gainst his love,
> Either in discourse of thought or actual deed,
> Or that mine eyes, mine ears, or any sense

Delighted them in any other form,
Or that I do not yet, and ever did,
And ever will—though he do shake me off
To beggarly divorcement—love him dearly,
Comfort forswear me. (155–63)

This time, Iago does not respond, does not jibe with the word. She is left the more isolated, when his reassurance—calculated to diminish Othello, and to deflect Emilia's indignation, but also to patronize and disable Desdemona's concern—ends in both texts in the mildest assurance:

IAGO I pray you, be content. 'Tis but his humour.
The business of the state does him offence,
And he does chide with you.
DESDEMONA If 'twere no other!
IAGO It is but so, I warrant. (169–73)

If 'Here I kneel...' is Desdemona's equivalent of the Propontic speech, it is tellingly contrasted with it in being focused on the facts of the case (her given word is assertory, Othello's blindly promissory), in seeking to resolve harm, not expunge it by revenge, and also in being directed towards the intimacies of the relationship, not out into the world of elemental forces and oriental adventure. Her utterance is analytical as well as assertory. She uses it actively to think through what could have gone wrong between her and the Moor, how she might have contributed to the conflict. His is almost escapist, taking him already out of marriage to the bracing, male world that lies along the conflict line between Christendom and the turbaned Turks. For all that, the two speech acts elide as stage tableaux. There is superimposition as well as contrast, as though a single, three-handed, oath-bound plot were being realized in two exposures, both centred on kneeling to Iago.

* * *

A step had already been taken towards these twists on the group revenge oath in the commitments given in *Titus Andronicus*. Tableaux of kneeling and judgement are so plentiful and impressive in this early tragedy that an unusual, contemporary sketch depicts a compound version of the scenario.[7] Like the kneeling sequences in *Othello*, those in *Titus* can be experienced as superimposed. Closest to the concerns of this chapter, however, is 3.1. This is the long, painful scene in which Martius and Quintus, Titus' sons, are led to execution, before Lavinia is brought in to her father, minus hands and tongue. In a vain attempt to ransom his sons, Titus is tricked into having one of his own hands chopped off by the villainous Moor, Aaron. It simply adds to his losses. A messenger soon comes on stage to return the rejected hand along with the heads of Martius and Quintus. In this extremity of abuse and abjection, Titus vows revenge within the corpus of the group. He is clipped round by his kin as Othello and Iago are by the elements.[8]

> You heavy people, circle me about,
> That I may turn me to each one of you
> And swear unto my soul to right your wrongs.
> [MARCUS, LUCIUS, *and* LAVINIA *circle* TITUS. *He pledges them*]
> The vow is made. Come, brother, take a head
> And in this hand the other will I bear.
> And Lavinia, thou shalt be employed.
> Bear thou my hand, sweet wench, between thy teeth.
> As for thee, boy, go get thee from my sight.[9]

'*He pledges them*', added in the Norton, is more in line with the dialogue than '*They make a vow*' in the Arden,[10] but both point to aspects of the scene. This is a collective corporeal oath even if Titus makes most of the moves. The body is at issue not so much by being articulate as by being dismembered of just those features which are in classical rhetoric held to be the chief means of expression (tongue, hands, heads) but which are reinvested with eloquence by virtue of their dismemberment—as when Lavinia carries Titus' hand, like a tongue, in her mouth.[11] Heads lopped of their trunks, like trunks lopped of hands, can be drawn into a vow. Revenge tragedy, we are reminded, is about the body because, often enough, it is about the body in parts, or skeletons (in Chettle's *Hoffman*, Middleton's *The Revenger's Tragedy*) or (as in Goffe's *Orestes*) a handful of a father's bones.

We cannot know exactly how the vowing sequence of 3.1 was performed on the Elizabethan stage, but the German adaptation of *Titus* (1620) gives a vivid account of how English travelling players enacted it:

> *Titus takes up his hand, raises it and looks up to heaven, sighs, mutters vows* [schweret heimlich], *strikes his breast, and puts down the hand after having sworn. Thereupon he takes up the heads and swears by each of them singly* [schweret bey einem jeglichen besondern]; *finally he approaches the kneeling Andronica* [*i.e. the Lavinia-figure*] *and swears by her as before. This done, they all rise again.*[12]

It is an astonishing, bizarre touch that Titus should pick up his own hand and raise it to heaven (he raises his hand) to make a prayer or vow. He turns the dead limb—the actor playing Titus turns a false limb—into a rhetorical prosthesis. Equally dramatic is his muttering in a confidential, homely way—the most forceful of declarations since the secrecy and intimacy underscore his determination. The Andronici become parties to the plot by hearing an oath rather than by saying it; they are gestured into revenge as Titus' own hand is manhandled into vowing.

The disposition of the 1620 text suggests an analytical style of performance. The original, German stage direction is heavily punctuated, recording a formal, ritualized action, almost like a dumb show: 'TITUS *nimpt seine Hand / helt sie und siehet gen Himmel / seufftzet / schweret heimlich...*'[13] Attaching an oath to each of the physical and emotional injuries inflicted on the family, Titus enumerates his own motives for revenge. This is consistent with Shakespeare's conception of the scene ('That *I* may *turn me* to each one of *you*'). In performance, though, the effect must always have been cumulatively to bind the group. The sequence yet again varies the group revenge formula. Titus remains the controlling patriarch, but he draws the Andronici together, and, of course, as one of the mutilated, he finds kinship with his kin. Titus' vows and vowings are *incorporated* into a pledge, the more bodily because bodies are disabled. The Andronici resemble the fused, disabled, multiple figures made by the Chapman brothers rather than the heroic, distinct Horatii swearing their oath in David's great picture.

The eloquence of Titus' severed left hand, and the work he does with his right, could prompt a revaluation of the scene in *Julius Caesar* where the conspirators are forbidden to swear. Before telling them that oaths are for priests and cowards, Brutus says, 'Give me your hands all over, one by one' (110). Shaking hands in Roman culture, like raising a hand or killing a pig, was a ritual element in pledging.[14] So Brutus' ban is incomplete. In place of words he admits an articulate, communicative gesture, as binding as any oath. The early modern view was not so different. Starting from the position that, since 'words are but interpreters of things conceived in the minde', which things can be 'signified by other means, as writing, nods, signes',[15] Robert Sanderson goes straight on, in his treatise on oaths, *De Juramento*, to an example that illuminates the situation of Lavinia, when she is drawn into the vow of revenge:

> So mutes, they who have had their tongues cut out, and such as lie speechlesse...use by nods, by lifting up the hands or other signes, to signifie their answer unto the question asked. Which signification is no lesse valid unto all intents and purposes of the Law, then if it had been expressed by word. And it is the very same in an oath,...according to that verse which *Stobaeus* bringeth out of an old *Comedian*.
>
> *The oath is firm, if I but give a nod.* (150–1)

Heads will do, a hand for a tongueless mouth. Exactly the body parts highlighted by their loss and use at this point in *Titus*.

The revenger's body enters into his oath or vow because the body communicates with and around words, but the corporeal is also active when its concreteness is used to secure what is slippery in language. The desire to return to this fixity feeds back into the language of swearing itself: 'by this hand', 'by these ten bones', 'by Pharaoh's foot', or, finding the body in the Divine, ''Swounds' (God's wounds), 'God's bodikins' (God's little body, the eucharist). Corporal oaths, so aggravating to the Godly,[16] could be grounded in a sword, a prayerbook, and other items sworn on but also used to inflict death (by stabbing or poison). Most obviously, in revenge oaths the body that is caught up in swearing is also the body that is going to take revenge. The oath is adapted to exploring the relationship between intention and act because it is not just a volitional utterance. The swearing body is bound.

So interested is *Titus* in all this that the matter returns in Act 4 after Lavinia has used a staff to replace her tongue and written down her rape and the names of those who inflicted it in the sand: '*Stuprum*—Chiron—Demetrius' (4.1.77). This time Marcus tries to manage his brother's rage and distress by conjuring another, more explicitly group revenge oath:

> My lord, kneel down with me; Lavinia, kneel;
> And kneel, sweet boy, the Roman Hector's hope,
> [*All kneel*]
> And swear with me—as, with the woeful fere
> And father of that chaste dishonoured dame
> Lord Junius Brutus sware for Lucrece' rape—
> That we will prosecute by good advice
> Mortal revenge upon these traitorous Goths,
> And see their blood, or die with this reproach. (86–93)

The disabled Lavinia is part of a circle that includes a one-handed old general and a little boy. Oaths in general, and revenge oaths in particular, are in early modern as in ancient drama almost always male. There is a male-bonding ritual in the scenes we have been looking at which builds a patriarchal order in excess of the needs of revenge. The presence of Lavinia gives the group oath a new torque, as though Lucretia had come back to life and joined Brutus and Collatine in vowing. Equally irregular is the presence of the boy urged to swear like heroes of the Roman republic. A child's oath was not held to bind in early modern England or classical Rome, but young Lucius, caught up in the group, does not disappoint with his judgement against

Chiron and Demetrius: 'Their mother's bedchamber should not be safe | For these base bondmen to the yoke of Rome' (107–8).

The entering of the corporeal into a vindictive purpose is typically combined with a narrowing, a dedication of mortal powers to a point. That is the work of the oath or vow, to focus the obligation. At the same time, in such plays as *Hamlet*, it swings open the supernatural. It brings inner and outer, decision and Divine witness, into a fused conjunction, yet it is damaged through loss, incomplete or maimed until revenge discharges the obligation and dims the motivating purpose. This is one reason why early modern stage revengers die. It is less a Divine punishment to reflect Christian disapproval of revenge than a necessary extinction, once a bloody oath is honoured and the job is done. The alternative would be another oath or vow. That is what happens at the end of *Antonio's Revenge*, a play that was performed by choristers only yards from St Paul's Cathedral. Antonio and his co-conspirators announce that they have taken vows to live a religious, cloistered life, so they move from one devotion (the murderous one) to another, unpunished—a nicely blasphemous conceit from Marston, who would a few years later leave the world of the theatre and give his oath and promises according to the Book of Common Prayer[17] to become a minister in the Church of England.

* * *

The oath proposed by Marcus is deflected by his brother; the great build-up of kneeling fails to deliver a declaration. Shakespeare presents a group revenge that almost follows the formula but does not quite close up its circle, as Titus, taking charge, announces another plan. Tamora, he warns the Andronici, is dangerously in league with Saturninus, so they must opt for a waiting game. '*Stuprum*—Chiron—Demetrius' must be written in something more durable than a 'sandy plot':

> come, I will go get a leaf of brass
> And with a gad of steel will write these words,
> And lay it by. The angry northern wind
> Will blow these sands like Sibyl's leaves abroad,
> And where's our lesson then? (101–5)

Like Hieronimo in *The Spanish Tragedy* (*c.*1587), Titus is short of proof and denied access to royal justice. He can only issue threats (arrows shot into the court) which do little but warn his enemies. The plotting is under-articulated, but this phase allows Titus to exemplify the philosophical patience which is as much a feature of 'Senecan' characterization as are fury and excess. Like Pandulph in *Antonio's Revenge* he is an exemplar of Stoic virtue with a potential for brutal violence.

What of the conflicting appeals of the oral and the written? Why should the utterance of an oath give way to a leaf of brass, filed away in an archive? This was a period when the authority of binding language was perceived as shifting from neighbourly utterance into script and print. Such a perception went back, of course, to at least the thirteenth century, when communally witnessed agreements began to be trumped by written contracts, and greater formalism crept into legal process. In his well-documented study *A Crisis of Truth*, Richard Firth Green shows how extensively this was complained of in the medieval period,[18] but the same theme and story were replayed in the sixteenth century:[19] old honesties and community were being replaced by legal bondage; trust and reciprocity were being lost to commercialism and greed.

One appeal of revenge oaths in drama, at such a historical juncture, is that they reinvest with power the oral, the somatic, and the communal, bringing binding language back to its supposed base in the body and in group agreement—even when (the more empathetically when) the group has been unjustly treated. There is something radically satisfying about oaths of this sort, vindicating solidarity even as they aim at vengeance. Yet words are but wind, as the early modern proverb puts it, so the impulse to fidelity in revenge plotting still makes writing attractive. This is one reason why Lavinia's voice hardens into staff and script when she comes out with the testimony which constitutes a revenge motive against Chiron and Demetrius. But writing in the sand is only one degree more permanent than speech; which is why Titus proposes to engrave his daughter's words on a sheet of brass. In the same way, Hamlet reaches for his tables, his notebook, to set down his revenge (1.5.107–11)—though he actually sets down an evasive commonplace, that one may smile and smile and be a villain, so writing is not always the answer. Group solidarity can be more effectively mnemonic.

The collective nature of the revengers' oath has a political dimension. Titus and his family make a league against tyranny that will support the return of true Roman values, even though—since this is Shakespeare, and nothing is unmixed—they will be brought in by an army of Goths led by Lucius. Titus' faction resembles the opponents of Piero in *Antonio's Revenge*, and, less convincingly, Brutus and the conspirators in *Julius Caesar*. There is a similarity between the oaths that hold such revengers together and the Bond of Association sworn by Protestant gentlemen in 1584, which committed them to 'revenge' against anyone who attempted to assassinate Queen Elizabeth (as Pope Gregory XIII had encouraged Catholics, in 1580):

> we . . . do . . . vow and protest, as we are most bounden, and that in the presence of the eternal and ever living God, to prosecute such person or persons to death with our joint and particular forces, and to take the uttermost revenge on them . . . And to the better corroboration of this, our loyal Bond and Association, we do also testify by this writing that we do confirm the contents hereof by our oaths corporally taken upon the Holy Evangelists, . . .[20]

The Bond has been discussed in relation to *Hamlet* because it vindicates 'revenge' by individuals.[21] It is the more relevant, however, to revenge plays because signatories were 'bounden' together. They constituted a loyal subculture turning into a revenge conspiracy.[22]

The opportunity for the Andronici, bound into their association, to fight back against the corruptions of Rome arrives when Tamora makes the mistake of coming to Titus' house disguised as Revenge with Chiron and Demetrius dressed as Rapine and Murder (which is madly what they are). As we began to see in Chapter 2, she wants to persuade him to sup with the emperor, which will give her the chance, she vainly imagines, to turn the army of Goths against the Andronici, and make herself and the emperor safe. Titus, still obsessed with writing, says that 'what I mean to do, | See here, in bloody lines I have set down, | And what is written shall be executed' (5.2.13–15). But he is not so fixed on his script that he misses the opportunity for violence. He sees how he can recycle the revenge of Atreus, Philomel, and Progne (see p. 65), and of many another tragedy revelling in a bloody banquet. There are classical precedents as well as pre-existing injuries to crowd the scene.

So the choreography of revenge is that of a group action, not just in the sense that binding and butchering the miscreants needs more hands than Titus' one, and Lavinia's none, or that cooking the meal and serving it as a feast is a stylized, social act. It is so dramaturgically and verbally as the couplets of the climactic sequence (5.3.45–65) draw Tamora and Saturninus on the one side and Titus, Lavinia, and Lucius on the other into a zigzag of violence. The act of rhyming is a riposte, a retaliatory response by Titus to Saturninus, Tamora, Saturninus again, then by Lucius to the emperor. The conspirators' bond of association pitches them against an evil faction. With the killing of the emperor in revenge for the murder of Titus in revenge for the stabbing of Tamora, a couplet answers itself—the 'bonds' or 'bands' tighten (pp. 57, 65–6)—by extending into an internally rhymed triplet, a perverse crystallization of order:

SATURNINUS Die, frantic wretch, for this accursèd deed!
  [*He kills* TITUS]
LUCIUS Can the son's eye behold his father bleed?
There's meed for meed, death for a deadly deed.
  [*He kills* SATURNINUS. *Confusion follows*] (5.3.63–5)

The assertion of order involves not just a cleansing of the state but an extirpation of what is deformed within the revenge group. The honour-killing of Lavinia by Titus lops mutilation from the Andronici, while the stabbing of Titus by Saturninus frees them from a one-handed patriarch. There is a return at the level of the *domus* as well as Rome itself to the dream of wholeness projected by the revenge oaths. It is reaffirmed after the bloody banquet in Marcus' celebrated lines:

O, let me teach you how to knit again
This scattered corn into one mutual sheaf,
These broken limbs again into one body. (69–71)

Lucius addressing the people, like Coriolanus in the later tragedy, says that he is scarred. These are marks of war-service, though, not of mutilation. They back up his eloquence, make him reliable, without vitiating a return to health: 'My scars can witness, dumb although they are, | That my report is just and full of truth' (113–14). His asseverative competence is sealed by these signs of healing on his wholeness. Marcus, relatedly, declares that, if the truth is not accepted, the Andronici 'Will hand in hand all headlong hurl ourselves' down upon jagged stones (131). In a play that so deftly handles hands and capitalizes on heads, this underlines the full complement of anatomically and rhetorically capable extremities now sported by the family. A clinching rhyme and handclasp create a rhetorical, mutual bond that is designed to persuade, and does: 'Speak, Romans, speak, and if you say we shall, | Lo, hand in hand Lucius and I will fall' (134–5).

* * *

We saw in Chapter 2 that the action of *Hamlet* has parallels with that of *Antonio's Revenge*, and that both have somewhere behind them *Titus* and *Thyestes*. Comparison leads to contrast. Like Antonio, the prince is challenged by the ghost of his father to take revenge, and like Antonio he commits an intermediate murder which elicits the re-appearance of the ghost.

In Elsinore, however, the victim is not a piece of the usurper's flesh and blood, and the stabbing of Polonius behind the arras sets in train a counter-action that destroys Hamlet before he unambiguously achieves his revenge. For all that, the killing of the counsellor is (like the murder of Marston's Julio) a warped anticipation of revenge against Claudius, which is one reason why Hamlet asks Gertrude whether he *has* killed Claudius ('Is it the King?' (3.4.25)). In Belleforest's *Histoires tragiques*, which is the play's source,[23] or source-at-one-remove, and, we may assume, in the *Ur-Hamlet* of the late 1580s, the prince returns to Elsinore from England to a feast laid on to deplore and celebrate his execution. This is reduced in Shakespeare to the ceremoniously ordered cups of wine which the king and Gertrude drink to Hamlet at the fencing match with Laertes. Yet the structure of a disrupted feast remains. The king's cups are filled with blood-red and poisoned wine (in *Thyestes*, as in *Catiline*, blood is mixed into wine).[24] The drink is the vehicle of Gertrude's death, and one of the instruments that kills Claudius. It is a bloody enough banquet.

So much for the outlines. Once detail begins to fill in, it becomes apparent how much of Shakespeare's divergence from *Thyestes*, *Titus*, and *Antonio's Revenge* has to do with the revenge oaths that are sworn. In pursuing this, we need to start from a damaged body, a *corpus* that in *Titus* would be a victim becoming revenger, and that in Marston becomes a generic, blood-drinking spirit. In *Hamlet* the ghost is multi-faceted: martial, stately on the battlements, an old mole, an actor clambering about under the stage. What he also creates for the prince, in his long narrative speech, is a forensic body. This is how he starts:

'Tis given out that, sleeping in mine orchard,
A serpent stung me. So the whole ear of Denmark
Is by a forgèd process of my death
Rankly abused. But know, thou noble youth,
The serpent that did sting thy father's life
Now wears his crown.
HAMLET O my prophetic soul! Mine uncle? (1.5.35–40)

The psychologizing bias of commentary attributes to the prince resentments that prompt him to suspect his uncle. The rhetoric of proof points another way. 'Sleeping in mine orchard', Old Hamlet announces, he was poisoned, through the ear, by his brother. It was a

leperous distilment, whose effect
Holds such an enmity with blood of man
That swift as quicksilver it courses through

The natural gates and alleys of the body,
And with a sudden vigour it doth posset
And curd, like eager droppings into milk,
The thin and wholesome blood. So did it mine;
And a most instant tetter barked about,
Most lazar-like, with vile and loathsome crust,
All my smooth body. (64–73)

The vitality and lucidity of this passage makes it a textbook example of the effectiveness of the rhetorical rules for pleading an 'honest cause'.[25] What makes it a *dramatic* success, however, is how it counters what is 'given out'.

The audience will be struck by the contrast between the invulnerability of the ghost, the worked surface of his 'complete steel' (1.4.33) which is also lighter than the air, and the pathos of his mortal body, tettered over with a scabby crust. In *2 Henry VI*, Warwick infers murder from the blackened face of Duke Humphrey, with his eyeballs starting out (3.2.168–9). He commits to his deduction with 'A dreadful oath, sworn with a solemn tongue' (153–9). Had Warwick been at Elsinore, what would he have read from the signs on Old Hamlet's body? They do not sound like the effect of snakebite. Contrast the barely visible 'vent of blood, and something blown' on Cleopatra's breast and arm after she has been bitten by the asps.[26] It strikes me as obvious—though I have not found it in the criticism—that anyone who saw the king's corpse would have doubted the official account. Hamlet was at Wittenberg. Even to the distant ear, the story does not ring true. The only poisonous snake to be found in northern Europe is the adder, which is only mildly venomous, and not known for attacking people napping in their gardens.[27] A murder has been smoothed over, by influential figures, to suit ambitions at court.

Yet tokens are not proof, and it is not surprising that the prince's commitment to revenge is so evasive. When the ghost of Andrugio appears to Antonio, revenge is asked for and sworn. With Hamlet, although it is asked for, it is taken up with only brief intensity (1.5.29–31), while the ghost's final words, 'Adieu, adieu, Hamlet. Remember me' (91), become the grounds of a demanding speech about this commandment living alone within the book and volume of the prince's brain. In an early modern context, the commandment of a king and father should 'bind', as does an oath.[28] But Hamlet, knowing that the injunction to revenge is not 'lawful' because contrary to the Decalogue ('Thou shalt not kil'),[29] chooses to take the dread command to be to 'remember', not to 'revenge', and gives his word accordingly.[30] Even when Hamlet swears, or says that he *has* sworn, the audience does not hear anything as demonstrative as Antonio's triple oath (p. 47):

> Now to my word:
> It is 'Adieu, adieu, remember me'.
> I have sworn't. (111–13)

There is no performative speech act, only a repetition of what was not really the king's injunction. The stage tradition that has Hamlet swear on his sword makes sense; as in *Titus*, 3.1, the oath can be gestural, corporeal, but it is also somewhere in the prince's head, with whatever degree of fervour or mental reservation. In a play as encouraging of scepticism as *Hamlet*, it has to matter that the audience does not actually hear him swear. After all, we do not, except in the most oblique sense, see him take revenge. The eventual killing of Claudius is more than at least ostensibly payback for his manipulation of the duel between Laertes and the prince and his reckless poisoning of the queen (p. 233).

The case has been made that in honour-based, retributive societies, and consequently in Hamlet's Denmark, remembrance *means* revenge.[31] Shakespeare sets up, however, as is his way in plot construction, a contrast between the prince and Laertes. He is Hamlet's foil not just in how rapidly he sweeps to his revenge, but in how he commits himself, vaulting over the casuistical and psychological complications that cluster around even simple oaths, and dedicating himself to his will. Squaring up to Claudius, he dismisses binding language, along with conscience and grace (as Hamlet dismisses other commandments that are in the book and volume of his brain), including sworn fealty and vows:

> To hell, allegiance! Vows to the blackest devil!
> Conscience and grace to the profoundest pit!
> I dare damnation. To this point I stand,
> That both the worlds I give to negligence,
> Let come what comes. Only I'll be revenged
> Most throughly for my father. (4.5.127–32)

An Elizabethan audience might have found this refreshingly direct after the prevarications of the prince; as Claudius goes on to say, however, there is no point in pursuing revenge if you do not know who your enemies are.

Hamlet is right to be troubled by the lack of evidence of Claudius' guilt, but his evasiveness with his oath suggests, among other motives, a reluctance to bind himself to a purpose. Early modern commentators knew that constancy and constraint were integral to the oath. William Gearing, for example, says that 'the Latin word *juramentum, a jure manente*, plainly sheweth unto us, that our oaths must be stedfast and constant: and so much the Greek word *horkos* importeth to us whether we understand it *quasi horkos* a hedge, or *quasi horkos*, a bound or limit, because the swearer hath hedged himself about with Gods truth, and is so bounded and limited, that he must of necessity perform what he hath sworn.'[32] Though a modern classicist would find the Christian overtones of this unhelpful, *horkos* is associated in Greek with boundaries and limits. To swear an oath can be liberating, empowering, and full of risk, but it then becomes a fetter. You are trapped by your word, either by making a promise to another person, or ghost, which annexes part of your agency, or by making God a witness, which obliges you not to disgrace God by failing to deliver your promise.

Of course, to make a vow is also to reinforce your agency, to have a mission, a standing different from all the people who have not taken vows. This is attractive to Hamlet, of whom it might be asked, 'Why seems it so particular with thee?' (1.2.75). Yet revenge is an ideal theme for exploring how oaths make life rigid and reduce options. The word *oath* has even been traced to 'the same Indo-European base as ancient Greek *oitos* fate, lit[erally] "what is to come" '.[33] The oath can be *so* rigorously set on an objective that the passage of time becomes indifferent, and fatalism wells up. 'If it be now, 'tis not to come', as Hamlet very wisely says. 'If it be not to come, it will be now. If it be not now, yet it will come' (5.2.158–60). The thrust of a promissory oath thus generates a counter-tendency, in the making of commitments to suspend them. The oath becomes a device for foreclosing an imposed responsibility, even, as we have seen with the pledge, earnest of what need not be done yet.

Trying to get at what 'should be counted as *treating* people in some way', the philosopher Derek Parfit wonders about 'breaking a promise to someone who is dead'.[34] The question of whether Hamlet forgets to revenge or to remember is compounded by his oath being sworn in favour of one such figure. If you break a promise to a living person or one that affects such a person, you might have to deal with him or her, which is a sanction, whereas, with the dead, the challenge is less palpable yet potentially more awesome. The ghost is the better to think with because he is not quite 'someone who is dead'. When Hamlet puts aside or forgets his promise, the ghost comes back, in the closet scene, 'in his habit as he lived' (3.4.126), to whet the prince's almost blunted purpose. We know that, in early performances, he wore a nightgown,[35] but this uncanny touch makes his return no less fearful. Compare the *Oresteia*, where the Erinyes or Furies pursuing Orestes are both the spirits of revenge and guarantors of oaths, who dog perjurers and oath-breakers. As the action of *Hamlet* goes on, revenge and promise slide away together. At the end of the play the ghost returns, as we shall see in Chapter 8, in effects more atmospheric than spectral—the dead still not quite dead, as though a fading promise kept it alive.

If Hamlet's 'I have sworn't' were the end of the matter—and his perfect tense suggests a desire that it should be—the revenge oaths of the play would be less interesting. Instead 1.5 flows into a complex group action which shows the dynamics of collective swearing in a new and volatile way. We need not have an exaggerated view of the privacy of memory to notice that, in his encounter with the ghost and his oath-taking, Hamlet is isolated. Antonio starts his revenge action equally alone, but Shakespeare's prince never arrives at the Gordian knotting of a group that provides one climax in Marston (p. 56). The opportunity is there—almost too promptly to be taken up—in the arrival of Horatio and Marcellus immediately after Hamlet's exchange with the ghost, but the prince, empowered yet bewildered, meets them with evasion and injunctions to secrecy.

Secrecy often attaches to revenge in plays about the punishment that should fall upon tyrants. We saw this in the German *Titus*, where the protagonist only mutters vows that are not set down in Shakespeare's script. Immediately before *Hamlet*, *Julius Caesar* explores more extensively the importance and the difficulty of maintaining secrecy in a plot. Too honourable to swear himself into a conspiracy, Brutus is not so honourable that he denies news of it to Portia, and she finds this hard to contain. Secrecy is also important in the protection of the revenge mission in Belleforest, and it was probably, as it is in *The Spanish Tragedy*, a feature of the *Ur-Hamlet*.[36] In Shakespeare's play, however, not only is the expected group oath entirely about secrecy, not revenge, it is not clear what there is for the potential conspirators to be secret about. Hamlet twice urges Horatio and Marcellus, with the resonant support of the ghost, never to make known what they have seen. But then they are sworn 'Never to speak of this that you have heard' (1.5.161), which draws attention to how little they have heard. Only Hamlet has spoken to the ghost; all that his associates hear from the spirit is the injunction to 'Swear' to secrecy. The informed, collective oath that we get in *3 Henry VI*, *Lucrece*, and *Titus* is essentially voided.

To bring this out more conclusively, contrast *The Revenger's Tragedy* (1607–8), a play deeply influenced by *Hamlet* and performed by the King's Men, Shakespeare's company. In the fourth scene of Middleton's play, a group of gentlemen swear on a sword to revenge the wife of Antonio, who took her own life after she was raped and whose body lies on the stage before them. It is, in other words, the Lucrece situation, with the wronged corpse acting as both victim and oath-sacrifice:

HIPPOLITO Nay then, step forth, thou bribeless officer.
[*He draws his sword*]
I bind you all in steel to bind you surely.
Here let your oaths meet, to be kept and paid,
Which else will stick like rust, and shame the blade.
Strengthen my vow, that if at the next sitting
Judgement speak all in gold and spare the blood
Of such a serpent, e'en before their seats,
To let his soul out, which long since was found
Guilty in heaven.
ALL We swear it and will act it.
[*They swear upon the sword*][37]

Being part of a group makes it easier to swear to danger. The characters are carried along and endorsed in their common purpose. The perpetrator of the rape, the Duchess's youngest son, has been given hope of acquittal. The revengers are sworn in as an incorruptible jury, a bond of association, tied by the sword as icon of justice. What rusts a sword is lack of use, which would here mean unredeemed, vengeful oaths. Like revenge, such an oath can only be effected by being paid, put into action.

Middleton has scripted a scene of energetic stasis. In *Hamlet*, by contrast, as we began to see in the Introduction (pp. 37–9), Horatio and Marcellus move around, from pillar to trap, one side of the stage to the other, as though trying to find a point of rest, whether away from the ghost or summoned to wherever he wants them to 'Swear'. To the end of the sequence, there is this volatile, difficult dynamic—hysterical enough to trouble an audience about the status of Hamlet's oaths, since, as we have seen, the oaths of madmen were believed not to bind. Like the ghost, though on different pathways, the prince moves in and out of participation in the group. Does he lead Marcellus and Horatio around the stage following the voice of the ghost to make him part of the conspiracy, or try to reassure by moving them away, so that swearing becomes a way of placating and shaking off the ghost? The actors can clarify this, but never definitively.

Julia Reinhard Lupton has recently argued that 'This band of "friends, scholars, and soldiers"—a cohort bound by education, vocation, conversation, affection, and consent—shelters and supports Hamlet's loneliness as he grudgingly shoulders the burden of the paternal past.'[38] This is a strong thought but sentimental. It takes the group to be pre-existing, pre-bound, but when Hamlet says, 'And now, good friends, | As you are friends, scholars, and soldiers' (1.5.144–5) there is a brittle ingratiation which shows the fragility of the 'band'. His dependence on the others for secrecy is shown by compliments which mark his distance. Differences in occupation and rank do not make for a circle of affinity, the basis of a group revenge. Later, having learned to trust him, Hamlet will tell Horatio what the ghost has said. With hindsight, that makes 1.5 partly about cutting out Marcellus.

Lupton's view stems from her Judaic premises: 'To be elected by God as a nation is to enter into forms of election and representation among the Jews as a covenanted group. So, too, in *Hamlet*, the prince returns from a precipice overshadowed by the Ghost to rejoin and reconfigure his circle of friends' (85). As we have seen, group revengers can have something of the Bond of Association about them. Those who took the National Covenant in Scotland (1638) or the Solemn League and Covenant in Scotland and England (1643) saw themselves as bearing God's sword to defend religion and state against a crypto-Romanist monarchy (even, tyranny). They drew their inspiration from the chosen people of the Old Testament. But the oaths in *Hamlet* 1.5 are sworn to a sinful spirit, hot out of purgatory. They are not sworn to God, nor set down as a list of principles and demands, shared by the participants. It is hard to see much that is covenant-like about the sequence. There is, on the contrary, anxious repetition, fragmentation, relocation, the search for an oath that will bind sufficiently to satisfy the ghost. Will Marcellus' and Horatio's 'in faith' not do (149)? 'Swear', cries the spirit, and so on.

The scene ends with Hamlet trying to get his associates together but being left alone with his burden. The suspicion grows in an audience that despite the carapace of conspiracy, he wants whatever he has taken up to be *his* task, the better, perhaps, for the task to be lost without the securing force of witness and reiteration:

So, gentlemen,
With all my love I do commend me to you,
And what so poor a man as Hamlet is
May do t'express his love and friending to you,
God willing, shall not lack. Let us go in together, ... (183–7)

These formulaic civilities are worthy of Osric. Such a connection as there is has been precariously created *by* oaths, which itself enlarges unease. Horatio and Marcellus have sworn to be secret, but still the prince enjoins them (cf. p. 39). How much belief does this show in the likelihood that promissory oaths will be kept—including his own?

> And still your fingers on your lips, I pray.
> The time is out of joint. O cursèd spite,
> That ever I was born to set it right!
> Nay, come, let's go together. (188–91)

The prince splits away, then draws the others back to him, not so much out of affinity as to keep them confidential.

In the sequence that we began with, in *3 Henry VI*, vows bind together the dead, the afflicted, and the ambitious. Word and gesture draw out a vindictiveness that is already there to be stirred and articulated. This is often the way in Elizabethan and Jacobean drama, from *Titus Andronicus* to *The Revenger's Tragedy*. The dynamic in *Hamlet* is different: the group is not a given, not tied by joint injuries or a covenant, but is made out of an uncanny experience that runs into the prince's attempts, abetted by the ghost, to bind by the flux of words. The mobility and friability of the bond is typical of the play, from whatever 'I have sworn't' means, through Hamlet's broken vows to Ophelia. It is not, however, that questions of binding language slip from sight, or become uncoupled from revenge. On the contrary, as we shall see in Chapter 8, oaths play a part in shaping and investing the action all the way to the end of the revenge plot, in the exercise with foils which turns into a duel and unleashes the bloody enough banquet.

6

Time and Money

The Comedy of Errors and *The Merchant of Venice*

As the action of *Errors* winds into a crisis, in the first scene of Act 4, a merchant comes on stage with an officer to press the goldsmith, Angelo, to repay a debt:

Enter [SECOND] MERCHANT, [ANGELO *the*] *goldsmith, and an* OFFICER
SECOND MERCHANT [*to* ANGELO] You know since Pentecost the sum is due,
And since I have not much importuned you;
Nor now I had not, but that I am bound
To Persia, and want guilders for my voyage.
Therefore make present satisfaction,
Or I'll attach you by this officer.
ANGELO Even just the sum that I do owe to you
Is growing to me by Antipholus,
And in the instant that I met with you
He had of me a chain. At five o'clock
I shall receive the money for the same.
Pleaseth you walk with me down to his house,
I will discharge my bond, and thank you too. (4.1.1–13)

This is typical of the coincidences and mishaps that make *Errors* tick until twins match, couples reunite, and all debts are off. But it also shows the contours of early modern debt. Money has been due (both owed and due in time) since Pentecost (debts were often dated to feast days of the Church), yet although the Second Merchant has reminded Angelo of what he owes a few times it has all been handled in a relaxed way since there was thought to be credit and charity in leaving a debt until the debtor could readily pay.[1] Now, though, landing on a word that will be used in various contexts, from the obligation to pay to the physical binding of the supposedly mad, the merchant says that he is *bound* by the demands of a voyage and that requires him to have his *bond* repaid. Within moments, we will be told that his ship is ready to sail. Debts may wait upon men, but wind and tide do not.

The situation, however, is complex, since, as often in the early modern period, debts create metaphorically the sort of chain that is at issue in the bond. Angelo says he will repay the merchant once he in turn is repaid by Antipholus of Ephesus for the chain that he has made him to give to his wife (and that is later given to a courtesan). Debt could be stressful because you were not in a position to repay it until someone else paid you a debt, or because you were surety for the debt of someone who might continue to be prodigal. As Antipholus quips in reply, complaining that he never received the goods, and cannot now 'trust' in Angelo: 'Belike you thought our love would last too long | If it were chained together' (25–6). Money or goods were often supplied in this way—as in *The Merchant of Venice*, where Antonio borrows money from Shylock for Bassanio, and falls into jeopardy as a result, while Shylock, according to him, borrows money from his fellow Jew Tubal. Being bound by other people's debt, by surety or inherited liability, could be the stuff of nightmare.[2] There was the fear of public arrest, and humiliation, as in the case of Antipholus, and of being dragged away to debtors' prison, where a man could easily die from malnutrition and disease, with no income from employment, leaving his family destitute. To avoid this train of disasters, you had to give *satisfaction*, which was personal, civic, and honour-based (as in fighting a duel) and which also had religious overtones. *Errors* is a volatile mix of Roman comedy with Christian features, ending in the loosing of all by an Abbess. It matters to *The Merchant of Venice*, though not in a pious way, that Christ stood surety for humankind and gave satisfaction for our sins.

What emerges most strongly from the Second Merchant/Angelo episode is the critical role of time. The events are not so much shaped by the passage of the hours as punctuated by moments when things become *due*. 'I pray you see him presently discharged,' says Angelo, to which Antipholus responds, 'I am not furnished with the present money', but adds, go to my house, and 'Perchance I will be there as soon as you' (32–9). Haste is essential, to catch at occasion, making sure you have 'time enough' (41). Antipholus accuses Angelo of 'dalliance', and the Second Merchant says: 'The hour steals on. I pray you, sir, dispatch' (48, 52). However urgent, transactions still need to be in the right temporal sequence. To Angelo's demand for the money,

Antipholus replies that none is owed until the chain is delivered. Having mistakenly handed the chain over to Antipholus' identical twin, the merchant impatiently says: 'You know I gave it you half an hour since' (65).

When Dromio of Syracuse (not Ephesus), 'running fast'—not just on his feet, but like a newly wound, Elizabethan watch—goes to get money for Antipholus' 'redemption', the pressures on time become even more insistent (4.2.30, 46). 'Tell me,' Adriana asks,

was he arrested on a bond?
DROMIO OF SYRACUSE Not on a bond but on a stronger thing:
A chain, a chain—do you not hear it ring?
ADRIANA What, the chain?
DROMIO OF SYRACUSE No, no, the bell. 'Tis time that I were gone:
It was two ere I left him, and now the clock strikes one.
ADRIANA The hours come back! That did I never hear.
DROMIO OF SYRACUSE O yes, if any hour meet a sergeant, a turns back for very fear.
ADRIANA As if time were in debt. How fondly dost thou reason!
DROMIO OF SYRACUSE Time is a very bankrupt, and owes more than he's worth to season.
Nay, he's a thief too. Have you not heard men say
That time comes stealing on by night and day?
If a be in debt and theft, and a sergeant in the way,
Hath he not reason to turn back an hour in a day?
Enter LUCIANA [*from the Phoenix, with the money*]
ADRIANA Go, Dromio, there's the money. Bear it straight,
And bring thy master home immediately. (49–63)

Virtuosic in the 1590s but confusing for modern audiences accustomed to reliable clock time—whatever the ebbs and folds of everyday temporality[3]—this extraordinary passage sets the agenda for this chapter, in its implication of time in money.

It matters that the clock is heard. 'To *talk* of time on the Elizabethan stage is a significant part of *presencing* time,'[4] but the hours also spoke in the church bells, around and beyond the theatre. You were never far from audible time in early modern London.[5] People counted the clock rather than reading it, as in Sonnet 12: 'When I do count the clock that tells the time.' As we shall see, it matters that *count* and *tell* were often used to describe the adding-up of coin. The chiming of bells and chink of money went together in shops and taverns. That different clocks gave different times, varying again from sundials, made time approximate, even negotiable, but no less urgent.

The clock ticked and rang inside schedules that were already shaped by the time taken to do pieces of work and by the movement of sun and moon (*The Comedy of Errors* is framed by the need for Egeon, father of both Antipholuses, to pay a fine of a thousand marks by sunset or be executed). The historians of time make the point too blandly: 'People appear to have coped quite comfortably with several coexisting temporal frames whether metric like clock time or much looser and more flexible. As public signalling of hours spread, people commonly made opportunistic use of public time-signals for diverse organizational purposes of their own.'[6] *Errors* finds an unsettling comedy in how the experience of time was geared to both erratic clocks and debt. That the play is not alone in this[7] is a measure of the extent of the perplexity on which Shakespeare was able to draw.

Many sociologists since Weber have argued that changes in attitude towards time and money were mediated by religion. Evidence of this can readily be found in early modern England. Thomas Powell's *The Art of Thriving* (1636), for instance, calls time 'the hinge of all thriving, . . . if Debts . . . fling not all off the hooks. . . . thinke the losse of a minute more dear than the losse of a pound; for certainly of all expences, the expence of Time is the costliest'.[8] For Powell, this requires of his readers an account book-keeper's view of time: 'that thou maist know how to take and redeeme thy Time, I have here set before thee, a table of each minute of thy life, this is the first leafe, and now I passe to the next, having not time to speake of Time' (A3r–v). The idea of *redeeming* time, so recurrent in English Protestantism, was at its origins economic. 'Walke circumspectly', urges Paul, 'Redeeming the time: for the days are euil' (Ephesians 5: 15–16). As later editions of the Geneva Bible note, this is 'an image taken from the merchants'.[9] The Greek word translated as 'redeeming' is *exagorazomenoi*, from *ek* ('from') and *agorazō* ('I purchase'). The word for 'time' is *kairon*, time not as sequence but as occasion, crisis, due, the moment of redeemed debt.

The danger of missing your due date was made to sound like imperilling your soul. In the dedication to Henry Wilkinson's *The Debt Book* (1625), for instance, we read: 'Debt not duly and seasonably paid, falles heauy vpon a mans outward estate, yea, and reflecteth bitterly, sometimes vpon the conscience.'[10] Five things make it undesirable—reasons that carry us beyond Antipholus and Angelo towards Antonio and Shylock: 'First, because debt consumes many a mans estate, by the hard conditions vpon which they are constrained to borrow; as upon vsurious contracts, or vpon cruell bargaines, or vpon such pawns and Morgages and Obligations as vtterly vndoe a man in the forfeiture.' Second, 'in many cases it is a seruile thing to be indebted'. You become a bondslave to your bond. As many commentators noted, and even more borrowers felt, the agreement to lend and borrow may be a mutual covenant but once the money is lent the borrower is the party bound: 'the *vsurer* hath bounde the borrower', declared Miles Mosse, in a treatise that Shakespeare may have read,[11] '*with bandes and pawnes as it were with fetters*'.[12] Third, 'by long continuance of a debt, freely lent, the Lender may be damnified[13] greatly by the Borrower'. Fourth, there is discomfort to the Conscience, and fifth the fruitless expenditure of serving usury (4–7). When all is said, a man should be 'exact and punctual in keeping day; not keeping time makes a iar in payments, as well as in musicke' (59).

This is the set of issues that the present chapter will unpack. I am interested in the bonds of debt and how they relate to time—what is *due* in a double sense. What energizes the intrigue of *The Comedy of Errors* is even more troublingly active in *The Merchant of Venice*, where the emergent, capitalist belief that 'time is money' (Benjamin Franklin) finds its most challenging form in usury, where time is sold until a debt becomes due. Other Shakespeare plays could be cited. We have already noted, in *Love's Labour's Lost*, a conjunction between the demand for quittance of a royal debt and the choosing time of marriage, counterpointed with arithmetical jokes. Linda Woodbridge has brought out the account-book ethos of revenge drama, which shows through in *Titus Andronicus* and *Hamlet*.[14] Though *Timon of Athens* is looked at from another angle in Chapter 13, the protagonist's tragedy is precipitated by having debts due. Beyond Shakespeare the list of works that could be discussed is large, from Robert Wilson's 'usury play', *The Three Ladies of London* (pub. 1584), to the city comedies of Marston and Middleton. This is not surprising given that the problems adduced in this chapter were ubiquitous in the early modern culture of credit.

To bring out what was systemic and traumatic, recall Shakespeare's early life. When his father got into difficulties after lending money and standing surety, he lost control of property that had come into the family on his marriage to Mary Arden. In 1580, the Shakespeares sought to redeem a mortgage on a house and forty-plus acres at Wilmcote that had been taken out to secure a loan to them from Edmund Lambert. The payment was late or incomplete, and the Lamberts retained possession of the property, despite a court action taken against them in 1588–90. These awkward proceedings—the Lamberts were relatives of the Shakespeares—would have been formative enough in the dramatist's life if that had been the end of it. On 24 November 1597, however, a complaint against John Lambert was filed in

Chancery under the names of John and Mary Shakespeare. The dramatist himself was surely involved, with his lodgings and theatre not far from the court, and this around the time that he was writing *The Merchant of Venice*.[15]

⋆ ⋆ ⋆

What was the orthodox, Christian model for lending? In his *General Discourse Against the Damnable Sect of Vsurers* (1578), Philipp Caesar explains that it is all about bonds:

> Euerie man as well the wicked as the godly is my neighbour, and that firste by reason of creation: secondlie, because of likenesse: thirdlie in respecte of humane societie. And although this triple bonde, whereby all men are tied together, is à greate cause, why one should benefite an other: yet is there a greater couplyng together of Christians. For there is a common callyng of all Christians, whereby we are called to the vnitie of the spirite in the bonde of peace.... I saie nothyng of that bonde, whereby all men in this worlde are debters one to an other.[16]

Nowadays a 'triple bond' is a bond between two atoms involving six bonding electrons. For Caesar, the allusion is to Ecclesiastes 4: 12: 'a threfolde coard is not easely broken'. As the marginal note explains: 'Al men are detters vnto God, and euerie one oweth a duetie to another.' Mainstream commentators agreed that there should be bonds, compacts, and covenants tying men together for the use of money, but that such bonds should be compatible with the bonds of charity. Mutually involved, they are not quickly broken. 'Debt is whatsoeuer is performed to another,' *The Debt Book* explains,

> vpon any bond or reasonable consideration: Now as is the obligation, such is the debt; obligations are of three sorts, of Nature, of Grace, and of Ciuill contract. Bonds of Nature and Grace are perpetuall, so long as the parties remaine, as a child oweth a perpetuall respect to the Parents, and they to him, euen by nature: so Christians are vnited in the bonds of grace, which must not faile but ought to continue. Yet the ciuill bonds of debt, which come by borrowing and lending, by buying and selling, or any interchangeable duties and seruices, doe then cease when they are payed and performed. (2–3)

The civil bonds of debt are temporary; they become due and are discharged—perfect matter, in their ins-and-outs, for the two hours traffic of the stage. Those of nature and grace are permanent, providing a matrix of charity within which time and money take their place.

Christ's injunction at Luke 6: 35—'lend, loking for nothing againe' (i.e. in return)—was sometimes a cause of difficulty, and not just for those who wanted to argue in favour of usury. There was a touch of the wastrel about

Jesus, giving without looking for return. Commentators dealt with this by saying that loans should be repaid even if those lending were charitably willing not to have their money back. The general view was that of Caesar:

> Lendyng is à contracte, whereby one manne giueth his right of à thyng to an other, without any price at all, but vppon condition that the same thyng in kinde be repaied. Herein two thynges should bee considered of the godlie, an Equalitie, and Obligation. Equalitie, to restore faithfully without fraude as-muche either in measure, weight, or goodnesse as was receiued. The Obligation is of twoo sortes, Naturall, and Christian. (fol. 8v)

At this point, Caesar modulates bonds from the obligations that tie us together through debt and charity into the language of Divine law. The ten commandments, the word of Christ, and other Christian principles bind men to be bound together with virtuous lending and repayment:

> The naturall is whereby we are bounde by the lawe of nature to lende to sutche, as lacke our helpe. The Christian Obligation is whereby God doth binde hys to lende to the needie, ... For he saith, *Lende, looking for nothyng thereby.* Here Christe doth not speake of liberall giuing, or of almes, but of lending, wherby the borrower is bounde to restore that whiche was lent hym, ... This lawe is contrarie to the malicious myndes of the Iewes, and the corrupt interpretyng of *Moses* lawe. The law commaunded to lende: but the Iewes tooke the same with this exception, *Lende, but not without respect to all, but onely to sutche as maye doe the like againe.* (fols 8v–9r)

According to Caesar, Shylock's people were guilty of worse than expecting a return on their loans. They drew out of the Law of Moses a distinction between lending between themselves without interest and their right to lend to Gentiles with usury (Deuteronomy 23: 20): 'Vnto a stranger thou maiest lend vpon vsurie, but thou shalt not lend vpon vsurie vnto thy brother.'[17] For Christian moralists such loans were incompatible with charity, creating bonds which severed bonds. As Caesar put it, catching the anti-social effect of Shylock's insistence on having his bond: 'an Vsurer ... doth take away and abolish the cheifest bonde of humane societie' (fols 34v).

The definition of a charitable loan depended critically upon time, and for two reasons. First, while the money was held by the borrower it was his, not the lender's. This was a deeply rooted contention, going back to the scholastic philosophers, though as Roger Fenton indicates in his *Treatise of Vsurie* (1611) it was coming under pressure from those who, like

Francis Bacon, thought that usury was justifiable. 'Those are much deceiued then,' wrote Fenton, 'who thinke that Vsurie is iust, because the vse of money for a time is worth money; ... during the time of loane whose is the principall? thine or the borrowers? It was thine before thou lent it, and it shall be thine at the day of payment; but during the time of loane, it is the borrowers.'[18] Second, time is critical because once a loan was due, and its ownership reverted to the lender, he was entitled to charge interest (which was technically not the same as usury) for the loss of its use, if the money was not repaid. 'The true and verie Interest indeede, whiche cometh to the lender,' wrote Caesar, 'is, when damage ariseth through not keeping daie' (fol. 23r).[19]

If time is critical in Christian lending, it is the more so with the usury that remained, strictly speaking, illegal in Elizabethan England, but which was tolerated up to 10 per cent per annum after the Usury Act of 1571. Usury grew out of the principal during the period of the loan, escalating debts with time. 'If the Creditour be an Vsurer,' Wilkinson reminded readers of *The Debt Book*, 'then the debt is nothing mitigated, but doubled by continuance, ... the burden will encrase howerly' (104–5). The usurer did nothing to bring about this growth. He did not labour in the sweat of his brow.[20] He was, as the scholastics had objected,[21] selling time. Thus Thomas Wilson: 'Usurye is also saide, to be the price of tyme, or of the delaying, or forbearing of moneye.'[22] Mosse concurs 'that the vsurer selleth the time and the ayre' (79).

To get around the Usury Law, loans often took the form of overvalued goods which had to be sold on by the borrower—the sort of device that ensnares Master Rash, in *Measure for Measure*, when he procures a commodity of ginger and brown paper.[23] With such tricks afoot, it could be hard to work out whether a commercial exchange was usurious or simply a hard bargain. Commentators argued that the test was whether time was sold, which it was only God's to sell: 'Some will not take Vsurie,' wrote Henry Smith in 1591, 'but if you haue not present money to pay for their wares, they will set a high price of them, for the forbearing of the time, and so they do not onely sell their wares, but they sell time to: that is, they do not onely sell their owne, but they sell Gods owne.'[24] You could sell things for more than they cost you if the market price went up[25]—as close as most commentators got to the problem of inflation, a late Elizabethan fact of life that inevitably encouraged usury—but you were not to mesh your bond with time. If money was put to use in this way, the whole economic system became an enormous clock. As Gerard Malynes put it in *Consuetudo, vel Lex Mercatoria* (1622):

> This intollerable Vsurie is effected by the Brokers selling old apparell and houshold stuffe, which doe take after diuers rates, but all of them excessiuely,... Most of these Brokers haue their money masters, to whom they pay twentie in the hundreth, or at the least; for some of these money masters pay themselues ten in the hundreth vnto others, so that one thing driueth or inforceth another. Like as in a clocke where there be many wheeles, the first wheele being stirred driueth the next, and that the third, and so forth till the last that moueth the instrument that strikes the clocke:...[26]

The good thing about buying time from a usurer was that you could in theory pay your debts early and get a reduction on the interest. As Malynes notes, 'it is lawfull and accustomed, that although one hundreth pounds were taken vp for one whole yeare, after the rate of ten vpon the hundreth; the Debtor or Taker vp of it, may discharge the same at three moneths, if he will, paying one hundreth and two pounds ten shillings' (102). Often enough, though, there was a catch. The passage continues:

> vnlesse the Bill made for the same be made paiable at a time limited, with a penaltie of a summe of money, called by the Ciuilians *Poena Canonica*, which with vs in England is done vpon a Bond, with a forfeiture of halfe or double the summe of the principall, wherewith the interest is also ioyned without distinction, which may not exceed the rate of ten vpon the hundreth for the yeare, in the computation whereof, diuers things are to [be] obserued, as we shal declare hereafter.

This was another way in which time was a critical factor to usury. As with a Christian loan, the due date of a bond, suitably sworn and sealed, brought with it the requirement to pay. In usurious, bond-tied arrangements, the penalty at that point could be massive—half or double the principal.

In some cases, the usurer would tempt clients into a free loan, reckoning that the forfeit would be more profitable than 10 per cent on the debt. The lender would secure what was borrowed with a penalty, which might be property in pawn or mortgage. It was a recipe for deceit, much favoured in city comedy. Fenton, for instance, describing how forfeits work, outlines a situation that would play well on the stage:

> A yong Gallant would borrow an hundred pound for a yeere; the Vsurer in kindnesse will lend him so much freelie for three moneths. The Gentleman glad to finger the money, accepteth his kinde offer. The Vsurer takes sure bonds, knowing that he who is so hungrie for a yeere, will not be in case to

> pay at three moneths; then shall the forfeiture of the bond pay the Interest of the money with aduantage; only, forsooth, because the Creditour is exceedingly damnified in being disappointed at the time. This were vsurie, if the craftie purpose of the Vsurer were discouered.[27]

Lenders were entitled to security, Mosse conceded, provided that the 'bandes, obligations, penalties, and forfeitures' were not used as a cloak for usury (24). In more pragmatic, worldly terms, Bacon argued that usury should be legalized—as it more or less would be in 1624—on the grounds that, without it, extortionate bonds would be worse: 'As for Mortgaging, or Pawning, it will little mend the matter; For either Men will not take Pawnes without *Vse*; Or if they doe, they will looke precisely for the Forfeiture. I remember a Cruell Moneyed Man, in the Country, that would say; The Deuill take this *Vsury*, it keepes vs from Forfeitures, of Mortgages, and Bonds.'[28]

This is where Shylock comes in. He gives Antonio a free loan with forfeiture. This may be (as he puts it) 'kind' (1.3.137), but it is also sinister. It is usurious in the extreme, yet not. The pledged pound of flesh is of no financial value, but of huge symbolic value (since it puts Shylock's enemy into his power) and of even greater psychological and moral value because he either gets credit for being a gentle Jew if he is repaid, or the ultimate payback, which is revenge, if he is not. Sure enough, at the due date, he does 'looke precisely for the Forfeiture'. The tables are only turned when Portia shows that he is not looking precisely enough: he is allowed a pound of flesh, but no more nor less, and not a drop of blood. Those quibbles, however, are last-minute. What the play most takes from time is the warping imminence of the due date.

⋆ ⋆ ⋆

Given the vigour and circulation of the debate about usury, Shakespeare's early audiences would have found their bearings without difficulty in Antonio's first, great scene with Shylock:

Enter BASSANIO *with* SHYLOCK *the Jew*
SHYLOCK Three thousand ducats. Well.
BASSANIO Ay, sir, for three months.
SHYLOCK For three months. Well.
BASSANIO For the which, as I told you, Antonio shall be bound.
SHYLOCK Antonio shall become bound. Well. (1.3.1–5)

Sum, time, and bond are equally addressed. But Shylock is forgetful about time in a way that exudes craft. Once Antonio is on stage he needs to be told again: 'But soft—how many months | Do you desire?' (53–4). Eight lines later Antonio sets out the terms, 'And for three months', and Shylock adds 'I had forgot—three months' (62–3). Either he is bad at his job, or there is something slippery about this. Meanwhile the audience is reminded that the period of a loan is at least as important as the amount of money loaned. In the end, time will be decisive, because the success of Bassanio's visit to Belmont means that there is no shortage of cash to repay the debt. What catches Antonio is the due date.

If Antonio were accustomed to taking and paying interest, perhaps the Christian friends who fail to come forward to save him from Shylock might be more inclined to help him. He would be bound by lucrative credit. As it is he takes a line of almost scholastic purity, as Shylock complains in an aside: 'He lends out money gratis, and brings down | The rate of usance here with us in Venice' (39–40). Antonio quickly confirms that 'I neither lend nor borrow | By taking nor by giving of excess', but is willing to make an exception, because of Bassanio's 'ripe wants' (57–9). It is a beautifully chosen expression of season and natural due-ness, standing against the unnatural artifice of a bond with forfeit. But he still has to borrow money.

This gives Shylock an opening to tell his marvellously complex story about Jacob grazing Laban's sheep. I shall start unpacking it here, though matters remain for Chapter 7:

Mark what Jacob did:
When Laban and himself were compromised
That all the eanlings which were streaked and pied
Should fall as Jacob's hire, the ewes, being rank,
In end of autumn turnèd to the rams,
And when the work of generation was
Between these woolly breeders in the act,
The skilful shepherd peeled me certain wands,
And in the doing of the deed of kind
He stuck them up before the fulsome ewes
Who, then conceiving, did in eaning time
Fall parti-coloured lambs; and those were Jacob's.
This was a way to thrive; and he was blest;
And thrift is blessing, if men steal it not.
ANTONIO This was a venture, sir, that Jacob served for—
A thing not in his power to bring to pass,
But swayed and fashioned by the hand of heaven.
Was this inserted to make interest good,
Or is your gold and silver ewes and rams?
SHYLOCK I cannot tell. I make it breed as fast.
But note me, signor—

ANTONIO Mark you this, Bassanio?
The devil can cite Scripture for his purpose. (73–94)

There are half a dozen reasons why this Old Testament story (Genesis 30: 31–43) figures at this point. First, as we have seen, lending involves, implicitly or actively, a 'contracte', 'couenant', or '*mutuall agreement*'.[29] An early audience would have been alert to this in 'compromise', which means 'co-promise, co-agree'. The case of Jacob and Laban was often cited to show how binding language bound agreements. It was used, for instance, to support the taking of oaths of office, in front of the magistrate.[30] It was also cited by those who wanted to think about bonds between those with different beliefs. So William Perkins asks whether sworn bonds are binding when one party is not a true believer:

> *Ans.* They doe bind in conscience. For example: Iacob and Laban make a couenant confirmed by oath. Iacob sweares by the true God, Laban by the god of Nachor, that is, by his idols. Now Iacob, though he approoue not the forme of this oath yet he accepts it for a civil bond of the covenant: and no doubt, though Laban beleeued not Gods word reuealed to the Patriarks, yet he was bound in conscience to keep this oth euen by the law of nature, and though he knew not the true God, yet he reputed the false god of Nachor to be the true God. Gen. 31. 53.[31]

The compromise between Jacob and Laban was the template of any agreement between the true-believer and the false. Whether Antonio or Shylock was rightly the successor of Jacob was a matter of huge controversy between Christianity and Judaism, as we shall see, in relation to this passage, in Chapter 7.

The answer turns out to depend on what happened to God's promise to Abraham, Jacob, Noah, and the rest of the chosen people, after the birth of Christ. Embedded within that argument was the vow given by Jacob—a reiteration of Abraham's covenant—in a section of Genesis that almost immediately precedes the story of Laban. The vow was effectively to pay 10 per cent interest to God: 'Then Iaakob vowed a vowe, saying, If God wil be with me . . . then shal the Lord be my God. . . . and of all that thou shalt giue me, wil I giue the tenth vnto thee' (Genesis 28: 20–2). The passage was often argued over in debates about the funding of the English Church, which—to the displeasure of hotter Protestants—was supported by tithes. Could you, for instance, vow to give God something that was (by definition) already God's?[32] Was tithe-taking a form of usury? The resemblance between both exactions, to which I shall return when discussing the end of *Timon of*

Athens, was the more troubling because tithes were marketable (Shakespeare, as a long-term investment, bought a half-share of the Stratford tithes[33] around the time he was co-writing *Timon*). Briefly put, however, two lots of lucrative promises run through Jacob's 'compromise'. He does a deal with Laban but gets streaked and spotted lambs after vowing a vow to God to pay Him 10 per cent (Genesis 28: 20–1, 31: 11–13).

That Jacob is one of the chosen people, and Laban is a Gentile, raises questions about religious (and ethnic) difference in relation to God's promise that are best pursued in the next chapter. More immediately, however, it has a bearing on Deuteronomy 23: 20 (see p. 152). Jews took this as allowing usury on loans to Gentiles but not on those to fellow-Jews. The money that Shylock borrows from Tubal to lend to Antonio will not carry interest. The Christian view was that this distinction had been swept away by the Gospel. All men were now brothers (though a few theologians argued that Christians were now the brothers, making it legitimate to charge interest to Jews).[34] Shylock's parable sounds as though it is about the legitimacy of charging interest altogether, but it incorporates the discriminatory assumption that Shylock/Jacob can take interest from a Gentile or pagan like Antonio/Laban.

It is time to edge back to time. As every student of the play should know, Shylock's speech is also about *tokos*, the breeding of money out of money. It is an ancient objection to usury. Here is Aristotle:

> usury is . . . hated, because its gain comes from money itself and not from that for the sake of which money was invented. For money was brought into existence for the purpose of exchange, but interest increases the amount of the money itself (and this is the actual origin of the Greek word: offspring resembles parent, and interest is money born of money); consequently this form of the business of getting wealth is of all forms the most contrary to nature.[35]

Early modern commentators liked to exaggerate the unnaturalness by saying that the breeding of money produced monsters. Here is Wilson in an influential formulation (recycled for instance by Malynes):[36]

> And I pray you, what is more against nature, then that money should beget or bring forth money? . . . And therefore Aristotle saieth, that such money as bringeth forth money through vsurie, is an vgly beast, that bringeth forthe monsters from time to time, suche as are not in nature. (97)

Shylock jokes his way around this by shifting attention from the unnaturalness of usury ('is your gold and silver ewes and rams?') to the time-scheme that it shares with good husbandry ('I make it breed as fast'). It is a help to him in evading Aristotle's objection that his monsters, though streaked and pied, are natural, organic products, and also that they are chosen by God for Jacob. They are marked out as distinctive, aberrant in fleece or garb, like Shylock and his tribe contrasted with the Christians. As importantly, notice Wilson's insertion of 'from time to time', which is not in Aristotle.[37]

For Shylock's speech, obviously, makes much of time. The rams come to the ewes and after several months the ewes give birth to the striped and spotted lambs. Shakespeare says more about the period of gestation than does the Book of Genesis, which simply reads 'and *afterward* broght forthe yong of party colour' (30: 39). Elsewhere in the plays, the gestation period of lambs is in itself a measure of time. When Henry VI contemplates the pastoral life, in which time slips away calmly, he imagines being a shepherd calculating, 'So many days my ewes have been with young, | So many weeks ere the poor fools will ean.'[38] This overlaps with the Sonnets, where the topic is, at least initially, the breeding of children. Scholarship has under-explored how the conflict between time and the young man which breeding is urged to overcome *brings in* usury. If the youth is 'contracted to [his] own bright eyes' (1.5) he is not only neglecting to secure and commit to a marriage contract, and so the generation of children, but (in a mischievous turn) not engaging in productive usury either. He is keeping his beauty and neither spending nor lending it to advantage:

> Profitless usurer, why dost thou use
> So great a sum of sums yet canst not live?
> For having traffic with thyself alone,
> Thou of thyself thy sweet self dost deceive.
> Then how when nature calls thee to be gone:
> What acceptable audit canst thou leave?
> Thy unused beauty must be tombed with thee,
> Which usèd, lives th'executor to be. (4.7–14)

The whole sequence of sonnets starts from the point that 'increase' of the sort that Shylock aims at is sought 'From fairest creatures' (1.1). Even those against economic usury would accept that natural increase is permissible. Fenton wrote: 'We must not therefore meddle with the vsurie of nature, that most innocent and primitiue increase which the earth yeeldeth in fruite vnto man for his seede sowne; *some thirtie, some sixtie, some an hundred fold. Terra nunquam sine vsura reddit quod accepit:* The earth (saith *Tullie*) neuer returneth that which it hath receiued, without vsurie.'[39] One of the clever points of Shylock's speech is that he deals with natural reproduction yet subtly introduces skill and guile. In the Sonnets, where husbandry is a topic, it is as though, wittily or cheekily—and perhaps not unexpectedly from a poet whose father was accused of usury,[40] and who himself made a margin on transactions[41] and took debtors to court[42]—the poet is paralleling, Shylock-like, the production of children from a fair youth with the 10 per cent usury that was tolerated in England. But why not ten for one, 'an hundred fold' in Cicero and Fenton's phrase?

> That use is not forbidden usury
> Which happies those that pay the willing loan:
> That's for thyself to breed another thee,
> Or ten times happier, be it ten for one;
> Ten times thyself were happier than thou art,
> If ten of thine ten times refigured thee. (6.5–10)

This is remarkable not so much because it leans into sophistical arguments in favour of usury but because it sheds another light on Time. These sonnets, we might say, are not primarily incitements to breed based on fear of mortality, though that fear is there. Breeding and usury *both* bring in Time. If it were not for the analogy between breeding and usury the sequence would not go on to deliver such majestic accounts of the destructive power of Time as Sonnets 55 and 65. What the sequence starts from is increase, and that leads to thoughts of usury, and that brings in train Time for all early modern writers in a Christian tradition where God had special rights over time.

On the back of the Jacob and Laban speech, Shylock prepares to offer a loan with a pro-rata payment of interest. It might be, as it were—he does the working out in his head—10 per cent per annum, which means two and a half per cent for three months:

> SHYLOCK Three thousand ducats. 'Tis a good round sum.
> Three months from twelve—then let me see the rate.
> ANTONIO Well, Shylock, shall we be beholden to you?
> SHYLOCK Signor Antonio, many a time and oft
> In the Rialto you have rated me
> About my moneys and my usances. (99–104)

Shylock has in mind the discounting of interest by time that we noted in Malynes's *Consuetudo*. Antonio's interruption, however, covers or triggers a slide from the *time* of the loan and its 'rate' to 'many a time' and 'rated'.

The Jew's resentment surfaces. He has been treated like a dog. His working week, his experience of 'time', is marked by contempt and rudeness:

> Shall I bend low, and in a bondman's key,
> With bated breath and whisp'ring humbleness
> Say this: 'Fair sir, you spat on me on Wednesday last;
> You spurned me such a day; another time
> You called me dog: and for these courtesies
> I'll lend you thus much moneys'? (119–24)

Interestingly, it is Antonio who raises the prospect of a forfeit, a penal or conditional bond. Recycling the Aristotelian arguments of the usury tracts, he asks, 'when did friendship take | A breed of barren metal of his friend?'[43] and proposes that Shylock lend to him as an enemy, 'Who, if he break,'—break promise, but also the due date—'thou mayst with better face | Exact the penalty.' Not at all, says Shylock,[44] I want to be your friend and will 'take no doit | Of usance for my moneys'. There will be a forfeit, but an essentially meaningless one:

> Go with me to a notary, seal me there
> Your single bond, and, in a merry sport,
> If you repay me not on such a day,
> In such a place, such sum or sums as are
> Expressed in the condition, let the forfeit
> Be nominated for an equal pound
> Of your fair flesh to be cut off and taken
> In what part of your body pleaseth me.
> ANTONIO Content, in faith. I'll seal to such a bond,
> And say there is much kindness in the Jew.
> BASSANIO You shall not seal to such a bond for me.
> I'll rather dwell in my necessity. (128–51)

So many editors and critics have been baffled by 'single bond' that the Norton deserves applause for glossing it 'Bond signed by the debtor alone (Antonio) without additional guarantors'. In early modern usage, a 'single bond' ties up one person, without sureties.[45] Shylock knows that, with his ships at sea and his credit running out, Antonio could not readily find others to guarantee the loan, so he is doing him a favour—though this also makes responsibility for the debt fall entirely and ominously on his enemy's head. Because lending on a 'single bond' was a sign of trust, such a bond might well not carry conditions[46]—but conditions are then imposed in the surely-not-serious form of a pound of flesh.[47]

Whether 'single bond' is primarily heard as about not needing sureties or (associatively) being without conditions, the more enticing features of the deal are put first. Generosity shades into entrapment. Like Jacob tricking Laban—a matter to be pursued in the next chapter—Shylock deceives Antonio; like the Jew of anti-Semitic legend, he draws his victim into an injurious pledge. The wording of the bond ('in such a place, such sum or sums') is worryingly legalistic. It is framed with the sort of care that ought to make Antonio cautious. Bassanio is, but his protest is faint. He says that he would rather dwell in a state of necessity, yet he does not *need* the 3,000 ducats, merely wants them for his venture to Belmont, to pay other prodigal debts. Notice how Shylock's bond draws on the traditional language of good lending. It is 'equal', like Caesar echoing the scholastics on 'Equalitie',[48] though equal to what is not clear.

Shylock and Shakespeare are nothing if not subtle, and it is worth recognizing that, just as a bond without usance could be generous, so many of those opposed to extortion would find nothing wrong with the proposed bond *as such*. Exacting the forfeit, or planning to, is what would be wrong. This was a loophole that attracted much casuistical comment. Some allow a creditor to set an extreme forfeit, Fenton notes, 'to preuent fraud in the debtor: prouided that hee neither exact the bonds, nor intend to exact them:... So that vpon the point *Zanchie* will giue a man leaue to be an Vsurer in parchment, but not in heart: to couenant for his best securitie, yet neuer intend to execute his couenant. But this, me thinks, is too too cunning, plaine dealing were the best.'[49] It certainly gave scope to duplicity on as well as offstage. In Middleton's *Michaelmas Term*, Quomodo draws in Easy by protesting that 'bonds lie forfeit in my hands'. Those who owe him money 'know I have no conscience to take the forfeiture, and that makes 'em so bold with my mercy' (2.3.124–30).

There would be something duplicitious about the bond even if there were no intention to exact the pound of flesh because it imposes a forfeit that would not then be taken. Like many an unwary debtor, Antonio disregards the condition because he thinks he has plenty of time.

> Why, fear not, man; I will not forfeit it.
> Within these two months—that's a month before
> This bond expires—I do expect return
> Of thrice three times the value of this bond. (152–5)

Shylock will have no use for his flesh, he adds, agreeing to 'seal unto this bond'. The deal is quickly concluded:

SHYLOCK Then meet me forthwith at the notary's.
Give him direction for this merry bond,
And I will go and purse the ducats straight,
See to my house—left in the fearful guard
Of an unthrifty knave—and presently
I'll be with you. (167–73)

The emphasis on speed is telling, perhaps incriminating. Shylock is eager to get this done, and now. He is also keen to get the bond secured. At a notary's a bond would be sworn to as well as sealed.[50] The audience would understand that, but Shakespeare also wants to bring out the binding role of the oaths—the very Jewish oaths, as we shall see in the next chapter—that Shylock puts on top of the 'compromise'. At all events, it matters that the sequence ends with time, the due date of a debt. In response to Bassanio's doubting comment 'I like not fair terms and a villain's mind', Antonio replies with a couplet that is the more wishful for casting the future in the simple present: 'In this there can be no dismay. | My ships come home a month before the day' (175–7).

* * *

What Shylock calls 'thrift' in Jacob, Antonio calls a 'venture'. The Jew is *shy*, meaning wary,[51] and inclined to *lock* things up; Antonio is a merchant venturer, a child of luck not lock. The contrast is more thematic than culturally diagnostic. The Venetian Rabbi, Leone da Modena, whose autobiography tells us much about how a 'real-life' Shylock would have lived, was virtually addicted to gambling (he called it the 'sin of Judah', alluding to Jeremiah 17: 1)—so much so that one year he took a vow to avoid it until the next Passover.[52] These, however, are the contrasts that structure the comedy, and that enable ironic reversals. The word 'hazard', which is used more often in *The Merchant* than in any other of Shakespeare's plays, is associated with the Christians and especially Belmont. Shakespeare could have presented Shylock as weighing up the risk of lending money to Antonio, but the language of his decision leans towards the security of forfeit. He prefers, in Bacon's phrases, the 'Certaine gaines' of the 'Trade of *Vsury*' to the 'Gaines of Hazard' sought by merchants.[53] If he does take chances himself, it is only in the sense that trying to be too safe is always a risk. The pound of flesh offers maximum security, but he ends up gambling 3,000 ducats against a pound of unmarketable flesh if he wins.

There were some who argued, as Malynes appears to, that the usurer always takes risks,[54] since he gambles on the reliability of those that he invests in. As Mosse explains, however, this is to say little, for 'euery man *aduentureth* his goods, . . . yea euen he that kéepeth his money fast lockt in his cofers: for they may be burnt, or stollen, or by cousenage conueyed away. . . . And yet I trowe no man will say that hée doth aduenture his money, who taketh for it sufficient pawne in hand, or who kéepeth it by himselfe vnder locke and key in his owne closet.'[55] This sounds very like Shylock, who 'kéepeth his money fast *lockt* in his cofers' and takes no risks. 'Fast find, fast bind', he urges Jessica (2.5.52). As safe as houses can be, he is not, given the human condition, absolutely secure. He keeps his valuables locked in a casket that is 'stollen, or by cousenage conueyed away', even the turquoise ring given to him by his late wife, Leah.

While Shakespeare makes Shylock the epitome of what fast-binding can contain, he does what he can to maximize Antonio's exposure to hazard. What could have protected him, the play takes away. He is at the limit of his credit so no one is willing to come to his aid when he is due to repay Shylock. Nor does he insure his ships, as Elizabethan merchants did and as Venetians had been doing for generations.[56] Perhaps he is so committed to the scholastic view of usury that he sees this as resisting the hand of heaven. It can be argued, as it was argued in the late middle ages, that permission to insure was the thin end of the wedge when it came to sanctioning usury.[57] Antonio's lack of insurance has been tentatively related to the fact that, during the 1590s, the Venetian and the London insurance markets were not functioning well.[58] Altogether more likely it was a dramaturgical decision, to heighten the contrast with Shylock.

According to conventional accounts, the merchant gains moral superiority from his exposure to risk, while the usurer is damaged by his security. Fenton writes: 'The husbandman lookes vp to the cloudes, and prayeth for seasonable weather: The Merchant obserues the winde, and prayeth God to deliuer him from tempest and wrack.'[59] Shakespeare puts this into the play, but keeps it fresh by having Solanio and Salerio wonder why Antonio is not 'Plucking the grass to know where sits the wind' and worrying about storms and shallows (1.1.18–36). The merchant himself, sunk in melancholy (1.1.1–7), cannot access these anxieties. As for the grasping lender, Fenton says, 'only the Vsurer of all others hath least need to say his prayers: be it wet or drie; be it tempest or calme; . . . he will be sure of his money' (96). His support is not God, nor even other people's efforts, but time: 'for time onely worketh for him; all the daies in the Calender be set a worke to worke out his gaine; yea Sabbaths and all' (96). Usury erases the natural and religious, shared contours of time. As Antonio waits for Bassanio, while Bassanio tarries in Belmont, taking far longer to choose the caskets than he need, every tick of the clock brings Shylock's gruesome profit closer.

Explaining how 'the *vsurer* neuer *hazardeth*', Mosse addresses a linguistic point which the defenders of usury turn to their advantage: 'That which is lent forth they commonly call the *principall:* in *latine* they call it *Sors:* which is as much to say, as *hazard*, or *chance*, or *lotte*' (53). We should not, Mosse argues, be deceived. The Latin word only fits usury in the way that 'men by speaking one thing, will vnderstande the cleane contrarie'—like calling a penal bond a merry one. Properly understood, '*To cast lottes* (in which, things are put vpon chance) *is nothing else, but to doe some acte, by the euent whereof wee may finde out some thing which is* hidden or *vnknowne.* According to which description, the *vsurer* is farre enough from *lotte* or *aduenturing*' (53–4). We shall look more deeply into lots and their relationship with oaths and sortilege in Chapter 8, on *Hamlet*. What Mosse more immediately points us to is the contrast between Shylock's casket and the gold, silver, and lead caskets at Belmont. The love-test with these caskets is twice called a 'lottery' (1.2.25, 2.1.15) and each time one is opened a suitor and the audience '*finde out something which is* hidden or *vnknowne*'. What is in the caskets is the future for the suitors, each of whom has been tied into his 'chance' and 'hazard' (2.1.43–5) by swearing oaths in Portia's temple not to marry, in a sort of anti-marriage vow (they have to risk something to take their chance).

With hindsight the choice of caskets is obvious. Gold and silver are the metals of cash. They are tradeable and public, and much too close to what Shylock wants. Lead by contrast, though used for tokens,[60] has nothing to do with wealth. A lead casket would typically be used for burying a body, whereas gold and silver flatter us with the hope of health and happiness. When Bassanio chooses the leaden casket, as Freud pointed out, he accepts mortality.[61] But it also attracts him as a fortune hunter, who is best placed to win Portia because he does not care about money. Recklessness and charm are his assets, not thrift. She has so much money that she can afford to be indifferent to its value, as when offering to save Antonio from Shylock; he has so little that he has to borrow it. They represent twin faces of the noble economy, so often, as *Timon of Athens* reminds us, extravagant and/or indebted.

There is another clue to Bassanio's choice in what is inscribed on the caskets. Morocco explains:

> This first of gold, who this inscription bears:
> 'Who chooseth me shall gain what many men desire.'

> The second silver, which this promise carries:
> 'Who chooseth me shall get as much as he deserves.'
> This third dull lead, with warning all as blunt:
> 'Who chooseth me must give and hazard all he hath.' (2.7.4–9)

The gold and silver caskets make promises. Bassanio's own flexibility with promises—as when he gives away Portia's ring to Balthazar (Portia in disguise) having vowed that he would always keep it—makes him intuitively aware of how equivocal they can be, how little to be trusted. In the casket test that Shakespeare found and adapted in the *Gesta Romanorum*, the gold and silver vessels bear inscriptions resembling those in the play, but the lead reads 'Thei that chese me, shulle fynde [in] me that God hathe disposid.'[62] The play heightens risk into warning: 'Who chooseth me must give and hazard all he hath.' Bassanio is not giving or hazarding much, except Antonio's money. But prodigality and a willingness to throw good money after bad goes back to his first exchange with his friend (1.1.140–52). Giving, as we shall see, is almost as important to the play as hazarding, and both are part of the Christian ethos of charity opposed to the security of usury and forfeit.

* * *

While Bassanio feasts in Belmont, Antonio's life is in danger. Like the Second Merchant, Angelo, and Officer, at a similar point in *The Comedy of Errors*, Antonio comes onstage with Shylock, Solanio, and a Jailer.

> ANTONIO Hear me yet, good Shylock.
> SHYLOCK I'll have my bond. Speak not against my bond.
> I have sworn an oath that I will have my bond....
> ANTONIO I pray thee hear me speak.
> SHYLOCK I'll have my bond. I will not hear thee speak.
> I'll have my bond, and therefore speak no more.
> I'll not be made a soft and dull-eyed fool
> To shake the head, relent, and sigh, and yield
> To Christian intercessors. Follow not.
> I'll have no speaking. I will have my bond. (3.3.4–17)

The audience will not be surprised. We have seen Shylock react to the news of Jessica's extravagance in Genoa by ordering that an officer be paid and ready to arrest Antonio a fortnight before his due date. Debtors were often allowed a period of grace between the due date and claiming of a debt. Three days was common. Having been pre-emptively prompt, Shylock is now fixed and repetitive, like the chiming of a clock. And it is not even

Antonio's debt. After Shylock rejects him, he says, 'Pray God Bassanio come | To see me pay *his* debt.'

Antonio's borrowing to lend to Bassanio is not unlike Angelo being responsible for giving money to the Second Merchant that Angelo is owed by Antipholus. If you lent to or went surety for a friend, you were at risk of losing more than the sum in question. It may be that John Shakespeare was unable to meet in full and on time the debt secured by the land at Wilmcote (p. 150) because he lost a bond of £10 that he stood for a debt of £22 owed by his brother Henry.[63] Edmund Lambert himself owed £5 to a baker called Roger Sadler, borrowed to lend to John Shakespeare. Justly or not—which makes the topic dramatically attractive—you often had to break both your promise and your date when others let you down, or were obliged to let you down. This was as demoralizing and problematic as it was socially binding, and potentially a solvent of integrity. It is a drawback of Christian orthodoxy that too many people in Venice expect someone else to pay their bills (Bassanio obviously, but Lorenzo too, and Lancelot Gobbo). It is a mentality sustained by the doctrine of the Atonement—a structure of substitution reflected in Antonio's willingness to pay Bassanio's debt with a pound of his flesh, his death in anticipation like that of Christ on the cross. Bassanio has a thoroughly Christian way of feeling entitled. Shylock's relationship with the Divine is more demanding; he feels that, like Jacob, he must be thrifty and clever to be blessed.

Even for mainstream Christian commentators surety was not straightforward. Luther denounced it as claiming too much for man: we should put our trust in God, not in a mortal being who pledges what is not in his power.[64] Others warned that standing surety—which was not always an act of charity, but could be a service to be sold[65]—was often more foolish than virtuous. William Burton, for example, agreed in *A Caueat for Suerties* (1593) that it was right in principle 'To become Suertie for mens persons'.[66] Yet it was so perilous to be bound in surety that some people bound themselves *not* to stand surety. Burton doubted whether it was 'lawfull for a Christian to binde himselfe by vow, or by oth, or by bond from a dutie so necessarie, so charitable, and so Christian' (B8r), but he urged readers to combine charity with prudence, and not risk lives and living. Shakespeare varies this by making Antonio a challenge to Christian charity. His willingness to sign away his life for Bassanio is self-neglecting or worse, the product of melancholy or consciousness of being in his sexuality a 'tainted wether' (4.1.113). His *caritas* smacks of *amor*, and is masochistic; it gives him something to be in danger for the man he loves.

In the circumspection recommended for standing surety, there was an analogy with taking vows. Burton writes: 'As in vowes to God, men must consider whether it be in their power or no, to performe that which they vow, so in making of promises to men' (C6v–7r). Never rule out the possibility that you will pay for another man's debt to the extent of death: 'in regard of thy person, take heede what thou doest promise, lest thou become a murtherer of thy selfe' (C7v). Solomon warns against standing surety (Proverbs 6: 1). The world is full of snares: 'as easily shall the Doe escape out of the hunters hands, and a bird out of the hand of the fowler, as thou shalt get out of some mens bonds,... some hunt for the goods, some for the offices, some for the liuings, and some for the liues of men' (F2r). He might as well be thinking of Shylock. 'Some by extreme couenants and bargaines do seaze vppon goods, lands, bodies and liues too' (F3v). Such reminders of what standing surety entailed make the denouement of *The Merchant of Venice* seem less of a folk tale. The murderous pound of flesh is a concentrated emblem of the experience of the many Elizabethan debtors who wasted away or died of horrible diseases when dragged off to prison by officers.

Early modern drama, beyond Shakespeare, does not neglect incarceration for debt.[67] What he saw in Shylock's bond, however, was its potential to combine the arc and crisis of a plot with the economic catastrophe of a forfeit. Yet the play would be much cruder if this were its only drive. The fixity of Shylock's payback is basic. Vengeance typically plays with time, contriving delay, looking for opportunities, and improvising.[68] It chooses its own time. Shylock, by contrast, is bound by time to his own bond. He does show flair, however, at what the Duke calls 'the last hour of act' (4.1.18). He is buoyant, quick, and impatient. 'We trifle time', is his cry (293). This dynamic is the more powerful in the theatre because the audience wants the trial to stop for the Jew's sake as well as Antonio's. His alacrity goes with the punctiliousness of his payback. A merely implacable performance misses out too much, as Henry James recognized, when he wrote of Irving as Shylock: 'The actor struck us as rigid and frigid, and above all as painfully behind the stroke of the clock. The deep-welling malignity, the grotesque horror, the red-hot excitement of the long-baffled, sore-hearted member of a despised trade, who has been all his life at a disadvantage, and who at last finds his hour and catches his opportunity—these elements had dropped out.'[69]

Surety is an issue beyond Antonio getting into debt for Bassanio. When Portia is asked what she thinks of the Scot among her suitors, she quips that 'he hath a neighbourly charity in him, for he borrowed a box of the ear of the Englishman and swore he would pay him again when he was able. I think the Frenchman became his surety, and sealed under for another' (1.2.65–9). At the end of the action, she makes Antonio surety for Bassanio's faith when the ring she gave the latter before marriage is returned to him (5.1.253–4). The most loaded sequence comes, however, in the trial scene, when Bassanio attempts to save his friend by promising to pay Shylock up to 30,000 ducats, offering his body as surety against delivery of the cash. 'Is he not able to discharge the money?' asks Portia, as the lawyer Dr Balthazar.

BASSANIO Yes, here I tender it for him in the court,
Yea, twice the sum. If that will not suffice
I will be bound to pay it ten times o'er
On forfeit of my hands, my head, my heart. (4.1.203–7)

That Shakespeare's interest in this sort of relationship extended well beyond *The Merchant* is clear from Sonnet 134, where the poet tells the dark lady:

> Myself I'll forfeit, so that other mine
> Thou wilt restore to be my comfort still.
> But thou wilt not, nor he will not be free,
> For thou art covetous, and he is kind.
> He learned but surety-like to write for me
> Under that bond that him as fast doth bind.
> The statute of thy beauty thou wilt take,
> Thou usurer that putt'st forth all to use,
> And sue a friend came debtor for my sake;... (3–11)

This is the obverse of the opening sonnets, which play with the legitimate usury of marriage and childbearing. The poet urged the youth to put forth all to use, but now that is debased into the emotionally and perhaps financially exploitative bond, where the lady enjoys the friend's pound of flesh in sexual form. In *Il Pecorone*, the Jew threatens to take the pound of flesh by castration, a fear which must have stirred in an Elizabethan audience when Shylock bears down on Antonio wielding his knife, like the medieval monster-Jew who was believed to circumcise his victims before killing them as a human sacrifice.

There are complexities enough in the sonnet.[70] Those in the play go almost inordinately beyond the divided feelings about surety to be found in

Elizabethan commentators. For a start, when Bassanio makes his offer—as though discharging his debt to Antonio—he must know that it will not be taken up, because Shylock is set on destroying his friend (or, more largely, paying back Christian Venice) and because, as an expert in getting other people to pay, Bassanio knows that he is now master of all the wealth of Belmont. Portia has already offered 'double six thousand, and then treble that' (3.2.299), so there are easily 30,000 ducats in her caskets (choose lead, and you get gold and silver). But the shallow Bassanio is deep enough to feel for Antonio, and Portia recognizes, as the audience must, that, if Antonio pays the forfeit, Bassanio will never be free of the bond, even though it has been cancelled. Antonio will take *his* pound of flesh, the heart in Bassanio's breast. This is why *The Merchant of Venice* has an Act 5, all about confirming marital bonds and establishing an appropriate place for Antonio in Bassanio's relationships.

Shylock, as we have seen, wants to seize the occasion: 'I pray thee pursue sentence,' he urges Portia as Balthazar (4.1.293). She by contrast has the leisure of her nobility and of a woman with all the right cards in her hand. She comes from a place in which the rituals of oath-taking and choosing caskets predominate over linear time. Decision is unattractive in Belmont, either because it will give her the wrong husband, or because Bassanio, in choosing, might choose wrongly and have to leave. She asks him to 'tarry. Pause a day or two | Before you hazard', for that reason (3.2.1–2). As Shylock prepares to strike, she re-uses that characteristic word, which no one else in the play has: 'Tarry a little. There is something else' (4.1.300)—pointing out that he can't take any blood with his pound of flesh. When Shylock, alert to the moment, says that that he will have thrice the bond instead, Bassanio is eager to pay (as you would be, with someone else's money) but Portia slows events again, saying that the Jew must cut off an exact pound of flesh: 'if the scale do turn | But in the estimation of a hair, | Thou diest' (325–7).

Now Shylock must tarry. It is a long, difficult moment, given his zest in the scene, and how time is supposed to serve the usurer, bringing him, effortlessly, the double payback of profit and penalty. 'Why doth the Jew pause?' Portia almost mocks, with another Belmont word ('pause'), found four times in her part:[71] 'Take thy forfeiture.' His response cues the actor to strike a note somewhere between the wheedling and the crushed: 'Shall I not have barely my principal?' (330, 337). He is still trying to bargain (like a 'Jew') but only to get his money back. His question anticipates refusal, so humiliates him since he loses even his scrap of dignity in asking. In any case, he must stay upon his bond. He has sealed to a free loan and a forfeit, if the principal be lost, and that means only the forfeit is available. 'Thou shalt have nothing but the forfeiture | To be so taken at thy peril, Jew' (338–9). He has to be made to see—to be humiliated into seeing—that he is in the sphere of risk also. Still insouciantly in command, 'Tarry, Jew. | The law hath yet another hold on you', Portia, the siren of mercy, says that, because he has plotted, as an alien, to kill a Venetian, his wealth, in Graziano's phrase, is 'forfeit' and his life lies at the mercy of the Duke (341, 360). Even when his life is spared, he is forfeit, not Antonio, because, as he protests, now like an anti-usuring pamphlet, a forfeit can deny you life by taking that by which you live (369–72).

Shylock is coerced into Christianity, following the path set by his daughter (something to come back to in Chapter 7). As for money, the Duke begins by saying that half his wealth will go to Venice and half to Antonio. The latter, prompted to mercy by Portia, asks the court to let Shylock keep half his money (not even reduced to a fine) so long as it is left to Lorenzo and Jessica while he keeps the other half 'in use' for them (378). Use, not usury. Shylock must be converted to the official ethos of charity. In the idiom of the lead casket, he must give after hazarding all he hath (as he does in the trial scene). Antonio says that he should 'record a gift | Here in the court of all he dies possessed | Unto his son, Lorenzo, and his daughter'. This Portia insists on: 'Clerk, draw a deed of gift.' It is charity as extortion, a completion of the theft of his goods by Lorenzo and Jessica. Shylock's 'merry bond' was a revenge disguised as a gift (a loan free of usance). Much the same could be said of the 'deed of gift' that ends the trial. Both are disadvantageous engagements. Shylock says, 'Send the deed after me, | And I will sign it' (383–93). '*Deedes, (Facta)*', explains John Cowell, 'signifie in our common law wrightings that containe the effect of a contract made betweene man and man, which the ciuilians call *(literarum obligationem)*.'[72] Dr Faustus writes a 'deed of gift' in his own blood, promising to give himself to the devil in twenty-four years so long as a set of 'conditions' are met.[73] A bond is payable if conditions are *not* met whereas a deed of gift is payable if conditions *are* met. Shylock's death is a condition that will be met. The deed and conversion are Shakespeare's related additions to source. They are followed persistently, as at the end, where Nerissa tells Lorenzo: 'I *give* to you and Jessica | From the rich Jew a special deed of *gift*' (290–1). The usurer takes, the charitable man gives; that is the orthodoxy travestied by the outcome of the trial. As Wilson says about time-selling: 'wil these idle men sell the sunne, the ayer, and the tyme for theire proper gayne? howe can hee bee of god that so dothe. God geeueth, and the vsurer withholdeth.'[74]

★ ★ ★

Looked at from a distance, the outcome of *The Merchant of Venice* resembles that of *Errors*. Antipholus and Dromio of Ephesus are 'bound and laid in some dark room' (4.4.89), with the encouragement of Adriana the wife and Dr Pinch the exorcist. The officer will not release Antipholus because, surety-like, 'If I let him go, | The debt he owes will be required of me' (112–13). Meanwhile, Egeon's life is in danger. He needs the thousand marks to avoid distraint of all his goods and execution, and although the Duke has given him a day—the period of the comedy—in which to beg or borrow there is no one willing to pay. The whole play is framed, as Plautus' *Menaechmi* (its main source) is not, by the need to 'quit the penalty' (1.1.22). As the sun sinks towards the late hour when debts traditionally fell due,[75] there is merry mayhem around binding and unbinding, not just because of the literal binding of Antipholus and Dromio of Ephesus but because both Dromios are slaves. The father, thus, asks the unrecognized twin of Antipholus of Syracuse:

is not that your bondman Dromio?
DROMIO OF EPHESUS Within this hour I was his bondman, sir,
But he, I thank him, gnawed in two my cords.
Now am I Dromio, and his man, unbound. (5.1.288–91)

The passage of time has so fretted body and voice that Egeon is unrecognizable to master or to man. As Dromio's wordplay anticipates, however, the comedy ends with a reaffirmation of social, familial, and civic bonds through unbinding. Egeon is released from his penalty by an overruling of the law amid the recognitions and resolutions of the plot. Out of a most un-Plautan priory comes Egeon's long-lost wife, the Abbess, to effect the final loosing:

DROMIO OF SYRACUSE O, my old master, who hath bound him here?
ABBESS Whoever bound him, I will loose his bonds,
And gain a husband by his liberty.
Speak, old Egeon, if thou beest the man
That hadst a wife once called Emilia... (339–43)

As in *The Merchant of Venice*, a merchant is freed by female intervention, with overtones of Christian redemption.

It is a major difference between the plays, however, that the freeing of Antonio comes at the end of Act 4. There is a long section to follow in which the oaths sworn by Shylock give way to those sworn by Bassanio and Graziano. All this binding language has to be undone, before it can be adequately renewed; bonds are not simply loosed in the trial scene. Marriage, as in *Errors*, still has its claims to make, but they are developed more complexly, and—as we shall see—in even more intricate counterpoint to the Shylock plot than has been noticed. The Jew's bond is replaced by another form of charitable coercion. The working out of this is pursued in Chapter 7.

7

Shylock and Wedlock

Carnal Bonds

One of the most spectacular sequences in early modern drama comes in the final scene of Ford's *'Tis Pity She's a Whore*, when the young, intense Giovanni, 'proud in the spoil | Of love and vengeance', bursts into a family banquet with his sister Annabella's '*heart upon his dagger*'.[1] It is a ghastly, visible consummation of an incestuous relationship that began with mutual, kneeling vows (1.2.252–67) and advanced to a hidden affair. Giovanni has to 'vow' and 'swear' repeatedly to the onstage audience before his scandalous confession is believed (31, 56), but these formal asseverations are merely the aftershocks of an action structured and pivoted by binding language. The mock betrothal of brother and sister is echoed in oaths and vows when Annabella is forced by her family and pregnancy to marry the noble Soranzo (3.6.50–5, 4.1.1). This 'contract', far from ending her relationship with Giovanni, enables further pleasure (5.3.6), but at the price of stoking jealousy. The impaling of Annabella's heart is an act of possessiveness and revenge, unjustly punishing her for being 'treacherous | To your past vows and oaths' (5.5.4–5), but it is also cannibalistic. Giovanni describes the heart as 'food' (5.6.24), and he brings it into a feast. In a play as thickly patterned as any work of Shakespeare with oaths, vows, and betrayals[2] it seals the bond by incision.

It seems outrageous to compare this outrage with Shylock's stepping forward, knife in his hand, in the trial scene of *The Merchant of Venice*, to 'have the heart of' Antonio (3.1.105–6). Yet the paradigm of irregular marriage is as relevant to their relationship as others that have been invoked: the Jew of medieval legend who circumcises then sacrifices his victim; the Jew who plans to cut himself a pound of Christian flesh to eat as a (kosher)[3] treat; Antonio like the crucified Jesus with the knife/lance at his breast. No doubt those grisly motifs are compatible with the scene. But Margaret Atwood is right to say, in *Payback*: 'Shakespeare is a very dodgy writer: ambiguity is his middle name. Did he realize that Shylock and Antonio are each other's Shadow figures? They are the only two characters who are left alone and uncoupled at the end of the play: everyone else marries someone. Are Antonio and Shylock married in a sense to each other?'[4] The usurer and the 'tainted wether' (4.1.113) make an odd couple but not an unprecedented one. The barren breeder of metal and the homosexual male had long been thought of together.[5] More immediately, Antonio and Shylock are joined by the carnality of their legal bond.

Violent courtship and enforced marriage are not hard to find in Tudor and Stuart drama. There is *The Yorkshire Tragedy* (where it ends in husband-killing), *The Miseries of Inforst Mariage* (all in the title), the predicament of Penthea, in Ford's other great play, *The Broken Heart*, who starves herself after marriage to Bassanes when she considers herself wedded to Orgilus. Shakespeare gives us Petruccio's bullying of Kate in *The Taming of the Shrew*, and Juliet, already married to Romeo but told that she must have Paris. Mammon usually plays a part. In *The Merry Wives of Windsor*, Fenton pursues Anne Page for her money, only then (he says) falling for her qualities. The vows of lovers were geared to dowries and inheritances, their carnal bonds meshed with financial contracts. Even when joined by affection, their promises were thought to resemble 'a promise of a future Sale or Payment', their 'Contract of Matrimony' a 'Bond or Assurance'.[6]

The orthodox line on enforced marriage is given by the Earl of Suffolk in *1 Henry VI*, when he argues (for self-interested reasons) that the king should be free to marry Margaret since he wants her: 'For what is wedlock forcèd but a hell, | An age of discord and continual strife . . . ?' (5.7.59–63). The word 'wedlock' carries a charge because it is rarely used (ten times) in Shakespeare, but also because its semantics reach beyond matrimony into ancient ideas about contract. A 'wed' was a pledge. 'Wedlock' in *The Merchant* is linked the more firmly to its rhyme-word 'Shylock' because the Jew and Antonio are pledged or wedded by their bond. The bond, in turn, parallels the rings given by Portia and Nerissa to their lovers, which come, through exchange, visual emblem, and wordplay, to stand for the carnality of sex. To make sense of the core relationship between Shylock and Antonio we must think about all the lovers but especially Jessica and Lorenzo. We must also cut a path into early modern ideas about Jewish oaths, a topic that has been neglected in accounts of *The Merchant of Venice*.

★ ★ ★

Let us return to the big speech about Laban and Jacob, discussed in Chapter 6. No sooner has Shylock begun than he glances aside:

> When Jacob grazed his uncle Laban's sheep—
> This Jacob from our holy Abram was,
> As his wise mother wrought in his behalf,
> The third possessor; ay, he was the third— (1.3.67–70)

Antonio reasonably asks what this has to do with charging interest. Shylock quickly continues, but the genealogical point has been made. Jacob's mother had Jacob blessed by his father Isaac in place of the first-born Esau by putting goat skins on his arm and neck.[7] There was trickery in Jacob's line, but also descent from the patriarch. Shylock goes on:

> Mark what Jacob did:
> When Laban and himself were compromised
> That all the eanlings which were streaked and pied
> Should fall as Jacob's hire, the ewes, being rank,
> In end of autumn turnèd to the rams, ... (73–7)

We have seen that, like the author of the Sonnets, Shylock is defying a commonplace when he represents usury as being as natural as breeding (pp. 158–60). Equally striking is the hint of miscegenation in the 'compromise' that generates the lambs, so many of them streaked and spotted. What else could be expected from a bond between Jew and idolator, Shylock and Antonio (the Catholic). Jessica and Lorenzo are not the only ones to engage in inter-ethnic pairing.

Nor is the 'compromise' of Jacob and Laban the only covenant at stake. As we saw when discussing Jacob's vow about the tithe, he is the beneficiary of God's promise. This bond, or covenant, was first made with Abraham at the near-sacrifice of Isaac. For Jews the promise descended in the line that went through Jacob, and remained with the chosen people (pp. 157–8). As Marlowe's Barabas contemptuously tells the Christian Lodowick, 'unto us the promise doth belong'.[8] The descent of the promise to the Church was a major point of doctrine for English Protestants, and it was lodged in the Book of Common Prayer (p. 13); but the topic remained contentious. John Foxe is representative of the reformers when he resists both the Roman Catholic claim to have God's promise because the ecclesiastical hierarchy inherits the keys by apostolic succession from Peter (Matthew 16: 19) and the Jewish assertion that they alone derive the promise from 'our holy Avram'. This is set out in a sermon that Foxe preached to celebrate the conversion of a Jew, Nathaniel:[9] some argue (he says) that the covenant was broken and God's promise lost because of the sinfulness of the Jews; however you look at history, the Christians have inherited the promise. God chose the Jews, Nathaniel declares in a confession of faith reprinted by Foxe, 'because he would keepe the othe which he had sworne vnto our fathers *Abraham, Isaac*, and *Iacob*' (B1r). Citing Jacob's vow in Genesis, Nathaniel says that 'the Scepter and gouernement was continued in the house of *Iudah*, as our fathers accord, vntill the comming of this man Iesus', who is 'our promised King and *Messhiach*' (B2v–3r, B7r).

So the Christian view of Jacob and Laban is that from Jacob descend all the Christians who eschew the paganism of Laban. Jews like Shylock are superseded in that genealogy or miscreant from it. They remain locked in the Old Testament. This fuelled the belief that the Jews are given to bloody penalties, an eye for an eye, a tooth for a tooth. The law of the talion in Exodus, Leviticus, and Deuteronomy sets a limit to retribution, but Christ's message of forgiveness made it look like tribal revenge.[10] Shylock exemplifies this severity; but he also comes, post-biblically, from a people that was believed to want to murder Christians. It was supposedly a Talmudic precept that Jews were to murder the best of the *goyim*.[11] This is reflected in the boasts of Barabas in *The Jew of Malta*, that he has killed sick people groaning under walls, poisoned wells, and so on. His usury goes along with this, because, as he goes on to brag, he drives people mad or makes them hang themselves by dragging them into debt with high rates of interest (2.3.191–9).

Marlowe's anti-Semitism is knowing and comic but he draws on myths about Jewish blood-lust which the general absence of Jews from England between the expulsion of 1290 and readmission under Cromwell[12] did little to moderate. In Thomas Calvert's preface to his translation of *The Blessed Jew* (1648), we are told that 'some of their Rabbies' read 'such Lectures as these, *A Jew may murder or slay a Baptized Jew without sin*. So much are they bent to shed the blood of Christians, that they say a Jew needs no repentance for murdering a Christian; and they add to that sinne to make it sweet and delectable that hee who doth it, it is as if he had offered a *Corban* to the Lord.'[13] A *corban* is a vowed gift or devoted offering to God (given a bad name by Jesus at Mark 7: 11). Isaac was a sort of *corban*, designed to seal the covenant, distantly resembling, in a Hebraic sphere, the classical oath-sacrifices discussed in Chapter 2. A confused idea of the *corban* was one root of the blood libel that Jews kidnapped and ritually killed Christians.

During Shakespeare's lifetime, there were hair-raisingly horrible updates. In Nashe's *Vnfortunate Traveller* (1594), for instance, Jack falls into a Jew's cellar, is locked up in a dark cupboard, kept and fed, and sold on for use in anatomy lessons.[14] Later, Zadoch swears and plans to blow up the city of Rome (315). His 'oath' is not incidental. What has been overlooked in the many studies of anti-Semitism is the association between the blood libel and what can be called 'the oath libel', the notion that Jews take oaths to effect the destruction of non-Jews. An early, influential example of the blood libel shows exactly this feature. It is an episode in Apion's first-century AD *Aegyptiaca* which early modern readers would have known from a refutation in the works of Josephus. That Shakespeare knew Josephus' *The Jewish War* is likely. Beyond the Bible, it was the obvious source to consult about Jewish history, and it was published in English every few years from 1558 right through the seventeenth century. As others have noted, according to Josephus, one of the Jewish leaders in Babylon who fought against the Roman general Antonius was called Shiloch (Antonio v. Shylock).[15]

In *Against Apion*, Josephus reports Apion's account of a Greek man who was trapped in a synagogue and fattened up with dainty foods. When he asked why he was being kept in this way, a Jew told him that it was their custom, in accordance with a secret law, to take a Grecian stranger, upon an appointed day, 'and feede him a yeere, and then to carrie him to a wood; and there to kill him, and sacrifice him according to their rites and ceremonies, and to taste and eate of his entrailes, and in the sacrificing of the Grecian, to sweare to bee enemies vnto the Greekes'.[16] The similarity of this to the plight of Nashe's Jack needs no remarking. Josephus pours scorn on the anecdote. Why should Jews conspire against the Greeks, he asks (why not the Egyptians, who had enslaved them)? How could thousands of Jews all eat of the entrails of one man? (787–8). The claim about the oath is nonsense, he says, more than once: 'He also belieth vs concerning the oath which he saith we Iewes doe take, swearing by the God of heauen and earth, and sea, neuer to fauour any stranger, and especially the Greekes.' There have been Greek converts to Judaism, some persisting, others not, 'yet none of them will say that he heard this oath spoken amongst vs, but it should seeme that onely *Apion* heard of it, in that he himselfe indeed forged it' (798). The refutation is convincing, yet it paradoxically gave circulation to the libel. During his campaign to have the Jews readmitted to England, half a century after *The Vnfortunate Traveller*, Menasseh ben Israel repeated the story—'in the offering up of this Greek they enter into a solemn oath'[17]—and repeated Josephus' rebuttal.

Christianity sustained the blood libel because of the structural position of Christ as a sacrifice (to God, to atone for sin). The Jews became the agents of this sacrifice by insisting on his death rather than that of Barabas. Through the figure of Judas, who betrayed Christ for thirty pieces of silver, the Jews were open to the greater charge of buying and selling the Messiah. The sufferings of the Jews—not least at the hands of Christians—proved how bad they were (how deserving of persecution) because the vengeance of God had fallen upon them, for a bond sealed for blood. 'As in times past they bought the blood of Christ,' declares the Preface to *The Blessed Jew*, 'so are they now fain to buy their own tears.' Buying Jesus from Judas, they put a price on the life of a man, as Shylock puts a price on Antonio's by making 3,000 ducats 'equal' to a murderous pound of flesh:

> See how miserably they are used at *Alexandria,* and in other places,... and we may conclude with a question to the Jew; *O wretches, is not this some payment of that Bond which you sealed, when you said, His Blood be upon us, &c? you desired a murderer, do's not the Lord give you murderers enough?* It will be long ere your blood will ever bee shed sufficiently for the Blood of Christ. (28–9)

In *The Merchant of Venice* a Jew seals a bloody bond to take a pound of Christian flesh, inviting retribution. The bond, you could say, is a *berit*, the Hebrew word for the covenant between God and Abraham, and that between Jacob and Laban, which troublingly for English Bible translators binds by virtue of *cutting* ('the biblical treaty is "cut" '),[18] most radically into the flesh, as in circumcision or animal/human sacrifice.[19] 'Cut' and 'cutting' are used of the bond eight or nine times in *The Merchant*.[20] So the play grafts debt deeply into the legacies of anti-Semitism; yet its bloody rationale has wider, ancient resonances. Thus the forfeit makes legal sense given the history of using the body as a pledge. Nietzsche writes vividly about this, in relation to ancient Egypt, Roman law, and the innate cruelty of punishment ('the creditor could inflict all kinds of dishonour and torture on the body of the debtor,... cutting as much flesh off as seemed appropriate for the debt').[21] A. W. B. Simpson more soberly remarks, in his *History of the Common Law of Contract*: 'The penal bond for securing performance was a sophisticated form of self-pledge, and Shylock's bond with its forfeit of a pound of flesh neatly illustrates the fact that the best pledge of all is the body of the contractor, which in early law he could have used as security.'[22] It needs to be understood how directly Shylock's bond is a commitment to cutting off flesh. In the late sixteenth century, when 'penal bonds' were widely employed and unpopular, such a document undertook to pay the creditor a specified forfeit; that was the agreement;[23] the condition designed to prevent this, e.g. payment of 3,000 ducats, would be written underneath the promise or even (out of sight) on the back of the bond.[24] The promise *on* the bond gives Shylock virtual payback for all the bad things Antonio has done—spitting on his Jewish gabardine, calling him dog, and so on.

We began to see in Chapter 6 how Shylock resembles a revenge protagonist. That the interest-free 'merry bond' can look, from one point of view, like the kindness he says it is, yet also licenses violence, gives it the element of disguised intention that is a common feature of revenge plots. It has a kind of poetic justice, in that Antonio brings the penalty down on his own head, knowing, as he does, that Shylock is malicious and admires Jacob's outwitting of Laban. Perhaps most radically, there is convergence between the revenge trajectory of the bond and the payoff of oaths and self-cursing. For Antonio to break his due date is to break his promise to pay and be punished for it by a sworn agreement to be cut into by the Jew. The oath libel is modulated into the neatest, most troubling form, by being a mutual 'compromise'. Shylock *has* this bond; it is not taken from him by Jessica when she steals the casket of jewels and coin (perhaps he sleeps with it under his pillow and keeps it in his gabardine). As the member of an oppressed minority, dependent on the good will of the Christians, he now has purchase on them, some control of his narrative. He can wave the bond about on stage, or pull it slyly from his pocket. To some extent the audience will take Shylock's wish for his deed, indulging in the fantasy of his violence. The stereotype of the murdering Jew is almost stronger than Shylock's being thwarted. Hence the Quarto title page: 'With the extreame crueltie of *Shylocke* the Iewe towards the sayd Merchant, in cutting a iust pound of his flesh'.

* * *

How far Shakespeare could enter the world of a Venetian Jew is, of course, questionable. He will not have known the *Shevu'ot*, that intricate discussion of how oaths should be kept (if I take an oath not to eat, then eat earth, more or less than the size of an olive, do I deserve the punishment for oath-breaking?).[25] Nor will he have known the *Nedarim*, the rabbinical treatise about vows. How aware was he that Jacob 'cuts a deal' in Scripture? Even if he learned some Hebrew at grammar school in Stratford, as the boys did at Merchant Taylors' School in London,[26] he will not have acquired the fluency that allowed Christian Hebraists at universities in England and on the Continent to enrich their students' and readers' understanding of scripture. There is, however, so much evidence from the play that Shakespeare wanted to give Shylock oaths and vows that would sound Jewish that it is worth pausing to investigate what an audience would know about Hebraic binding language.

Elements of rabbinical thought passed into general circulation through the work of influential reformers. The Italian humanist and Oxford professor of Divinity Peter Martyr Vermigli, for example, repeatedly draws in his *Common Places* on the Torah, Talmud, and Aramaic Targum when discussing oaths and vows.[27] His opening definition is typical: 'The Hebrues call an oth by the name of *Nischba,* being a noune deriued of *Schaba,* that is, seuen; by which number is expressed the power of the holie Ghost, séeing whosoeuer sweareth, let him vnderstand that he is bound and tied by that oth.'[28] Disagreeing with Calvin's account of Hebrew terms in the third commandment,[29] Vermigli declared: 'An other thing that is to be blamed in an oth, is, if a man doo not sweare, but forsweare. Which sinne is so gréeuous, as of that onelie, among the ten commandements, you find written, *Lo Iinke,* He will not forgiue him, He will not hold him guiltlesse. For God is highlie offended, when we abuse his name to confirme our lies.'[30] To emphasize the gravity of perjury, he adds: 'this the Hebrues, in a certeine Apollogie of theirs doo declare; who write, that when the tables were giuen vpon mount *Sina,* so soone as the lawe was made concerning periurie, the whole world was shaken.'

Vermigli was interested in the Nazirite (or Nazarite) vow. The Reformers had to be, because this vow to leave hair uncut, and to avoid wine and contact with the dead,[31] was regarded by Catholics as a precedent for the cloistered vows of monks. Significant figures in scripture, including Samson and John the Baptist, were known to have been Nazirites. What was the drink *sicera* from which the devoted were bound to abstain? 'The *Chaldaean* interpretation', in the Talmud, Vermigli noted, 'calleth *Sicera,* Old wine' (Pt III, 179). It is unlikely that when Shylock dismisses Bassanio's invitation to dinner by saying, 'Yes, to smell pork, to eat of the habitation which your prophet the Nazarite conjured the devil into!' (1.3.28–9), he is characterizing Jesus as anything more than a man from Nazareth. It is not impossible, however, given that Jesus was sometimes believed to have taken a version of such a Nazirite vow when he told the apostles, at the last supper, 'Verely I saye vnto you, I wil drinke no more of the frute of the vine, vntil that day, that I drinke it new in the kingdome of God' (Mark 14: 25).

More controversial even, and bearing closely on Shylock, because of the death he wishes upon Jessica when he hears of her prodigality after eloping with Lorenzo (3.1.74–6), was Jephthah's vow to make a burnt offering of the first thing he saw coming out of his house on his return from victory against the Ammonites. Did Jephthah really, as Judges 10–12 appears to say, sacrifice his daughter to keep this vow? If so, was he as virtuous as Abraham when he showed himself willing to sacrifice Isaac? Hamlet, rather famously, believes that Jephthah did the deed. Accusing Polonius of putting Ophelia in harm's way by introducing her into the game of cat and mouse being played out between himself and Claudius, he says, 'Oh Jephthah, judge of Israel, what a treasure hadst thou!' (2.2.385–6), and so on for a dozen lines. Others, as Vermigli notes, argue that Jephthah was not a killer,

> but onelie punished hir with ciuill death; namelie, in separating hir from the common conuersation, so that she liued onelie vnto God, by giuing hir selfe to praiers onelie, and by liuing apart from the companie of men. And they séeme to affirme that that was the vow *Cherem:*... euen as a féeld or house dedicated by the vow *Cherem,* could not be reuoked to the first owner: so (saie they) this maiden being once dedicated vnto the Lord, could not returne vnto hir old state.[32]

The *cherem* is an act of banning, separating from society, even anathematizing. It is sometimes compared to excommunication, but it imports a distinctively Hebraic understanding of Jephthah's vow.

Vermigli cites two rabbis, David Kimhi (1160–1235) and Levi Ben-Gershon (1288–1344), who agree that Jephthah did not kill his daughter, largely on the basis of the ambiguity of the Hebrew letter *vau*, which, 'being a coniunction copulatiue,... dooth make a proposition alternatiue'.[33] Vermigli, however, rejects their arguments. Like Hamlet, he believes that Jephthah killed his daughter, and without the excuse of Abraham—obedience to God—since he was responsible for his own rash vow. In support he cites yet more rabbis, including 'the *Chaldaean* paraphrast', i.e. the Aramaic Targum, 'which among the Hebrues is almost of the same estimation and authoritie that the holie scriptures be' (183). In this he was far from unique. William Perkins, for instance, brings 'the Hebrewe Doctors' in aid of his translation of cruxes in the Jephthah story.[34] John Donne took pride in the freedom of Protestant scholars to learn from the rabbis, noting that Azorius confessed himself '*bound* (that is, by the oath of the Trent Councell) *to expound Scriptures according to the sense of the Fathers*' so reluctantly found Jephthah guilty.[35] In practice, Catholics like Robert Parsons cited the rabbis extensively, to consolidate Romanist orthodoxy.[36] Jeremy Taylor invoked 'The Doctors of the Jews' to construct a distinctively Anglican interpretation of Jephthah, arguing that Church and State should work together: 'because *Jephthah* was a Prince in *Israel,* he would not goe to *Phinehas* the high Priest to have had his vow interpreted, commuted, or released. Neither would *Phinehas* goe to him, because he was not to offer his help till it was implor'd.... In the mean time the Virgin died, or, as some say, was kill'd by her Father.'[37]

How familiar would the original audience of *The Merchant of Venice* have been with these rabbinical names and arguments? It is worth remembering *The Alchemist* (1610), where the prostitute Doll Common, in a pretend fit of pious raving, draws on the Hebrew-saturated works of Hugh Broughton and speaks of the '*Talmud skill*' and of '*rabbi David Kimchi, Onkelos, | And Aben-Ezra*'.[38] The joke would be lost if her list of rabbis meant nothing to an audience. There is nothing as precise as this in Shakespeare, whatever Hamlet says about Jephthah, nor as scholarly as Jonson telling Drummond about the emendation of a Jewish oath in Martial's *Epigrams*, XI.xciv.[39] Doll's speech is an indication, however, that audiences in the public theatre had some sense of Jewish tradition.

* * *

Yet the streams of information about Jewish oaths and vows that Shakespeare might have come across from scriptural and rabbinical sources were polluted by anti-Semitic legend. For one thing, the binding utterances were thought to be typically malicious. Here is *Purchas his Pilgrimage* (1613), a useful compendium of beliefs in early modern England about Jewish religion and custom:

> Doctor *Rainolds* sayth, That the Iewes, as they were prone to vngodly vowes, so this was an vsuall vow amongst them, and they would bind it with an oath, That such or such a man should haue no profit by them.... The Iewes vsed to bind their vowes with a Curse, as they which vowed *Paules* death, vsing yet to suppresse the Curse it selfe,... Thus the Talmud (sayth he) the booke of their Canon Law, and Schoole-Diuinitie, sayth, That a man is bound to honour his father, vnlesse he vow the contrarie.[40]

For this obdurate people, an oath or vow was more binding than the Decalogue. A formalistic interpretation of Numbers 30: 3 ('Whosoeuer voweth a vow vnto the Lord, or sweareth an othe to binde him selfe by a bonde...'), supposedly in the Talmud, overrode 'Thou shalt not kil' and 'Honour thy father and thy mother' (Exodus 20: 12–13). A marginal reference points us to Acts

23: 'certeine of the Iewes made an assemblie, and bounde them selues with an othe, saying, that thei wolde nether eat nor drinke, til they had killed Paul' (v. 12, cf. 14). The Geneva Bible in turn glosses this 'othe' in the margin: 'The worde signifieth cursing, as when a man either sweareth, voweth or wisheth him self to die, or to be giuen to the deuil, except he bring his purpose to passe.' The oath to kill Paul does not just throw fuel on the fire of the oath libel, it reinforces the evidence of the Old Testament, that the characteristic Hebrew oath is grounded in a curse which can be used to stand for the whole.[41] Hence the form of the oath in Shylock's first, embittered speech about Antonio—'How like a fawning publican he looks'—which combines a binding, conditional self-curse with the stubborn animus against Christians, and reluctance to forgive, associated with his people: 'Cursèd be my tribe | If I forgive him' (1.3.36–47).

While the oath or vow of a Jew was believed to be rigid, it was also open to the slur of being slippery and deceptive. The trickiness of Jacob in his 'compromise' with Laban[42] is but one symptom of this. Peter Martyr Vermigli would no doubt say to Shylock, 'If there be an oth made, guile must not be vsed.'[43] The unreliability of a Jewish word was held to be the outgrowth of a more radical dishonesty. Running together charges that were already half-fused, Luther says in *The Jews and their Lies* (1543) that 'their Talmud and their rabbis record that it is no sin for a Jew to kill a Gentile, . . . Nor is it a sin for a Jew to break his oath to a Gentile. Likewise, they say that it is rendering God a service to steal or rob from a Goy, as they in fact do through their usury.'[44] As *The Blessed Jew* puts it: 'In their Talmud they say, It is not murther if a Jew kill a Gentile; nor is it perjury if he falsifie his promise to him, confirmed by oath' (187).[45]

Jews pushed back against these libels. Leone da Modena, for instance, whose autobiography I mentioned in Chapter 6, writing about the rites and customs of the Jews, in Venice, around 1616, in a treatise prepared for the English ambassador and friend of poets Henry Wotton, denied that they used oaths to deceive Christians (or, worse, took an oath to deceive Christians):

> And those men, that have given out . . . that they swear every day, (and account it a godly work,) to endeavour to defraud, and cheat the Christians, is a most Grosse Untruth, and scattered abroad by these men, onely to render them more Odious among the Nations, then they are. Whereas, in truth, many of the *Rabbines* have commanded them the clean contrary, in their Writings: [saying] that it is a far greater sin, to defraud one that is not a Jew, then to defraud a Jew; . . .[46]

Modena does admit that there are Jews who have lapsed from truthfulness because of the hardships they have endured, but their deceptions are contrary to teaching. Menasseh ben Israel takes the same line. Jews are not allowed to lie to Gentiles, he says, though some are tricksters because they have had to live that way. 'The *Iewes* are bound not to defraud, nor abuse in their accounts, negotiation, or reckonings, any man whatsoever.'[47] Looking at the sort of 'compromise' that obtains between Jacob and Laban, he underlines the rabbinical position:

> After the same manner they command, that the oath which they shall make to any other nation, must be with truth, and justice, and must be kept in every particular. And for proof thereof, they quote the history of *Zedekias,* whom God punished, and deprived of his kingdome, because he kept not his word, and *oath,* made to *Nebuchadnezzar, in the name of God,* though he were a *Gentile,* as it is said, 2 of *Chronicles,* cap. 36.13. *And he also rebelled against Nebuchadnezzar, who made him swear by God.*
>
> These are the laws and obligations which the *Iewes* hold. So that the Law that forbids the *Iewes* to *kill* any *Gentiles,* forbids them also to *steal* from them. Yet every one must look to it, for the world is full of fraud in all Nations.[48]

Ideas about Jewish duplicity were fed by *Kol Nidrei* (or *Kol Nidre*), the declaration that begins the Jewish Day of Atonement. Here is a scholarly translation from a ninth-century prayerbook; it represents the utterance as it prevailed across much of the Jewish world through the medieval and early modern periods:

> All *nedarim, isarim, shevuot, kiyumim* and *charamim,* [vows, prohibitive vows, oaths, contracts, and vows of dedication], which we have vowed, imposed, declared, sworn, and obligated upon ourselves under oath from the previous Day of Atonement until this Day of Atonement which has come to us, we retract all of them and we come before our Father in heaven [to say]. If we uttered a *neder,* this no *neder.* If we bound ourselves by an *isar,* now there is no *isar.* If we declared a *cherem,* now there is no *cherem.* If took a *shevuah,* now there is no *shevuah.* If we made a *kiyum,* now there is no *kiyum.* Now there is no *neder,* no *isar,* no *shevuah,* and no *kiyum.* Now there is pardon, forgiveness, and atonement as it is written in Your Torah, 'The whole Israelite community and the stranger residing among them shall be forgiven, for the entire people acted in error' (Numbers 15: 26).[49]

Yom Kippur is about wiping the slate clean, so it is easy to understand the role that it gives to *Kol Nidrei.* The cantor tells believers that they can be released from such rash and pernicious oaths, vows, and curses as wishing your daughter dead at your feet or contracting for a pound of flesh (engagements made with the stranger). The ability to erase undertakings was, however, open to misconstruction.

Kol Nidrei underwent changes.[50] In the twelfth century, when Christian disapproval of it may have contributed to the expulsion of the Jews from England,[51] the period covered by the chant was changed, from oaths past to those to come, since it was held to be irrational to revoke a given word. *Kol Nidrei* now declared, 'From this Day of Atonement until the next Day of Atonement may it come upon us for good.'[52] This change was not widely accepted by the Ashkenazim until the seventeenth century, and never by the Sephardic Jews of Spain and Portugal.[53] While it removed what could be seen as the immorality of revoking a commitment, it gave Jews a free hand—so anti-Semites argued, and do argue to the present day—to lie. In the nineteenth century, Reform Judaism took *Kol Nidrei* out of Yom Kippur (or inverted it, 'calling not for the annulment of vows, but for divine assistance in fulfilling them');[54] but the haunting power of the traditional melody and the consistency of the utterance with the desire for atonement led to a revival.

Kol Nidrei was widely discussed in Europe during Shakespeare's lifetime.[55] Here is *Purchas his Pilgrimage*:

> Before they beginne praiers, thirteene of the principall Rabbies, walking in the Temple, giue licence to all, both good and bad, to pray. And the *Praecentor* or Reader fetcheth the Booke out of the Arke, and openeth it, singing a long prayer, beginning all compacts, vowes, and oathes, &c. insinuating, that all the vowes, promises, oathes, and couenants which euerie Iew had that yeare broken, be disanulled and pardoned: and that, because now all haue power to pray and praise GOD. (176)

This is the old, retrospective version of *Kol Nidrei*, varied by 'which euerie Iew had that yeare broken'. This might reflect rabbinical objections to the validity of revoking vows, promises, oaths, and covenants, and a turn towards Divine forgiveness. Even if that is so, there is an insinuation of dishonesty. The passage evidently draws on a widely read book by the Christian Hebraist Johann Buxtorf the Elder, *Juden-Schul* (1603), which circulated in Latin as *Synagoga Judaica* (1603).[56] After his account Buxtorf remarked, 'Whence every Christian may see how little they esteem of an oath, especially made unto one of us'—in the words of the 1657 English translation of the *Synagoga*, which could not desist from adding: 'A very papistical indulgence.'[57]

That Purchas does not include Buxtorf's comment scarcely reduces the effect of 'had that year broken'. Readers would assume what Buxtorf makes explicit, that *Kol Nidrei* encouraged Jewish swearers to be unreliable. Rather as Protestant accusations about Jesuitical equivocation had some basis in Catholic casuistry, so *Kol Nidrei* had problematic features. Rabbis reminded their congregations that the oaths and vows it covered were only those made between individuals and God. That the advice was given repeatedly indicates that many Jews must indeed have understood the text as allowing flexibility in 'both vows to God and vows made to others—including vows made before a court or to the government'.[58] It was partly on those grounds that *Kol Nidrei* had Jewish opponents. Leone da Modena, for example, disapproved,[59] and his account of Yom Kippur in *The History of the Rites*—a book that refutes many of Buxtorf's criticisms of Judaism[60]—does not mention it, as either discreditable or too hard to justify to Christian readers. Modena does note, however, that—beyond *Kol Nidrei*—Jews can be let off an oath or vow when this is not prejudicial to a third party:

> They have a Tradition also, that, if a Man, or a Woman, make a Vow, or take any Oath whatsoever; if it be not to the Prejudice of any Third Person, that it should be broken; and if it may, upon any tolerable pretence, or reason, be wisht unmade again; in this Case any one of the Principal *Rabbines,* or any other Three men, though they have not any Title of Dignity, may absolve, and discharge them from it. So that, He that would be absolved from any Vow, by him made, goeth either to a *Rabbine,* or to any Three other Men; and they, hearing his reasons why he repents himself of having made such, or such a Vow, if the thing seem but Reasonable, they say unto him thrice, *Be thou absolved from this Vow,* &c. and so he is discharged.[61]

So when Shylock says that he has sworn an 'oath in heaven' to have his bond (4.1.223), how bound is he? The question will be answered in a moment, but it is worth filling out first some of the prejudices attached to Jewish oaths by early modern Christians. For the widely held Jewish belief that *Kol Nidrei* had the power to annul interpersonal and official vows 'was not lost', as Stuart Weinberg Gershon writes, 'upon the Gentile European society in which the Jews lived. Considering the oath of a Jew to be untrustworthy, Christians compelled Jews throughout the Middle Ages to take a special Jewish oath (*More Judaico*) declaring that the oaths they swore in Christian courts would not be annulled by *kol nidrei* or by a Jewish court' (97). The oath had a long afterlife. In the municipal courts of Amsterdam, during Shakespeare's lifetime, a Jew was required to 'swear by the living God Almighty, who created heaven and earth, and by the Law he gave Moses, honestly and truthfully to answer the questions put to you', adding that 'if you answer falsely or incorrectly ... you should be plagued and punished now and forever with all the curses, plagues and such sufferings that God visited upon Israel'.[62]

Although the Amsterdam oath can be read as adapted to the realities of religious difference, the *More Judaico* was more often discriminatory, stressing the self-curse that characterizes Old Testament oaths and the Jewish oath to kill Paul, and tending to travesty. The notorious Frankfurt oath, initiated in 1392, for instance, required a Jew to swear standing on a sow's skin, with the Torah set before him.[63] Theodor Reik, one of the most perceptive modern commentators on *Kol Nidrei*, cites another example:

> The Jew had to put a girdle of thorns around his loins, stand in water, and spit three times on his circumcised penis, then he took the oath in the following form, 'By Barase, Baraa, Adonai, and Eloit, who led Israel dry-shod through the Red Sea, etc. By the law which Adonai decreed, by the spitting on the circumcised penis, and by the thorns with which I have girded my loins I swear not falsely the name Sabaot. If, however, I swear falsely then cursed be the descendants of my body; I will tap the wall like a blind man and fall like one who has no eyes. Besides this, may the earth open its mouth and devour me like Dathan and Abiram.'[64]

The oath becomes a mockery of Pharisaical formality and self-cursing. The Jew has to become more Jewish, be forced to insist on his difference, that is, on the very grounds for disbelieving him, at the moment when he is required to be believable.

As a psychoanalyst, Reik notes with purpose 'the particular sanctity and inviolability of oaths in all Jewish laws' (173). Religious Jews often refuse to swear at all, he observes, so seriously are oaths and vows taken. We know that early modern Yeshuvas forbade swearing by the Lord.[65] Leone da Modena is a Jew of his time when he says that swearing was one of the sins that brought the plague into the Venetian ghetto.[66] For Reik, the *Kol Nidrei* is not just a device for getting out of misguided oaths (something that Christianity also provides, as we see at many points in this book). It is a reaction generated by the high esteem in which oaths and vows are held, a revolt against caution and conscientiousness. With a gesture towards the theories about primal, tribal parricide in Freud's *Totem and Taboo* (1913) and *Moses and Monotheism* (1939), he concludes that *Kol Nidrei* 'has the character of a wish ... to break oaths, vows and promises, ... deep down, there stirs the unconscious wish to carry out anew the ancient deed of violence' (203).

Whatever explanations we accept for its tenacity, *Kol Nidrei* reinforced the belief, which spread far beyond those who knew anything about the Day of Atonement, that early modern Jews were both formalists and slippery experts in the bending of oaths and vows (one way of reading the scruples of *Shevu'ot* and *Nedarim*). It fed the accusation, from Luther through Schopenhauer to Hitler, that the Jews are liars.[67] We need not imagine Shylock, as Heine did, among the Jews of Venice, at the synagogue for Yom Kippur,[68] and we should not think of Shakespeare poring over the *Kol Nidrei*. Jewish and Christian reaction to it, however, and the spin-off charges of lying, filtered down the centuries into such readily available models as Barabas in *The Jew of Malta*, who tells Abigail his daughter to encourage the Christian Lodowick's suit, even though she does not want him:

> Use him as if he were a Philistine.
> Dissemble, swear, protest, vow to love him;
> He is not of the seed of Abraham. (2.2.229–31)

In the case of Barabas, and even more that of Shylock, the association between Jews and usury reinforced the reputation of the chosen people for intransigence and deception. There was, of course, a historical basis. Excluded from other professions, and enabled—most commentators agreed[69]—by Deuteronomy 23: 20 (see p. 152), Jews were allowed or encouraged by Christian princes and doges to lend at interest. There was a ready elision between the Jewish reputation for lying and the reputation of usurers, which goes back to classical antiquity. 'Usurers ly', says Plutarch: 'neither are there any that practise more falshood and deceit in their day debt bookes wherein they write.'[70] Elizabethan usurers are repeatedly characterized as cheating and mendacious.[71] Because the law discouraged the taking of interest, schemes such as the sale of commodities had to be found for allowing it (see pp. 153–4), which encouraged the impression of mendacity. '*Musculus* ioyneth *Vsurie*', wrote Mosse in 1595, 'with *Deceit* and *Periurie*.'[72]

Also mutually reinforcing was the association between the oath and blood libels and the reputation that usurers had for swearing people into debts that would kill them. When Bacon reports men saying 'That *Vsurers* should haue Orange-tawney Bonnets, because they do *Iudaize*', this was part of the slur on both money-lenders and Jews, that even the Christian agents of this 'Iewish kind of practise'[73] were binding men to a slow death. '*Cicero* doth compare Vsurie to manslaughter', wrote Philipp Caesar, 'And therefore as it is against nature to kill à man, so is it to take Vsurie.'[74] Like the bogey Jews of medieval legend, usurers were sadists who would rather kill than recover the money they had lent.[75] Word origin was invoked, to anti-Judaic effect. 'Let vs go to the very word of vsury in the hebrue tong', enjoins Thomas Wilson: 'It is calledde a bitinge, of this woorde Neshech, whiche is nothinge else but a kind of bityng, as a dog vseth to bite or gnawe vpon a bone.'[76]

⋆ ⋆ ⋆

It is time to look more closely at the oaths, vows, and curses that Shylock piles on top of his bond. Though Shakespeare did not, like John Selden, undertake scholarly research into Hebrew, he gives Shylock formulations which reflect what was widely believed—not always wrongly—about Jewish oaths. For one thing, Shylock does not swear by God. He might have said 'By Jehovah', but Shakespeare makes him swear 'By Jacob's staff' and 'by our holy Sabbath' (2.5.35, 4.1.35) to emphasize his tribal attachment while avoiding any risk of taking the Lord's name in vain. Second, he knows how to curse. We have seen that, when he first encounters Antonio, he swears an oath in which only the stump of a curse is left: 'Cursèd be my tribe | If I forgive him' (1.3.46–7)—meaning, 'I swear I will not forgive him and if I do may my tribe be cursed.' As Vermigli, among others, noted of the Israelites: 'There be also oths made of cursings:... in the holie scriptures of the old testament, they sware in a maner alwais by that particle *If:* and there wanteth the expressing of the cursse, which must be alwaies supplied of vs.'[77]

Yet this curse is also calculated to remind the audience of the Christian belief that the Jews were cursed for crucifying Christ. Shylock, one might think, is saying, the tribe is *not* cursed, and will only become so if he ever forgives Antonio. It is a measure of the pain of his journey that, when he hears of Jessica's extravagance in Genoa, spending what she stole from him, he says to Tubal: 'The curse never fell upon our nation till now—I never felt it till now' (3.1.72–3). The curse is brought upon him by Jessica going over to the Christians and adopting their prodigal ways. The effect is painfully divided, but it is hard for the audience to conclude, as anti-Semitic, early modern writers do, that the ill treatment of Jews by Christians simply fulfils God's anger against the former. It has agents and reckless causes.

As though prompted by his talk of the curse, Shylock pronounces his *cherem* against Jessica. It has been deplored even by those writers, often Jewish, from Heine to Reik, who understand how far it is fuelled by love and grief at his daughter's loss, not by fury at the money she wastes. 'I would my daughter were dead at my foot and the jewels in her ear!' he cries: 'Would she were hearsed at my foot and the ducats in her coffin!' (74–6).

As John Gross notes, this is 'A terrible curse—but it *is* a curse, and not an expression of greed. On the contrary, the jewels and ducats are to be buried along with the girl who took them. In his self-punishing, self-pitying fury, Shylock calls down destruction on everything that he has lost.'[78] How sharp a distinction should be made in any case between Jessica and the jewels and ducats? Shylock has provided for Jessica (and suffered indignities for it), as Portia's father provided for her. Now that purpose for accumulating wealth has gone. He has already lost his wife Leah to death, his servant Lancelot Gobbo to Bassanio. Losing Jessica leaves him with only his tribal attachment. Her social death kills him a little. In the treatise on vows, the *Nedarim*, we read: 'A man who is childless is accounted as dead, for it is written, Give me children, or else I am dead.'[79] It is a Hebraic view of the family that Shakespeare would have found in many parts of the Old Testament.

The actor playing Tubal can colour his few lines with any mixture of sympathy, relish, and rebuke when describing Jessica's runaway excesses. Has he gone in search of her out of loyalty to his community or to get back the money that Shylock has (if Shylock can be believed) borrowed from him? Jessica's elopement shames her father in front of a Jew of high status. The community still matters to him, perhaps the more so now Jessica has gone. To justify killing Antonio he engages in rationalization, saying that it will be good for business, either to bring Tubal round or to defend himself from the charge of being vindictive: 'I will have the heart of him if he forfeit, for were he out of Venice I can make what merchandise I will. Go, Tubal, and meet me at our synagogue. Go, good Tubal; at our synagogue, Tubal' (105–8).

The synagogue was where Jews were said to go to vent and swear their hatred of Christians. One of the best readers of *The Merchant* declares that 'While Bassanio is sailing, courting, and choosing for three months, Shylock is . . . taking a solemn oath in the synagogue to have his bond.'[80] The text does not actually say this, but an early audience might well assume it. This is not the first oath that he has taken among other Jews, for we soon hear Jessica, in Belmont, report that

> When I was with him I have heard him swear
> To Tubal and to Cush, his countrymen,
> That he would rather have Antonio's flesh
> Than twenty times the value of the sum
> That he did owe him; . . .   (3.2.283–7)

With the obstinacy attributed to a people who were regarded as having resisted conversion to the truth of the Gospel,[81] 'a blind, hard-hearted, stiff-necked people',[82] Shylock sticks to his bond by piling up such oaths.

When Antonio comes to him for grace, he insists: 'I'll have my bond. Speak not against my bond. | I have sworn an oath that I will have my bond' (3.3.4–5).

The Duke begins the trial scene by confronting this recalcitrance. Anticipating a refusal, he says that everyone expects Antonio to be released not just from the forfeiture but half the principal of 3,000 ducats: 'We all expect a gentle answer, Jew' (4.1.33). Edged with threat and insult ('an answer such that Gentiles would give'), this provokes not just sworn stubbornness but a reported Jewish oath that asserts cultural difference:

SHYLOCK I have possessed your grace of what I purpose,
And by our holy Sabbath have I sworn
To have the due and forfeit of my bond.
If you deny it, let the danger light
Upon your charter and your city's freedom. (34–8)

'Our' is pitched to exclude despite being an inclusive pronoun. Jews were known to venerate their Sabbath, one day before the Christian one. 'Due and forfeit' sounds legalistic in its obstinacy, but the city has its own sort of bond, its charter, to which the Duke is obliged to stick.

Shylock's next oath is his most resonant and metaphysically loaded. When offered three times his principal, he replies:

An oath, an oath! I have an oath in heaven.
Shall I lay perjury upon my soul?
No, not for Venice. (223–5)

What is 'in heaven' is beyond dispute, like God's Law at Deuteronomy 30: 12. To swear 'by heaven' is commonplace in Shakespeare; 'an oath in heaven' is more securely and strangely lodged. An oath sworn 'by heaven' stays on the earth, though it briefly invokes a Divine witness; one kept 'in heaven' cannot be erased. The wording implies a distinct, Hebraic view of where an oath should be, and how permanently. At the same time, and relatedly, Shylock avoids any possibility of taking the Lord's name in vain. As the expurgation of plays after the Act to Restrain Abuses often shows, to swear 'by heaven' is metonymically or by substitution to swear 'by God'.

Alert to this reticence, the poet Anthony Hecht once wrote:

> The solemnity with which he takes that oath is the more awful in that it respects one of the Ten Commandments. And it is the more devout in its conspicuous contrast to virtually all the other oaths in the play, which are made with ease and broken with impunity. Indeed, Shylock's fealty to his oath has a

> dark and lonely courage about it, a kind of inverted nobility that would be heroic if it were not perverse...[83]

As we shall see, Hecht is correct to compare, if not entirely to contrast, Shylock's oaths with others in the play. Whether the solemnity of his oath gives it weight is, though, another matter. Its almost incantatory stubbornness ('An oath, an oath... an oath') and the grandeur of its appeal to heaven do not so overwhelm the audience as to preclude another reaction. Up to and including this passage, we do not actually hear Shylock swear to have his bond. He merely reports his oath or oaths. That we have to take his word for his having given his word leaves open a margin for duplicity that is the less surprising because any oath on top of the sworn bond is a device for getting his forfeit. Whether or not he wants the pound of flesh, he is now obliged—he says—to take it.

Hecht is right that the wording of Shylock's oath scrupulously respects the third commandment, but it is aimed at breaking the sixth ('Thou shalt not kil') by insisting on the pound of flesh. That such an oath could not bind was a given in rabbinical—as in Christian—teaching. Perjury, as we have seen, is a serious matter in Judaism. The Hebrew doctors argued that Mount Sinai trembled at forswearing. They believed, however, in keeping all ten commandments (the *Aseret haDibrot*), not just the third. At this point Shylock exemplifies the Christian view that the Jews condemned by Jesus are more committed to their oaths than the spirit of the Law.[84] As Vermigli puts it: 'The doctrine of the Pharisies was so corrupt, as they iudged themselues to fulfill the lawe throughlie, if they performed the thing which they sware.'[85]

Shylock now insists on his pound of flesh, with an oath. Shakespeare has held back, for maximum effect, the moment when the audience actually hears him swear that he will have his bond.

> Proceed to judgment. By my soul I swear
> There is no power in the tongue of man
> To alter me. I stay here on my bond. (4.1.235–7)

As he ties the knot of the oath, the actor will be caught by contrary energies. On the one hand Shylock has the push and pace of a man who knows that his due is due. He more or less commands the court, as though taking a line from the Duke ('Proceed'). On the other, his fixed presence, unmoving and unmoved, is a rebuke to the wasteful flux of Venice, an insoluble, inconvenient block, unalterable in his Jewish obstinacy: 'I stay here on my bond.'

How seriously and how sacredly should we take Shylock's 'By my soul'? After quoting these lines, in an essay on translation, Derrida unpacks the perplexities of a speech which says that speech has no power to undo a speech act:

> Thus the oath is, *in* the human tongue, a promise that human language, however, cannot undo, control, obliterate, subject by loosening it. An oath is a bond *in* human language that the human tongue, as such, insofar as it is human, cannot loosen. *In* human language is a *bond* stronger than human language... The oath, the sworn faith, the act of swearing is transcendence itself, the experience of passing beyond man, the origin of the divine or, if one prefers, the divine origin of the oath.... No sin is more serious than perjury, and Shylock repeats, while swearing, that he cannot perjure himself; he therefore confirms the first oath by a second oath in the time of a repetition. This is called fidelity, which is the very essence and vocation of an oath. When I swear, I swear in a language that no human language has the power to make me abjure, to disrupt, that is to say, to make me perjure myself. The oath passes *through* language, but it passes beyond human language.[86]

This is what you might argue if you did not believe in the soul as prior to language and if you were willing to run the bond of 'By my soul' into the written 'bond' through the 'tongue of man'. Shylock and his audience would have understood these interrelations—on which the denouement will casuistically turn—but also the differences in moral quality. For the Jew to swear on his soul involves a step-up in commitment from swearing 'By Jacob's staff'. To have sworn an oath 'by our holy Sabbath', 'in heaven', and then to swear 'By my soul', is not just to redescribe or allude to a stream of oaths that it would be perjury to break,[87] it is to escalate the commitment. Shylock could tear the bond without perjury, merely releasing Antonio from his promise, but not this oath on his soul.

The perplexity that arises is not the one that Derrida identifies. Shylock's 'By my soul' is exactly the sort of oath that could be expunged by *Kol Nidrei* (a wicked oath, to murder) or by consulting rabbis. Many of the rabbis who warned against using *Kol Nidrei* as a way of getting out of interpersonal contracts picked out in the declaration 'which we have taken upon our souls'. As Reik explains: 'The significance of these words is clear. The *Kol Nidrei* formula does not concern oaths valid at law regarding other persons, but it concerns obligations, oaths, vows, etc., which one imposes upon oneself' (176). The more Shylock turns the bond into a matter between himself and God, the more loosely he is bound, and open to the appeal of mercy. Shakespeare has identified a paradox in a religion that takes oaths so seriously that it most needs a way out of binding language when the Highest Power is tied into the bond.

Actually Reik's comment concludes 'imposes upon oneself, therefore a contract with one's own ego'. A rabbi might say 'for "ego" read "Jehovah"', but a note of self-bound isolation is struck in 'no power... To alter me' and 'I stay here on my bond.' The grandeur of the oath is reduced by the shrinking into egotism and the slender piece of paper against which a man's life is balanced. Yet the fluency and superficiality evoked by 'the tongue of man' give solidity to the written bond, as does the almost unbroken train of monosyllables from 'By my soul' to 'I stay here on my bond.' As the oaths become more transcendental (sabbath, heaven, soul) they also become less palpable, and the value of the bond becomes clearer. The importance of written contracts among the Jews was known to the learned, and might be inferred by the dramatist. It stemmed from their lack of integration into a society that still regarded them as aliens, from the fact that they were themselves so often fleeced by the Christians to whom they lent. So it is not simply the case that the bond is overtaken by the oaths. They could fly away on the tongue of man, but the bond looks to be irrefutable.

When Portia concludes that Shylock is entitled 'to the penalty | Which here appeareth due upon the bond' (4.1.243–4), we are halfway to the simplicities of *A New Song, Shewing the Crueltie of Gernutus a Iew, who Lending to a Marchant a Hundred Crownes, Would Haue a Pound of his Flesh* (*c.*1620), a ballad which has been cited as an analogue of the play,[88] but we are not beyond the law and what it was obliged to test, because illegal conditions on a bond were actionable even if evil ones were not. As Coke writes on Littleton, 'it is commonly holden that if the condition of a bond, etc. be against law, that the bond itself is void. But herein the law distinguisheth between a condition against law for the doing of any act which is *malum in se*, and a condition (that concerneth not anything that is *malum in se*) and therefore is against law because it is either repugnant to the state or against some maxime or rule of law.'[89] The audience is asked to decide whether Shylock's condition is *malum in se* or merely against a rule of law. John Stubbs had his right hand hacked off and William Prynne his ears cut off and nose slit—by order of the Queen's Bench and Star Chamber—for writing against the authorities (1579, 1637). If such appendages for words, why not a chunk of flesh for debt? The scene acts on our proven, sadistic ability to accept small atrocities, not to mention our ability to scale up to larger ones. The later history of the Jews in Europe sufficiently reminds us of that.

Yet human weakness slips in, and Shylock does not keep his oaths. Hecht is wrong to contrast him as entirely as he does with the play's loose swearers. There *is* a power in the tongue of man to prevent him from having his bond; it lies in Portia's pleading, in the law that forbids an alien to take the life of a Venetian citizen, and in the language of the bond itself. 'We must look to the contract', Selden said, quite likely with the Talmud behind him: 'if that be rightly made, we must stand to it.'[90] Shylock's bond is not rightly made because it is not proof against the law about aliens but it is not rightly made to secure what Shylock wanted in any case, because of the ambiguities of its wording, even its making use of language at all. Feste's jest in *Twelfth Night*, 'words are very rascals since bonds disgraced them' (3.1.18–19), turns out to be wrapped around another jest: no one trusts a given word since it became fashionable to insist on bonds; bonds have proved so slippery that words themselves are in disgrace. The ambiguities in Shylock's bond are easily exploited by the tongue of man, or at least by a boy pretending to be a woman disguised as Dr Balthazar.

Portia explains to Shylock that he can take his pound of flesh but 'no jot of blood' (4.1.301). If he spills but a drop of that, his lands and goods are 'by the laws of Venice, confiscate | Unto the state of Venice' (306–7). Moreover, she adds, after Shylock puts in for compensation, if he takes more or less than a pound by 'the division of the twentieth part | Of one poor scruple', he will be executed and his property seized (324–7). This turns against Shylock the words of Jesus answering the Pharisees in their own coin in the Sermon on the Mount, when Christ declared that he had come not to destroy the Law but to fulfil it: 'Til heauen, and earth perish, one iote, or one title of the Law shal not scape, til all things be fulfilled' (Matthew 5: 18). We heard Shylock rehearsing the language of the instrument even before it was signed (1.3.141–7), but he was legalistic rather than legally literate. Portia's captious finding is a conclusion that he set in train himself, when he said that he would 'compromise' (uncompromisingly, it turns out) for an 'equal' pound of flesh. Flesh is not blood and what is equal must be exact. The trick that he played by claiming medieval, scholastic purity for his loan—that it would be an 'equal' loan—rebounds upon him precisely. The primary driver of the scene is Shylock's payback being paid back, but the further-reaching point is that, because Shylock is thwarted of his oaths, and does not plunge a knife into Antonio regardless, his unbindable binding language is brought closer to the adaptable oaths sworn by the Christian lovers.

* * *

Portia, it will be recalled, gives Bassanio all her goods and household authority with a ring:

> I give them with this ring,
> Which when you part from, lose, or give away,
> Let it presage the ruin of your love,
> And be my vantage to exclaim on you. (3.2.171–4)

He answers her with a vow which soars partly because, as a prodigal deeply in debt, he can only match her generosity by giving all he can, which is a promise of fidelity: 'when this ring | Parts from this finger, then parts life from hence. | O, then be bold to say Bassanio's dead' (183–5). Along with the gift of the ring, this vow completes a spousal, though an expert on betrothals—such as Henry Swinburne—might wonder whether Bassanio's words focus too much on his own faith to be mutual.[91] The lack of an oath-formula does not detract from Bassanio's promise, not just because, as Swinburne goes on to note, 'some Spousals be confirmed by an Oath, and some contracted without an Oath' (11), but because the betrothal is almost immediately confirmed in the temple, where vows will be made. Graziano, by his own report, was closer to swearing. He says to Portia and Bassanio, of Nerissa: 'With oaths of love, at last—if promise last— | I got a promise of this fair one here' (205–6).

If promise last is a dodgy joke with an aftershock. The susceptibility of all new love to trial is something that has to be lived with until more than promising sustains a relationship: hence the ring trick. This is often presented as a tidy piece of intrigue designed to show the men the importance of fidelity and to promote Portia above Antonio in Bassanio's heart. It complicates such a view that the trick is framed by Portia reporting a false, holy vow, designed to parallel Shylock's reported 'oath in heaven' to have his bond but also to diminish the severity of Bassanio's and Graziano's offence when they fail to keep their oaths and vows. After her husband has gone back to Venice, to try to save Antonio in the trial, as Portia is about to exit, she tells Lorenzo:

> I have toward heaven breathed a secret vow
> To live in prayer and contemplation,
> Only attended by Nerissa here,
> Until her husband and my lord's return. (3.4.27–30)

She could have contrived another alibi or even pretended to the same one without lying about a vow. To face what she says with plausibility, and to claim more for the 'secret vow', she says that she is going to somewhere like Shylock's synagogue, where votive utterances are indulged: 'There is a monastery two miles off, | And there we will abide' (31–2).

Refusing to give Dr Balthazar Portia's ring after the trial, Bassanio shows a punctiliousness that is also slightly deceptive: 'when she put it on she made me vow | That I should neither sell, nor give, nor lose it' (4.1.438–9). Strictly speaking, the audience did not see this happening, but heard Bassanio volunteer his vow. That he ups the level of pressure under which he gave his word is understandable given the aim of graciously withholding the ring, but it sustains an elasticity. Portia happily recognizes the way of the world when Nerissa proposes to emulate her mistress's success in getting the ring:

[*Aside to* PORTIA] I'll see if I can get my husband's ring,
Which I did make him swear to keep for ever.
PORTIA [*aside to* NERISSA] Thou mayst; I warrant we shall have old swearing
That they did give the rings away to men.
But we'll outface them, and outswear them too. (4.2.13–17)

'*Old* swearing' is happily familiar. Oaths are easy, worn-out stuff—as she might well complacently say after the crash of Shylock's oath on his very soul. For someone regarded by so many critics as a paragon, Portia verges on the unprincipled. Shylock's futile rigidity with oaths is contrasted with her worldly recognition that they can be fruitfully broken, that they are manifestations of a human desire to have more than we should wish for, better for being tempered by failure.

The outfacing goes nicely. Portia even manages to be light about Antonio's bond (which is fair enough since she got him out of it). 'This is the man,' says Bassanio, respectfully,

this is Antonio,
To whom I am so infinitely bound.
PORTIA You should in all sense be much bound to him,
For as I hear he was much bound for you. (5.1.133–6)

But there is a problem for comedy to resolve. We saw in Chapter 6 that Portia has to uncouple Bassanio from Antonio's surety. It can only be done by unravelling the betrothals, and showing Bassanio what is at risk, before re-rebinding them. There is some enjoyable awkwardness in store for the audience. We hear Graziano swearing to Nerissa by the same fickle moon that Juliet urges Romeo not to swear by: 'By yonder moon I swear you do me wrong; | In faith, I gave it to the judge's clerk' (141–2). He attempts to argue that the hoop of gold did not matter in itself, dismissing it as the more commonplace because inscribed with a conventional posy (as lovers' rings often were): 'Love me and leave me not' (149). Unfortunately for Graziano, the formulaic motto makes the ring more manifestly a token of betrothal, of the oaths and vows that bound the couple.[92] As Nerissa buoyantly berates him:

> You swore to me when I did give it you
> That you would wear it till your hour of death,
> And that it should lie with you in your grave.
> Though not for me, yet for your vehement oaths
> You should have been respective and have kept it. (151–5)

Nerissa does not outswear Graziano quite, but she comes as close to an oath as a maid should with 'God's my judge' (156). He is more insistent, swearing by something palpable, the very hand, presumably, that wore the ring: 'Now by this hand, I gave it to a youth' (160).

It is a measure of the density of the issues drawn together at this point in the action that Portia's rebuke demands full quotation:

> You were to blame, I must be plain with you,
> To part so slightly with your wife's first gift,
> A thing stuck on with oaths upon your finger,
> And so riveted with faith unto your flesh.
> I gave my love a ring and made him swear
> Never to part with it; and here he stands.
> I dare be sworn for him he would not leave it,
> Nor pluck it from his finger for the wealth
> That the world masters. Now, in faith, Graziano,
> You give your wife too unkind a cause of grief.
> An 'twere to me, I should be mad at it. (165–75)

Again this is outswearing with female decorum—'I dare be sworn' and 'in faith'—but any failure on Bassanio's part will now have made Portia swear a false oath too, and because of her trust in him. The carnality of the lovers' bond, with its cumbersome, abrupt finality ('stuck on . . . riveted'), is replicated as well as represented by a ring that is nailed to or pulled off the flesh. What is sacramental about marriage owes much, it seems, to the sacrament of an oath that provides through word or token external, sensorily accessible, 'inartificial proof' of fidelity.[93] Bassanio's response to what Portia says does not make light of the situation but the situation is made light of by what might be the instrument of his oath—perhaps, like Graziano's, held up on stage: 'Why, I were best to cut my left hand off | And swear I lost the ring defending it' (176–7). The only way out, he senses, is to swear another oath, though it is hardly a promising prospect.

Since denial is useless—there is his hand without the ring—he tries to ring the changes on the ring. Unfortunately, there are no changes, just a ringing of the binding word:

Sweet Portia,
If you did know to whom I gave the ring,
If you did know for whom I gave the ring,
And would conceive for what I gave the ring,
And how unwillingly I left the ring... (191–5)

As many have noted, the repetition of 'the ring'—which goes on for six more line-endings—recalls, in a comic key, Shylock's repeated 'I'll have my bond' in 3.3. Just as *The Merchant* has far and away the highest count of 'bond' in Shakespeare, so it rivals *All's Well* with 'ring', and largely by virtue of this exchange. More will be said in a moment about why the rings are also like the bond. What needs to be noted immediately is something that has never, to my knowledge, been picked out by critics, though early audiences, with their ears attuned to the gradations of binding language, would have been alert to the irony. When he counters Portia's rebuttal, 'I'll die for't but some woman had the ring', Bassanio echoes Shylock, at the moment when he swears in court, in saying, 'No, by my honour, madam, *by my soul*' (207–8).

It is an oath that Bassanio is obliged to repeat, because he is forced now to stretch as far as oaths will go. Portia declares that she will become as free with her favours as Bassanio, given his betrayal of what he did swear to keep. Where can he go beyond oaths? The answer in this play is nowhere:

BASSANIO Portia, forgive me this enforcèd wrong,
And in the hearing of these many friends
I swear to thee, even by thine own fair eyes,
Wherein I see myself—
PORTIA Mark you but that?
In both my eyes he doubly sees himself,
In each eye one. Swear by your double self,
And there's an oath of credit.
BASSANIO Nay, but hear me.
Pardon this fault, and *by my soul I swear*
I never more will break an oath with thee. (239–47)

This is climactically weak. What kind of an assurance is an oath not to break another oath? 'By my soul' did not hold Shylock's oath, and there is no reason for it to secure Bassanio's either.

Antonio now steps up to declare that not all the onstage friends who hear Bassanio swear are merely passive witnesses. In another, glancing echo of Shylock, he stakes his soul on a binding forfeit:

I once did lend my body for his wealth
Which, but for him that had your husband's ring,
Had quite miscarried. I dare be bound again,
My soul upon the forfeit, that your lord
Will never more break faith advisedly.
PORTIA Then you shall be his surety. Give him this,
And bid him keep it better than the other.
ANTONIO Here, Lord Bassanio, swear to keep this ring.
BASSANIO By heaven, it is the same I gave the doctor!
PORTIA I had it of him. Pardon me, Bassanio,
For by this ring, the doctor lay with me. (248–58)

The substitution is a restitution, even a continuity, as though the ring had never been given away, which it almost has not been. In this it resembles the pound of flesh that was given to Antonio by Dr Balthazar without being taken, when Shylock's bond was judged binding and then not. Look at how 'by this ring, the doctor lay with me' turns a binding oath, by a ring which is an emblem of truth, into an untruth, or a part truth. What Portia says is literally true ('by means of this ring') but it means something different from the proffered oath. It is like the bond which forbids the pound of flesh because it forbids the spilling of blood.

This is the sort of casuistry that Portia excels in. If Shylock tricks Antonio into accepting his bond, Portia inveigles Bassanio into getting out of his—but not to dispose of it for ever. Love and society depend on the tearing up of bad bonds and the renewal of good ones. Portia is not a lord of misrule, but she has a light touch with tough love. Oaths and vows in themselves do not secure trust, but rather point to where the trust should be that marriage needs. This is what the end of *The Merchant* is about for Portia, Nerissa, and their lovers. They test their bonds, before they are consummated, with the rings that were given in betrothal. The one-fleshing of the marriages is deferred yet put to proof. The word 'band' does not seem to have meant 'ring' in early modern England, as it can today. But the rings are like the bond in being pledges of contract, not just sworn or vowed contract in themselves, but piled up with breakable oaths by Bassanio, Graziano, and Shylock.

The double-plotted parallels go deeper. Although the rings are exchangeable they are not interchangeable. They resemble the bond because each is tied to the person—to the flesh and blood—of Antonio and of the women. Some early modern writers argued that bonds should be saleable, as they were on the Continent. This was not, however, how 'bills of debt' were regarded. 'The Common Law of England, is directly against this course; for they say there can bee no alienation from one man to another of debts; because they are held, *Choses en Action*, and such whereof no propertie can passe by assignement or alienation.'[94] The bond sealed by Shylock and Antonio is specifically for a pound of *his* flesh. The rings are likewise not marketable. Dr Balthazar has no difficulty in rejecting Bassanio's proposal that he seek out and buy for him the most expensive ring in Venice as a substitute for the ring on his finger (4.2.430–6). The rings are not replaceable with ducats because they are so intimately bound up with the physicality of the women's honour. As Graziano bawdily quips in the last line of the play, his challenge as a husband will be 'keeping safe Nerissa's ring'.

* * *

At this point we must return to the marriage of Shylock and Antonio, through the parallel offered by that other Jewish–Gentile carnal bond, the relationship between Jessica and Lorenzo. This means hearing the echo of the 'compromise' between Jacob and Laban, as Jessica anticipates escape:

> O Lorenzo,
> If thou *keep promise* I shall end this strife,
> Become a Christian and thy loving wife. (2.3.18–20)

'Strife' will strike most audiences as a self-justifying, exaggerated word for such discord as we witness in her father's house. Shylock, as his name implies, is keen on getting Jessica to shut doors and windows against the world: 'Fast bind, fast find—| A proverb never stale in thrifty mind' (2.5.52–3). He means, 'if you lock everything up, you'll find all your goods in place when you come back', but there are psychological and verbal connections with his trust in the legal bond, which, like his house, pillaged by Jessica, is not fast bound for long. Though Shylock imagines himself as Jacob, he has a touch of the unenterprising Laban. In Genesis, when Rachel runs away with

Jacob, she distresses Laban her father by stealing his goods and idols (Genesis 31: 19, 33–5), as Jessica and Lorenzo run off with Shylock's casket.

Given that Lorenzo is like Bassanio a fortune-hunter, we might mistrust the durability of his 'promise'. His friends assume that he is late for their rendezvous because his ardour has already cooled.

SALERIO O, ten times faster Venus' pigeons fly
To seal love's bonds new made than they are wont
To keep obligèd faith unforfeited. (2.6.5–7)

The discouraging judgement is there, in part, to keep alive the parallel with Antonio and Shylock. As the Jew's bond with the merchant shows, no one rushes with alacrity to keep obligèd faith. The irony is that Antonio will be the more harried for the resulting forfeit as a result of Lorenzo and Jessica sealing their own love-bond.

Are they represented as committed by vows? Jessica asks a question that probes further than Lorenzo's mask in the darkness:

JESSICA Who are you? Tell me for more certainty,
Albeit I'll swear that I do know your tongue.
LORENZO Lorenzo, and thy love.
JESSICA Lorenzo, certain, and my love indeed,
For who love I so much? And now who knows
But you, Lorenzo, whether I am yours?
LORENZO Heaven and thy thoughts are witness that thou art. (2.6.26–32)

As one might expect in a script so intensively structured by the keeping and breaking of bonds, Jessica's search for affection is represented as a seeking out of faith (she does not presume on Lorenzo's love). She 'will' swear, because, as a woman, she should not actually swear, and he invokes Heaven and her thoughts, since she ought to believe that he loves her, as witnesses to his binding language. Yet a shiver of doubt remains. Money is awkward when a lover does not have it, though Portia makes it less so at Belmont; Jessica's response to his reassurance looks like a reward and his declaration a sort of incitement: 'Here, catch this casket. It is worth the pains' (33). Worth the trouble of catching but hardly worth the pains that catching it will cause her father. Contrast the paternal caskets kept and obeyed at Belmont.

Interestingly, when Lorenzo calls Jessica away, she lingers for divided reasons. On the one hand, almost bizarrely, she stops to follow Shylock's instruction to 'make fast the doors' (49), rather as Portia bends, more fully, to her father's instructions regarding the love-trial. Throwing the casket of jewels and ducats out of the window to her lover contrasts sharply and no doubt deliberately—as others have pointed out—with the scene in *The Jew of Malta* where the faithful Abigail throws a chest of treasure out of their house (now a nunnery) to Barabas. But affinity with her father remains. The compulsion to lock the doors does not owe everything to the anxiety caused by leaving the house. Second, she stays to 'gild' herself 'With some more ducats', to make herself more attractive to Lorenzo; like Portia, giving herself to Bassanio, she wants to be more rich even more than to be more fair (3.2.154). In Shakespeare, gilding is always close to guilt. Jessica unwittingly gives herself a touch of the golden casket, all superficial promise. Meanwhile, adding to her store makes her something of a usurer, reminding audiences of the early modern commonplace that usury is (more or less lawful) theft.[95] In *The Merchant*, we might say, the daughter of a thief is a thief; more forgivably, she pays a thief back by stealing from him, yet takes what ought to be hers as a marriage portion.

Antonio's plight is mixed up with this, because Shylock wants revenge for what is a double taking of his treasure. Antonio has 3,000 of his ducats, Lorenzo a casket of money and jewels. The former allows revenge for the latter (see 2.8.12–26, where Solanio acts out Shylock's outrage). More interestingly, the bond makes him the owner of a pound of Antonio's flesh and this he will take because his other collop of flesh and blood (Jessica) has gone.

SHYLOCK My own flesh and blood to rebel!
SOLANIO Out upon it, old carrion, rebels it at these years?
SHYLOCK I say my daughter is my flesh and my blood. (3.1.30–2)

Shylock's characteristic insistence, refusing to get the joke, makes what is metaphorical oddly literal. It is as though he owns Jessica because she is a piece of his body matter. This is a point that Salerio pursues:

> There is more difference between thy flesh and hers than between jet and ivory; more between your bloods than there is between red wine and Rhenish. But tell us, do you hear whether Antonio have had any loss at sea or no?
>
> SHYLOCK There I have another bad match. A bankrupt, a prodigal, who dare scarce show his head on the Rialto; a beggar, that was used to come so smug upon the mart. Let him look to his bond. He was wont to call me usurer: let him look to his bond. He was wont to lend money for a Christian courtesy: let him look to his bond. (3.1.33–42)

Salerio's laboured insistence on flesh *and* blood, which in Shylock's mouth was initially a stock phrase, points the audience—especially when it is repeated, and more when viewing of the play is repeated—to see what is in the bond. Shylock is forgetting about blood. When he recasts Salerio's phrase and speaks of '*my* flesh and *my* blood' he is not just shown to be possessive but wrong-headedly inclined to assume that flesh-and-blood are distinct. To the cry, 'let him look to his bond' the audience might respond, 'look to your bond yourself'. Meanwhile, the cry is self-binding, since, whatever the technicalities about the bindingness of repeated oaths, the more often he speaks of it the more bound Shylock is to his action. Most importantly for the structure of the comedy, Shylock has two bad matches. One is his 'compromise' or fleshly pledge with Antonio, the other the match he now has for his daughter. Each match reflects on the other, for they are both carnal bonds.

The play's good matches are secured by rings that are given away and returned. Lorenzo and Jessica exchange no rings, but shamelessly barter for a monkey the ring that Shylock had of Leah (the name of Jacob's first wife, in scripture) when he was a bachelor.[96] By early modern custom, compatibly with Jewish practice, this turquoise will have firmed up Shylock's betrothal; now it is frivolously disposed of, not used to bind. But then, the audience might wonder, why was Shylock not wearing the ring? Why was it kept in the casket? Was it for safe-keeping, because it meant so much to him, or miserliness? Has the binding function of the ring become less important to him than its value? Or is it that, in hostile Venice, he has come to lock up everything that matters to him, from his wife's ring to his daughter? Different performances of the role will stir in different audiences varying shades of question and answer—some more sympathetic to Shylock, others less so—but the vectors all go back to the bindingness of the ring.

Do Lorenzo and Jessica have a ring of their own? That Bassanio/Portia and Graziano/Nerissa make such play with theirs makes the lack of it being mentioned more than a way of underlining how excluded the mixed couple are from integration in Belmont. Much depends on the body language of the actors, but the possibility of seduction and abandonment unbound by any ring is real. When Lorenzo is late for the rendezvous, Graziano asks, 'Who riseth from a feast | With that keen appetite that he sits down?' (2.6.8–9). There is talk of a 'prodigal' and the 'strumpet wind' (14–16). Contrast the formal elaboration of contracting with a ring, in front of a rabbi, and so on, in Leone da Modena's *Rites* (174–5). This is what Jessica has shunned by running away from home (many Elizabethans would have a sense of what Selden explores in depth, the solemnity of Jewish marriage customs).[97] Jessica and Lorenzo may, like the be-ringed other couples, have vows. But how much can they be relied on given the slidingness the audience is shown in both the Shylock/Antonio and the Christian lovers' plots?

The question becomes explicit in the last scene of the play, as Jessica and Lorenzo rehearse their tales of betrayal and loss.[98] Everyone in Shakespeare's audience with even the rudiments of a classical education would recognize how mutually yet troublingly they catalogue love affairs that went wrong through broken vows (Cressid, Dido abandoned by Aeneas) or death (Thisbe, Medea gathering herbs bloodily to renew old Aeson). Their own tale is one of theft and vowing:

LORENZO In such a night
Did Jessica steal from the wealthy Jew,
And with an unthrift love did run from Venice
As far as Belmont.
JESSICA In such a night
Did young Lorenzo swear he loved her well,
Stealing her soul with many vows of faith,
And ne'er a true one.
LORENZO In such a night
Did pretty Jessica, like a little shrew,
Slander her love, and he forgave it her.
JESSICA I would outnight you, did nobody come. (5.1.14–23)

This can be played with the teasing confidence of lovers who are sure for now of their love. They enjoy testing the tolerances within their intimacy, knowing what outsiders might say about their being a bad match. But there is another implication. Jessica's 'outnight' minutely recalls Portia's 'outswear' (pp. 198–9). This is a subplot version of the contesting of oaths around the ring trick.

At this point the pair break off, with the entrance of the minor figure Stephano. 'I bring word', he says, that

> My mistress will before the break of day
> Be here at Belmont. She doth stray about
> By holy crosses, where she kneels and prays
> For happy wedlock hours. (28–32)

The servant reminds us of the pretend-vow, the 'secret vow', taken before Portia went to Venice as Balthazar (see p. 197). 'Stray about' hints at the errancy of what kneeling in front of crosses would amount to for Protestant audiences even if her imaginary prayers were not a deception. Yet the reported devotion has enough allure to make the trading of rings and oaths in which Portia has been engaged seem bluntly pragmatic. Around 'wedlock', as in other areas, there is a falling-short of Christian values, not unlike Shylock's fall from the Judaic dignity of his oath in heaven. The audience—reminded by this passage—will not forget the falsity of Portia's 'secret vow' and the doubts that spread out from it as far as Lorenzo's 'vows of faith'. The pledge-word 'wedlock' no longer seems so fast bound.

This is not quite the last that we see of Jessica and Lorenzo. The Shylock plot, largely over an act earlier, resumes with the delivery of the deed of gift that we looked at at the end of Chapter 6. In keeping with the charitable economy theoretically practised by the Christians, Nerissa presents the legal instrument to Lorenzo and says:

> There do I give to you and Jessica
> From the rich Jew a special deed of gift,
> After his death, of all he dies possessed of. (290–2)

On stage the deed rhymes visually with Shylock's (other) bond, in the trial scene; this is a late extension of the parallels between the Antonio/Shylock and Lorenzo/Jessica plot-lines. It secures the marriage of Jessica and Lorenzo, on confiscated money, filling pockets now emptied of stolen jewels and ducats. There is no doubt a suggestion that Jessica is heading for the destitution that moralists liked to say awaited the children of usurers. 'If God be true ... he will take the riches which they haue vnlawfully gathered, from them, and from their house, and from their children.'[99] The audience can deduce their poverty from Lorenzo's gracious, disgraceful thanks: 'Fair ladies, you drop manna in the way | Of starvèd people' (293–4). This is the clearest case of a Hebrew word being used in the dialogue, but *manna* had long been expropriated by Christians to describe a free gift.

Manna can be heard as grating pun on *money*, much as Portia sounds like *portion* ('marriage *portion*'), which is a large part of what she is to Bassanio. Audiences would be sympathetic to Lorenzo and Jessica's expectation of a portion, a dower, from Shylock; but they would also feel for a father required to hand over assiduously piled-up cash to a spendthrift son-in-law. Shakespeare himself, most likely writing *The Merchant of Venice* shortly after the death of his only son Hamnet, cannot have contemplated with enthusiasm leaving so much of what he had worked for to the future husbands of his daughters Judith and Susanna. He would be right to be concerned. Susanna, the older sister, married well, to the physician John Hall; but Judith's romantic life had a less satisfactory outcome. The dramatist left a 'marriage porcion' to Judith in his will. The exact time-scale is unclear, but it looks as though, a few weeks before his death, he had the will revised to remove a reference to her husband Thomas Quiney, who had (it emerged) fornicated with and impregnated Margaret Wheeler, soon to die in childbirth with her infant. Called to answer for this in the Stratford bawdy court, Quiney would later be fined for swearing and allowing drinking in his premises at forbidden hours.[100] Shakespeare was signalling disapproval and probably trying to make it harder for the scapegrace son-in-law to get his hands on his property. What would happen in 1616 is not written into *The Merchant of Venice*, but it shows how fraught life could get when carnal bonds came to incorporate financial deeds.

8

Mighty Opposites

2 Henry VI to *Hamlet*

In the third scene of *2 Henry VI* (*c.*1591), Queen Margaret and her favourite, the Duke of Suffolk, are waylaid as they cross the stage by a group of supplicants, among them Peter Thump, the armourer's man, who presses forward to give Suffolk a petition

> Against my master, Thomas Horner, for saying that the Duke of York was rightful heir to the crown.
>
> QUEEN MARGARET What sayst thou? Did the Duke of York say he was rightful heir to the crown?
>
> PETER That my master was? No, forsooth, my master said that he was and that the King was an usurper. (1.3.28–34)

The comic mistaking shows, with a gratuitous, Shakespearean twist of insight, how muddled and emphatically careful ordinary people become when put on the spot by those in authority. Perhaps it also suggests how weak King Henry now is, that an apprentice might think it could be thought that his master would harbour royal ambitions. It is Margaret, however, who starts the confusion by pressing Peter to implicate York in treason. Within moments, Suffolk and she have moved against their enemy by having Horner summoned for questioning.

Called upon to explain himself in front of the king, Horner denies saying that York is heir to the throne and Henry a usurper. This is more than an opportunity for master to disagree with man. It is a formal legal occasion, and both make their deposition with oaths:

> An't shall please your majesty, I never said nor thought any such matter. God is my witness, I am falsely accused by the villain.
>
> PETER [*raising his hands*] By these ten bones, my lords, he did speak them to me in the garret one night as we were scouring my Lord of York's armour. (1.3.191–6)

Recognizing that he is the one under suspicion, York, with scant regard for Horner's denial, calls for the dunghill villain to be executed. The armourer, however, persists, saying that he can bring a witness to prove that Peter has a grudge against him and wants to get even:

> Alas, my lord, hang me if ever I spake the words. My accuser is my prentice, and when I did correct him for his fault the other day, he did vow upon his knees he would be even with me. I have good witness of this, therefore, I beseech your majesty, do not cast away an honest man for a villain's accusation. (201–6)

Like Peter, bolstering his evidence by placing his conversation with Horner in a garret while scouring York's armour, Horner circumstantiates his testimony. Whether or not Henry and the rest can imagine Peter making a vow on his knees, the revenge motive is plausible, and so is Horner's offer to bring a witness to prove it. Unfortunately, what he cannot do is produce a witness to the exchange in which he said or did not say that York was heir to the crown. So the king, on Gloucester, the Protector's, advice, does what was often done during the middle ages, in the absence of a confession or witnesses: he declares that Peter and Horner must undergo a judicial combat to establish which of their sworn statements is true. Although this gives Peter an immediate, physical opportunity to get even with his master, he is not keen to take it up, because Horner is bigger and stronger. He is caught up in the process, though, and Gloucester insists, 'Sirrah, or you must fight or else be hanged.' The king fixes a date for the wager of battle (220–7).

When we next see Horner and Peter they are coming onstage to fight using staffs with sandbags attached. This is not a parody of chivalric lances and shields but standard weaponry for the task. The point of judicial combat was to establish through Divine judgement which party had sworn the truth. Lethal violence—execution, at the king's command—could then follow. Though the combat in *2 Henry VI* lacks the elaborate routine set out in such sources as Henry of Bracton's *De Legibus et Consuetudinibus Angliae* ('On the Laws and Customs of England')—widely read in England, from the thirteenth century through the lifetime of Shakespeare—it has a degree of formality. 'A God's name,' Henry cries, 'see the lists and all things fit; | Here let them end it, and God defend the right' (2.3.54–5). Decorum is more demotically observed by the neighbours who ply Horner with sack, charneco,[1] and beer—prompting him to 'pledge' them all—and by the prentices who pledge Peter but cannot get him to drink (59–83). The basics of legal process are followed. Above all, Horner gives a commoners' version of the traditional, sworn declaration of why he is there to fight:

> Masters, I am come hither, as it were, upon my man's instigation, to prove him a knave and myself an honest man; and touching the Duke of York, I will take my death I never meant him any ill, nor the King, nor the Queen; and therefore, Peter, have at thee with a downright blow. (89–93)

The fight that follows can be protracted and entangled, if the actor playing Horner combines unbeatable strength with self-defeating intoxication, but it ends with the fatally wounded armourer crying, 'Hold, Peter, hold—I confess, I confess treason' (95). York says out of self-interest what most members of an early audience would think, that drink helped Peter's victory, though he does not exclude Divine involvement. Henry more directly invokes *judicium dei*:

> Go, take hence that traitor from our sight,
> For by his death we do perceive his guilt.
> And God in justice hath revealed to us
> The truth and innocence of this poor fellow, . . . (101–4)

The oaths sworn by Horner and Peter ('God is my witness', 'by these ten bones') carry into the process something of the religious, ritual structure that in earlier literary and legal instances is provided by the laying of relics around the combatants,[2] by preliminary prayers and oaths uttered in front of icons,[3] and by the blessing of shields and swords.[4] In Bracton, as we shall see, the wording of the oath to be sworn before wager of battle indicates the use of relics. In such contexts, the 'sacrament' of the oath[5] had a quasi-religious function, and opened up combat to God's judgement. Like trial by ordeal—dipping a hand into boiling water, then seeing whether it heals, carrying a piece of hot iron—and like trial by drawing lots (which was a widely practised, early medieval form of judgement), wager of battle was underpinned by a belief in Divine immanence and vengeance.[6] What Shakespeare characteristically adds is the unofficial, only-too-human use of judicial combat to get revenge: Peter Thump's desire to 'be even' with Horner, Hereford's aim, as we shall see, in *Richard II* (1595?), to retribute Mowbray for the murder of his uncle, Woodstock, even Laertes' attempt—at the end of this chapter—to murder Hamlet in the exercise with foils in revenge for the killing of Polonius.

In this the ungainly, vicious fight between Horner and Peter Thump resembles the Wars of the Roses. From one point of view, the wars are so much pointless thumping and horning, unconvincing one-to-one combats with old-fashioned long swords and bucklers, feuds, infidelities, and an urge to get even. Yet the possibility of Divine judgement does hang over the conflict, as over the apprentice's fight with his master. The battles of the first tetralogy do not just test prowess, but who keeps and who breaks oaths (of fealty, above all). It is a drama of promise-breaking and false witness, with vengeance—as we saw in Chapter 2—caught up in it. God punishes sworn lying as surely as he retributes murder. In Judaeo-Christian tradition, perjury attracts the same law of the talion as injury and murder: 'If a false witnes rise vp against a man to accuse him of trespasse, . . . thine eie shal haue no compassion, *but* life for life, eie for eie, tothe for tothe, hand for hand, foote for foote' (Deuteronomy 19: 16–21). To the end of the tetralogy, this principle is dramatically potent, though attenuated as a religious truth. In *Richard III* (1592–3), false oaths and testimony thus bring down retribution. After Clarence dreams of being punished for breaking his oath of fealty to Henry VI as well as for stabbing Prince Edward (1.4.44–56), his murderers self-excusingly say that they bring him God's 'vengeance . . . For false forswearing, and for murder too' (189–90). Before the final battle, Richard accuses himself of 'Perjury, perjury, . . . Murder, stern murder' (5.5.150–1), and expects to be punished for both—as he is.

* * *

Though a judicial combat was arranged in Tothill fields in 1571 and another was fought to the death at Dublin Castle in 1583,[7] wager of battle—like its sibling, trial by ordeal—had fallen out of use by the time of Shakespeare. It was already becoming a curiosity in the reign of Henry VI. Yet the decline of *vadium bellum* did not reduce its fascination. Interest ran high because judicial combat was seen as the native, historic basis of the duelling code that became fashionable in late Elizabethan England. The duello owed much to contemporary Italy,[8] but affronted men liked to say, 'Thou doost not proceede in this case like a Gentleman, neither according to the honorable custome of Knights.'[9] That rebuke comes from *Vincentio Sauiolo his Practise* (1595), a treatise that Shakespeare read before writing *Romeo and Juliet*. But a related curiosity about ancient, honourable custom was satisfied by such works as *The Booke of Honor and Armes* (1590), which sets out the rituals of wager of battle.[10] This account, which Shakespeare quite likely knew, was recycled in Segar's *Honor Military, and Ciuill* (1602) and in John Despagne's *Anti-Duello* (1632).

Among the texts that appeal to a late Elizabethan interest in judicial combat is *Richard II*, where challenge, pledging, and wager of battle are displayed and explored at length. This is how the play begins:

> *Enter* KING RICHARD II, JOHN OF GAUNT, *with* [*the* LORD MARSHAL,] *other nobles, and attendants*
> KING RICHARD Old John of Gaunt, time-honoured Lancaster,
> Hast thou according to thy oath and bond
> Brought hither Henry Hereford, thy bold son,
> Here to make good the boist'rous late appeal,
> Which then our leisure would not let us hear,
> Against the Duke of Norfolk, Thomas Mowbray? (1.1.1–6)

It has been said that Richard invokes the fealty sworn to kings.[11] The specificity of 'thy oath and bond' more likely points to an earlier stage in the story—as set out in Holinshed—where Hereford accuses Mowbray of treachery and Mowbray calls this a lie, Gaunt is ordered to be arrested by the king to ensure Hereford's compliance in judgement, and the Duke of Surrey and Duke of Aumerle 'vndertooke as pledges bodie for bodie for the duke of Hereford'.[12] Richard's speech declares, then, that the 'appeal' or charge against Mowbray is now formally to be heard. Whatever the Elizabethan audience made of 'oath and bond', they would be prompted by the phrase (which Shakespeare added, at this point, to his sources) to notice that the whole situation is framed by oaths.

The king, quite properly, according to the medieval rules, asks Gaunt whether his son

> appeal the Duke on ancient malice
> Or worthily, as a good subject should,
> On some known ground of treachery in him? (9–11)

Is the trial going to be about the alleged treachery or be driven by a longer-standing grudge? Unconvincingly, since a history of hostility is going to emerge, Gaunt assures the king that Hereford is impelled by 'some apparent danger' against Richard, not by 'inveterate malice'. The king calls in the parties, and denunciations are made. Hereford says that he will prove with his body (in combat) that 'Thou art a traitor and a miscreant, ... With a foul traitor's name stuff I thy throat' (39, 44). Mowbray responds with equal, strident formality, saying that, were it not for the king's presence, he would return 'These terms of treason doubled down his throat. ... most falsely doth he lie' (57, 68). Speech acts morph into action, as Hereford issues a challenge which puts at stake a piece of his honour, throwing down his gauntlet as a pledge:

Pale trembling coward, there I throw my gage, . . .
If guilty dread have left thee so much strength
As to take up mine honour's pawn, then stoop. . . .
MOWBRAY [*taking up the gage*] I take it up, and by that sword I swear
Which gently laid my knighthood on my shoulder,
I'll answer thee in any fair degree
Or chivalrous design of knightly trial; . . . (69–81)

As we shall see from Bracton, it is in accordance with the legal conventions that appellant and defendant should confront one another before saying what their dispute is about. It also makes strong theatre. Hereford charges that Mowbray kept for his own lewd uses 8,000 nobles given him to clothe the king's soldiers. In case that accusation is too narrow, he says that he was behind all the treason plotted in the kingdom for the last eighteen years. This charge is both a screen, and prepares the ground, for what he is really after. He wants to revenge the death of his uncle, Woodstock:

Further I say, and further will maintain
Upon his bad life, to make all this good,
That he did plot the Duke of Gloucester's death, . . .
Which blood, like sacrificing Abel's, cries
Even from the tongueless caverns of the earth
To me for justice and rough chastisement.
And, by the glorious worth of my descent,
This arm shall do it or this life be spent. (98–108)

Richard's response to this oath, 'How high a pitch his resolution soars!', is more defensive than judicial. In the very next scene, the audience will be told what many would have recalled from the chronicles and the anonymous play *Woodstock*: that the king was implicated in Gloucester's death. When the Duchess of Gloucester warns Gaunt that unless he 'venge' Woodstock his own life will be in danger, he replies that 'revenge' against the king can only be taken by heaven. For Gaunt and the house of Lancaster, judicial combat with Mowbray is not just a means of establishing the untruth of his denials but of getting even. 'O, set my husband's wrongs on Hereford's spear,' the Duchess cries, 'That it may enter butcher Mowbray's breast!' (1.2.36, 40, 47–8).

For now, revenge smoulders, while Mowbray rebuts Hereford. The money was mostly spent properly. 'For Gloucester's death, | I slew him not, but to my own disgrace | Neglected my sworn duty in that case' (1.1.132–4)—another oath, also not in Holinshed, to add to Richard's 'vow' at this point that he will not favour his kinsman, Hereford. Mowbray admits that he once laid an ambush for the life of Gaunt, but he has confessed it and begged pardon and hopes he had it (from which we might infer a feud). He then flings a few insults at Hereford for being a villain and a traitor, 'Which in myself I boldly will defend, [*He throws down his gage*] | And interchangeably hurl down my gage' (145–6). Promising, as William Kerrigan points out, often dilates into braving and boasting.[13] The king tries to manage the quarrel, but the men would rather throw themselves at his feet for permission to fight than drop or give up the other's gage. Richard therefore, with some loss of authority, announces that they will fight with swords and lances 'At Coventry upon Saint Lambert's day' (199).

By drawing out the essentials of Holinshed in this scene of appeal and defence, Shakespeare stays close to the oath-rich procedures of medieval law. In Bracton, we read:

> Let the defender first give gage for defending and then the appellor for deraigning[14] the appeal. Then let the defender first swear a denial, denying the felony imputed to him absolutely and by negative words; then the appellor shall swear an affirmation, affirming in affirmative words that everything he alleges against the appellee is true. The form of the oath is this: 'Hear this, O man, whom I hold by the hand, who call yourself A. by the name of your baptism, that I did not slay your father (or "your brother" or some other, such a one) nor did I deal him the wound with a weapon of such a kind by which he is alleged to be farther from life and nearer to death, nor did you see it, so help me God and these holy relics.' And in his oath let him make mention of the year, the day and the place in accordance with the terms of the appeal. And afterwards let the appellor swear to the contrary...[15]

The charges and rebuttals are less formulaic in Shakespeare, and the throwing down of gages builds a more potent dynamic. The legal symmetries are maintained, however, in a way that draws attention to the inadequate, suspect role of the king, who goes through the motions with style but gives the whole process an air of masquerade.

When it comes to the combat at Coventry, Holinshed is positively cinematic, giving richly detailed, close-up descriptions of heraldic devices and weaponry, and unstageable dramatic action:

> About the houre of prime came to the barriers of the listes, the duke of Hereford, mounted on a white courser, barded with gréene and blew veluet

> imbrodered sumptuouslie with swans and antelops of goldsmiths woorke, armed at all points. The constable and marshall came to the barriers, demanding of him what he was, he answered; I am Henrie of Lancaster duke of Hereford, which am come hither to doo mine indeuor against Thomas Mowbraie duke of Norfolke, as a traitor vntrue to God, the king, his realme, and me. Then incontinentlie he sware vpon the holie Euangelists, that his quarrell was true and iust and vpon that point he required to enter the lists. Then he put vp his sword, which before he held naked in his hand, and putting downe his visor, made a crosse on his horsse, and with speare in hand, entered into the lists, and descended from his horsse, and set him downe in a chaire of gréene veluet, at the one end of the lists, and there reposed himselfe, abiding the comming of his aduersarie. (VI, 494)

Shakespeare could have worked some of this into a report, but he chose to focus, almost austerely, on the oaths of Hereford and Mowbray. He may have been encouraged to do this by the prominence that oaths are given in the account of wager of battle in *The Booke of Honor and Armes*,[16] but the explanation must be dramaturgical, and to do with the potency of words and ritual in this play.

Certainly, he set aside the sorts of dramatic potential that he would usually have worked with. The signs of impatience in Hereford, for instance, swearing his oath 'incontinentlie' (immediately) and requiring to enter the lists before the king even arrives. In the play, he holds back until after the entrance of Richard with his entourage—indeed, he does not step across the stage and swear until after Mowbray, which is not just contrary to Holinshed but to the order of oaths by appellant and defender set out by *The Booke of Honor*, though it provides a dramatic crescendo. What we get is an echoing of voices, from king to herald (not in Holinshed) and then to Mowbray, all reduplicated for Hereford and reinforced by the sort of minute articulation of space that was routine in the Elizabethan theatre but that was also encouraged by the sources (proclamation made from all four corners of the lists that no one should come within four feet of them,[17] or touch them,[18] and so on).

This is how the sequence ends up, starting from a stage direction that has to be elaborate:

> *The trumpets sound, and* KING [RICHARD] *enters with* [JOHN OF] GAUNT, BUSHY, BAGOT, GREEN, *and other nobles. When they are set, enter* MOWBRAY *Duke of Norfolk, defendant, in arms, and a* HERALD [*to Mowbray*]

RICHARD II Marshal, demand of yonder champion
The cause of his arrival here in arms.

Ask him his name, and orderly proceed
To swear him in the justice of his cause.
LORD MARSHAL [*to* MOWBRAY] In God's name and the King's, say who thou art,
And why thou com'st thus knightly clad in arms,
Against what man thou com'st, and what thy quarrel.
Speak truly on thy knighthood and thy oath,
As so defend thee heaven and thy valour!
MOWBRAY My name is Thomas Mowbray, Duke of Norfolk,
Who hither come engagèd by my oath—
Which God defend a knight should violate—
Both to defend my loyalty and truth
To God, my king, and my succeeding issue,
Against the Duke of Hereford that appeals me;... (1.3.7–21)

The reduction of a jousting field to a few square yards of stage gives an air of unreality to the formal questions required by the procedure: who is the newly arrived champion (evidently Mowbray)? ask him (though he can hear me) why he has come? As often when Richard is on stage, there is a performative aspect to the proceedings. Yet the work of initiation still has a ritual power: the emergence of name, title, and bond as though from nowhere are steps into social agency; they go along with Mowbray's (and later Hereford's) physical approach to the place of swearing. The journey is only a few steps long, from the edge or back wall of the stage, but psychologically large, since it goes from 'yonder' to 'arrival'. It is also culturally deep. We still walk or step up to the witness stand, to swear on the Bible or Koran. The orderly transition into the zone of commitment and truth is as necessary in framing such an oath as the verbal formulae that surround it. The origins of the word conceivably encode this sort of ritual process. According to the *Oxford English Dictionary*, the word *oath* 'may perhaps have arisen from the walk of the oath-taker to the place of oath-taking being seen as part of the solemn ceremony (... Swedish *edgång* oath-taking, lit. "oath-walking", Old Swedish *ganga eþ* to swear an oath, lit. to "walk an oath"...)'.[19]

The formal oaths of the combatants are not the only binding words. Hereford talks of a vow which reflects the coming together of the men as they share the same space of combat, and honour one another for the sake of the honour they owe themselves: 'For Mowbray and myself are like two men | That vow a long and weary pilgrimage.' Now, though, Hereford reasserts his innocence, as does Mowbray, 'However God or fortune cast my lot'—a phrase to remember (48–9, 85). The combatants are given their lances, heralds recapitulate the accusation of treachery and rebuttal, trumpets are sounded, but then, as they are about to charge, the king stops the combat by throwing down his warder. His judgement is one of exile upon both. They are indeed vowed on a long pilgrimage, Bolingbroke (i.e. Hereford) to ten years abroad, Norfolk to lifelong expulsion, which he proposes to turn into a crusade to the holy land. Then, Shakespeare stages yet another oath, sworn on the royal sword, that the two men will not conspire, nor even meet, abroad (172–85).

Conflict in *Richard II* repeatedly breaks through ceremony only to become in turn ritualized, while scenes that appear recapitulative often register change. So it is in the leap from 1.3, in front of Richard, to 4.1, in front of Bolingbroke. Because none of the allegations have been tested in a trial of proof, the question of murder has rumbled on and it erupts again after Hereford returns from exile and ousts Richard. Aumerle is accused by Bagot of contriving Woodstock's death, and of resisting Hereford's return. How can the honour machine process this accusation of a nobleman by a commoner? In Holinshed, the quarrel builds with the throwing down of 'hoods' as 'pledges' (VI, 512). To echo and sustain the argument from 1.1, Shakespeare has gauntlets thrown down instead: 'There is my gage, the manual seal of death', Aumerle tells Bagot: 'I say, thou liest' (4.1.24–5). Bolingbroke, showing more authority than Richard in the opening scene, and presenting himself as a defender of nobility, successfully bids Bagot not to take it up. Fitzwalter then seconds Bagot's accusation and throws down 'my gage, Aumerle, in gage to thine' (33). Percy joins in too: 'Aumerle, thou liest. . . . there I throw my gage' (4.1.43–5). Defiance is flung back, another Lord joins Bagot's party and throws his gage (though only in the quartos), but Surrey joins with Aumerle. The repeated giving of the lie, more sketchily present in Holinshed, connects medieval *defiance*, which is an accusation of faithlessness (see p. 17), with the duello, which was fought over the accusation of lying and the dishonour of not being trusted with an oath. The act of challenge became a matter for revenge since, in most cases, giving the lie injured the swearer by denying his faith and honour.

SURREY Dishonourable boy,
That lie shall lie so heavy on my sword
That it shall render vengeance and revenge,
Till thou, the lie-giver, and that lie do lie
In earth as quiet as thy father's skull;

In proof whereof, there is my honour's pawn
[*He throws down his gage*]
Engage it to the trial if thou dar'st. (56–62)

Although the scenes of defiance and combat give Elizabethan audiences a gratifyingly full account of the supposed origins of their honour code, there is a testing of the conventions to the point of parody. Surrey's quibbling on 'lie' drives the charge against him down into the grave which waits for Fitzwalter, but turns the word into wordplay. His opponent's reassertion of the literal seems frustrated and petulant:

> I dare meet Surrey in a wilderness
> And spit upon him whilst I say he lies,
> And lies, and lies. There is my bond of faith, . . . (65–7)

And Aumerle, in a remarkable moment, says that he has run out of gauntlets to throw down, even though he has twice as many pledges available as his equivalent in Holinshed, who has to borrow a hood: 'Some honest Christian trust me with a gage. | . . . Norfolk lies' (74–5). The chivalric code is not going to hold, when even a forfeit has to be borrowed. It hardly did with Hereford and Mowbray. Now the gages are piling up on stage and Bolingbroke has to show command, to manage the growth of faction. 'These differences shall all rest under gage', he declares, 'Till Norfolk be repealed' (77–8). The accusations and uncertainties will remain suspended, under gage, like an untested wager. Perhaps Bolingbroke already knew that Norfolk, i.e. Mowbray, could not be recalled from exile since he had died in Venice, as the Bishop of Carlisle now reports. Conveniently, he must draw a line and move on to his coronation.

Richard II tells us that the age of chivalry is over; yet its return was repeatedly mooted during Shakespeare's lifetime, from the pageantry of Gloriana's tournaments to the ethos associated with the Earl of Essex and the Protestant, Arthurian knighthood of Prince Henry. In *The Booke of Honor* and the duelling pamphlets there is a similar attempt to harness tradition, though the notion that what is tested is the truth of what is sworn to is tilted towards fighting over the capacity of a man to give an oath, and thus his honour, the honour put in jeopardy when he is given the lie. As Saviolo puts it, 'The summe of all therefore, is in these cases of honour, that hee vnto whome the lie is wrongfullie giuen, ought to challenge him that offereth that dishonour, and by the swoorde to proue himselfe no lyer' (R4r). Saviolo and his ilk are wittily travestied in *As You*

Like It, where Touchstone lists the grades of giving the lie, from 'the Retort Courteous' through the 'Quip Modest' to 'the Lie Circumstantial, and the Lie Direct' (5.4.67–75). It can be said, in Saviolo's defence, that his taxonomy is often perceptive. What matters, in any case, is the twist that he shows the honour code giving to binding language. Oaths may be binding, but so (in a peculiar way) is an accusation of lying. The dishonour is such that you are obliged to disprove the lie, as the accuser is to maintain it. So, in 'Of Lies certaine', Saviolo writes: 'lyes speciall, . . . assuredlye binde the parties vnto whome they be giuen' (whereas, of 'the Lye in generall', he says 'no man is bound to answer the same') (S3r, S4r). That particular lies 'binde', that the person uttering them is 'bound' to prove them by combat (as oaths are proved by combat), and that the object is 'bound' to answer them, is a notion that recurs in his 'Treatise of Dementies or giuing the lie', as it does in Book I of *The Booke of Honor.*[20]

What about those cases where the falsehood of a lie is so transparent that there is an accusation without an injury, or where a deed is so evidently villainous that it stands self-condemned? Saviolo's advice, rather surprisingly, is that the wronged man should not be drawn:

> But perhappes some man wyll aske me if in this case hee shoulde put vp this iniurie without reuenge? To whome I aunswere, that Combat was ordayned for iustifieng of a truth, and not to laye open a waie for one man to reuenge him of another, for the punishment of suche thinges resteth in the Prince . . . (Z3v–4r)

Saviolo is in line with the medieval view that the duel/judicial combat is for proof not revenge. Such a view, however, is more principled than realistic. As a play such as Chapman's *Reuenge of Bussy D'Ambois* (1610?) reminds us, duelling was often regarded as the least bad way of pursuing revenge when punishment was otherwise unobtainable. It was a course the more honourable because it left your opponent a fair chance to defend himself physically—as Montsurry defends himself, after some prevarication, in his duel with Clermont D'Ambois; it also gives a fair chance to God or fortune to decide whether the defender should be retributed with death.

Even in Saviolo, revenge slips in through the back door, as when he discusses the case—pertinent to Clermont[21]—of a man who is slighted and denied the right to correct a wrong because he is of lower status than those who have injured him. For Saviolo, all noblemen should be part of the honour community, and so have a right to revenge:

> We haue shewen great inequalitie of noble men, wherby the lesse cannot binde the greater to answere him in person: but because no mans greatnes can make it lawfull for him vniustlye to oppresse the lesser, without leauing him sufficient meanes to reuenge himself, and no man ought to make the shadowe of his nobilitie a pretence to be able secretlye to commit defectes, without yeelding reason for them. (Gg3r)

He goes so far as to say that a prince (including a sovereign) should agree to fight with one who is merely noble. He would in other words back the right of Laertes to fight Hamlet for real, though not, of course, while concealing that his rapier is for real because unbated: 'a Prince with his subject is bound to fight in person:...and whensoeuer one man shall oppose vnto another, any defect of promise and faith, ... the accuser is to trye the quarrell in person with the accused' (Gg4r). Saviolo is keener on legal recourse than one might expect from an advocate of the duel, but Claudius' protection of Hamlet after the killing of Polonius would make a challenge legitimate. Saviolo would certainly not be surprised to find vengeance woven into the process—to which we must now turn.

* * *

The title of this chapter comes from Hamlet's exchange with Horatio, on the prince's return from the voyage to England. He is justifying his little plot to have Rosencrantz and Guildenstern executed in his place, despite the lack of evidence that his former friends knew what was in the commission sent by Claudius to the English king. They were like men, he says, who dawdle between the rapiers of two opponents in a duel, himself and Claudius. ''Tis dangerous when the baser nature comes | Between the pass and fell incensèd points | Of mighty opposites' (5.2.62–3). This is often, and understandably, extrapolated into an image of the whole play as a contest between Hamlet and Claudius. As my argument will show, much about the tragedy can be learned by thinking in such terms. But *The Tragedy of Hamlet* (*c.*1600) is framed by two actual duels, and it is worth looking at them both. One belongs to the pagan prehistory of *judicium dei*—that between Old Hamlet and Old Fortinbras, described by Horatio near the start of the play—and the second is the exercise with bated rapiers, by the prince and Laertes, which turns lethal in Act 5.

This is what Horatio says about Old Hamlet's combat:

> Our last king,
> Whose image even but now appeared to us,
> Was as you know by Fortinbras of Norway,
> Thereto pricked on by a most emulate pride,
> Dared to the combat; in which our valiant Hamlet—
> For so this side of our known world esteemed him—
> Did slay this Fortinbras, who by a sealed compact
> Well ratified by law and heraldry
> Did forfeit with his life all those his lands
> Which he stood seized on to the conqueror;
> Against the which a moiety competent
> Was gagèd by our King, which had returned
> To the inheritance of Fortinbras
> Had he been vanquisher, as by the same cov'nant
> And carriage of the article designed,
> His fell to Hamlet. (1.1.79–94)

We cannot be sure how much of this passage was imported from the *Ur-Hamlet*, but pieces of the story found in Belleforest's *Histoires tragiques*—the originating source of Shakespeare's play[22]—do find their way into the speech. Like Fortinbras, Collere, the King of Norway in Belleforest, was encouraged by 'emulate pride' to fight with Old Hamlet. In both texts, the antagonists pledge an agreement. Horatio describes, however, not the oral pact between Collere and Horvendile (Old Hamlet), 'the most renouned pirate' of the north (in Belleforest),[23] but a full, early modern covenant, legally secured, recognized by the heralds who supervised wager of battle, or bearing on its seal heraldically correct devices. The stake is larger, also, than the shipfuls of treasure in Belleforest. The two kings wager territory. Old Fortinbras forfeited to Old Hamlet 'all those his lands | Which he stood seized on'—most likely land taken from Norway, part of the territorial mosaic that constituted the Scandinavian kingdoms, that were sometimes distinct in the medieval and early modern periods, sometimes pulled into union. Old Hamlet, meanwhile, kept the moiety (half, piece) of territory that he had 'gagèd'—which means both 'engaged (by the compact)' and 'thrown down like a gage' (as his pledge), and thus, given the etymological closeness of *gage* and *wager*, 'put up as his stake'.

A single combat between monarchs may sound less likely to a modern ear than the fight between a rover king of Norway and the pirate Horvendile that Belleforest inherited from Saxo Grammaticus, but Shakespeare's audience would not have been surprised. In *Antony and Cleopatra*, Antony offers to fight Octavius. An early medieval combat between kings was staged in *Edmund Ironside* (*c*.1590), a play that has been implausibly attributed to Shakespeare. There Canute the Dane and Edmund the Saxon resolve their differences without risking the lives of their followers. Emma, Ironside's stepmother, tries to persuade him that he should not 'hazard the loss of all upon the chance | of fickle fortune, since the better man | is sooner killed by overhardiness than an advisèd coward'.[24] Edmund replies, in the language of *judicium dei*, that he does not fear to fight, 'my cause being good | and justice on my side... the God in whom I trust will succour me' (lines 1946–52). In the event, Edmund begins to prevail, and Canute offers either his hand or his sword, friendship or enmity. As is the way, or one way, combat induces accord. They agree to divide the country between Anglo-Saxony and Danelaw, and the rest is history.

Shakespeare did not so much drop Horvendile's piracy, made abundantly clear in Belleforest and possibly the *Ur-Hamlet*,[25] as bring it back in the form of the pirates who fight with the prince on the sea voyage to England, take him captive, do some sort of deal with him, then accompany him back to Elsinore, where (Hamlet tells Horatio) 'I am to do a good turn for them' (4.6.11–23).[26] This is more than a case of re-deploying source material to produce a turn-around in the action. It was a classic point of dispute in moral philosophy whether undertakings given under duress to pirates should be kept. Cicero argued that 'an othe is manye times to be kept with our enemie' but that 'if you bring not the summe of money, that ye promised rouers for your life: ther is no deceiuing in it: no, though, beyng sworne therto, ye do it not. For a pirate is not counted in the noumber of enemies to ones countrey, but a common enemie to all men.'[27] Most early modern moralists, from Bodin[28] to Jeremy Taylor,[29] disagreed. Your word was your bond, even to robbers and pirates.[30] Hamlet seems to share their view. Despite his patchy record when it comes to keeping his word to the ghost and vows of love to Ophelia, he sets about keeping this promise, enabling the pirates/sailors to give letters to the king.

Meanwhile, as Horatio makes clear, Old Hamlet put both himself and his lands in jeopardy when he made his gage/wager with Old Fortinbras—creating risks for Denmark which run on into the tragedy. We might think of a promissory oath as fixing a course, but you do not actually know that you can deliver until you have. You gamble on your oath working out, doing what you can (as in combat), but under the reign of chance or God (as in combat), to redeem your word, your gage, your pledge, your bet. There is something grandly reckless about the staking of territory (and sovereignty) on a duel, but there is also a staking of life and reputation, so the gamble is not just made on a pledge of fine dirt. It is often the same with oaths. The prince's 'I have sworn't', when he takes up the commandment of the ghost, is more elusive (p. 140). Once steps are taken against him, though, he unavoidably has skin in the game. The play does become a duel between Hamlet and Claudius as 'mighty opposites'. The stakes are nowhere clearer than in the combat with foils between Hamlet and Claudius' champion, or instrument, Laertes.

This combat has its roots in *judicium dei* and its branches in the duello; but Osric, the anonymous Lord, and Hamlet (twice) call it 'play'. In Chapter 3, on *Love's Labour's Lost*, etymology helped us educe some of the connections between play and binding language. More can now be said. *Plegan*, the Germanic root of 'play', means *inter alia* 'stake, risk. It is the source also of the verbs "pledge" and "plight"... from Old English *pliht*, danger, peril.'[31] It rings true that play, when serious, should put the player in danger, at stake. In Hamlet's 'play' with Laertes, he finds in himself a touch of his father. How far the combat recapitulates that between Old Hamlet and Old Fortinbras is something to get to soon. Meanwhile, although 'plighted' is a *Love's Labour's Lost* word, its role is taken in *Hamlet* by 'pledge', 'lot', 'odds', and by the *Richard II* terms *gage* and *wager*. 'Gaged' in Horatio's speech about Old Hamlet occurs only twice in Shakespeare;[32] 'wager' is used more often in the tragedy than anywhere else in his works. What do these twin words mean? '*Gage, (vadium)* commeth of the French *(gager....)*', notes John Cowell in his legal glossary of 1607: 'It signifieth with vs also a pawne or pledge.... *Wage (vadiare)* proceedeth of the French *(Gager....)* and signifieth in our common lawe the giuing of securitie.'[33]

Hereford and Mowbray utter their oaths and in a connected, emphatic action throw down their gages to assert guilt or innocence. Giving your word can extend into or be replaced by a gesture and pledge. For an oath or vow has some of the properties of a thing, in a medieval or Tudor society where so many engagements were given with or took the form of objects (bent coin, rope, stick, ring, glove, 'carved knitting needles, spindles, and bobbins'[34]). In Holinshed, as we have seen, Aumerle and the rest throw down their hoods; in the play they throw down gauntlets. It was the word, gage, or wager manifest in the object that made the pledge. In high medieval actions, the oath or gage was held as a forfeit, a surety—which could be a kinsman, or his substitute—against the appearance of challenger and defender to have their truth tested. When Hereford turns up to fight Mowbray, in Holinshed, he comes to defend his accusation but also to acquit the forfeit of his father substituted by the Constable and Marshal who are his 'pledges'.[35] In *Edmund Ironside*, two Saxon noblemen left with Canute, and known simply as '1 Pledge' and '2 Pledge', have their noses and hands chopped off because their fathers have rebelled against the Danes.

Among the meanings of *pledge* are the drink taken to salute someone, wish them health, or secure an agreement. This is important in *Hamlet*. The prince gives his word to the ghost against the raucous background noise of Claudius drinking pledges with cannon being fired to mark the achievement. This is the king's way of making *his* commitments while Hamlet makes his. The sequence is carefully prepared. When the prince agrees to stay in Elsinore, in 1.2, and not go back to study at Wittenberg, the king calls this an 'accord'. He will seal it with drink, even if the fastidious prince is not going to join him:

> This gentle and unforced accord of Hamlet
> Sits smiling to my heart; in grace whereof,
> No jocund health that Denmark drinks today
> But the great cannon to the clouds shall tell,
> And the King's rouse the heaven shall bruit again,... (1.2.123–7).

Whether this is wise behaviour in a court that goes in fear of attack by the son of Old Fortinbras, reported by both Horatio and Claudius to be in arms to get the lands lost by his father back, is doubtful. Compare *Othello* 2.3, where the Moor is angry that the alarm bell has been rung, after a scene of drunken revelry, when there is still fear of a Turkish invasion. Hamlet explains:

> The King doth wake tonight and takes his rouse,
> Keeps wassail, and the swagg'ring upspring reels,
> And as he drains his draughts of Rhenish down
> The kettle-drum and trumpet thus bray out
> The triumph of his pledge.
> HORATIO Is it a custom?
> HAMLET Ay, marry, is't,
> And to my mind, though I am native here
> And to the manner born, it is a custom
> More honoured in the breach than the observance. (1.4.9–18)

Claudius' 'pledge' looks feeble compared with Old Hamlet's gage, when the warrior-king's prowess defeated the Norwegians.

As we have begun to see, early modern drinking was about more than indulgence. Wassails and healths had an 'Art and Order', meshing alcohol into the routines of good neighbourliness (Horner and Peter), legal education, gambling in taverns, adolescent rites of passage, and parodic hierarchies.[36] Rounds, drinkers matched in threes, bets about who could drink most, were part of this culture, along with the ugly fallout in abuse and revenge for honour. There were 'wager cups' designed for drinking bouts, including a cup for pledges that had a die built into the stem.[37] You shook the cup to find out how many times it should be filled up. Drink loosened tongues as well as tempers. In the *Othello* sequence, Iago and the soldiers egg Cassio on (2.3.25–146). Swearing and wine go together in his self-loathing tipsiness, as they do in the denunciation of drinking practices by moralists.[38] There is not just a risk of blasphemy, though, when a man drinks healths over cards. There is a deep congruence between pledges, oaths, and gambling.

Before we get to that, in the exercise with foils, it is worth noticing another overspill of the combat in Belleforest between the King of Norway and Horvendile. These are Norsemen fighting it out on the coast of Scandinavia, which is exactly where the institution of the duel was believed to come from. Selden, for instance, writes in his *Duello*: 'the Normans, alias North mans (being by their first ofspring from the Norwegian coast, where this custome as before is shewed, had his breeding) were the first authors of it in this their conquered kingdome.'[39] This is the reason—unnoticed by Shakespeare scholars—why, when Claudius and Laertes conspire, and grope their way towards the plot against Hamlet's life, they make so much of Lamord, who admired Laertes' abilities as a swordsman, in France, being 'a gentleman of Normandy'. 'A Norman was't?' 'A Norman' (4.7.67–76). This is not in Belleforest, and there is no reason for it to have been in the *Ur*-play. That Claudius within a few lines of his first mention refers to Lamord as a Frenchman shows how little Shakespeare was interested in his ethnicity once the idea of a duel going back to its origins in the world of Horvendile had been registered. In keeping with his heritage, Lamord appreciated Laertes' abilities as a fencer. 'This report of his | Did Hamlet so envenom with his envy | That'—like the emulous Old Fortinbras, we might say—he wanted a trial of 'play' with Laertes (84–7). If 'envenom' plants the seed of a plot against Hamlet, 'wager' continues it. The king will draw him on with a 'wager on your heads', and Hamlet, being nonchalant, will not check the foils, so Laertes can 'choose | A sword unbated' (106–10). Now the apparently honourable Laertes shocks the audience by proposing to 'anoint' his sword with poison. Not to be outdone Claudius will poison a 'chalice' from which Hamlet will drink: 'We'll make a solemn wager on your cunnings... If he by chance escape your venomed stuck, | Our purpose may hold there' (112, 127–33).

Lest the audience miss the wagering, between the fighting and drinking, it is spelled out to Hamlet by the stilted Osric: 'his majesty... has laid a great wager on your head', and again, 'The King, sir, hath wagered with him six Barbary horses, against the which he imponed, as I take it, six French rapiers and poniards,... Three of the carriages, in faith, are very dear to fancy' (5.2.99–100, 108–11). Hamlet's baffled question 'What call you the carriages?' gets a simple answer ('The carriages, sir, are the hangers') and the prince goes on rather fogeyishly about how carriages would be more appropriate if we could carry cannon by our sides. The word has been used only once before in the play, in the terms of Old Hamlet's combat with Old Fortinbras: 'by the same cov'nant | And carriage of the article designed.' The micro-echo is revealing of purpose in the contrast it points up. The combat between the fathers was epic, open, and princely in what was at stake. Hamlet has to get his mind around a complex as well as a fashionable wager. The basics are: six horses against six swords, 'that's the French bet against the Danish' (119–20). But beyond this, there are what Mowbray calls *odds*, when he boasts, in their flyting, that, to maintain his rebuttal of Hereford, 'I would allow him odds'.[40] In *Hamlet*, the odds are built into the bet: 'The King, sir,' Osric explains, 'hath laid, sir, that in a dozen passes... he shall not exceed you three hits. He hath laid on't twelve for nine, and it would come to immediate trial' (122–5). A fair bit of ink has been spilled on the question of just what calculation the king has made. Suffice it that he takes Laertes to be the better swordsman, but is prepared to back Hamlet: a nicely judged mix of challenge and encouragement.

This is not the only Shakespeare play in which betting is a point of attention. In *Antony and Cleopatra*, for instance, the soothsayer tells Antony that, when Caesar is with him, his genius—his guardian spirit—is afeared. It is true, Antony reflects: 'If we draw lots, he speeds.... His cocks do win the battle still of mine... and his quails ever | Beat mine, inhooped, at odds' (2.3.33–6). Caesar is, in a play much given to chance, 'full-fortuned' (4.16.25). *Hamlet* is almost as concentrated in its focus. We have noted its heavy use of *wager*; the lines quoted above give us Shakespeare's only use of *bet*. A bet is a speech act, like an oath or vow; it is one of Austin's basic examples of a performative utterance;[41] more than most promises (all of which involve risking some honour or social capital), it requires a stake to be put down, like a pledge. It is a forfeit against something *affirmed*[42]—'Horse *x* will win the three o'clock at Aintree'—rather than an undertaking or money pooled and then taken by the winner. This relates conceptually to the idea of life as a series of existential bets (very much a *Hamlet* idea), the self repeatedly hostage to situations in which it finds itself—certainly so for a revenger, who has not chosen his *lot*.

When the king enters 5.2 he puts Laertes' hand into Hamlet's. This is a gesture of reconciliation which also inaugurates conflict, or, rather, renews the struggle which they begin when fighting in Ophelia's grave, a struggle which the practice with foils is officially meant to regulate and allay. The same gesture can be found in *The Booke of Honor*, where the constable requires those fighting to 'take one the other by the hand' before swearing their third oath (79). The potential for reconciliation through conflict is there, as with Ironside and Canute. The handclasp is an ancient gesture of accord. Whether prompted by the queen through the Lord who follows Osric as messenger in the Second Quarto, or spontaneously, as in the Folio, Hamlet takes up the opportunity:

> Give me your pardon, sir. I've done you wrong;
> But pardon't as you are a gentleman.
> This presence knows,
> And you must needs have heard, how I am punished
> With sore distraction. (163–7)

It was his madness, not himself, that wronged Laertes, he formally protests, like shooting an arrow over the house and hurting his brother. The latter's reply needs careful listening.

> I am satisfied in nature,
> Whose motive in this case should stir me most
> To my revenge. But in my terms of honour
> I stand aloof, and will no reconcilement
> Till by some elder masters of known honour
> I have a voice and precedent of peace
> To keep my name ungored;... (181–7)

On the one hand Hamlet offers an apology of sorts, and exculpation. If Laertes is looking for retribution, the prince has already been punished, by the very madness that drove him to commit the deeds that Laertes wants to revenge. On the other, Hamlet's asseveration, placed just before the fight that he now calls 'this brothers' wager' (190), resembles the sworn rebuttal traditionally given before judicial combat. The prince's word will be tried by the wager of battle. Laertes says that he has *satisfaction* of a sort, but reserves his position on *reconcilement* by declaring that he'll consult the experts. These words belong to the Elizabethan discourse of duelling, as does the plan to consult *pareri*, the back-up masters in honour.[43] Hamlet's apology is less socially determined, but uncomfortably casuistical. Shakespeare would not have needed Montaigne to grasp the point, but he would have found it in the *Essayes*. For once sounding like Polonius ('Beware | Of entrance to a quarrel, but being in, | Bear't that th'opposèd may beware of thee' (1.3.65–7)), Montaigne deplores such apologies:

> he that enters lightly into a quarrel, is subject to leave it as lightly.... Most agreements of our moderne quarrels, are shamefull and false: Wee onely seeke to save apparances,... The excuses and reparations, or satisfactions, which dayly I see made; promised and given to purge indiscretion, seeme to me more foule than indiscretion it self. Better were it for one to offend his adversarie againe, than in giving him such satisfaction, to wrong himselfe so much.[44]

In his own account of 'satisfaction', Saviolo takes a more positive line, disagreeing with the many who 'are of opinion, that satisfaction cannot be made by words for offences by deeds' (Hh4r). Yet he issues a salient warning. It is dangerous to offer symbolic satisfaction—as in fighting a duel against an angry opponent with bated rapiers. He gives the example of 'Satisfaction done to one in Burgundie' in which it was agreed that, to pay back an insulting box on the ear, the injured party would strike his antagonist on the shoulder, and say 'I am satisfied, wee will be friends'. Unfortunately, the wronged man broke the agreement and gave his antagonist 'a sound blow on the eare', which prompted his opponent to run him through. Saviolo concludes, in a passage that lights up Laertes' keywords:

> My opinion concerning these reconciliations is, that it were not good in the making of them to allow any signe of reuenge, to passe betwixt the parties that are to be reconciled, so that if satisfaction in the treating of any peace betwixt two fallen out, can be made by words, me thinks it were not amisse that euen all tokens or signes of reuenge were auoyded... (Kk1v–2r)

As we have seen, with Peter v. Horner, Hereford v. Mowbray, and Clermont v. Montsurry, combat is absolutely a 'signe of revenge'. It is often enough its vehicle. And so it proves in *Hamlet*.

It could be said that play with bated rapiers is hardly duelling; yet wager of battle, as we have seen, was not, at least officially, about killing—nor, necessarily, was the duello—but testing the truth of an utterance. What the duel tested, Saviolo insists, is the truth of the word of honour, the untruth of giving the lie. This lends the oath or asseveration, of the sort that Hamlet makes to Laertes, an unusual temporal reach. For the most part, assertory oaths ('by Heaven, *x* is true now') contrast with promissory oaths ('by Heaven, I will give you *y* next week'), but judicial combat tests an assertory oath through time. It stretches time—we fight in slow motion—as it stretches through time, and the speaker or his champion has to prove its truth. Part of the psychology is that if you do not believe in your truth you will be the less committed to combat, and fear God's wrath, and perhaps that is Laertes' problem, since, against the odds, he keeps losing. When he has a chance to strike at Hamlet between bouts, he says, 'And yet 'tis almost 'gainst my conscience' (5.2.240): he would be breaking the rules of the game to lunge, but he also knows more radically that he is untrue in using an unbated, poisoned rapier.

Even when the weapons are chosen, distrust is in the air. The prince's sworn complimenting cannot placate Laertes—eager as he is to justify his treachery to himself:

LAERTES You mock me, sir.
HAMLET No, by this hand.
KING CLAUDIUS Give them the foils, young Osric. Cousin Hamlet,
You know the wager?
HAMLET Very well, my lord.
Your grace hath laid the odds o'th' weaker side.
KING CLAUDIUS I do not fear it; I have seen you both.
But since he is bettered, we have therefore odds. (195–201)

There it might be left (with some uncertainty as to the odds), but Hamlet has one of his many questions as they choose their weapons: 'These foils have all a length?' (203). It was usual before a judicial combat or duel, to compare the length of the weapons, as a matter of fairness and ritual.[45] Touchstone once measured rapiers for a duel, then parted.[46] Hamlet is halfway, but not far enough, towards acting on Saviolo's advice that one should never underestimate the animus of an opponent, even if a friend or kinsman (E2r–v).

There is another preliminary, entirely the king's but not unexpected. As in Act I we already know that he plans to drink a pledge to Hamlet. Now he sets out the rules:

> Set me the stoups of wine upon that table.
> If Hamlet give the first or second hit,
> Or quit in answer of the third exchange,
> Let all the battlements their ordnance fire.
> The King shall drink to Hamlet's better breath,
> And in the cup an union shall he throw... (205–10)

This is getting mathematical, as tends to be the way—treatises show—with wagers and drinking games, though the complication helps Claudius slip in mention of the 'union' (a pearl, actually his capsule of poison) as part of the routine. The pledging will also be amplified, drum speaking to trumpet, he goes on to say, trumpet to cannoneer, cannons to the heavens, the heavens to earth. This is designed to project the health-pledge with all the falsity of court percussion—and the audience hears it after the first bout, when Hamlet succeeds in giving Laertes a palpable hit.

> KING CLAUDIUS Stay. Give me drink. Hamlet, this pearl is thine.
> Here's to thy health.—
> *Drum [and] trumpets sound, and shot goes off*
> Give him the cup.
> HAMLET I'll play this bout first. Set it by a while.— (225–7)

In such revenge plays as *Antonio's Revenge*, the ghost is present in the scene of payback (see p. 57). The ghost of Old Hamlet is notoriously absent from the catastrophe. But drum, trumpet, and cannon recreate the sound-world of his appearance to Hamlet on the battlements. The ghost fades out of the tragedy (see pp. 141–2), but his presence can still be felt as the revenge plot comes to a crisis.

Pledging with cups of wine was a friendly act that could be coercive; moralists complained that it was competitive and even aggressive in requiring reciprocation. 'Whosoeuer... wyll sweare and compel other men at his banquets to drinke', wrote Gascoigne, 'shalbe guiltie at the day of iudgement both for himselfe, and for other men.'[47] Claudius is exploiting the convention against refusing to return a pledge to pressure Hamlet into drinking from the poisoned cup, which, like the unbated rapier, is a weapon.

Even without the poison, drinking the wine would weaken the prince, and expose him to Laertes' sword. As we saw in *2 Henry VI*, drinking pledges proposed by his neighbours incapacitates Horner. Given what he said about drink on the battlements, an audience will not expect Hamlet to succumb to Claudius' pledging, but there is more involved in the rejection than fastidious distaste.

How deep are the roots of his refusal? In a wide-ranging study of drink-pledges in early modern Augsburg, B. Ann Tlusty looks a long way back:

> The forming of a bond or brotherhood through sharing a drink was a custom as prevalent among the symposiums of ancient Greece as it was to the communal drinking bouts of the Germanic tribes. In these societies, alcoholic beverages were described as containing a spirit or a demon that inhabited the body of the drinker upon consumption of the wine.... The spirit of the drink became a supernatural witness to the pact who could be angered and seek revenge if the pact were broken.[48]

This anthropologizing claim hangs suggestively over Hamlet's refusal of the cup, since drinking Claudius' wine would deny his pledge to the ghost ('I have sworn't') and haunt or possess him with a new bond. Less speculatively, Tlusty notes the 'nearly universal association between wine and blood' (104). In early modern Germany, 'as both parties in the contract shared the drink... both also shared in pledging a part of themselves' (106). By denying Claudius, Hamlet refuses a connection that has already become toxic—refuses to be of Claudius' blood, we might say—at a pitch of social symbolism that is easily interpreted by the court. His resistance is the more sympathetic because Claudius' ritual is perverted, even damnable. When he holds the union above the cup, the king is like a Catholic priest celebrating the eucharist, with a piece of the host between his fingers above the 'chalice' (Claudius' word). The 'association between wine and blood' takes on blasphemous, cannibalistic overtones. On the one hand, the table, cups, and host-like union recall the masses and blessings over relics associated with medieval judicial combat. On the other, it invokes the sort of bloody, cannibal banquet that could be expected at the climax of a revenge play.

Hamlet and Laertes fight until the latter nicks the prince—the merest touch of chance—and the queen, drinking from the poisoned cup—not stopped by the self-preserving Claudius—staggers. Duels were sometimes fought to first blood,[49] honour then being satisfied, but this is the point where the duelling really begins, or rather, in many productions, where the balletic order of fencing turns into a ruthless struggle. The king tries to calm the stage by calling for the fighters to be parted, like Richard throwing down his warder, but the combat has its own momentum. In wager of battle, the truth was meant to come out. Some of it does, when Hamlet sees the blood drawn out of him by Laertes' sword, and more is seen and heard when the queen warns him that the drink is poisoned and Laertes cries, 'the King's to blame' (263). The 'mighty opposites' of the duel do turn out to be Hamlet and Claudius. So the prince, in whatever way the actors play it, wrests the unbated rapier from Laertes, turns it upon the king, and then, to make payback doubly sure, forces him to drink from the poisoned cup.

A few stoups of wine might seem a modest banquet—though banquets, in the Elizabethan period, were more dessert-like than substantial. The sequence does rest, however, on a saga-sized 'banket' in Belleforest. There, Hamblet gets back to Elsinore from England to find the court eating and drinking. As the king's men sink into drunken sleep, the prince bundles them up into wall-hangings, sets them on fire, and goes off to destroy the king. Once in Fengon's bedchamber, rather than kill him asleep he 'layd hand upon the sword of his fathers murtherer, leaving his own in the place, which while he was at the banket some of the courtiers had nailed fast into the scaberd'. When Fengon leaps out of bed to defend himself, he is only mocked by the chance of defence, 'taking holde of Hamlets sworde, that was nayled into the scaberd, which as hee sought to pull out, Hamlet gave him such a blowe upon the chine of the necke, that hee cut his head cleane from his shoulders'.[50] This really nails revenge. In contrast with the scuffling hazard introduced by Shakespeare, it turns upon Fengon the trick played on Hamblet by his courtiers. In Belleforest, death is certain. *Hamlet* lets in what the duelling pamphlets call 'the vncertaine chances of the field'.[51]

* * *

It is tempting to attribute this revision of the story to the *Ur-Hamlet*'s or Shakespeare's desire to follow the usual arc of tragedy, through catastrophe to clarification. But there is a deeper conjunction between chance, wager, duel, and their relationship with binding language. For this reason we should go back to Hamlet's exchange with Horatio, when he first discusses the proposed 'trial' (Osric's word) with Laertes:

HORATIO You will lose this wager, my lord.

HAMLET I do not think so. Since he went into France, I have been in continual practice. I shall win at the odds. But thou wouldst not think how ill all's here about my heart[52]—but it is no matter. . . .

HORATIO If your mind dislike anything, obey it. I will forestall their repair hither, and say you are not fit.

HAMLET Not a whit. We defy augury. There's a special providence in the fall of a sparrow. If it be now, 'tis not to come. If it be not to come, it will be now. If it be not now, yet it will come. The readiness is all. Since no man has aught of what he leaves, what is't to leave betimes? (5.2.147–61)

This self-consciously noble speech is often taken as Hamlet giving himself up to Providence. That would be an orthodox, Protestant manoeuvre; but in practice, as Brian Cummings has noted, the lines are preoccupied with chance. For Cummings this is because Protestantism has plenty to say about mortality: Hamlet knows 'that he is implicated in a wager with death. . . . he may be lucky or he may not, but he can't know now, and there is nothing he can do to change the luck he is about to have'.[53] Even this strikes me as more fatalistic than it need be. Hamlet has choice,[54] skill, and practice. Like his father, fighting Old Fortinbras, he opts to gage his wager. We have to grasp how the idea of the duel takes us to lots and so to hazard and Divine direction.

In the middle ages, as we have seen, the rights and wrongs of a case could be tried by casting lots, as well as by wager of battle. There was, however, debate about the practice. Aquinas opens the question of 'Whether divination by drawing lots is unlawful?' by quoting Augustine on Psalm 30: 16:[55] 'It is not wrong to cast lots, for it is a means of ascertaining the divine will when man is in doubt.'[56] In both Testaments, Aquinas notes, 'we find holy men practising the casting of lots.' Judicial combat, he goes on, along with trial by fire and water, seems 'to come under the head of sortilege, because something unknown is sought by their means'. In this respect it resembles divination, rightly regarded as wrong. Yet *vadium bellum* is on balance 'lawful', which is why David 'engaged in single combat' with Goliath. Ordinary duels, on the other hand, that lack a judicial purpose, are like 'the common kind of sortilege' and unacceptably tempt God. This presents with Aquinas's usual clarity what remained orthodox for centuries. Thus James VI advised Prince Henry in *Basilikon Doron* (1599): 'neither committe your quarrel to be tryed by a Duell, for it is a committing of it to a Lot, and there is no warrant for it in the Scripture sen the abbrogating of the old Law.'[57] A couple of decades later, noting that many justified the duel as 'one kind of Lot, and by consequent practicable', John Despagne objected, 'if it chance that this fatall Lot fall vpon the innocent [i.e. if the wrong man dies]; can the Conscience of the Iudges find reasons sufficient for their excuse?'[58]

As a wager that tempted God in the sense of asking Him to make known something that was unknown, judicial combat was an extension, and testing, of the oath, which did the same thing. Misarticulation of an oath, whose protocols and formulae acted like lie-detectors, could prejudice your case as badly as losing your sword in combat. You could wage your law (through compurgation, having oaths sworn on your behalf) as well as wage by battle, or be put through an ordeal by fire or water or a casting of lots. All are forms of trial, bets upon the soul. Furthermore—to get back to Hamlet—oaths and lots both tempt God to intervene with a 'special providence'. As the puritan James Balmford complained in a 1593 treatise against games of chance: 'a Lot in the nature therof doth as necessarily suppose the special prouidence and determining presence of God, as an oth in the nature therof doth suppose the testifying presence of God. Yea so, that (as in an oth, so) in a lot prayer is expressed or to bee vnderstoode, 1. Sam. 14.41.'[59] Lots should not be used as a way of revelling in hazard. On the contrary, 'the proper end of a Lot (as of an oth, Heb. 6.16.) is to end a controuersie' (A5r). Lots are to be 'be vsed religiously, ... and not to be vsed in sport: as wee are not to pray or sweare in sport' (A5r). This yoking of lots with oaths was commonplace, though not unchallenged.[60]

So Hamlet's lines to Horatio are not just prompted by a fear of death, or reconciliation with the inevitability of death: the association between judicial combat, the duel, oaths, and lots moves the prince's mind from Laertes and the king's wager through 'We defy augury' (combat as sortilege) and 'There's a special providence in the fall of a sparrow' (God is tempted by combat as by lot to decide who will die) to 'The readiness is all.' The fight with Laertes, as Osric says, puts the king's wager 'to immediate *trial*', as it also tries Hamlet's asseveration of innocence (his apology to Laertes) and the skill of both young men. The process of testing the truth is drawn into the action. The duel manifests Hamlet's uneasy conscience and Laertes' treacherous guilt. You could say that, historically, and as reflected in Shakespeare's historical vision, the ritual of formulaic swearing that preceded judicial combat in the medieval period—as with Hereford and Mowbray—gave way to a subtler process of apology and satisfaction embedded in the duel itself.

In his study of duelling in early modern France, François Billacois finds related evidence 'that the oath was becoming anachronistic and that the fight itself was taking over the role of the oath in duels'.[61] To fight a duel is, in this sense, not to abandon pleading and contradiction, 'it is to try out a metalanguage. It is to use a sacred language which takes over from profane language in a discontinuity which is not an end' (201). That profane language in a stronger sense went with duelling is, of course, undeniable. Drinking and quarrelling led to swearing and fighting. There is the blasphemy uttered by a man striking or receiving a death blow. Along with these profanities, however, went the enactment of 'the sacred vow' in a duel[62]—sacred, at least, to masculinity, if not in the eyes of the Church. So the scaling down of oath rituals was a matter of shedding the inessential. 'Like the oath, the duel is a form of trial', as Billacois puts it, 'the armed combat was itself an oath. A silent oath, beyond all speech, which "would tell the truth", made by the reciprocal and decisive touch of two living and mortal bodies' (201–2).

Shakespeare always escapes the sociological diagram. *Hamlet* does not neatly end with the prince being tried and found wanting in a combat which is a tacit oath. The struggle which first turns away from its apparent object to focus on Claudius takes another twist with the arrival of Fortinbras. What looked like a duel between the mighty opposites of prince and king was really a resumption of the fight between Old Fortinbras and Old Hamlet. Shakespeare solders the connection by giving fathers and sons—as Belleforest does not—the same names. Another bout is played, and this time Norway wins. Like his father in Saxo and Belleforest, Young Fortinbras agrees that his opponent should have honourable burial ('Go, bid the soldiers shoot' (5.2.347)).[63] The audience knows that, encouraged by the demise of Old Hamlet, Fortinbras was seeking to win back the lands lost by his father. With his uncle old and sick, he has strengthened his claim to the throne of Norway by waging war and winning a patch of ground from the Poles—a victory which, tellingly, recapitulates Old Hamlet's defeat of the Polacks, as well as his victory over Old Fortinbras. At the end of the play, it turns out that the lands that Old Hamlet won in Norway were a Trojan horse in Denmark, giving Young Fortinbras an excuse to claim the whole. 'I have some rights of memory in this kingdom,' he announces, 'Which now to claim my vantage doth invite me' (5.2.332–4). Advantage Fortinbras; checkmate. The language of duelling and gaming often turns on *vantage* (*OED*, 3a).[64] The coup concludes Old Hamlet's and Old Fortinbras's contest. The tragedy of the prince is overtaken by chronicle history. The wager is played out and the audience has its lot.

9
Oaths, Threats, and *Henry V*

Enter Mac Morris and Fluellin. 'By Crist, my Honey Dear,' says the Irishman to his friend, 'it is a great Shame to be talking, and talking, when there is no Wars, nor no Disciplines, nor no Pates to be broken. There ish the *Irish*, and the *French*, the *Turks* ish all at Peace upon one another; and by my Shoul it is a great Shame to be prating, and to be after doing of nothing.' This is, evidently, not quite Shakespeare's MacMorris, but the same character filtered through eighteenth-century politeness and the peace that followed the Treaty of Utrecht, in Charles Molloy's *The Half-Pay Officers* (1720).[1] Molloy is an intriguing figure: an Irishman in London, a Jacobite, and an anti-ministerial journalist. But he matters chiefly to theatre history because he was the first dramatist to put elements of *Henry V* (1599) back on stage after a gap of more than a century. Self-conscious, we may infer, about what it meant to meet the British, to be a stage Irishman in London society, Molloy gave a leading role to Mac Morris, along with a revised Fluellen, in his light, romantic comedy. This is symptomatic of a longer history. The background of *Henry V* in Tyrone's Rebellion (1594–1603) has often been pointed out, and from Orrery's *Henry V* (1664) to the formative, critical arguments between Hazlitt, Dowden, and Yeats,[2] Ireland and its problems have contributed to the renewable energy of this English-patriotic play.

As the author of a book that devolves early modern, anglophone literature,[3] I find it gratifying to discover that when *Henry V* slipped back onto the English stage, it was not initially in the heroic form of Aaron Hill's 1723 adaptation, which cut out the Celtic fringe entirely, but in the main plot of a drama that writes back to the centre from the Jacobite margins of the archipelago, and that, for all its easy ethnic stereotyping, presents sympathetic rewritings of MacMorris and Fluellen. Gallant soldiers and friends, they end *The Half-Pay Officers* marrying wealthy women. Molloy's play is worth revisiting later. What interests me about these characters in Shakespeare is less the appearance of such headline motifs as MacMorris's fiery, Irish temper and Fluellen's patriotic leek than the working of these elements into patterns of speech and action that are both more ubiquitous and more loaded than we are inclined to recognize. Let me start, then, by declaring that what MacMorris originally said about the disciplines of war is, if not exactly a key to Shakespeare's play, so densely consistent with one of its preoccupations as to render him a decisive indicator.

In *Henry V*, Fluellen's invitation to discuss the disciplines comes not in the calm of a long peace but in the context of a crisis in the mines at Harfleur, which MacMorris has been given the responsibility of supervising. Understandably, the ruin of his work by the sounding of a retreat makes the Irishman tetchy:

> By Chrish law, 'tish ill done. The work ish give over, the trumpet sound the retreat. By my hand I swear, and my father's soul, the work ish ill done, it ish give over. I would have blowed up the town, so Chrish save me law, in an hour. O 'tish ill done, 'tish ill done, by my hand 'tish ill done. (3.3.31–5)

An astonishing amount has been written about MacMorris's few lines of dialogue. In our eagerness to answer his later question, 'What ish my nation?' (61),[4] however, we have overlooked the obvious, that this is the heaviest concentration of swearing in all of Shakespeare, swearing both in the formal sense of oaths sworn by *x* or *y* and in the everyday sense of profanity. It is not just repetitively but deeply sworn: this is the only *by Christ* in the corpus, and 'by... my father's soul' is heavy enough for Hamlet. The use of such language in the Folio text—the 'four captains' scene is not in the 1600 quarto—is the more striking because it runs counter to a broader, uneven pattern of expurgation in the Folio, prompted by the Act to Restrain Abuses (1606).[5] MacMorris, moreover, is not supposed to be saying any of this. Profanity was out of order in the field. In the *Lawes and Orders of Warre Established for... Seruice in Ireland*, issued by the Earl of Essex in 1599, we read, 'Let no man blaspheme Gods holy Name, or vse vnlawfull othes or execrations,...vpon paine of losse of his pay, imprisonment, and such further punishment as a Marshall Court shall thinke his offence deserues.'[6]

From Spenser to Molloy and beyond, the Irish were represented as great swearers. The presence of 'By Crist' in *The Half-Pay Officers* is exceptional in its time.[7] It may be a hang-over from Shakespeare, but it is also a sign that profanity was still attributed to the stereotype. Perhaps this does go back to cultural realities. Camden disparagingly observes, '*At every third word it is ordinary with them to lash out an oth, namely* by the Trinity, by God, by

S. Patrick, by S. Brigid, by their Baptisme, by Faith, by the Church, by my God-fathers hand, and by thy hand.'[8] The Irish, it was said—and this is a point to return to—would swear to almost anything except loyalty to the crown, never mind keep that, when they did.[9] Swearing by the hand, as MacMorris does several times, is not just the habit of Hibernian characters from Mackener in *Captaine Thomas Stukeley* to the Irish visitors in Jonson's *Irish Masque*;[10] it is attested by such commentators on Ireland as Spenser, H.C., and Barnabe Rich, who note that swearing by your lord's or your gossip's hand is peculiarly binding for the Irish[11]—a belief that might be traced back to the 'hand of the prince' motif in bardic poetry.[12]

You can find comparable traits in Fluellen, however, who swears 'By Cheshu' (in Molloy as well as Shakespeare), 'God's plud', and 'God's will',[13] and in the Scottish captain, Captain Jamy, who says 'gud feith', 'By the mess', and 'Marry'.[14] This context for MacMorris is as significant as the concentrated profanity of his own lines, not just because of the unreformed or old-fashioned tenor of all these oaths, with their reminders of cultural difference, but because he represents in heightened form a broader presence of swearing in the play. What MacMorris has in common with the other captains he also shares with Pistol, and, in a more exalted way, with King Henry, whose rousing St Crispin's Day speech, and response to Mountjoy's offer of ransom, are stiffened with such phrases as 'by the mass', 'God's will', 'By Jove', 'faith' and 'God's peace'[15]—respectively old, bold, expurgated, mild, and euphemistic oaths. Soldiers were notoriously given to swearing. Remember Jaques on the ages of man: 'Then, a soldier, | Full of strange oaths and bearded like the pard, | Jealous in honour, sudden, and quick in quarrel.'[16]

Oaths can be aggressive and forceful, like blows struck by the word. The rips they tear in civility assert a willingness to do physical damage. It follows with irascible logic that, after assailing Fluellen with oaths, MacMorris threatens to decapitate him as the Irish rebels supposedly did their foes:[17] 'So Chrish save me, I will cut off your head' (3.3.70–1).[18] In other words, an oath can be threatening not just because it insists on a truth and gives no quarter to contradiction, or because it asserts an implacable intent, but because of the associated, linguistic violence of at least incipient profanity. But oaths, vows, and engagements also mortgaged honour, so the use of them was a serious matter. They were significant in relation to status. You could hear MacMorris's swearing, like that of Pistol and Nim, as a vehement demand for respect, a demand that those more routinely honoured are able to make less insistently. Is his ability doubted, as an Irishman? 'By Chrish', he will not accept that. The phatic, Hibernian 'law'[19] that follows 'By Chrish' and 'so Chrish save me' in his opening lines makes a related claim, to be heard out and not interrupted. MacMorris shows his anxiety about this by himself interrupting Fluellen, when the Welshman says 'there is not many of your nation—' and he rushes in with 'What ish my nation?', assuming an insult, or that an insult is coming, before Fluellen has said what he means (3.3.60–1). The question is more about picking a fight than an invitation to discuss national identity; on the scale of quarrelling points set out by Touchstone, it is roughly equivalent to level four, 'The Reproof Valiant'.[20] But swearing is serious, secondly, because honour is not the same as honesty. You swear to something because it might be doubted, though this frequently heightens doubt. You make your honour, your status, the stake of your word, yet honour can be held in the breaking of a word if it brings honour by other means. The military treatises of the time, many of them dedicated to Essex, are clear that soldiers should keep their word, but also that such undertakings could, 'vpon iust cause', be broken.[21]

⋆ ⋆ ⋆

Does binding language bind? As we have already shown, the answers to that question were so complicated during the early modern period and so woven into the fabric of life that plays could appeal to audiences by harking back to a time, allegedly historical, when everything had been much simpler. One such play, of importance to *Henry V*, is the partly Shakespearean *Edward III* (1592–3?). This presents the wars fought against the Scots and the French by the royal grandsire of both the Lancastrian and Yorkist lines. It is a patriotic work, though there is greater sympathy in it for the French than can be found in *Henry V* because its source is Froissart rather than Hall and Holinshed.[22] Thus, one strand of binding language concerns the safe passage to Calais given to the Earl of Salisbury through the agency of his French captive Villiers, who is released on oath to get him a passport. The passport must be respected not just by the Duke of Normandy who issues it but by his father, the King of France. The machinery of honour is tested but it holds. This plot is a foil to the familiar episode in which Edward, despite some reluctance, keeps his promise to the burghers of Calais to spare their city if they surrender with nooses around their necks. More importantly, it echoes an earlier sequence in which Edward attempts to seduce the Countess of Salisbury before setting sail to France.

This sequence is the more fascinating because it is the section of *Edward III* which is generally agreed to have been written by Shakespeare.[23] What his sources gave him was this.[24] Edward, going north to defeat the Scots, falls for the Countess of Salisbury, a young and beautiful noblewoman, who refuses to become his mistress. Without disclosing the source of his problem, Edward makes her father, Warwick, swear to do whatever he can to alleviate his suffering. Warwick duly swears, then feels obliged to keep his oath by urging the king's suit, dishonourably, on his daughter. This is the sort of drama produced by conflicting oaths that is familiar from the first tetralogy of history plays, so it is not surprising to find Shakespeare reduplicating the double bind by having Edward, at the start of the episode, make the Countess swear to help him before revealing what he wants. Because the Countess's husband, the Earl of Salisbury, is still alive, she cannot keep her oath without breaking her marriage vows. The knots of conflicting obligation are only untied, or cut, when the Countess, after the scene with Warwick, pulls out her marriage knives and threatens to take her own life if Edward does not back down. Respecting her constancy, he does.

So many references are made to the victories and sovereign legitimacy of Edward in *Henry V* that a good case can be made for seeing Henry's campaign in France as a re-run of this earlier drama. Whether that makes the young king equally faithful to his word is far more questionable. Conservative critics like to see him as a truth-teller who puts behind him the slipperiness of his father, the Bolingbroke who betrays the oaths he makes not only to Richard II but also to his own supporters about not seeking the crown.[25] They take Harry at his own estimation, as a man 'Who never promiseth but he means to pay'.[26] Even within the *Henry IV* plays (1596–8) this is hard to accept. The prince's first soliloquy shows a subtle intelligence loosening the bonds of language. When he puts his prodigal youth behind him, he says, 'And pay the debt I never promisèd,' he will show the doubting world 'By how much better than my word I am'. The prince is certainly above his word when he solemnly informs the Sheriff ('I do assure you')[27] that Falstaff is not in the Boar's Head tavern, though he is dozing behind an arras. Does he tell his father the truth after he takes the crown from beside him as he sleeps in Jerusalem chamber?[28] Once he becomes king, Henry has more pressing reasons for binding himself only pragmatically to facts and futures constructed on the wheels of political interest. We find him, for instance, early in *Henry V*, leaving the Archbishop of Canterbury to take upon himself, with clerical reticence about swearing by God, the conditional self-curse that traditionally lay at the heart of oaths. After sitting through Canterbury's long, tendentious account of the operation of Salic law, he asks, 'May I with right and conscience make this claim?', and the archbishop declares, 'The sin upon my head, dread sovereign'—may the sin fall upon my head if what I swear be not true (1.2.96–7).

What of binding coercion? Within a few minutes, Henry is declaring: 'by God's help | And yours, the noble sinews of our power, | France being ours, we'll bend it to our awe, | Or break it all to pieces' (222–5). The firmness of this promise, backed by the oath-like appeal, and the constancy with which it is prosecuted, have again attracted the admiration of the king's scholarly apologists. The lines might, rather, remind us that a formal asseveration can be designed less to bind the speaker than to rally good opinion among its auditors—still unsure of Hal's reformation—and to function as a threat. This comes out the more plainly when the assurance is given again over the Dauphin's tun of tennis balls: 'We will in France, by God's grace, play a set | Shall strike his father's crown into the hazard' (262–3). As we noted in the Introduction, oaths, prayers, and promises are rarely just self- or Divinely addressed; they are social utterances, pitched to persuade, cajole—or intimidate. Here the piety of the phrasing ('by God's grace') grotesquely but realistically sustains the lethal import that it should counter. Whether in Eastcheap or before the walls of Harfleur, oaths that are threats can get things done in this play.

Part of the problem is that commentators are being naively unhistorical when they assume that binding language ought always to bind. Consider the French-backed conspiracy, which comes to light in Act 2. According to the Chorus, Cambridge, Scrope, and Grey are 'hollow bosoms, which [France] fills | With treacherous crowns' (2.0.21–2). 'By their hands'—by virtue of their oath, gestural, or handwritten, which blurs into the violent act that they swear to commit *with* their hands—'this grace of kings must die' (28). We have seen that homilies and treatises argue, reasonably enough, that you should not swear to do bad things, such as killing a monarch, but that, if you do swear, you should not keep your word.[29] Henry shows some courage in leaving this conspiracy to ripen while his army goes to Southampton, ready to embark. He might be murdered before he sets foot in France. Or is he just waiting for the evidence he needs to clinch his show trial? When that comes, he makes good use of written bonds to discredit his opponents. Cambridge has, 'for a few light crowns lightly conspired | And sworn unto the practices of France'; Grey 'hath likewise sworn' (2.2.86–90). They go to execution, as they came together, a sworn fraternity.

How threatening the whole plot is, is opened to parodic doubt when, in the scene that follows the Chorus's first mention of it, we are shown, not the three noble conspirators, but Bardolph telling Nim and Pistol that *they* are 'three sworn brothers to France' (2.1.10). They are 'sworn' because soldiers took oaths to their captains, creating the camaraderie that Henry will invoke when he calls himself and his men 'we happy few, we band of brothers' (4.3.60). The Quarto text reads 'bond of brothers', which is not just a spelling variant.[30] Much was made in treatises of the antiquity and virtue of these oaths. As the author of *Certen Instructions, Observations and Orders Militarie*, put it: 'soldiors of euery different sort of weapon,...should vow to liue and die together, as if they were but one...society and Camerada.'[31] How different the reality could be is shown by the quarrelling between Fluellen and MacMorris, but also, much earlier, by the row in Eastcheap between the 'three sworn brothers'.

Pistol, the audience gathers, has married Mistress Quickly, despite Nim being 'troth-plight to her' (2.1.16–17). Bardolph tries to contain the fallout from her contradictory vows by offering to buy the rivals breakfast, then urging and cajoling. Oaths and insults, oaths as threats, fly. 'Faith', 'by my troth', 'Pish', 'pardie' (12–43). Money is offered, withdrawn, and haggled over. The quarrel about Mistress Quickly turns out to be caught up in a gambling debt left unpaid (a wager, another verbal bond). Modern audiences are likely to be left with a general impression of roistering, but those in the Curtain or the Globe would have picked up on the variety and gradation of binding words and actions (waving swords, shaking hands), the swagger of colourful oaths (such as Pistol's 'by Gad's lugs').[32] All this is consistent with what we know about Elizabethan quarrelling, but it is also completely in line with the play's preoccupation with binding language.

'Hear me what I say', cries Bardolph, drawing his sword,

> He that strikes the first stroke, I'll run him up to the hilts, as I am a soldier.
> PISTOL An oath of mickle might, and fury shall abate.
> [*They sheathe their swords*]
> [*To* NIM] Give me thy fist, thy forefoot to me give.
> Thy spirits are most tall.
> NIM I will cut thy throat one time or other, in fair terms, that is the humour of it.
> PISTOL *Couple a gorge*,
> That is the word. I thee defy again. (56–65)

This is thickly embedded in the idiom of the play. 'As I am a soldier' will later be used by Henry when he threatens Harfleur with an oath.[33] In the same line, he says 'defy' to the citizens: 'Defy us to our worst. For as I am a soldier…' (3.3.82). The word does not just mean 'resist, affront'; as we have seen, etymologically and technically it implies defeasance, a breaking of faith.[34] 'Forefoot' plays on 'forfeit', something *given up*, or *risked*, as a fine, when the word is broken in oath-breaking.[35] As for 'I will cut thy throat' and '*Couple a gorge*', these do not just loosely recall Henry's threats against the French; they will literally become his 'word' at Agincourt.

'The word' is tortured in Pistol's mouth. The formulaic nature of his asseveration, which helps give it authority as a speech act, slides away between French and English (as so often in *Henry V*) and leaves the audience to work out what '*Couple a gorge*' means. 'By this sword,' swears Bardolph, threatening those about him, 'he that makes the first thrust, I'll kill him. By this sword, I will.' To which Pistol responds, 'Sword is an oath, and oaths must have their course' (2.1.89–91). Does he really think that ''s word', an abbreviated form of 'his word' or 'by God's word', is the same as 'sword'? Can a man be bound by an oath the meaning of which he does not understand? This is the sort of question that fascinated casuists.[36] But then, how fixed can anyone's word be in this play of comic language lessons and Babylonish signifiers, where 'pardie' counts as English, 'permafoy' counts as French,[37] and 'Cheshu' sounds bizarrely like the joke Welsh staple, cheese? As in *Henry V* as a whole, oaths turn out to be potent when they are backed by force—your sword *is* your most binding word—and helped along, sealed, by money as payment or earnest. Nim has repeatedly asked Pistol for the eight shillings he won of him at betting. 'A noble shalt thou have, and present pay,' Pistol expansively promises: 'Give me thy hand' (2.1.95–102). Nim cannot be happy that a noble is two shillings short of eight. On the other hand, it does sound good. A noble, like a crown, is the sort of word for a coin that can make a mercenary settlement seem like the acquisition of honour. And this is but a foretaste of the 'profit' that Pistol says Nim will share when he becomes 'sutler' to the camp (100–1). It seems worth a handshake. As deals go, it is as viable as the credit most people had to get by on[38] in the early modern economy.

* * *

What, though, is the relationship between Eastcheap and the historical plot? Pistol may be unreliable, but is not Harry constant? Let us test his truthfulness by focusing on another scene which presents three 'brothers' in arms: John Bates, Alexander Court, and Michael Williams. In their encounter with the disguised Henry, the night before Agincourt, Bates and Williams talk about the justice of the king's cause. For Williams, the king has a heavy reckoning to make if his cause is not good because soldiers leave wives and children in need, debts unpaid, die swearing and calling for a surgeon. Henry's reply is tangential. A king is no more responsible for the good or bad death of his soldiers, he says, than a father whose son taking his merchandise sinfully miscarries at sea, or a master who sends his servant on a journey only for the servant to be murdered. Every soldier's soul, he concludes, is his own (4.1.118–72). As a contribution to just war theory this is unimpressive. Yet again, the king offloads blame for the effects of his military policy. The level of risk in war is much higher than that of even an early modern journey; soldiers are recruited to kill or be killed. In any case, his conclusion ignores the problem that Williams has presented, about the lack of provision for wives, children, and creditors.

Bates's response is surprisingly tractable. And what provokes Williams to scorn is Henry's further, manipulative observation, 'I myself heard the King say he would not be ransomed.' When the soldier, realistically, replies, 'when our throats are cut, he may be ransomed, and we ne'er the wiser', Henry declares, 'If I live to see it, I will never trust his word after', and Williams mocks the thought that his private displeasure would count: 'You may as well go about to turn the sun to ice with fanning in his face with a peacock's feather. You'll never trust his word after! Come, 'tis a foolish saying.' This becomes 'a quarrel' between them. The king asks for 'any gage' to wear, and, hands being important to bonds in this play, Williams (in an empty handshake) exchanges gloves with him. 'This will I also wear in my cap', he says: 'If ever thou come to me and say, after tomorrow, "This is my glove", by this hand I will take thee a box on the ear.' To this Henry promises, 'If ever I live to see it, I will challenge it...though I take thee in the King's company.' 'Keep thy word,' the soldier urges (177–205).

The problem posed by the scene is the same as the one dramatized in the confrontation between Bagot and Aumerle, in *Richard II* (see p. 218), of how contestants so unequal can exchange gages, uphold an engagement. The difference in rank troubles but also indurates Henry in the soliloquy that follows the quarrel. 'O hard condition, ... subject to the breath | Of every fool, whose sense no more can feel | But his own wringing' (215–18). Elizabethan audiences would have been less shocked than we are by that unfair description of Williams, but Henry's pique must have registered. They would also have been alert, as we are not, to the link between the king's ransom and his gage. As we saw with the help of a legal glossary in Chapter 8 (p. 224), a *gage* is 'Something of value deposited to ensure the performance of some action, and liable to forfeiture...; a pawn, pledge, security.'[39] It is a pledge held to ransom, like a prisoner. And ransom is caught up with honour, as in the Villiers plot of *Edward III*, but also with hard cash. This the play will pursue not just in the Henry–Williams quarrel but Pistol's ransoming of Le Fer.

Encountering Williams, after the victory at Agincourt, the king asks who gave him the glove in his cap: 'An't please your majesty, a rascal, that swaggered with me last night—who, if a live, and ever dare to challenge this glove, I have sworn to take him a box o'th' ear; or if I can see my glove in his cap—which he swore, as he was a soldier, he would wear if a lived—I will strike it out soundly' (4.7.114–18). What was an engagement has now become an oath. 'What think you, Captain Fluellen?' asks the king: 'Is it fit this soldier keep his oath?' (119–20). In Shakespeare's late plays, this sort of retrospective promotion of a binding word tends to be the product of the 1606 Act, which made full-blooded oaths harder to script. Here, though, something more interesting is going on. Swearing may incline to formal, ritual encapsulation, as though Divinely or self-empowering, but its potency turns out to depend on the interpretative slant of the agents involved, their witnesses, their status and intentions. For Williams the quarrel is a point of honour; for the king it has shrunk into a jest. Compare the young Harry in *Richard II*, reportedly saying that he will wear a whore's glove as a favour and unhorse any challengers (5.3.16–19). That declaration was sympathetic because it mocked an outdated code. Here the scenario is less palatable because Williams's fidelity and honour are discounted. Given the difference in rank, which is the issue at stake in the quarrel, the soldier can only find a viable opponent if the king passes on his gage. Which he duly does to Fluellen.

* * *

In his preface to *The Half-Pay Officers*, Molloy declares that 'The Character of Fluellin has been esteem'd, (next to that of Sir *John Falstaff*) the best and most humorous, that *Shakespear* ever wrote.' He was certainly a popular figure in the mid-to-late eighteenth century,[40] until concerns about low stereotyping, and, it may be, anxiety about British–Irish disharmony during the French revolutionary and Napoleonic wars, reduced the role and drove his quarrel with MacMorris from the stage.[41] More recently, critics have regarded Fluellen less as an entertaining, walk-on Welshman and more like the subversive Falstaff.[42] This revisionism can go too far. He is more often the butt of comedy than Falstaff would allow himself to become. But his uses by Shakespeare are disruptive, not least in the Henry–Williams plot and its successor, Pistol and the leek. He is also more profane and turbulent than older discussions give him credit for, coming into the play, as he means to go on, with a fulsome 'God's plud',[43] and starting the scene with MacMorris by subverting the disciplines of war, when he refuses to obey an order from the Duke of Gloucester to come to the front line to discuss the state of the mines (3.3.1–4).

The glove in Williams's hat is half a handshake, which can move around the action. This forfeit, standing in for a 'forefoot', migrates from the king's hat to Fluellen's, because, as Williams had predicted, a private displeasure cannot be pursued against a monarch. Does the gage have its own course to run, regardless of the participants ('oaths must have their course', as Pistol put it), or does it mean something different, when on Fluellen's hat not Henry's? In one sense, Henry has ensured that the gage means as much as it can on the Welshman's cap of what it would mean on his own. The two have already discussed, in the wake of Agincourt (4.7.89–96), how the king wears a leek in his hat on St David's Day, like Fluellen, to assert his mock-Tudor Welshness (he was born in Monmouth). Henry now arranges for his countryman to become a down-market version of himself by wearing the leek-like glove in his cap. Gloves were often given and exchanged as tokens of amity.[44] Hence the whore's glove in young Harry's cap. There is a potential for affectionate respect in the king's plot with the gage.

So much for the shell of a situation which could have been about good fellowship, the populism of a royal general, but which, in its execution, is problematic. Of the glove accepted from Williams, Henry tells Fluellen: 'If any man challenge this, he is a friend to Alençon, and an enemy to our person' (143–4). This is ironic enough given the king's impending alliance with the French, but it is, more simply, mendacious, and it only partly absolves the king in the eyes of the audience that it shows the Prince Hal in him wanting to come out and play. It is not just that, as Henry tells Warwick and Gloucester, 'The glove . . . is the soldier's. I by bargain should | Wear it myself' (157–60), but that the eventual showdown with Williams (4.8.36–56) could be managed with better grace. The king 'thou-s' Williams, calls him 'soldier', 'sirrah', and 'fellow', never asking his name. His fidelity to the quarrel becomes a proof of his guilt, when, indeed, the king's handling of it shows Williams to have been correct about rank and the absence of fellowship.

It would be humourless to pick through the dialogue, accusing Henry of hypocrisies which are also, and which can be played up as, jokes between the king and the audience. But when Henry pulls rank, putting on the royal *we*, there is menace as well as mockery: 'It was ourself thou didst abuse.' And when he gives the command, 'Here, Uncle Exeter, fill this glove with crowns', the gesture is troublingly reminiscent of the filling of the hollow bosoms of the conspirators with treacherous crowns.[45] It is, in a way, a measure of Henry's achievement at Agincourt that Williams's 'treason' (as Fluellen calls it) is unreal, as Scrope's was not, and that he can now afford to reward, or buy off, what minor threat there is to his authority.[46] But Williams's resistance to taking a shilling from Fluellen, in the sequence which immediately follows, is a sign of the resentment that is left when the king breaks his word.

Between his encounter with the three soldiers and the comedy played out with Williams, Henry repeats the promise which the soldier said could not be proven. When Mountjoy comes to him, for the second time, before Agincourt and offers him, before his troops, ransom, he replies: 'Come thou no more for ransom, gentle herald. | They shall have none, I swear, but these my joints' (4.3.123–4). Is this, then, definitive? Has he been reinforced in his determination by Williams's scepticism? Mountjoy says that he will not renew the offer, but Henry, significantly, adds, 'I fear thou wilt once more come for a ransom' (129). If so, his swearing is not final. He will have another chance, if in the course of the battle he ends up circled by French steel, huddled on the stage beneath the royal standard. And, of course, his very success means that we shall never know whether Williams was wrong. We can, though, gauge the likeliness of his being right by the way the glove intrigue ends. Henry's willingness to pay the soldier off shows that he is indeed prepared to break his word to the troops and buy himself out of a quarrel, to avoid injury by paying a ransom.

This implies that the Williams intrigue is a subplot to the main historical action, a Shakespearean addition to Holinshed, but the layering of oaths in the play goes further down than that, since the little drama involving Fluellen and Williams reverberates hollowly in the sequence in which the Welshman makes Pistol eat a leek. Before we get to that scene, often orphaned in accounts of the play, we need to recall an earlier sequence in which ransoming figures. We also need to remember, as we consider Pistol's seizure of Le Fer, that, as Hall and Holinshed acknowledge, many Englishmen went to France during the Hundred Years War to make money from ransoming and pillage.[47] Sir John Fastolf's followers (historians tell us) became rich.[48] When Pistol leaves Eastcheap, he reminds Mistress Quickly of what we have already seen in his reconciliation with Nim, that money seals the deal:

> Look to my chattels and my movables.
> Let senses rule. The word is 'Pitch and pay'.
> Trust none, for oaths are straws, men's faiths are wafer-cakes,
> And Holdfast is the only dog, my duck.
> Therefore *caveto* be thy counsellor.[49]
> Go, clear thy crystals.—Yokefellows in arms,
> Let us to France, like horseleeches, my boys,
> To suck, to suck, the very blood to suck! (2.3.40–7)

This is a theme that continues. When Pistol assaults Le Fer, calling him 'Seigneur Dew' because he misunderstands his French oath (4.4.7), he thinks only of cash. Wrenching language, he finds money everywhere. When Le Fer speaks of '*moi*', Pistol assumes that this is a denomination of coin; '*bras*' he hears as 'brass', and is insulted to be offered base currency (12–18). He turns against the Frenchman the threat levelled at him by Nim: '*couper la gorge,* [*permafoy*]'. Only when he is offered *écus*, which the boy translates as crowns, is he satisfied. Molloy replaces Pistol with a character called Culverin. It is true that Pistol's name primarily suggests a firearm ('Pistol's cock is up' (2.1.46)), but a *pistole* was also a Spanish gold coin. He is the incarnation of acquisitiveness. Yet he then kills his prisoner, with whatever degree of reluctance. The scene shows us Henry's willingness to break the terms of an engagement between Pistol and Le Fer which everything suggests Pistol would keep. 'The French have reinforced their scattered men,' Henry declares, 'Then every soldier kill his prisoners. | Give the word through' (4.6.36–8). To which Q adds Pistol's cry, 'Couple gorge,'[50] a reading that is the more plausible given that, seven lines into the next scene, Gower happily declares that 'the King most worthily hath caused every soldier to cut his prisoner's throat'. Whether or not we see the French prisoners killed on stage, this is a shocking moment, often and rightly described as a war crime.[51] It is telling that, when Henry commands Pistol and his fellows to break their gages, he echoes the ensign's line in Eastcheap, '*Couple a gorge*, | That is the word.' He turns an oath into an order (two strong meanings of *word*), a low threat into military policy.

In *The Half-Pay Officers*, the boastful, ineffectual Culverin is beaten on two separate occasions, by Mac Morris and by Fluellin. The Fluellen–Pistol plot in *Henry V* was evidently too inviting for Molloy to resist, and repeating it did have the merit of underscoring his point that the Irishman and the Welshman are in accord. In Shakespeare the beating of Pistol is less superficially farcical, and it is calculated to reflect on Henry's binding-language plot with Williams. The leek is agreed by Fluellen and Henry to be a 'memorable honour' of the 'good service in a garden' done by Welsh soldiers during the French campaign of the exemplary Edward III (4.7.89–95). However true that point of history, Pistol reportedly dishonours this badge or pledge of achievement by bringing Fluellen bread and salt and inviting him, on St David's Day, to eat the leek in his cap. In 5.1, Fluellen strikes back, cudgelling Pistol in front of Gower. 'By Jesu', he thunders, 'I will make him eat some part of my leek, or I will peat his pate four days and four nights.'[52]

How does this mesh with the Williams plot? First, it shows Fluellen yet again standing in for the king. In the conflict with Williams he was the king's proxy in wearing the glove. In the Pistol plot, he defends the honour of the leek that Henry, self-amusingly, wears as proto-Tudor propaganda, which has the additional advantage of linking his campaign with that of Edward III. Second, more visually and immediately, the leafy leek in Fluellen's cap resembles the glove worn earlier. This makes play with the interchangeability of gages that goes back to the scene in *Richard II* where the gloves pile up on stage and Aumerle has to borrow one. The pledge of honour remains, but problematized by the displacement of the object, as the gage becomes a leek, much as it was problematized by the displacement of the bearer, Henry to Fluellen. Now, moreover, the leek becomes the mocking incarnation of a threat that the promissory oath as word-object always entails. As Pistol is forced to eat, the vegetable, or twist of green paper, combines sacred word with punitive thing.[53]

To bring home the satirical echo of the sequence in which Williams is paid and required to stifle his desire to thump Fluellen if not the king, Fluellen contemptuously gives Pistol a groat for plaster to heal his head. 'Yes, verily, and in truth you shall take it', he insists, 'or I have another leek in my pocket which you shall eat' (5.1.55–6). Leeks, like gloves, it seems, come in pairs.[54] The groat is a gift as insult, a reward that is really a punishment, in a spirit of beggary but also as earnest. Insult the leek again, the groat-pledge declares,[55] and you know what will happen. The bond is tied by a threat. What of the modest oath, 'verily, and in truth'? This is almost puritanical in its mildness, compared with Fluellen's customary *Cheshus* and *'s pluds*. In performance, this will strike us as an ingenuously mocking reminder that the vehemence of an oath is likely to be in inverse proportion to the power of the person uttering it. Like those of the assertive MacMorris, Pistol's oaths have been colourful ('by Gad's lugs') as well as unreliable. Now they are empty and stifled, choked on what disempowers him. 'By this leek,' he protests, 'I will most horribly revenge— [FLUELLEN *threatens him*] I eat and eat—I swear' (42–3). Those of Fluellen, by contrast, can be minimal because they carry a big stick. The cudgel first threatens Pistol and then enacts the Welshman's speech acts. '*Quiet* thy cudgel', Pistol cries, 'thou dost see I eat' (46).

Yet the ensign has the last word, which is, predictably enough, about unreliable oaths. Once Fluellen has left the stage, and Gower has finished rebuking him, Pistol tells the audience that he is old and is done with fighting. He will steal back to England and turn to stealing purses, 'And patches will I get unto these cudgelled scars, | And swear I got them in the Gallia wars' (79–80). The lines may well recall Gower's earlier dismissal of Pistol, now back in our minds, as the sort of cowardly soldier who, once he returns to England, claims the credit due to valour by lacing his discourse with 'new-tuned oaths' (3.6.69–71). More disconcertingly, they echo the buoyant St Crispin's Day speech, where Henry imagines a veteran of Agincourt, grown old, back in England, showing 'his scars' (however acquired) and 'remember[ing], with advantages, | What feats he did that day' (4.3.47–51). Should God, or report, be credited with the magnitude of the victory at Agincourt? Can the chronicles be believed when they draw on the testimony of such veterans as Pistol? Shakespeare does not follow the lead of those among his contemporaries who highlighted the military factors that made it convincingly possible for the king's small force of seasoned men to defeat a much larger army[56] but reproduces with ironical wonder the most astonishing of the casualty figures he found in Holinshed.[57] He gives us the word of History demonstrably 'with advantages' when it comes to the Gallia wars. Pistol's resilient epilogue provides a thought-provoking, troublesome link into the final scene of the play, where oaths are again at issue.

★ ★ ★

The last act of *Henry V* has not had many friends. Dr Johnson objected to its 'emptiness and narrowness'.[58] The Fluellen–Pistol scene, the wooing of Princess Catherine, and the treaty arrangements with France are prepared for in the body of the play, but they can seem supplementary. They will not do so, however, if we recognize the importance to the play of oaths and threats, of oaths becoming threats. If there is 'emptiness and narrowness', it comes from what has happened to binding language over the course of the first four acts.

There is no point in lingering over Henry's courtship of the princess, thick though it is with the ploys and coercions of assertory obtestation and engagement. The king slips fluently through different modes, from the 'I'faith' and 'Marry' appropriate to conversation with a princess to bluff, mock-English directness: 'Give me your answer, i'faith do, and so clap hands and a bargain' (5.2.98–129). This is the Henry who shamelessly declares, 'I have no cunning in protestation—only downright oaths, which I never use till urged, nor never break for urging' (141–2), but there is—as one would expect—a great deal of flexibility in his plainness. It is shown, for instance, in the way promising is recast not as a dragon at the gate of the future but a way to make consent easier in the moment: ''tis hereafter to know, but now to promise' (199). The king clearly remembers how to be better than his word.

Throughout the play, Henry's adroitness in the use of binding language throws into relief the stiltedness of the French. When roused, they are given to such banalities as '*O Dieu vivant!*', '*O diable!*', and '*O Seigneur!*' (3.5.5, 4.5.1–2). The limit of their eloquence is 'By faith and honour!' (3.5.27). The fixedness of the phrasing insists not just on their foreignness (as in a cartoon) but on the rigidity of their code,[59] rendering faintly absurd the momentousness of the utterance.[60] Yet however comparatively engaging, Henry's versatility has a threatening assurance. Claiming to know Catherine's mind, he directs her to 'avouch the thoughts of your heart with the looks of an empress' (219). Kissing her lips, against French custom, to plight the troth she is slow to give, compromises her into consent. It is true that the peace of the kingdoms is advanced through this playful, iron-fisted courtship. Yet the binding language of the sequence cannot, by now, reassure us. Oaths are not magic spells that secure truths and futures. Vows, articles, ransoms, and gages function in relation to larger forces, subject to displacement, performance, and error.

What, then, of the oaths, associated with the Anglo-French treaty, with which the whole play ends? Before addressing them, let me return, as anticipated, to Irish oaths, then introduce Sir Francis Bacon, not as the author of Shakespeare's plays but as someone who often helps us understand them.

First, recall that allusions to Ireland accumulate in the fifth act of *Henry V*, starting from the reference in the chorus to the hope that our general, Essex or possibly Mountjoy,[61] will return with 'rebellion broachèd on his sword', continuing with the Queen of France's greeting of Henry as 'brother Ireland', a glance at English sovereignty in Ireland after 1541 that cannot be dismissed as a slip of Shakespeare's pen given the king's later promise that, by marrying him, Catherine will become queen of England, Ireland, and France.[62] The effect of these allusions is to alert audiences to the parallels between Henry's war in France and the hoped-for conclusion of the Tudor wars in Ireland.

The divergences are obvious enough; but Henry does lead like Essex an expeditionary force into sieges and guerrilla warfare, facing a daunting enemy whose otherness is already intimate. And we should not miss the contextual pressure of the giving, taking, and breaking of oaths in the Irish wars as instruments of faction, policy, and terror. Accounts are full of this. Lord Deputies like Sir Henry Sidney swear and are reported as swearing that they will hunt down rebels; the Irish conspire against them with oaths.[63] When they are defeated, Sidney notes in his *Memoir*, the rebels submit 'with oath and hostage', 'promise and oath', 'charge and oath', 'pledges or prisoners', 'upon [their] bond', 'sw[earing] allegiance to her majesty'; yet their word is unreliable, despite what gages they give, not least because the tide of war makes it so easy for them to turn.[64]

Sidney spent decades in Wales, as president of the Council in the Marches, managing the likes of Fluellen, but when he wrote his *Memoir*, in the hope of recompense from Elizabeth, it was the relatively few years he had committed to the refractory men beyond the Pale that took up his attention. Men like the MackMorris, whose English surname was Prendergast, who submitted to Sidney in Galway;[65] or the notorious M'Maurice born James fitz Maurice Fitzgerald (d. 1579), who rebelled twice against the crown before he was killed in a quarrel and decapitated by his own men lest his head fall into the hands of the English;[66] or Padraigín FitzMaurice Mac Muiris, 17th baron of Lixnaw and Kerry (son of the sometimes loyal, sometimes rebellious Thomas FitzMaurice), who accompanied Sidney to London as a youth, but who fought against Essex's army in 1599 (while *Henry V* was being performed) and died in 1600;[67] or his son Thomas, who joined the rising against the Munster Plantation and held out until, in April 1603, we read: 'None in Munster are in action, saving M'Morris, whose force is but seven horse and 12 foot, and they have fed on garrans' flesh [horseflesh] these eight days' (by 1604, he was at James's court, making his submission, though his loyalty remained in doubt).[68] I am not about to argue that Shakespeare's Irish captain should really be called Prendergast, as they say Falstaff should be Oldcastle. My point is rather that the presence of MacMorris, the name and its reputation as well as his fluent, unreliable swearing, which aggressively smothers over whatever disservice he has done at the mines, and which leads into his rebel-like threat to chop off Fluellen's head, shows an interest on Shakespeare's part, heightened by the Irish wars, in enemies sworn into friends, who might then turn back into enemies, and in oaths of fealty to the crown, as a seal of victory that comes unstuck, once the power of binding words is unsupported by swords.

The contextual pressure from Ireland would have had less effect on the last act of *Henry V* if it did not so readily cohere with how binding language was regarded—after Machiavelli, as it were[69]—when it came to affairs of state. In his essay about the Styx, the river in the underworld which the classical gods swore by, because it was crooked and fatal, Bacon declares:

> This Fable seemes to pointe at the Leagues and Pactes of Princes, of which more truely then opportunely may bee said, that bee they neuer so strongly confirmed with the solemnity and religion of an oath, yet are for the most part of no validity: insomuch that they are made rather with an eye to reputation, and report and ceremonie, then to faith, security and effect....[I]t is an easie thing for Princes to defend and couer their vnlawfull desires and vnfaithfull vowes, with many outwardly seeming faire pretexts,...Therefore there is no true and proper thing made choice of, for the confirmation of faith, and that no celestiall power neither, but is indeed *Necessitie* (a great God to great Potentates) the perill also of State, and the Communication of profite.[70]

True safety comes, he concludes, from military superiority. Oaths, agreements, and pacts are subject to the necessity of the state.

At the end of the anonymous *Famous Victories of Henry the Fifth*, a play well known to Shakespeare, Henry requires the King of France and the Dauphin to swear fealty on his sword. As we saw in the Introduction (pp. 36–7), it was a moment celebrated enough for Nashe to remember in *Pierce Penilesse*. In Shakespeare, this does not happen.[71] It may be that by Act 5, with his army gone back to England, Henry can no longer project his power—the sword behind the word—strongly enough to seize the crown,[72] but we might also feel that the manipulativeness of rule, the Henry–Williams plot, and the dissonant voices of Eastcheap have brought too many doubts to bear on the authority of oaths. A lot of words have been given and broken since Hereford swore to Richard that he would not conspire against him in exile.[73] Henry tells Burgundy that, on his wedding day, 'we'll take your oath, | And all the peers', for surety of our leagues'.[74] But we do not see the oath uttered. And a note of caution is sounded in Henry's next, final couplet of the play, as he and the French royal house come together, without joining, on the stage: 'Then shall I swear to Kate, and you to me, | And may our oaths well kept and prosp'rous be.' The epilogue reminds audiences that the hope was vain, that the enemy's oaths were broken (as Henry Sidney and Bacon would have predicted), and that the English nobility under Henry VI 'lost France and made his England bleed, | Which oft our stage hath shown'.

10

Troilus, Cressida, and Constancy

Dryden took a firm line with Shakespeare in the Preface to his adaptation of *Troilus and Cressida* (1679):

> 'Tis true, that in his later Plays he had worn off somewhat of the rust; but the Tragedy which I have undertaken to correct was, in all probability, one of his first endeavours on the Stage.
>
> The Original story was Written by one *Lollius*, a *Lombard*, in *Latin* verse, and Translated by *Chaucer* into *English*: intended I suppose a Satyr on the Inconstancy of Women:.... For the Play it self, the Author seems to have begun it with some fire; the Characters of *Pandarus* and *Thersites*, are promising enough; but as if he grew weary of his task, after an Entrance or two, he lets 'em fall: and the latter part of the Tragedy is nothing but a confusion of Drums and Trumpets, Excursions and Alarms. The chief persons, who give name to the Tragedy, are left alive: *Cressida* is false, and is not punish'd.[1]

This is wrong in almost every particular, from the early dating of *Troilus* (written *c.*1601–2), through the identification of 'the Original story' (Lollius is Chaucer's invention) and the quality of *Troilus and Criseyde* (too sympathetic to be a satire), to the notion that Shakespeare lets Pandarus and Thersites 'fall' (they persistently, even stubbornly, figure in the final acts of the play). It is also, as we shall see, wrong about the structure of the 'latter part of the Tragedy', and simplistic, to put it mildly, about Cressida being 'false, and... not punish'd'.

As usual, however, even when misguided, Dryden's criticism is substantial and trenchant enough to be worth thinking about. *Troilus* does work with and against received ideas about 'the Inconstancy of Women', and it is instructive to see how extensive Dryden's revisions had to be in order to free Cressida from the taint. In his version she is driven to show her constancy by stabbing herself in front of Troilus and Diomedes on the battlefield of the stage, though the outcome is still problematic and contrary to poetic justice ('Cressida,' we might cavil, 'is constant, and is not rewarded'). To make Cressida's purity more convincing, Dryden also felt obliged to rewrite all the female roles in the play. That of Andromache, Hector's loyal wife, is enlarged, Helen (unfaithful to Menelaus) never appears, and neither does the troublesome Cassandra, whose willingness to contradict Hector we encountered at the start of this book.

What of the inconstancy that Dryden imputes to the play and its author? It may be misguided to say that Pandarus and Thersites start 'promisingly' and are then dropped, but the play *is* dominated by characters who start with heroic promise and disappoint expectation (e.g. Troilus and Hector), who are introduced but then 'let fall' (Calchas, Antenor), and of plots that lead nowhere (notably, Ulysses' attempts to get Achilles to fight). Moreover, while some of the characters show an all-too-human inconsistency, others (e.g. Thersites and Ajax) are consistent with a reductiveness or stupidity that gives constancy a bad name. Dryden irons out these irregularities, recasting Hector, Troilus, and Achilles as the protagonists of heroic tragedy. He knits together plot-lines that Shakespeare left parallel or broken, and unpacks motives. Driving all this is a precept that he twice cites from Horace in his Preface: 'The last property of manners is, that they be constant, and equal, that is, maintain'd the same through the whole design: ... *Servetur ad imum, qualis ab incæpto processerat, et sibi constet*.'[2]

Dryden's neoclassical elision of constancy in the representation of manners with the representation of characters as constant gives his play a theatrical (and verse) dynamic entirely different from Shakespeare's. He leaves scope for villainy, virtuous dissimulation, and tragic misunderstanding, but the truth of Cressida's truth is never, for the audience, in doubt. The tragedy is that Troilus takes so long to recognize it. Hence the subtitle of the adaptation: *Truth Found too Late*. In Shakespeare, by contrast, Cressida's dilemmas are caught up in wider patterns of reversal, flux, and inconsistency, a proliferation of effect that, in the verse writing as well as the dramaturgy, may be, as Hazlitt gratefully complains, 'too various and flexible; too full of transitions, of glancing lights, of salient points. If Chaucer followed up his subject too doggedly, perhaps Shakespear was too volatile and heedless.'[3] As critics are now quick to register, not just Cressida's truth to Troilus but truth itself is relativized and fragmented by multiple points of view, disruptive scurrility, the ironizing effect of multiple, warped plot-parallels, and the situational ambiguities of language.

This is not to say that 'the Inconstancy of Women' dissolves as an issue. For Troilus, quite the contrary. The fear that Cressida might be subject to the general mutability of attachment and valuation leads him perversely to woo her with a massive declaration of doubt:

> O that I thought it could be in a woman—
> As, if it can, I will presume in you—
> To feed for aye her lamp and flames of love,
> To keep her constancy in plight and youth,
> Outliving beauty's outward, with a mind
> That doth renew swifter than blood decays;... (3.2.145–50)

Hearing these lines onstage, any Cressida must be taken aback. But this is only one of several moments where Troilus—fearful of going the way of Menelaus—insults Cressida by harping on this theme. He is, of course, the heir of centuries of medieval and early modern misogyny that genders constancy and fickleness on physiological grounds.[4] 'To bee borne a manchilde', announces Thomas Wilson, in a treatise on *The Arte of Rhetorique* that Shakespeare drew on when writing the Sonnets and *A Lover's Complaint*, 'declares a courage, grauitie, and constancie. To be borne a woman, declares weakenes of spirite, neshenes of body, and fikilnesse of mynde.'[5] Beyond that, however, Shakespeare classicizes the Troilus that he found in Caxton, Lydgate (probably),[6] and Chaucer by giving him the ancient, Stoic regard for constancy that was becoming fashionable in the late sixteenth century.

Relevant sources are not hard to find. There are Lipsius' *Two Bookes of Constancie*, translated into English in 1595, which Shakespeare may have read, and Montaigne's *Essaies*, which he consulted around the time he was composing *Hamlet* and *Troilus* (*c.*1600–2). The *Essaies* are drawn to constancy in rather conventional, Stoical terms, but there is also a sceptical recognition that the constancy of humankind is a slow, '*wauering dance*', that we are inherently inconstant.[7] The Stoic ideal of constancy is explored, and gendered, in the Roman play written just before *Troilus and Cressida*, where Brutus advocates 'formal constancy', Caesar claims to be 'constant as the Northern Star', and Portia, Brutus' wife, has to fight against her sex to prove and claim the virtue:

> I have made strong proof of my constancy,
> Giving myself a voluntary wound
> Here in the thigh. Can I bear that with patience,
> And not my husband's secrets?[8]

This style or model of constancy did reach Shakespeare with a Senecan accent. But Roman Stoicism has its roots in third-century BC Athens, and it was imposed on Greek texts of even greater antiquity by Renaissance scholars, including Chapman in his versions of Homer. The origins of the Greek council scene, for instance, in *Troilus and Cressida* 1.3, lie in two of the seven books of the *Iliad* translated by Chapman in 1598, and especially the sequence in Book IX where Diomedes says that Agamemnon lacks 'fortitude' when he proposes giving up the siege of Troy. It is true, he says, that Jupiter has been 'Inconstant', in breaking his promise to the Greeks that they would conquer Troy, but this is a test of resolve, not a reason to be 'inconstant' in turn: 'Inconstant *Saturns* son hath giuen inconstant spirites to thee.'[9] This is how the equivalent speech, reattributed to Agamemnon, begins in the play:

> Princes, what grief hath set these jaundice on your cheeks?
> The ample proposition that hope makes
> In all designs begun on earth below
> Fails in the promised largeness....
> Do you with cheeks abashed behold our works,
> And call them shames, which are indeed naught else
> But the protractive trials of great Jove
> To find persistive constancy in men? (1.3.1–20)

This could be inflated further. Dryden, prizing constancy, rewrites the speech yet again to have Agamemnon praise 'heroique Constancy in Men' (1.1.10). But Shakespeare's general is, if not out of conviction then out of policy, sufficiently Stoic. The 'promised largeness' of success is no longer, as in Chapman's Homer, Jupiter's promise of victory to the Greeks, but the incorrigible, misplaced optimism of man, to which the philosopher must not succumb. Only through constancy, trial, and proof in the teeth of misfortune will the fine metal of manhood ('rich in virtue and unminglèd' (29)) be found. This is a commonplace of Neostoic thought,[10] and it leaves its mark on Troilus. In a play where love and war are deeply entangled and awkwardly fused, this classical, Stoic-inflected mentality informs his outlook as a lover. It shapes, or at least rationalizes, a defensive, unhealthy desire to be proven in his constancy and to see Cressida put to the test.

Troilus speaks of Cressida *keeping* her constancy, not just to characterize a virtue maintained through active perseverance, but as a woman would 'keep' a promise. This implication is brought out by 'in plight and youth' (3.2.148). Constancy is like (as it would feed into) a faith, a troth, a plight. The phrasing shows, among other things, that Troilus is hankering for the security of binding language that, in the first part of the scene, Cressida has conspicuously not offered. Recall, from the Introduction, the widely known sentence in Cicero's *De Officiis*: 'Fundamentum autem est iustitiae fides, id est dictorum conventorumque constantia et veritas.'[11] This was translated by schoolboys: 'But the foundation of Iustice is faithfulnesse: that is to say, a constancy and truth of words and couenants.'[12] Constancy is a quality of mind, 'stedfastnesse' in Grimald's translation of Cicero's *constantia*,[13] but also a property of words and covenants when they are uttered with truth. Out of that comes a rarer, but indicative, meaning of *constancy*, which leaves its trace in *Troilus*: a firmness of thought that yields certainty.[14] Steadfastness is esteemed in the early modern 'economy of obligation' because it makes for predictability and thus reliability in oaths and engagements.[15] Rather as the Latin word *fides* extends from trustworthiness through faith of utterance to a given word or token, so *constancy*, like *faith* and *truth*—words conspicuous in *Troilus* because those qualities are so desirable but often in doubt—implies not just an inward consistency but something to be kept, held to, and *plighted*. In any case, constancy cannot be known to be constant until it is tried and tested, so it must be visible, palpable, and social if its existence is to be proven.

So *plight* can mean a given word and hand, as in *King Lear* ('That Lord whose hand must take my plight shall carry | Half my love with him'),[16] but also a token, like the sleeve and glove exchanged between Troilus and Cressida, on which so much of this chapter will turn. And here we have to remember that Cicero—never one to recommend the vagaries of erotic love[17]—was describing an ideal social condition, in which *constantia* would inform word and deed. *Troilus* presents a more emulative, competitive, even Hobbesian world than a classical-humanist dream of truth.[18] Even virtuous 'Perseverance'—as in Ulysses' speech to Achilles about valour (3.3.144–84)—is incited by opinion (the great Stoic enemy of self-determined constancy),[19] by reputation-hunting rather than true honour, and the action is overarched by the enemies and bastard rivals of true asseveration and promise: fear, prophecy, desire, and giddy expectation. This is why Troilus says, 'keep her constancy in plight', meaning not just 'uphold the faith of her word' but 'keep her fidelity in circumstances of danger'.[20] Her *plight* is an 'unfortunate condition', a predicament,[21] because 'youth' is a time of sexual appetite and importunity. The danger does not just lie in the challenge to Cressida's constancy. When *plight* is used to mean a faith or engagement, it is, the *Oxford English Dictionary* also notes, one that involves hazard: 'An undertaking (of a risk or obligation); a pledge (esp. one made under risk of forfeiture).'[22] We could legitimately hear further into the word and take the plight as *including* the risk of betrayal that threatens its constancy. To swear or accept an oath is dangerous because if it is broken one loses not just whatever was bound, but hope in the *plight* as a bastion against selfishness and flux.

Oaths, engagements, and the like are the more called upon in *Troilus*, and especially *by* Troilus, because they stand in for what constancy should keep (Troilus would solicit no vows from Cressida if women's constancy needed no proof), yet they are peculiarly susceptible to being incomplete, self-serving, and unreliable. All assertory and promissory declarations have an element of uncertainty, since they might be false or broken. But plights in this play become objects of constancy that are surrounded by and mortgaged to risk, dangerous things to rely on as a stay against confusion. Given or taken as a bulwark against untruth, invoking, in many cases, the gods who are supposed to govern the fate of Troy (sworn by Jove, Venus, Mars, and so on), they offer the sort of surety (a loaded, ambivalent word in the play)[23] that steadfastness ought to provide; but they are caught up in broader exchanges of money, trophies, hostages, reputation, and sexual favour, and put plighters in a worse plight because they have staked more, and visibly, on them.

* * *

Dryden's *Troilus and Cressida* is not the first play on the subject to have been written under Shakespearean influence. An earlier response can be found in Thomas Heywood's two-part drama *The Iron Age* (comp. 1610–13?). In Part I, we see the lovers plight their troths:

TROILUS Daughter to *Calchas* and the pride of *Troy*,
Plight me your hand and heart.
CRESSIDA Faire Heauen I doe.
Will *Troilus* in exchange grant me his too?
TROILUS Yes, and fast seal'd, you gods, your anger wreak
On him or her, that first this vnion breake.
CRESSIDA So protests *Cresida*, wretched may they dye,
That 'twixt our soules these holy bands vntye.[24]

This is more straightforward than the equivalent scene in Shakespeare because the lovers exchange vows without the destabilizing, background presence of the unfaithful Helen in Ilium (at this point in Heywood, Paris has not yet gone to Menelaus' court), but also, more importantly, because the troth is plighted without preliminary exchanges passing through the hands of Pandarus. In Shakespeare's first scene between Cressida and

Pandarus, Troilus' boy comes to Pandarus and asks him away, and he says he will return with 'a token from Troilus'. 'By the same token', Cressida quips,

> you are a bawd.
> *Exeunt* PANDARUS [*and* ALEXANDER]
> Words, vows, gifts, tears, and love's full sacrifice
> He offers in another's enterprise;
> But more in Troilus thousandfold I see
> Than in the glass of Pandar's praise may be.
> Yet hold I off. Women are angels, wooing;
> Things won are done. Joy's soul lies in the doing. (1.2.258–65)

A motif that will turn out to be central (oaths, vows, tokens) is set up in a minor key, and open to wordplay. Swearing by Troilus' token that Pandarus is a bawd, Cressida says that she will prove the validity of her oath by means of this same token, by the token which will, on his bringing it, prove him a bawd. Behind this lies a larger concern about proof and constancy, that men are more constant before a plight is trothed. Once a woman has been won, a lover is less likely to tarry. This is what happens the morning after faiths are exchanged and Troilus sleeps with Cressida. There are reasons for his letting her go, but then, there always are. One dramatic interest of the play is to explore how he can abandon her while believing that he is the more constant because so bound by truth.

Go-betweens were common in early modern courtship.[25] It is not in itself irregular that Pandarus should carry tokens between a prince and the daughter of a priest, or utter proxy vows. He is, though, peculiarly, even kinkily, involved. Given the conventions of early modern betrothal, Shakespeare's lovers should be more firmly bound than Heywood's because when they come to plight their troth they do so in front of a witness. Yet this is not how it works. The commitments in Heywood are mutually reinforcing, those in Shakespeare are pre-empted and dispersed by Pandarus.

> [*to* CRESSIDA] Come, come, what need you blush? Shame's a baby. [*To* TROILUS] Here she is now. Swear the oaths now to her that you have sworn to me. [*To* CRESSIDA] What, are you gone again? You must be watched ere you be made tame, must you? (3.2.38–42)

Pandarus is so intimate in their coupling that he takes the words out of their mouths, then turns the deeds back into binding language:

> Words pay no debts; give her deeds. But she'll bereave you o'th' deeds too, if she call your activity in question. [*They kiss*] What, billing again? Here's 'in witness whereof the parties interchangeably'. (53–6)

David Bevington glosses those final words as follows: 'a legal formula used in indentures, to which the two parties to the contract set their hand and seals on each half of the document, after it had been divided in two along a jagged edge so that the fit of the two halves could not be reproduced by any other document....The phrasing also imperfectly recalls the betrothal ceremony in the Book of Common Prayer.'[26] If Pandarus' legalistic language prompts us to wonder why the two do not marry with proper rites, it also draws attention to the uncomfortable overlap between marriage, doing a deal, and, as yet incipiently, prostitution. A similar willingness to link marriage with the making of bargains can be found in such impeccably orthodox works as Henry Swinburne's *Treatise of Spousals* (composed around 1600), but Pandarus makes the conjunction uncomfortable. We have the carapace of an Elizabethan betrothal, which brings out (as Heywood does not) how far the lovers are from a socially sanctioned bond, from the public recognition that would make it impossible for the Trojan council to send Cressida to the Greeks without consulting Troilus.

Troilus' soliloquy before Cressida's arrival is full of desire and anxiety. Now, he is scarcely less worried, and deals with her talk of 'fears' (64) by appealing to the security of vows. Yet his attempt at levity makes light of their bindingness. There is nothing 'monstrous' in love, he assures Cressida, 'but our undertakings, when we vow to weep seas, live in fire, eat rocks, tame tigers, thinking it harder for our mistress to devise imposition enough than for us to undergo any difficulty imposed' (71–5). This is agreeably self-mocking but unlikely to reassure. First, because it presents lovers' vows as a spur to valiant action, not devotion. A lover taming a tiger will not have much time to think about his lady. This is consistent with the chivalric ethos elsewhere in the play, as when Hector, fresh from chiding Andromache, offers to fight with any Greek who believes he has a better mistress (a challenge in which the lover's vows are revealingly called 'truant vows', distractions from warrior commitments).[27] Second, while Troilus' jokes satirize the conventions of courtship and love poetry (as do in part the Sonnets), he lets slip that lovers vow more than they know they can do, because the vow is meant to impress, to be ardent in its impossibility. This is not an auspicious way to introduce a scene of vowing and plight.

What makes it the more awkward is that Troilus reveals an anxiety about the sexual performance that the vows are designed to enable. Cressida is sometimes accused of inadvertent bawdy, but she is usually, as here, picking up something current in the discourse of the men. 'This is the monstruosity in love, lady,' Troilus says, that the will is infinite and the execution confined; that the desire is boundless and the act a slave to limit.

CRESSIDA They say all lovers swear more performance than they are able, and yet reserve an ability that they never perform: vowing more than the perfection of ten, and discharging less than the tenth part of one. They that have the voice of lions and the act of hares, are they not monsters? (3.2.75–82)

This doubly stings Troilus, because Cressida identifies that what is monstrous in lovers' vows is not so much the absurdity of what is promised as the let-down of the vows not being kept, and because she brings out an apparent admission of inadequacy (lack of total potency) in Troilus' words—which is not the sort of thing you want to have said before a first night together:

TROILUS Are there such? Such are not we. Praise us as we are tasted; allow us as we prove. Our head shall go bare till merit crown it. No perfection in reversion shall have a praise in present. We will not name desert before his birth, and being born his addition shall be humble. (83–7)

Cressida has bounced Troilus into saying that he will not fall short in his performance, but be true to his vows (eating rocks and taming tigers?) and no doubt a lion in bed. On the defensive, he asserts himself with 'Such are not we', which causes editors some trouble; this is either a princely 'we' or a men-in-general 'we'; it does not include Cressida among the true. The fixation with being tested in his truth until it is *proved* begins to emerge, and narrowingly. Bevington glosses 'the perfection of ten' out of Onions's *Shakespeare Glossary*, 'the accomplishments of ten worthy lovers', and 'No perfection in reversion ... present' as 'No promise of some future achievement should be celebrated now'. This is accurate, except that Troilus reiterates 'perfection' as 'thing done' for a reason. He wants not to promise (though he so clearly does want to, and does) but to *prove* (both be tested, and now, show *evidence* of) how perfect in the common sense of the word he is.

The psychological and ethical basis of Troilus' thinking owes something to a conjunction made by Proteus in *The Two Gentlemen of Verona*, when, penitent at his oath-breaking 'Inconstancy', he overturns misogynistic orthodoxy and declares: 'were man | But constant he were perfect' (5.4.108–11). Troilus' desire to be perfect and proven as such motivates his fetishization of constancy. The difference, as we shall see, is that, whereas Proteus' faithlessness to Julia makes him imperfect, Troilus' hanging on to constancy becomes his vice and his way of being unfaithful. Shakespeare has constructed a distinctively Elizabethan but still recognizable type: a lover who leaps to the security of binding language because he cannot cope with the flaws and uncertainties that are part of any new relationship. Meanwhile, thinking of what might be glued together in bed, perfectionism of this sort does not mix well with having a sex life. The pressure is on for an unsuccessful night. All this means that Troilus' anticipated humility rings hollow. There is a fine line between modest, tautologous faith, played out as Cratylic ('as true as Troilus'), and the overweening claim that not even truth will be truer than he: 'Few words to fair faith. Troilus shall be such to Cressid as what envy can say worst shall be a mock for his truth; and what truth can speak truest, not truer than Troilus' (87–90). Wordplay of this sort puts the word into doubt. We have already heard this tautology in Cressida's riposte to Pandarus about Troilus' complexion:

PANDARUS Faith, to say truth, brown and not brown.
CRESSIDA To say the truth, true and not true. (1.2.89–90)

The giving of the word might be all a play of words. Cressida is right to doubt, and, it may be, to regret that she has not followed her self-counsel to hold off, as offering greater security than plight.

As the lovers prepare to go into the tiring house, to consummate their relationship, vows and constancy come up again. This time there is a leaning pressure on Cressida to swear too. Pandarus instructs her to 'Be true to my lord. If he flinch, chide me for it,' and Troilus adds, 'You know now your hostages: your uncle's word and my firm faith' (3.2.94–7). *Hostages* are pledges between enemies designed to ensure that a promise is honoured. They are war-pledges, in that sense, coercions that substitute for trust. This is a straw in the wind. Whether because she is reluctant to swear or because her commitments are pre-empted by Pandarus, Cressida does not respond, but her uncle says, 'Nay, I'll give my word for her too. Our kindred, though they be long ere they are wooed, they are constant being won' (98–100). Pandarus speaks for Cressida, as earlier he had given Troilus' word to Cressida, but also becomes her voucher, swearing on her constancy. This does not quite convince Troilus, as Pandarus hopes. Rather, it points on to the lines about 'constancy in plight' from which this discussion started.

After insulting Cressida with his belief that women are inconstant, though the plays of Shakespeare are full of examples to the contrary, Troilus continues in the same vein. If only persuasion could convince me, he says,

That my integrity and truth to you
Might be affronted with the match and weight
Of such a winnowed purity in love.
How were I then uplifted! But alas,
I am as true as truth's simplicity,
And simpler than the infancy of truth.
CRESSIDA In that I'll war with you.
TROILUS O virtuous fight,
When right with right wars who shall be most right. (152–9)

The level of insult to Cressida, though driven by anxiety (which might subside), as well as second-hand misogyny (for which he might be forgiven), and a misplaced, rhetorical desire to enhance his own claim to truth by contrast, is remarkable. For him to be simply true is for him to be incapable of believing that a woman could be constant. This provocation secures in some form the commitment that Troilus seeks. It is, however, couched in combative terms. This both distances Cressida and shows that she knows her world well enough to provide what her lover wants. Troilus warms to the exchange when told that it resembles a war. It is a rivalry played out in the extensive not-quite-vows that are the climax of this scene—a vignette that may look like an Elizabethan troth-plight but which has aptly been called 'trope-plighting'.[28]

Here, leading off, is Troilus:

True swains in love shall in the world to come
Approve their truth by Troilus. When their rhymes,
Full of protest, of oath and big compare,
Want similes, truth tired with iteration—
'As true as steel, as plantage to the moon,
As sun to day, as turtle to her mate,
As iron to adamant, as earth to th' centre'—
Yet, after all comparisons of truth,
As truth's authentic author to be cited,
'As true as Troilus' shall crown up the verse
And sanctify the numbers.
CRESSIDA Prophet may you be! (160–70)

Promising does have a family resemblance to the forms of prophetic utterance that animate *Troilus and Cressida*, notably in the roles of Cassandra and Ulysses.[29] But Cressida brings out the extent to which Troilus has not given an undertaking to her or to a deity but has leant entirely on the futurity of a vow. Like his lines on the monstrosity of lovers' vows, it is a nice piece of literary satire, but it takes almost as much from binding language as it gives.

What it most resembles is boasting. It is not just the competitive militarism raised by Cressida that sets up this exchange to mirror the confrontation between Hector and Achilles when they meet in the Greek camp. Their promises to fight each other are full of boasts, and escalation—as when Hector responds to Achilles' menaces with this self-confessed 'brag':

> Henceforth guard thee well.
> For I'll not kill thee there, nor there, nor there,
> But, by the forge that stithied Mars his helm,
> I'll kill thee everywhere, yea, o'er and o'er. (4.7.137–41)

You could say that Troilus mocks boasting. Or rather, that, as a literary mocker, he resembles Biron in *Love's Labour's Lost*, showing his mastery of exaggerated conceits the more convincingly to be believed in the 'honest kersey' of his truth. But boasting slips through when he says that to claim to be as true as Troilus will 'sanctify' and 'crown' poetic numbers.

In one sense, comparison with Hector's and with Achilles' more lethally restrained vaunting breaks down: Cressida refuses to 'war with' Troilus by matching his catalogue of hyperbole; nor can she join in his mock-modest game of Cratylism by saying that she will be 'as true as Cressid'. Yet she is not entirely free in what she does say. We feel that a declaration is required of her, and that the requirements of rhetorical variation force her, going second, into the disadvantages of envisaging failure. What he says is more a threat to herself than a boast. It is as though the self-assurance of a promissory oath had been denied her by Troilus, leaving the self-curse typical of such speech acts retrospectively to blight her. 'If I be false, or swerve a hair from truth,' she declares:

> When they've said, 'as false
> As air, as water, wind or sandy earth,
> As fox to lamb, or wolf to heifer's calf,
> Pard to the hind, or stepdame to her son',
> Yea, let them say, to stick the heart of falsehood,
> 'As false as Cressid'. (3.2.171, 178–83)

In Dryden's revision, Cressida says that she will only take Troilus if he swears that 'the holy Priest | Shall make us one for ever' (3.2.84–5). Pandarus jovially urges him to agree on the grounds that women always ask for this but never expect a man to keep his oath. Some critics still worry that Shakespeare's lovers go to bed without getting married,[30] but a more challenging point for an audience is why Troilus is so fixated on a plighting of troth, a declaration of constancy, when Cressida does not expect marriage. Why would she, as a traitor's daughter, who needs a protector and knows she must fall upon her back to defend her belly (1.2.240)? This is not to say that the betrothal framework is inactive; it is satirically intrusive. Pandarus' urging of 'a bargain', acting as 'witness', and initiating 'Amens' makes the action flit unstably between a romance in ancient Troy and a clandestine, Elizabethan betrothal (never a secure arrangement, always shadowed with a suspicion of whoredom):

> Go to, a bargain made. Seal it, seal it. I'll be the witness. Here I hold your hand; here, my cousin's. If ever you prove false one to another, since I have taken such pains to bring you together, let all pitiful goers-between be called to the world's end after my name; call them all panders. Let all constant men be Troiluses, all false women Cressids, and all brokers-between panders! Say 'Amen.' (184–90)

This is what they affirm, with biblical force.[31] The stress on *proof* is striking. The lovers will not know what they are until they are proven—which makes the leaning into anticipated betrayal the more ominous, and the reinscription of the assumptions that Dryden noted in Lollius and Chaucer the more provocatively (on Shakespeare's part) unjust. If the affair goes wrong, there is no prospect of false men being called Troilus; constant men will be Troiluses and false women will be Cressidas. But is not Troilus already false in trying to keep the relationship hidden, debasing the value of the bond? The secrecy of this known-about affair (Aeneas expects to find Troilus sleeping at Pandarus' house) seems to be crucial for him, though why is never explained. The audience is left to speculate about inequality of status, the scandal of consorting with a traitor's daughter, and Troilus' fear that, given women's inconstancy, he risks sharing the disgrace of Menelaus. All these adumbrations render the future insecure.

The need to compensate, over-insist, and, we might say, mislead is strong, and the audience hears this from more than Troilus. Pandarus brings together legal process, retribution, and being pressed to death while maintaining secrecy, in a horrible image of sexual pleasure:

> Amen. Whereupon I will show you a chamber with a bed—which bed, because it shall not speak of your pretty encounters, press it to death. Away!
>
> *Exeunt* [TROILUS *and* CRESSIDA]
>
> And Cupid grant all tongue-tied maidens here
> Bed, chamber, pander to provide this gear. *Exit* (193–7)

Having urged Cressida bedwards with quasi-marital imagery, Pandarus now more frankly addresses the audience. How tongue-tied has Cressida been? Her eloquence was remarkable. The line is there for the quibble on 'tied by the tongue'. Unlike the image of security adduced by 'Seal it' (the kiss a validating mark on a bond), this is now a slippery connection, constancy glued only by tongue-tangled kissing.

⋆ ⋆ ⋆

The emphasis on 'Words, vows, gifts' sets Shakespeare's play apart from earlier, extant versions of the story. He is likely, for example, to have added the scene of troth-plighting which then figures in Heywood and Dryden. Chaucer does include more than one loaded scene of troth-giving. Troilus speaks of his *trouthe* when uniting with Criseyde.[32] Next morning, she speaks of her *trouthe* to him (III.1492–512). The great set piece, however, comes when the lovers have to part and Criseyde is resisting Troilus' idea that they should elope.[33] She is backed into protesting her faith as a way of resisting his proposal, which she believes would be bad for both of them. In Shakespeare, the parting is brief, but equally intense. Once again, Troilus claims most stage time, and he certainly does not suggest that he is willing to elope, thereby leaving his status in Troy behind him. There is, rather, a sense that parting is at once a desirable challenge to his valour and a test of her constancy.

It is typical of the dissonance of the play that, just as the first round of troth-plighting is anticipated by dialogue that casts doubt on the bindingness of vows, so Shakespeare precedes the parting troths with destabilizing turns of phrase. This time, however, the disruption is registered more obliquely. When Aeneas arrives at Pandarus' house, looking for Troilus, Pandarus, playing the innocent, declares, 'By my troth, | I knew you not. What news with you so early?' (4.2.48–9). As is customary with him, especially in the company of his betters, Pandarus indulges in nice, effeminate asseverations. More significantly, they are false. When Aeneas insists that he knows the prince is there, Pandarus says: 'Is he here, say you? It's more than I know, I'll be sworn. For my own part, I came in late. What should he do here?' (53–5). Aeneas knows the lie, but the way he responds to it is telling: 'you'll do him wrong | Ere you are ware. You'll be so true to him | To be false to him' (56–8). This is a paradox worryingly transferable to Troilus' truth to Cressida.

Such ironic details an audience might not pick up until they know the play well, but the exchange creates an atmosphere of trivial dissembling which detracts from the parting to come.[34] When Aeneas tells Troilus that

Cressida is to be exchanged for Antenor, his capitulation is immediate. They must be separated, he tells Cressida. Their 'dear vows' must be strangled in the birth of their labouring breaths, as he puts it, with sexual, infanticidal intensity (4.5.36–7). We have witnessed Troilus only a few scenes earlier standing up to Priam and Hector—not to mention Cassandra—on the Trojan council, and prevailing. That he does not rush to Ilium to talk to his father has persuaded many, and presumably on some level Cressida, that he is not as devoted to her as he wants to believe.[35] What he is committed to is his constancy, his plight, to being as true as Troilus, which effectively means being committed to his externally arbitrated image, to what Ulysses, urging Achilles to fight, calls 'reflection' (3.3.90–118). He cannot leave constancy alone. He asks Cressida, yet again, to be true. Do not react badly to my over-insistence, he says, '"Be thou true" say I, to fashion in | My sequent protestation: "Be thou true, | And I will see thee"' (4.5.64–6). The problem is only partly that this weakly discounts what we know to be the all-important 'Be thou true' as an incidental; it is also that the declaration appears to come out more conditionally than is intended, though it is true to how Troilus will act. He sees her, as he assumes, being untrue, with Diomed in front of Calchas' tent, and does not come to see her.

Cressida makes her own promise with an incidental matter-of-factness that contrasts with Troilus' insistent vowing. She lets her concern for his safety push her declaration of truth into a secondary position, as though taken for granted:

CRESSIDA O you shall be exposed, my lord, to dangers
As infinite as imminent. But I'll be true.
TROILUS And I'll grow friend with danger. Wear this sleeve.
CRESSIDA And you this glove. When shall I see you? (4.5.67–70)

Troilus' 'And' is gallantly eliding but still detectably conditional. Her 'And' is coupling. These subtleties are going to matter, as the sleeve becomes contentious. Even at this point, the tokens provide a striking tableau in performance. They do not, however, necessarily stand out from the other unnamed token or tokens that have been sent by Troilus to Cressida. The exchange is sudden, with no break in the verse lines for elaborate gestures of handing over or adornment. Cressida's focus is on seeing her lover again. Like Desdemona with the handkerchief, she does not realize that a crucial marker of faith has been laid down, or at least a marker that will be retrospectively invested with huge significance, that he will want this sleeve to be kept as firmly as her faith.

In his edition, Bevington slides in the stage direction, *'as they exchange favours'*. This is likely as to timing, but are the glove and sleeve strictly 'favours'? In the vocabulary of *Troilus*, 'favour' is used of the face, advancement, and being well disposed, but not of anything given or exchanged. These are 'tokens', serving as remembrances, that will later become 'pledges'. If they were gifts, they would be less impromptu. Troilus cannot wear Cressida's small glove, nor can Cressida attach his manly sleeve to her gown with points. She can only wear it as a sign, and an unwieldy one at that. On practical grounds alone—and Troilus is rarely practical—it is not surprising that she is not wearing it when she meets Diomed at Calchas' tent. Contrast Dryden's version, where Cressida wears a—more conventional—ring, as token of her faith. Recent work has found gloves and sleeves cited as love gifts in early modern England, but in pairs, thoughtfully selected and fit.[36]

The glove and sleeve are more like (in Pandarus' word) *hostages*, awaiting reunion with their pair when the lovers are reunited. That is a positive, probably over-extrapolated way of dealing with the point that, like the couple's troth-plights, 'this sleeve' and 'this glove' half-rhyme but do not match. Also in this resembling the troth-plights, Troilus goes first with the sleeve and Cressida is obliged to reciprocate. Troilus re-plights his troth 'by the same token' (as Cressida quipped to Pandarus), i.e. by his sleeve, and Cressida by her glove, as Hector will swear 'By Mars his gauntlet' and 'by Venus' glove' in the passage where he mocks Menelaus (4.7.61–3). These are textile plights handed over like spoken faiths. Where do they come from? A director might ask Cressida to carry gloves as a matter of course, as she does in Caxton, letting Diomed take one from her when she arrives at the Greek camp.[37] But Troilus has no space in the dialogue to unpick a sleeve. It must be, in performance, a sleeve left over from their hasty dressing, which also means their hasty undressing the night before. The glove and sleeve can carry an erotic charge, as well as the pathos of being empty. They are reminders of the shape of the lover's body as near as can be kept in their absence.

This is not the end of the plighting. Troilus promises to sustain his faith by breaking the faith of others: 'I will corrupt the Grecian sentinels | To give thee nightly visitation' (4.5.71–2). Once again, vowing is mixed up with boasting and a desire not to underperform. We must admire Troilus' sexual prowess, proposing to be at it nightly, but also note that it is raising the stakes on him keeping his word. He is pledging the over-ambitious to make it a more galvanizing objective. Ulysses will later urge him away from Calchas' tent where they eavesdrop on Diomed and Cressida by saying that the place and time are dangerous and deadly (5.2.36–7). It is not just Cressida who fears that he will be exposed to dangers infinite. Troilus promises so much, almost to the extent of fighting tigers, to insist on the value of the constancy that he doubts in Cressida. 'But yet, be true', he urges, to which, at a loss, she replies: 'O heavens! "Be true" again!' She tries to counter, 'O heavens, you love me not!', which is well pitched to encourage an audience to suspect that she is right, though it does not follow. And she asks him directly whether he thinks she will be tempted: 'Do you think I will?' (73–93).

This time there is scope for a half-line pause which an actor would be reluctant to overleap, though it should not hang too archly. Then comes his reply, followed by what could be even longer hesitation[38] before he says yes under the sign of no:

No, but something may be done that we will not,
And sometimes we are devils to ourselves,
When we will tempt the frailty of our powers,
Presuming on their changeful potency.
AENEAS [*within*] Nay, good my lord!
TROILUS Come, kiss; and let us part. (94–8)

It would be over-ingenious to hear 'Presuming' as a scrambled form of 'Promising'. Yet it amounts to the same thing. Cressida does try to turn the tables in the exaction of faith, by asking 'My lord, will you be true?' But the prince is only too fluent in his response:

Who, I? Alas, it is my vice, my fault.
Whiles others fish with craft for great opinion,
I with great truth catch mere simplicity;
Whilst some with cunning gild their copper crowns,
With truth and plainness I do wear mine bare.
Enter [PARIS, AENEAS, ANTENOR, DEIPHOBUS, *and* DIOMEDES]
Fear not my truth. The moral of my wit
Is 'plain and true!'; there's all the reach of it. (101–8)

This is what Troilus calls 'truth tired by iteration'. It is one of those moments when an audience will weary of the mock-humble prince. Truth becomes empty and obsessive, a citation, a formula. All is set for Troilus to be so true to Cressida that he'll be false to her.

* * *

In Chaucer's *Troilus and Criseyde*, there is an agony of waiting for Troilus to see whether his mistress will be faithful, while she falls in love with Diomed. We later hear that Diomed woos Criseyde and takes a glove from her, and then that she gives him further gifts including

> the faire baye stede
> the which [s]he ones wan of Troilus;
> And ek a broche—and that was litel nede—
> That Troilus was, she yaf this Diomede.
> And ek, the bet from sorwe him to releve,
> She made hym were a pencel of hir sleve.[39]

Later again, when the Trojan Deiphoebus seizes Diomed's coat in battle, we learn that this brooch (worn under Diomed's collar) was given by Troilus to Criseyde on their parting. 'Who shal now trowe on any othes mo,' asks the dejected Troilus.[40] One of Shakespeare's most brilliant innovations was to telescope this part of the action, bringing together the handing over of Troilus' sleeve to Diomed with Troilus' discovery of betrayal (if that is what it is), in the layered eavesdropping scene at Calchas' tent, where Cressida gives Troilus' sleeve to Diomed, Troilus and Ulysses observe and comment, and Thersites overlooks the others, darting in his poisonous cynicism. For its mastery of the stage, and volatility of tone, it is one of the most celebrated scenes in Shakespeare, and it deserves attentive scrutiny, because, consistently with the play, it is full of binding language, given, broken, pledged, and hedged.

It must have been admired as early as the seventeenth century because both Heywood and Dryden imitate the scene. In Heywood, however, it is not used to frame Cressida's betrayal of Troilus. That is decided over a banquet with Calchas, where he pressures Cressida with his prophetic knowledge that Troy is bound to fall into taking up with Diomedes.[41] The eavesdropping scene is played out, instead, in Part II of *The Iron Age*, where Sinon persuades Diomed to test his belief that Cressida is 'constant'—a word repeatedly used, as it is not elsewhere in the plays. Initially, Cressida is repelled by Sinon. To make his triumph the more complete, he tells her that he breaks his oaths because he is a politician, only for her to take his word that he will care for her (Diomed, he points out, has a queen back in Greece). Shown to be 'inconstant', Cressida is cast off by both men. When we next see her in *The Iron Age*, she has become (as in Henryson's *Testament of Cresseid*) a leper.[42] Dryden went the other way entirely. He keeps the outline dramaturgy of Shakespeare's scene, but posits it on the need for

Cressida to go along with Diomedes by showing interest in him, and giving him Troilus' ring, on her father Calchas' advice, to ensure that they are taken care of long enough to escape to Troy. Unlike Shakespeare's Cressida, she shows no trace of succumbing to Diomed. The situation is one of tragic misunderstanding.

Thought about between these extremes, the complexities of Shakespeare's scene are easier to grasp. Interpretation is difficult because the meaning of what is seen and heard is so much in the eye and ear of the beholders, readily disillusioned in the case of Troilus, cynical for the misogynistic Ulysses, reductive for Thersites, and divided for the audience. There is encouragement to conclude that Cressida is attracted to Diomed and false in succumbing to him, but also for believing that Dryden drew out what is already there in the Shakespeare, that, with Calchas more a cipher than a protector, Cressida can only temporize and does hold off her suitor. Ulysses and Troilus are the two witnesses required for something to be judged a crime in the Old Testament (Deuteronomy 19: 15) and Roman law. But proof of troth-breaking is harder to find than most critics (the children of Lollius) assume.

Troilus is startled to see Cressida come out of Calchas' tent and seek 'a word' with Diomed (5.2.7). It turns out, however, that she is aiming to preempt a demand, based on an oath that she has given, or had forced out of her, that she will allow him more intimate access. What looks like alacrity is containment. Diomed is impatient and exclamatory:

DIOMEDES Fo, fo! Come, tell a pin. You are forsworn.
CRESSIDA In faith, I cannot. What would you have me do?
THERSITES [*aside*] A juggling trick: to be secretly open.
DIOMEDES What did you swear you would bestow on me?
CRESSIDA I prithee, do not hold me to mine oath.
Bid me do any thing but that, sweet Greek. (22–7)

It is not just that Cressida is in danger of breaking her vows to Troilus, but that she now has conflicting engagements. She is put in the same position as Achilles, who, as we saw in the Introduction (pp. 4–5), promises to fight with Hector but is then reminded by letter (from Hecuba) and token (from Polyxena) of his 'major vow' not to fight the Trojans (5.1.32–9). There is no course for either Cressida or Achilles that does not involve a broken word; it is a matter of pressures and priorities. There is an escape-route available to Cressida, however, which she is quick to spy. And if Diomedes is, as Thersites gleefully insists just before the scene begins, a notorious promise-breaker

(5.1.80–6), she has found the right person with whom to pursue an exit-strategy. It was an available—though not the only—view that '*An oath may be released by him unto whom it is made*.'[43] Is this a matter of Cressida throwing herself on Diomed's mercy? She is represented with Shakespearean resourcefulness as cleverer than that. It is a way of offering to put herself into Diomed's debt which intimates that she will look on him the more kindly if he lets her off. He would make progress, she hold off.

Diomed's response is brutally to give her what she asks for: 'Good night' (5.2.28). This does not so much let Cressida off the hook as refuse to insist on her oath at the price of leaving her unprotected.[44] 'Nay, but you part in anger', she says, calling him back and stroking his cheek (43–9). She can only secure his loyalty by promising again, which whets his appetite for results. All this creates consternation in Troilus, who shows himself much less possessed of the Stoic virtues than he would wish. 'Hold, patience!', he cries. But 'You have not patience', Ulysses replies, trying to draw him away. Without patience, how can Troilus be constant?[45] 'Stay', he deeply swears: 'By hell and all hell's torments, | I will not speak a word.' It is the start of a sequence of oaths sworn ('By Jove ... By Jove') not to speak, which he breaks, and less and less convincing promises of 'patience' (29–86). These broken oaths form a jangling counterpoint to Cressida's similarly hard-pressed, conflicted, perjured, or temporizing promises.

As a woman, her repertoire of oaths has to be less full-blooded than Troilus', but she pushes 'In faith' hard. In response to Diomedes' dismissive 'Fo, fo! Adieu. You palter'—which is even stronger than 'Good night', a threateningly final goodbye—she protests, 'In faith, I do not. Come hither once again', then, after unheard whispering, in response to his challenge 'But will you then?', where 'then' might be heard as 'therefore' but more likely sets a later date, she adds 'In faith, I will, la. Never trust me else' (47–57). 'La' is a light emphatic, used elsewhere in Shakespeare to give such phrases as 'i' faith' point.[46] 'Never trust me else' is another stock asseveration, but it does pick out a word which is striking in its absence from her exchanges with Troilus. I have noted the importance of such words as *faith*, *truth*, and *constancy* in the play's lexicon. *Trust* is a word that only occurs three times; this is equally telling.

Diomed presses the advantage: 'Give me some token for the surety of it' (58). He will only seem superficial if we imagine that he is asking for the sleeve he is about to be given. He wants something to bind the contract. Perhaps he means by this (it can be in the actor's body language), let me have a physical taste of you, earnest of what is to come, as a warrant that I will enjoy you. Perhaps he does not have to know what he means, only that he needs more than words. He must bring something from the encounter to prove that he is making progress. She responds, 'I'll fetch you one', and after some promise-talk between Ulysses and Troilus ('You have sworn patience'), which splits Troilus as Cressida is being split ('I will not be myself, nor have cognition | Of what I feel'), she re-enters to Thersites' crowing cry: 'Now the pledge! Now, now, now' (59–64). It is almost as though Thersites knows. If the audience is not familiar with the play, it might be braced for a shocking parallel with the scene where Cressida gives a glove to Troilus, but the token could still be anything. Now, even worse, it is his sleeve. It matters that a 'pledge' can be a verbal promise as well as a token. Since the sleeve is a portable reminder of her binding word to Troilus, it is ironic that it should be dubbed a 'pledge' at the very moment that it is given away, the word broken—or, would Cressida say, re-directed? The pledge is a sign of the vows between Troilus and Cressida that now becomes a sign of the promise given by Cressida to Diomedes.

In Chaucer, Diomede is given Criseyde's sleeve to wear as a banner or pennon. Here, more awkwardly, we have a woman giving a man a man's sleeve. There are options and opportunities in performance. The coup could be slow to unfold. At first, the sleeve might be taken (even by the audience) as something of Cressida's own, crumpled up. Once it is handed over (65), Diomed inspects it whether suspiciously or not and looks to her for clarification, which comes a few lines later with 'He loved me' (70). What will an audience imagine is going through her mind? That she already feels let down by Troilus, who has left her so exposed? That she does not want to give Diomedes something of her own, of her self? That she wants to see the situation (as partly it is) as one of two men in competition over her, as much as for her? When Troilus ringingly declares that it is his, and goes out to fight for it (5.3.99), he confirms that, and indeed he could not fight for it as Cressida's because that would be to accept that he has nothing really to fight Diomedes for since he ought to accept her choice.

Yet it is not entirely Troilus'. When he gives it, it is a man's sleeve, unloosed from his clothing, perhaps torn, fraying from his shoulder. An emblem of disjoined faith, it begins the process of unravelling that will bring it into conjunction with Thersites' comparison of Patroclus to 'an idle immaterial skein of sleave-silk' (5.1.25–6), a useless, airy loop of silk thread. Before it gets to that, however, it becomes a token of physical access, something tactile of hers, to be possessed (for the psychoanalytically minded an emblem of her sexual organs). You could argue that handing it over is the acceptable staging of her infidelity; but the moment of that is not 'Now', in Thersites' word. Men want instant results—which is one reason why they are attracted to full-blown, promissory oaths (e.g. 'I'll kill thee everywhere'), that give pre-emptive satisfaction—when there is always more to come, more uncertainty, if not worse upon worse. So the sleeve changes in meaning not just because second- or third-hand (more handed around, as Cressida will be) but because female. If so, it is a peculiarly empty token, open at both ends, mouth and vagina, a cast-off, and re-useable by any man since it can be tied on by points but is useless because ill matched.

Cressida presents the sleeve with more ceremony than she did the glove (she has to make it count, if she is to keep Diomed at bay, which means secure him by holding off): 'Here Diomed, keep this sleeve' (65). As I have not kept it, an audience might silently add. 'Keep this sleeve' as you might say keep your word, your constancy. After Cressida's half verse-line, Troilus and Ulysses have a brief exchange which requires the actor to do something with the sleeve. Cressida could be suddenly reluctant, or drape the sleeve around Diomed while he takes a good look at it. The sleeve is once again given as a token of her faith, and given as a way of requiring something of him (keep the sleeve, keep me). Yet it is the very handing of it over in faithlessness that makes it a stronger pledge. Cressida is not just giving a favour but enacting a wrong, that of abandoning an existing relationship to satisfy Diomed. So the actor playing the latter would be right to convey a sense that he is being given something that counts.

It is ironically eloquent, though a little obvious, if, as in some productions, Troilus, looking on, is wearing Cressida's glove in his hat. She, meanwhile, goes on: 'You look upon that sleeve. Behold it well. | He loved me—O false wench!—give't me again' (69–70). This compunction might consciously or not be a way of freighting the sleeve with significance, to make it the more plausible a substitute for actually sleeping with Diomedes. More strikingly, 'Give't me again' creates the reciprocity that she had in the exchange of tokens with Troilus. In place of that reciprocity there are now two 'bad' moves, to give the sleeve away and to have to snatch it back. Diomed's response, 'Whose was't?' shows him warming to the surety. An audience is likely to assume that he knows perfectly well whose it was, since he has seen Troilus with Cressida at their parting; the pressure for information is to seek a greater betrayal and therefore more of her. 'Was't' also conveniently pushes

Troilus into the past (though Cressida did that with 'He loved me', choosing to forget that he still might well love her):

CRESSIDA It is no matter, now I ha't again.
I will not meet with you tomorrow night.
I prithee, Diomed, visit me no more. (72–4)

This is what he has already offered, and now she says that she wants it. Much depends on the actors. You could say that the sleeve has after all stirred memory and faith. She is turning him away. You could also say, she is now empowering herself by claiming the right to say she will be isolated. Unfortunately, you could equally well say what Thersites does at this point: 'Now she sharpens. Well said, whetstone.'

This is indeed how Diomedes responds. He says, 'I shall have it.' Now that the sleeve is not to be given but to be taken by force, the warrior in him is interested. He can take something, if not her chastity, and show that he has power over her. Cressida, sensing the threat, pretends not to know what he means: 'What, this?' What else could it be? Her body (yes, in some sense). It can also be played belittlingly: what, this little thing? Now Diomed is sure that it matters, 'Ay, that' (76–8). Shakespeare cues the actor to show how keenly Cressida feels the coercion by scripting a miniature, sentimental reverie (that may sharpen Diomedes further). Cressida is having to create for herself a tenderness that she knows she will not get from him. A further meaning of *pledge* in early modern English is 'child'. The sleeve is the only offspring she has from her union with Troilus. Should the actor cradle and stroke it?

O all you gods! O pretty pretty pledge!
Thy master now lies thinking on his bed
Of thee and me, and sighs, and takes my glove
And gives memorial dainty kisses to it—
As I kiss thee.[47]
[*He snatches the sleeve*] (79–83)

To judge from Diomedes' snatching, Cressida does whet him by kissing Troilus' token, as she has whetted Troilus by stroking Diomed's cheek. 'As I kiss thee' could, as it were, be a phrase uttered to Diomed, but not a bit of it (she uses a wary, respectful *you* for him):

Nay, do not snatch it from me.
He that takes that doth take my heart withal.
DIOMEDES I had your heart before; this follows it.
TROILUS [*aside*] I did swear patience.

CRESSIDA You shall not have it, Diomed. Faith, you shall not.
I'll give you something else.
DIOMEDES I will have this. Whose was it?
CRESSIDA It is no matter.
DIOMEDES Come, tell me whose it was?
CRESSIDA 'Twas one's that loved me better than you will.
But, now you have it, take it.
DIOMEDES Whose was it?
CRESSIDA By all Diana's waiting-women yond,
And by herself, I will not tell you whose. (83–93)

There is a lot going on here, partly articulated by the play with the sleeve in ways that the dialogue does not fully represent. ''Twas...will...now' shows the drifting of Troilus into the past, her knowledge that Diomed will not love her well, and the live turning of the theatre moment on 'now'. 'He that takes that...' may 'capture the magical power of a piece of clothing to absorb its wearer'.[48] But 'now you have it, take it' is both paradoxical (how can you take what you have?) and a step back from 'Here Diomed, keep this sleeve.' She is no longer giving, and she no longer hopes to be kept. There is progress of a sort for him, but not enough; which is why he pushes again for disclosure. 'By all Diana's waiting-women yond, | And by herself' (i.e. by the stars and the moon) is a strong oath for a woman, much weightier than 'In faith'. Her resistance to naming Troilus becomes a sticking-point she can use to self-exculpating advantage, a substitute in her mind for the sexual loyalty that she should preserve but feels increasingly she will have to abandon. In Dryden, Diomed replies to this, 'Why then thou lov'st him still' (4.2.309). That may be too heavy a cue to the audience not to doubt Cressida's constancy. But the oath is in Shakespeare as well as in Dryden an indication of some level of faith. It also feels, however, like a resentful sort of substitution. If the secrecy of her relationship with Troilus mattered to him so much that he was not even willing to appeal to the Trojan council in order to keep her, then let him have what he most valued, not her but her secrecy. Yet the oath is also a joke against Cressida herself. First because she is invoking Diana as sacred to virginity yet is already a fornicatress on the way to becoming promiscuous. Second because we are within earshot of Juliet in *Romeo and Juliet*, 'O swear not by the moon, th'inconstant moon' (2.1.151), and of Cleopatra, seeking to be worthy of Antony in his Stoic-Roman death-mode: 'I am marble-constant. Now the fleeting moon | No planet is of mine' (5.2.236–7). The moon is a veritable emblem of 'the Inconstancy of Women', and Cressida makes it her own.

Troilus, Ulysses, and Thersites have been observers of and commentators on Troilus' exchanges with Cressida. Now a new couple emerges, for the wider, theatre audience. The token given by Troilus to Cressida becomes not just a pledge of faith but a pledge as forfeit in a challenge—like a gage thrown down to propose a fight, if an opponent is bold enough to take it up.[49] Troilus is defiantly willing, responding unheard in a balanced distich:

DIOMEDES Tomorrow will I wear it on my helm,
And grieve his spirit that dares not challenge it.
TROILUS [*aside*] Wert thou the devil, and wor'st it on thy horn,
It should be challenged. (94–7)

Yet the action is not quite ready to slide across to Diomedes and Troilus. Cressida self-dividedly declares, 'Well, well, 'tis done, 'tis past—and yet it is not. | I will not keep my word' (98–9). This is extraordinary, utterly Shakespearean in the way the simplest phrase is loaded with the perplexities of the play. It is like the Cretan Liar paradox. 'I will not keep my word': I promise not to do what I promise. Any audience that wants her to be constant will be enticed by 'and yet it is not' into hoping that she will break her word. But then, if she does not keep her word to Troilus she will keep her word to Diomed (and so on).

Diomed reverts to a threat of departure and insists on a time to return. By now, Troilus is not responding to Cressida, but peeling away into dialogue with Diomedes. In response to his 'I do not like this fooling', he says, 'Nor I, by Pluto—but that that likes not you | Pleases me best' (102–3). In both Quarto and Folio texts this is given to Thersites. It clearly does belong to the trajectory of Troilus' oaths, and to his growingly explicit animus. One taste of male rivalry and he has been knocked out of his youthful idealism into Thersitean contempt and pettiness. Diomedes' final lines in the scene also contain an interesting crux:

DIOMEDES What, shall I come? The hour—
CRESSIDA Ay, come. O Jove, do come. I shall be plagued.
DIOMEDES Farewell till then.
CRESSIDA Good night. I prithee, come. (104–6)

Q has a dash after Diomedes' 'the houre', F a full-stop. Modern editors either follow Q, taking 'Ay, come' as an interruption, or add a question mark to F. But Q allows Cressida's 'Ay, come' to cut her suitor off without specifying a time, while F allows her more evidently not to answer his question. The hour is not specified, but a degree of reluctance is, before the more ardent or careful encouragement of 'O Jove, do come'. What cannot be edited away is the invitation that was revoked to return 'tomorrow night'. That, though, is also a double-edged commitment, and not just because it defers the 'now'.

The soliloquy which Cressida has on Diomed's departure is slanted towards leaving Troilus. Her commitment to him has to be defeasible (see p. 5), given the circumstances she is now in. Yet, to take 'my heart' in the opening lines as a shameless admission that, in opting for Diomed, she would be following her fickle emotions shuts down too many undecidables. She is still oscillating between her suitors, adjusting to her predicament; her heart's outlook is not final. In any case, she is entitled to make what she now feels pressurized to do as compatible with her self-respect as possible. She can try out the thought of a new lover once Diomed has exited. The speech is scripted in balanced couplets, which, as in her first soliloquy (1.2.260–73), parade commonplaces—misogynistic ones this time—with a degree of bitterness. This is not soliloquy as self-expression (it never really is in early modern drama) but a sort of choric monologue that is looking for a point of balance in self-description and rationalization. Not that she is helped in the audience's eyes by Thersites' scathing couplet, which caps her own by saying, out of Troilus' idiom, that she has *proved* herself inconstant:

Troilus, farewell. One eye yet looks on thee,
But with my heart the other eye doth see.
Ah, poor our sex! This fault in us I find:
The error of our eye directs our mind.
What error leads must err. O then conclude:
Minds swayed by eyes are full of turpitude. *Exit*
THERSITES [*aside*] A proof of strength she could not publish more
Unless she said, 'My mind is now turn'd whore'. (107–14)

Yet if this soliloquy offers the 'proof' that Troilus had looked for, it does not entirely convince him. He has a major adjustment to make. 'Shall I not lie in *publishing* a truth?', he asks, taking over Thersites' word,

Sith yet there is a credence in my heart,
An esperance so obstinately strong,
That doth invert th'attest of eyes and ears,
As if those organs had deceptious functions
Created only to calumniate.
Was Cressid here? (119–25)

We are prompted to heed the 'invert'. Troilus' fearful, philosophically rigid idea of constancy is making his eyes and ears 'attest' (formally asseverate) calumnies against Cressida because his hope has expected more of her than most unprotected women under Diomed's coercion could deliver. She has held Diomed off with the promise of an assignation tomorrow, not entirely secured. She is set on a wavering course that could still be changed. If Troilus were true to her, his esperance would make him believe that she has kept Diomedes away in order to give him (as certainly she is giving him) the chance to honour his promise to bribe the guards and come to her nightly. This he has begun to do, but not persisted in, because he is so true to what he takes constancy to be that his eyes and ears tell him she has swerved a hair's breadth from truth. His patience is selective. Right to the end of the play Cressida does not sleep with Diomed, who sends her persuasive (as he hopes) tokens from the battlefield. Sexually speaking, she is no more false to Troilus in Shakespeare's play than she is in Dryden's. The audience may assume that she will go the way of Lollius' and Chaucer's Criseyde. Even the way of Henryson's and Heywood's. As we shall see, 'I shall be plagued' can grimly mean, without her knowing it, Diomedes will give me the pox, and I will become a leper. But this depends on negative expectations of 'the Inconstancy of Women', not any basis in 'proof'. A sympathetic audience will feel that, if Shakespeare's Cressida turns into Henryson's, a large part of the fault lies in Troilus' abandoning her to his truth.

By now, he has a more interesting subject than Cressida to think about—the philosophical make-up of vows:

TROILUS This, she? No, this is Diomed's Cressida.
If beauty have a soul, this is not she.
If souls guide vows, if vows be sanctimonies,
If sanctimony be the gods' delight,
If there be rule in unity itself,
This is not she. (137–42)

What he shared with Cressida has unravelled, the binding sleeve airily reduced not just to an 'immaterial skein of sleave-silk' but to the warped trace in his speech of 'Ariachne's broken woof' (152), probing for an opening between his and Diomed's Cressida. How can unity not be single, when the point of a silken thread cannot slip into the division between them (150–2)? Without the sacred bonds of language, the *fides* that Cicero makes so much of, not just the social order but the order of heaven (where vows are heard) will collapse.

What is the source of this extraordinary passage, to gloss which would take many pages—the literary source? Chaucer's Troilus is eloquent about love constituting the 'holy bond of thynges'.[50] In the play, the bonds are binding faiths, vows, oaths, heavenly because tied by Divine authority but also the fabric of Troilus' vision of the world. The speech is wildly exalted, even impressive in its way. But its corrupt, jealous driving-force is shown in the Leontes-like closing lines, where Cressida's taking of Diomed's hand (witnessed, or imagined, a recapitulative demolition of Troilus and Cressida's troth-plight) becomes repulsive:

> Instance, O instance, strong as Pluto's gates:
> Cressid is mine, tied with the bonds of heaven.
> Instance, O instance, strong as heaven itself:
> The bonds of heaven are slipped, dissolved, and loosed,
> And with another knot, five-finger-tied,
> The fractions of her faith, orts of her love,
> The fragments, scraps, the bits and greasy relics
> Of her o'er-eaten faith, are bound to Diomed. (153–60)

Q less forcefully reads 'giuen to Diomed'. In F, which is usually regarded as the later, revised text, the bonds which are solemn plights bind her in the sense of making her a prisoner. It is, roughly, how Troilus has conceived of it all along. Now, he arrives at the constancy of a known, proven truth: 'O Cressid, O false Cressid! False, false, false' (178–9). Or maybe not.

* * *

Believing that 'the latter part' of *Troilus and Cressida* was 'nothing but a confusion of Drums and Trumpets, Excursions and Alarms', Dryden streamlined Shakespeare's battle sequence and gave it a climax not in the killing of Hector but in the suicide of Cressida. She tells Troilus, on the battlefield, that she was never false but pretended love to avoid being held 'in hated bonds' (5.2.218). When Diomed mocks Troilus with the ring ('this pledge'), using it to claim that he enjoyed Cressida's body, she kneels to Troilus and swears her constancy, 'by all those holy vows | Which, if there be a pow're above, are binding, | Or, if there be a Hell below, are fearful' (242–4). This is a restatement of binding language in all its sanctimony, but Troilus' belief is frayed. Discredited by Diomed, Cressida can only secure her word by death. Even in that, her innocence is not proven. As Dryden's Troilus says:

> This were too much, ev'n if thou hadst been false!
> But, Oh, thou purest, whitest innocence,
> (For such I know thee now, too late I know it!) (267–9)

Only Diomed's taunting him with having believed an enemy (290–4) provides the last piece of evidence. The scene then collapses into combat: 'Troilus *singling* Diomede, *gets him down and kills him; and* Achilles *kills* Troilus *upon him. All the* Trojans *dye upon the place,* Troilus *last.*' Compared with this shapely, absurd conclusion, the last few scenes of Shakespeare's play do indeed seem loosely sequential, as well as full of boasts, epic catalogues, and scorn. But we should resist any temptation to assume that Cressida is dropped from the story. This is *Troilus and Cressida* to the end.

After the eavesdropping scene, Troilus is obsessed with going out to fight. He has already said he hates Diomed as much as he does Cressida love, and has vowed, Hector-like, terrible triumph over his enemy (5.2.165–76). As he goes out to battle, this priority is restated. Faith to Cressida, and the complication of her words, have become an unwelcome distraction from what is now his 'major vow':

TROILUS They are at it, hark! Proud Diomed, believe
I come to lose my arm or win my sleeve.
Enter PANDARUS
PANDARUS Do you hear, my lord, do you hear?
TROILUS What now?
PANDARUS Here's a letter come from yon poor girl.
TROILUS Let me read. (5.3.98–103)

Among the play's syncopated parallels, this resembles the letter sent from Hecuba (with Polyxena's token) to Achilles: one between Troy and the Greek camp, the other in reverse. It also has, since letters could be regarded as tokens,[51] something in common with glove and sleeve. It is another token of their plight, but not one that he can now trust:

TROILUS Words, words, mere words, no matter from the heart.
Th'effect doth operate another way.
Go, wind, to wind: there turn and change together.
My love with words and errors still she feeds,
But edifies another with her deeds.
PANDARUS Why, but hear you—
TROILUS Hence, broker-lackey! Ignomy and shame
Pursue thy life, and live aye with thy name. *Exeunt* [*severally*] (110–17)

What deeds are those? This is the morning after the eavesdropping scene and only a token has been taken. If he kills Diomed in battle, nothing more will happen. So even though he has broken his troth by not truly seeing her, only eavesdropping, even though he has been so unbending in his notion of constancy that he has cast her off before she is false, he could still preserve her faith. The audience is never told the contents of the letter (though it is, we gather, lovingly worded). 'Where were you last night?' 'Ransom me before I am forced'? The eloquence of Troilus on the bonds of heaven is plunged into petty dismissiveness in his rejection of the letter as merely words.

Achilles receives from Troy a letter and a token. These double items figure in the Troilus plot too. From Cressida's letter we move to the token, as derisively introduced by Thersites on the battlefield as it was outside Calchas' tent:

> Now they are clapper-clawing one another. I'll go look on. That dissembling abominable varlet Diomed has got that same scurvy doting foolish young knave's sleeve of Troy there in his helm. I would fain see them meet, that that same young Trojan ass that loves the whore there might send that Greekish whoremasterly villain with the sleeve back to the dissembling luxurious drab of a sleeveless errand. . . .
>
> *Enter* DIOMEDES, [*followed by*] TROILUS
>
> Soft, here comes sleeve and t'other.
>
> TROILUS [*to* DIOMEDES] Fly not, for shouldst thou take the river Styx
> I would swim after.
>
> [...]
>
> THERSITES Hold thy whore, Grecian! Now for thy whore, Trojan! Now the sleeve, now the sleeve!
>
> [*Exit* DIOMEDES, *driving in* TROILUS] (5.4.1–21)

'Now the pledge! Now, now, now', as he cried outside Calchas' tent. But this time the contest is entirely between the warriors, who will take the sleeve and who will keep it. There is nothing here of the discretion of the brooch worn under Diomed's collar, in Chaucer. The pledge is an open, competitive challenge. And Troilus promises fidelity to (his conflict with) Diomed by invoking the river that the ancient gods swore by. It is a displaced version of the tokens given to and taken from Cressida.

In Dryden, Troilus had said to Diomed, on the battlefield, of Cressida's ring upon his finger:

> You must restore it *Greek*, by Heav'n you must:
> No spoil of mine shall grace a Traitors hand.
> And, with it, give me back the broken vows
> Of my false fair; which, perjur'd as she is,
> I never will resigne, but with my Soul. (421–5)

This shows what Shakespeare could have given Troilus to say. He does not mention Cressida. He does not say he still loves her and will not give her, or her vows, up, even if false. Why bother with the sleeve? The sign of rivalry is turning into an idiotic fixation, the meaning of where it comes from so secondary as to have been lost sight of. One thinks of the glove in Williams's cap in *Henry V*, which Fluellen challenges without any regard for the back-story of its bearer (4.7). In the play's vigilant, not always unadmiring depiction of Henry's ability to delegate or shuffle off responsibility, he is shown as flexibly able to give up on a troublesome, honour-bound token. In *Troilus* there is only compulsion, as the sleeve becomes an excuse for two competitive men to try to kill each other (something that, to add a further absurdity, they would, as leading enemies, be doing in any case). The symbolic value of the sleeve is translated from love token to a pledge of rivalry.

Through the sleeve Cressida remains spectrally present. That Troilus does not admit to Diomed that he wants the sleeve makes little difference: from his hostility, and from earlier in the play, Diomed, like the audience, knows that he does, and why. As a result, when Diomed wins Troilus' horse—an unseen, offstage prize, even more notional than the sleeve—he can demonstrate to Cressida that he has breached the guard of her strongest oath, to conceal the identity of her lover. He knows it is Troilus and can show it. So she has nothing to hold back on.

> Go, go, my servant, take thou Troilus' horse.
> Present the fair steed to my Lady Cressid.
> Fellow, commend my service to her beauty.
> Tell her I have chastised the amorous Trojan,
> And am her knight by proof. (5.5.1–3)

Note the importance, once again, of proof. As he does in Chapman's Homer, Diomed shows 'persistive constancy' in the face of fortune. His winning of the horse is in Caxton. But in Chaucer, as we saw, Diomed had been given it earlier by Cressida, who won it of Troilus, in an amiable bet. In the play, the horse is Diomed's reciprocation for the sleeve, taking Troilus' place in the exchange of tokens with Cressid.

The next time they wheel out on stage, Troilus is being hotly pursued, because he has done such killing work among the Greeks. Rivalry between Troilus and Diomed is now compounded by rivalry between the fellow-Greeks, Diomed and Ajax, about which of them should fight him. When Troilus boldly enters, there is yet more reciprocal nonsense: 'O traitor Diomed! Turn thy false face, thou traitor, | And pay the life thou ow'st me for my horse' (5.6.6–7). This would be merely ridiculous did it not display Troilus' projection of his shame at losing Cressida onto the man who is dislodging him. Diomed has promised Troilus nothing, so he cannot be (as he calls Cressida) 'false'. And he is certainly not a traitor (a good word for a traitor's daughter, going over to the Greeks). The sleeve was a ghost of Cressida. The horse is an even lighter recollection of Troilus' bond with her in Chaucer. Now her presence is reduced further, lending an edge to rivalry. When he rejects Ajax's claim to fight Troilus, Diomed says: 'He is my prize; I will not look upon' (5.6.10). From such small, contrasting touches, what we call character is constructed. If only Troilus had been as eager to act when he 'looked upon' Diomed taking Cressida. Sleeve, horse, now Troilus himself are prizes (and beyond them, Cressida). This is almost the last we see of the men's rivalry. But there is another, telling echo of it when Menelaus and Paris come on stage fighting and Thersites cries: 'The cuckold and the cuckold-maker are at it.—Now, bull! Now, dog!' (5.8.1–2). The same words could be applied to Troilus and his cuckold-maker. We are taken back to the fight between Paris and Menelaus at the start of the play, about which Troilus had been disparaging.[52] And to Troilus having become the Menelaus he feared to be.

'All's done, my lord', says Ulysses to Troilus, after the eavesdropping scene (5.2.115). In Shakespeare, that is rarely true. Even after the death of Hector, after Troilus has rallied (as best he can) the Trojans, his plight with Cressida still reverberates, though Pandarus is all that remains of what held the lovers together. It is obtuse of Dryden to say that Shakespeare lets Thersites and Pandarus 'fall', when Thersites is so busy during the battle scenes and Pandarus so tenacious. Dryden ended the role of the latter in Act 4, shortly after the eavesdropping scene. In Shakespeare, in both Q and F, he keeps turning up, like a bad penny. Some scholars have argued that a duplication in F indicates that, in one early version of the play, his last appearance (with or without speaking what is now the epilogue) was meant to be in 5.3, where he gives Troilus the letter.[53] Even that theory leaves open, however, the version of the ending that stands in both Q and F:

PANDARUS But hear you, hear you.
TROILUS Hence, broker-lackey. [*Strikes him*] Ignomy and shame
Pursue thy life,[54] and live aye with thy name. *Exeunt* [*all but* PANDARUS]
PANDARUS A goodly medicine for my aching bones. O world, world, world!—thus is the poor agent despised. O traitors and bawds, how earnestly are you set a work, and how ill requited! (5.11.31.1–7)

Directors are often reluctant to leave the end of the play entirely in Pandarus' hands. Trevor Nunn and Peter Stein[55] are among those who have given Cressida another entry, to supply one last meeting with Troilus. Yet the lovers are already present in spirit around the epilogue:

[PANDARUS] Good traders in the flesh, set this in your painted cloths:
As many as be here of Pandar's hall,
Your eyes, half out, weep out at Pandar's fall.
Or if you cannot weep, yet give some groans,
Though not for me, yet for your aching bones.
Brethren and sisters of the hold-door trade,
Some two months hence my will shall here be made.
It should be now, but that my fear is this:
Some gallèd goose of Winchester would hiss.
Till then I'll sweat and seek about for eases,
And at that time bequeath you my diseases. *Exit* (31.14–24)

The play has repeatedly focused on what brought the lovers together: vows, tokens, pledges, and the go-between of their plight. Pandarus is what remains of their bonds, once the sleeve has been given away and the letter torn up. Broker, traitor, bawd. The 'and' in *Troilus and Cressida*. Now he enters poxy and blighted, marked with the lesions that were passed between intimates in an age before antibiotics.

Recall 'I shall be plagued', after Cressida promises to see Diomed again. He might take this as saying that she will be plagued with waiting, full of desire. A sympathetic audience will take it rather as anticipating the plague of conscience that Cressida fears she will suffer if she does abandon Troilus. Metadramatically, it apprehends the plague of disapprobation that will disfigure her reputation down the ages. But it also prompts the audience to remember that, in other versions of the story, including those of Henryson and Heywood, Cressida contracts leprosy. As we saw in Chapters 3 and 4, the plague was viewed as a punishment for the abuse of oaths and forswearing ('Thus pour the stars down plagues for perjury', as Biron puts it).[56] What Pandarus adds are the sores known as 'tokens' that were associated with syphilis and thus (given Elizabethan confusion) with leprosy and the plague. Compare Ulysses on Achilles: 'He is so plaguy proud that the death tokens of it | Cry "No recovery"' (2.3.166–7). To be 'tokened' with plague sores is a common image. It occurs in *Antony and Cleopatra* (3.10.9–14) and Shakespeare plays on the similarity between love- and plague-tokens near the end of *Love's Labour's Lost* (5.2.419–24).[57] The marks of Pandarus' diseases are the most sordid pledge of venery. All he can do now is seek relief from the symptoms.

In promising to bequeath his diseases to us some two months hence, Pandarus might be alluding to a never-written or lost sequel (as Heywood wrote an *Iron Age, Part II*), to be staged, it may be, after the passage of an eight-week term at the Inns of Court; but the more pressing, obtuse reference is to a last will and testament that will bequeath to the audience the ailments that drive the bawd to his death bed. It should be understood that, in Protestant England, a testament was not just an allocation of property but 'a promise made by a man about to die, by which he assigns his inheritance and appoints heirs'.[58] Pandarus leaves us with the promise of that promise, and the most durable of bonds—love's ultimate, sick tokens, to be circulated through the brothels and playhouses after he has gone.

11

Binding Language in *Measure for Measure*

The fourth scene of *Measure for Measure* opens with Isabella—who is about to take her vows as a novice—talking to the nun Francesca:

And have you nuns no farther privileges?
FRANCESCA Are not these large enough?
ISABELLA Yes, truly. I speak not as desiring more,
But rather wishing a more strict restraint
Upon the sisterhood, the votarists of Saint Clare. (1.4.1–5)

'Votarists' is an unusual word, unrecorded before Shakespeare, and it is placed here in an admiring, supplementary way, to point up the fact that the Daughters of St Clare are bound to their routine by vows (from Latin *votum*). Whether Isabella is taken aback by what Francesca has told her, or would 'Yes, truly' welcome greater austerity, depends on how the actor plays the lines. But the strictness of the restraint becomes almost comically apparent when Lucio, bringing the news that Claudio has impregnated Juliet, calls from offstage 'Ho, peace be in this place!' 'It is a man's voice', Francesca anxiously declares:

Gentle Isabella.
Turn you the key, and know his business of him.
You may, I may not; you are yet unsworn.
When you have vowed, you must not speak with men
But in the presence of the prioress.
Then if you speak, you must not show your face;
Or if you show your face, you must not speak. (6–13)

Shakespeare often uses the word *vow* interchangeably with *oath*. In *Measure*, however, his focus on binding language makes for precise, loaded distinctions, which condition our understanding of specific utterances in religious as well as secular contexts. Early modern writers sometimes call oaths 'confessional' because they invoke the Deity as witness; including an element of 'prayer' they could be categorized as a form of worship.[1] With vowing, we are even more closely involved with the rites and ties of religion—a word derived by Elizabethan scholars from *religio*, 'I bind' (p. 11). *Votum* is a religious promise, a votive offering or prayer.[2] We have seen that, unlike an *oath*, a *vow* can be directly addressed to God. It can also be cerebral or passionate (*votum* as 'wish, desire'). Yet the higher the speech act, the harder, more dramatic its fall. *Measure* will show vows being broken, false, base, and no more reliable than dicers' oaths.

Religious vows of the sort that Isabella and Francesca discuss would have been attractive to some in Shakespeare's audience. In 1598, the first nunnery for English Catholics was founded on the Continent. Another was set up at Saint-Omer in 1604, the year when *Measure for Measure* was composed and performed (on 26 December) at court. But the reformers were opposed. They could accept the validity of Nazirite vows, such as those taken by Samson, and the baptismal vows approved by Christ. They also, for the most part, admitted holy, personal vows taken for specific purposes,[3] breakable when circumstances changed. For Luther, Calvin, Tyndale, Peter Martyr Vermigli, and the rest, however, cloistered vows were Judaic, mechanical, absurd—as with Francesca—and by promoting works over faith they flew in the face of the Gospel.[4] 'According to the doctrine of S. Paule', Beza declared, 'wee rest in the libertie wherin Jesus Christ hath set us, without farther binding vs to mens bondages. And therefore if wee make any vowes or promises vnto GOD, they must haue their ground from his worde, that he may like and allowe of them.'[5] Behind this is the celebrated passage in which the apostle rebukes the Galatians for reverting (like the Catholic Church) to 'bondage vnder the rudiments of the worlde' (4: 3), when they ought to stand 'in the libertie wherewith Christ hathe made vs fre, and be not intangled againe with the yoke of bondage' (5: 1).

Measure for Measure uses multiple parallels to force comparison and baffle resolution. While Isabella is joining the votarists, the Godly, precise Angelo is devoting himself to 'study, and fast' (1.4.60), and Duke Vincentio is putting on the habit of a Franciscan—male equivalent of the Little Clares. 'By the vow of mine order', he dubiously assures the Provost, when attempting to save Claudio.[6] Still in the garb of a friar he explains to Isabella that he cannot attend the occasion of the Duke's return to Vienna because 'I am combinèd by a sacred vow'—another unusual word in which the *combination* of the friars is fused with the *binding* vows that unite them.[7] More immediately, while Isabella heads into 'strict restraint', her brother, who has equally not yet taken his full vows (of marriage), is under the 'restraint' of arrest thanks to Angelo's revival of Vienna's 'strict statutes'.[8]

Once again there is a Pauline background. The audience has already seen Lucio encountering Claudio in the street, crossing the stage under arrest: 'Why, how now, Claudio? Whence comes this restraint?' 'From too much liberty, my Lucio,' he replies, 'liberty' (1.2.104–5). Paul warned the Galatians: 'brethren, ye haue bene called vnto libertie: onely vse not *your* libertie as an occasion vnto the flesh' (5: 13). Having slipped with Juliet, Claudio has fallen into what Angelo will call 'the manacles | Of the all-binding law' (2.4.93–4). It is not the least of the play's textual problems that the Folio (there is no quarto), at this, the only point where the word 'binding' can be found in Shakespeare, reads 'all-building-Law'. Without being too neoclassical, we can say that, locally, 'binding' sounds right after 'manacles'. As should already be clear, however, the stronger argument for emendation is that the play is preoccupied with binding language, and thus with loosing and associated paradoxes.

Think beyond Paul to the Duke as Friar and sovereign. One of the best-known verses in Matthew (16: 19) has Jesus saying to Peter: 'I wil giue vnto thee the keyes of the kingdome of heauen, and whatsoeuer thou shalt binde vpon earth, shalbe bound in heauen: and whatsoeuer thou shalt lose on earth, shalbe losed in heauen.' Reformers interpreted the keys as the Gospels, but Catholics held to the medieval belief that they were the power invested in the Pope and lesser clergy to dispense from vows and to absolve sins in confession. 'O merciful God', a typical Jacobean, Catholic prayer begins, 'as at the wordes of thy Angel, the chaines and fetters, fell from S. *Peter*, and he immediately was loosed, *Actes. 12.* so graunt, deare Lord, that by the wordes of this holy Sacrament, pronounced by the Priest, the chaines and fetters of my sinnes may be vnbound.'[9] Catholics argued that the requirement to confess made for social discipline and encouraged people to take their oaths more seriously.[10] You were 'bounde' to speak the truth in confession,[11] as you were in the tribunal of your oath, if you wished to be absolved or acquitted.

That the name and nature of the sacraments were grounded in the Roman military oath or *sacramentum*, for Tertullian, Augustine, and other Church Fathers, was well known after the Reformation.[12] The sacrament—for Catholics—of confession was isomorphic as well as etymologically identical to the ritualized structure of 'sacrament' in the early modern as well as classical sense of *oath* (*OED*, sacrament, *n.* 4). As a Friar, the Duke hears Juliet's confession, sealing her asseveration with a *benedicite* (2.3.41), and offers ghostly counsel to Claudio (3.1). He says he has been confessor to Angelo, and has been so to Mariana. As we shall see when we get to Act 5, it probably matters that the status of confession as a scene of binding and loosing was topical in 1604 because of controversy at the Hampton Court conference about the survival of pre-Reformation wording about absolution in the Book of Common Prayer.[13]

So much for the Duke as Friar. Within the same scriptural framework, Vincentio as magistrate is obliged to put into effect those 'all-binding laws' that establishment-minded Protestants keyed to the power of the state. Here is Jeremy Taylor, as though praising Shakespeare's 'Duke of dark corners' (4.3.147): 'God... confirms the laws of men, and he binds in heaven what they bind on earth, and he also knows in earth what is done in the most secret corner, and judges accordingly.'[14] But what is binding about the law if the law has itself been bound?[15] The question had some urgency in 1603–4, when King James sought to impose statutes neglected under Elizabeth. He issued, for instance, a proclamation warning that he would revive the hunting laws.[16] Angelo, rather less fairly—though any reimposition raises doubts—issues a proclamation that instantly, even retrospectively, reanimates old laws against sexual irregularity. The Duke tells a Friar that he is putting Angelo in charge because the 'strict statutes' have been gathering dust. When the Friar points out that 'It rested in your grace | To unloose this tied-up Justice', he replies that it would have been tyrannous of him to have done so, and that it would have led to 'slander'—criticism of the powers that be, whether accurate or not (1.3.31–2, 43). This elliptical, characteristic observation carries us into the heart of a set of early modern, sociolinguistic issues that I want to pursue in this chapter.

Of all the plays of Shakespeare, *Measure for Measure* is the most dizzying in the inventiveness with which it articulates and connects in patterns, from the sexual and legal on the one hand to the sacramental and allegorical on the other, the over- and undertones of *binding*. The scope of what is said, shown, and suggested is at its most astonishing in Act 5, though a number of the tropes and institutions involved have already been mentioned. For now, it seems important to narrow discussion down by returning to the names in play when Lucio comes to the nunnery. Isabella means 'vowed to God'.[17] Lucio suggests 'Lucifer' (as Angelo is a fallen Angel, and as Satan is the father of lies, the seasoning, as we shall see, of slander).[18] Lucio does shed light (*luce*) on Vienna's darker vices. But mostly he is 'Loose-io',[19] the antithesis of a votarist's restraint. Some critics have expressed surprise that he does not offer to stand bail for Claudio and refuses it to Pompey, but this is to be expected in a character who would hate to 'bind' himself for another's 'forth-comming'.[20] Lucio is not just sexually loose, getting Kate Keepdown with child, but psychologically and dramaturgically so, shifting around the action, constantly on the edge of scenes, and also in speech, not keeping his promises to Kate, forswearing her before the Duke, and spraying out perjuries and slanders, which are, in early modern thought, inseparable from the oaths and vows that give detraction a superficial, ingratiating credibility.

This is a decisive point. Lucio is central to *Measure* as a play not just about sexuality but about the loose, binding language that is meant to control it. He haunts the taverns and bawdy houses in which libels were bred and consumed, along with ale and tobacco.[21] We should not always think of oaths and vows as free-standing, load-bearing speech acts. Swearing can go with the flow, sliding into abusive practices that include lying and defamation—scandalous talk, whether true or false—the argot of the insubordinate. In the Folio dramatis personae, 'Lucio, a fantastique' is associated with '2. Other like Gentlemen'. Though singular, he is the voice of a group, a subculture of profanity and rumour. As the churchman William Perkins puts it in *A Direction for the Government of the Tongue*:

> It woulde make a mans heart to bleede, to heare and consider how Swearing, blaspheming, Cursed speaking, Railing, Backbiting, Slandering, Chiding, Quarrelling, Contending, Iesting, Mocking, Flattering, Lying, dissembling, Vaine and Idle talking overflowe in all places.[22]

Oaths are abused by such people not just to garnish slurs and lies but to insist on their veracity. This is important to *Measure*. As a loose habit of language, swearing laced speech to win assent to slander, then sealed it; the instruments of truth turned into devices for lying. Catholic tracts denounce the spectrum of impious, perjured language, noting how dangerously addictive the habit could be,[23] but it was a favourite theme of the Reformed.[24] The king himself warned Prince Henry, in *Basilikon Doron* (a treatise which Shakespeare must have known): 'And especially, beware to offend your conscience, with vse of swearing or lying, suppose but in iest; for oathes are but an vse, and a sinne cloathed with no delight nor gaine.'[25] 'The spirit of Detraction and Periury', William Vaughan noted, was one and the same, and

God's disapproval of it could be demonstrated by quotations from the Bible against swearing.[26]

Isabella's vows represent the 'bondes of Truth'[27] at their most exalted. But vows can be abused, as they are by the Duke/Friar, and sink from rigidity into profanity and error. To the speaking names Isabella and Lucio we can add that of Deepvow, who is mentioned by Pompey in his soliloquy about the inhabitants of the prison, along with Master Rash, who swore himself to a bond for a commodity of brown paper and old ginger, not to mention wild Half-can who brutally stabbed Pots (4.3.1–16). Editing *Measure* in the Oxford Middleton, John Jowett argues that this speech was interpolated.[28] We are urged to compare the phrase 'deep oath' in Middleton's (?) *Nice Valour*. Though it is likely enough that the duplicate opening of Folio 1.2 was added by Middleton, I see nothing else in the play that requires such explanation. One might as well compare Brutus' 'deep vow' in *The Rape of Lucrece* (line 1847) or 'deep oaths of thy deep kindness' in Sonnet 152. From one angle you could view the soliloquy as a pile-up of material prompted by the subplot of Shakespeare's main source, Whetstone's *Promos and Cassandra* (1578), in which the deputy's officer, Phallax, cheats people by making them swear to disadvantageous bonds. For now it is enough to note that Master Deepvow is doubly bound in prison. As she prepares to become a deep vower behind the bars of holiness, little does Isabella know what company she keeps.

* * *

So far so likely. Yet the play is not called *The Adventures of Rash and Deepvow*. It takes its title from the Sermon on the Mount:

> Iudge not, that ye be not iudged.
>
> For with what iudgement ye iudge, ye shal be iudged, and with what measure ye mette, it shal be measured to you againe.
>
> And why seest thou the mote, that is in thy brothers eye, and perceiuest not the beame that is in thine owne eye?
>
> Or how saist thou to thy brother, Suffer me to cast out the mote out of thine eye, and beholde a beame is in thine owne eye? (Matthew 7: 1–4)

This informs the Duke's warning in the final scene of the play that Angelo deserves to die for sending Claudio to execution: 'Like doth quit like, and measure still for measure' (5.1.403). He should be sentenced for the beam in his own eye having sentenced Claudio for the mote in his. It matters, however, that Christ's injunction turns not just on seeing but on speech: you should not uncharitably defame, by remarking on the mote in your brother's eye.[29] As a result, early modern commentary is often intimately connected to what is said about another set of verses, earlier in the Sermon, about the limits of asseveration. This has been quoted in the Introduction (p. 12) and selectively in Chapters 3 and 4 (pp. 75, 114), but it is so central that it bears repetition:

> Againe, ye haue heard that it was said to them of olde time, Thou shalt not forsweare thy self, but shalt performe thine othes to the Lord.
>
> But I say vnto you, Sweare not at all, nether by heauen, for it is the throne of God:
>
> Nor yet by the earth: for it is his fote stole: nether by Ierusalem: for it is the citie of the great King.
>
> Nether shalt thou sweare by thine head, because thou canst not make one heere white or blacke.
>
> But let your communication be, Yea, yea: Nay, nay. For whatsoeuer *is* more then these, commeth of euil. (Matthew 5: 33–7)

The precepts in these passages were 'binding' in the sense that Christ's injunctions—especially his negative ones—were held to 'bind' the conscience.[30] How all-binding his new law was may, of course, be doubted. To read commentaries and sermons on the Sermon on the Mount from Luther, Calvin, and Tyndale to Perkins and John Carter is to find it said that judgement by a magistrate is necessary to the Godly commonwealth, though it should not be 'rash' or hypocritical—there should be no beam in the magistrate's eye—and that oaths, again not 'rash' ones, should be sworn as required by the authorities. For all that, a great deal of scope was left for objecting to 'rash iudgement' by individuals, especially when it took the form of 'carping, and slaundering' (Calvin) which gave wings to defamation and was itself a disparagement of God.[31] Charity requires us to avoid being curious about others' deficiencies, and to shun perjury by cutting out oaths and vows and only mildly averring, as Isabella does when she says to Francesca 'Yes, truly'. As Perkins puts it in *Direction*: '*let us take heede that we judge not or condemne any mans saying or doing rashly*.'[32] It begins to sound as though Master Rash was a shrewdly chosen associate of Deepvow.

This set of arguments goes back to Augustine. In his own sermon on the Sermon on the Mount, he connects licentious language and the lying about which he is so severe in his treatises on mendacity with rash, habitual oaths and profanity, and both with uncharitable judgement. As it happens, his sermon also includes the earliest recorded version of the story on which *Measure* is based, of a rich man who coerces a woman to sleep with him by saying that, if she does, he will give her enough gold to free her husband from the death penalty imposed by a stormy, oath-swearing governor.[33] When the woman succumbs, the rich man pays her with a bag full of earth not gold. Augustine presents Acindynus' rash swearing as the trigger to this set of events, which is only partly redeemed when the woman is rewarded with ownership of the land from which the earth was taken. This ancestor of the Isabella plot is symptomatically placed just before the chapter in Augustine's sermon on asseverating by yea and nay.

Slander and not judging become major, linked issues in the last scene of *Measure for Measure*.[34] But questions about them, and thus about swearing and perjury, bleed through the dialogue. Take the scene in Act 2 where Isabella, egged on by Lucio, presses Angelo to spare her brother. Unexpectedly to the modern audience, she finds her way through the question of profanity to the mote and beam argument that urges the deputy to substitute himself for Claudio, a development which, unfortunately, encourages him to want to fornicate with the would-be nun. 'Great men may jest with saints', she says, ''tis wit in them, | But in the less, foul profanation' (2.2.130–1). This means that the high and mighty can get away with jesting with the virtuous when it would be counted blasphemous for ordinary people to do so. But 'jest with saints' also means swear by saints in jest, as the Duke does, when disguised as a Friar, he falsely swears by St Francis: 'by the saint whom I profess' (4.2.165). Compare the wording of the Act to Restrain Abuses (1606), which forbade actors 'iestingly, and prophanely [to] speake, or vse the holy Name of God, or of Christ Iesus, or of the holy Ghost, or of the Trinitie'.[35] This undertow becomes more explicit:

That in the captain's but a choleric word,
Which in the soldier is flat blasphemy.
LUCIO [*aside to* ISABELLA] Art advised o' that? More on't.
ANGELO Why do you put these sayings upon me? (2.2.133–6)

These are commonplaces, Angelo protests. As Lucio senses, however, Isabella is on the right track. The point about jesting with saints leads into 'Iudge not': the mote which is a captain's rash word is a beam of blasphemy in the soldier's mouth: 'Go to your bosom; | Knock there, and ask your heart what it doth know | That's like my brother's fault' (139–41).

What shows through as an issue here leaves many marks in the language of *Measure*. Beyond the modest, specific incidence of such words as 'oath' and 'vow',[36] there is a high count of 'marry', 'by heaven', 'i' faith', and so on. The volatility of binding language can be felt: on the one hand, serious vowing to God, on the other, profanity that enables perjury and sticks defamation to its object. Yet the text as we have it is reduced. The script played before James would have been stronger (more swearing 'by God', 'by the mass', and so on) before the Act of 1606 led to expurgation. It is as though the surviving text of *Measure*, worked over—editors agree—for a revival, had gone to Angelo for licensing. Shakespeare can hardly have meant the bawdy Pompey to sprinkle his lines with such Isabellan phatics as 'very well', 'Truly', 'indeed', and 'Pray', nor have meant Barnardine to refuse execution with the palpably substitutive declaration: 'I swear I will not die today' (4.3.52). If an unexpurgated quarto had been published it would have stood in relation to the Folio text as Q *Othello* does to F. It would have resembled *Promos and Cassandra*, where the low-life version of yea and nay is 'Nay gogs foote,... Yea, gogs h[e]art.'[37] The changes are most damaging in the case of Lucio, whose profanities are spurred on by defamation, by the *iniuria* that tied 'Iudge not' to 'Sweare not'. Lucio now says 'Yes' where we would expect ''Sblood', then 'Come', 'indeed', 'Why', and even 'O sir', where, in other cases of expurgation, the earlier, extant text has 'zounds', 'i' faith', 'fore God', 'swounds', and 'by the masse'.[38] It is an index of the importance of loose, binding language to early audiences of *Measure* that so much of it should have been purged. That we have to read the text with X-ray attention to deleted profanities explains why commentators have missed its significance.

* * *

Licentious language, from swearing to slander, and the implication of each in the other, was a live issue throughout Shakespeare's lifetime. It was peculiarly topical, however, during the months in which *Measure* took shape, before its performance at court. In his speech at the Prorogation of Parliament, on 7 July 1604, the new king complained about the Lucios in the Commons: 'where many are some must needs be idle heads, some rash, some curious, some busy informers.... where there is a like liberty the worst likely carries away the best.'[39] Invoking Proverbs 10: 18–19 ('he that inuenteth sclandre, is a foole. In manie wordes there can not want iniquitie') he objected to the loose talk: 'Some had an itching humour ever to be talking,... *in multiloquis non deest peccatum*.' Curiosity, he keeps saying, was the fault. In Scotland, 'I was heard not only as a king, but, suppose I say it, as a counsellor. Contrary, here nothing but curiosity from morning to evening to find faults in my propositions.' Like the Duke disguised as a Friar, offering spiritual advice to Claudio and Mariana, James wanted to counsel his people. Instead his tolerance was abused. 'You have done many things rashly,' he concluded. 'I wish you would use your liberty with more modesty in time to come.'

This theme long held the king. Liberty in speech was acceptable, within the limits approved by scripture, and by the Protestant reformers, who knew that language like the flesh could run from liberty to licence.[40] But speech was always too free when it incited commoners to pry into and judge royal decisions. Then criticism was slurred into slander. As late as 1620, James issued *A Proclamation against Excesse of Lauish and Licentious Speech of Matters of State*, which warned against 'libertie of discourse' that proceeded 'out of rashnesse'. In July 1621, troubled by popular discussion of war in Europe and relations with Spain,[41] he issued a further proclamation with the same title, rebuking 'inordinate libertie of vnreuerent speech' among the vulgar. This conjunction reinforces the claim made by the Oxford editors of Shakespeare and Middleton that the passage at the start of 1.2 in which Lucio and a couple of gentlemen irreverently discuss the likelihood of war between the Duke and the King of Hungary was added in 1621.[42] *Measure*, we shall see, was an apt play to revive at times of official sensitivity about loose language.

Lucio, as I have noted, is the strongest instance of language running loose through curiosity, slander, swearing, and forswearing. When he first meets Vincentio disguised as a Friar, he is all agog for news, then digs into criticism of the authorities. 'It was a mad, fantastical trick of [the Duke] to steal from the state,' he opines (3.1.340–1), and, as for Angelo's campaign against lechery, 'Yes, in good sooth'—one of his expurgated oaths—'the vice is of a great kindred' (347). If Lucio simply spoke truth unwittingly unto power he would be less amusing. He would not even be an early modern slanderer. As the historian Laura Gowing notes, 'Slander was a creative project',[43] in which the likely modulated into the entertaining. Lucio thus goes on:

> They say this Angelo was not made by man and woman...Some report a sea-maid spawned him, some that he was begot between two stockfishes. But it is certain that when he makes water his urine is congealed ice; that I know to be true. And he is a motion ungenerative; that's infallible.
>
> DUKE You are pleasant, sir, and speak apace. (349–57)

We can safely assume that Lucio does not know this to be true. Perjury designed to please was held to be typical of slander—as was speaking apace, when we should follow the Sermon on the Mount, and James's speech at the Prorogation of Parliament, and say little, not have an itching tongue. It is one of Lucio's neatest ploys that, after promising to disclose the reason for the Duke's absence from court, he deepens the innuendo by purporting to be a man of discretion: 'No, pardon, 'tis a secret must be locked within the teeth and the lips' (375–6). This mockingly recycles a commonplace about the physiology of linguistic restraint.[44]

The Duke/Friar wants to make Lucio answerable for his slanders. Saying that he plans to call him to account in front of Vincentio, he invokes his vows as Friar and his obedience to the prince: 'I am bound to call upon you.' He rightly suspects, however, that Lucio will not be bound but will 'forswear' his defamations, including those of the Duke (394–5, 401). This is detraction of the state, for the sake of good fellowship. As Vaughan scornfully put it: 'Hee is no Politician (quoth *Peter pleaseman*) that will not pledge the world in the cup of *Detraction*'[45]—where pledging enacts an oath. The man who wants to please will back up and even heighten profanity and rumour: 'If thou hearest them blaspheme, or blazing out nouelties, indeuor thou to verifie the same, or to requite their familiar conference with some additions of thine owne inuention.'[46] Such a pattern of speech is dangerous. To slander for the sake of popularity leads to a curious probing of authority:

> By this meanes thou shalt make thy company precious vnto them, and also prie (like an insinuating intelligencer) into the inward state of all thy countrey. By this means thou shalt learne their seuerall and secret inclinations, who be... *corrupt* Magistrates, who be carousers, fornicators,... (236)

It is hard for us to feel that there could be anything wrong with the exposure of corrupt magistrates, even by detractors in alehouses; but this sort of disparagement was regarded as contrary to scripture. As *A Plaine Description of the Auncient Petigree of Dame Slaunder* declares, we should not 'backbite the Judges, nor... speake euill of the superiors that gouerne the people'.[47]

According to the *Plaine Description*, 'Sclaunder... standeth on three persons, euen like as matters of Commedies doe, that is, by the Accuser, and by him that is accused, and by the hearer of the accusement' (B7v). In the scenes between the Duke/Friar and Lucio, those roles are conflated. The point of the comedy is that the hearer of the accuser is the accused, and the audience enjoys his discomfiture. We are in the theatre to be pleased, so our response to Lucio's licentious speech cannot be the lofty one of the Protestant moralist. But neither, on the other hand, does the play promulgate anything like a modern defence of free speech. Rather, it complicates orthodox disapproval of Lucio by making some of what he says self-evidently, buoyantly incredible, and, as others have noted, by giving the fantastical Duke some of the same qualities as the fantastic. Both are curious, sniffing out scandal, and going into dark corners to shed some light. The Duke, it may be objected, is not a slanderer. In the final, climactic scene, however, still in the role of Friar, he does, in the words of Vaughan, uncover the secrets of corrupt magistrates, denouncing Angelo and through him the Duke, and prompting Escalus to accuse him of 'Slander to th' state!' (5.1.317).

More intriguingly, in early modern treatises, the slanderer was compared to the confessor (which will lead us back to binding). Both are in a position of judgement, and can be agents of repentance. 'As sone as any man shall backbite vs, or mocke vs, or make vs as it were a tale and laughingstocke', urged Calvin, we should accuse ourselves and probe our guilt so that defamation can lead to penitence.[48] Moreover both slanderer and confessor spread scandalous intelligence. Lucio, for instance, shops Mistress Overdone ('this is one Lucio's information against me' (3.1.427–8)), and the Duke/Friar confirms the Protestant stereotype that Catholic clerics broke the seal of confession (no wonder the play was excised from the copy of the Folio held in the seminary at Valladolid).[49] As Vaughan puts it: '*Detractours* measuring our actions by the ell of their owne guiltie consciences, and vsurping the Popish partes of Ghostly Confessors, doe parley in priuate among themselues.'[50] The Duke/Friar falsely informs Claudio that Angelo does not intend to sleep with his sister, adding, 'I am confessor to Angelo, and I know this to be true' (3.1.167–8). He tells Isabella, in 4.3, that he knows from parleying in private that the Duke is due home tomorrow ('One of our convent, and his confessor, | Gives me this instance' (4.3.120–1)). More plausibly, though disconcertingly, Mariana says that the Duke/Friar has been her confessor, and in the final speech of the play he assures Angelo that, having been so, he knows her virtue. Why, apart from the Duke's incorrigible desire to revel in curiosity and control his subjects' thoughts, does he reassure him in that way? The answer takes us deeper into loose, binding language.

* * *

Historians have shown that actions for defamation—often pursued in the ecclesiastical courts[51]—increased in the late sixteenth century and were voluminous during Shakespeare's lifetime.[52] They have also shown how mistaken it is to see defamation as simply the problem and legal process the solution. Taking defamation to court could be a way of escalating a quarrel.[53] One of the paradoxes that Shakespeare was aware of is that testimony and trial could generate slander rather than resolve it. This is thrashed to a conclusion of sorts in the final scene of *Measure*; but it is anticipated in its first legal action, the examination of Froth and Pompey by the magistrates Angelo and Escalus—in accordance with the Marian statutes[54]—where testimony is given to the latter with many a 'Marry' and 'Truly'. The constable, Elbow, declares that Pompey and Mistress Overdone and their bawdy house are 'respected'. The bawd counters the malapropism by swearing 'By this hand, sir, his wife is a more respected person than any of us all' (2.1.145–9). To discredit Elbow more explicitly, how truly we may wonder, he says that Mistress Elbow 'was respected with him before he married with her' (153)—i.e. she did what Juliet did with Claudio, contrary to the strict statutes.

That the Duke is sensitive to slander is indisputable.[55] It would be a mistake, however, to take this as royal vanity and roll it into an anti-Duke account of the play—commonplace though they have become—as though Shakespeare were satirizing the King James of the 1604 Prorogation.[56] Loose, binding language and the 'opprobrious slanders' it impelled were regarded by Jacobean commentators as 'firebrands of priuat and open grudges',[57] and they have negative effects in Vienna far beyond Mistress Elbow. Recall the beginnings of the bed-trick, when the Duke/Friar asks Isabella, 'Have you not heard speak of Mariana, the sister of Frederick, the great soldier who miscarried at sea? (3.1.205–7). Interestingly, she replies: 'I have heard of the lady, and good words went with her name.' Mariana's reputation, then, was sound. 'She should this Angelo have married,' the Duke/Friar explains: 'was affianced to her oath' (208–11). This precise, odd Folio reading, often wrongly amended,[58] catches the intensity of Mariana's devotion to her word and its emptiness as Angelo slips the knot. Not 'affianced *by* her oath' or 'affianced *to*' her lover, but 'affianced to her *oath*'. For she lost 'her combinate husband' (218)—another neologism that compresses *binding*—when her dowry went missing at sea along with Frederick. Failure to deliver on a promise of material goods was not unknown in the period as grounds for breaking off a betrothal.[59] What the Duke/Friar stresses, however, is that he evaded marriage by saying that Mariana was accused of levity. He 'swallowed his vows whole, pretending in her discoveries of dishonour' (221–2). Since the Duke has heard of this imputation, Angelo has been guilty of slander. This was the licentious language that loosened the bond of his vow.

Mariana, about to be substituted for Isabella in the bed-trick, is the more closely paralleled with her because the latter risks losing her brother. She will be protected only by the cloisters of the Daughters of St Clare, much as Mariana has retreated to the grange (a monastic farm-building)[60] at St Luke's. Lack of support from her family has left Mariana, like other early modern spinsters, reduced in her ability to counter defamation,[61] even were she not still unhappily in love with Angelo—as we see from the song that starts Act 4:

MARIANA, [*discovered with a*] BOY *singing*
BOY Take, O take those lips away
That so sweetly were forsworn, . . .

That the song has been attributed to Fletcher—unconvincingly in my view[62]—does not detract from the work it does with binding language. Does 'forsworn' mean that you lied to me when swearing (or silently kissing) your faith or that you swore a faith that was later broken? Either way, your lips remained sweet to me even in betrayal.

And those eyes, the break of day
Lights that do mislead the morn;
But my kisses bring again, bring again,
Seals of love, though sealed in vain, sealed in vain. (4.1.1–6)

What will the audience infer about Mariana from this song? She does not want to lose lips or eyes, but the injunction to take them away (when they have already been taken away) touchingly gives her some say in the matter, within the frame of the song. It also recasts the separation as a lovers' parting at dawn which the returns of a relationship can repair. The Mariana of the song insistently yet fadingly asks for her kisses back 'again'. From her point of view, the bed-trick will resume something broken off, which gives emotional content to the Duke/Friar's questionable stratagem. Though kissing may feel like an exchange, however (and my kisses only exist by virtue of the lips I kiss), to get your kisses back is impossible. They go away with your lover. Seals were specific and authenticating (only Angelo's lips would do). In principle they confirmed oaths, and made promises binding.[63] Warm, red, and adhesive, like waxen seals being fixed in place, the reciprocating lips of Angelo resemble the 'scarlet ornaments' that 'have . . . sealed false bonds of love' in Sonnet 142. The kissing left no trace, except in the betrayal of

Mariana's heart. No betrothal witnesses are mentioned. The intensity of the intimacy draws on its end-stopped covertness.[64] What the seal of the kissing most oddly resembles is the seal of secrecy in confession.

When her actual confessor, the Duke/Friar arrives, Mariana instructs the boy: 'Break off thy song, and haste thee quick away.' There are a number of rapid entrances and exits in the play, often exits and re-entrances. Cumulatively, these serve to highlight the privacy of key exchanges. But there is an immediate reason for the boy's exit: as her lines make awkwardly clear ('Let me excuse me' (12)), Mariana is embarrassed to be found in circumstances so lacking in piety; rendered anxious by slander, she fears that even such a song might put her reputation in doubt. The Duke/Friar also obsesses. A number of scholars have wondered whether the notably short soliloquy that he utters while Isabella and Mariana negotiate the bed-trick should not follow his scene with Lucio, scores of lines further back. The question misses the point, that the Duke is brooding about slander:

> O place and greatness, millions of false eyes
> Are stuck upon thee; volumes of report
> Run with their false and most contrarious quest
> Upon thy doings:... (56–9)

He is right to be concerned.[65] Soon enough, Lucio returns, as rumour always does. Tellingly, given the Mariana plot, the Duke/Friar gets him to swear to the truth of his having forsworn what Mistress Overdone has disclosed, that 'Mistress Kate Keepdown was with child by him in the Duke's time; he promised her marriage. His child is a year and a quarter old come Philip and Jacob. I have kept it myself' (3.1.428–30). Lucio now admits to at least the basics of this, saying to the Duke/Friar:

> I was once before him for getting a wench with child.
> DUKE Did you such a thing?
> LUCIO Yes, marry, did I; but I was fain to forswear it. They would else have married me to the rotten medlar.
> DUKE Sir, your company is fairer than honest. Rest you well.
> LUCIO By my troth, I'll go with thee to the lane's end.... (4.3.158–63)

Lucio swears that he forswore ('marry'), a liar telling the truth ('By my troth'). It is an abuse of binding language, even when it is reduced to this tame, expurgated form. Defamation comes with that. We do not know that Kate Keepdown was a rotten medlar when he promised to marry her,[66] or forswore her and the child, though we might conclude from her taking up with Mistress Overdone that she is sinking into prostitution. If so, she was driven to it by being cast off when pregnant before marriage and by slander. The assumption is strong among critics that Kate is and was a whore. But we have no reason to think that, given the way men slander the women with whom they have broken vows. Whores are made not born. Let me qualify that. Kate's child, brought up by Mistress Overdone, is unlikely to avoid the profession (Pompey was born a bawd (3.1.319)). The legacy of loose, binding language can descend to the third and fourth generation.

* * *

Both *Measure* and *Promos and Cassandra* deal with truths sworn to and vowed. In Whetstone the very name of the Angelo-figure reminds us of the *promise* that he gives to Cassandra. As he admits, in soliloquy, after sleeping with her, Promos was 'bounde with oathe' to spare her brother and to marry her, and he should now 'keepe my vowe'. He has a get-out, however: 'I to *Cassandra* sware: | But no man else is privie to the same.' There is no evidence of his promise, and none that he bedded her. So he decides to 'unsweare the oathe' and have Andrugio's head sent to his sister with a casuistical commendation: 'To *Cassandra*, as *Promos* promist thee, | From prison, loe, he sendes thy Brother free.'[67] The whole history of 'monstrous othes' and 'perjurd *Promos*' is recapitulated by Cassandra when, at the end of the play, the matter comes to trial. At this point also, the subplot, centring on abusive bonds, reaches a crisis, as Phallax looks for knights of the post to swear to his innocence, in an old ritual of compurgation known as wager at law.[68]

In *Measure* this outline is kept. Isabella and Mariana testify against Angelo, who swears his innocence. As in *Promos* the importance of oaths is heightened by the inadequacies of evidence. Shakespeare, however, works this further back into his play. In the scene where Escalus tries to find out what actually happened to Mistress Elbow when she came to Mistress Overdone's house, energy is dispersed in an investigation that takes in a dish of stewed prunes, that was a good dish but not china, Froth sitting in the snug called 'the Bunch of Grapes', and so on. The wily Pompey realizes that by stacking up circumstantial evidence ('I hope here be truths'), he can bolster his authority as a witness—he offers to take an oath—and at the same time deflect attention from a charge that Elbow is too incompetent to articulate (2.1.112–71). It has been argued by Barbara Shapiro and others that, increasingly over the early modern period, legal action involved the pursuit of evidence in a culture of fact.[69] That goes nowhere in Vienna. In the case of the bed-trick, the Duke pointedly asks Isabella, concerning her deal with Mariana, 'Are there no other tokens | Between you 'greed concerning her observance?' and she replies 'No, none, but only a repair i'th' dark' (4.1.38–40). This is not *All's Well*, where the ring given by Bertram to Diana is proof of what has gone on. We might expect Isabella's knowledge of the maze-like geography of Angelo's house and garden to have an evidential role. In Thomas Lupton's *Too Good to Be True* (1581), another version of the story, the Gentlewoman's ability to describe 'the priuie staires', 'sheetes, pillowes, couerings, and curtains of the bed' where the wicked Judge forced her, convinces the council.[70] But although Isabella's description of Angelo's walled garden, in Act 4, with vineyard, gate, and little door, adds to the surreptitious, neurotic quality of the deputy's coercion,[71] it is not cited in the final trial scene.

Lorna Hutson has argued that there was a move in the late sixteenth century towards a drama of 'evidential uncertainty'.[72] *Measure for Measure* reflects this, but its final scene resolves doubt, as *Promos and Cassandra* does not, by including the well-informed, controlling Duke. Should this be taken (as Hutson implies) as a sign of Shakespearean caution, an avoidance of dramaturgical risk? It is better understood, I believe, as consistent with the weight he so often places on the testing of binding language. In the absence of evidence Isabella and Mariana have only their word to stand on. The philosopher Richard Moran has recently argued that testimony does not derive its authority from evidence, as centuries of Anglo-American empiricism lead us to assume, but from acceptance of the illocutionary commitment and accountability of the person that utters it.[73] From an early modern point of view, where the reputation and credit of witnesses—susceptible to slander—is always to the fore, this is a recognizable perspective. The divergence from *Promos and Cassandra* (and Cinthio, and other versions of the story)[74] lies partly in the fact that Angelo is a liar who does not even equivocate. This squares, one might feel, with the anti-puritan aspect of the play, and of Shakespeare's work as a whole. When he breaks his promise to Isabella, then lies about it to the Duke, the precise, hypocritical deputy is like the puritans that James denounced, in *Basilikon Doron*, 'whome ... neither oathes or promises binde'.[75] Equally striking, however, and integral to the play's account of defamation, set loose by binding language, is the point that, whereas Cassandra tells the King what she takes to be the truth (though her brother has survived), Isabella and Mariana engage in perjury and slander.

Thus, when she denounces Angelo, at the Duke's grand entry into Vienna, Isabella gives false testimony, in a speech that ironically starts from the accusation that Angelo is an oath-breaker:

> Most strange, but yet most truly, will I speak.
> That Angelo's forsworn, is it not strange?
> That Angelo's a murderer, is't not strange?
> That Angelo is an adulterous thief,
> An hypocrite, a virgin-violator,
> Is it not strange, and strange? (5.1.37–42)

This sounds like the sort of puzzling that we have at the end of *All's Well*. Any redemptive potential, however, is buried under captious and knowing falsities. 'Someone hath set you on,' the Duke disingenously declares, since his is the hidden hand, 'Confess the truth.' Avowing perjury, not holy vows, the would-be novice is consigned to the cage of prison, not the cloisters, for venting 'scandalous breath' (112–23). Friar Peter says that Friar Lodowick will swear an 'oath' to the deputy's innocence (155). But the case against Angelo mounts with another round of riddling testimony, drawing on the language of confession.

'I do confess I ne'er was married,' Mariana declares, 'And I confess besides, I am no maid' (182–3). Angelo is the one who needs to confess, given his loosening of binding language:

> This is that face, thou cruel Angelo,
> Which once thou swor'st was worth the looking on.
> This is the hand which, with a vowed contract,
> Was fast belocked in thine. (202–5)

Angelo does confess a little. 'My lord', the deputy admits, 'I must confess I know this woman.' He did not marry her, he says, because 'her promisèd proportions | Came short of composition' and, 'in chief | For that her reputation was disvalued | In levity . . . Upon my faith and honour'. Thus he gives *his* oath. What faith, what honour? It sounds bad to modern ears, but, as we have already noted, it was common to break off a betrothal if the promised proportion did not materialize (Mariana broke promise too); and it may be that her reputation was dented. Perhaps a Lucio started to talk—only the Duke says that Angelo began the rumour, whereas defamation is insidious and systemic. Perhaps the deputy thought it levity to listen to such songs as 'Take, O take'. Mariana rebounds and rebinds by insisting on her knees that 'I am affianced this man's wife, as strongly | As words could make up vows', and that their betrothal was consummated in Angelo's garden-house (221–30). Outwardly, the Duke is unimpressed. Mariana can jest, he says, and as Isabella would say, with saints, but not discredit Angelo:

> Thou foolish friar, and thou pernicious woman
> Compact with her that's gone, think'st thou thy oaths,
> Though they would swear down each particular saint,
> Were testimonies against his worth and credit
> That's sealed in approbation? (238–42)

Vincentio enforces the point that has recurred in this chapter, that slander runs into perjury and is typically confirmed with oaths. This problem with binding language makes it problematic even when true.

Escalus and Angelo are given the task of sorting out 'these slanderers' (256). When the Duke returns as Friar Lodowick, in one of the play's rapid exit/returns, it is with a double reference to confession and slander from Escalus (283–4). The Duke/Friar, however, proves recalcitrant, exposing, with Shakespearean vivacity, the double standard built into early modern codes of slander, which allow only the powers that be to criticize the state. When the Duke-as-Lodowick recites the same complaints about disorder and neglected statutes that had figured in the Duke's speeches in Act 1, he is accused of slander by Escalus and threatened with a tousing on the rack—another bed-trick (305–18). The Duke has found a way of bringing slander and perjury to a head by committing against himself the most serious form of abuse, according to Jacobean, legal commentators, the *scandalum magnatum*.[76] Denying Lodowick speech, Escalus has him bound with chains and taken away (339–40). The action has reached an active, visibly binding climax. For once Lucio unhoods the Friar, the Duke arranges for Isabella and Mariana to be loosed, and for Lucio himself to be bound. It is Angelo, however, swiftly offering his 'own confession', who is more radically bound. The Duke sends him off to be married to Mariana.

At this point we arrive at the play's most direct encounter with the Sermon on the Mount. You must pardon Angelo, the Duke tells Isabella, for the attempt upon your honour, but for 'promise-breach' and for executing Claudio, he must die. 'Or how saist thou to thy brother, Suffer me to cast out the mote out of thine eye,...?' Angelo's condemnation of her brother, who was also *his* brother, when he had a beam in his own eye, was an uncharitable utterance, an abuse of language, which now speaks the law back to him:

> The very mercy of the law cries out
> Most audible, even from his proper tongue,
> 'An Angelo for Claudio, death for death'.
> Haste still pays haste, and leisure answers leisure;
> Like doth quit like, and measure still for measure. (397–403)

The Duke's speech rhetorically weighs out and exemplifies measure; its judicious unpacking of wrongs answers the concern of such moralists as Vaughan: 'Rash iudgement hurts...him, that so rashly iudgeth.'[77] Yet the Duke knows Claudio to be alive, so perjury still hangs in the air, around the play's most sacred quotation.

As the ending turns towards tragicomedy, however ill sorted and unresolved, there is a mingling of real with specious, factitious faults. It is not just that Claudio is alive, but that the condemnation of Angelo is set against the less plausible interrogation of the Provost. 'How came it', the Duke suddenly asks, 'Claudio was beheaded | At an unusual hour?' (449–50). The Provost did not have special warrant, so, as he admitted at the time,[78] he acted contrary to his 'oath' of office. 'Give up your keys,' the Duke demands (454). These are the tools of the Provost's office but also its emblems. They visibly remind the audience of the power of the law to bind—as in the quotation from Jeremy Taylor above (p. 293)—but they also, as we have seen, have sacramental overtones, which the language of confession has begun to prepare. Hence the appearance of Claudio 'muffled', as the Duke tells us (480), brought in bound with Barnardine. As his hood and bonds are removed, the authority of the tribunal to judge remains but there is a shift from punishment to absolution. 'I find an apt remission in myself,' declares the Duke (492).

The word 'remission' edges us towards confession in the fully sacramental sense—and so does binding and loosing. To be loosed from the bond of sin ('te absolvo ab omni vinculo', in the words of absolution)[79] was the central purpose of a rite 'in the which by the ministery of the Priest, all actuall sinnes are remitted, and all bonds dissolued, which concerned sinne'.[80] For this reason, figures of absolution were found in scripture, not just, as we have seen, in the freeing of Peter from his shackles but in the raising of Lazarus.[81] The Duke has just imagined Claudio breaking the 'pavèd bed' of his grave to come back to haunt Isabella (427). When he enters now, hooded and in bonds, he is for her, Angelo, and others like a man brought back from the dead: 'Then he that was dead, came forthe, bounde hand and fote with bandes, and his face was bounde with a napkin.

Iesus said vnto them, Lose him, and let him go' (John 11: 44). It is often claimed that Shakespearean dramaturgy has been influenced by the medieval cycle plays. If that is true anywhere it is (where it has not been noted) in Claudio's unhooding and unbinding. In the Towneley cycle, for instance, Jesus says: 'Com furth, Lazare, and stand vs by;... Take and lawse hym foote and hande, | And from his throte take the bande, | And the sudary [shroud, hood] take hym fro.'[82] In Whetstone, the Claudio figure has been living incognito but in freedom. He does not come on stage from prison bound to be loosed in this way.

Confession in the legal sense was held to be the strongest testimony.[83] When Angelo confesses his faults, it resolves the problem of probation where loose-binding oaths cannot. The play explores the dramatic as well as the legal value of such moments of confession. Yet the questions that stir in an audience, about how penitent Angelo is when he asks for instant death, show the imminence of a more religious set of questions about binding and loosing. The readiness with which the legal slips into the religious can be understood in relation to the survival after the Reformation of the ecclesiastical courts, which so often dealt with contested betrothal vows and defamation. In medieval England, confession provided a spiritual tribunal to match the public judgement provided by these courts.[84] During the sixteenth century, while confession was abolished (or reduced to Godly counsel) for Protestants, the court system underwent complex changes. If we must look for analogues, the bringing of complaints by women straight to Duke Vincentio, combined with the pressure on Angelo to swear his own innocence—which was not permitted in common law courts—more closely resembles the procedures of the Court of Requests[85] than it does the ecclesiastical courts. But the persistence of the latter is a reminder of how often crime, trial, and punishment were thought about in terms of sin, confession, and penance. In *Promos and Casssandra*, this burden is felt when Phallax, on trial, admits 'of force I must sing *Peccavi*,... I am in fault, I must confesse, [and] with repentaunce redresse'.[86] Confession and remission are only one framework provided for the audience in a trial that seems worryingly like the bed-trick in its combination of the rigorous with the expedient and the lax. It does provide, however, a strong perspective.[87] Shakespeare fully articulates the religious frequencies of his denouement by bringing friars and nuns into the story, and by putting a cowled confessor into the judgement seat in the role of Duke.

Now I get to the endgame. However Divinely forgiving or royally manipulative Vincentio may be, he declares that he 'cannot pardon' Lucio (493). After Claudio is loosed from his bonds, much of the denouement concerns men being bound by marriage vows—Angelo with Mariana, Claudio with Juliet, the Duke as he hopes with Isabella. Lucio must not be left loose, though not just because he has forsworn Kate Keepdown. 'You, sirrah,' the Duke tartly demands,

that knew me for a fool, a coward,
One all of luxury, an ass, a madman,
Wherein have I so deserved of you
That you extol me thus?
LUCIO Faith, my lord, I spoke it but according to the trick.... (494–8)

By recycling Lucio's slanders the Duke brings out yet again the dangerous ability of defamation to circulate; yet, over-confidently and comically, he aims to bolster his authority by facing it down. Lucio's response is more prompt than exculpating,[88] though even Augustine agreed it was allowable to tell lies when they were evidently jokes.[89]

Lucio begins his reply with the mild half-oath 'Faith', presumably not because of expurgation this time but because he would be wise not to provoke. He cannot, however, escape from the binding consequences of an earlier oath and broken vow. 'As I have heard him swear himself there's one | Whom he begot with child', the Duke declares,

let her appear,
And he shall marry her. The nuptial finished,
Let him be whipped and hanged.
LUCIO I beseech your highness, do not marry me to a whore. (504–8)

For the first time in the judgement sequence, the Duke himself rises to something like an oath:

DUKE Upon mine honour, thou shalt marry her.
Thy slanders I forgive, and therewithal
Remit thy other forfeits.—Take him to prison,
And see our pleasure herein executed.
LUCIO Marrying a punk, my lord, is pressing to death, whipping, and hanging.
DUKE Slandering a prince deserves it. (511–17)

This is an edgy piece of scripting, not the brisk tying-up of a plot-line. The Duke's high-minded assertion of honour and forgiveness crumbles as he is tested one last time by Lucio's unbidden speaking-up—an abuse of language, in front of a magistrate[90]—and he testily contradicts himself. 'Thy slanders I forgive' but 'slandering a prince' deserves the marriage.

Why does Lucio have to marry Kate? Practically, as the historians tell us, because the primary driver of sexual regulation was money. Illegitimate children need to be paid for, not left to the parish or Mistress Overdone.[91] Without Vincentio's (and, before him, Angelo's) rigour what would happen to future Juliets—or even to Juliet herself, given that Lucio's friend (in debauchery?) Claudio says nothing to and little about her, except to declare that sexual desire resembles the appetite of a rat ravening down its proper bane (1.2.108–10). The couple come on stage together in the final scene but nothing is said between them nor of them that indicates intimacy. In some productions they stand well apart, the shell-shocked semi-libertine and the pregnant, unmarried woman whom he has left exposed to defamation. But the larger point is that both slander and the abuse of binding language converge on Kate Keepdown's case. For her to be married is to fulfil Lucio's promise but also to correct his imputation that she is a punk by making her a married woman. Optimistically, we might recall that the ecclesiastical courts sought through compurgation, and Star Chamber through apology and request for forgiveness, the restoration of complainants' standing in cases of defamation.[92] More negatively, there is a punitive logic. Like Angelo, in a minor key, Lucio is required to marry a woman whom he has damaged with his own slander, so the defamation rebounds to reduce him. In that sense he gets measure for measure, for lack of charity. Yet the punishment does not fix the crime. If Lucio's wife were to wander, in Act 6, into a brothel (where early modern husbands could, to their chagrin, find their wives),[93] she would be, like Mistress Elbow, 'respected'—open to casual, sworn defamation. The Duke may shackle up slander, but its ability to exploit loose, binding language cannot be abolished by the uneasy ending of the play.

12

Knots, Charms, Riddles

Macbeth and *All's Well That Ends Well*

That Middleton's tragicomedy *The Witch* (1616) has been influenced by *Macbeth* (1606) is agreed. The impact on it of a very different play, *All's Well That Ends Well* (1605–7), does not seem to have been noticed. How these connections should be understood is one matter pursued in this chapter. I shall not be taking up the theory—which I doubt—that Middleton helped write *All's Well*,[1] though it has to count for something that songs and dialogue written for *The Witch* can be found in abbreviated form in the Folio text of *Macbeth* (which is the only text that we have). Directly or not, Middleton had a hand in the tragedy. My interest lies rather in the circumstances and ethos of the two Shakespeare plays. To pursue this line of enquiry leads to an early Jacobean crisis in oath-taking and blasphemy, via the religious and magical terminology used to designate a great deal of early modern binding language. I want to think about oaths and vows in relation to plots and conjurations—links that would have been intuitive for early audiences, but that escape the categories we bring to Shakespeare from philosophy of language and speech-act theory.

The story can begin with 1.2 of Middleton's play,[2] where a disappointed lover, Sebastian, comes on stage to seek the help of the witch Hecate and her followers to prevent the consummation of Isabella's marriage with Antonio. He has women's 'faithless vows' on his mind (115) because he was contracted to Isabella before he went to war as a soldier, and she was deceived into marrying Antonio by news of his death. With the sinister foreknowledge of her kind, Hecate is expecting Sebastian; she reminds her fellows of their covenant with Satan, which requires them to labour for those who can be tempted into evil: 'We're all sworn | To sweat for such a spirit' (127–8). The witches' pact was widely depicted in continental and

Scottish demonology, but it was only just beginning to find its way into English texts.[3] *Macbeth* is one of the earliest plays to be alert to it—thanks to what the tragedy draws from the pamphlet *Newes from Scotland* (1592) and King James's *Daemonologie* (1597).[4] Middleton's Hecate reinvokes the pact, after Sebastian has left the stage carrying knots of serpent skins to use as a charm. ''Tis for the love of mischief I do this', she vaunts, 'And that we're sworn to—the first oath we take' (180–1).

Hecate and the witches are bound by oath to the devil, but the binding does not go all one way, because the charm that Sebastian is given has the power to fix and compel. When Hecate hands him the snake-skins, she declares,

> So sure into what house these are conveyed,
> Knit with these charmèd and retentive knots,
> Neither the man begets nor woman breeds,
> No, nor performs the least desires of wedlock
> Being then a mutual duty.... (155–9)

Hecate is the triple deity of ancient witchcraft. But she is also, in the play, the sort of '*bad Witch*' that was known in the Jacobean period as a '*binding Witch*'.[5] Here what is bound is Antonio's sexual performance. The knotted snakes are a black-magic remedy for the untied knot of betrothal between Sebastian and Isabella. In place of that tie,[6] Sebastian has knots in hand that will bind and frustrate desire. Like Bertram in *All's Well*, refusing with a pun to consummate his marriage with Helena, he plans 'to make the "not" eternal' (3.2.21).

During the lifetimes of Shakespeare and Middleton, Godly commentators argued that the power of a spell derived from the devil, not from the spell itself.[7] In the eclectic world of *The Witch*, however, older, wilder forces are at work. Hecate's charm draws on the knot magic of the classical, Old Testament, and Islamic worlds. Twists of energy, digital mnemonics, folk-survivals of the rosary, knots were widely employed in early modern magic, and still figure in occult practice.[8] The Jacobean physician John Cotta, who was troubled by something that I shall return to—the difficulty of establishing a boundary between witchcraft and medicine—noted that 'Some practise also Sorcery by tying knots.'[9] *Macbeth* alludes to the belief that witches tied winds up in knots and sold them to sailors.[10] Most relevant to *The Witch* is the classical Roman idea that a knot-charm could make a man impotent.[11] Jean Bodin describes the persistence or recurrence of this magic (the tying of knots in codpiece strings) in sixteenth-century France.[12] James VI cites the spell in *Daemonologie* (12), but the practice was widely known. It was so troubling—especially for men—that whoever enlarged Reginald Scot's inclusive *Discouerie of Witchcraft* (1584) for the 1665 edition called it 'notorious' but not 'fit to be openly described'.[13]

When it is tied to desire, knot magic can go either way, attracting rather than frustrating. Moments later in *The Witch*, a second character, Almachildes, comes onstage to consult Hecate and the witches. Seeking a spell to make the Duchess's maid Amoretta fall in love with him, he is given an amulet that is knotted in triplicate. When he puts this charm to use, it proves stunningly effective, till it slips out of Amoretta's dress and the maid recovers her disdain. Like other spells in the period, this one is written in Latin—not, as so often, Latin derived from medieval, Catholic prayer, but from Virgil's eighth Eclogue:

> What's this? O, 'tis the charm her hagship gave me
> For my duchess' obstinate woman, wound about
> A threepenny silk ribbon, of three colours.
> '*Necte tribus nodis ternos Amoretta colores*'
> —Amoretta! Why, there's her name indeed!—
> '*Necte, Amoretta*'—Again! Two bouts! [i.e. knots]—
> '*Nodo et Veneris, dic vincula necte.*'
> Nay, if veneries be one, I'm sure there's no dead flesh in't. (2.2.9–16)

The blundering mistranslation goes on:

> '*Necte tribus nodis*'—'Nick of the tribe of noddies'—
> '*Ternos colores*'—that makes 'turned colours'—
> '*Nodo et Veneris*'—'goes to his venery like a noddy'—
> '*Dic vincula*'—'with Dick the vintner's boy'!
> Here were a sweet charm now, if this were the meaning on't,
> and very likely to overcome an honourable gentlewoman! (22–8)

Almachildes' guessing paraphrase is reductively physical. The original is more linguistic: 'Wind together three coloured ribbons in three knots, Amoretta'—Virgil has 'Amaryllis'; 'Just twine them... and say "I twine the bonds of Venus."' The Latin makes much of bonds (*vincula*) and knots (*nodi*). As we shall see, it matters that *vinculum* and *nodus* can mean 'oath', 'vow', binding language as a 'tie'.

One of Almachildes' knots cannot be found in Virgil. There is a 'nodo' for 'modo' error in the Latin[14] that identifies as Middleton's source a book that may have gone into *Macbeth* as well:[15] Pierre Le Loyer's *A Treatise of Specters or Straunge Sights*. Le Loyer ends his treatise with an account of a young man who was prosecuted for using 'scroles or papers, and such like charmes' to attract a woman.[16] In the course of his trial it emerges that he wrote his spells on parchment made from the skin of an unbaptized child. You would expect that to be compelling for a dramatist—like the finger of a birth-strangled babe, that gets into the cauldron in *Macbeth*.[17] Middleton, however, side-stepped Le Loyer's main narrative and picked up on his digression: '*Virgil* reporteth and setteth downe the very woordes which were vsually spoken to entangle and entrappe in the snares of love, . . . ioyned and vsed with a ceremonie of certaine knows [i.e. knots] made in a riband' (143). This variety of knot magic, designed to attract not render impotent, is as old as Greek and Assyrian antiquity.[18] In the comical Almachildes plot, as in the Sebastian story, *The Witch* has deep roots.

That *nodus* could mean knot, bond, oath, and the tangled band of a charm anticipates the intricacy of *knot*, which the *Oxford English Dictionary* defines as *inter alia* a 'bond or obligation; . . . a spell that binds'.[19] The word 'knotte' could mean 'othe'[20] as readily as a knot could be a charm. A spell binds the other as an oath or vow binds the self. The charms used by sorcerers and binding witches to call up the dark powers were explicitly called 'bonds'.[21] Spirits were summoned and bound by what Scot and others call a *conjuration*. The word meant 'constraining by oath' as well as 'magical incantation'. As a swearer is bound by an oath, and as a witch who calls up Satan is caught into the system of evil (a pact can be recursively imposed by the spell),[22] so a charm can bind devilish spirits[23] or entrap an enemy with knots.

The concatenation of charm, knot, and plot reaches deep into *Macbeth* and *All's Well*, and goes via oath and vow to *riddle*. That is the trajectory that my analysis will follow between tragedy and tragicomedy, whatever the chronology of composition (though I would myself date *All's Well* after *Macbeth*). Riddles resemble oaths and vows because they are exactingly tied-up word-bundles of truth and promise. Once unbound, they lose their power to compel and become a form of words. That they are perplexities of meaning explains their traditional role in knotting and resolving plots. The riddles of Diana and Helena in the final act of *All's Well* bind the ability of the King and the court to act until answers are found and they are loosed. The affinities between *charm* and *riddle* open up another angle. As Northrop Frye once noted,

> the riddle is essentially a charm in reverse: it represents the revolt of the intelligence against the hypnotic power of commanding words. In the riddle a verbal trap is set, but if one can 'guess', that is, point to an outside object to

which the verbal construct can be related, the something outside destroys it as a charm, and we have sprung the trap without being caught in it.[24]

Like the charm, doubling and troubling, a riddle has hypnotic power. Macbeth repeats, as though conjuring, the assurance of the powers of darkness that 'none of woman born' can harm him (4.1.96). The witches slip with ominous ease between charms and prophetic riddles.

Of course, there is a difference. The riddle is a juggled or conjured-with knot of information. The charm is a binding speech act that brings about change or protects us from evil. But the two can overlap because of the promissory element in prophecy, which is typically puzzling and oracular. Macbeth says that the witches and their masters 'keep the word of promise to our ear' (they keep their word, as a word) though they 'break it to our hope' (5.10.21–2). Birnam Wood does come to Dunsinane, Macduff was not of woman born. The riddle is a verbal trap that crushes Macbeth inside it. Likewise, Bertram is caught by his promise to Helena, which becomes a riddling prophecy of the bed-trick: 'When thou canst get the ring upon my finger, which never shall come off, and show me a child begotten of thy body that I am father to, then call me husband' (3.2.55–7).

In setting out this forcefield it is important, finally, to note that *conjuration* as 'Constraining by oath' was typically used of oaths of conspiracy.[25] The bond that brings up dark forces was also an oath of sedition mutually imposed on members of what was called (yet again) a *knot*, in the early modern sense of 'cluster, band or company'—as when the conspirators in *Julius Caesar* are called by Cassius a 'knot', and when Ford in *The Merry Wives of Windsor* says that 'There's a knot, a gang, a pack, a conspiracy against me'.[26] This accords with the Jacobean impulse to see witches and necromancers as conspiring with the powers of darkness and binding themselves into a pact. Of more pressing relevance to this chapter are the dramaturgical consequences, visible on the stage after the Essex rebellion (1601), the Main and Bye Plots (1603), and beyond the Gunpowder Plot (1605). Plots as narratives are generated from plots as conspiracy, and the latter knots are darkened by irreligious, blasphemous oaths. From the Faustian pact in *The Diuils Charter*[27] to the blood-drinking, sworn conspiracy in Jonson's *Catiline* that we looked at in Chapter 2,[28] scenes of this sort are as easy to find as they are lurid. Whether it is dated to the late Elizabethan period, to 1605, or (as I think likely) *c.*1607, *All's Well* owes much to this moment, though it is *Macbeth*, written in 1606, after the interrogation and trial of the Powder plotters, that shows most vividly how the ethos and its atmospherics stem from the value placed on binding language.

* * *

'When shall we three meet again?' In *Macbeth*, as in *The Witch*, three is the magic number, tying the witches into an onstage knot, a conspiracy against the health of Scotland:

FIRST WITCH When shall we three meet again?
In thunder, lightning, or in rain?
SECOND WITCH When the hurly-burly's done,
When the battle's lost and won.
THIRD WITCH That will be ere the set of sun.
FIRST WITCH Where the place?
SECOND WITCH Upon the heath.
THIRD WITCH There to meet with Macbeth. (1.1.1–7)

This is an invocation, a conjuration, of the action. Prophecy slides into promise, simple statements become equivocal ('When the battle's lost and won'), and there is a choric knotting of dialogue into the rhymes that contemporaries called a 'band' or 'bond'.[29] As the witches agree to meet again, plot as conspiracy turns into a plot as process.

When the witches do parley with Macbeth, by tying him into their secrets they implicate him in their plot. Their device is prophecy, heard as promise: 'Do you not hope your children shall be kings', Macbeth will shortly ask Banquo, 'When those that gave the thane of Cawdor to me | Promised no less to them?'[30] Meanwhile the agents of Satan bewilder with their mischief. One has been killing swine. Another has gone after a sailor whose wife would not share her chestnuts. Showing their skill in knot magic, the other witches offer her winds, and she says that, like Antonio, the sailor's strength will be sapped. As they dance around the stage, the witches revel in their triplicity.

ALL (*dancing in a ring*) The weird sisters, hand in hand,
Posters of the sea and land,
Thus do go about, about,
Thrice to thine, and thrice to mine,
And thrice again to make up nine.
Peace! The charm's wound up. (1.3.30–5)

The winding-up of the charm recalls those early modern spells against tetter-worm, bleeding, or scalding that end 'In the name of the Father, Son and Holy Ghost'.[31] What could be a prayer is corrupted into magic, the charm-world of triple Hecate. The witches' threefold triple knot is blasphemously Trinitarian.[32]

Their damnable style is similar in the necromantic scene that influenced, and includes material from, *The Witch*. It is often said that 4.1 was written with King James in mind, and it does climax in a vision of the descendants of Banquo stretching out to include the king and his successors. More immediately, it chimes with the advice given by James to Prince Henry: 'Consult therfore with no Necromancer nor false Prophet, vpon the successe of your warres, remembring on King *Saules* miserable end.'[33] Macbeth comes to the witches—who are led at this point by the probably Middleton-scripted Hecate—like Saul visiting the Witch of Endor to talk to the spirit of Samuel,[34] when he is given the prophetic news that he will be defeated by the Philistines. The spirits that speak to Macbeth are as obscure as the witches are duplicitous:

ALL Double, double, toil and trouble,
Fire burn, and cauldron bubble.
SECOND WITCH Cool it with a baboon's blood,
Then the charm is firm and good. (35–8)

Scale of dragon, tooth of wolf, the liver of a blaspheming Jew—all go into the pot, like a riddle turning into a charm.

If spells and charms absorb fragments of prayer, they scatter their energy into other forms. 'The riddle and the metrical charm', writes Daniel Tiffany in *Infidel Poetics*, 'became part of a vital and complex vernacular tradition: spells, oaths, lullabies, and nursery rhymes; yet also curses, toasts, tongue twisters, namings, recipes, work songs.'[35] 'Double, double' is a recipe and a work song, with a mocking twist of nursery rhyme, a halloween game. What goes on in the scene is beyond generic definition. Doubled, folded, tied, binding, the spells are verbal knots in which words turn into things, thrown into the cauldron along with choice, horrific morsels in a Black Mass of speech and object. They exemplify, in Tiffany's phrase, 'the binding properties of lyric obscurity', an obscurity which lies in their 'way of *doing things with words*'.[36] The slanted allusion to Austin seems right.[37] The doubling and troubling sink into the darkness of what is done: 'A deed without a name' (65).

When Macbeth arrives he utters a conjuration, contrary to Divine imperatives as well as, more prosaically, the 1604 'Act Against Conjuration, Witchcraft and Dealing with Evil and Wicked Spirits' (2 James I, c. 12):

I conjure you by that which you profess,
Howe'er you come to know it, answer me.
Though you untie the winds and let them fight
Against the churches, though the yeasty waves
Confound and swallow navigation up,
Though bladed corn be lodged and trees blown down,
Though castles topple on their warders' heads,
Though palaces and pyramids do slope
Their heads to their foundations, though the treasure
Of nature's germens tumble all together
Even till destruction sicken, answer me
To what I ask you. (66–77)

The subjunctive account of disorder is almost a charm to effect the chaos. The recurring sweep of the syntax has the gusty force of an unleashed gale. The speech makes precipitous use of the set-piece account of what witches do that Shakespeare, like Scot and Middleton, found in Ovid.[38] The whole vista is, however, more windy than it is in *Metamorphoses*. As Middleton presumably noticed, this is another speech about knot magic. Macbeth speaks of *untying* the winds that the witches have bound up in their knots. By *conjuring* he joins the witches in a sworn conspiracy with evil. He binds them by swearing *by Satan* ('by that which you profess'), a blasphemous, occult speech act, which raises the dark question of whether he is swearing himself into a pact. As oath and invocation it is one of those 'blasphemous coniurations' that are deplored in the witchcraft pamphlets because they lead to damnation.[39]

The widely read Calvinist divine William Perkins, systematic about the pact because it provides a confirming inversion of the promise of salvation that covenant theology finds in scripture, says that sorcerers and witches can have either an explicit or an implicit covenant with Satan.[40] We have already heard Macbeth talk about bonds, ahead of the ambush of Banquo and Fleance:

Come, seeling night,
Scarf up the tender eye of pitiful day,
And with thy bloody and invisible hand
Cancel and tear to pieces that great bond
Which keeps me pale! (3.2.47–51)

This conjuration has been interpreted as being about the baptismal covenant.[41] Yet why would that great bond keep Macbeth *pale*? 'Seeling' plays on the sealing of a bond which will go unread in the scarf-like (seeling) darkness. Night is urged to hide from daylight—which would show murder to be pitiful, and discourage it—the killing which night will bring, the killing that will tear and thus cancel before it is due the bond (like a bond of debt) that Macbeth and Banquo have with the witches. This is a bond which, appallingly for Macbeth, promises in the future a line of kings descended from Fleance. Recall the end of the conjuration scene, where Macbeth decides to murder Macduff:

> I'll make assurance double sure,
> And take a bond of fate thou shalt not live,
> That I may tell pale-hearted fear it lies, . . . (4.1.99–101)

He will double, double, toil and trouble to kill Macduff and his household. This will secure him a promise from the future which, rather than make him pale, will allow him to tell his own fear that it lies. When he takes the bond, however, and puts Macduff's family to the sword, he binds himself to evil. His actions, Perkins might say, make his implicit covenant explicit. He is like the necromancers of *Daemonologie* who 'become in verie deede bond-slaues to their mortall enemie' (11).

Saul was told by Samuel that he was doomed to lose the battle against the Philistines. Macbeth is given more equivocal advice, though he still loses his battle. The ambiguity of the riddling prophecies is orthodox enough.[42] But the idea goes deep in *Macbeth*, because of Satanic enticement. James in *Daemonologie* describes the tricksiness of the necromancer, servant of the devil: 'he will make his schollers to creepe in credite with Princes, by fore-telling them manie greate thinges; parte true, parte false: For if all were false, he would tyne[43] credite at all handes; but alwaies doubtsome, as his Oracles were' (22). So the riddling nature of the prophecies in the tragedy is partly to do with temptation. But there is another reason why the oracular should figure, why the fiend that keeps the 'word of promise' should find its place in a play informed by an early Jacobean crisis in the giving of the word. That has to do, of course, with equivocation, and that has to do with oaths.

* * *

James's accession to the throne had been anticipated by many prophecies, some of them published with official blessing in *The Whole Prophesie of Scotland, England, and Some Part of France and Denmark* (1603). Nothing in that book, however, compares with the opacity of the prophecy that troubled the authorities a few months before *Macbeth* was composed. It was written into a warning letter sent to Lord Mounteagle on 26 October 1605, as the Gunpowder Plotters were preparing their attack on the House of Lords: '*they shall receiue a terrible Blow this Parliament, and yet they shall not see who hurts them.*'[44] James realized, or was credited with realizing, that '*Blow*' pointed to the blast of an explosion and he ordered that the cellars under the House be searched, with what results everybody knows. The insight was celebrated.[45] In *His Maiesties Speach* we are told of James's 'fortunate Iudgement in cleering and soluing of obscure riddles' (F3r). He was credited with the sort of holy, divinatory inspiration that in *Macbeth* is attributed to that virtuous foil of the witches, Edward the Confessor: 'then commeth *God* againe [and puts] a very *divination*, a very *oracle, in the King's lipps*,... made him, as *Joseph*, the revealer of Secretts, to read the riddle.'[46]

When it comes to the Plot itself, the *Speach* makes much of the vow or oath taken among the conspirators, in a lodging in Butcher's Row. They swore upon a primer and sealed their secrecy by taking the eucharist. Reportedly, it was a blasphemous conjuration of the Trinity: '*You shall sweare by the blessed Trinitie, and by the Sacrament you now purpose to receiue, neuer to disclose directly nor indirectly, by word or circumstance, the matter that shall be proposed to you to keepe secret, nor desist from the Execution thereof vntill the rest shall giue you leaue.*'[47] The oath was highly irregular, since it committed the knot to concealing they knew not what, which then proved unlawful. The result was a baleful bond, a parody of legitimate oath-taking.[48] The conspirators were a wicked conclave, compact with the powers of darkness, contriving a 'diabolicall *Domesday*'.[49]

Sedition was often said to be blasphemous because it set words to work against the Divinely appointed order,[50] but the prominence of blasphemy as a charge against the plotters owed much to their oath and sacrament. Reproducing the oath, Francis Herring's verse narrative *Mischeefes Mysterie* (translated and dilated by John Vicars) accuses the conspirators of 'blasphemous fowle crimes'.[51] They left their conclave, he says, 'hauing with blasphemous hearts... receiued the *Sacrament*, | And ta'ne an oath' (23). They were guilty of a triple blasphemy, like Cerberus with his three throats (60). Lancelot Andrewes's first Powder sermon presents the oath as almost the worst thing about the conspiracy. He is appalled that 'so *abominable and desolatorie* a plott' was 'Undertaken with an *holy oath*; bound with the *holy Sacrament*... hallowing it with *orison*, *oath* and *Eucharist*; this passeth all the rest.'[52] For Andrewes it is sweet that the very mouths that swore themselves into complicity betrayed the secrecy sworn to. This showed the hand of

God: 'they shall *sweare*, they shall take the *Sacrament* not to doe it; and yet, contrarie to all this, it shall come out by themselves' (155).

False in being traitorous, the conspirators' oaths were also treacherous because in the other way false—self-betraying, deceptive, spawn of the father of lies. The charge of blasphemy in conspiracy modulated into accusations of blasphemous equivocation[53] when the plotters were put on trial and they were tested under oath. The official account of the proceedings, *A True and Perfect Relation* (1606), condemns the oaths of conspiracy,[54] but it follows through with the prosecutor, Coke's, objections to

> their perfidious and periurious Equiuocating, abetted, allowed, and iustified by the Iesuites, not onely simply to conceale or denie an open trueth, but Religiously to auerre, to protest vpon saluation, to swear that which themselues know to be most false, and all this by reseruing a secret and priuate sense inwardly to themselues, whereby they are by their Ghostly fathers perswaded, that they may safely and lawfully delude any question whatsoeuer.[55]

For Coke, equivocation, which was advocated in a treatise by the plotters' ghostly father, their confessor, Father Garnet,[56] was an 'Art of cousning' (I1v). It gave equivocators, for instance, a way out of marriage as unscrupulous as that of Bertram when he tries to sleep with Diana by saying he did not consent to his marriage with Helena:

> one being conuented in the Bishops court, because he refuseth to take such a one to his wife, as he had Contracted with *per verba de praesenti*, hauing Contracted with an other priuily before, so that hee cannot bee husband to her that claimeth him, may answere that hee neuer Contracted with her *per verba de praesenti*, vnderstanding that hee did not so Contract that it was a marriage, . . . (I2r–v)

Anti-papists like Coke were not the only ones to protest. The crypto-Catholic Northampton, eager to distance loyal Catholics from the plotters and the Jesuits,[57] descants in the *True Relation* on the sanctity of oaths, citing out of St Gregory the promises that God swears to man as a model of how we should keep our oath and allegiance to the sovereign (Yy1v). By contrast, the plotting 'Gallantes', like vulgar blasphemers, abused the name of God 'in binding faith and promise one to another by solemn oathe' (Aaa2v). Their testimony was equally suspect. Garnet eventually admitted that he and Francis Tresham, one of the plotters, had equivocated. By wriggling out of the meaning of an oath, and leaving God, Jesus, the Holy Ghost, or the Trinity to hang loose, as witnesses enlisted to deceive, equivocation *created* blasphemy. This is how Coke represents the doctrines of Father Garnet: 'wherein vnder the pretext of the lawfulnesse of a mixt proposition to expresse one part of a mans mind, and retaine another, people are indeed taught not onely simple lying, but fearfull and damnable blasphemie' (T2r).

More incisively than has been recognized, this bears on the Porter scene in *Macbeth*, where oaths and unbound language figure in a scene of mock-conjuration:

> Knock, knock. Who's there, in th' other devil's name? Faith, here's an equivocator that could swear in both the scales against either scale, who committed treason enough for God's sake, yet could not equivocate to heaven. . . . (2.3.7–10)

The joke formula ('Knock, knock', 'Who's there?') sets up an expectation of a quibble, as when a Jesuit takes an oath, and the directness of the question slides into equivocal profanity ('in *th' other* devil's name'). Like stale jests about drink and impotence, equivocation had a well-understood relationship with wit. Though Protestant commentators were against it as a trick of casuistry, they could be indulgent towards it when 'the amphibology or equivocation be not insolent and strange, but such as is usual in forms of witty speech'. Lying, Jeremy Taylor went on, is wrong, 'but if by intrigues of words and actions', as in a 'Comedy', 'a man have entercourse', it can be legitimate to mislead.[58]

Equivocation in *Macbeth* is not just troublingly comic; it is blasphemously and damnably so, caught up in the unravelling of oaths. If it ripples, as I hope to show, through *All's Well*, it reaches into darker places in the tragedy. Its ominous ambivalence is felt not just in the Porter scene but in the exchange between Lady Macduff and her son, as we wait for them to be murdered; a traitor, we are told—like a Powder plotter, schooled by Jesuits—is 'one that swears and lies' (4.2.47). This is a Jacobean intensification amounting almost to a redefinition of the medieval and Tudor view that it was treachery to refuse or break the oaths of fealty that were sworn by subjects to the monarch.[59] The Oath of Allegiance controversy was waiting in the wings.

* * *

The reaction of the authorities to the Gunpowder Plot went much further than the execution of the conspirators. A war of oaths began, and with it came a debate: against the plotters' oath on primer and sacrament, James and

Parliament introduced an Oath of Allegiance in 1606, designed, the king argued—though how truly it may be doubted, given the divisiveness of the oath's wording[60]—to allow Catholics to show their loyalty by asserting the authority of the crown rather than the Pope in affairs of state. That this oath was to be taken 'without any equivocation or mental evasion or secret reservation'[61] will not have prevented some Catholics from swearing and lying when they took it. Perhaps Shakespeare's daughter Susanna, charged with recusancy in 1606,[62] was one such. There were heavy penalties for refusal; to reject the oath twice constituted a misprision of treason (see p. 371). Meanwhile, and relatedly, new impetus was given to a long-running campaign against swearing as blasphemy.

In response to the Oath of Allegiance, the Pope issued two briefs, urging Catholics not to take it, on the grounds that it challenged the authority of the Church in matters of faith, and these were followed by a letter from Cardinal Bellarmine. James responded with a treatise called *Triplici Nodo, Triplex Cuneus: An Apology for the Oath of Allegiance* (1607). The Latin of his title ('a triple wedge for a triple knot') alludes to Erasmus' *Adagia* I.ii.5 which in turn cites Jerome: 'Malo nodo malus quaerendus cuneus' ('A hard wedge must be sought for a hard knot)'.[63] Knotty questions, too hard to untie, have to be wrenched apart.[64] The three missives sent from Rome deserve this treatment, three times over.

James's wordplay goes further, alluding to the 'triple vow' of the Catholic orders (poverty, chastity, obedience). These *nodi* should be countered by the one, conscionable oath that is called, in *Triplici Nodo*, 'the maine knot of true allegiance'.[65] The Jesuits were obvious scapegoats for the Powder Plot, not just because of the zeal with which these triple-sworn priests pursued their oath-bound, covert mission to England but because, as Donne points out in *Pseudo-martyr* (1610), they were 'tied...in [a] knot' of 'obedience' to their superior, and by a supernumerary vow of loyalty to the Pope,[66] when they should be 'fastned with a new knot' (the Oath of Allegiance) to the king.[67] *Pseudo-martyr* was a relatively early contribution to a European-wide argument about oaths that drew in such weighty figures as Lancelot Andrewes, William Barclay, Francisco de Suárez, and Marco Antonio De Dominis. As we shall see in Chapter 15, the controversy lies behind Shakespeare and Fletcher's *Henry VIII* (1613?).

On the home front, the war around oaths took a turn that was equally calculated to assert the Godliness of Protestant England. There had been Elizabethan sermons and tracts against swearing as the bad obverse of legitimate oath-taking.[68] A succession of bills designed to curb profanity and blasphemy was brought to Parliament, but they always ran into resistance, including, it appears, from bishops wanting to protect the use of *ex officio* oaths in ecclesiastical courts.[69] From what we have seen already, it is unlikely to be accidental that legislation against swearing—the Act to Restrain Abuses (1606)—finally got onto the statute books in the heated aftermath of the Powder Plot. Though this Act was narrower in scope than the bills that preceded it,[70] it made it illegal (as we have seen) 'in any Stage-play, Interlude, Shew, Maygame, or Pageant, iestingly, and prophanely [to] speake, or vse the holy Name of God, or of Christ Iesus, or of the holy Ghost, or of the Trinitie'.[71] The puritan inspiration shows in the Act not troubling to mention Our Lady or the saints. It was a putting into law of the Decalogue: 'Thou shalt not take the Name of the Lord thy God in vaine: for the Lord wil not holde him giltles that taketh his Name in vaine' (Exodus 20: 7).[72]

How purposeful it was as a piece of legislation may be doubted. Characters in Elizabethan plays are not inclined to swear by the Father, Son, or Holy Ghost or 'by the Trinitie'. By identifying the theatre as a site of blasphemous swearing, however, as sulphurous as a knot of Powder plotters, the Act must have gratified the Godly. The implications for the writing of plays were, strictly speaking, limited, but concern about the law could lead—think of the Folio text of *Othello*—to damaging expurgation. Research is still needed into how extensive the expurgation was. But we should not be so focused on the effects of the Act on dialogue[73] as to overlook how imaginatively dramatists could get around the law. Recall the witches in *Macbeth* staging a blasphemous subversion 'of the Trinitie' without the word ever being uttered.

It is easy to see why blasphemy would be associated with the players, who swore by God and Jesus without meaning to be bound. There are other, overlapping reasons why it was associated with witches and plotters. That the oaths of Catholic extremists would be construed by the orthodox as blasphemous requires no explanation. More interesting is the impulse to self-driven excess. As David Nash notes in his study of *Blasphemy*: 'The temptation to blaspheme must have come frequently to the dispossessed and the poverty-stricken. Just as the powerless genuinely believed that they had made a pact with the devil, so blasphemous words and actions performed a similar function.'[74] The blasphemer wants to harness the power of an oath despite the danger of breaking a commandment—or even for the sake of that jeopardy, risking his soul for his faith, like Catesby and Guy Fawkes sworn to what Catholic leaders called a 'scandalous and desperate'[75] plot. The pamphlets show us alienated old women who were enticed by the devil to blaspheme,[76] or whose blasphemy brought the devil to their elbow, drawing them into a pact. Given the frequency with which this sort of unwary conjuration is described, you could see witchhunts from one point of view as a subset of the campaign against blasphemy. There was a witch-hunt against blasphemy in which persecuted women were caught up, the evil that they did proving the hellish origin of their swearing. 'Everywhere', as Alain Cabantous notes, 'blasphemy and sorcery were made equivalent.'[77]

Certainly, in England, the witchcraft pamphlets slide between blasphemy and pact, between irreligious oaths and the arrival of a familiar. Take the case of Mother Sawyer, who is almost sympathetically depicted in Rowley, Dekker, and Ford's play *The Witch of Edmonton* (1621). In the pamphlet version of her life, she confesses,

> The first time that the Diuell came vnto me was, when I was cursing, swearing and blaspheming; he then rushed in vpon me, and neuer before that time did I see him, or he me: and when he, namely the Diuel, came to me, the first words that hee spake vnto me were these: *Oh! haue I now found you cursing, swearing, and blaspheming? now you are mine.* A wonderfull warning to many whose tongues are too frequent in these abhominable sinnes; . . .[78]

The warning is reiterated, and the 'Conclusion' gives the moral—not to avoid witchcraft, or dogs that talk, but rather to avoid blasphemy, because 'it brings the Diuell to you: for it seemed that when shee so fearefully did sweare, her oathes did so coniure him' (D3r). The play puts greater responsibility on Mother Sawyer's neighbours. It is because she is so badly treated that she wants to learn to blaspheme; but the Dog still says to her, 'Thou never art so distant | From an evil Spirit, but that thy Oaths, | Curses and Blasphemies pull him to thine Elbow.'[79]

⋆ ⋆ ⋆

To link this into *All's Well*, I must return to where we left *Macbeth*: with Macduff fled to England. His exchanges with Malcolm, much preoccupied with swearing and lying, culminate in a speech about Edward the Confessor that strikes modern audiences as tangential. King Edward, Malcolm explains, is able to cure the scrofula by praying and hanging a gold coin around the patient's neck:

How he solicits heaven
Himself best knows, but strangely visited people,
All swoll'n and ulcerous, pitiful to the eye,
The mere despair of surgery, he cures,
Hanging a golden stamp about their necks,
Put on with holy prayers; and 'tis spoken,
To the succeeding royalty he leaves
The healing benediction. (4.3.150–7)

It is often said that this passage was included to flatter James, in his new, post-1603 guise, as another ideal, English king, succeeding to Edward's throne. From the perspective of royal policy, however, it could just as easily be seen as a rebuke, since the king was initially reluctant to take up Queen Elizabeth's practice of touching to cure the king's evil, the scrofula. He was troubled by the resemblance between this supposedly Divine healing and superstitious magic. The dangling of a specially minted 'angel' around the neck of the patient was all too like the folk-magic hanging of spells on bits of paper around the necks of the afflicted.[80] The distinctions were uneasily blurred between witchcraft, medicine, and the royal touch.

That Edward is woven into *Macbeth*, as a play deeply concerned with illnesses of the mind and body, is one way in which the tragedy intersects with *All's Well*, where the narrative leaps forward when Helena heals the King of a debilitating fistula in Act 2. The incantatory lines in which she promises a cure sound in performance like a spell—although, unlike the witches, she procures the 'help of heaven' and speaks of health without ill intent:

Ere twice in murk and occidental damp
Moist Hesperus hath quenched her sleepy lamp, . . .
What is infirm from your sound parts shall fly,
Health shall live free, and sickness freely die. (2.1.151, 162–7)

Some in the audience would remember what another female healer had achieved. In his *Right Frutefull and Approoued Treatise* on the king's evil (1602), William Clowes praises the cure of physicians above the 'exorcismes and the Illusions of certaine Charmes' but also celebrates Elizabeth's ministrations.[81] Helena treats a fistula, the location of which is unclear. In the diagnostics of the period, scrofula blurred into fistula. Clowes writes of a patient 'sore troubled with diuers pernitious *Cancerous Fistulous Vlcers*' who was cured by the touch of the queen (G4v). Helena's magically capable touch will be reasserted at the end of the play when she undoes the 'not' tied by Bertram.

Let us advance into the action by going back to Middleton's *The Witch*. One of several points at which it remembers *All's Well* comes in 3.1:

> *Enter Duchess, leading Almachildes blindfold* [*with scarves*]
> ALMACHILDES This's you that was a maid? How are you born
> To deceive men? I'd thought to have married you:
> I had been finely handled, had I not? (1–3)

Almachildes believed that his love charm had worked on Amoretta and that she was willing to sleep with him. Instead she substituted, apparently, her mistress, the Duchess. When the blindfold comes off, he discovers that he has been in a bed-trick—a thoroughly *All's Well* motif. Yet the trick is worse than he realizes. He has actually slept with a whore. 'A common strumpet!', Almachildes cries at the end of the play: 'This comes of scarves: I'll never more wear | An haberdasher's shop before mine eyes again' (5.3.121–3).

The obvious source for this is Paroles, when he heads out to recover the regimental drum, and is captured, blindfolded, and interrogated by soldiers who are his friends. This in turn recapitulates the fate of Bertram, who is hoodwinked (Cupid is blind)[82] into sleeping with Helena when he thinks he is deflowering Diana. It all happens when 'night', in Macbeth's words, has 'Scarf[ed] up the tender eye of pitiful day' (3.2.47–8). Why does Lafeu, from the outset, make such a big deal of Paroles's scarves (2.3.197–9, 214–15)? At first, they are an example of gallant, unruly frippery.[83] It looks as though, in Italy, when Bertram acquires a mistress, Paroles's scarf takes on a knot (4.1.300–1). The knot pretends to be an amorous favour,[84] a charm tied by a mistress who wants to hold him fast. It speciously and even touchingly declares Paroles to be a man of intrigue and a ready blade (knots were used to carry weapons). Most likely—it is up to the actors—the knotted scarf is also the bond in which he is later tied and hoodwinked. Lafeu anticipates as much: 'If ever thou beest bound in thy scarf and beaten thou shall find what it is to be proud of thy bondage' (2.3.214–15).

When setting up the conspiracy or scarf-trick against Paroles, the Second Lord assures Bertram that he will betray the secrets of his own side. Bound, he will break the bonds he shares 'with the divine forfeit of his soul upon oath' (3.6.27–8). This is not an isolated flash of *Macbeth*-speak. The last act of *All's Well* is shot through with references to the Divine, the demonic, and the blasphemous, and the spiritual perils of oath-breaking are brought out in the sequence where Diana rebukes Bertram for proposing to break his vows to Helena by sleeping with *her* and promising her marriage:

> What is not holy, that we swear not by,
> But take the high'st to witness; then pray you, tell me,
> If I should swear by Jove's great attributes
> I loved you dearly, would you believe my oaths
> When I did love you ill? This has no holding,... (4.2.24–8)

An oath that asserts what is true is a *nodus*, a holding knot. An oath that can be untied is more like a gypsy's knot, proverbial in this period for an oath that is equivocal, playing fast and loose. The easily verbal Bertram is willing to have but not hold. The passage subtly registers, in the wordplay about swearing not, an implication of *knot* with *not* that will generate a number of perplexities in the final scenes of *All's Well*, not just, at bottom, because the words were near-homophones in early modern English[85] but because a knot as oath or bond is tied or spoken of at moments when doubt and perjury impend, when the *knot* compels attention to the *not* that it carries.

The plot against Paroles is more derisive than tragic, but the 'band' of conspirators who 'bind' him (4.1.13, 3.6.21) gabble like the witches of *Macbeth* a hubble bubble speech. At one extreme of the word, of *parole*, is an oath or order or password, at the other is what the Second Lord calls 'choughs' language, gabble enough and good enough' (4.1.18). The gallants expect Paroles to 'return and swear the lies he forges' (21). He does swear and lie—he is overheard planning what he will swear to—but we also hear blasphemous gabble:

SECOND LORD DUMAINE *Throca movousus, cargo, cargo, cargo.*
SOLDIERS [*severally*] *Cargo, cargo, cargo, villianda par corbo, cargo.*
[*They seize and blindfold him*]
PAROLES O, ransom, ransom, do not hide mine eyes. (58–61)

Soldiers were notorious blasphemers. '*Cargo, cargo, . . . par corbo*' ('by God'?) is one way of representing this that will not fall foul of the 1606 Act. It is less vehemently the idiom of Paroles, whose faith is outrageous and profane. When told that the enemy will spare him if he spills the secrets of his camp, he promises to cooperate. 'But wilt thou faithfully?' the Interpreter asks. 'If I do not, damn me' (81–2).

Without blasphemy and talk of damnation it would seem a tonal lurch for Bertram to denounce Paroles like Macbeth berating the witches: 'this counterfeit model... has deceived me, like a double-meaning prophesier'

(4.3.95–6).[86] But there are repeated reminders in this phase of the comedy of the sacrilegious aura of conspiracy and treason, as when Paroles commits himself with the assurance, 'I'll take the sacrament on't' (132). The First Lord rubs Bertram's nose in the treachery of his friend: 'This is Monsieur Paroles, the "gallant militarist"... that had the whole theoric of war in the knot of his scarf' (136–9). Paroles's military accomplishment lay entirely in his clothes. His knot showed what he was not. But the comedy is richly complicated by the punctiliousness of his false truth-telling (e.g. 155–6) and by the way he unwittingly but unerringly turns the tables on his tormenters by telling truths about their louche ways, and especially their oath-breaking.

In his pocket, for instance, is found a letter that shows he was already a truth-teller about Bertram's abuse of oaths, to Diana: 'When he swears oaths, bid him drop gold, and take it. | After he scores he never pays the score' (211–12). He is a sort of rival, in his use of binding words: 'Thine, as he vowed to thee in thine ear, Paroles' (219–20).[87] Of Dumaine, Paroles says: 'He professes not keeping of oaths; in breaking 'em he is stronger than Hercules. He will lie, sir, with such volubility that you would think truth were a fool' (238–40). It is telling that, in the scene derived from this one, in Jasper Mayne's *Amorous Warre* (probably written in the 1630s), those who are blindfolded and shown up as cowards swear not to the truth of what they divulge but more conventionally not to fight against the enemy.[88]

When Paroles is unblindfolded, we hear about the knot again (the scarf becomes a noose: treachery was a hanging offence):

INTERPRETER You are undone, captain—all but your scarf; that has a knot on't yet.
PAROLES Who cannot be crushed with a plot? (300–2)

Bertram certainly can be. The parallel is pursued by Helena with her substitute in the bed-trick, Diana. Both work under cover of darkness. Both turn on a knot. 'Why then tonight', Helena says,

> Let us essay our plot, which if it speed
> Is wicked meaning in a lawful deed
> And lawful meaning in a wicked act,
> Where both not sin, and yet a sinful fact. (3.7.43–7)

'Where both *not* sin': this is her equivocal riposte to Bertram's equivocation, 'I have... sworn to make the "not" eternal' (3.2.20–1). They will knot in a sinful act, tangling up their bodies, yet, because they are married, will not sin. The lovers will be bound together like Othello's toads that 'knot and gender'[89] when they tie the marriage knot and breed in Diana's bed. An audience can only hear this as uncomfortable and deceptive. We have already seen Helena's capacity to juggle and palter[90] when she pursues Bertram by pretending to or actually breaking a 'sainted vow' to go on pilgrimage to Compostela (3.4.7), a vow that was known to require a special annulment from the Pope to undo it.[91] Now her plots so thicken that the end of the play will become—like the revelation that Macduff is not of woman born—the birthing of a riddle.

So the equivocations around the knot are carried into the finale. When the King presses Paroles on whether Bertram did pursue and seduce Diana, he replies, 'Faith, sir, he did love her, but how?... He loved her, sir, and loved her not', to which the royal response is 'As thou art a knave, and no knave. What an equivocal companion is this!' (5.3.245–51). By now equivocation is necessary if the truth is to be told. Bertram loved Diana sexually, but did not want to live with her. He loved her virgin knot. Once it was unknotted, he did not. This is to puzzle with an oath ('Faith, sir') in dialogue that is drawn to riddling. Paroles's leaning into speech as he gives his word makes him one of nature's Jesuits because he is a figure of mental reservation as well as equivocation:

DIANA [*to* PAROLES] Do you know he promised me marriage?
PAROLES Faith, I know more than I'll speak.
KING But wilt thou not speak all thou know'st?
PAROLES Yes, so please your majesty. I did go between them, as I said; but more than that, he loved her, for indeed he was mad for her and talked of Satan and of limbo and of Furies and I know not what. (254–60)

The wordplay on know/no is subtly sustained by 'Yes', which also shows Paroles cautiously scaling down his 'Faith'. Note the strange extremity of 'Satan and of limbo and of Furies', which edges us, yet again, into the world of *Macbeth* so that Paroles can cover his saying that he does not know what Bertram said.

The play's denouement—i.e. its 'unknotting'—turns on equivocations compacted into incantatory, charm-like riddles, as when Diana testifies to the King, 'By Jove, if ever I knew man 'twas you', then says this of Bertram:

he's guilty, and he is not guilty.
He knows I am no maid, and he'll swear to't;
I'll swear I am a maid, and he knows not. (284–8)

This is the riddle as a knot of nots, sealed ('By Jove') with an oath. 'I quit him', Diana goes on:

He knows himself my bed he hath defiled,
And at that time he got his wife with child.
Dead though she be, she feels her young one kick.
So there's my riddle; one that's dead is quick.
And now behold the meaning.
Enter HELEN *and* WIDOW
KING Is there no exorcist
Beguiles the truer office of mine eyes?
Is't real that I see? (296–303)

From the point of view of the King, and most of those onstage, 'Nothing is | But what is not' (1.3.140–1)—as Macbeth confusedly says when he is hailed as Thane of Cawdor. The 'knot' of intrigue that Helena has tied strikes those not privy to her scheme as devilish or impossible. As in the castle at Inverness, scene of the air-drawn dagger, what is seen cannot be believed and calls for an exorcist.

Even more *Macbeth*-like is the riddle that the dead are quick, Helena's child a knot of woman born, a quick tangle of limbs. Her quotation from Bertram's letter turns what it seemed could not be (Birnam Wood coming to Dunsinane) into a conditional prophecy, fraught with such equivocations as 'get this ring' (i.e. 'take this virgin knot, conceive').

> 'When from my finger you can get this ring,
> And are by me with child,' et cetera. This is done.
> Will you be mine now you are doubly won? (309–11)

Legally, a spousal was void if attached to impossible conditions ('*If thou shalt touch the Skies with thy finger*', or the like); possible conditions, even unforeseeably possible ones, were not disabling.[92] Helena, one could say, proves in the most literal way the ostensibly impossible possible. But the resonances of her language go beyond the law and its appetite for facts, to the witches and Lady Macbeth. 'Doubly won' rhymes with 'done'—'done double'[93] with toil and trouble. Doubly as in duplicitous. Done as final, a bond of fate: 'What's done cannot be undone.'[94] Whether by cleverness or magic, Bertram is undone by what is done.

It is not anachronistic to call this untying a denouement, though that word comes into English from French in the mid-eighteenth century. The *Oxford English Dictionary* records from Chaucer onwards *knot* meaning: 'the complication in the plot of a tale or drama'.[95] Way back, in the *Poetics*, Aristotle uses *desis* ('binding together', 'tying in bundles') to describe complication in plots, and *lusis* ('loosing') for resolution.[96] Latin *nodus* was employed in Renaissance drama theory to designate the 'whole knot of errors' into which comedies led.[97] This is what Shakespeare evokes when Cesario/Viola declares in *Twelfth Night*, 'O time, thou must untangle this, not I. | It is too hard a knot for me t'untie' (2.2.38–9). The use of riddles at the end of *All's Well* makes explicit what is tied into its oaths and vows and is riddling about its plot. As the editors of *Untying the Knot*—a study of the riddle—point out, there is

> an affinity between the riddle form and narrative in general, . . . The riddle, looked at in a forwardly evolving direction, is a story structured around a knot; untie the knot, and the unbounded enigma lies in ambush. Once again, however, we may detect an illusionary investment in this form.[98]

The riddling builds towards the revelation of the bed-trick, which is the clinching of marriage vows but also so banal as to be, like the equivocal prophecies in *Macbeth*, a bathetic black joke. The riddle has an illusionary investment which creates an aura, until it is solved.

The comedy of sexual banality and riddling fascination is sophisticated and uneasy at the end of *All's Well*, and shadowed by disappointment. As Northrop Frye observes: 'The riddle is also connected with the very common type of recognition scene which turns on a shift of identity, where, say, the heroine is proved to have been stolen by pirates in infancy, so that her present social status is lower than the one she ought to have.'[99] *All's Well* ends as a problem play because both the audience and Bertram already know who and what Helena is: this physician's daughter is not going to turn into a princess. Now that she carries his child, however, Bertram is in a double bind. To accept Helena as his wife, to be bound having tied the knot, is to take up a family but also be defeated. He is heading into the sort of bondage described in the tight little prose poems of R. D. Laing's book about relationships, *Knots*. 'The patterns delineated here', he writes, 'have not yet been classified by a Linnaeus of human bondage. . . . Words that come to mind to name them are: knots, tangles, fankles, *impasses*, disjunctions, whirligogs, binds.'[100]

The comedy of plots, equivocation, and riddling in *Macbeth* is in another key to *All's Well*. Yet the links are strangely insistent, and come back to binding language. Why does Angus say, that, like Paroles, Macbeth is guilty of 'faith-breach' (5.2.18)? Does he have in mind his broken fealty to Duncan, or his coronation oath, or is it—more likely—some reflex of Shakespeare's double, double-plotting to impute to the character the false faith of the witches? Why should 'th'equivocation of the fiend, | That lies like truth' (5.5.41–2) infect what might have been cheerful, humiliating comedy in the plot against Paroles, whom the audience is led to see as 'palter[ing] . . . in a double sense',[101] who undoubtedly lives a lie, and swears to truths to be false? The answers should be looked for in the dramatic opportunities created by a crisis in binding language in the years around the Powder Plot.

13

Benefits and Bonds

King Lear and *Timon of Athens*

In the second scene of the academic comedy *Timon*, usually dated to about 1601, a dissolute youth called Eutrapelus comes on stage pursued by the 'gryping Vsurer' Abyssus. Having pursued his prey like a bloodhound, the fiend now threatens to deprive him of food, sleep, and liberty unless he pays back a loan of four talents. Eutrapelus tries to repel Abyssus with a stream of oaths which are almost a curse:

> By greate *Bellonas* sheild by th' thunderbolt
> of *Panomphæan Ioue*, by *Neptunes* mace
> By the *Acroceraunian* mountaines
> and by the glistering Iemms of thye redd nose
> Goe hence, or els I'le crush thee like a crabb ...[1]

Not surprisingly, the usurer is not shaken by these 'bugbeare wordes'. You would need an MA to understand them (the play was probably written for performance at the Inns of Court). 'Thou showld'st haue paid the ffirst of the *Calends*', is his blunt response: ''Tis now the third day.' Only Timon's willingness to lend Eutrapelus four talents—'yea take ffyue, while I haue gouuld | I will not see my ffreinds to stand in neede'—gets him off the hook.

That *Timon* influenced *Timon of Athens* is generally, though not universally, agreed. It certainly looks as though the Eutrapelus–Abyssus episode fed into the scene in which Shakespeare's Ventidius sends to Timon for five talents to save him from prison, and Timon pays[2]—or rather (since this is a play about bonds) promises to 'send his ransom'. As the messenger more than courteously says, 'Your lordship ever binds him' (1.1.105–6). That Ventidius is not explicitly under the thumb of a usurer might seem to support the view, which became lodged in twentieth-century criticism, that

Shakespeare's interest in Timon centred on his generosity, his abandonment by such friends as Ventidius when he runs out of money, and his Lear-like tirades against injustice out in the woods in Acts 4 and 5.[3] Even in more recent scholarship, it tends to be assumed that usury and debt were brought into the play by Shakespeare's collaborator, Thomas Middleton, directly or by example.[4] Usury is conspicuous, however, in Shakespearean parts of the script, where it is tied into arguments about superfluity, charity, and making something out of nothing that are also pursued in *King Lear*. You could argue that Ventidius is kept off stage, as Eutrapelus was not, to avoid pre-empting the scenes written by Shakespeare in which the servants of the usurious senators, beneficiaries of Timon's largesse, come to reclaim the money that they have lent to him. Usury in this play is not just the breeding of coin, to be contrasted with noble gift-giving. As in *Lear*, there is a larger problem, a difficulty with excess in the binding language of benefits.

Both tragedies show Shakespeare thinking about how societies can function without Christian values; although the dialogue is coloured by the religious beliefs that saturate Jacobean English, and although scriptural allusions are made, a sustained attempt is made to strip away transcendental consolation and to focus on the social animal. In the case of *King Lear* the result is an anachronistically feudal, ancient Britain, where Jove, Juno, and Apollo are called upon to witness oaths, but the most potent divinity is Nature. *Timon of Athens*, by contrast, starts from classical ideas that were influential in the early modern period: Aristotle on moderation, Seneca on benefits and gratitude, and—in a source that has been neglected—Plutarch on usury. Plutarch's *Moralia* is cited in such Christian anti-usury tracts as Lodge's *Wits Miserie* (1596).[5] His ideas were widely diffused. It seems likely, however, that Shakespeare read the 1603 translation by Philemon Holland before writing *King Lear* and *Timon of Athens*—probably in 1605 and 1607–8 respectively, though some have dated *Timon* to 1603–5. His reading in the *Moralia* merged with what Plutarch briefly says about Timon in the *Lives of the Noble Grecians and Romans*, in the course of his *Life* of Antony, and about Alcibiades—who leads an army against Athens in Shakespeare's play—in the *Life* that Plutarch puts in parallel with that of Coriolanus.

The *Moralia* stresses that money is typically borrowed not to cover necessities but for 'foolish and riotous expenses'.[6] Plutarch might be describing the home life of Timon when he declares: 'marke how usurers do not ordinarily put forth their money unto those who are in necessity and distresse, but to such as be desirous to purchase and get that which is superfluous' (283).

The cynical philosopher Apemantus carps about waste in *Timon*, but it is a core-topic in *Lear* also, where the relationship between necessity ('O, reason not the need!') and superfluity ('the superfluous and lust-dieted man') is argued out around benefits and cascades down into charity.[7] The woodland scenes in *Timon* push the protagonist beyond material (though not psychological) excess, to find out man's necessities—edible roots turn out to be more valuable than gold. Lear, similarly, is stripped and strips himself of entourage and fine array, forced to look for what distinguishes humanity from the poor, bare, forked animal.

To avoid getting into debt, Plutarch says, you should not eat off silver but use 'vessel[s] of earth and pottery, which . . . cary not the strong smel nor unpleasant sent of usury' (283). Simple dishes 'will not put thee in minde daily of the calends and new moones, which being in it selfe the most sacred and holy day of the moneth, is by meanes of the usurers, become odious and accursed' (283). As in the academic *Timon*, usury distorts time: 'calends' is desacralized and becomes merely a due date. It would take us back too squarely to the matter of Chapter 6 to show how temporally determined is the fate of Shakespeare's Timon, brought down by 'broken bonds' and 'long-since-due debts' (2.2.37–8). Although his name has relevant meanings in Greek—'honour', 'offering', 'payment', for a start[8]—what it tells an English audience is that Timon is a creature of time.[9]

Usury is unnatural. In terms that might have caught the eye of the future author of *Lear* ('Nothing will come of nothing'),[10] Plutarch says that usurers 'laugh at natural philosophers, who holde this Axiome, That of nothing can be engendred nothing: for with them usurie is bred of that which neither is, nor ever was' (285). Classical authors accept that the natural world generates increase (see p. 159); as Plutarch points out, however, 'The swallowes are not in the usurers booke, the pismiers pay not for use of money' (286). To avoid honest toil—and Shakespeare's protagonist never does any, in contrast to Lucian's Timon—we take on the shackles of debt, and the absurdity is that we feast the very usurers who enslave us. Usury and prodigality go together because they are both agents of excess, and we end up with ingratitude:

> because we would be free (God wot) we care not to thrust our selves into debt, we pay for the use of money, we flatter vile and base persons, we give them presents, we invite and feast them, we yeeld (as it were) tribute underhand unto them; . . . excesse it is and deintinesse, which hath ingendered usurers; . . . and many times wee receive no other fruit of all our cost and labour, but ingratitude. (286)

Yet if austerity were the answer, the cynical Apemantus would be the hero of *Timon of Athens*. As we saw in the case of Ventidius, Timon's largesse can be socially constructive. He goes on to give money to a faithful servant so that he can marry a rich man's daughter, whose dowry needs to be matched: 'To build his fortune I will strain a little, | For 'tis a bond in men' (1.1.147–8). Timon means that his gesture will forge a social bond, but it also involves, as often in the play, binding language. 'Pawn me to this your honour,' the Old Athenian says, 'she is his.' The actor playing Timon must respond by reaching out, and he might well pause on the rhyme: 'My hand to thee; mine honour on my promise' (151–2). This commitment will strike an audience as liberal in the right sort of way. Only once his friends fall away might we recall that his generosity has had the effect of leaving him with one follower fewer. For now, like Lear before the love-trial, set to endow his daughters' marriages, he exemplifies purposeful bounty.

Even when Timon is excessive, we should not assume that early modern life was all about balancing the books (though gifts were often recorded in account books, alongside columns of credit and debt).[11] Seneca's *De Beneficiis*, widely read and a source for this play,[12] emphasizes the importance of generosity even when met with ingratitude. 'What I haue lost in this man, I will recouer in another,' is how the treatise ends, in Golding's 1578 translation, 'Yea I will doo the same man good still: and lyke a good husbandman, I will ouercome the barrennesse of the soyle, with composte and tilth....'[13] There was a great deal of Protestant-humanist writing that disapproved of waste, and sometimes that waste was found in the extravagances of antiquity,[14] but there was also a tendency to argue that the exchange of benefits could be left asymmetrical, within a structure of reciprocity, for the sake of reinforcing bonds. 'There were those who professed it was indeed best to avoid trying to offer requitals in full,' notes Ilana Krausman Ben-Amos,

> in order to ensure that the gratitude and indebtedness owed to or by patrons, dependants and friends remained durable and intact... to avoid the 'wiping out of obligations' as Timothy Burrell, the Essex gentleman, put it, they deployed a language steeped with notions of reciprocity of the kind cited by writers of manuals and courtesy books used to educate men of their position throughout the period.[15]

Yet the benefit system was complicated, even contradictory. It enhanced the status of a patron to bestow benefits, but it could also be princely to receive and not reciprocate. By giving so freely, Timon risks undermining his nobility and becoming a prodigal. His lack of interest in what he gives—contrast, for example, Sir Epicure Mammon's infatuation with luxury goods[16]—is a sign of his virtue; in line with Seneca, he recognizes that a true benefit lies in the mind not the thing.[17] But his disregard makes him look indifferent to what he gives, and so careless of the party who receives. When he refuses reciprocation from others, or neutralizes gifts by returning more than he receives, he pays interest on benefits in order to enlarge himself. It was a standard view in antiquity that benefits should be returned above the value of the gift. For Aristotle, this was a way of protecting the status of the receiver, who would otherwise become subordinate.[18] Though alert to the element of 'rivalry' in the exchange of benefits, Seneca took the more generous view that, this side of extravagance (a line he never cogently draws), to give in overplus was noble (I.iv.2–4). From Hesiod to Cicero,[19] Lucian,[20] and on to Aquinas,[21] returning more than you receive was the advice, if only because an exchange could only be made equal when the responder acknowledged the commitment that went with initiating an exchange with no guarantee of a response.

That Timon inhabits an Athens dominated by usury—with a senate full of usurers, as Alcibiades will later protest—gives the play a language for representing this asymmetry in damaging terms. 'He pours it out', says the Second Lord,

> no meed but he repays
> Sevenfold above itself; no gift to him
> But breeds the giver a return exceeding
> All use of quittance. (1.1.275–9)

'Breeds' takes us back to Aristotle on usury and the Jacob–Laban story in *The Merchant of Venice* (pp. 156–60). The words 'use' and 'quittance' are also drawn from the money-markets. To pay back sevenfold is an extortionate rate of self-imposed interest, resembling, in its twisted way, the acceptance of commodities in lieu of cash made by foolish gallants in city comedy. The elision of usury with benefits is a running motif. A Senator says, 'If I want gold, steal but a beggar's dog | And give it Timon, why, the dog coins gold' (2.1.5–6). When Timon realizes how he has been exploited, he asks Flavius, the faithful steward, who brings him money in the woods—in lines apparently written by Middleton—'Is not thy kindness subtle, covetous, | A usuring kindness, and, as rich men deal gifts, | Expecting in return twenty for one?' (4.3.500–2).

What throws this conjunction into sharper relief is the dramatically productive irony that Timon's bounty is sustained by debts that are subject to usury by the very friends who are gifted in excess. As Flavius repeatedly tells the audience, his master is giving away what he does not own and forfeiting his estate. The liberality that might count as virtuous in the old, noble world of bounty looks different when kept going by debt. Like so many members of the Jacobean elite, Timon maintains a façade of inherited wealth on the shifting sands of usury. It is symptomatic that, when he runs out of money, he does not just ask his friends to reciprocate their benefits—a natural thing to do, given that early modern friendship (heavily influenced, among the educated, by classical writings about *amicitia*) 'was embedded within notions of reciprocity and exchange . . . suffused with concepts of giving and receiving; of benefits and requitals'.[22] Ignominiously, Timon must ask for loans, which are refused because he has no assets or credit to secure them. When others prove faithless, there can be no faith in his ability to service his debts. Timon and his flattering friends exchange horses and hunting dogs but the play ruthlessly exposes the base of this reciprocity in the cash nexus. In a passage probably written by Middleton, we even hear of coin infiltrating noble benefits. When Lucius is backing away from helping Timon he says that he has 'received some small kindnesses from him, as money, plate, jewels and suchlike trifles' (3.2.17–18). The objection to money is not just to its general circulation, its passing through mercenary hands without the select appropriateness of a gift, but to its links with corruption. Give a man a jewel and it stays in his cap to remind him of you—or it should, though Timon finds it to the contrary;[23] give him coin and care is needed lest it look as though you are trying to buy him.[24] Hence the sensitivity of Timon's fair-weather friends, in the senate, to Alcibiades' charge that they are not just usurers but can be bribed.

Timon's excess first looks undeniably like folly when he refuses repayment from Ventidius. He has already given Ventidius more than he asked for (as the protagonist does in the academic *Timon*) by promising to support him after his debt has been paid. When Ventidius comes to Timon, less than two hundred lines later, having inherited from his father, he says

> as in grateful virtue I am bound
> To your free heart, I do return those talents,
> Doubled with thanks and service, from whose help
> I derived liberty. (1.2.4–7)

This is an exemplary reciprocation: gracious and prompt, even if—and in part because—the return is doubled only by 'thanks and service'. Timon's response is to reject the repayment, and the more patronizingly to call Ventidius 'honest', like an upright citizen:

> O, by no means,
> Honest Ventidius. You mistake my love.
> I gave it freely ever, and there's none
> Can truly say he gives if he receives. (7–10)

These lines are probably Middleton's, but they are consistent with what Shakespeare shows us as the role develops. Wherever the border runs between generosity and extravagance, Timon has crossed it, almost to the point of engaging in a potlatch—the competitive, triumphalist gift-giving much-discussed by anthropologists.[25] It is worth noting, even so, that Ventidius says of him, 'A noble spirit!', rather than taking offence (13).

From one point of view, the hyper-noble Timon can be thought of as utopian. A. D. Nuttall has suggested that he is prompted, in the first place, to give Ventidius more than the talents he asks for by that line spoken by the messenger: 'Your lordship ever binds him.'[26] 'Bound | To your free heart' might have a similar, chilling effect. How can a heart be free (liberal but also independent) when it is bound by others' obligation, even just by gratitude? Timon needs his gift to be gratuitous to be a true gift. Perhaps he gives so much to ensure that his friends are thankless. As Derrida provokingly puts it, if giving is even fractionally gratifying, if what is given becomes a gift, it is not a gift:

> If the gift appears or signifies itself, if it exists or if it is presently *as gift*, as what it is, then it is not, it annuls itself... The truth of the gift is equivalent to the non-gift or to the non-truth of the gift. This proposition obviously defies common sense. That is why it is caught in the impossible of a very singular double bind, the bond without bond of a bind and a non-bind. On the one hand,... there is no gift without bond, without bind, without obligation or ligature; but on the other hand, there is no gift that does not have to untie itself from obligation, from debt, contract, exchange, and thus from the bind.[27]

Timon's unbinding bonds continue to dysfunctional effect. When Lucullus sends him 'two brace of greyhounds', he commands that they 'be received | Not without fair reward' (1.2.184–6). Flavius complains that his lord asks his men to 'give great gifts... out of an empty coffer' (187–8), but there is a prior solecism. As many commentators on the gift note, immediate reciprocation is an insulting cancellation. It ties the gift back into what Derrida calls 'debt, contract, exchange', or, in the words of *De Beneficiis*, 'to send something back at once, and to wipe out a gift with a gift is almost a repulse.... He who hastens at all odds to make return shows the feeling, not of a person that is grateful, but of a debtor' (IV.xl.2–5). Much of Seneca's effort goes into showing how like debt and repayment the exchange of benefits can be and how important it is for the encouragement of gratitude to maintain the difference between the cash and gift economies.[28]

Only a score of lines later, the incorrigible Timon says to the First Lord:

> And now I remember, my lord, you gave good words the other day of a bay courser I rode on. 'Tis yours, because you liked it.
>
> FIRST LORD O I beseech you pardon me, my lord, in that.
> TIMON You may take my word, my lord, I know, no man
> Can justly praise but what he does affect.
> I weigh my friends' affection with mine own.
> I'll tell you true, I'll call to you.
> ALL LORDS O, none so welcome.
> TIMON I take all and your several visitations
> So kind to heart, 'tis not enough to give.
> Methinks I could deal kingdoms to my friends,
> And ne'er be weary. (1.2.205–16)

What looks to us merely impulsive would (once again) have struck a Jacobean audience as not all bad. Timon is thinking, in his way, about the person he is obliging; and the gift is not unconditional, in that he warns the recipient that he'll 'call to you', and expect something back one day—though this sounds like a piece of gift theory, not secured by a judgement of likelihood. More strikingly, binding language is folded into the exchange of benefits. For the Second Lord to 'give' good words earns a courser; he may 'take' Timon's 'word' for that. It is a tying of the language of gifts into knots of reciprocal words, except that the asymmetry leaves Timon at risk. The lords acknowledge their obligation. They should be bound by stating their bond. Yet any audience will sense that words for them are cheap:

> FIRST LORD We are so virtuously bound—
> TIMON And so am I to you.
> SECOND LORD So infinitely endeared—
> TIMON All to you. Lights, more lights! (221–4)

It cannot last. Lights, and more lights, burnt, burn out.

As we shall see in the final section of this chapter, the topic of empty promising rises to a climax when Timon is in the woods. Yet the issue is introduced earlier, by Middleton, after the reward is pledged to Lucullus:

His promises fly so beyond his state
That what he speaks is all in debt, he owes
For every word. He is so kind that he now
Pays interest for't. His land's put to their books. (1.2.192–5)

Is Timon a promise-breaker? Not exactly; he promises what he only thinks he has—a lesser offence—and pays for it with his land. Furthermore, the promises are given to people who have already profited. Timon's prodigality is not victimless; his servants are cast adrift when he runs out of funds, with only a small pay-off held back for them by the faithful Flavius. But the creditors that he cannot satisfy when they harry him with bonds have been prepaid, to excess, with gifts. This is a narrowly produced version of what debt was like in the early modern period. Unless the Senator of 2.1 is one such,[29] independent creditors damaged by Timon's excess are not shown and nor does anyone stand surety.[30] At the heart of a culture of credit, the protagonist is left almost experimentally disconnected. This is one reason why the play never opens into tragedy, for all the rage and scope of Timon's big speeches, because his actions do not have consequences that hurt others and for which he must reproach himself. The energies of the situation rebound into satire and agonized narcissism.

Timon makes big, even unrealizable promises because he is so recklessly generous. His false friends are so base that they make promises they do not intend to keep, even though they could. They flatter him by saying 'none so welcome' and 'We are so virtuously bound'. Apemantus brings out the centrality of binding words in his mock-grace before Timon's great feast (that most emblematic of early modern benefits):[31] 'Grant I may never prove so fond | To trust a man on his oath or bond' (1.2.63–4). As the First Servant puts it, after the second, mock banquet of water and stones:

his familiars to his buried fortunes
Slink all away, leave their false vows with him
Like empty purses picked;... (4.2.10–12)

Having picked his pocket, and emptied his purse, the false friends have left him only hollow promises. These are the vows of deference and service that, as early modern letter-writing shows,[32] those put under an obligation customarily made to their benefactors. Offers of reciprocation are given which prove to be mere words. As we shall see, it is ingratitude and the betrayal of bonds that ravages Timon more than being left without material benefits. Deprivation is a misanthropic pleasure by comparison.

That a play about benefits should gravitate to oaths, bonds, and false vows is not surprising. *De Beneficiis* starts with broad brush strokes about generosity, but human nature being what it is Seneca quickly turns to sifting the sophistries of promise and agreement. What happens if the person promised a benefit is discovered to be an ungrateful person? Should we keep back what we have promised? What happens if circumstances change between promising and being able to give? What if I am beset by robbers on the way to keep a promise? And what of reciprocation? How, and how quickly, should we repay 'a debt of gratitude'. Seneca addresses these questions with his usual determination to keep gift-giving distinct from debt, yet he contrives both to regret that debt is not more like gift-giving and to accept that feedback from debt to gift has corrupted benefits:

> Would that no compact marked the obligation of buyer to seller, and that no covenants and agreements were safeguarded by the impress of seals, but that, instead, the keeping of them were left to good faith and a conscience that cherishes justice! But men have preferred what is necessary to what is best, and would rather compel good faith than expect it. Witnesses are summoned on both sides. One creditor, having recourse to factors, causes the record to be made in the books of several people; another is not content with oral promises, but must also bind his victim by a written signature. O, what a shameful admission of the dishonesty and wickedness of the human race!... The only thing that avarice lacks now is that we should not even give benefits without a bondsman![33]

Seneca's condemnatory, satirical pulling together of gift and debt, a dynamic which is so variously and dramatically active in *Timon of Athens*, is dangerously close to common sense for modern readers. We inhabit a marketized world in which everything has its price. The value of almost any birthday present can be checked online, and often is. So the calculus we apply to Timon has little scope for nobility and largesse. One symptom of our modernity is the argument of the most influential treatise on benefits to have been written since Seneca: Marcel Mauss's *Essai sur le don* (1925). This account of how benefits are exchanged in traditional societies stresses rivalry and the requirement to reciprocate. From group gifts, Mauss argues, societies advance to the giving of pledges, and on to bonds, contracts, and money. The gift carries with it the spirit of the giver, as does, more residually, the pledge. It is driven by 'the obligation to give',[34] posited on the assumption of reciprocity, and, of course, to return. Binding words narrow the connection made by objects. This would be a fable of the Fall—and becomes so, in such studies as Lewis Hyde's *The Gift* (1979)—did Mauss not so greatly respect the principle that your word should be your bond.

He tells readers, indeed, at the outset, that his treatise stems from work done by Georges Davy and himself on sworn words of faith.[35] 'For years our attention has been concentrated on both the organization of contractual law and the system of total economic services operating between the various sections or subgroups that make up so-called primitive societies' (3). Because Mauss's treatise grows out of Davy on 'La foi jurée', it is not entirely surprising that his account of the early, gift economy looks like a projection back from the oaths and bonds that were judged to follow it. This is one reason why the book reads so persuasively; it starts from a system familiar to us, and finds its back-story. Mauss even argues, in the style of a bank manager, that when a gift is not reciprocated the assets of those who default can be distrained by the giver. Anthropologically this is inaccurate; the Trobriand islanders who give a *kula* and do not get one in return are only entitled to take a *kula*-type item (not all benefits are fungible).[36] Imagine a version of *Timon* in which the protagonist could send his men around to the houses of his false friends and reclaim goods to the value of what had been given. Unless a gift is different from a debt, yet closely resembles it, there is no tragedy. Similarly, we might hazard, Mauss projects back the idea of interest. He calls the potlatch 'essentially usurious', and goes on to specify a rate: 'normally, the potlatch must be reciprocated with interest, as must indeed every gift. The rate of interest generally ranges from 30–100 per cent a year' (8, 53). This again is dubious, generalizing gifts from the potlatch, and taking as normative a practice in NW America that was already under European influence.[37]

The point of this highly compressed critique is to suggest that, like Mauss, and with greater justification, Shakespeare and Middleton located in ancient Athens a society in which the predicates were contemporary, Jacobean ones, showing an old order of noble benefits being corroded from within by oaths and interest. Certainly, these writers are attracted to classical antiquity for similar reasons. Mauss sees the early Roman republic and (more sketchily) classical Greece as the historical moment in which the gift economy gave way to bonds and contracts and the forfeiture of the human body as currency of last resort. It is another area in which his scholarship is derivative and unreliable. We do not, in practice, know much about the Roman *nexum* on which his narrative turns:[38]

> it is precisely the Romans and Greeks, who . . . invented the distinction between personal and real law, separated sale from gift and exchange, isolated the moral obligation and contract, and in particular, conceived the difference that exists between rites, laws, and interests. It was they who, after a veritable, great, and admirable revolution, went beyond all the outmoded morality, and this economy of the gift. It was too dependent on chance, was overexpensive and too sumptuous, burdened with consideration for people, incompatible with the development of the market, commerce, and production, and, all in all, at that time was anti-economic. (69)

Mauss reveals explicitly his liking for modern law, for the 'admirable revolution' that led to bonds and commerce. *Timon of Athens* offers a more divided and humanly convincing fable of how the gift economy is supplemented and ravaged by the market. We shall return to the tragedy in a few pages' time, after thinking about *King Lear.*

* * *

Over the last couple of decades, scholars have shown that Lear's plan to divide his kingdom, or kingdoms, is more sensible than was assumed by critics of an earlier generation. Given the refusal of the House of Commons to accept a union of Scotland with England and Wales in 1604–7—English MPs insisting that the kingdoms should remain divided—there was a geopolitical as well as a dynastic logic in Lear proposing to give power to Goneril and Albany (Scotland), Regan and Cornwall (the Celtic lands to the West), and Cordelia (effectively, England) in the absence of a male heir who could, like James VI and I, hope to command the whole of Britain.[39] We are also better informed than we were about the frequency with which older men and women made *inter vivos* gifts to their children, handing out marriage portions and shaking out wealth while expecting to be looked after in old age.[40] Legal guidance could easily be found. William West's widely read *Symboleography* (1590, etc.), for example, includes among its sample documents 'A gift of goods and chattels, with couenants to find the donor necessaries'.[41] Lear may not make a covenant—it would have to take the form of a treaty—but he does make clear his conditions, his reservation of a hundred knights, the name and all the addition of a king. He will later have to learn just how few necessaries subsistence needs.

What has not been thought about sufficiently is the word that heads that document: 'A *gift* of goods and chattels . . .'. *King Lear* is, like *Timon of Athens*, deeply concerned with the giving of benefits.[42] We are repeatedly told, by the Fool, Lear himself, and others, when the king is ill treated, that he *gave* his lands away, *gave* all to his daughters. To give away kingdoms might seem beyond largesse; and it is true that Lear's liberality raises the question of whether the crown has the right to sell or give away pieces of the realm (in practice, English monarchs did, in some measure).[43] In his own eyes, however, in the love-trial, Lear is like Antony in Cleopatra's description, so full of bounty that isles and realms fall from his pocket.[44] What he expects in return is gratitude, with what likelihood we know from *Timon of Athens*. He speaks of extending his 'largest bounty' to the daughter who loves him most—'bounty' is a *Timon* word[45]—and sends Cordelia to France without 'benison' (1.1.49–50, 263 [49–50, 266]). We might remember Timon himself: 'I could deal kingdoms to my friends' (1.2.215). No doubt, if he had them, he would give them away, and with less justification than Lear.

Whatever the wisdom of dividing the state, and of Lear's retirement plan, the love-trial is a dangerous way of putting these schemes into effect. Designed to display his generosity to Albany and Cornwall, who are already bound to him as king and father and who should now be bound to him by gratitude, and perhaps appropriate for the granting of dowries, late in the day, to Goneril and Regan, the contest is also, we quickly realize, a way of coercing and appearing to bribe Cordelia into saying how hugely she loves her father in front of her suitors France and Burgundy. 'Great rivals in our youngest daughter's love', Lear calls them, revealing his own role in the scene (44 [44]). In the best of the few discussions of gift-giving in *King Lear*,[46] Andrew Zurcher rightly notes that, just as three women are made to compete for the love of Lear, so three men—Burgundy, France, and Lear—compete for the love of Cordelia. It further muddles the process that the roughly equal division of realms (which reflects early modern custom, in mitigating the effects of primogeniture)[47] should be geared to judgement by merit, both rashly in rewarding flattery and more justifiably by earmarking the most opulent territory for Cordelia. By introducing competition and quantification, the king ensures that the playlet will become a specious display. There is an insidious corruption in the exchange of words for benefits. Goneril and Regan resemble the lords who flatter Timon in order to extract greater bounty.

That the performance is one of performatives is evident in the pledging. Goneril and Regan do not utter but 'profess' their love (1.1.70 [71])—a word which in Jacobean English means 'avow' or 'vow', and which carries relevant, post-Reformation implication of 'merely profess' (e.g. the profession of friars to poverty and chastity).[48] Lear responds to his elder daughters with speech acts that bestow land and power: 'To thee and thine hereditary ever | Remain this ample third of our fair kingdom' (1.1.77–8 [78–9]). We know that Goneril and Regan are wedded to their lords, and that Cordelia soon will be to hers. They are bound by vows as well as the marital rites that produce hereditary futures. The bond between the king and his daughters is equally, or even more, a natural one, but the strands of blood and filiation are entwined with the feudal obligations which Shakespeare anachronistically puts into ancient Britain—bonds which tie the Dukes of Albany and Cornwall to the king. As E. Catherine Dunn has shown, in the still-standard study of ingratitude in English Renaissance thought, benefits reinforced social bonds *along with* oaths and allegiance in the medieval and early modern periods: 'Largesse was . . . a kind of additional bond, superimposed upon the fundamental bond of fealty.'[49] Historically, medieval princesses did not swear allegiance to their royal fathers,[50] whatever the fealty of their lords. When urging on the wind and rain in 3.2, however, Lear says: 'I tax not you, you elements, with unkindness. | I never gave you kingdom, called you children. | You owe me no subscription' (15–18 [15–18]). The *Oxford English Dictionary* glosses 'subscription' here as 'the action of acknowledging allegiance to someone; submission. . . . allegiance, fealty'. The gloss is justified. 'Subscribe' carries this meaning in the source play *King Leir*.[51]

Goneril and Regan initiate the play's impulse to excess when they declare that they love their father 'Dearer than eyesight, space, and liberty', and then some (1.1.54 [54]). Cordelia stops the competition by saying 'Nothing' (more than once in the Folio). When pushed on what she means, she famously declares: 'I love your majesty | According to my bond, no more nor less' (1.1.85–91 [86–92]). There is a touch of Shylock in this. What she says is designed in its minimalism to rebuke her sisters' flattery, in a scene of sibling rivalry that no doubt goes back to childhood,[52] as between Edmund and, Edgar eventually realizes, his legitimate brother. Yet, the chime of *according* with *Cordelia* must at least subconsciously register. In *Leir*, the Gallian King speaks of 'deare *Cordella*, cordiall to my heart'.[53] Cordial can be heard in 'Cordelia'.[54] *Cor-* also suggests *cœur*, heart. When Lear madly remembers the love-trial in the hovel scene, he sees his daughters as the little dogs Tray

(Goneril's betrayal), Blanch (Regan as whited sepulchre), and Sweetheart (Cordelia) (3.6.19 [58]). But *Cor-* goes on to *Cord*, as in bond.[55] Cordelia enshrines, in that sense, the bond that she advocates.

What is at stake at this point, and how are the characters tied to it? Edmund unscrupulously tells Gloucester that he reminded Edgar 'with how manifold and strong a bond | The child was bound to th' father' (2.1.46–7 [48–9]). A belief in such bonds is of radical importance in the play, where they are taken back into the suffering, strung physicality of life, as when Kent denounces Oswald: 'Such smiling rogues as these, | Like rats, oft bite the holy cords a-twain | Which are too intrince t' unloose' (2.2.67–9 [65–7]). The holy cords are the bonds of family, allegiance, and state that tie together (wholly) the body politic, and tie bodies into the polity. Meanwhile, *according*—in 'According to my bond'—signifies 'in accordance with something previously stated'.[56] Cordelia will stick to her bond, be bound by its language. But *according* also suggests 'concordant, harmonious... obedient, compliant',[57] all softening a nature which in this declaration seems hard. *Cord-* is itself an aphetic form of the verb *to accord*, meaning 'To bring to agreement, reconcile',[58] which is the use to which Cordelia puts her bond in the latter acts of the play. If we must look ahead, however, the word is a premonition of Cordelia's death. In Shakespeare's most horrible, literalistic parody of being bound by bonds, Cordelia is hanged at Edmund's command to make her death look like suicide. *Cord* is 'A rope for hanging; the hangman's rope'.[59]

Unclenching a little, Cordelia explains what she means by her bond. It is reciprocal, creating ties by exchange:

Good my lord,
You have begot me, bred me, loved me.
I return those duties back as are right fit—
Obey you, love you, and most honour you.
Why have my sisters husbands if they say
They love you all? Haply, when I shall wed
That lord whose hand must take my plight shall carry
Half my love with him, half my care and duty. (1.1.93–100 [94–101])

This is scarcely less challenging for being expansive. What Cordelia says about her sisters' marriages resists Lear's quantification of love, but she also brings out the importance of the *plight*, a vowed bond. Language does not simply report emotional states, as Goneril and Regan purport in their pledges. Truly to give a plight is actively to create a bond, and so to generate love, which is taken by the hand that clinches the deal. The speech acts and articulate gestures help create the holy cords.

Cordelia's speech is valid but peremptory. Her lucidity sounds like ingratitude, which stirs the insecurity that any early modern patriarch would feel when relinquishing his power and throwing himself upon the good will of his daughters. At this date, relationships within the family were 'systems of exchange whereby parents not only offered substantial gifts and support, but also received much in return', and although material benefits tended to flow from parents to children, returns included care in age and such non-material goods as respect and a willingness to please and reassure.[60] This ran along with, but sometimes counter to, the command based on the Decalogue that children should honour their father and mother by being obedient, that the father had power, for instance, to commit to vows on behalf of daughters below the age of adulthood. On either model of the family, Cordelia seems to be deficient. What the king fears in her—lack of care, of respect and honour—will come with Goneril and Regan, but she has begun the process of humiliation.

Lear's reaction is extreme, fed by shame and a bitter foretaste of the powerlessness to come. 'Let it be so', he declares;

> Thy truth then be thy dower;
> For by the sacred radiance of the sun,
> The mysteries of Hecate and the night,
> By all the operation of the orbs
> From whom we do exist and cease to be,
> Here I disclaim all my paternal care,
> Propinquity, and property of blood,
> And as a stranger to my heart and me
> Hold thee from this for ever. (106–14 [108–16])

Though sometimes referred to as a curse,[61] this is an oath. Like the lines this chapter started with—though in an entirely different key—it is an oath that wants to be a curse, as Lear's oaths will become. For now it can be an oath because the king is able to put what he says into practice, at least by disowning Cordelia. That he cannot make her a 'sometime daughter' by hacking through the bonds of blood with words (118 [120]) does not prevent his assault from hurting the filial connection. If the lines show his later tendency to declare something done which cannot be done, as though he can command the wind to blow and crack its cheeks, they also foreground a key concern of the tragedy, in showing how bonds can be cut into by binding language, especially when oaths morph into curses.

Kent expostulates by invoking his own oath and bond: 'Good my liege—' (118 [120]). The matrix of subscription is reinforced and extended by this reminder of his fealty. The drama unfolds in a space of bonds that is partly natural and affective but that requires consolidation by duty and dutiful speech. The king's authority lies in his word. For him to be challenged in this is an affront to his power but also to his royal inability to go back on an oath. The king has sworn 'by the sacred radiance of the sun'—i.e. by Apollo—and now Kent, as he will do again later, when he is in the stocks,[62] challenges his authority by throwing back his oath as words:

LEAR Now, by Apollo—
KENT Now, by Apollo, King, thou swear'st thy gods in vain.
LEAR [*making to strike him*] O vassal! Miscreant! (157–9 [160–1])

Interrupting—perhaps to stop Lear saying anything worse—Kent makes the king's oath his own, as though to imply that it means as much in his mouth as in Lear's, and consequently does not mean much. There is a metatheatrical touch in '*thy* gods' for an audience at court or in the Globe just ahead or in the wake of the Act to Restrain Abuses; Kent disarms the oath by saying that it has no potent God or Trinity to witness it (see p. 8). Note the force of 'by Apollo, *king*'. We saw in Chapter 3 that it was a 'sayngе... amonge men / that the word / promes or othe / of a kynge shulde stande'.[63] The royal oath should not be gainsaid, as Kent both urges and effects. There is also the prior point that a king should not have to vow or swear, because his word alone is reliable and potent.[64] Kent exposes the weakness that is revealed by the king's rising to an oath, as well as its appalling folly, in the hope that he will revoke it. That Lear is attacked at the verbal root of his authority leads him to cry out 'O vassal', since the king is not just Kent's liege lord but his superior (vassalage was service owed and confirmed by oath).

Kent's next piece of loyal disobedience is to declare 'Reuoke thy doome' in Quarto and 'reuoke thy guift' in the Folio.[65] The F reading may reveal Shakespeare's awareness that he had written a tragedy of benefits. As often in revision, the text moves away from the source. Leir says in the old play: 'Cease, good my Lords, and sue not to reverse | Our censure, which is now irrevocable' (lines 505–6). Not wanting to revoke, he adds, 'We have dispatched letters of contract | Unto the Kings of Cambria and of Cornwall; | Our hand and seale will justify no lesse: | Then do not so dishonour me, my Lords, | As to make shipwrack of our kingly word' (lines 507–11). In *King Lear*, letters are important, but there are none on display at this point;

weight is thrown instead upon binding utterance, and the impossibility (for the king) of revocation. Lear reverts to Kent's oath of fealty, 'on thine allegiance hear me!', and offers him a perverse benefit, a 'reward' (as he puts it) of the most negative kind. Like other leading figures in Shakespeare—Shylock, for example, or Othello—he declares his hands to be tied by an oath that he has sworn: 'thou hast sought to make us break our vows, | Which we durst never yet.' He asserts his waning authority by exiling Kent's 'banished trunk' with another oath, that moves higher up the scale of the gods, from Apollo to Jove himself: 'Away! By Jupiter, | This shall not be revoked' (164–76 [168–80]).

An important word and experience in both *Lear* and *Timon of Athens*, being *banished* is rooted in *ban*, which meant, as late as the fourteenth century, 'summon', 'proclaim'—as in the declaration of *banns* before marriage; but that older sense gave way to the once-strong but now faded meaning 'To curse, anathematize, interdict'.[66] In Jacobean English 'to banish' had its modern sense but this was coloured by *ban* as 'curse' or 'address with angry and maledictory language'[67] (a banished person is cast out, anathematized in some sense). 'Banning' as 'cursing' was standard usage; it features in treatises against swearing[68] as well as in Shakespeare's plays. ''Ban, 'ban, Cacaliban' in *The Tempest* is an obvious example (2.2.175); the slave knows how to curse (1.2.367), though editors still refer to this line as 'a nonsense refrain'.[69] Suffolk wants to 'curse and ban' in *2 Henry VI* (3.2.321). Later, he declares, with wordplay between banning and banishment: 'You bade me ban, and will you bid me leave? | Now, by the ground that I am banished from, | Well could I curse away a winter's night' (3.2.335–7). In *Lear*, Edgar joins the 'Bedlam beggars who, . . . Sometime with lunatic bans, sometime with prayers | Enforce their charity' (2.2.171–7 [2.3.14–20]). The king himself, when he becomes a beggar, is one such, denouncing ingratitude in his bans, while he looks for shelter from the storm. Both *Lear* and *Timon* make much of banishment, mixing those who endure and undo it (Kent, Alcibiades, in a way Cordelia) with those who choose it (Timon, Edgar, the Fool). Both plays lay bare the conditions of exposure and isolation that lead to massive curses that protest and attempt to punish.

* * *

Cordelia's refusal to win the love contest gives Lear a sample of the ingratitude that he will experience at the hands of Goneril and Regan. His response is punitively reciprocal; it was a commonplace that ingratitude provokes revenge.[70] 'Ingratitude challengeth reuenge by custome', noted John Bodenham in 1597, 'and is a vice most hatefull both before God and man.'[71] Vindictiveness can already be heard in Lear's rejection of Cordelia, when he tells Burgundy that she is 'Dowered with our curse and strangered with our oath' (1.1.201 [205]), but it mounts to a passion in the curses uttered against Goneril when she shows herself to be 'Ingratitude, thou marble-hearted fiend' (1.4.220 [236]) by proposing to reduce his train of knights. The king's rage is premature, but consistent with the play's Senecan ethos. *Ira* in Senecan tradition is the engine of revenge as ingratitude is a bad payback for benefits. The ingratitude of Goneril and Regan might even be construed as revenge for the many years in which their father preferred Cordelia.

We have noticed the pre-shock of banning in Lear's oath against Cordelia. Oath turns into curse in what he says to Goneril. He invokes the goddess Nature as a witness—paradigmatic of an oath—but then makes Nature a stand-in for himself, able to inflict the revenge that he cannot. There is a dire largesse, a horrible excess, to his language. His spiralling tirade draws increase out of itself and makes it the theme of the curse.

> Hear, Nature, hear, dear goddess, hear:
> Suspend thy purpose if thou didst intend
> To make this creature fruitful.
> Into her womb convey sterility.
> Dry up in her the organs of increase,
> And from her derogate body never spring
> A babe to honour her.[72]

The curse is bent on destroying the bonds that link father and daughter, yet in a powerful counterflow, generated by the desire for payback, Lear registers himself as one who is accursed while cursing—similar effects can be found in Timon. He imagines Goneril as a version of himself, wrinkled, afflicted, and tearful, the parent of a child who will not repay *benefits*:

> If she must teem,
> Create her child of spleen, that it may live
> And be a thwart disnatured torment to her.
> Let it stamp wrinkles in her brow of youth,
> With cadent tears fret channels in her cheeks,
> Turn all her mother's pains and benefits
> To laughter and contempt, that she may feel—
> That she may feel
> How sharper than a serpent's tooth it is
> To have a thankless child. (1.4.243–52 [258–66])

Storming off the stage, Lear re-enters immediately, against all the conventions, to resume his curse:

Blasts and fogs upon thee!
The untented woundings of a father's curse
Pierce every sense about thee! (262–4 [276–8])

It is an astonishing instance of the unbounded bindingness of the curse. Meant to be final and cathartic, it has only the power to go on. As Björn Quiring puts it, in *Shakespeare's Curse*, though from another angle, 'The curse is cursed with the need for its own endless repetition.'[73]

Lear's curse has biblical precedents. A Jacobean audience might think of Jesus cursing the fig tree with sterility,[74] or the 'Comminacion Againste Synners' that was added to the Book of Common Prayer in 1552, from Deuteronomy: '*Minister.* Cursed is he that curseth father or mother. *Aunswere.* Amen.'[75] Overall, however, it owes more to the classical curse that Shakespeare would find exemplified in such texts as Ovid's *Ibis*. The mode is elucidated in Peacham's *Garden of Eloquence*:

> *Ara* called of the Latins *Imprecatio*... is the fit instrument of speech to expresse the bitternesse of the detestation within vs against some euill person, or euill thing, and forasmuch as it sendeth forth the flame of reuenge kindeled in our affections, it may well be compared to the casting of wildfire, or poysoning of shotte, to destroy the enemie.[76]

The flame of revenge is blazingly audible in Lear's curse, the more terrible, and mountingly so, for being known to be ineffectual and thus humiliating for a king, accustomed to command. This does not stop him wanting to reclaim his gift ('To take't again perforce—monster ingratitude!') as his vengefulness takes bizarre, fantasy forms in Acts 3 and 4. He wants to arm a thousand men with red burning spits, or to shoe a troop of horse with hoof-muffling felt, then to kill six times over.[77]

Lear's desire for revenge becomes explicit when Regan proposes that he return to Goneril, and he rounds again on his eldest child:

All the stored vengeances of heaven fall
On her ingrateful top! Strike her young bones,
You taking airs, with lameness!
CORNWALL Fie, sir, fie.
LEAR You nimble lightnings, dart your blinding flames
Into her scornful eyes. Infect her beauty,
You fen-sucked fogs drawn by the pow'rful sun
To fall and blister. (2.2.327–33 [2.4.155–61])

Long-inclined, we might suspect, to the tyrannical, Lear becomes increasingly imperious in the sense of using imperatives.[78] The more he bans, however, the more he relies on the vengefulness of natural forces which might not grace him with favour, however imposing they begin to seem in this scene, as theatrical thunder rattles the rafters of the playhouse. Lear's vehemence locks into the self-driven violence of a rant, though his banning never becomes, like that of Timon in the woods, a generalized venting of spleen.

Regan reasonably but provocatively says that Lear will curse her too 'when the rash mood is on'. Lear reassures her otherwise. Goneril has broken the 'bond of childhood... dues of gratitude'. Regan will not forget 'Thy half o'th' kingdom... Wherein I thee endowed.' (2.2.333–46 [2.4.162–74]). He is still relying, of course, on quantity, and gratitude, but has no quantity left for himself. His problem, as the Fool points out, is that he has nothing left to earn gratitude with now he has given everything away. In one sense, though, Lear is right. He does not curse Regan. Instead, he swears in the only way left to him that can be potent, not commanding Regan but himself by abjuration. 'Return to her, and fifty men dismissed?', he asks, 'No, rather I abjure all roofs, and choose | To be a comrade with the wolf and owl' (2.2.372–4 [2.4.202–5]). It is binding language at its most resolute because Lear can ensure its outcome. However damaging to his welfare, it gives him the consolation of a return to verbal potency.

* * *

When he leaves Athens in disgust and poverty, Timon becomes like Lear a self-banished man. Like the king he responds to ingratitude by looking for revenge, first by hateful cursing then by funding an army. Perhaps this turn of events was always latent in his name, since *timē* can mean in Greek 'compensation, satisfaction, penalty'.[79] At first, his raging resentment is too comprehensive to hit any targets. As he shouts at the distant city, at the tiring house from the open stage, he declares that he wants Athens to be punished by becoming worse than it is ('Matrons, turn incontinent! | Obedience fail in children' [4.1.3–4]). His 'multiplying bans' (34) lose force. We are closer to Puttenham than to Peacham on the classical imprecation:

> This made the auncient Poetes to inuent a meane to rid the gall of all such Vindicatiue men: so as they might be a wrecked of their wrong,... And this was done by a maner of imprecation, or as we call it by cursing and banning of the parties, and wishing all euill to a light vpon them, and though it neuer the sooner happened, yet was it great easment to the boiling stomacke:...[80]

The *ara*, in this account, is a way of letting off steam, and it never makes anything happen a moment sooner than it otherwise would.

What does make things happen, in the final acts as in the first, is gold. In an astonishing sequence, the tattered and hungry Timon, digging about on the bare boards for roots, comes upon a hoard:

> What is here?
> Gold? Yellow, glittering, precious gold?
> No, gods, I am no idle votarist:
> Roots, you clear heavens. Thus much of this will make
> Black white, foul fair, wrong right,
> Base noble, old young, coward valiant.
> Ha, you gods! Why this, what, this, you gods? Why, this
> Will lug your priests and servants from your sides,
> Pluck stout men's pillows from below their heads.
> This yellow slave
> Will knit and break religions, bless th'accursed, . . . (4.3.25–35)

He has found the alchemy he needs to make matrons, children, all, turn against their virtues and bonds. 'No idle votarist' will strike the audience as meaning, 'I'm not praying frivolously for roots.' But there is an implication, also, of the votive as a vow; he is not the sort of hermit who has taken vows idly to live and die by gold. Though he would much rather have roots, he acknowledges the gold's fascination. Divisive yet fusing, it knits and breaks, is a 'common whore of mankind' (43). Most brilliantly, as a stage effect, just after he finds the gold, we hear a drum beat, a '*March afar off*', which comes closer. 'Ha! a drum!' he exclaims, 'Thou'rt quick' (45). The gold has a life of its own in its instant capacity to pull in false friends. The isolation of the misanthrope is invaded in the most stage-crowding fashion by an army and its camp-followers:

> But yet I'll bury thee.
> [*He buries gold*]
> Thou'lt go, strong thief,
> When gouty keepers of thee cannot stand.
> [*He keeps some gold*]
> Nay, stay thou out for earnest.
> *Enter* ALCIBIADES *with* [*soldiers playing*] *drum and fife, in warlike manner; and* PHRYNIA *and* TIMANDRA (46–8)

Directors have to decide how to stage the gold. It is tempting to make it nodular, dirty, raw, like the roots that Timon wants to dig up, but it is yellow and glittering in the script, so should include rings or goblets and coin. On the one hand it can suggest what Gloucester in *King Lear* calls 'The bounty and the benison of heaven' (4.5.218 [4.6.220]). As Seneca writes in *De Beneficiis*: 'God has planted in the earth countless mines, has drawn forth from its depths countless rivers that over the lands where they flow carry down gold' (IV.vi.1). On the other, it must include cash, because, after Timon gives gold to Alcibiades, he does the same to Phrynia and Timandra, and they relentlessly ask for 'more money' (165). Gold is ductile, fungible, category-defying. Even as coin it can be hoarded as convertible metal, but its value was meant to be standardized by the authority of the state in the Jacobean period, so it was turning for early audiences into what coin has become for us, a sign or token of value.[81] The tableau reflects the pressures on gold between the gift economy in which it is beaten into vessels and jewels and the early modern market for cash. Quoting Timon's speech in *Capital*, Marx illuminates the allure of gold by noting how, once commodities and money begin to circulate, there is a 'passionate desire to hold fast to the product of the first metamorphosis . . . its gold-chrysalis. . . . money is petrified into a hoard'.[82]

Recognizing a kindred spirit, another man banished from Athens, Alcibiades asks Timon what 'friendship' he may do him (70). The misanthrope is at bay, but not because of a lack of human warmth, or shelter, or nourishment; his feelings of mistrust are concentrated into the betrayal of binding language that goes with a failure to reciprocate:

TIMON None but to maintain my opinion.
ALCIBIADES What is it, Timon?
TIMON Promise me friendship, but perform none. If thou wilt not promise, the gods plague thee, for thou art a man. If thou dost perform, confound thee, for thou art a man.[83]

It might seem that promising is not that important in an economy based on gifts or cash. You reciprocate or you do not, and other agents take note. But the time between promising a benefit and giving it is as critical (Seneca reminds us) as the time between giving it and repaying it, and equally important is the time between promising to reciprocate and doing so.[84] If a benefit is withheld too long, the promise begins to rankle. We are back with the false friends' vows like empty purses (p. 344). The human animal promises you friendship but does not perform the actions of a friend. If you promise to help me, he tells Alcibiades, be cursed with the plague—the plague associated with oath-breakers[85]—because you are acting like a man (who will not deliver). If you do perform, confound you, as you confound your nature, because you are not being human.

The protagonist in the academic *Timon* falls in love with Callimela, who turns to a richer suitor when his merchant ships are wrecked. In Shadwell's adaptation of Shakespeare (1677–8), the protagonist abandons Evadne for the delectable, trivial Melissa, who responds to his fall by taking up with Alcibiades once he returns from exile.[86] Shadwell puts romantic attachment, its challenges to faith and liberty, at the heart of the play. Shakespeare's tragedy is different. Even before he goes into the woods, Timon is isolated. In Simon Russell Beale's performance, at the National Theatre (2012), the protagonist avoided physical contact at the height of his popularity. His journey was not a long one from wealth to lonely tomb. As many critics have noted, the only women in Shakespeare's play are a group of Amazon masquers and the whores who accompany Alcibiades—none of them good models of heterosexual bonding. Timon warms to the whores, if at all, because of their capacity to destroy.

When they ask Timon for gold, he showers it into their aprons—the ultimate, monetized sexual act—without even giving them a chance to utter their mercenary oaths:

> Hold up, you sluts,
> Your aprons mountant.
> [*He throws gold into their aprons*]
> You are not oathable,
> Although I know you'll swear, terribly swear,
> Into strong shudders and to heavenly agues
> Th'immortal gods that hear you. Spare your oaths;
> I'll trust to your conditions. Be whores still, . . . (4.3.134–9)

Timon quibbles on the conditions attached to oaths and the innate condition of whoredom. He will later give the faithful Flavius gold, 'thus conditioned', that he will avoid men, do no charity, and so on (4.3.516–21), but he knows, with Poor Tom, that you should never trust 'a boy's love, or a whore's oath'.[87] What they *can* be relied upon to do—in this sense they are utterly reliable—is spread disease through sex, a vicious payback through reciprocity. The impulse to revenge is barbed with just deserts. Venereal disease will 'Crack the lawyer's voice' and put a stop to his false pleading. Lear denounces the 'rascal beadle', who lashes the whore that he 'hotly lusts to use';[88] Timon imagines a priest being ravaged by the pox even while he preaches against the flesh. 'Hoar the flamen', is how he puts it: make his hair turn white—with a vindictive quibble on 'whore' (4.3.152–6).

The most closely fought, and for audiences the most baffling, exchange comes between Timon and Apemantus, who quarrel about which of them has the more justifiably negative view of the world. Which of these men is better equipped to live (like Lear) on 'the mere necessities'? The contours of debate are frayed, but audiences are rightly impressed by the rapidity and rhetorical ease with which Timon shifts from abusive flyting to a lyrically anticipated resolution, and then on to a further analysis of the division-in-bonding of money that caught Marx's attention:

Rogue, rogue, rogue!
I am sick of this false world, and will love naught
But even the mere necessities upon't.
Then, Timon, presently prepare thy grave.
Lie where the light foam of the sea may beat
Thy gravestone daily. Make thine epitaph,
That death in me at others' lives may laugh.
[*He looks on the gold*]
O, thou sweet king-killer, and dear divorce
'Twixt natural son and sire; thou bright defiler
Of Hymen's purest bed; thou valiant Mars;
Thou ever young, fresh, loved, and delicate wooer,
Whose blush doth thaw the consecrated snow
That lies on Dian's lap; thou visible god,
That sold'rest close impossibilities
And mak'st them kiss, ... (4.3.367–81)

In an early Notebook, Marx quotes this address to the gold and writes: 'If *money* is the bond which ties me to *human* life and society to me, which links me to nature and to man, is money not the bond of all *bonds*? Can it not bind and loose all bonds? Is it therefore not the universal *means of separation*? It is the true *agent of separation* and the true *cementing agent*, it is the *chemical* power of society.'[89] Given how the play develops, there is indeed a case for thinking money the bond of all bonds in *Timon*, if not elsewhere in Shakespeare. It is among its other powers a magnet to sociability, drawing Timon into contact that repels. This is the light in which we should interpret Apemantus' own little revenge on Timon: 'I'll say thou'st gold. | Thou wilt be thronged to shortly' (386–7).

In *Lear*, the idea of superfluous benefit modulates into charity. Thinking about the ingratitude of his daughters, the king calls down curses first on them and then on other wrongdoers, such as the rascal beadle, and questions his own rectitude, the more keenly now that he is himself a poor half-naked wretch. 'O, I have ta'en | Too little care of this' (3.4.32–3 [33–4]). Though he finds sympathy with Poor Tom through the self-obsessed belief that he must have given all to his daughters, it becomes the basis of care. In Seneca's *De Beneficiis*, Shakespeare found the thought that 'It is only through the interchange of benefits that life becomes in some measure equipped and fortified against sudden disasters. Take us singly, and what are we? The prey of all creatures, ... the covering of man is a frail skin ... his safety lies in fellowship ... it is this that has checked the assaults of disease, has made ready supports for old age' (IV.xviii.1–3). Early modern commonplaces, these have an evident bearing on the ragged, mutual knot of Lear, Fool, Caius, and Gloucester, who give benefits and thanks to one another.

Beyond benefits, are there bonds? What of Poor Tom, and his inability to reciprocate? Senecan arguments, broadly construed, were open to extension. Because we are enabled by Nature to assist one another, Cornwallis wrote in his *Essayes*, 'therfore is the vngratefull man to be termed a monster. Pitty and humanity, where benefits binde not, must binde.'[90] 1601 saw the introduction of the Elizabethan Poor Law, which is often correlated by historians with a hardening of opinion against charity and the making of ungenerous distinctions between the worthy and unworthy poor.[91] There were undoubtedly arguments in favour of prudence and desert in Jacobean discussions of charity, but recent work has shown that there was a continuing praise of good works and a consensus that the superflux should be shaken to the needy in a way that harmonized with broader beliefs in the virtue of benefits among the better sort: 'notions of reciprocal obligations between patrons, clients and friends supplemented and considerably broadened their sense of religious obligation and beliefs in the merits of good works as well as the imperative to give that were evident in the numerous small charitable donations they gave throughout their lives'.[92]

The vagrant, idle, and disguised in *Lear* all seem worthy of charity compared with most of those who come to Timon. The first visitors brought in by Apemantus' news are thieves. Timon gives them gold because they will despoil Athens, like Alcibiades and his army, but also because the trade which they practise while denying to is universal:

> The sun's a thief, and with his great attraction
> Robs the vast sea. The moon's an arrant thief,
> And her pale fire she snatches from the sun. (4.4.429–31)

This is a reciprocity of taking not giving, the way of the world that Timon believes he has discovered in Athens. The thieves are called *Bandetti* in the Folio ('*Enter the Bandetti*')—an unusual word in the period, found only once elsewhere in lines usually attributed to Shakespeare,[93] who more often writes of thieves and outlaws. *Bandetti* contains *ban*, of course, as in banished, proclaimed, outcast,[94] and bandits clump into a *band* or *bond*. Banded together to rob, Timon encourages them to 'Rob one another' (438), to mirror the cosmic kleptocracy.

Timon of Athens tends to satire because the protagonist's refusal to give charity in the woods is never confronted by real need. This effect is at its sharpest in the vacuous return of the Poet and Painter who were seen at the start of the play flattering Timon by presenting him with their uninspired works of art. This time they bring nothing but a promise of objects to come and the gift of their visit. This outrageously weak gambit allows for the keenest test of promising in the play:

POET What have you now to present unto him?
PAINTER Nothing at this time, but my visitation; only I will promise him an excellent piece.
POET I must serve him so too, tell him of an intent that's coming toward him.
PAINTER Good as the best.
Enter TIMON *from his cave* [*unobserved*]
Promising is the very air o'th' time; it opens the eyes of expectation. Performance is ever the duller for his act, and but in the plainer and simpler kind of people the deed of saying is quite out of use. To promise is most courtly and fashionable. Performance is a kind of will or testament which argues a great sickness in his judgment that makes it. (5.1.17–28)

Since this has misled commentators not attuned to its modish tone, a paraphrase is in order. 'Promising is quite the thing these days; it provides the pleasure of anticipation. Delivering on a promise is always duller for having been done (the deliverer appears stupid for having been so crass as to honour his promise, and the thing delivered lacks the spice of expectation). Only ordinary and dim people now say this or that; the courtly and with-it promise things or say "I promise you" when they just mean say or tell (like Edmund to Edgar, "I promise you, the effects he writes of succeed unhappily", or the Third Lord to Timon, "I promise you, my lord, you moved me much")...'[95]

How unusual is this apologia? The Ciceronian/Christian view of promising was strict. 'Promise is debt', writes Henry Wilkinson in *The Debt Book* (the phrase was proverbial), 'and must bee performed though to our hindrance. Faithfulnesse in promises is the bond of humane contracts.'[96] Yet the orthodoxy was not rigid. It was acceptable to be conditional and qualified in order to encourage aspiration and good behaviour, though we must be careful to avoid empty promising: 'Circumspect promises are of vse I know to assure true mens words,' Wilkinson goes on, 'to secure good mens hopes, to encourage industry, and make it liuely in well-doing; but then wee must beware wee bee not like *Antigonus*, ... *That wil giue*; ignominiously so called, because forward in promising, but slacke in performing. Promises are as vowes, much better neuer made, then not made good' (94). Luke Wilson has suggested that the Painter's speech draws on Shakespeare's awareness as he drafted a play that might never be performed that he was being forward in the art of promising.[97] It is just as likely that he thought of the text as earnest of dispersed, reciprocal benefits, between collaborating playwrights, scribes, a promptbook keeper, and actors—a matrix of promises and performances, any part of which might slip.

That promise continues to matter is shown by the arrival of one last delegation: senators who have given a 'promise to th' Athenians' that they will ask Timon to fund the defence of their city (5.2.5). Characteristically, they offer a 'recompense' over and above their 'render' that sounds usurious: 'such heaps and sums of love and wealth | As shall to thee blot out what wrongs were theirs, | And write in thee the figures of their love' (34–9). Timon rejects this calculated excess, preferring isolation even in death. 'Say to Athens', he declares,

> Timon hath made his everlasting mansion
> Upon the beachèd verge of the salt flood,
> Who once a day with his embossèd froth
> The turbulent surge shall cover. (99–103)

This is a lovely evocation of a not-for-profit exchange, a place of harmless visitation, where the gilt-embossed ceilings of the rich are replaced by the sway of the tide ('embossed' as 'swelling'). Later we see a soldier finding Timon's tomb in the woods, though in the final lines of the play he is once again said to be 'Entombed upon the very hem o'th' sea' (5.5.67). No doubt this confusion would have been revised away before the manuscript of the play became a promptbook. But the two sites share a rationale; like wooded common land, the shore, as the hem of the sea, was often regarded as beyond ownership.[98] Timon so far rejects the Athenian market-place that he is buried where money cannot reach him.

In Plutarch, Alcibiades is banished because he 'wickedly mocked the two goddesses, *Ceres,* and *Proserpina*'.[99] Shakespeare and Middleton change this to integrate his story with that of Timon. In 3.6 we see him pleading with the senate for the life of a captain who killed a man in a duel. When they resist, he allows charges of bribery and money-marketeering to slip into his indignation (in lines probably by Middleton): 'Banish me? | ... banish usury | That makes the senate ugly' (96–8). I have fought their enemies, he tells the audience, 'While they have told their money and let out | Their coin upon large interest' (105–6). This is the background to his attack on Athens, and it makes the less surprising not just the nature of their offer to Timon but what they offer the general himself:

> March, noble lord,
> Into our city with thy banners spread.
> By decimation and a tithèd death,
> If thy revenges hunger for that food
> Which nature loathes, take thou the destined tenth,
> And by the hazard of the spotted die
> Let die the spotted. (5.5.29–35)

Shakespeare will have read in Plutarch about the Roman custom of culling the ranks of a cowardly legion by decimation.[100] Here a parallel is drawn with the payment of a tenth part of a man's income to the Church—a payment traced back to Jacob, who vowed the tithe to God (see pp. 157–8). Decimation, tithe, interest at 10 per cent; beyond that, the bloody overlap between debt collection and destroying a man that goes from ancient legal practice into the trial scene in *The Merchant of Venice*. This is how a senate of usurers thinks about human worth. The analogy between usury and a tithe was often noted, as in Bacon's account of why people objected to paying 10 per cent to a money-lender: 'They say, that it is Pitie, the Deuill should haue Gods part, which is the *Tithe*.'[101]

Lear ends with fragmentary echoes of the love-trial and division of Britain. Edgar's duel with Edmund is like the formal, pledged combats discussed in Chapter 8, but it is also a contest of sibling rivalry. Gloves are cast down, words exchanged. Edgar is qualified to fight his brother by 'the privilege of mine honour, | My oath, and my profession' (5.3.119–20 [128]). Each, in Bourdieu's terms, makes a gift of honour to the other by fighting an unworthy rival (Edgar appears as an unknown knight, Edmund is a bastard),[102] and the competition—like that between Lear's daughters—turns out to be a struggle to the death. Rather as Cordelia has two suitors, Edmund has sworn 'reciprocal vows' with both Goneril and Regan, great rivals for his love.[103] On the outcome of the duel hangs the fate of their realms. Albany tries to divide the kingdoms, as though nothing had been learned. Whoever inherits the realm (Albany in Q, Edgar in F), the resolution of the plot brings a return to a political system that has been unable to contain ambition and lust. The Folio king rouses himself to a last few imperatives over the afflicted body of Cordelia: 'Look on her. Look, her lips. | Look there, look there' (5.3.285–6 [309–10]). He returns to the pledges of the love-trial but hears her say nothing rather than 'Nothing'.

The wheel comes full circle more conclusively in *Timon of Athens* where Alcibiades is absorbed into an ethos that proved destructive to the protagonist. Doing a deal with the usurers of the city, who are as willing to decimate their friends as they are prepared to let debtors die in prison, he pledges himself, like a soldier. 'Throw thy glove,' a Senator says, 'Or any token of thine honour... till we | Have sealed thy full desire' (5.5.49–54). He promises that only Timon's and his own enemies chosen by the Athenians will be killed: 'Descend, and keep your words' (65). It would be hard for them to break their words given that Alcibiades is marching in with an army. It is if anything a sign of their weakness that they propose to let him into the city. This is evident to any modern audience with a sense of the reality of power. What we can miss is the particular Renaissance interest in the part that promises could play both to knit together enemies and deceive.

Parleying was always parlous. As Montaigne observes in his essay 'That the Houre of Parlies is Dangerous':

> no man ought to expect performance of promise from an enemie, except the last seale of bond be fully annexed thereunto, wherein notwithstanding is then much care and vigilancie required, and much adoe shalbe found. And it was ever a dangerous counsell to trust the performance of word or othe given vnto a Cittie, that yeelds vnto gentle and favourable composition, and in that furie to give the needie, bloodthirstie, and pray-greedy Souldier free entrance into it, vnto the free choise and licence of a victorious armie.[104]

The last scene of Timon has often struck critics as cursory. This is to misunderstand what Montaigne makes plain. Far from wrapping up a play about broken promises that has already reached its conclusion in Timon's extinction, the exchange between Alcibiades and the senators stages a life-and-death instance of how a 'word or othe' still matters. Timon has urged Alcibiades to visit upon Athens the bloodshed and devastation anticipated by his imprecations; the general has retributive reasons of his own to unleash destruction. The play gestures, nonetheless, in what can only be an imperfect cadence, towards Alcibiades as a promise-keeper and limited exactor of payback—a fidelity and continence that are his own way of defying the usurious senate. This is in weighty contrast with Timon's rejection of oaths and bonds.

While Alcibiades commits to promises, Timon stays with curses. Promises make bonds, curses reject and sever them. When the soldier brings onstage a wax impression of what is inscribed on Timon's tomb, Alcibiades reads out '*the Epitaph*' which is two curses:

> 'Here lies a wretched corpse,
>   Of wretched soul bereft.
> Seek not my name. A plague consume
>   You wicked caitiffs left!
> Here lie I, Timon, who alive
>   All living men did hate.
> Pass by and curse thy fill, but pass
>   And stay not here thy gait.' (5.5.71–8)

Both are found in Plutarch, the latter supposedly by Callimachus.[105] When Shakespeare or Middleton, or the company scribe, revised the text, one would have been cut, but the excess is typical of a character who terminally announces, 'let four words go by, and language end' (5.4.105), then rhymes another line with that and adds a further couplet. In any case the curses do complementary as well as contrary things. The former curses others, the latter invites the passer-by to curse Timon, consistent with his conclusion that all deserve to be cursed, and making doubly sure that his bonds with his kind are cut. His last gift to the world still looks for reciprocation.

14

Reformation I

King James, *King Johan*, and *King John*

The imposition of the Oath of Allegiance on English Catholics in 1606 precipitated a European-wide controversy. The debate was of some importance in rearticulating the relationship between monarchs, republics, and the Roman Church in the aftermath of the Reformation and the growth of nation states. It can also be seen, more questionably, as an episode in the appropriation of the power of oaths by secular authorities.[1] Most of the many treatises that appeared between James VI and I's *Triplici Nodo, Triplex Cuneus: Or, An Apology for the Oath of Allegiance* (1607) and his final statement on the matter, in the *Remonstrance* (1616) that he co-wrote with Pierre du Moulin, returned to sources in scripture and the early councils of the Church.[2] Many of them explored the history of the medieval papacy. Some again, especially those written by Jesuits, were acutely casuistical, and found new things to say about bonds under the pressure of debate. Argument centred on whether James had required his subjects to swear against points of Catholic doctrine, and on whether the Pope could use the power of the keys (Matthew 16: 19) to dispense with oaths, excommunicate monarchs, and free subjects from their allegiance; yet discussion of these exalted topics often swooped down into analysis of everyday binding language.

Overarching the controversy was argument about the relationship between oaths, vows, and the laws of God and man. The status of the Decalogue and of natural and positive law thus provides one focus of this chapter. A related line of enquiry leads to obedience, while a third, less developed, turns on the sacraments, especially baptism. All three themes, but especially obedience and baptism, are pursued in Chapter 15, which is very much a sequel to this one. It is worth stating clearly that, although the Oath of Allegiance is both a starting-point and recurrent point of reference, this oath cannot be understood without appealing, as Jacobean controversialists did, to the Oaths of Succession (1534) and Supremacy (1535)—really a cluster of variant oaths—that were imposed by Henry VIII. These were the oaths that drew the English Reformation out of the loins of a monarch whose relationship with Protestantism was initially hostile and never warm. Chapters 14 and 15 thus combine attention to the Henrician period—both what historians now tell us about it, and the record as it was distorted in Jacobean controversy and drama—with scrutiny of the fractious, sometimes opaque relationship between King James and his Catholic subjects after 1603, in which the Oath of Allegiance was a defining though not definitive issue.

That a significant amount of Jacobean debate and drama was grounded in Henrician texts and events should not obscure the importance of the stream of arguments about doctrine, conformity, and obedience that ran into the reign of James from the later sixteenth century. Many of the points of contention brought up after the Oath of Allegiance had circulated decades earlier: after the papal bull *Regnans in Excelsis* (1570) declared the queen a heretic, excommunicated her, and released her subjects from their sworn allegiance; during the Jesuit mission of the 1580s and 1590s; and after the Armada of 1588. Sometimes the same controversialists were active under both Elizabeth and James—notably, the formidable Jesuit Robert Parsons. Sometimes controversy went along with milder attempts at conversion, as in Parsons's *Booke of Christian Exercise*, first published in Rouen in 1582 and later enlarged as *A Christian Directorie*.[3] This work, which went through forty editions by 1640, and found large audiences right into the eighteenth century, had influence far beyond the often embattled, internally divided community of English Catholics. These continuities and cross-currents matter to a dramatist whose conscience and artistry were formed in the 1580s and 1590s, even if one resists the view that his upbringing and ongoing sympathies were Roman Catholic.

Throughout this period, recourse was often made, in arguments about Church and State, to medieval history. How and why this happened is thrown into relief in the present chapter by looking back through a series of representations of King John. To sketch out the development of the Oath of Allegiance controversy is quickly to find oneself inspecting the celebratory depiction of John in James VI and I's and du Moulin's *Remonstrance*. To go back to the Henrician period, as Jacobean controversialists urge, is to find the protagonist of Bale's *King Johan*: a play about the Reformation written and performed *during* the Reformation. Finally, there is Shakespeare's *King*

John, composed *c.*1596, at a time of renewed debate about royal and papal power. The second half of this chapter is entirely devoted to that play. In Chapter 15 the focus is on the Henrician Reformation as it was represented in two collaborative dramas: *Sir Thomas More* and *Henry VIII*.

⋆ ⋆ ⋆

The oath of 1606 was not a new phenomenon. By calling it an Oath of *Allegiance*, the king was harking back to feudal oaths of fealty sworn to a lord or the crown. For Coke, in *Calvins Case* (1607), the 'oath of Ligeance at the Tourne and Leet was first instituted by King *Arthur*' in the mists of British antiquity.[4] Precedent was set more immediately by the Oaths of Succession and Supremacy. There were other Henrician oaths, beyond the scope of this chapter. As Jonathan Michael Gray has shown, 'The English Reformation was as much about oaths as it was about Henry's marriage, succession, and headship over the English Church.'[5] Shakespeare could hardly miss this, because of the popular and learned arguments that swirled around the Elizabethan Oath of Supremacy (1559) that was inherited by James, as well as the Oath of Allegiance. Oaths and the obedience they exact are in his Reformation-related plays far more important than such points of faith as the sale of indulgences, transubstantiation, or predestination.

The basis for Shakespeare's interpretation of the period can be found in Holinshed, Hall's *Chronicle*, Foxe's *Actes and Monuments*, and the other historical sources that he consulted. Hall, for instance, describes a scene which he probably witnessed in person, when Henry VIII, in the midst of his struggles with convocation about the Great Matter of his divorce from Katherine of Aragon, summoned Thomas Audley and a dozen members of the Commons, and said: 'welbeloued subiectes, we thought that the clergie of our realme, had been our subiectes wholy, but now wee haue well perceiued, that thei bee but halfe our subiectes, yea, and scarce our subiectes: for all the Prelates at their consecracion, make an othe to the Pope, clene contrary to the othe that thei make to vs, so that thei seme to be his subiectes, and not ours, the copie of bothe the othes, I deliuer here to you, requiryng you to inuent some ordre, that we bee not thus deluded, of our Spirituall subiectes.'[6] According to Hall, 'The openyng of these othes, was one of the occasions, why the Pope within two yere folowyng, lost all his iurisdiccion in Englande.' Foxe identified it more definitively as 'the occasion that the Pope lost al his interest and iurisdiction heere in Englande'.[7]

Whatever the truth of those judgements, oaths and the conflicts around them were agents and catalysts of change. For such religious conservatives as Thomas More, the oaths that Henry introduced to clarify the allegiance of churchmen and then of his servants and other subjects were an assault on the order of Christendom. Others, such as Thomas Cromwell, saw them as an adjunct of the crown's imperial authority, which bound together those bound to the king: 'this realm of England is an empire, . . . governed by one supreme head and king . . . unto whom a body politic, compact of all sorts and degrees of people . . . be bounden and owe to bear, next to God, a natural and humble obedience.'[8] Others again, such as Bishop Gardiner—all three, figures who appear in the Shakespeare plays—took oaths under Henry, forswearing their obedience to Rome, then returned to office under the Catholic Queen Mary. Gardiner's *De Vera Obedientia*, one of the best, most scholarly defences of the royal supremacy, written in 1536, was translated into English and printed in 1553 to expose his 'double periurie'; but his leading tenet, that truth and obedience take priority over unjust oaths, was armour-plated against changes of regime, and shame.

After many orthodox pages on the merits of obedience, Gardiner thus lets his opponents be heard. They ask

> what caused me to be so hardye / as to write one worde / concerning any maner of obedience / namely true obedience / seing I neuertheles / entreprising to teache obedience / disclose myne owne dis obedience / and geue the onsette against his power and autoritie / for whose defense I was called ones to be a patrone / and bounden by myne othe to defende and maitene his autoritie to my possible power? wher is the keping of othes become / saye they? Wher is fidelitie? What maye a man beleve now a dayes? Whom maye a man trust? For he was made a bishop and by the priuilege of the Bishop of Rome / admitted in to the ordre of Bishoppes / and consecrated by his commaundement / and sworne vpon the holy euangelistes to defende the rightes of the churche of Rome: all which thinges he willingly and with al his hearte obeyde / and permised to performe. . . .[9]

We have already heard Gardiner arguing, along traditional, Catholic lines that a wicked oath should not be kept. His new piece of artillery is the aggressive, Henrician thought that new obedience itself makes an old oath unlawful. Since 'obedience' (as Christ showed) is 'full of truthe', what could be more virtuous than to 'faithfully sticke vnto it' (H2v). This takes Gardiner to an extreme position, but it is only one instance from the period. Perjury and abjuration in matters of faith were, it seems, widespread under Henry—

as they had been during the persecution of the Lollards[10]—and principles needed to be found both to make binding language stick and to loosen it. The legitimacy of state oaths, and of *ex officio* oaths in heresy trials, and the morality of swearing in general, became a focus of contention during the 1530s and 1540s. When James wrote *Triplici Nodo*, he found himself arguing about More and the Oaths of Succession and Supremacy, and recommending Henrician tracts, including *De Vera Obedientia*.

Catholics had hoped for toleration under James. Early in his reign there was talk of a revised Oath of Supremacy that would not challenge the authority of the Pope.[11] This was a moment when moderate Catholics could have reached an accommodation with the government. That changed with the Gunpowder Plot (1605), which prompted the Oath of Allegiance, and the assassination of Henry IV of France in 1610, by the Catholic zealot Ravaillac, which led James to promulgate the Oath more widely, requiring women and peers of the realm to take it. For many Catholics, swearing the Oath was less troublesome than the charge of misprision of treason[12] and the fine for *praemunire*[13] that fell on those who refused it twice. They could take the Oath to be, as the king insisted it was, a test of civil obedience. This was the line adopted by a number of Benedictines and secular priests, anti-Jesuit in outlook, including the polemical monk Thomas Preston.[14] It was a long and untidy oath, however, and at points deliberately provocative. There is little doubt that some of it was calculated to divide and oppress the Catholic community.[15] Most tellingly, when it mentions obedience, the word is lodged in sentences that denigrate the Pope.

This is how it begins:

> I A.B. doe truely and sincerely acknowledge, professe, testifie, and declare in my conscience before God and the world, That our Soueraigne Lord King IAMES, is lawfull King of this Realme, and of all other his Maiesties Dominions and Countreys; And that the Pope neither of himselfe, nor by any authoritie of the Church or Sea of Rome, or by any other meanes with any other, hath any power or authoritie to depose the King, or to dispose any of his Maiesties Kingdomes, or Dominions, or to authorize any forraigne Prince, to inuade or annoy him, or his Countreys, or to discharge any of his Subiects of their Allegiance, and obedience to his Maiestie, or to giue Licence or leaue to any of them to beare Armes.[16]

Elizabethan difficulties with Rome and Spain are writ large rather than laid to rest. Loyalty is tied to reminders of papal support for the Northern Rising of 1569 and the Armada of 1588. Even more confrontationally, we get: 'I doe from my heart abhorre, detest and abiure, as impious and Hereticall, this damnable doctrine and Position, That Princes which be Excommunicated or depriued by the Pope, may be deposed, or murthered by their Subiects, or any other whatsoeuer.'[17] This formal abjuration—an oath against, within the oath for—is aimed at *Regnans in Excelsis*, which incited the murder of Elizabeth. A similar threat of violence hung over James, or so his supporters claimed.

The formality and performativity of oaths contribute to their credibility. Truth is claimed by the mode of utterance, whatever the speaker's motives. In the case of the Oath of Allegiance, this was brought out and duplicity was ostensibly excluded. The swearer had to testify that he or she was swearing 'according to the plaine and common sense and vnderstanding of the same words, without any Aequiuocation, or mentall euasion, or secret reseruation whatsoeuer'.[18] The oath was presumably drafted in this way to minimize the opportunity for equivocation, but it would be impossible to know whether this clause was itself sworn with mental reservation.[19] As Catholic opponents pointed out, why would anyone sinful enough to plot regicide be put off by taking an oath? They would swear and lie. The answer, that oaths were such sacred bonds that even the wicked would not perjure themselves,[20] could not be offered with much conviction, not least because it was at odds with the stereotype of Catholic treachery. Moreover, as Parsons pointed out, Catholics were not allowed to equivocate in any oath regarding matters of faith,[21] and since, *pace* the king, the Oath touched on points of faith—notably in relation to the power of the keys, which brought with it a papal power to dispense with oaths and vows or pardon their breach—it could not be equivocated away: 'And I doe beleeue, and in conscience am resolued', the Oath went on, 'that neither the Pope, nor any person whatsoeuer, hath power to absolue me of this Oath, or any part thereof, . . . and doe renounce all pardons and dispensations to the contrary.' Taken together these passages are not plausibly designed to bolt the stable door after the horse of truth has galloped. They draw the attention of those swearing to what Protestants believed was the unreliability of Catholic swearing. Casuistical, equivocal, and dissoluble, the binding word of a papist could be slipped off like a monkey's collar; the Oath would only be sworn for as long as the Pope thought obedience politic,[22] at which point a dispensation would be issued. From that point of view the Oath was a slur on the Catholics who were forced to take it, not just because it required of them an obedience which most already demonstrated[23] but because it iterated a lack of belief in their capacity to take the Oath.

It is not surprising, then, that, shortly after the Oath was published, admonitions against taking it were issued in two papal briefs ('it conteines many things, which are flat contrary to Faith and Saluation')[24] and in a letter from Cardinal Bellarmine to the head of the English clergy, the Archpriest George Blackwell, who had denounced the Oath, then allowed it, then fallen in with the Pope, and then sworn it under duress in prison. The arguments rippled out, from Rome through Paris and Venice. On the king's side were Thomas Morton, James Montague, and William Barlow, but more coruscatingly John Donne, then at the start of his clerical career, whose treatise *Pseudo-martyr* (1610) is one of the most incisive texts to emerge from the controversy. The king also found support from a Scottish Catholic writer in Paris, William Barclay, who had a heavyweight exchange with Robert Bellarmine, and from the Jesuit-trained Marco Antonio De Dominis. Ranked against him were a regiment of Catholic clerics, including the great scholastic philosopher Francisco Suárez, whose *Defensio Fidei Catholicae* was answered by being publicly burned in 1613. Many of the tracts were closely argued, and aimed at educated Europe (*Triplici Nodo* itself quickly went into French and Latin). But there was a popular wing to the debate. One officially sponsored tract, *God and the King* (1615), reduced James and his argument to two essentials, and repeated them: 'That receiuing *authority immediately from* GOD, *hee hath no Superiour to punish him, or chastise him, but God alon*', and '*The bond of his subiects in obedience vnto his Maiesty is inuiolable, and cannot be dissolued*.'[25]

* * *

Obedience was the key. The Oath of Allegiance was even called (by those on the king's side) the Oath of Obedience.[26] Across the field of political argument, the two words were in practice understood to have different histories and implications. The distinctions would be wedged open during the 'Engagement controversy' that followed the execution of James's son, Charles I, in 1649, when some royalists argued that they owed obedience to the Republic, as the victorious, de facto government, but allegiance to the Stuarts.[27] To understand obedience and the Oath of 1606, however, one must, like James in *Triplici Nodo*, go backwards, to the Reformation. The 'Tudor ideology of obedience'[28] was fostered by the state in the 1530s and 1540s for the same reason that the Oaths of Succession and Supremacy—followed by oaths along similar lines (1536, 1544)—were imposed: to bolster authority in a realm that threatened to split along confessional lines.

'Obedience' was the better able to take the strain because it had ecclesiastical implications but was also associated with passages in scripture repeatedly cited to show that kings and magistrates should be obeyed. In the medieval world, *obedientia* was primarily used of submission to the Church and its demands, as in clerical vows. At the Reformation, 'obedience' shifted away from the religious orders, the Catholic Church centred on Rome, and a vision of salvation through works, to the notion that the fourth commandment, 'Honour thy father and thy mother' (Exodus 20: 12), required under God's own law the obedience of the subject to what Paul called 'the higher powers' (Romans 13: 1).[29]

From Tyndale's *Obedience of a Christen Man* (1528) to William Perkins's *A Discourse of Conscience* (1596), reformers stressed the obligation to be obedient to the monarch, particularly if the alternative was obedience to the Pope. This injunction was posited, however, on the belief that the object of obedience should always be God's law. We should obey the powers that be, as Paul said, 'not because of wrath onely, but also for conscience sake' (Romans 13: 5). In addition to fear of worldly punishment, the subject was bound in conscience to obey his ruler because the authorities were Divinely appointed.[30] It is to this verse that Bellarmine appeals when he argues, to the annoyance of James in *Triplici Nodo*, that 'obedience due to the Pope, is for Conscience sake. But the obedience due to Kings, is onely for certaine respects of Order and Policie' (108)—an ambitious extrapolation from medieval views of the papacy that was alien to reformed opinion. The model of obedience based on Paul's Epistle to the Romans allowed Protestants to be obedient to God's law rather than to even a Divine-right monarch if the latter went against the former, and to argue about observing statutes and common law over matters that were indifferent, not set down in scripture.[31] For Catholics, Mosaic law and the commandments of Christ could be extended and refined by canon law and papal decree. Those laws could again take priority over the demands made by kings.

The background difference goes deeper. Protestants were incipiently paradoxical when they stressed obedience, whether to God or to the king, because they believed that works of obedience were never enough to save the soul; mankind would always be fallen, retrievable only through grace and faith. In some versions of this train of thought, it was reassuringly said that, because of our innate sinfulness, merely the desire to be obedient would suffice. 'God regardes not the outward pompe of the action or the doer', Perkins wrote, 'but obedience and especially the obedience of the heart ... God will accept of our imperfect obedience, if it be sincere: yea he accepts the will, desire, and indeauour to obay for obedience it selfe is not certain.'[32] For certainty one needed to look to God's promises to Abraham and to the elect, promises that He had sworn to (pp. 12–13). It is an astounding thought that God would *bind* Himself to save anything as worthless as man, and it leads to the doctrine of the Atonement, where the obedience required for salvation cannot be man's but must be that of Jesus, in his perfection: 'Christ ... himselfe shed hys owne blood: he himselfe was the Sacrifice: for he offred himselfe obediente to hys Father vnto death: by which obedience he toke awaye the disobedience of man.'[33]

When James defended the Oath, he invoked, as we have seen, a number of defences of Henrician obedience, including *The Institution of a Christen Man* ('the Bishops' Book') and Tunstall's sermon on the supremacy.[34] The arguments of these tracts Shakespeare would have been exposed to early and often. He would have heard Cranmer's 'Exhortacion to Obedience', in the Edwardian book of Homilies, and the further, Elizabethan homilies 'Agaynst Disobedience and Wylful Rebellion' in which he more likely than not first encountered the story of King John. He would have learned in Holy Trinity Church how the king was excommunicated for refusing to accept Stephen Langton, the Pope's candidate, as Archbishop of Canterbury, when he preferred John de Grey, how the Pope discharged his subjects of their oath of fidelity, how the king was forced to give up his crown to the papal legate, Pandolphus, when the Pope leaned on the French to punish John, and the English nobility and people rose against him, and how he was crowned again swearing allegiance to Rome. If only the English had supported their king, the homily says, in the rousing, patriotic manner of the Bastard's final speech in Shakespeare's play, and resisted.[35] It was something they would do—in large measure—in the face of the Armada.

James, for reasons of his own, which have much to do with his Scottish background, accented the Divine Right of Kings, but he subscribed, in broad terms, to the 'ideology of obedience'. In *The True Lawe of Free Monarchies*, he writes: 'out of the Law of God the duety, and allegeance of the people unto their lawful king, their obedience, I say, ought to be to him, as to Gods Lieutenant in earth, obeying his commands in all thinges, except directly against God.'[36] The margin for conscience was left, but, even before the Powder Plot, there was Jacobean pressure towards an Erastian coupling of Church to State. In its title as well as its argument, *Obedience: Or, Ecclesiastical Union*, by the king's chaplain William Wilkes (1605), is exemplary. The royal line is reflected in the statute that imposed the Oath of Allegiance, in the following year, declaring its purpose to be 'the better trial how his Majesties subjects stand affected in point of their loyalty and due obedience'.[37] Recurring in the Oath, obedience is repeatedly invoked in *Triplici Nodo*. The king said that he 'intended no persecution against [his Catholic subjects] for conscience cause, but onely desired to be secured of them for Ciuill obedience, which for Conscience cause they were bound to performe'. He did not, that is, want to trouble their conscience over matters of faith, but required that they obey the powers that be for conscience sake.

It would take another book to sift the repetitive accounts of obedience given in defences of the Oath. Occasionally, there are sharper insights. Donne, for instance, who knew from his upbringing what obedience meant for Catholics,[38] is penetrating in *Pseudo-martyr*, where he dedicates a chapter to 'A comparison of the Obedience due to Princes, with the seuerall obediences requir'd and exhibited in the Romane Church'.[39] In every case, obedience turns on oaths and vows. First, there is 'that blind Obedience, and stupiditie, which Regular men vowe to their Superiours' (166). This sort of devotion cannot be as potent, Donne says, as the obedience that all men owe by the law of nature to their prince. His third target is the supernumerary vow of loyalty to the Pope taken by Jesuits. This goes beyond traditional teaching (as many Catholics complained) and is unjust. Between these comes a second, less predictable obedience. Catholic enemies of the Oath, such as Bellarmine, write 'of that vsurped obedience to which they pretend by reason of our Baptisme, wherein we ar said to haue made an implicite surrender of our selues and all that we haue, to the Church' (166). The vows and profession of faith that are part of the rite of baptism are the agents of this surrender. Donne is dealing with the belief, that goes back to Tertullian,[40] that the first sacrament, baptism—and following on from that the other sacraments—*were* in some sense oaths. We touched on the conjunction between sacraments and oaths while thinking about confession in *Measure for Measure* (pp. 292–3); it is time to get to the root of this in baptism, in preparation, not least, for the baptism of the infant Queen Elizabeth at the end of *Henry VIII*, in Chapter 15.

The Greek New Testament uses the word *mystērion* to describe baptism, the eucharist, and so on; in the Latin Vulgate, and other early Christian writings, this was translated as *sacramentum*, which means 'oath', specifically the military oath of obedience sworn by Roman soldiers to their captain, consul, or emperor.[41] Baptism did resemble this. Girded by the godparents' vows and profession, it was a declaration of allegiance to the Church, an initiation into the army of militant Christians. There was a thought, readily extendable to confirmation, orders, and the last rites, that oaths and sacraments alike turned on a testifying and promising of faith. An element of the sacred (Latin *sacer*) was present in both. As Peter Cramer notes: 'The idea of the sacred had already coloured the Roman sense of legal oath, and at the same time had made *sacramentum* a suitable term of entry into religious societies.'[42]

The idea of baptism as a *sacramentum* had an obvious appeal to Jesuits as soldiers of Christ, but it was embraced across the spectrum. As the Presbyterian Matthew Henry (1662–1714) put it, a century after Bellarmine's letter: 'Baptism is an oath, which must be made good. A s*acrament* is a military oath; an oath of allegiance, to be true and faithful to the Lord Jesus; and having *sworn*, we must *perform* it. An oath is a tie upon conscience: and this is an oath, to which God is not only a witness (as to every oath), but a party principally concerned: for to him are we sworn.'[43] Cautionary notes were sounded. Calvin, for instance, said that the early Christians translated *mystērion* as *sacramentum* without regard to everyday usage. They gave the word a 'new signification, whereby they signified onely holy Signes'.[44] He argues this partly because it is so important for him, and for other reformers, to maintain that what is promised by a sacrament—attached to scripture as a seal is attached to and signifies something about a document—is God's promise of salvation (91). Even Calvin does not abandon the idea, however, that those who are baptized swear themselves to, avow their faith in, God (103). He wants the promising to go both ways, and finds evidence for this in the Church Fathers. The sacraments, he says, 'be againe on our behalfe markes of profession, by which we openly sweare to the name of God, for our partes bynding our Faith vnto him. Therefore Chrysostome in one place fittly calleth them couenantinges wherby God byndeth hymselfe in league with vs, and we be bounde to purenesse and holinesse of life, because here is made a mutuall forme of couenanting betwene God and vs' (97).

Donne follows his king in rejecting as a 'novel' doctrine Bellarmine's contention that 'In our supernaturall birth in Baptisme wee are to conceiue of a secret and implied oath . . . to yeelde obedience to the spirituall Prince, which is Christs Vicar.'[45] He agrees with the Catholics that, in a finely tuned phrase, we owe 'obedient confidence' (as in *fides*) to the Church, 'yea, it is *spirituall Treason*, not to obey her' (181). But this is not to say 'that in my baptisme I haue implied a confession, *That the Bishop of Rome is so monarch of the Church, that he may depose Princes*' (181). Rejecting the papal claim that this second obedience entails, Donne appeals again to natural law, declaring 'that obedience which is *Naturall* and *Certaine*' to be obedience to the king (187). The role of a Christian monarch was not to determine doctrine (though James had showed an inclination to do that when controverting Bellarmine)[46] but to govern the Church. This he undertakes to do in his coronation oath, which—*contra* the example of King John, we might add—commits him to resist papal interference. Donne writes, in accordance with Church of England orthodoxy: 'The king therefore defends the *Liberties* of the Church, as the nature of his office, which he hath acknowledged, and Declar'd, and seal'd to his Subiects by an Oath, binds him to do, if he defend the Church of England from foraine vsurpation' (188).

⋆ ⋆ ⋆

The swearer of a state oath is submissive, becoming, as the words are uttered, an emblem of obedience. Swearing requires a performance of the very obedience that an oath of supremacy or allegiance requires. Jonathan Michael Gray argues that 'oaths were paramount in coercing and convincing Henry's subjects to be obedient'.[47] This is radically true: without an element of coercion the oath would not display the power relations that obedience requires. Yet an oath must bind the conscience if it is to be more than a mere performance. For believers, it brought with it the threat of Divine punishment if broken. However legalistic in formulation a state oath might be, it raised the fear in most takers of being a self-cursing oath-breaker. This is evidently important in the context of post-Reformation state oaths, where religious belief, as well as civil obedience, was at stake. People brought their faith to the oaths, as acts of Divine witness, related to prayer, which is why some—though not many—were prepared to endure the heaviest retribution for keeping or not taking them. Finally, state oaths were not just designed to split off traitors, but to tie up loose branches, link the wavering to the crown, and create verbal bonds that reached into the network of obligations that knit society.

The thinking was that with connection would come a change in conduct. 'Obedience', Thomas Starkey noted, 'hath euer ben reputed, the chiefe bonde and knotte of all vertue and good ciuilitie, . . . the mother of al vertue and honestie.'[48] To enshrine obedience in an Oath of Allegiance was to strengthen—it was hoped—the *liganda* that bound together the social order, the body of the commonwealth. Although the word 'allegiance' does not actually derive from *ligare* (to bind), many thought it did, and the false etymology registers an aspiration. It reinforced the tendency to see oaths as an articulation of a pre-existing, natural duty[49]—one reason why Catholics felt aggrieved at having to swear to an allegiance that their opponents told them was a given. As the historian David Martin Jones says of early modern state oaths in general:

> As a device long recognized both by common law and the unpaid local functionaries that enforced it, the oath secured the vital *liganda* of the body politic. The oath also acted as a bond of conscience, at a time when group and individual conscience had been heightened by a new awareness of the word. Finally, with the extension of equity as a legal jurisdiction that also came to constitute the conscience of the state, the oath, as both a religious and a secular bond, united the two sides of the triangle that constituted the ecclesiastical polity. Significantly, those who challenged the character of this inclusionary corporation secured by oaths, resisted it in terms of a shared vocabulary of conscience and law.[50]

The role of conscience in relation to law does need to be drawn out at this point. What did Paul mean when he told the Romans to be subject to 'the powers that be...for conscience sake' (Romans 13: 1–5)? In the late medieval sense of determining the right course of action on the basis of scripture, natural, and canon law, conscience was an exercise of reason. It was tested and arbitrated through Church councils, papal decrees and dispensations, and the ecclesiastical courts. The Reformation removed parts of that superstructure, and decision-making became for many a less institutionally determined process. For all that, over the course of the sixteenth century, the continuities are such that the Calvinistic Perkins would agree in the 1590s that conscience was 'a part of the vnderstanding'.[51] It was a spark of judgement, *synderesis*, a piece of God put into man, shared knowledge with the Divine (*con-scientia*), that acted as both witness and judge.

Already apparent in the writings of Thomas More, supposed guardian of the late medieval, scholastic, collective conscience, and explicit in later, Protestant treatments, is an emphasis on individual conscience, which can become a source of affliction.[52] The operation of the conscience, intimate with or loaded with affect, brought inner quiet or distress, while reaching into the world. This is the double orientation of anyone who swore the Oath of Allegiance, both 'in' and 'before': 'I A.B. doe truely and sincerely acknowledge, professe, testifie, and declare in my conscience before God and the world.' For More there could be no peace of mind without obedience, yet he could not obey both God, working through the Church, and the king. In later, Protestant treatises, causality can go both ways. Perkins says that 'obedience ... is the signe or fruite of good conscience', but William Ames declares that 'peace of Conscience doth depend upon our Obedience'. We are 'bound', he writes, to obedience,[53] though the justification that we have by Christ overarches our failures.[54]

Scholars of all shades of belief agreed that conscience binds us to keep, and is in turn bound by, God's laws. They would also, with different emphases, add natural law, and, for Catholics, canon law. Yet there is another layer of binding language, almost as potent. 'The binder of conscience', explains Perkins,

> is either proper or improper. Proper is that thing which hath absolute and soueraigne power in it selfe to bind the conscience. And that is the worde of God written in the books of the old and new Testament ...
>
> The improper binder is that which hath no power or vertue in it selfe to binde conscience: but doth it onely by vertue of Gods word or of some part of it. It is threefold, Humane lawes, an Oath, a Promise.[55]

That oaths and vows are banded below the bonds of God's law should not be seen as a demotion; Perkins puts them into the same category as positive law. For thinkers of this sort, state oaths are the more exalted, because an everyday oath or promise is elective whereas Oaths of Supremacy and Allegiance were passed by Act of Parliament and legally enforced by the king. They were required by the powers that be, and therefore had a claim on the conscience. An oath has authority for Perkins not so much because the speech act is potent in itself (he would regard that as magical thinking), or because of the social sanctions that might be triggered by breaking a bond, but because God's laws require you to keep oaths. This is why, writing in 1596, at about the date of Shakespeare's *King John*, he calls it erroneous divinity 'when the Pope frees the subiects of this land, as occasion is offered, from their sworne allegiance and loyaltie to which they are bound, not onely by the law of nature, but also by a solemne and particular oath to the Supremacie, which none euer deemed vnlawfull but such as carrie traytors hearts'.[56]

Did the Oath of Allegiance bind Catholics to the obedience required by Romans and natural law, or unjustly entrap their consciences? James was furious with Bellarmine for saying that it did the latter because it was the Oath of Supremacy all over again.[57] Not at all, he replied in *Triplici Nodo*, to

Parsons as well as Bellarmine:[58] in the Henrician oath (which he reproduces) 'is conteined the Kings absolute power to bee Iudge ouer all persons aswell Ciuill as Ecclesiasticall, excluding all forreigne Powers and Potentates to be Iudges within his Dominions; Whereas this last made Oath containeth no such matter, onely medling with the Ciuill obedience of Subiects to their Soueraigne, in meere Temporall causes.'[59] For a topic supposedly irrelevant, the validity of the supremacy was argued tenaciously on both sides, notably in the writings of the Jesuit Martin Becan and his opponents.[60] Becanus called defenders of the Oath of Allegiance Henricians, and said that they made the supremacy central to their divinity.[61] James found himself drawn to the theme in the *Premonition* that he addressed to fellow kings and rulers in a new edition of *Triplici Nodo* (1609).[62] In reality, both sides were redrawing the boundaries of papal power. Pulling back from medieval excesses, Bellarmine argued that the Pope was entitled to exercise 'indirect' power in temporal affairs, intervening in the secular sphere to protect true religion. James invokes medieval history—including the reign of John—to argue that kings and emperors should not be subject to the deposing power, and that the king should govern the Church.

These arguments were revived by James and du Moulin with a French inflection in 1616. The situation across the channel, and the line taken by the Sorbonne and the Estates-General, were relevant not just because the assassination of Henry IV in 1610 sent a shock-wave through Protestant Europe but because the kingdom had a long tradition of resisting the encroachments of Rome. Gallicanism had a history and an even bigger future. In his *Remonstrance*, James again resists the claims of a cardinal (this time Cardinal Perron) by drawing on the medieval chronicles. Popes if anything owe allegiance to emperors and the papacy abuses oaths of allegiance, and dispensation. 'The whole auncient Church' showed obedience to the emperors.[63] As loyal Catholics knew under Elizabeth, it does not matter if your Caesar has a different set of beliefs.[64] Obedience remains obligatory. James cites Romans 13.

The *Remonstrance* ends up discussing the exemplary cases of two English kings. The first, inevitably, is John. James reports Perron as saying that '*When King Iohn of England, not yet bound in any temporall recognizance to the Pope, had expelled his Bishops, &c.* His Lordship means, that King Iohn became so bound to the Pope not long after. And what may this meaning be, but in plaine tearmes and broad speach, to cal me vsurper and vnlawfull King?' (253). Some Catholics said that, by receiving his crown from Pandolphus,

John put the English throne ever after at the disposal of the Pope. James and du Moulin retell the story, emphasizing, for their French readers, that even the King of France, Philip II, refused to act against his fellow monarch for the reasons urged by the Pope.[65] Then, implicitly conceding that the Oath of Supremacy lay behind so much of the Allegiance controversy, they present Henry VIII as a model king, reversing John's defeat: 'Greater blessings of God, . . . were neuer heaped vpon my Great Brittaine', James writes, since she 'hath shaken off the Popes yoke; since shee hath refused to receiue and to entertain the Popes Legats, employed to collect S. Peters tribute or Peter-pence; since the Kings of England, my Great Brittaine, haue not beene the Popes vassals to doe him homage for their Crowne, and haue no more felt the lashings, the scourgings of base and beggarly Monkes'.[66]

⋆ ⋆ ⋆

It should already be clear how Shakespeare's Reformation plays relate to all this. When he reworked the anonymous play *The Troublesome Raigne of Iohn*, contributed to the revision of *Sir Thomas More*, and wrote *Henry VIII* with Fletcher, he was one of a number of dramatists who brought these issues alive. So many plays have been lost between *The Troublesome Raigne* (probably written *c.*1589) and Dekker's *Famous History of Sir Thomas Wyatt* (1602; pub. 1607) that it is impossible to say how distinctive Shakespeare's contributions are. But there is a decisive emphasis on obedience—the word occurs more often in these three plays than in any others in the Shakespeare canon[67]—and on oaths, and on both running together. Contrapuntal elements, such as the assertiveness of the Bastard in *King John*, and the insubordination of Falconer in *Sir Thomas More*, sharpen the topic. In their preoccupation with obedience, however, the plays that Shakespeare wrote or co-wrote are in a line that goes back to the 1530s and 1540s, even while they refuse (e.g. in the sympathetic depictions of More and Katherine of Aragon) the crude anti-Catholicism that can be found in a string of related works, from Bale's *King Johan* to *The Troublesome Raigne*.

The connection made in the *Remonstrance* between John and Henry VIII was anticipated by the early reformers when they praised the kings and emperors who had resisted papal authority. *King Johan*, first performed in Cranmer's household in the Christmas season of 1538, though revised in 1558 and later, is a conspicuous example. From the opening lines, it is also more or less a Morality Play transcript of the sympathetic treatment of John, and the doctrine that went with it, in Tyndale's *Obedience of a Christen Man*:[68]

Bothe Peter and Pawle makyth plenteosse utterauns;
How that all pepell shuld shew there trew alegyauns
To ther lawfull kyng Christ Jesu dothe consent,
Whych to the hygh powres was evere obedyent.[69]

The character called England knows that John is a Divinely appointed monarch, to whom 'allegeance' is owed, but Sedition declares that 'no prince can have his peples obedyence, | Except yt doth stand with the Popes pre-hemynence' (lines 219–20). This bad eminence is sustained by oaths already sworn. When John defies the Church, Nobility says that it is 'sworne' by a 'great othe whan I was dubbyd a knyght | Ever to defend the Holy Churches ryght' (lines 362–3). Clergy knows that 'Owre kyng to obeye the Scriptur doth us bynde', but it is also tied to Rome. To counter this, the king must impose another bond of conscience: 'Ye shall fyrst be sworne to God and to the crowne | To be trew and juste' (lines 519–20).

Throughout, however, the clergy hold the secret weapon of the keys. When Nobility asks how they can break the oath they have given to the king, they reply, 'The keyes of the Church can all soche materes of shake.' 'What call ye those kyes?', Nobility naively asks: 'Owre Holy Fathers powre and his hygh autoryte' (lines 620–1). What the keys, with their power to 'bind and loose', meant to Jesus and Peter, in Palestine, is still discussed by biblical scholars, who look to the Book of Isaiah and to Aramaic idiom.[70] For the early Protestants, 'Owre Holy Fathers powre' was exactly what the keys were not. They were the word of God, the promise of salvation (what Tyndale called 'the privey membre of God'),[71] what admitted you to election, or, for many, including King James,[72] the remission of sin. Nobility, then as now, is easily bamboozled by a little learning: 'Well, I can no more say', he tells Clergy: 'ye are to well lernyd for me' (line 623).

It has been argued that the Henrician elevation of state oaths brought in its train denunciations of casual swearing.[73] This can be overstated: there had been campaigns against profanity in the late middle ages. Profanity is, however, castigated in conjunction with praise for dutiful oaths in such treatises as Henry VIII's *A Necessary Doctrine* (1543)[74] and Bale's own *A Christen Exhortacion vnto Customable Swearers* (1543)—unless it is by Coverdale—where the exhortation against bad oaths extends to those sworn to the wrong thing and to papal dispensations, as when the subjects of 'good king Iohan' were turned against him by Rome.[75] That profane oaths pour out of the mouth of Sedition in *King Johan* makes his encouragement to break oaths of obedience and allegiance the less surprising.

Meanwhile, the oaths sworn to John are underpinned by theology. Bale wrote a play called *God's Promises*, about the covenant and promises of salvation given to Adam, Noah, Abraham, and the rest. The lesson of *King Johan* is that, if we keep our oaths to the king and obey God's laws, God will fulfil his promises. This remained a main plank of orthodox, reformed thought into the Jacobean period. 'The promises of God are the ground of obedience,' Anthony Hugget repeats time and again in his Paul's Cross sermon of 1615.[76] Yet there is no promise for voluntary works, as England says at one point (line 2154), just as there is no papal right to dispense with binding language.

At the end of Act 1, John is praised as the Moses of the Reformation and Henry VIII as its Joshua (lines 1107–13). But the promised land is not easily taken from the Canaanites. Clergy uses the power of the keys to draw wealth into the Church and to 'assoyle'[77] Nobility 'from the kynges obedyence'; to be relieved of obedience is like being given absolution in confession: '*Auctoritate romani pontyficis ego absolvo te*' (lines 1184–6). While Nobility is loosed, England is put into the 'band' of a papal interdiction, and the common people are assoiled of their sworn obedience to the crown (lines 1205–6, 1372). What makes this more unjust is that Nobility, Clergy, and Civil Order tell John that they cleave to the Pope because they are bound by oaths (lines 1471–9). The king responds with an argument familiar from Gardiner and others, not least Tyndale:[78] unlawful oaths, including oaths inappropriately sworn to the Pope and his minions, need not be kept (lines 1479–87). Yet John is outmanoeuvred. Excommunicated, he accepts Stephen Langton as archbishop. Sedition gloats: 'Unto Holy Churche ye are now an obedyent chylde' (line 1805).

Veritas, who respects obedience,[79] saves the day. As the disaffected estates promise allegiance and reverence, John is replaced by Imperial Majesty—the allegorical manifestation of Henry VIII—and the sequence culminates in a version of the Oath of Supremacy. 'Than must ye be sworne to take me for your heade', Imperial Majesty declares. 'We wyll obeye yow', Civil Order replies, 'as our governour in Gods steade' (lines 2435–6). Dramatic energy comes not from any turbulence in the reformers' message, which is represented as tending entirely to obedience and order. It comes, at the level of intrigue, from the unreliability and Vice-like scheming of the agents of Rome. Even after Imperial Majesty has apparently won over the realm, not all is resolved: there is yet another plot by Sedition and Clergy. This is a recurrent feature of plays about obedience, where its obverse proves so hard to suppress. The result is a tendency to dramatic action that is episodic, cyclical, and repetitive—a characteristic that could not be clearer in the case of *Henry VIII*, and that is evident to some extent in the much earlier *King John*, to which we now turn.

* * *

Shakespeare's version of John is doctrinally less committed than Bale's.[80] The play is not so much about religion as about Church/State relations and the politics of Anglo-French war. The king does make the Church pay for his campaign in France, and the Bastard Falconbridge ransacks the monasteries—though we do not see this happen, as we do in *The Troublesome Raigne* where a nun is scandalously found inside a chest in a monastery.[81] The king is poisoned by a monk, but this does not become an excuse for anti-Catholic bigotry. For all that, it would be hard—though it has been attempted—to fit the play into the view that Shakespeare was a Roman Catholic. Such attempts at categorization inevitably lead to distortion, not just because of the mercurial, sceptical quality of the playwright's creative intelligence, but because, by the late sixteenth century, although religious polemic is not hard to find[82] (we shall return to Parsons soon), and although anti-Romanist prejudice is often luridly active in the drama,[83] there was, as we are coming to recognize, a fair degree of interactivity and toleration between moderate Catholics and Protestants (not to mention the many churchgoing papists) in local communities.[84] Whatever the mixed, confessional background of *King John* and its audiences, it can be said with some clarity that it exposes what is unreliable and dangerous in the Tudor system of oaths and obedience but is unsympathetic to papal manipulation.

The play quickly moves into the sort of crisis in marriage arrangements and oaths of fealty that we find in the *Henry VI* plays. King Philip of France is 'divinely vowed' to support Arthur's claim to the English throne.[85] But John's mother, Eleanor, sees an opportunity to knit a marriage between his niece, Blanche, and the dauphin, Louis, that will trump any vow to support Arthur. A deal is done, with John offering provinces and cash. France, as Constance, Arthur's mother, keeps telling us, is 'forsworn' (2.2–3.1). There is a strong, if slightly static, layering of situations—a scenario that Shakespeare by the mid-1590s had proven expertise in managing—with the actor playing Constance locked into a posture of choric complaint.[86] The transactions of expediency, what the Bastard calls 'commodity', seem to be complete, but a further twist is given—the play becomes a Reformation drama—with the arrival of Cardinal Pandolf seeking obedience from John in the form of the appointment of Stephen Langton. To get this he requires a selective devotion to oaths and offers dispensation for the rest.

The writing of this scene is nothing if not overt. By the standards of late Elizabethan or early Jacobean Shakespeare, too little is left to implication. Yet modern audiences can still miss what is contentious, even tendentious. That is highlighted by mid-seventeenth-century markings in a copy of the Second Folio once owned by the English College at Valladolid (it is now in the Folger Shakespeare Library).[87] The deletions made by the censor foreground the play's bias against Catholic views of binding language. Dismissing Pandolf's commands, John is contemptuous of the Pope ('slight, unworthy, and ridiculous'—in a phrase crossed out at Valladolid) and sends this message to Rome:

> no Italian priest
> Shall tithe or toll in our dominions;
> But as we, under God, *are supreme head,*
> So, under him, that great supremacy
> Where we do reign we will alone uphold
> Without th'assistance of a mortal hand.
> So tell the Pope, *all reverence set apart*
> *To him and his usurped authority.* (3.1.76–86)

Apart from the gratuitous, final swipe, this is entirely in line with the principles set out in the Henrician Oath of Supremacy, which had only been lightly adapted (to the grief of many Catholics) by Elizabeth. It clearly aggravated the censor in Valladolid, who scored out all the phrases in italics. No doubt he agreed with King Philip's response:

> Brother of England, you blaspheme in this.
> KING JOHN Though you and all the kings of Christendom
> Are led *so grossly by this meddling priest,*
> *Dreading the curse that money may buy out,*
> And by the merit of vile gold, dross, dust,
> *Purchase corrupted pardon of a man,*
> *Who in that sale sells pardon from himself;* . . .
> PANDOLF Then by the lawful power that I have
> Thou shalt stand cursed and excommunicate;
> And blessèd shall he be that doth revolt
> From his allegiance *to an heretic;*
> *And meritorious shall that hand be called,*
> *Canonizèd and worshipped as a saint,*
> *That takes away by any secret course*
> *Thy hateful life.* (87–105)

This is a grand reprise of English Protestant objections to Rome. John attacks the sale of pardons. The cardinal releases his subjects from their allegiance and encourages regicide. By 'cursed' Pandolf means that John will be subject to the 'ban' of excommunication. He will bind the king *in vinculo anathematis*, expelling him from the Church until he is absolved and readmitted. The procedure was 'abhominable' to the reformers, who asked, with Tyndale, 'Who gave you auctorite to commaunde God to curse?'[88] Pandolf does not ban John 'with boke bell and candle' (Tyndale again)[89] but the audience would have this rite or anti-sacrament in mind, as does the Bastard, when, instructed by the king to 'shake the bags of | Hoarding abbots', he declares: 'Bell, book, and candle shall not drive me back' (3.3.712). In the full ritual, an anathema would be pronounced at the altar, a bell would be rung (like a death knell), the Bible would be closed (separation of the sinner from the Church), and candles would be snuffed out and knocked over (extinguishing of the soul). Meanwhile, Pandolf strips John of the allegiance of his subjects, dissolving the power of an Oath of Supremacy or of Allegiance to bind Catholics to the crown. This is *Regnans in Excelsis* taken back to the twelfth century. Any follower of Rome who secretly murders the king will be regarded as a saint.

Although it is mortally—indeed, eternally—threatening, this execration is cooler and more legalistic than the unofficial curses which Constance adds at this point, piling grievance and abuse upon the enemies of her son.[90] For the cardinal and the kings, her powerless, maternal complaint, though it becomes forensic as well as copious,[91] is a distraction from dilemmas that require disagreeably supple argument. Philip asks Pandolf whether he should obey the Pope when he has sworn a peace with John and tied it with the promise of a marriage that has led to the exchange of vows between his son and Blanche. Pandolf is insistent; the Church demands vow-breaking, and war. As in *King Johan*, the power of the keys can be used in almost any way that advances the interests of Rome. When Philip persists with his case of conscience he gets a full-blown casuistical response. Though it lacks theatrical appeal, it is a rhetorical and, in the right hands, a dramatic *tour de force*:

KING PHILIP I may disjoin my hand, but not my faith.
CARDINAL PANDOLF So mak'st thou faith an enemy to faith,
And like a civil war, sett'st oath to oath,
Thy tongue against thy tongue. O, let thy vow,
First made to heaven, first be to heaven performed;
That is, to be the champion of our Church.
What since thou swor'st is sworn against thyself, . . .

It is religion that doth make vows kept;
But thou hast sworn against religion;
By what thou swear'st, against the thing thou swear'st;
And mak'st an oath the surety for thy troth:
Against an oath, the truth thou art unsure
To swear: swear'st only not to be forsworn—
Else what a mockery should it be to swear!—
But thou dost swear only to be forsworn,
And most forsworn to keep what thou dost swear;
Therefore thy later vows against thy first
Is in thyself rebellion to thyself, ...[92]

Reformation problems flow into this speech, because it involves swearing an oath against an earlier Church-approved oath. The cardinal's lines may sound like those of Biron in *Love's Labour's Lost*, excusing the men for breaking their academic oaths. In the comedy, however, as in most early Shakespeare, oaths are sworn or forsworn out of self-interest. One outcome of the Reformation was the taking of oaths that involved a choice between conflicting principles, or a holding to principles at odds with obedience. The casuistry that was required to avoid a bad conscience was widely disseminated and widely discussed,[93] and this had cultural consequences. That 'the use of oaths of allegiance to exact commitment and allegiance' helped drive a wedge between 'inner and outer'[94] may be doubted, but casuistical discourse did provide new, extreme materials for representing duplicity and evasiveness. Pandolf's masterly, devious syntax has a late Elizabethan texture. It strikes the ear of an audience rather differently from the unreliability of language—fostered by equivocation and mental reservation—in *Macbeth* and *All's Well* (see Chapter 12). But his tortuous complications still echo in the casuistry associated with the Oath of Allegiance a decade after *King John*. As the king wrote of Bellarmine's advice to Catholics who had sworn the Oath: 'they must now renounce and forsweare their profession of obedience already sworne, and so must, as it were at the third Instance, forsweare their two former Oaths, first closely sworne by their birth in their naturall Allegiance; and next, clearely confirmed by this Oath.'[95]

* * *

Pandolf pointedly alludes to Philip's coronation oath: 'thy vow... to be the champion of our Church.' This is another 1590s topic that—as we have seen in *Pseudo-martyr*—was carried into the reign of James. We find it, for instance, in Robert Parsons's influential *Conference about the Next Succession to the Crowne of Ingland* (1595) where King John repeatedly figures. Parsons focuses on his reign because he believes he can trace a line of succession from Constance (and Blanche) to Isabella, the Infanta of Spain, a potential Catholic monarch for England after Elizabeth.[96] Her descendants were barred by Salic law from taking the crown of France, but not that of England (31–2, 150)—a topic which recurs in *Henry V*, where the king's claim to France, supposedly blocked by Salic law, distracts from the weakness of his claim to the English throne.[97] The reign also features, however, because of the evidence it gives of rule by consent. John was made king 'by admission of the realme' (134), in preference to Arthur, son of his brother Geoffrey, who had a better claim by blood, while his own son, the future Henry III, would have been passed over in favour of Louis, to whom the barons swore fealty and obedience (155), 'for the fault of King John his father', had the king not suddenly died (177–8). The fault in question was, of course, disobedience to the Pope, who exercised his power to depose at the request of John's subjects. Each major turn of events in this tangled story was tied by oaths. And what entitled the nobility and commons to act against John was the breach of his coronation oath.

Parsons's resourceful trawl through the coronation oaths of kings and emperors shows that there is nothing innovative in the weight he gives this commitment. He argues that monarchies have long been bound by oaths between sovereign (i.e. the coronation oath) and subject (allegiance, fealty).[98] The Homilies, like King James later, argued that the punishment of bad kings should be left to God. Not all Protestants went along with that, but Tudor orthodoxy, needless to say, abhorred rebellion (especially oath-bound rebellion).[99] Parsons is less passively interested in '*how othes doth binde or may be broken by subiects towards Princes*' (63). For a monarch is subject to the same conditions governing oaths and vows as anyone else. Parsons's civil lawyer (one of the personae in his tract) explains:

> the power and authority which the Prince hath from the common wealth is in very truth, not absolute, but *potestas vicaria or deligata*, ...a power delegate, or power by commission from the common wealth, which is giuen with such restrictions cautels and conditions, yea, with such playne exceptions, promises, and othes of both parties, (I meane betwene the king and common wealth at the day of his admission or coronation) as if the same be not kept, but wilfully broken, on ether part, then is the other not bounde to obserue his promise nether, though neuer so solemly made or sworne, for that in al bargaines, agreements and contracts, wher one parte is bound mutually and reciprocally

> to the other, by oth, vow, or condition, ther, if one side go from his promise, the other standeth not obliged to performe his: ...(73)

This is radical enough, for all its continuities with mainstream, English medieval thought.[100] What made it declared high treason to have a copy of this *Conference* in your house was that Parsons, the dangerous Jesuit, took his argument one step further, giving the disobedient subject permission to judge the monarch. Princes could be deposed, he argued, not just if they broke the terms of their coronation oath, but if their conduct 'should turne to the notable damage of the weale publique' (76). One example would be 'the depriuation of Childerike the last king of France, of the first lyne of Pharamond'. This break in the royal succession is mentioned, of course, in the Salic law speech of *Henry V*. Childeric was relieved of his throne after the Bishop of Würzburg appealed 'to Zacharie the pope, for his deposition, and for the election of Pepin in his place' (76).

Parsons's agenda is clear. He is interested in consent because he wants to allow the English people to choose a monarch congenial to the Catholic cause, and he enlarges the possibility of deposition to create an opening for the Pope, who would reassert his medieval authority. In his account of coronation oaths Parsons accordingly brings out a recurrent deference to Rome. Of the Holy Roman Emperor, for instance, he writes: 'the conditions which he sweareth vnto presently after his election, *Are, to defend the christian and catholique religion, to defend the pope and church of Rome, whose aduocat he is*' (90). Parsons goes on to reprint the coronation oath of Philip II of France—on whom Shakespeare's Philip is based; it commits him to the obedience that Pandolf speaks of in the play. It is also, Parsons points out, the oath of the French king to this day (109). The king of England's oath is similar. 'He sweareth ... *That he wil during his life, beare reuerence and honor vnto almightie God, and to his Catholique church, and vnto his ministers, and that he wil administer law and iustice equally to al, and take away al vniust lawes*' (116).

We can edge back to Shakespeare's play by noticing how, for Parsons, King John was beneficially held in check by the Pope. He avoided deposition for bad government 'by resigning his crowne into the handes of Pandulfe the popes legate' (56), which led to a second coronation. Protestant commentators regarded this as outrageous meddling. King James and du Moulin have an indignant passage in the *Remonstrance* about Pandolphus' contempt for royal authority.

> The King now the Popes vassall, and holding his Crowne of the Pope, like a man that holds his land of an other by Knights seruice, or by homage and

> fealty, doth faire homage for his Crowne to the Popes Legat, and layeth downe at his feete a great masse of the purest gold in coyne. The reuerend Legat, in token of his Masters Soueraigntie, with more then vsuall pride fals to kicking and spurning the treasure, no doubt with a paire of most holy feete. Not onely so; but likewise at solemne feasts is easily entreated to take the Kings chaire of Estate. (255)

Shakespeare passes over the chance to write this up in the style of Bale, but the same shift in power is enacted at the start of Act 5 of *King John*. In a sequence that is little discussed by commentators because it depends on stage time and action for its effect rather than dialogue on the page, and because its political sensitivity for Elizabethan audiences is often simply missed, he represents the second coronation.

Here is the opening of the sequence:

[*Flourish.*] *Enter* KING JOHN *and* [*Cardinal*] PANDOLF, [*with*] *attendants*
KING JOHN [*giving* PANDOLF *the crown*] Thus have I yielded up into your hand
The circle of my glory.
PANDOLF [*giving back the crown*] Take again
From this my hand, as holding of the Pope,
Your sovereign greatness and authority.
KING JOHN Now keep your holy word: go meet the French,
And from his Holiness use all your power
To stop their marches 'fore we are enflamed.
Our discontented counties do revolt,
Our people quarrel with obedience,
Swearing allegiance and the love of soul
To stranger blood, to foreign royalty. (5.1.1–11)

This exchange—the exchange of the crown—would have struck early audiences as momentous, the more so because the gesture is so swiftly and easily executed (slipped into an unbroken, divided verse line). It bears comparison with the 'deposition scene' in *Richard II* that was never printed (nor perhaps staged) during Elizabeth's lifetime (4.1.145–308). In some respects it is more troubling. When Richard gives his crown to Bolingbroke, there is an orderly, if constitutionally dubious, transition of authority; in *King John*, the crown is given to the cardinal, and returned as an empty O because the power remains with Rome. That said, John's alacrity and pragmatism leave open the thought that the momentous is also momentary, not a permanent, disabling submission.

The exchange is about faith in both its Reformation-related meanings. On the one hand, the giving and handing back of the crown represents the fealty paid by John to the Pope. This is humiliating enough; a few lines later Pandolf tells John to remember that he is going to persuade the French to call off the invasion of England that dominates the latter part of the play because of or conditionally 'Upon your oath of service to the Pope' (23).[101] On the other hand, the giving away and return of the crown represents a ceding of authority to Rome in matters of faith in the sense of 'belief'. Much ink would be spilled during Shakespeare's lifetime—some of it by King James himself—about where the border should run between secular and religious authority, but this is clearly a dereliction on the part of John, and it turns, itself, on a failure of faith in the sense of the 'obedience' and 'allegiance' that the English people are removing from John and 'Swearing' instead to the King of France.

* * *

The relationship between oaths and obedience is pointed up by parallel plotting: John's tangled relationship with Rome is matched by the loyal disobedience of his servant Hubert. We are told that Hubert has sworn not just the usual oath of service but a 'voluntary oath' to the king (3.2.23); this being 'the more binding',[102] John feels encouraged to use him to dispose of Arthur. Hubert implicitly consents by saying, 'I am much bounden to your majesty' (29). With Shakespearean, literalizing irony, being bound becomes an element in the assault on Arthur. There is only one reference to him being 'fast bound' in the sources,[103] but it recurs in what is onstage a vicious, loquacious scene: 'bind the boy . . . Fast to the chair', 'bind him here', 'let me not be bound' (4.1.4–5, 74, 77). Hubert binds because he is bound: 'I have sworn to do it' (58). He tries to tie Arthur with a promise not to speak. But the boy does speak persuasively, saving himself from being blinded with a hot iron and killed. It is a test of Hubert's conscience. He recognizes that Divine law can justify disobedience to the king.

The word 'conscience' slides into John's speeches at the same point in the action. When Arthur goes missing, Salisbury says, 'The colour of the King doth come and go | Between his purpose and his conscience' (4.2.76–7). Regretting the murder (as he thinks), the king tells Hubert that he should have followed his conscience. Hubert shows him the warrant: 'Here is your hand and seal for what I did' (216). This John is no sort of Reformation hero. He says it was Hubert's fault for being there to tempt him, and for taking up his thought. There is a rebellion within the king himself: 'Hostility and civil tumult reigns | Between my conscience and my cousin's death' (248–9).

The actors are alone onstage; in a good production, the space of performance folds in upon the secrets of the king and his loyal, disloyal servant. When Hubert reassures him that Arthur lives, John (with telling opportunism) wants the news taken immediately to the peers to curb their rising against him: 'make them tame to their obedience' (263).

In accordance with Tudor theory, obedience is part of a network. Hubert's good service revives the obedience of the barons. At least, it would if he were believed. Because Arthur has flung himself from the wall of his prison—perhaps leaping from the musicians' gallery—and lies dead upon the stage, the barons disavow their allegiance. Arthur's death, says Salisbury, with more than a trace of truth, is 'The practice and the purpose of the King; | From whose *obedience* I forbid my soul' (4.3.63–4). Accompanied by the strikingly named Bigot (which means 'by God'),[104] he vows revenge:

Kneeling before this ruin of sweet life,
And breathing to his breathless excellence
The incense of a vow, a holy vow,
Never to taste the pleasures of the world,
Never to be infected with delight,
Nor conversant with ease and idleness,
Till I have set a glory to this hand
By giving it the worship of revenge.
PEMBROKE *and* BIGOT Our souls religiously confirm thy words. (65–73)

Hubert protests and later swears that he did not kill Arthur ('Upon my soul' [126]), but the damage to obedience has been done.

Potent though this is onstage—and characteristically Shakespearean in the way the determination of the vow does not entirely fit the facts of the crime—this is not the climactic oath sequence in the play. That comes when the English nobles swear with Louis to fight against John. Louis, however, or Lewis in the Folio, is *loose*, as his name suggests, and treachery impends.[105] The oath is sacramental. It is sworn at the altar of the monastery at Bury St Edmunds, and sealed by taking the eucharist (5.2.6–7). Like Hubert, with his 'voluntary' oath to John, the English nobles 'swear | A voluntary zeal and an unurgèd faith' (9–10). This is bad news for the country, but there is honour among the French. Melun's declaration to the English barons shows conscience working against oaths and obedience. Betraying a bad oath, he urges the English nobility to give up their rebellion because the French king means to chop their heads off if he wins the day:

Thus hath he sworn,
And I with him, and many more with me,
Upon the altar at Saint Edmundsbury,
Even on that altar where we swore to you
Dear amity and everlasting love. (5.4.16–20)

This is one of those neat symmetries that you find in revenge plots, a blasphemous breach of faith. It gives history shape, in a play that generally inclines to the inconsequentiality and disorder created by disobedience and oath-breaking.

Melun goes on to insist:

I say again, if Louis do win the day,
He is forsworn if e'er those eyes of yours
Behold another daybreak in the east; . . . (30–2)

The audience might well wonder what Louis being 'forsworn' would amount to. If he invoked his oath to kill the barons as a reason for having to do so, he could only achieve this by erasing the prior, holy vow. The play ends by raising as many questions about oath-taking as it does about obedience, even though the Bastard Faulconbridge's submission and oath of service to John's successor Prince Henry (5.7.100–5), which precipitates a round of kneeling in allegiance by Salisbury, Pembroke, and Bigot (106–7), does cut through casuistical complication and set a patriotic course beyond papal and French predation, in line with his celebrated, final speech. Philip breaks his word to the Pope (good) then to John (bad); Hubert breaks his word and obedience to kill Arthur (good); Melun breaks his word and obedience to his king (dubious); while Salisbury and the other barons break their word to Louis (good). With hindsight, Pandolf's involved oration about setting the word against the word sounds less like a stand-out instance of Romanist casuistry and more like a devious grappling with problems that are central to the play.

15

Reformation II

Sir Thomas More and *Henry VIII*

Sir Thomas More has an unusual place in the Shakespeare canon. On the one hand, it is a patchwork, collaborative work, unfinished in manuscript and apparently unperformed. This was not a play that Shakespeare either initiated or made his own; he only became involved, it seems, when objections by the Master of Revels, Edmund Tilney, to an earlier version of the play, possibly written 1593/5 though quite likely around 1600,[1] by Anthony Munday (actor, popular writer, and persecutor of Catholics), led to a revision by several hands, which Shakespeare, with his theatre contacts and court associations, was well placed to assist.[2] Even with his input, the script seems not to have not satisfied the licenser. For all that, because the manuscript includes what are generally agreed to be pages in Shakespeare's own hand, the play has become peculiarly central to our image of the author.

If as now seems probable 1603–4 was the date of the revision,[3] it coincides with attempts by the Appellant (anti-Jesuit) wing of English Catholicism to agree with the authorities an oath of obedience that would avoid reference to the Pope but still satisfy the new king.[4] Discussion of what was at stake would have circulated beyond the royal bedchamber and Privy Council and out into London and the shires because James's overtures to the English Catholics, before and immediately after his accession, were controversial and became politically awkward. Thomas More was something of a hero for moderate Catholics,[5] because he had been true to his faith without disloyally opposing Henry VIII and Parliament.[6] At the same time, his appeal to conscience in the face of authority had its attractions for the mixed, predominantly Protestant, playhouse audience.[7] Protestant admiration would become explicit, as it did among the Anglican Non-Jurors who refused the Williamite Oath of Allegiance after 1688–9.[8] For reasons that will be taken up later, and that have much to do with oaths and vows, More could not accept Henry's divorce from Katherine of Aragon, or his supremacy in the Church. Yet William Warmington, one of the Catholic priests who defended the 1606 Oath of Allegiance, 'intimated that More would have taken it in obedience to royal command'.[9] Some of More's Catholic relatives and descendants did just that, or supported those who did, in the face of Jesuit opposition.[10]

The manuscript *Booke of Sir Thomas Moore*, held in the British Library, is almost an emblem of the royal supremacy. It is wrapped in 'a vellum wrapper taken from a manuscript of papal decretals', one of many pulled out of monastic libraries at the Dissolution and often sold as waste.[11] The text itself is more generally concerned with the supremacy than scholars have recognized. Like *King John* and *Henry VIII* it has much to say about the relationship between foreigners and English jurisdiction. It starts with the citizens of London being provoked by 'strangers'—Lombards, i.e. Italians, at Tilney's bidding—who do not obey English laws, taking goods and trying to take women as Rome took wealth from the realm.[12] The citizens would fight back, but George Betts the clown says he is 'curbed by duty and obedience' (1.57–8). Sherwin, a goldsmith, speaks of 'the strict obedience that we are bound to' (85). They do plan resistance, however, by signing 'a <bill> of our wrongs and the strangers' insolencies' (99–100). There are elements of sworn conspiracy: 'let's friendly go and drink together, and swear true secrecy upon our lives' (149–51). This is not found in Holinshed, where the bill is merely read out (as reportedly, in the play) in a sermon. The play is in various ways more tightly organized than critics have recognized. The rebelliously signed bill prefigures the Oath of Succession which More and Fisher disobediently refuse to subscribe later in the play.

In the pages written by Shakespeare, More suppresses a riot led by Doll, Lincoln, and others. It has carnivalesque features—jokes about parsnips and pumpkins—but the threat to order is real. More appeals to Tudor orthodoxy so closely that he might be reciting Cranmer's 'Exhortacion to Obedience'.[13] He says of the rebels, 'Whiles they are o'er the bank of their obedience, | Thus will they bear down all things' (6.47–8) and invokes their duty. He goes straight to the passage in St Paul that everyone from Tyndale to James makes much of: 'Let euerie soule be subiect vnto the higher powers: for there is no power but of God: and the powers that be, are ordeined of God' (Romans 13: 1):

how horrible a shape
Your innovation bears. First, 'tis a sin
Which oft th'apostle did forewarn us of,
Urging obedience to authority;
And 'twere no error if I told you all
You were in arms 'gainst <God>. (104–9)

Because of the accumulation of such passages, the present chapter, like the previous one, will focus on the connection between oaths and obedience that was reinforced by the English Reformation. Yet More's language is not entirely Henrician. What he says about God and the king is so much the message of *The True Lawe of Free Monarchies* that you might indeed suspect these pages of being early Jacobean:

For to the king God hath his office lent
Of dread, of justice, power and command;
Hath bid him rule, and willed you to obey. (112–14)

God himself 'Calls' the king 'a god on earth' (118), so to rise against the king is to rise against God, with obvious dangers to the soul. More harps on obedience so insistently that a later hand—known as Hand C—found the writing muddled and cut the following, elliptically Shakespearean lines:

To kneel to be forgiven
Is safer wars than ever you can make
Whose discipline is riot.
In, in, to your obedience! Why, even your hurly
Cannot proceed but by obedience. (125–9)

The common people come round with almost comical alacrity, and More gives his word that if they 'obey the magistrate, ... mercy may be found' (163–4). By the time Shakespeare and More are done with the riot, rebellion only matters as a foil to display obedience.

In an earlier scene, More had given his word to get a thief called Lifter out of trouble if he played a trick in court and cut the magistrate's purse (2.51–95). Now, once again, he promises to protect—and, as the audience might see it, foster—illegality. Doll does a deal with him: 'Give me thy hand. Keep thy promise' (6.189), but she, like others, is clear about the risk of trusting him. In the event, pardon comes too late for Lincoln, who dies regaling on- and offstage audiences with a rhymed restatement of the main theme: 'learn it now by me: | Obedience is the best in each degree' (7.57–8). Doll thinks that More has broken his word but pardon comes in time to save her. As it turns out, the fact that the rebels surrendered on his word was one of the reasons why the king was willing to let them off.

Shakespeare's More is a paragon of the 'Tudor ideology of obedience' (see p. 373), designed to appeal to the censor. In the design of the play, however, he comes across as more complex. Rather as Shakespeare's Ulysses foments unrest while preaching order,[14] so More suppresses it by indulging rebels. In *Triplici Nodo*, James would call More and John Fisher 'two Captaines and ringleaders to Martyrdome'.[15] It is an irony that resonates in the play—most intriguingly in relation to the figure of Falconer, who is brought to More after the Ill May Day riot is over, as 'A ruffian . . . that hath set half the City in an uproar' (8.57–8). Accused of stirring up a broil, Falconer says he was trying to stop it. He has also, it seems, taken a vow, of a perversely Catholic, eremitical kind, not to cut his hair.[16] At the edge of this sequence is the Reformation argument about Nazirite vows in scripture, one of which, as we saw in Chapter 7 (p. 181), required the devoted individual not to cut his hair. Catholics liked to argue that Nazirite vows foreshadowed those taken by monks, who shaved the 'crowne' of their heads in devotion just as Nazirites displayed their 'crowne' of hair.[17] That Falconer's unruly hair smacks of the old religion as well as lack of civility is suggested by the source in Foxe where we are told that he 'vsed to go with his haire hangyng about his eares downe vnto his shoulders, after a strange monstrous maner, counterfeiting belyke the wyld Irish men, or els *Crinitus Ioppas*, which Uirgil speaketh of'.[18] He has a touch of the artist (Iopas is a poet and singer in *Aeneid* I), but he is also like an Old Irish Catholic, papistical and rebellious.

In Holinshed, the magistrate who sends Falconer to prison is Thomas Cromwell, a much more likely representative of austere, civil discipline. Munday saw the chance of presenting More as the ruffian's *alter ego*,[19] half rebellious, half into a cloistered, penitential life. According to the Catholic, manuscript biography by Nicholas Harpsfield, which constitutes the play's main source, and which fed into other, Elizabethan accounts, when More was a young man he 'inclined . . . to take some monastical and solitary life', and spent 'four years and more . . . in great devotion and prayer with the monks of the Charterhouse of London', though 'without . . . profession or vow'.[20] In the original script of the encounter, before the licenser prompted changes, there is a comic allusion to a hair shirt[21]—More's hair shirt was already lodged in popular memory, and it was long kept, in pieces, as a relic.[22] As for Falconer's long hair, before his execution More has to have his beard cut so that he can be decapitated cleanly. Falconer also resembles More in being a wit and punster: 'How long have you worn this hair?'; 'I have worn this hair ever since I was born', and so on (8.99–100). Both have something of the jest-book about them. Finally, there is the vow, with its Catholic associations, which More appears to respect. He even says that he does not want Falconer to be shriven—absolved through the power of the keys—of his obligation to keep it, though he does offer a way out:

Vows are recorded in the court of heaven,
For they are holy acts. Young man, I charge thee
And do advise thee start not from that vow.
And for I will be sure thou shalt not shear,
Besides because it is an odious sight
To see a man thus hairy, thou shalt lie
In Newgate till thy vow and thy three years
Be full expired.—Away with him.
FALCONER My lord—
MORE Cut off this fleece, and lie there but a month. (117–25)

Is this 'vow' an excuse or a commitment? In Holinshed, when the ruffian 'was not able to yeld any reason for refuge of that his monstruous disguising, at length he fell to this excuse that he had made a vow'. Cromwell sends him to prison by way of a riposte. This is not the impression given in the play, where the vow is taken and held more seriously. The term of three years is not mentioned in Holinshed. In *Love's Labour's Lost*, as we saw in Chapter 3 (pp. 69–72), the vow to study for the same period recalls the matriculation oath. Here it is more penitential (Trinitarian), like a folk version of Catholic piety.[23] When More assures Falconer in the original text of the dialogue that he will not tamper with his vow, but send him to Newgate instead, to see whether his mind will change, the word that he uses is 'conscience'.[24] Surrey adds to the Catholic, monastic associations by saying that prison is 'A cell most meet for such a votary'[25]—monks lived and prayed in cells. Falconer thus anticipates the stubbornly Romanist More, who will be confined to his house in Chelsea (to give him time to reconsider) after refusing for reasons of conscience to sign the king's oath.

As we have seen from several angles, a vow is not an oath. The differences were well understood in medieval Europe, but the two types of commitment were wedged the more firmly apart at the Reformation because of the assault on monastic vows. The distinctions would later prove central to one of the most prestigious exchanges concerning the Oath of Allegiance.[26]

Hostile to cloistered vows, Protestants were conditional and tepid about individual vows also, which they tended to argue should not be held against a man's general or particular calling.[27] Since Falconer is a servant, his hair should not be growing to an uncivil length. Despite the differences, however, it was not easy to keep these two classes of speech act apart. As Jonathan Michael Gray observes:

> at precisely the same time as English reformers were echoing medieval Catholic rhetoric on the sanctity of oaths, they were also flooding the printing presses with attacks on monastic vows.... Although English reformers never explicitly applied this logic to the state oaths of the Henrician Reformation, the great similarity between vows and oaths... and the fact that much of this logic originated in oath theory itself meant that many people could and did apply these arguments to the oaths of the Henrician Reformation.[28]

The play certainly conjures with the parallels to potent effect. Munday was said by Meres to be 'our best plotter'.[29] This compliments his skill in managing the playhouse practicalities of construction,[30] but he is a good double-plotter in the modern, literary sense as well. Falconer gives up his vow in prison, becomes obedient, learns to conform, while More, apparently a pillar of the establishment, refuses to swear a state oath, even when arrested and confined, and is executed. It is clear which man is the more obedient to the powers that be, and also which is the more admirable, in ways that put some strain on the orthodoxy of the play. Given the tensions and problems it generates, this contrast has the potential to turn *More* into a full-blown drama, but the writing is so cautious—ahead of as well as after Tilney's intervention—that the sorts of complexity that Shakespeare brought out in his late Elizabethan history plays are left largely unarticulated. Up to a point, however, this makes *Sir Thomas More* even more fully a Reformation play—not in the propagandist style of Bale's *King Johan* (pp. 382–5) but in being, like so many writings from the 1530s and 1540s, and like *Henry VIII*, so careful with the language it uses, so opaque about action and motive.

For late Elizabethan or Jacobean audiences More's refusal to take the oath set by the king would be the defining thing about his life. It comes up between Bellarmine and James, when the former puts Blackwell in mind of the martyrdom and glory open to him if he resists the Oath of Allegiance, as another Oath of Supremacy, and the latter complains of his inaccuracy.[31] More and Fisher were not sent to prison over the supremacy, James explains, but for resisting the succession (and, in Fisher's case, for being mixed up with the Maid of Kent), and although supremacy became a question, as their obduracy provoked the king, they still died resisting the succession, which almost the entirety of the English Church had accepted. More knew that he was executed '*for that I would neuer*', in his own words, '*consent in the businesse of the new marriage of the King*'. It was, James tartly adds, 'but a very fleshly cause of Martyrdom, as I conceiue'.[32]

In the play, More is brought the (unspecified) oath to sign while he is at a meeting of the Council, protecting English interests in international affairs (Catholics need not be disloyal). He is not in Council in Munday's source for this scene, Harpsfield's *Life*.[33] The oath is a dramatic interruption, but its presentation is also formal. It is brought in '*with great reverence*'—something that might placate the censor, though it also helps mark this as a turning-point in More's life story:

PALMER My lords, his majesty hath sent by me
These articles enclosed, first to be viewed,
And then to be subscribed to. (*with great reverence*) I tender them
In that due reverence which befits this place.
MORE Subscribe these articles? Stay, let us pause.
Our conscience first shall parley with our laws.
My lord of Rochester, view you the paper. (10.68–74)

His conscience must parley with the laws because he has to decide whether he is bound by the statute that imposes the oath. Rochester refuses to subscribe and is sent to the Tower. More asks for 'time for to bethink me of this task', resigns his office, and is sent to his house in Chelsea. The other lords sign 'Instantly'. Surrey says, ''Tis strange that my Lord Chancellor should refuse | The duty that the law of God bequeaths | Unto the king' (86–107). More rather passively fails in what the commoner George Betts knows: 'duty and obedience' (1.57–8).

The Master of Revels read this scene with mounting unease. Though he did not demand that the oath be cut, he told the authors to 'All alter' More's refusal to subscribe and his resignation from office.[34] That the staging of state oaths was sensitive is suggested by their absence from *Henry VIII*, even though the issues and events around the Oaths of Succession and Supremacy are central to the play. But this is apparent from *More* as well, since, as we have noted, it is not clear from the dialogue just what oath More is asked to swear. Modern productions sometimes add a line or two, so that the audience can understand what is at stake.[35] It may be that early audiences thought they knew enough about the life of More to be clear what he was refusing; but the issues were probably cloudy, and some vagueness was theatrically useful, because it avoided alienating parts of the audience, along confessional lines, and left More's refusal to swear to resonate as an act of conscience. Harpsfield is himself confused about what the oath contained, and to this day, historians are not clear what More objected to in the Oath of Succession—perhaps with a preamble about the supremacy—that was put to him. Many assume, wrongly, that he refused the Oath of Supremacy. We think of oaths as fixed; in the absence (for most of us) of a retributive Deity, their determinate, formal make-up is the more important in explaining what remains of their power. During the Henrician period, however, oaths were adapted to make them more takeable, if that was advantageous to the authorities, or made more stringent,[36] or the taker might be allowed to tag on a reservation, as More's daughter, Margaret Roper, did when she took the Oath of Succession but added 'as far as the law of Christ allows'.[37]

It strikes me that obedience may have been the sticking-point for More. In its standard form, the Oath of Succession began: 'Ye shall swear to bear your Faith, Truth, and Obedience, alonely to the King's Majesty.'[38] Faith and truth in the secular senses, More could clearly promise. How though could he give all his obedience only to the king, when the Pope was supreme in matters of faith? Significantly, in More's own account of his celebrated exchange about the Oath with Cranmer—closely followed by Harpsfield[39]—an opening-up of doubts about conscience is seen as an opportunity to demonstrate obedience:

> My Lord of Canterbury takinge hold vpon that that I saide, that I condempned not the conscience of them that sware, saide vnto me that it apered well, that I did not take it for a very sure thinge and a certaine, that I might not lawfully swere it, but rather as a thinge vncertain and doubtfull. But than (said my Lord) you knowe for a certenty and a thinge without doubt, that you be bownden to obey your souerain lorde your Kyng. And therfore are ye bounden to leaue of the doute of your vnsure conscience in refusinge the othe, and take the sure way in obeying of your prince, and swere it.[40]

This is the version of the encounter that reached the dramatists through Harpsfield's paraphrase in his *Life*. Cranmer's position is not so different from that of Donne in *Pseudo-martyr*.[41] If taking the oath is a viable choice, why not do so for the sake of obedience? Apply Catholic casuistry to the problem, and you are allowed to do what is arguable even if it is not the most defensible course of action.

Allusions to conscience mount in the final act of the play. This reflects their prominence in the late writings of More, as he explicated his position on oaths.[42] You can see why he had to (in the words of the play) 'parley with our laws'. A state oath is required by statute, yet the taker must meet it in his conscience and decide whether to be bound in the eyes of God. To refuse the Oath of Succession was to commit treason by misprision, according to the relevant statute—as when refusing the Oath of Allegiance; yet to take it if it was contrary to faith was to put the soul in peril. The Reformation piled problems of conscience into the oaths of fealty and allegiance that had operated in the middle ages. As David Martin Jones puts it, in his study of *Conscience and Allegiance*:

> Through the process of Reformation, the English Empire acquired, amongst other things, a conscience. Prior to 1534–36, the matter at stake in relationship to the feudal oath was not primarily conscience, but honour and faith. . . . considerations of conscience were of essentially scholastic significance and only peripherally affected the political or legal obligation of an oath. This was a consequence of the pre-Reformation fact that the universal church acted as the official moral arbiter of a shared *consensus fidelium*.[43]

The Reformation changed that. Even Thomas More, so often seen as maintaining a Catholic, medieval vision of the universal Church, reflects his age. That his conscience was tested by state oaths did not mean that decisions were clear or fixed. Conscience was swayed by obedience, as the powers that be changed their complexion. But conscience had to have priority.

There is enough of Falconer the wit in the play's More for him to equivocate about the oath. As when he tells his family that he is ready to 'subscribe', but just means submit to go to the tower (13.172–5). Or when he jokes about the state of his urine, saying '<in very sober truth I swear,> | The man were likely to live long enough, | So pleased the King' (16.25–7). Or when he steps up to the scaffold saying, 'In sooth, I am come about a headless errand' (17.51).[44] It probably matters that these jests are tied by casual oaths. They show a dexterous wit and wordplay that could have turned his given word to words. He could have taken the king's oath equivocally, or taken it knowing that it did not count, because, with a change of royal policy (or regime and shift of obedience), it would be shown to be unlawful—as Bishop Gardiner so readily argued (p. 370) and as the historical More deplored.[45] He could have been like the play's original author, Munday, who apparently switched from Catholicism to Protestantism, and who was, it seems, a notorious forswearer. Sir John Davies's epigram, '*In Mundayum*', reads: 'Munday I sweare shalbee a hollidaye, | If hee forsweare himselfe but once a daye.'[46] The charisma of More's stand, in life and in the play, lies less in the scrupling of his conscience than in the decisiveness of his rejection and reticence about his motives. With obedience, casuistry, and equivocation providing reasons or excuses to swear an oath that would not stick, More's *not* taking the oath was perhaps the only way of reinvesting oaths with integrity.

* * *

Sir Thomas More gives us a fragmented snapshot of how the oath controversies of the 1530s appeared from the vantage point of late Elizabethan and perhaps early Jacobean London. What did the same, Henrician period look like, after the Powder Plot of 1605 and the introduction of the Oath of Allegiance a few months later? The answer is, naturally, different across the confessional spectrum, but often surprisingly complicated. Take the example of *Thomas Morus*, a Latin play written at the English College in Rome, for performance to a Jesuit audience, in 1612, around the same date as *Henry VIII* (1613?). The college that Munday satirized in *English Roman Life* (1582) was a place of superstition and hostility to Elizabeth. *Morus* might be expected to be a polemical, martyr play. But the representation of Henry VIII—who remains safely uncontroversial, offstage, in *Sir Thomas More*, but who is squarely in the foreground of *Morus*—is mixed; he is led astray by Cranmer, Cromwell, and Audley, who urge him to put aside conscience, law, and reputation.[47] In one notable scene, he asks each of them in turn to characterize the shortcomings of the others; withering judgements expose the rivalry and mistrust at the heart of a regime that is driven by ambition as well as heresy to the destruction of the Church (4.1).

Thomas Morus turns on an analogy between the Oath of Succession and the Oath of Allegiance as the audience in Rome understood it. It deplores the imposition of an oath that afflicts the conscience of Catholics and excludes them from public office—like the Elizabethan Oath of Supremacy. Though it nowhere suggests that More would have taken the Oath in 1606, it does show his reluctance to become a disobedient servant.[48] It is Cranmer who forces the issue, by pressing him, against the wishes of the king, to commit to an Oath of Succession that is edged into direct acceptance of the Anne Boleyn marriage. As in the Latin play about Fisher, *Roffensis*, written for the same audience a few years later (1618?), Henry is blamed less than the reformers. This conciliatory treatment presumably reflects the fact that Henry remained an orthodox Catholic, though it might also indicate a willingness to keep open the possibility of reconciliation with James,[49] who, even after the Powder Plot, often sought in his public pronouncements to be a moderate, unifying figure in Christendom.[50]

It is, at all events, a very different depiction of Cranmer from that presented by Shakespeare and Fletcher. He is tougher and more insistent, especially in his pursuit of More. 'Tangat volumen mysticum', Cranmer declares—'Let him put his hand to the Bible.'

Thomas Morus
Iurabit Annam iure divino torum
Licite tenere regis? Utriusque soboli
Diadema debitum Angliae?
MORUS Hoc, praesul, iubes
Ut deiearem?
CRANMER Publica hoc auctoritas,
Successionis iura, maiestas iubet
Haec summa regni et regis.
MORUS Excelsae fidem
Appello maiestatis. (3.1; lines 982–9)

[CRANMER ...Does Thomas More swear that Anne occupies the royal bed rightfully, in accordance with divine law? And that the crown of England is reserved for their offspring?

MORE You command me to swear this, prelate?

CRANMER Public authority, the right of succession, the supreme majesty of the realm bid you swear these things.

MORE I appeal to your lofty majesty's trust.]

Henry tells Cranmer that he does not want the peace disturbed, or More pressed on the queen's cause. He tells More to 'Go home, absolved now by my word, but in all respects an innocent man' (lines 997–8). The king lacks tenacity in controlling his advisers, and he harbours an oblique unease (as he discloses in Act 4) that he should not encourage disobedience in others by allowing More to live.

When Fisher refuses the same oath, once again pressed by Cranmer, he is sent to the tower. The Reformation advances down its double track of forcing oaths and denouncing vows. After Audley has called for the Minorites' convent (where Princess Elizabeth has just been baptized) to be pulled down, to make room for an enlargement of the royal palace, Cromwell says: 'Let a census be taken of our entire people, let the numbers of those bound by any vow and wearing a religious habit be totted up.... Let every man take his oath of loyalty'—'Iuratus fidem | Spondebit istis quisque.' To which 'Omnes' dutifully cry, 'Spondemus fidem' ('We pledge our loyalty') (3.3; lines 1061–71). Historically, this is baseless; the Oath of Succession was not a general oath. It looks like an allusion to the Jacobean Oath of Allegiance.

More accurately *Thomas Morus* shows the new theme of the polity to be unity, as in the Act in Restraint of Appeals (see p. 370). Straight after the oath of loyalty is sworn by *Omnes*, Cromwell says: 'Henry alone rules, and at last he alone wields the scepter.... Union is the strength of this realm, united power triumphs' (3.3; lines 1072–8). Norfolk, the old Catholic, knows that in discord royal authority will not hold the commonwealth together: 'Discordia studia civium sola licet | Unire religione' ('By tradition, the discordant strivings of its citizenry can only be united by religion') (lines 1079–80)—where religion displays its widely assumed root in *religare*, 'to bind'. The play offers a surprisingly pragmatic defence of the usefulness of the Catholic Church. In its alertness to the politico-theological practicalities, it comes closer than one might expect to the work that, in other respects, has such a different apprehension of the Reformation, namely *Henry VIII*.

★ ★ ★

The historical moment that produced *Henry VIII* extended, of course, beyond 1605–13. There were plays about Henry and his leading statesmen—some of them lost—in the late Elizabethan and early Jacobean periods.[51] The debate between Katherine Howard and Gardiner in Samuel Rowley's *When You See Me, You Know Me* (1605) takes us straight back to the early Tudor 'ideology of obedience' and the conflicting oaths sworn by prelates.[52] Yet interest in the mid-1530s after 1606 was stoked by the emergence of the Supremacy as a point of contention in debates about the Oath of Allegiance. That More is kept on the sidelines, and may even, through error, attend the marriage of the king and Anne Boleyn,[53] is a sign of Shakespeare and Fletcher shying away from any direct depiction of state oaths. But the situation that the Oath of Allegiance was designed to address—Catholic priests taking orders from Rome, conspiracy, and disobedience—is written deeply into the play.[54]

As we have seen, the Oath of Allegiance was revived after the assassination of Henry IV in 1610. Regicide was in the public mind, and certainly in James's,[55] as was the role of Catholic clerics in fomenting plots. It is significant, therefore, that Buckingham's plot to murder and replace Henry is steeped in clerical conspiracy. In a scene attributed to Shakespeare, the duke's Surveyor accuses his master of declaring, every day,

that if the King
Should without issue die, he'll carry it so
To make the sceptre his. These very words
I've heard him utter to his son-in-law,
Lord Abergavenny, to whom by oath he menaced
Revenge upon the Cardinal. (1.2.134–9)

This sounds like common ambition, tied by a vindictive oath, and pitched to appeal to the king's anxiety about the lack of a male heir. As the exchange unfolds, however, the role of priestcraft emerges:

BUCKINGHAM'S SURVEYOR He was brought to this
By a vain prophecy of Nicholas Hopkins.
KING HENRY What was that Hopkins?
BUCKINGHAM'S SURVEYOR Sir, a Chartreux friar,
His confessor, who fed him every minute
With words of sovereignty.
KING HENRY How know'st thou this? (147–51)

According to his Surveyor, the duke was led astray by

certain words
Spoke by a holy monk that oft, says he,
'Hath sent to me, wishing me to permit
John de la Car, my chaplain, a choice hour
To hear from him a matter of some moment;
Whom after under the confession's seal
He solemnly had sworn, that what he spoke
My chaplain to no creature living but
To me should utter, with demure confidence
This pausingly ensued: "neither the King nor's heirs",
Tell you the Duke, "shall prosper. Bid him strive
To win the love o'th' commonalty. The Duke
Shall govern England."' (160–72)

The matter of 'confidence' and trust is betrayed by the seal of confession. A sacrament that should be bound like an oath, a *sacramentum*, in Catholic doctrine, gave cover to sinful temptation, which used its seal to fix an oath of secrecy. This is treason by misprision, exactly the crime which those who twice refused the Oath of Allegiance were charged with, and behind them it was the crime of those who swore to keep the Powder Plot secret. James highlighted this in his account of the conspiracy in the *Premonition* (1609), shortly before the composition of *Henry VIII.*[56] He would complain, after the murder of Henry IV, that clerics still encouraged regicide; the *Remonstrance* (1616) that he wrote with Pierre du Moulin is bitter upon the matter.[57] When interrogated after the Powder Plot, the Jesuit Father Garnet admitted that he had been told about the conspirators' plans by Catesby's confessor, Father Tesimond, under the seal of confession but in ordinary conversation.[58] The Powder Plot lies behind the resemblance between the Buckingham story-line and the assassination of Henry IV by the would-be monk and rejected Jesuit Ravaillac.

The queen—aware that Wolsey is campaigning against Buckingham—warns the Surveyor against lying under oath. He firmly reports an oath, however: an Oath *against* Allegiance. It resembles the oath of the Powder Plotters (see p. 322). Shakespeare found in his main source what he needed: Holinshed says that Buckingham was heard 'swearing to confirme his word by the bloud of our Lord'.[59] He made the report more lurid, however, by adding an additional, regicidal oath. According to the Surveyor, Buckingham compared Henry to the villainous usurper Richard III, and treasonably imagined the murder of his king:

'I would have played
The part my father meant to act upon
Th'usurper Richard who, being at Salisbury,
Made suit to come in's presence; which if granted,
As he made semblance of his duty, would
Have put his knife into him.'
KING HENRY A giant traitor!...
There's something more would out of thee—what sayst?
BUCKINGHAM'S SURVEYOR After 'the Duke his father', with 'the knife',
He stretched him, and with one hand on his dagger,
Another spread on's breast, mounting his eyes,
He did discharge a horrible oath whose tenor
Was, were he evil used, he would outgo
His father by as much as a performance
Does an irresolute purpose. (195–210)

When Buckingham is put on trial, he is unable to resist his accusers' testimony. *Henry VIII* was known under the alternative title *All is True*. The audience is not clear at this point whether all is true or not (Buckingham is executed protesting his innocence). The circumstances recall those of Sir Thomas More, who was said by the Solicitor General, Richard Rich, under oath, to have spoken against the supremacy in prison.[60] This was something that More thought and might have said, but it was neither proven nor likely that he did. Even more immediately, the imputed conspiracy or shared plan to kill Henry recalls the Powder Plot against James and his lords, which was felt by many to have suited the authorities too well. Had it been confected, provoked, or helped along by *agents provocateurs*?

★ ★ ★

Gardiner said that, in taking the Henrician oaths, he plighted his troth to Dame Truthe.[61] *De Vera Obedientia* yokes true obedience to the king to the truth of God's law. Yet the scruples and complications of the 1530s could produce a version of truth that was much more legalistic and less knowable. Henry's tract about the royal divorce, *A Glasse of the Truthe* (1532), argues that the truth of anything is hard to establish in itself, so that what is agreed to be true by the powers that be, and what is deemed to be true, after oath and testimony in court (in this case, that Katherine of Aragon consummated her marriage with Prince Arthur), must be taken as the truth. The play-title, *All is True*, is well chosen for its 1530s subject matter because it has overtones of scepticism about truth while claiming to be realistic. Doubts about where truth lies are easy to hear and see in this play. In the case of the divorce, the king's disquiet about the papal dispensation which allowed him to marry Katherine are partly stirred up by the self-interested Wolsey and partly come from his desire to bed the young Anne Boleyn.

He is said (in lines written by Shakespeare) to have a 'scruple', 'a tenderness, | Scruple, and prick'[62]—an equivocal form of words, since late medieval Catholics argued against over-scrupulousness and Protestants echoed the thought that one could be over-impressed by a scruple, which is like a tiny stone in your shoe.[63] How much could a scruple matter when humanity is steeped in sin? James takes this line, about those who wrongly prioritize incidentals, when he writes of Catholics refusing the Oath of Allegiance 'not as seeming thereby to swarue from their obedience and Allegiance vnto his Maiestie, but onely being stayed from taking the same vpon the scrupulous tendernesse of their consciences, in regard of those particular words which the Pope had noted and condemned therein'.[64] Henry's scruple, however, proves, in a long speech written by Shakespeare, to have the potential to be violently felt. Like Perkins describing the affective impact of a bad conscience, he says that his doubts piled in 'with a spitting power, and made to tremble | The region of my breast' (2.4.180–1). He is now 'hulling in | The wild sea of my conscience' (2.4.196–7). This carries a sort of conviction, but Suffolk has already quipped that his pangs are really about getting the royal hands on Anne Boleyn: 'his conscience | Has crept too near another lady' (2.2.16–17). More prick than scruple. In Anne's scene with the Old Lady—another Shakespearean sequence—her 'soft cheveril conscience' (2.3.32) is the glove of sexual pleasure, playing with *con* as in Sonnet 151.[65]

More's conscience told him that, in the collective view of the Church down the ages, a divorce could not be granted to Henry because of the papal dispensation concerning Leviticus that had allowed the king to marry his deceased brother's wife. *A Glasse of the Truthe* rejects this. For reasons of Christian liberty we should not be 'bounden nowe to the groundsell and very foundacion of this lawe of Deuteronomy' (which allowed the marriage to Katherine); this would be 'seruitude and bondage' to ceremonies, to a Jewish law from which Christ freed us (B5r–6r). By contrast, Leviticus, which says that the marriage of brother and brother's wife will be barren, remains as a law of God and nature and it cannot be dispensed with by the Pope. Bringing in vows, Henry adds that the Pope cannot set aside a canon in support of Leviticus which he has vowed, by virtue of his office, to uphold (D5r–v). He 'is bounde to obey . . . the commandmentes statutes or ordinances' of the general councils of the Church (D6r).

So the Great Matter is a test of conscience regarding what laws and vows should bind marriage. The argument was not settled in the early seventeenth century, partly because the legitimacy of Elizabeth and to a lesser extent the Jacobean succession depended upon it. When Perkins, for instance, is distinguishing between Catholic and Protestant views of conscience, he says that the Pope is Antichrist 'when he takes vpon him authoritie to make such lawes as shall binde the conscience, as properly and truly as Gods lawes'.[66] Catholicism eases the conscience into self-betrayal through casuistry. What does the papal dispensation from the degrees of consanguinity forbidden in Leviticus show but 'that the Pope and Church of Rome doe sit as lords, or rather idols in the hearts and consciences of men. This will yet more fully appeare to any man, if we read popish bookes of *practical* or *Case divinitie,* in which the common manner is, to binde conscience where God looseth it, and to loose where he bindes.'[67] As with the 'proper' bonds of

God's law, so with the 'improper' bonds of human law, oath, and promise. The papacy keeps telling Catholics, as it did in 1606, the year in which Perkins published his treatise, that all these could be trumped by the dispensing power of the Pope. Catholicism put the soul into bondage by loosening the conscience.

Henry VIII is sympathetic to the loyal, markedly English, even anti-clerical Catholicism of Katherine—she will not, for instance, listen to speeches in church Latin—as the cardinals, Wolsey and Campeius, manoeuvre around the divorce. This material has long been ascribed to Shakespeare. She does not just show in her conduct 'obedience' to her husband and the crown.[68] From the outset, in 1.2, which is another Shakespeare scene, she tries to protect the 'Allegiance' and 'tractable obedience' of the king's subjects by denouncing Wolsey's taxes (63–5). The cardinal destructively fuses temporal and ecclesiastical powers. He has the Great Seal at his command but also the keys. Diplomacy he perverts to serve his papal ambitions. As Holinshed explains: 'The king of England had giuen vnto the said cardinall full authoritie, power, and libertie, to affirme and confirme, bind and vnbind, whatsoeuer should be in question betwéene him and the French king: and the like authoritie, power, and libertie, did the French king by his sufficient letters patents, grant to the same cardinall.'[69] Raking off money from the state, Wolsey fees his friends in Rome. His line on the Great Matter is just as self-serving, and bound to Romanist power. The outlook of the play on this point dovetails with that of *A Glasse of the Truthe*:

> the succession of this realme, ought nat to be ordered by forreins. . . . the kinges highnes and his parliament shulde ernestly prese the metropolitanes of this realme (there vniuste othe made to the pope nat withstandyng) to set an ende shortly in this. And to take a greatter regarde to the quietyng of his graces conscience and this realme: than to the ceremonyes of the popes lawe. For by goddes lawe they be bounde to the obedience of their prince, . . . (F2r–v)

Wolsey has his fall. Once Henry, by whatever means, finds in a bundle of papers an inventory of the cardinal's assets,[70] and a letter written by him to the Pope, he doubts that he is 'bound to us', brushes aside his 'allegiant thanks', and upbraids his disobedience with sarcasm: 'A loyal and obedient subject is | Therein illustrated' (3.2.166, 177, 181–2).[71] Wolsey has the archetypal Catholic vices. First, that of putting the Pope's law above the king's. Those who fell foul of the Oath of Allegiance were specifically fined for this. Both the offence and the statute and writ designed to prosecute it were known as *praemunire* (see p. 371), and Wolsey's misdemeanours 'Fall into th' compass of a praemunire'

(3.2.341). The queen highlights another trait: the equivocation that was already deplored in the Henrician period[72] but that became a public scandal after the trial of the Powder plotters and Garnet, and was picked out—as we have seen—in the Oath of Allegiance. Wolsey, she reports, would 'be ever double | Both in his words and meaning' (4.2.38–9).

* * *

The Cranmer plot, written by both Shakespeare and Fletcher, has often been criticized as an add-on. After the fall of Buckingham, the royal divorce, the fall of Wolsey, the marriage to Anne Boleyn and death of Katherine, why another episode in which Gardiner and his allies conspire against the new archbishop? As in *King Johan*, though without the polemic, we are shown that the Reformation is not easily secured. But the episode also resolves aspects of the Buckingham plot. It is another conspiracy orchestrated by clerics, though this time the king guides events to a happy outcome. Henry's experience with the Buckingham plot, where the sworn testimony of knaves brought down a great man, prepares him for the moves against Cranmer. When the archbishop, warned by the king, in a sequence attributed to Shakespeare, declares his allegiance ('Most dread liege') and his 'truth and honesty' (5.1.122–3), Henry reminds him of what happened to Christ:

> not ever
> The justice and the truth o'th' question carries
> The dew o'th' verdict with it. At what ease
> Might corrupt minds procure knaves as corrupt
> To swear against you? Such things have been done.
> You are potently opposed, and with a malice
> Of as great size. Ween you of better luck,
> I mean in perjured witness, than your master,
> Whose minister you are, whiles here he lived
> Upon this naughty earth?... (130–39)

This reinforces the audience's sense of Cranmer's almost unworldly virtue, but it also in some sense justifies the royal supremacy. Henry does not determine matters of faith, but his wise government of the Church is informed by his knowledge of scripture. If the Church is left to clerics, corrupt minds will undermine it from within. The king seals his faith in Cranmer with what is piously not quite an oath (a more Henrician than Protestant one): 'God's blest mother, | I swear he is true-hearted' (154–5).

Cranmer remains notorious for urging an oath on More. In the post-Reformation period he was equally well known for making a pre-emptive protestation that limited the obligation to Rome that would be implied by the oath of obedience that he swore to the Pope when he was made archbishop. From a Catholic point of view, this exceeded the infidelity of those, like Gardiner, whose obedience was adaptable. Pole said that Cranmer had committed a double perjury by being forsworn before he swore.[73] And this is before his abjurations under Mary, later rescinded in the fire of martyrdom. Against all that—and inconveniently for those who want Shakespeare to be a secret Catholic—*Henry VIII* supports the Protestant view that Cranmer is an improvement on Wolsey because he is not led astray by Rome. The character stands for true allegiance, and for the obedience that Cranmer himself advocated in his Exhortation. Hence his declaration (in lines written by Fletcher) of allegiance and detestation of disorder:

CRANMER Nor is there living—
I speak it with a single heart, my lords—
A man that more detests, more stirs against,
Both in his private conscience and his place,
Defacers of a public peace than I do.
Pray heaven the King may never find a heart
With less allegiance in it. (5.2.71–7)

The Act of Supremacy would not be passed for several months after the events dealt with in this sequence, but the plotting against Cranmer shows why it was necessary. The friends of Rome plan to execute an ecclesiastical coup, to deny the king his archbishop, and guidance of the Church, as King John was forced by the Pope to replace John de Grey with Stephen Langton. Henry, forewarned, comes out of concealment to castigate them for scheming to send Cranmer to the Tower. Even as Bishop Gardiner is repositioning himself, his use of 'obedience' betrays him:

Dread sovereign, how much are we bound to heaven
In daily thanks, that gave us such a prince,
Not only good and wise, but most religious.
One that in all obedience makes the church
The chief aim of his honour,... (5.2.148–52)

This 'flattery' (Henry's word), smuggles in the Catholic notion that kings should obey the Church in more than matters of faith (158). Henry requires the lords to respect Cranmer, whose mildness towards his enemies shows such Christ-like forbearance that an audience is likely to feel the greater need for royal government of the hierarchy.

The play climaxes in the baptism of Elizabeth, in which Cranmer has a leading part. This sacrament of vows and faith was anciently and often said, as we saw in Chapter 14, to constitute an *oath*. The Catholic *Ordynarye of Crystyanyte*, translated from the French in 1502 and frequently reprinted, writes of 'the vowe and sacrament of Baptem' (where 'sacrament' can mean *oath*).[74] Protestants reading the works of the influential Swiss theologian Zwingli found baptism, as in the Church Fathers, compared to a military oath, or pledge.[75] For Zwingli, however, as for other reformers, the rite imposed a mark or badge or sign, rather than being a channel of active grace.[76] It was God's promise, once again, that mattered. So Tyndale, who writes traditionally of 'the profession and vowe of oure baptyme',[77] goes on to say that 'washynge without the worde helpeth not: but thorow the worde it purifieth and clenseth vs.... The worde is the promise that God hath made.'[78] It was an account that ran headlong into the resistance of men like Thomas More, who takes it apart unsparingly in *The Confutacyon of Tyndales Answere*.[79] Iago, surprisingly, reflects the view of the reformers, when he speaks of Othello's 'baptism, | All seals and symbols of redeemèd sin'.[80]

Cranmer himself remained relatively conservative. God was active in baptism; it was not just a sign or symbol of his promises. Baptism brought remission of sins. Its covenant involved promises made on behalf of the child (a vow and profession) as well as promises from God. Hence the wording of the 1549 prayerbook[81]—passed into the Elizabethan prayerbook (1559) by which both Shakespeare and Fletcher (the son of a Protestant clergyman) were baptized:

> Ye haue hearde also that our Lord Jesus Chryst hath promised in hys gospel to graunt all these thynges that ye haue prayed for which promyse he for his part wil most surely kepe, and performe: Wherfore after thys promyse made by Christ, these infantes muste also faithfully for their parte promyse by you that be their suerties, that they will forsake the deuyll and all his workes, and constantly beleue gods holy word, and obediently kepe hys commaundementes.[82]

Baptism turned on the double promise of forsaking the devil but also obedience to God's commandments.

It was, of course, the godparents who gave the 'answers' when the priest asked whether the child would renounce the devil and all his works. This was neither an act of ventriloquism nor (as some of the more radical reformers proposed) merely an undertaking to educate the child—though that was one of the godparents' responsibilities. One effect of the Reformation emphasis on baptism as an exchange of binding language was to shift the focus of the sacrament away from the priest who sprinkled the child with water to godparents who, in the well-established terminology of Catholicism, were known as *sponsores, offerentes, fidejussores*—those who stand as 'sureties'. Historically most unusually, and in the play, an archbishop is surety for Elizabeth. 'You must be godfather', Henry tells Cranmer, 'and answer for her' (5.3.196).

We do not see the sacrament being enacted on stage. That would risk blasphemy. There is, however, a strikingly dramatic, ritualized moment of cohesion between Church and State which is not found in the play's sources. The king greets the infant Elizabeth after she is brought out of her baptism:

KING HENRY [*To the child*] With this kiss take my blessing—
[*He kisses the child*]
God protect thee,
Into whose hand I give thy life.
CRANMER Amen. (5.4.10–11)

This blessing is followed by Cranmer's prophecy of the glories of Elizabeth's reign, and the Jacobean succession. Almost certainly written by Fletcher, it is in line with the play's preoccupation with vowing and promising, now directed into the public sphere:

> This royal infant—heaven still move about her—
> Though in her cradle, yet now promises
> Upon this land a thousand thousand blessings... (17–19)

Cranmer's inspired speech caught the eye of the censor at Valladolid (see pp. 301, 386). Mostly he crossed out words and phrases in the play. When it comes to these lines on Elizabeth, however, whole sections are deleted.

Bale's *King Johan*, first performed—as we saw in Chapter 14—in the household of Cranmer, ends in its later, published form with praise for Elizabeth as the 'godly' prince of her 'liege people', suppressing superstition and idolatry.[83] Cranmer in *Henry VIII* strikes a similar note: 'Truth shall nurse her, | Holy and heavenly thoughts still counsel her... God shall be truly known' (28–36). Jacobean Catholics would have known how discriminatory the anti-recusancy laws had been under Elizabeth. Even the oath of baptism could be used to damn their reluctance to swear allegiance. As William Fulke mocked: 'if these men, doe sticke so firmely vnto their consciences and fayth sworne vnto God in their oth of Baptisme: then wil they as firmely for the same conscience, sticke vnto her Maiestie, if occasion should serue, in keeping their secondary faith and allegeance, sworne vnto her Highnesse as to the substitute of GOD.'[84] In the play, Elizabeth is celebrated as the first monarch to be baptized into an English Church free of Rome. The vows and profession of her baptism, put into the mouth of Cranmer, ensure her allegiance to something truer.[85] As the archbishop goes on to speak of the 'star-like' James, rising from the ashes of Elizabeth the phoenix (45–6), the rite of baptism becomes an act of succession, founding a line of Protestant princes.

As Holinshed's account makes clear, Elizabeth's baptism owed nothing to Geneva. The sacrament was performed 'with all suche solemne ceremonies as were thought conuenient'. Salt, chrism, silver font, the Friars' church hung with arras.[86] In 1533, you would expect nothing less. Henry was still the Defender of the Faith that he had been when he published the *Assertio Septem Sacramentorum contra M. Lutherum* in 1521. Luther and Henry VIII clashed dramatically over baptism, in large part because Luther, like other reformers, placed a high value on the rite. Henry denounced his enemy's serpent-like hissing, 'quo Baptismum non in aliud levat, quam ut premat Poenitentiam, et Baptismatis gratiam statuat impune peccandi licentiam' ('by which he extols *Baptism*, for no other End, but to depress *Penance*, and establish the Grace of Baptism for a free Liberty of Sinning').[87] It was a point that More would repeat in his *Responsio ad Lutherum*.[88] Luther put the Divine promise, and our faith in it, nourished by baptism, 'far above all the glitter of works, vows' and 'religious orders';[89] for him it was repugnant to see vows of poverty, chastity, and obedience being compared with baptism (75). That men would bind themselves to their religious superiors struck the reformers as absurd. Only a fool, Tyndale scoffs, would so abuse his God-given liberty.[90] 'For a vow is a kind of law', Luther went on, and 'When vows are multiplied, laws and works are necessarily multiplied... faith is extinguished and the liberty of baptism is [brought into bondage]' (75). This is why his celebration of baptism went along with his attack on pardons, indulgences, and on the keys used to loosen vows (79) or to bind by creating laws that put the Church into captivity (71).

In his own discussion of baptism Henry reacts against Luther's attack on vows and laws as bonds that threaten to displace the promises of the sacrament. Vows are the ecclesiastical version of what the king really wants to protect: his authority over the laws. 'After he has deprived the Sacraments of Grace', Henry says of Luther,

> he robs the Church of all Vows and Laws; nor does it at all move him, that God said, *Vow, and render to God your Vows*. . . . as for the Laws, . . . he robs Princes and Prelates, of all Power and Authority; for what shall a King or a Prelate do, if he cannot appoint any Law, or execute the Law which was before appointed; . . . Where then is that saying of the Apostle, 'Let every Creature be subject to the higher Powers'? . . . Where is also that, 'be obedient to your Governours' . . . ? (312–14)

Here once again is the Henrician obsession with obedience. Luther is not just doctrinally unsound on this, he does not show obedience himself: 'If he thinks [people] ought to obey, why is not he himself obedient?' (316).

The play adapts Holinshed. The procession to and from the baptism is both more Tudor-Protestant in its make-up and more questioningly framed. It is recast as a popular spectacle, while the crowd that gathers to watch it is described by the Porter and his man in terms that slyly comment on the irregular, incestuous qualities of the royal re-marriage and birth: 'what a fry of fornication is at door! On my Christian conscience, this one christening will beget a thousand. Here will be father, godfather, and all together' (5.3.33–6). The procession is stripped of the bejewelled chrism vessel, virgin wax taper, and the rest. There is no trace in the detailed stage direction of the clerics of the king's chapel in copes, mentioned in Holinshed. The tone of Church–State relations is set by the austere presence of Cranmer, and by overtones of obedience and order.

For if baptism is a rite of vows and profession, a sacrament that is an oath, it is also, as we saw in Cranmer's prayerbook, a locus of obedience.[91] This ancient, long-standing view underlies Henry VIII's transition in his *Assertio* from baptism through vows and laws to Romans 13 and 'be obedient to your Governours'—including governors of the Church. In an often-quoted passage, Isidore of Seville had declared, 'Two couenants there are which Christian men do make in baptism, the one concerning relinquishment of Satan, the other touching obedience to the faith of Christ.'[92] The Reformation encouraged clerics and scholars to narrow this obedience down to the faith of a particular Church. Some, such as the Jesuits rebuked by Donne (see p. 376), meant obedience to the Church of Rome; mainstream English Protestants thought sacramental obedience was owed to God's law, the commandments of Christ, and the ecclesiastical polity by law established.[93] So the baptism of Elizabeth at the end of *Henry VIII* is not just an excuse for spectacle. It shows the historical roots of the settlement to which the Oath of Allegiance bound James's subjects. It is resonant with implications of obedience to a reformed Church and State bound by oaths, vows, and laws.

16

Coriolanus Fidiussed

When Coriolanus returns to Antium, in the final scene of Shakespeare's tragedy, marching with drum and colours and accompanied by cheering Volscians, he looks like a victorious general. The audience knows, however, that this is a fragile triumph. We have seen Aufidius briefing the nobility against his rival, and he now springs his trap by accusing Coriolanus of treachery:

CORIOLANUS Traitor? How now?
AUFIDIUS Ay, traitor, Martius.
CORIOLANUS Martius?
AUFIDIUS Ay, Martius, Caius Martius. Dost thou think
I'll grace thee with that robbery, thy stol'n name,
'Coriolanus', in Corioles?
You lords and heads o'th' state, perfidiously
He has betrayed your business, and given up,
For certain drops of salt, your city, Rome—
I say your city—to his wife and mother,
Breaking his oath and resolution like
A twist of rotten silk, never admitting
Counsel o'th' war. (5.6.87–99)

This insolently effective accusation is mostly based on events that Shakespeare found and followed in Plutarch's *Life of Coriolanus*. In the *Life*, as in the play, Coriolanus succumbs with tears to Virgilia and Volumnia's plea that he hold back from attacking Rome, and the decision to spare the city is indeed made without counsel. The charge of oath-breaking, however, was added to the mix by Shakespeare. It belongs to a train of oaths, promises, and asseverations, almost entirely absent from Plutarch, that carry great weight in the drama.

In the vigorous, austere idiom of *Coriolanus*, repetition counts for a lot. 'Oath and resolution like | A twist of rotten silk' goes back to the opening lines of the play, where the hungry Roman citizens 'resolve' (i.e. agree) to have grain at their own price (1.1.3–4). 'Resolution' is also, however, the firmness of purpose that stiffens an oath and a soldier ('To bee a souldier, is to be resolute: Resolution is a vertue'),[1] so the accusation cuts deep. 'Rotten' recurs in the play, to characterize privilege, damp air, decrepitude, and marshy fens, and it meshes with other images of fusty, decaying perishables. Aufidius could have accused Coriolanus of shattering a cast-iron oath; it cheapens him further to say that his oath was only ever 'A twist of... silk'. Such feeble strength as it had came from its being perverse, deceitful, and the ornament of a courtier. Coriolanus has deplored 'the parasite's silk' (1.10.45). Fine as a thread or thick as a braid, a twist of silk will always be unsuitable for a warrior.[2]

'Perfidiously' heads the charges. It means 'wickedly' but more specifically 'guilty of breaking faith'.[3] This word we have heard as an undertone every time Aufidius is named. For names can speak in this play.[4] After noting how Martius acquired the name 'Coriolanus', when he defeated the Volscians in Corioles, Plutarch explains that such 'surnames' were given by the Greeks and Romans to reflect individual characteristics: '*Eudemon*: as muche to saye, as fortunate... *Niger*, blacke: *Rufus*, red: *Caecus*, blinde', and so on.[5] The particularity of 'Coriolanus' matters so much to Martius that, when he is banished from Rome, he refuses it (5.1.11–12), only to have it denied again by Aufidius. Yet the eloquence of the name stems partly from its irony: 'Coriolanus' can mean 'man of Corioles',[6] which is what Martius (cf. 'Mars-like, martial') becomes when he goes over to the Volscians. It also depends on its components. Scholars have found the *anus* at the end of 'Coriolanus',[7] and we have recently been alerted to the *cor* (Latin, 'heart') that starts it,[8] though not to why it is there—something that I plan to put right. More could be said about a name that contains both 'royal' and 'real', reflecting Martius' descent from Numa, the second king of Rome (2.3.226–33),[9] his potential to become a tyrant (3.3.1–2, 65–9), and his soldierly focus on essentials, as when he says that to heed to the hunger of the people distracts from 'Real necessities' (3.1.150).

As for Aufidius, in Plutarch he is thrice called Tullus Aufidius, never just Aufidius, and most often (some nineteen times) Tullus. In Holland's Livy, a secondary source for the play, he is Accius Tullus, not Aufidius.[10] In *Coriolanus*, by contrast, he is almost always Aufidius. To be more precise, the Folio reads 'Auffidius', and occasionally, in compositor B's stint, 'Auffidious'. The name conjures up *fides*, or, more fully, *Fidius*, the name of Jupiter as defender of truth or of a lesser power, Dius Fidius, god of oaths. From this springs the Roman oath, 'me dius fidius', 'by the god of truth'. But fidelity is in doubt, given an Aufidius who is on the look-out for advantage, and who betrays the trusting Coriolanus. What should be 'fidius' is ''fidious', i.e. 'perfidious'. The *Oxford English Dictionary* records *fidious* in this sense, citing James Shirley's *Arcadia*: 'Oh! fidious rascal! I thought there was some roguery.' Aufidius is All-'fidious.

We are cued to think about this name when Menenius and Volumnia exult over the news of Coriolanus' victory at Corioli, before he is exiled from Rome:

MENENIUS Has he disciplined Aufidius soundly?
VOLUMNIA Titus Lartius writes they fought together, but Aufidius got off.
MENENIUS And 'twas time for him too, I'll warrant him that. An he had stayed by him, I would not have been so fidiussed for all the chests in Corioles, and the gold that's in them. (2.1.113–18)

'Fidiussed' could be glossed, 'truly (by the god of truth) bashed into himself'. Yet there is another implication, picked out in R. B. Parker's edition: '(a) a nonce-word, making the past participle of a verb from Aufidius' name, (b) playing on the legal term "fidejussor", one who goes bail for another.'[11] 'Fidejussor' must be part of the joke, but 'one who goes bail' is unhelpfully put. In Roman law a *fidejussor* is a promise-maker (who might be a promise-breaker), someone 'who could make a promise in support of a bargain of any kind—a "real" or "consensual" contract, sale and so on'.[12] The usual early modern gloss was 'surety, pledge',[13] and 'He that confirmeth anything by an Oath... one that gives security to Faith.'[14] In English law, the *fidejussor* promises to pay what someone else owes, if that someone does not pay up. Note the proximity of 'all' in Menenius' speech, without which the play on the name would be incomplete: '*'fidius* stands as a surety for *all* the wealth of Corioli, yet what it amounts to is not worth the pounding he would have got from Coriolanus, had he not run away.' Not wanting to be truly thrashed, 'fidious abandons his *fides*. The word ties up with a series of *pledges*, *warrants*, *vouches*, *safeguards*, and *sureties* in the play.

⋆ ⋆ ⋆

From Livy, Cicero, and other classical writers, Shakespeare and many in his audience would know that *fides* could designate the assurance provided by speech acts ('othe', 'troth', 'promise') but also social virtues ('trust', 'protection', 'credite') and the integrity of individuals ('Constancie and faithfulness').[15]

They would additionally be aware that *fides* had a place in Roman religion, in the worship of Jupiter as truth-teller,[16] Dius Fidius, and the goddess Fides.[17] The cult of Fides went back to Numa, in whose *Life* Plutarch writes: 'It is he (as some saye) that first built a temple to *Faith* and *Terme*: and which made the ROMAINES vnderstand, that the most holy and greateth othe they could make, was to sweare by their faith, which they kepe yet at this daye' (77). Livy adds:

> And to Faith alone hee instituted a solemne yearely feastivall day, and erected a chappell. Vnto which hee commanded the Flamines to ride in an arched or embowed close chariot, ... with their hands covered and wrapped close to their fingers ends: signifying thereby, that faith is to bee kept and preserved ...[18]

The *Oxford Classical Dictionary* says of this passage: 'A pair of covered hands is indeed [Faith's] symbol, as often on coins commemorating the *fides* of the Augusti, the legions, etc., in imperial times. Since giving the hand is a common gesture of solemn agreement, the symbolism is natural.'[19] Recall the device in *Pericles*, written just before *Coriolanus*: 'an Hand enuironed with Clouds, | Holding out Gold, that's by the Touch-stone tride: | The motto thus, *Sic spectanda fides*.'[20]

Coriolanus is Shakespeare's most assiduously Roman play, his answer, as it were, to Ben Jonson. The centrality of *fides* follows. Critics have interpreted it as a study of the 'Herculean hero' or a dramatization of the Midland Rising of 1607. Such contexts have their relevance, but they overlook what drives the tragedy. Stanley Fish is closer to the mark in his account of *Coriolanus* as 'a speech-act play'.[21] He sees that Martius is drawn to refusing and promising, that 'promising ... is Coriolanus' favorite speech act, the one by which he defines himself'.[22] But Fish's analysis is limited by his Austinian belief that it is the utterance of a speech act that creates a moral obligation ('Coriolanus knows as well as Austin does that having an intention *is* "merely a matter of uttering words"').[23] In the tragedy, as in antiquity, *faith* goes wider and deeper, raising questions about the links between 'oath' and 'resolution', i.e. utterance, decision, and integrity. Fish misses the play's grappling with the paradox, familiar to antiquity, that it can be right *not* to keep a promise, and its exploration of the tragic potential of that for a man who defines himself by *fides*. In any event, to focus on refusing and promising neglects other aspects of faith.

Cicero's *De Officiis*, read in every Elizabethan grammar school, defines *fides* like this: 'fides, id est dictorum conventorumque constantia et veritas.'[24] 'Faithfulnesse', in Nicholas Grimald's translation, 'is in worde, and couenaunt, a trouth, and stedfastnesse.'[25] We think of asserting ('worde') and promising ('couenant') as having different temporal and logical structures, but the classical sources encouraged Shakespeare and his contemporaries to regard lying about the past or present as of a piece with lying about the future. You are bound to the truth of an asseveration as you are to the truth of a promise. When Aufidius accuses Coriolanus of breaking his 'oath and resolution', the rebuttal thus turns on the faithlessness of the assertion: 'Measureless liar, thou hast made my heart | Too great for what contains it' (5.6.104–5). We shall see later—and it has much to do with oaths—how this 'heart', angry and word-choked, is the *cor* in Coriolanus (who asks the Volscian lords to 'give *this cur* the lie', to help 'thrust the lie unto him' (108, 111)).

Relatedly, Menenius' joke about fidiussing is followed by a passage about the truth of Coriolanus' success:

VALERIA In truth, there's wondrous things spoke of him.
MENENIUS Wondrous, ay, I warrant you; and not without his true purchasing.
VIRGILIA The gods grant them true.
VOLUMNIA True? Pooh-whoo!
MENENIUS True? I'll be sworn they are true. (2.1.124–9)

This will strike a modern audience as mere exulting insistence, but the stress on asseveration—'In truth, warrant, true [five times], I'll be sworn'—makes it integral to a play about *fides*. Much the same could be said about the apparently digressive exchange in 5.2, where Menenius admits to the Volscian sentinels that he has sometimes exceeded 'verity' in praising his friend. 'Faith, sir, if you had told as many lies in his behalf as you have uttered words in your own, you should not pass here, . . . Howsoever you have been his liar, as you say you have, I am one that, telling true under him, must say you cannot pass' (20, 26–34).

That *Coriolanus* is concerned with both the assertory and promissory branches of *fides* does not make it a disquisition on Roman virtue. Compared with Jonson's *Catiline*—a tragedy which, with its solemn oaths, its patrician anti-hero going into exile, and its long transcripts from Cicero's speeches, almost reads like an attempt to show how *Coriolanus* should have been written—Shakespeare's last, great Roman play explores the difficulties and contradictions in the values he found in his classical sources. For Cicero, *fides* is a social virtue that flows from personal integrity. Shakespeare highlights the price that is paid by a man of 'Constancie and faithfulnesse' (as well as wrath, and lack of civility), when he bends the working of his heart to the requirements of social order. The value that he places on *fides* becomes Coriolanus' weakness. This is already known to the Tribunes, when they castigate the people for agreeing to elect him consul without exacting from him a 'gracious promise' to do something to their advantage that they could later press into effect or that would have enraged him with its burden (2.3.179–88). But this strength that is a weakness is most ruthlessly exploited in Aufidius' charge of perfidy. 'There is no Vice, that doth so couer a Man with Shame, as to be found false, and perfidious,' wrote Bacon.[26] To be fidiussed, in short. It triggers the angry self-assertion ('I | fluttered your Volscians in Corioles. | Alone I did it' (5.6.115–17)) that brings Coriolanus down.

Cicero regards the faithful, indomitable Regulus (about whom, more later) and the magistrate, Pomponius, who dropped a case because he swore to do so, even though he swore under duress, as exemplary figures from an earlier Rome.[27] 'For our annceters wer of this minde', he writes of them, 'that ther is no strayter bonde to bynde a mannes promes, than an othe.... So greatly was an othe had in regard, at those dayes.'[28] Livy strikes a similar note in his account of Brutus' oath to drive Tarquinius out of Rome, and the execution of Metius Suffetius for breaking 'allegeance, promise, and covenants'.[29] Commenting on an episode that took place not long after the expulsion of Coriolanus, when the Tribunes tried to stir up the people but the military oaths that they had taken made the people obey the consuls, he declares:'There was not as yet that neglect and contempt of the gods... which now reigneth every where...: neither did men interpret their oathes... to serve their own purpose.'[30] The passage was well known in the early modern period. Machiavelli, for instance, quotes it in his *Discourses upon Livy*.[31]

A similar sense of decline is not hard to find in England. If *Coriolanus* is Shakespeare's most profoundly Roman play, it is calculated to engage a London audience because a 'Ciceronian' model of civility and commonwealth[32] was perceived to be under threat. Hugh Oldcastle and John Mellis's *Briefe Instruction and Maner how to Keepe Bookes of Accompts* (1543/1588), for instance, praises

> the outwarde fayth or promise of a marchaunt that is iust in dealing, the which in time past hath bene incomparable, In so much, that their oathes in confirming the trueth, in great common weales were made in this maner: *Per fidem bonae et fidelis mercatoris*, which is to say: By the faith of a good faithfull marchant. For without fayth and fidelitie betwixt man and man, it is not possible that our labours and trauels can eyther be well maintained, continued or ended.[33]

In Shakespeare's London, as in *Coriolanus*, the market-place that should be a sphere of faith was becoming an encompassing arena in which all was up for sale, including a man's integrity, as Martius finds when he stands for election.

★ ★ ★

He comes into the tragedy firing off insults at the people. Curses and battle-cries are his *forte*, in a play that is full of clamour. The impulse to invective goes along with a willingness to swear binding oaths because one shatteringly vilifies the multiplicity of the plebeians while the other reinforces the construction of a singular, noble self. Both forms of utterance are absolute, symptoms of a need for certainty. When Coriolanus is sent into exile, he says that he leaves the people to their 'uncertainty' (3.3.128). It is a state that they live with rather happily, for a time, but that he would find intolerable. By the end of the play, he is forced to accept that his greatest source of security, war, is, as Volumnia reminds him, 'uncertain' (5.3.142). What this does to the character is, as we shall see, one of the most extraordinary things in Shakespeare, as his commitment to binding language is bent into pliability. Initially, however, his oaths, though made out of inherited formulae, are pitched to transcend the common lot of speech, which is to be chewed in every mouth, like the food that Martius disdains. There are collective oaths in Plutarch[34] and Livy,[35] but for Coriolanus they are individual. He makes words his own by giving them as his word, at junctures of his own life, with his own rattling intensity. The his-ness of the oaths distances them from the 'voices' of the people which echo unreliably around Rome.

In specificity and circumstantial uniqueness, the oath has something in common with the name, especially as described by Plutarch. Should we look for a connection between Coriolanus' 'By Jupiter' and 'By Jove'[36] and his proper surname? In *The Sacrament of Language*, Giorgio Agamben cites Wittgenstein's *On Certainty*, 'The security of the propriety of names conditions every other certainty', then adds:

> It is a certainty, or better a 'faith,' of this kind that is in question in the oath and in the name of God. The name of God names the name that is always and only true, that is, that experience of language that it is not possible to doubt. For man this experience is the oath. In this sense every name is an oath, and in every name a 'faith' is in question, because the certainty of the name is not of an empirico-constative or logico-epistemic type but rather always puts in play

> the commitment and praxis of men. To speak is, above all, to swear, to believe in the name.[37]

This is as questionable as a general thesis as it is persuasive about the faith that a man of *fides* might place in the propriety of his name and the potency of an oath; equally convincing is the thought that the certainty of an oath and a name is not absolute but mediated by 'the commitment and praxis of men'. This Martius comes to experience when his name fragments, and is taken from him, while oaths are qualified, interpreted, and challenged, after his expulsion from Rome.

Martius, from the outset, is self-confirmed as faithful. Urged to fight the Volscians under the leadership of Cominius ('It is your former promise') he agrees: 'Sir, it is, | And I am constant' (1.1.229–30). That he selects troops from Cominius' ranks and leads them against Aufidius, immediately after the fall of Corioles, might put this promise in doubt. The sequence does anticipate his troublesome ability to draw soldiers away from Aufidius, when they jointly lead the Volscians; but he gets Cominius' permission for his adventure, and seeks it with an appeal to mutual fidelity ('by th' vows we have made | To endure friends' (1.7.57–8)). So his faith is still unblemished when he pitches into Aufidius, crying, 'I'll fight with none but thee, for I do hate thee | Worse than a promise-breaker' (1.9.1–2). These words do not appear in the *Life of Coriolanus*, but, in the *Life of Alcibiades*, which is paired with it, Plutarch writes of Alcibiades' 'breache of promise which he often made', and the marginal note in North's translation reads '*Alcibiades a breaker of promise*'.[38] For Plutarch, Alcibiades was successful because '*more chaungeable then the Camelion*'.[39] This must have encouraged Shakespeare to represent Martius as, by contrast, dangerously 'constant'.

For an audience in the theatre, the parallel that claims attention is that between Martius and Aufidius. Plutarch does not mention Tullus until Coriolanus has been exiled from Rome. Shakespeare makes the parallel-with-differences almost continuous, and threaded by faith and perfidy. So, when Aufidius talks to the Volscian lords about the imminent campaign, he has a 'promise' of his own to keep:

> I speak from certainties....
> If we and Caius Martius chance to meet,
> 'Tis sworn between us we shall ever strike
> Till one can do no more. (1.2.31–6)

This is entirely Martius-like, in its need for certainty, alertness to military intelligence (cf. 1.1.218–19), but above all in commitment to an oath.

When does the 'fidious side of Aufidius show itself? Arguably when we first see him encounter Martius on stage. After much vaunting, they come to blows, but the outcome is unresolved, even bathetic:

AUFIDIUS Wert thou the Hector
That was the whip of your bragged progeny,
Thou shouldst not scape me here.
Here they fight, and certain Volsces come in the aid of AUFIDIUS.
MARTIUS *fights till* [*the Volsces*] *be driven in breathless* [, MARTIUS *following*]
Officious and not valiant, you have shamed me
In your condemnèd seconds. *Exit* (1.9.11–15)

Just what the Folio stage direction—everything not in square brackets after line 13—intends is debatable, but it looks as though Aufidius is meant to show his untrue colours by allowing Volscian soldiers, contrary to his oath, to join him in fighting Martius, most likely until they are beaten off and he utters the last two lines, with frustration, as an excuse. The audience will not be surprised, a hundred lines later, to hear him swear 'By th' elements' that, having failed to defeat Martius 'True sword to sword', he will now 'potch at him some way' (1.11.10–15).

Aufidius is preparing to cross a line that was much discussed by classical and Renaissance commentators. Watching how he crosses it is part of the fascination of the play. It was agreed, even by Christian moralists, that deception in war was permissible as it was not in the contract-making and civil conversation of peace. 'Lying', as Jeremy Taylor puts it, is 'an engine of warre'. When did acceptable guile turn into ignoble potching? The usual source of guidance was a distinction made by Ulpian between *dolus* and (predictably enough) *perfidia*. In Taylor's paraphrase: '*Dolus* and *perfidia* are extremely different... Craft against a thief or enemy is good; but not perfidiousness.' Adding to Ulpian another authority, the Roman historian Ammianus—though the point was an early modern commonplace—Taylor says that 'To bring warre to a happy end, you may use force or wit; but at no hand break a promise, or be treacherous.'[40]

What Aufidius says about potching is ominous enough, but the newly surnamed Coriolanus first has to deal with the more pressing complications of *fides* in Rome. 'By the faith of men', Menenius warns him and Cominius, when they return victorious from Corioles, there are 'some old crab-trees here... that will not | Be grafted to your relish' (2.1.173–5). He means, we understand, the Tribunes, who make the people such a force. They are confident that Coriolanus will not stand for Consul in the time-honoured way:

BRUTUS I heard him swear,
Were he to stand for consul, never would he
Appear i' th' market-place nor on him put
The napless vesture of humility,
Nor, showing, as the manner is, his wounds
To th' people, beg their stinking breaths.
SICINIUS 'Tis right.
BRUTUS It was his word.... (2.1.217–23)

By the time Volumnia has finished cajoling, Coriolanus feels obliged to stand for a consulship in the market-place wearing the vesture he abhors. If an audience concludes, having heard Brutus' report, that his resistance to putting on the gown, and his refusal to show his scars, partly stem from his not wanting to break a publicly known 'oath and resolution', it will take the measure of his capitulation as the more lamentably an anticipation of his succumbing to Volumnia in Act 5, when, with better reason, he agrees to pull back from Rome.

Yet he is not the only promise-breaker. The people break their word too. They do this in a market-place, where the election to the consulship is caught up in buying and selling ('You must think', the Third Citizen says to Martius, 'if we give you anything we hope to gain by you'),[41] not governed by what the *Briefe Instruction and Maner* calls 'fayth and fidelitie'. The relationship between sworn friend-enemies that Coriolanus has with Aufidius is not possible between him and the plebeians. 'I will, sir, flatter my sworn brother the people', he tells them (2.3.87–8). This has been compared with 'the "fratres jurati" of medieval chivalry, knights bound by oath to share each other's fortunes' and the 'sworne brethren' who model their friendships on Hercules and Iolaus in Plutarch's *Life of Pelopidas*.[42] But Shakespeare typically uses the phrase to suggest an easy, vulgar association, as when Prince Harry declares himself 'sworn brother to a lease of drawers' at the Boar's Head tavern.[43] How can 'the people' (a plural mass) be reduced to a singular 'sworn brother'? If there is any trace here of the democratic potential of sworn brotherhood, the replication of kin relations by means of an oath, that Derrida wrote about so hopefully,[44] it is as a foil to Martius' contempt. Unable to engage, he turns to scorn:

CORIOLANUS Most sweet voices.
Better it is to die, better to starve,

Than crave the hire which first we do deserve.
Why in this wolvish toge should I stand here
To beg of Hob and Dick that does appear
Their needless vouches?[45]

Yet, for all that this is dismissive, Coriolanus still assumes the viability of *fides*. He believes that the 'voices' of the people have hardened into 'vouches': promises, pledges, warrants. And their acclamation would carry, for Bible-reading, Jacobean audiences, asseverative force: 'Amen, amen. God save thee, noble consul!' (126).[46] The problem is, of course, that their binding words do not bind.

The historian Mark Kishlansky has shed light on the election in *Coriolanus* by comparing it with parliamentary selection in Jacobean England. 'In early modern parlance', he notes, 'electors gave voices rather than votes and spoke of having voices to give.' Election was secured by acclamation.[47] Kishlansky does not register, however, the importance to *Coriolanus* of a point that he makes when he has left the play behind and is discussing elections in general. Once a voter (from *votum*, 'one who has vowed')[48] had made a 'commitment' to a candidate, it was considered 'binding'. 'A pledge was not lightly given and could not ordinarily be withdrawn. The practice of revolting—of switching from one side to the other—was universally despised and gave rise to ugly accusations of dishonor and shamefulness, which suggests that the pledge of support was similar to an oath.'[49] The citizens shame and dishonour both themselves and Coriolanus when they cast away their oath-like vouches.

This throws Martius into a rage, and he rails against the plebs. ''Twere well we let the people know't', Sicinius provocatively observes:

MENENIUS What, what, his choler?
CORIOLANUS Choler? Were I as patient as the midnight sleep,
By Jove, 'twould be my mind. (3.1.87–9)

David Schalkwyk has argued that the tone in which speech acts are uttered onstage is irrelevant to their ethical force. This may be philosophically correct, in the moderate, even light of J. L. Austin, but what Schalkwyk finds in the curses in *Richard III* seems to hold for Martius' oaths, that the '*affective*' is hard to separate from the '*effective*'.[50] Defiant, percussive, exultant in the assurance of his constancy, 'By Jove, 'twould be my mind' is of a piece with the insults, curses, and indeed the physical blows that Coriolanus deals out on all sides.

Shakespeare has put 'choler' and 'patient' into the dialogue because he knows that the potency of Coriolanus' speech acts is inextricable from their vehement delivery and he wants to cue the actor to what he found in Plutarch's *Life*: 'he was so chollericke and impacient, that he would yeld to no liuing creature: which made him churlishe, vnciuill, and altogether vnfit for any mans conuersation' (237). This was among the qualities that attracted Shakespeare to Coriolanus, shortly after he wrote the parts of raging Lear and cursing Timon. Yet the excess is constrained; there remains a degree of circumspection. Martius does not spray out threatening oaths like the captains in *Henry V*, but has a Roman respect for the religious dimension of *fides*:

> No, take more.
> What may be sworn by, both divine and human,
> Seal what I end withal! (3.1.143–5)

And so he goes on, into his critique of popular power,

> where gentry, title, wisdom
> Cannot conclude but by the yea and no
> Of general ignorance, it must omit
> Real necessities,... (147–50)

'Yea and no' is not just the assent and dissent of the people; it presents their vouches as a puritan-plain, citizen oath. As we have recurrently seen, Christ told his disciples to give their word only by yea and nay (Matthew 5: 37) and the Godly followed his lead in early modern England. The phrase 'by yea and no/nay' or 'by the yea and no' occurs five times in Shakespeare, always as a pious or mild asseveration. It contrasts sharply with Coriolanus' self-determined, high-flown swearing, his damaged but noble resolution.

Menenius' defence of Coriolanus to the patricians is significantly phrased:

> His nature is too noble for the world.
> He would not flatter Neptune for his trident
> Or Jove for's power to thunder. His heart's his mouth.
> What his breast forges, that his tongue must vent,... (3.1.255–8)

There is something incongruous about Martius' choler, mixing up body parts; but at least there is no distance between heart and tongue. It is a coupling that recurs several times in Act 3, recalling a line from Euripides' *Hippolytus* that was widely quoted by the learned in early modern England: 'my tongue swore to, but my heart did not.' Austin cites this in support of his contention 'that *our word is our bond*'. If the speech act is not binding, regardless of intention, then you have left, he argued, a 'let-out' for the deceiver—as in the line from *Hippolytus*.[51] Behind Menenius, if not Austin, is a passage in the *De Officiis* which turns on the same line.

For Cicero, *fides* is so sacrosanct that 'the promes of an othe is manye times to be kept with our enemie'. As we saw, however, in Chapter 8 (p. 223), he notoriously adds that it is allowable to break faith with pirates, because a pirate is not a lawful enemy, if, when you swear, you did not intend to keep the promise. This is why it is misleading to propose, as Fish does, that 'Coriolanus knows as well as Austin does that having an intention *is* "merely a matter of uttering words"', for it bypasses the classical ethos of the protagonist. 'To sweare an vntruthe, is not to forsweare,' Cicero continues. What makes something 'periurie' is 'not to perfourm that, which according to the meaning of your hert ye haue sworn, as by our custome is exprest in a certein fourme of wordes'. The speech act has to have a recognized form, but this is secondary to the 'meaning of your hert'. 'For feately sayde Euripides: In worde I sware, but hert vnsworne I bare.'[52]

Cicero uses 'lingua' where Grimald has 'worde', and 'animi' and 'méntem' where the translation has 'heart'. The line from *Hippolytus* could be translated tongue/mind[53] but tongue/heart was also commonplace (Austin, after quoting the Greek, gives 'tongue' then both 'heart' and 'mind').[54] In Shakespeare's case, the *cor* that he found in 'Coriolanus' will have slanted him towards 'heart' when thinking about *faith*, in its classical and early modern senses, in relation to a given word. Martius can only be faithful, true to himself, if his tongue utters what his heart dictates. This is not about him having, as Fish assumes, an anti-social ideal of autonomy, which leads to a falsely privatized view of language, but about the integrity of *fides*, not flowing, as Cicero would like to believe, into social harmony, but tearing up the tissue of lip-service that civility requires.

Menenius starts using the figure, but Volumnia makes the same distinction when she tells her son to return to the market-place and speak to the people,

> Not by your own instruction, nor by th' matter
> Which your *heart* prompts you, but with such words
> That are but roted in your *tongue*, though but
> Bastards and syllables of no allowance
> To your bosom's truth. (3.2.54–8)

Knowing her son, she works with his absolute impulse to regard his every word as an index of his faith. Hence her gravitation to Cicero, Euripides, and the permissibility of what Martius would regard as perjury. Flatter the people, she counsels; it will not engage your bosom's truth. The persuasion is unscrupulous, but it gains purchase by dealing more explicitly in oaths. Volumnia urges her son to swear to the plebeians the sort of oath that cannot be taken to be binding because it is, like 'by the yea and no', a citizen's oath. It is *fides* reduced to sooth, the kind of empty-mouthed 'in good sooth' that Hotspur attributed to city wives (and that we hear in the near city-comedy sequence in which Valeria tries to persuade Virgilia to go gadding about while her husband fights at Corioles).[55] 'In asking their good loves', Volumnia advises, say that 'thou wilt frame | Thyself, forsooth, hereafter theirs' (84–5).

Coriolanus has been attentive. He plays back to Volumnia the *Hippolytus* distinction: 'Must I with my base *tongue* give my noble *heart* | A lie that it must bear?' (100–1). Must he be perjured, be perfidious, and 'surcease to honour mine own truth' (121)? When his mother's pressure overcomes him he agrees in terms that show the heart/tongue opposition seething away. He will use his tongue, he says—in an almost petulant turn—to deceive:

I'll mountebank their loves,
Cog their *hearts* from them, and come home beloved
Of all the trades in Rome. Look, I am going.
Commend me to my wife. I'll return consul,
Or never trust to what my *tongue* can do
I'th' way of flattery further. (132–7)

Whether or not it knows the story an audience knows that he will not be able to do this. What is in his breast will out. He must revoke his false promise—to flatter his way to the consulship and sooth or soothe his way out of trouble—and reclaim his heart's integrity.

So instead of addressing the charges levelled by the Tribunes against him, Coriolanus challenges the 'shame and dishonour' (in Kishlansky's phrase) that the disavowal of the 'vouches' has brought upon him:

CORIOLANUS What is the matter
That, being passed for consul with full voice,
I am so dishonoured that the very hour
You take it off again? (3.3.60–3)

As he works himself into a rage, provoked (as he will be in Antium) by the charge of being 'a traitor', Menenius has to remind him, 'Nay, temperately—your promise' (70). The rebuke is not enough. What affronts him in the Tribune is what he is forced to recognize in himself—a lying tongue—and he vehemently repudiates it:

> Within thine eyes sat twenty thousand deaths,
> In thy hands clutched as many millions, in
> Thy lying *tongue* both numbers, I would say
> 'Thou liest' unto thee with a voice as free
> As I do pray the gods. (73–7)

Even Brutus' concession, when he reduced his sentence from death to banishment, stirs him to outrage:

BRUTUS But since he hath
Served well for Rome—
CORIOLANUS What do you prate of service?
BRUTUS I talk of that that know it.
CORIOLANUS You?
MENENIUS Is this the promise that you made your mother? (87–90)

The rebuke is now humiliating, laughable, stifling. It is not just that a big strong warrior is shown up as deferring to his mother, but that, in the moment of being defiantly true to himself, Coriolanus becomes yet again what he hates, a promise-breaker. There has to be a world elsewhere. Yet why should prating of service offend him?

* * *

When he comes to Aufidius' house, Coriolanus hopes to turn sworn hostility into a bond of friendship. 'O world, thy slippery turns!', he declares: 'Friends now fast sworn... break out | To bitterest enmity. So, fellest foes... shall grow dear friends' (4.4.12–21). Reflecting, it may be, that, by going over to the Volscians, he will break his vows of friendship with Cominius, he clearly has it in mind that Aufidius will become an enemy-friend. Theirs is a volatile, dangerous intimacy, one that, when it becomes political, will put Coriolanus at a disadvantage. As Derrida suggests in *The Politics of Friendship*, 'the political... endlessly *binds* or *opposes* the friend-enemy/enemy-friend couple in the drive or decision of death'.[56] 'I'll enter', Coriolanus resolves; 'If he slay me, | He does fair justice; if he give me way, | I'll do his country service' (24–6). Strikingly, Aufidius' servants now come on stage, as they respond to a call for wine ('What service is here?' (4.5.1)). Coriolanus tells his rival that he has been banished despite 'painful service', and twice offers him 'revengeful services'.[57]

The word 'service' and its cognates are surprisingly plentiful in the play. Coriolanus aspires to military 'service',[58] one which allows him to reward his deeds in their doing and be the people's 'servant in my way' (2.1.189). Yet service of any sort, especially the mercenary service he offers to the Volscians, cannot easily shake off dependence. Think of the Earl of Essex, abjectly writing to Elizabeth on his departure for Ireland: 'From a mind delighting in sorrow, ... what service can your Majesty reap? Since my services past deserve no more than banishment and proscription...?'[59] Most servants were not generals, but menials, hired for pay; this is why Martius, the 'noble servant' of Rome (4.7.36), so vehemently resists staging himself in the market-place, like a cast servingman looking for a job. He does not want to be reduced to the status of Aufidius' men: nameless, bound by indenture or oral agreement (like the minor actors who played their parts in Shakespeare's company) but also by fidelity. At all levels, the bonds of service[60] were held to involve that '*Faithfulnesse*... whereby seruants doe well discharge that trust which is committed to them', in the words of William Gouge: 'Expresly it is commanded to seruants, *To shew all good faithfulnesse.*'[61]

Plutarch only refers to promising once in relation to Coriolanus, and it comes at this point: 'let my miserie serue thy turne, and so vse, as my seruice maye be a benefit to the Volsces: promising thee, that I will fight with better good will for all you, than eyer I dyd when I was against you' (250). When Nahum Tate adapted the play, in 1682, he heightened the offer of service, by adding 'this I avow'.[62] Shakespeare could have had Coriolanus utter here the 'oath and resolution' which Aufidius later accuses him of breaking. He kept the crucial oaths in *Coriolanus* offstage, however, not just to avoid the stiltedness of set-piece 'By Jove' moments, but to feed them into the action in reported, incomplete forms, merging into the wider 'commitment and praxis of men' (Agamben). By leaving inexplicit the 'oath and resolution' mentioned by Aufidius, Shakespeare allows it to be inferred through Martius' misgivings about being forsworn. The focus is on his struggle to keep his faith, once compromises become necessary.

Cominius' description of Coriolanus throned in gold, refusing to withdraw Volscian forces from the gates of Rome (5.1.63–7), grips the imagination. Because we are less alert than a Jacobean audience would have been to the role of oaths and binding rituals in securing leagues and treaties—adjuncts of faith that loom large in Plutarch and Livy[63]—we give less attention than we should to what follows:

> What he would do
> He sent in writing after me, what he would not,
> Bound with an oath to hold to his conditions. (67–9)

'Hold' is the emendation understandably adopted by the Norton Shakespeare, yet there is much to recommend the Folio's 'yeeld'. In Jacobean English, *yield* could mean 'comply'[64] as well as giving in. If Martius yields to his own conditions (i.e. sticks to, complies with them), he opens a window to giving in. Even before Volumnia's deputation arrives, he undoes his meanings through a mixture of dividedness and faith. We have heard a messenger telling the Tribunes 'that Martius, | Joined with Aufidius, leads a power 'gainst Rome, | And vows revenge' (4.6.67–9). If so, to allow 'conditions' means that holding is already a yielding.

When Menenius comes on his embassy, the sentinels send him 'back to Rome', saying 'You are condemned, our general has sworn you out of reprieve and pardon' (5.2.47–9). Whether this is the old, reported vow of revenge, or a hardening of Coriolanus' position once the holding/yielding conditions sent after Cominius are not accepted, scarcely matters. What is striking, again, is the mixture of obduracy with conditionality when Coriolanus tells Aufidius that he has 'once more offered | The first conditions' to Menenius,

> which they did refuse
> And cannot now accept, to grace him only
> That thought he could do more. A very little
> I have yielded to. (5.3.13–17)

Is yielding in the air? Shakespeare does not tell us what the indulgently re-issued first, or the possibly enhanced, conditions were. It is from Plutarch, and the later adaptations of *Coriolanus* by John Dennis and Thomas Sheridan, that we learn about the Volscian demand to have lands seized by Rome returned to them.[65] The omission does not so much make it harder for an audience to measure the extent of Coriolanus' flexibility as throw the weight of that judgement on what we see of his reactions to the delegations from Rome, how forsworn he admits himself to be, and what Aufidius, looking on, makes of this.

Coriolanus tries to discipline his yielding with oaths and vows. He now swears not in support of a promise but, more unusually and defensively, to avoid becoming a promise-breaker. Assuring Aufidius of his faith—that he remains, as he tells Menenius, 'servanted to' the Volscians (5.2.79)—he declares:

Fresh embassies and suits,
Nor from the state nor private friends, hereafter
Will I lend ear to.
Shout within
Ha, what shout is this?
Shall I be tempted to infringe my vow
In the same time 'tis made? I will not.
Enter VIRGILIA, VOLUMNIA, VALERIA, YOUNG MARTIUS,
with attendants (5.3.17–21)

It would indeed be awkward to be tempted, but no audience will be surprised that he is. He has already said that he knows neither wife, mother, nor son, when Menenius had not mentioned them (5.2.78). This is an approach that he has, we realize, been dreading. The absoluteness of the vow is itself disabling. To lend an ear to wife and mother, which it is almost impossible to avoid, is to break his vow, not to mention the promissory addition, 'I will not'. And further concessions beckon:

But out, affection!
All bond and privilege of nature break;
Let it be virtuous to be obstinate.
[VIRGILIA *curtsies*]
What is that curtsy worth? Or those dove's eyes
Which can make gods forsworn? (5.3.24–8)

If even the gods would be forsworn, would not he? It has to be easier to 'break' a verbal bond than those of nature.

What bonds, what privileges? As we noted near the start of this book (p. 14), Cicero influentially argued that the bond of society (*coniunctio*) is secured, in the first instance, by 'the felouship of al mankinde. The bonde wherof is reason, and speeche' ('Eius autem vinculum est ratio et oratio').[66] Such bonds, he added, develop most intensely within the family, then reach out to Rome and its institutions. Of the bond (*colligatio*) between kindred, the first (*coniugium*) is between spouses, the next between parents and children, the next within the household—'And this is ye original of a citie and as it were the seedplotte of a commonweale.'[67] The Latin used by Cicero meshes natural and social bonds with the ties made by binding language. *Vinculum* can mean 'oath', while *colligatio* contains a ligat-ure, as in *obligatio* ('contract, agreement'). English has its own mesh of usage (though Grimald uses *bound* and *bond* to translate these Latin words), and Shakespeare's audience would have been familiar with *bond* used of oaths, kinship, duty, friendship, service, and so on. Looking through books written around the time of *Coriolanus*, one finds, for instance, this denunciation of the Jesuits: 'their crie is, *dirumpamus vincula, proijciamus funes let vs breake their bonds, and cast away their cordes:* Noe bond of nature, consanguinitie, allegiance, alliance, affiance, wedlock, oath, sacrament standeth good, if they list to dissolue it.'[68]

Hence the huge tensions, between natural, social and verbal bonds, as mother kneels to son:

CORIOLANUS I beseech you, peace.
Or if you'd ask, remember this before:
The thing I have forsworn to grant may never
Be held by you denials. Do not bid me
Dismiss my soldiers, or capitulate
Again with Rome's mechanics. Tell me not
Wherein I seem unnatural. Desire not t'allay
My rages and revenges with your colder reasons. (5.3.79–86)

Do not bid or desire this, he urges, because—the banked-up negative imperatives concede—if you do, I shall weaken. The 'thing' that Volumnia wants, he has sworn against giving, so she and her deputation should not take as denials his denying it.[69] Yet 'forsworn to grant' edges beyond 'for-' as rejection or breaking off[70] into 'fore-, previously', making what was sworn-against already sworn and grantable. There is an implicit, dense prolepsis: 'I would be forsworn if I granted what you want so it cannot be.' Yet bringing it into view makes it likely.

For although nature plays its part, Shakespeare makes Volumnia—as others in the period thought her—politic and persuasive.[71] She commands the stage as she reminds her son that his wife and mother are *also* in a double bind:

Alas, how can we for our country pray,
Whereto we are bound, together with thy victory,
Whereto we are bound? (5.3.108–10)

This allows her to insinuate what she will later, potently, argue, that despite his commanding position, the outcome of war is 'uncertain' (142), and that, in his case, neither victory nor defeat can be good. He might 'as a foreign recreant be led | With manacles through our streets', or 'Triumphantly tread on thy country's ruin' (115–17). Why not be faithful to 'The Volscians whom you serve' (135), but save Rome, by agreeing a lasting peace? Anyway, he owes her everything: 'There's no man in the world | More bound to's mother' (159–60). After a hundred or so lines of this, the pressures are too great, and he '*holds her by the hand, silent*'.

It is an intense dramatic moment, but not an operatic one. There is no excuse for the theatrical habit of milking the silence, which turns the gesture into an end in itself. What makes it eloquent is its place in the argument of the play, which frames the gesture as one of natural affinity and need but also of agreement. Taking the hand, as we have seen, was an emblem of *fides*. Plutarch describes Coriolanus 'holding her hard by the right hande' (the Greek is 'tēn dexian piesas sphodra', 'pressing her right hand warmly'), which makes this even clearer, because the right hand was used by the Romans to seal their faiths.[72] A Jacobean audience would pick up awkward overtones, both classical and early modern, of mother–son marriage, a misplaced handfast.[73] As when he took the hand of Aufidius, however, in Act 4 (5.146), Martius is entering into an accord[74]—inappropriately, for Plutarch, because not with the official representatives of Rome[75]—that will be cemented when he drinks pledges with his family, at the end of the sequence, and sends them to the city with 'A better witness back than words'—a written treaty—'which we | On like conditions will have counter-sealed' (205–6).

In any case, the striking thing is not the gesture, nor even the lines of foreboding that follow it ('But let it come'), but the new note of pragmatism that Coriolanus finds in himself:

Aufidius, though I cannot make true wars,
I'll frame convenient peace. Now, good Aufidius,
Were you in my stead, would you have heard
A mother less, or granted less, Aufidius?
AUFIDIUS I was moved withal.
CORIOLANUS I dare be sworn you were. (191–5)

If he can no longer be true—in his wars, to his 'oath and resolution'—he must do what is *convenient*. It is impossible to think of Martius saying this in Acts 1–3, but he has to remake himself now around the uncertainty of war and the conditions that make for peace. Not that his dilemma is unprecedented. *De Officiis* grapples with the problem of how to reconcile the *utile* with the *honestum*; for Cicero, in a celebrated paradox, what is 'convenient' or 'expedient' (in Grimald's translation) can never be truly *utilis* unless it is honourable, virtuous, just.[76] The tragedy for Coriolanus is not simply that he is dragged by conflicting bonds into dealing with the expedient, but that the compromises he has to make—which show him to have larger capacities than he could access in the contentious, mother-dominated world of Rome—also carry him onto ground where the politic Aufidius is master. It is a bleak irony for the audience, which has seen Aufidius confiding that he will use what he knows about Coriolanus' management of the wars to bring him down, that he now seeks his rival's advice on the terms of peace—terms that can be used against him. Even as he does so, he senses Aufidius' distance, appeals to him by name thrice, and has to invoke his own faith immediately after breaking his word: 'I dare be sworn . . .' Can that be taken seriously now?

* * *

Why does Martius continue: 'I'll not to Rome; I'll back with you' (199)? Because he does not anticipate, what the audience will see in the next scene, the willingness of the Romans to unbanish him? Because he wants to mark his decision to spare the city as a concession to his family, not Rome? Because he returns, not so much *to* Antium as *with* Aufidius, loyal to an enemy-friend? All these motives circulate the more freely because of Shakespeare's decision not to give Coriolanus a late soliloquy. They are subsidiary, however, to the matter of *fides*, a matter that was clearer to the play's seventeenth- and eighteenth-century adapters than it is to modern audiences. In Tate, Coriolanus returns to Antium to 'have my Services approv'd'; in Sheridan, where Shakespeare's dialogue is intercut with material from James Thomson's *Coriolanus* (1749), it is to secure 'acquittal' from the Volscians.[77]

As for Shakespeare, in his adaptation of Plutarch he was also patently influenced by the models of Roman fidelity applauded in *De Officiis*. Immediately after quoting Euripides' *Hippolytus*, Cicero praises Regulus, who returned to the enemy city of Carthage because he was bound by an oath to do so even though he knew he was in jeopardy (he was tortured and killed): 'But it was not fitte for Regulus with periurie to disturbe the conditions, and couenaunts with his enemies, and of warre. For with a iust, and lawfull enemie the thing was done.'[78] Coriolanus returns to Antium to keep his covenants and to persuade the Volscians of the merits of the conditions that he has won from Rome. He is in this sense following through what his mother urged as better than victory, and what Plutarch criticizes him for endangering, the possibility of securing a durable peace. Cicero notes that Regulus could have stayed in his native land with his wife and children, enjoying the rank and dignity of an ex-consul.[79] Substitute gone home for stayed at home, and this is Coriolanus. Regulus was right to keep his word, Cicero says, because 'Whoso...stayneth his othe, he stayneth Ladie Faith: whom, as it appeares in Catoes oration, our auncetours would needs haue to stand in our Capitole, next vnto that great, and mightie Ioue.'[80]

We are back with the concept of *fides* that is as central to *Coriolanus* as it is absent from Plutarch's *Life*; yet quoting Cicero throws into relief how far Shakespeare's play is from inertly dramatizing Roman values. He focuses on difficulties and transformations: that keeping your *fides* can be socially isolating, rather than, as Cicero assumes, constitutive of a good commonwealth; that clinging to an 'oath and resolution', even one sworn from the heart, might not be just, since faith has to be kept with allies and enemies but also with wife, children, and (most importantly for Cicero) parents and native land;[81] that dealing with incompatible commitments can be the test of virtue and growth. The paradoxes run deep, as Coriolanus goes to Antium to keep an oath that he has broken. Evidently his courageous fear about what will be done to him makes return the better substitute for fully keeping his oath. He will face danger from the Volscians to be as true as he can.

Shakespeare continues to write the lives of Coriolanus and Aufidius in parallel. In 1.11, despising the conditions on which Corioles, as part of a treaty, could be returned ('What good condition can a treaty find | I'th' part that is at mercy?' (6–7)), Aufidius had wished he were a Roman, then later cursed the Volscians for their cowardice, and abandoned Corioles for Antium,[82] all actions shadowing events in the life of Coriolanus. Now he moves against his fellow general, who has bettered him in the eyes of the Volscians, but who also, from a politic, patriotic point of view, should not be trusted. 'Therefore should it be considerd', warned Machiavelli in his *Discourses*, 'how vaine their words and promises are, who are banished their Countries.'[83] Both men prepare documents to present to the Volscian Lords. Coriolanus' is the treaty sent to Rome, and sealed. But Aufidius gets his paper in first, asking his co-conspirators to bid the Volscian Lords

repair to th' market-place, where I,
Even in theirs and in the commons' ears,
Will vouch the truth of it. (5.6.3–5)

Aufidius we might expect to be a creature of the market-place. But Coriolanus also 'Intends t'appear before the people'. He wants to 'purge' himself, Aufidius to perjure himself (for his 'vouch' is as unreliable as that of the Roman plebeians). Aufidius unsparingly uses Martius' noble compromises to discredit his *fides*, complaining to the conspirators, 'I pawned | Mine honour for his truth' (7–8, 20–1).

Shakespeare's Coriolanus never shows himself to be, as he is in Livy, 'right politicke of advise',[84] but conflicting obligations do bend him into arguing for an honest, utile peace. Aufidius tells the Lords that Martius has denied them spoils, and made a treaty 'where | There was a yielding' (5.6.68–9). Coriolanus, however, makes his case judiciously, starting from the triumphal entry with which this chapter began:

Enter CORIOLANUS *marching with drum and colors, the Commoners being with him*

CORIOLANUS Hail, lords! I am returned your soldier,
No more infected with my country's love
Than when I parted hence, but still subsisting
Under your great command. You are to know
That prosperously I have attempted, and
With bloody passage led your wars even to
The gates of Rome. Our spoils we have brought home
Doth more than counterpoise a full third part
The charges of the action. We have made peace
With no less honour to the Antiates
Than shame to th' Romans. And we here deliver,
Subscribed by th' consuls and patricians,
Together with the seal o'th' senate, what
We have compounded on. (5.6.71–84)

This is one of the most remarkable, unexpected speeches in the play. Reassuring and deferring to the patricians, Coriolanus also brings the people with him. 'With bloody passage led your wars even to | The gates of Rome' is wisely put. The gates sound like a worthy objective; 'even' brings out the valour needed to fight with that degree of fidelity. Have the Lords got their money back? The question is not raised in Plutarch or Livy, and the Coriolanus we see in Rome would not have deigned to introduce it. The compression of the late style is momentarily unhelpful, but, whether the Lords have recovered a third of their costs or (more likely) enjoyed a profit of a third over their outlay,[85] the return is not great. Tate changed this to 'our Spoils brought home, | Ten time o're pay the Charges of the Action'.[86] What the revision loses is the evidence that Coriolanus is doing his expedient best to sell an imperfect victory, to show that despite everything he has been faithful.

Above all, he has secured a treaty sealed with *fides*. 'Compound' means 'agree, contract', usually with some substitution or softening of terms. So there has been a compromise. Nor are treaties unbreakable.[87] But he has not, he can believe, betrayed the Volscians' business, or given up Rome for certain drops of salt. He has got them the best terms by making the enemy sue ('What good condition can a treaty find | I'th' part that is at mercy?');[88] and because war is uncertain there was no assurance of conquest. As the audience saw, from the rejection of the terms sent after Cominius, Rome was not minded to surrender. It is possible that the city, explicitly defiant in Plutarch,[89] would have repelled his attack. In Brecht's adaptation of Shakespeare, the mobilization of the plebeians, and their manufacture of weapons, tips Coriolanus into withdrawing. But we need not look so far. Machiavelli, in his *Discourses*, rebutted Livy's claim that the Volscians' success under Coriolanus shows that good generalship is crucial for victory. Roman forces, he notes, could look after themselves without a Martius: 'wee see, in many places of his History, that Souldiers without any Captaine have given extraordinary proofes of their valours.'[90]

So this is a classical play, but not a neoclassical one. It does not centre on a Herculean hero who is unbending until he breaks. Nor does it, as Fish contends, so rigorously plot the consequences of 'the execution and mis-execution of illocutionary acts' that it is 'questionable whether or not it is a true tragedy or even, in the usual sense, a drama'.[91] Exploring the tragic potential of *fides*, it stages a protagonist torn apart because he breaks his word but also because he keeps it. By the same token, it deals in perfidy, and that brings intrigue and contingency. Coriolanus and Aufidius play for high stakes, but until the final moments there is still the possibility of escape. Livy presents alternative endings, with Martius either murdered or, as Fabius reports, living into old age, unhappy in his banishment. It is not inevitable that Coriolanus will be provoked—that requires Aufidius' skilful perfidy—or that the Lords will fail to calm the people or stop the conspirators killing him. Yet when Aufidius denies Martius the truth of his 'stol'n name' and his 'oath', robbing him of the 'certainty' (to recall Agamben) that names and oaths appear to provide, 'true tragedy' builds a momentum. Looking for security, Martius reverts to defiance ('I | Fluttered your Volscians in Corioles') and, once again brought down by an attempt to follow his mother's advice—to explain himself to the people, as in Rome—pitches into destruction.

17
Oath and Counsel
Cymbeline and *The Winter's Tale*

A young man hides behind an arras. Looking into the hall—as he might look onto a stage, from a curtained discovery space—he sees his beloved Luscinda, bound to him by 'a thousand oathes and promises', entering in her finery to be contracted to Don Ferdinando, as her father requires. He knows that she has a dagger, and he himself is armed; violence looks only too likely. 'The Curate of the Parish entred, and taking them both by the hand, to doe that which in such an act is required', said: '*Will you Ladie* Luscinda *take the Lord* Don Ferdinando *who is heere present for your lawfull spouse, according as our holy mother the Church commands?*' Though he wants to rush out and cry '*Luscinda* is my spouse, and I am her husband', the youth restrains himself:

> The Curate stood expecting *Luscindaes* answere a good while erre she gaue it, and in the end, when I hoped that she would take out the Poynard to stab her selfe, or would vnloose her tongue to say some truth, or vse some reason or perswasion that might redound to my benefit, I heard heere in stead thereof answere with a dismaied and languishing voice the word: *I will*: and then *Don Fernando* said the same, and giuing her the ring, they remained tyed with an indissoluble knot. Then the bridegroome comming to kisse his spouse, she set her hand vpon her heart, and fell in a trance betweene her mothers armes.

The youth's reaction is extreme: 'I rested void of counsell, ... burned throughly with rage and iealousie.' This torment does, however, keep him on the spot long enough to notice an important clue. As her mother unclasps Luscinda's bosom, 'there appeared in it a paper foulded vp, which *Don Fernando* presently seazed on, and went aside to reade ... with manifest signes of melancholy discontent'. At which point, the youth leaves the scene, without taking 'reuenge' on the couple, but unfortunately not staying to discover that the letter explains why Luscinda, already espoused in her heart, has resolved to take her own life.

This is the story of Cardenio, as told by himself, in Cervantes' *Don Quixote*.[1] When Quixote first encounters the youth he is running wild in the mountains, still jealous and vindictive. What he saw and now relates was not a full marriage by the rules of Counter-Reformation Europe but a *de futuro* spousal. Nor does it come with Luscinda's consent, though her '*I will*' gives a clear-enough agreement to perplex any canon lawyers reading the romance. Even so, Cardenio's jealousy is understandable. It is not until a second strand in the Don Ferdinand story, involving his seduction of a lower-status woman called Dorotea, is unpacked, in the pages that follow Cardenio's narrative, that the contents of Luscinda's paper will be disclosed, confirming her commitment to her 'thousand oathes and promises'.

Though we cannot know precisely how Shakespeare and Fletcher dramatized this sequence in the lost play *Cardenio*—as Lewis Theobald would later dramatize it, with variations, in the *Double Falsehood* (1727)[2]—it is not hard to see what drew Shakespeare to the story. *Cardenio* belongs to a group of late plays about jealousy, mis-seeing, the ambiguities of betrothal and marriage, misconstrued tokens of faith (ring, bracelet, hand-holding, letters), and, in varying degrees, counsel: *Cymbeline*, probably written in the summer or early autumn of 1610, *The Winter's Tale* (late 1610), and *Cardenio* (*c.*1613). All three stage, or must have staged, situations in which a man betrothed or married is presented with the spectacle of his partner slipping with awful tactility into what looks like another involvement. In *Cymbeline* the dramaturgy is both more attenuated and more conventional, since the jealousy of Posthumus is roused by Iachimo's false—yet almost true—report of his intimacy with Imogen in her bedchamber. In *The Winter's Tale*, we are thrillingly close to how jealousy infects the eye and feeds back into the mind. For Leontes, fixated on Hermione paddling palms with Polixenes, seeing is believing, except that what he believes he sees—as he will do again, more benignly, when his wife's statue comes to life.

This is where counsel comes in, modestly in *Cymbeline*, more substantially in *The Winter's Tale*, to throw into relief the problems of authority and perception. Cardenio was 'void of counsell' when he misconstrued Luscinda's '*I will*'. He had no external wisdom to temper his misjudgement. By the time Don Quixote, Sancho Panza, and the Curate find him, he is beyond advice. 'Doe not in vaine labour to perswade or counsel me,' he cries. Nevertheless, as Part III of the romance breaks off, 'the Curate was bethinking himselfe of some comfortable reasons to answer and perswade him' (279). To give counsel is the responsibility of a priest, as it is of an appointed (or self-appointed) courtier. In *Cymbeline*, counsel comes from the loyal, mature figure of Philario, but also the wicked Queen. When Shakespeare adapted Greene's *Pandosto*, in *The Winter's Tale*, he added three major figures: Autolycus, the vagabond emperor of lies, but also Camillo and Paulina, who are exemplars of honest counsel.

The importance of counsel in these plays has scarcely been noticed,[3] even though, as a topic, it goes back to (at least) Polonius in *Hamlet* and Kent in *King Lear*. This neglect is the stranger given that counsel figured so prominently in humanist political discourse—European-wide in its reach—and gained new urgency in Jacobean England as the king showed an unfortunate tendency to favour advisers brought down from Scotland, or young, glamorous favourites from Robert Carr to George Villiers, rather than the elders recommended by the treatises.[4] Entirely overlooked by critics is the further question of how counsel relates to binding language, both in early modern political theory and in Shakespeare's late romances. With counsel is meant to come honesty, truth, trust, and certainty, a set of attributes that are not just homologous with oaths and vows but expressible through them. Above all, with both come *fides*, fidelity, faithfulness, and in more religious terms *faith*. That the late plays—including *Henry VIII*—are caught up with matters of faith should not be news to anyone. Imogen, for half of *Cymbeline*, is disguised as a boy called Fidele. What deserves to be brought out is the connection between faith, counsel, and the oaths, vows, and covenants that are pivotal as well as accentual in *Cymbeline* and *The Winter's Tale*, as they must have been in *Cardenio*, even though their expression is deflected and reinvented as a result of the Act to Restrain Abuses which made blasphemous onstage oaths a fineable offence after 1606 (see pp. 8–9).

⋆ ⋆ ⋆

Let us start with the exchange that precipitates the main action of *The Winter's Tale*. Making an appeal to verity which turns out to be untrue, Polixenes has told Leontes that he will leave Sicily and return to Bohemia, 'Very sooth, tomorrow'. Called upon to make him stay by Leontes, in what proves to be a trial of her fidelity, Hermione says that she has been waiting for oaths to do their work: 'I had thought, sir, to have held my peace until | You had drawn oaths from him not to stay.' Warming to her task, she makes a distinction between saying and swearing which is not unknown in early

Shakespeare—as when Juliet asks Romeo to say rather than swear his love, because lovers' oaths and vows are so notoriously unreliable[5]—but which here seems loaded with the legacy of the Act because, on the contrary, it attributes an unspeakable potency to swearing. It is the first of several such say/swear manoeuvres in the play:

> To tell he longs to see his son were strong.
> But let him say so then, and let him go.
> But let him swear so and he shall not stay,
> We'll thwack him hence with distaffs. (1.2.17, 28–9, 34–7)

In another context, the audience might brood on 'longs to see his son'. Does Polixenes not have a queen? Apparently he does (1.2.78–84), though she is never so live a presence as to deflect Leontes' jealousy. What the lines chiefly signal, however, is a careful, warily quibbling relationship with oaths. This Hermione develops, exploiting the fact that, at this date, only asseveration or the mildest oath is permissible on stage. 'I may not, verily', replies Polixenes. 'Verily?', pounces Hermione, 'You put me off with limber vows' (46–8).[6] Taking advantage of the limitation set by the Act, she evens out the inequality which, across most of Jacobean society, allowed men to swear more potently than women. Polixenes must now draw his sooths from the same lady-like box as Hotspur's Kate (pp. 26–7). 'But I,' the queen playfully goes on,

> Though you would seek t'unsphere the stars with oaths,
> Should yet say 'Sir, no going.' Verily
> You shall not go. A lady's 'verily' 's
> As potent as a lord's. (48–52)

So will you be our guest or our prisoner? 'By your dread "verily", | One of them you shall be' (56–7). A gender imbalance remains. In the subtleties of Hermione's speech around these sensitive locutions, she still signals her modesty. She does not even propose 'verily', but picks it up from Polixenes[7] and echoes it back teasingly as both 'your' and 'dread'. In the event, he agrees to stay. The King of Bohemia's 'sooth' and 'verily', two of the commonest binding words in the play,[8] prove to be too fragile to resist even gentle urging.

Polixenes' pliability adds to Leontes' suspicion, but there are more powerful pressures at work, which are also vow-related. There has been much speculation about the sudden outbreak of the king's jealousy, with critics arguing that he fears losing Polixenes to Hermione, rather than the other way round,[9] or that he fears to be a father, so the crisis somehow turns on Mamillius.[10]

What the play shows and tells the audience is that it has to do—circularly, to a pitch of destruction—with his marriage, and thus with betrothal practices. In the early modern period, binding rituals evolve with happy or dangerous ease out of such everyday, friendly gestures as giving a hat or handkerchief or pledging with a cup of wine. People were vigilant about the potential for commitment in such exchanges, but sometimes not vigilant enough to avoid claims that came to the ecclesiastical courts. Polixenes and Hermione might think themselves free of the risk of any such misconstruction, given the queen's long marriage and pregnancy, but they are not.

As Leontes closely observes Polixenes and his wife, he splits Hermione between the woman who once gave him her hand and her word with delaying modesty (or was it, he now wonders, reluctance?) and the sexy immediacy of the onstage hand-clasp:

HERMIONE What, have I twice said well?...
LEONTES Why, that was when
Three crabbèd months had soured themselves to death
Ere I could make thee open thy white hand
And clap thyself my love. Then didst thou utter,
'I am yours for ever.'
HERMIONE 'Tis grace indeed.
Why lo you now; I have spoke to th' purpose twice.
The one for ever earned a royal husband;
Th'other, for some while a friend.
[*She gives her hand to* POLIXENES.
They stand aside]
LEONTES Too hot, too hot:
To mingle friendship far is mingling bloods....
But to be paddling palms and pinching fingers,
As now they are,... (92–118)

It is not just the excluding, physical contact which tips Leontes into derangement, nor the suggestive ambiguity of 'friend',[11] but the implication that Hermione's espousal, her handfast, is being reprised, one vow overlaying another. Leontes sees his 'contracting... re-enacted', as Anne Barton puts it, 'his own role in it usurped by Polixenes'.[12] It is the same dilemma as Cardenio's, at the spousal of Luscinda and Don Ferdinand, with 'rage and iealousie' again the result.

Gentlemen, noblemen, and princes were believed to have '*perceptual competence*'.[13] This was a major reason why they were supposed to be better qualified than the vulgar to be truth-tellers. Though not explicitly presented as a counter-example to this orthodoxy, Leontes is clearly accustomed to assuming the authority that goes with his status, and in the case of Hermione and Polixenes he believes more than there is to see. One of the paradoxes on which his role turns, however, is that, precisely *because* of his status, he is liable to misjudge. After the shocking death of Mamillius, he gives up his accusation of Hermione and says, 'I have too much believed mine own suspicion' (3.2.149). The tone is self-exculpatory, but it does reflect what contemporaries might say about his jealousy, which is that kings are predisposed, and understandably, to suspicion.

Cornwallis catches this pithily in his *Essayes* (1601–2). In 'Of Suspicion' he might have Leontes and Polixenes in mind:

> Suspition cannot detract from acted Aduise which is example. What this humour doeth vndirected, it vndoeth: what directed ful of preseruation. Suspition will accuse a friend, and fearing enemies, make an enemy: Wisedome knowes Trust ought heere to be applied, and makes Suspition iealous of loosing him, not loosing him by Suspition: . . . Suspition out of smiles, and courtesies, can picke dangers, and Distrust venome out of sugar: but thus if not gouerned she wil go too farre, and starue her selfe with suspecting all thinges daungerous: but Wisedome applies it selfe to the place, and time, and out of them frames the allowance, or disallowance of Suspition.[14]

Unless managed by advice, wisdom, and trust, suspicion is highly dangerous, but, Cornwallis adds, it is incident to princes:

> it seldome lights vpon things not precious in estimation, as among poore men iealouse of their wiues: but no where so conuersant and powerful, as among Princes, vnto whom to say rightly, it rightly belongs: for how soeuer they are, they haue enemies: If good, enuious: If euil, some that lay holde vpon that occasion: Yea, euen their friends are doubtfull, not beeing easily to bee discerned whether louers of them, or of their fortunes. (D5r–v)

The point is not that Shakespeare might have read Cornwallis, though that is likely enough, but that these are commonplaces. Hence the account of the Leontes-figure at the start of *Pandosto*. Jealousy, Greene writes, is 'sawsed with suspitious doubtes, and pinching mistrust, . . . Yea, who so is payned with this restlesse torment doubteth all, dystrusteth him-selfe, is alwayes frosen with feare, and fired with suspition.'[15] To distrust yourself is to lack a secure relationship with your faculties, not to distrust your own distrust and keep suspicion at bay. What a suspicious prince needs (to repeat what was often repeated) is advice, wisdom, and trust—the characteristics of good counsel. As Cornwallis writes in his essay 'Of Advice': 'if the safest purchase of goodnesse bee counsayle, if counsaile without scarres be most profitable, why eschew wee the blessing of Aduise?...I see nothing more decay the fairest braunches of our Commonwealth, then this neglect' (C1v–2r). Advice he regards as personal, counsel is more public and offered to the state.[16] This is a track that *The Winter's Tale* follows, from the initial probing of what Camillo saw, to the near-sworn asseveration of Leontes' counsellors that his jealousy is misplaced.

Camillo's advice to the king is grounded in perceptual competence. When asked, he gives a blow-by-blow account of the sequence that educed Leontes' jealousy. He has seen and processed it all, particularly anything that might redound to the discredit of his master ('He would not stay at your petitions, made | His business more material' (1.2.215–16)). What he has not seen is any evidence of impropriety. Leontes however continues madly to overreact, finding confirmation of his suspicion in the merest ambiguity in Camillo's words ('satisfy'), then denying his ability to advise:

I have trusted thee, Camillo,
With all the near'st things to my heart, as well
My chamber-counsels, wherein, priest-like, thou
Hast cleansed my bosom, I from thee departed
Thy penitent reformed. But we have been
Deceived in thy integrity, deceived
In that which seems so.
CAMILLO Be it forbid, my lord.
LEONTES To bide upon't: thou art not honest;... (237–44)

Leontes' rebuke incidentally lets an audience know the extent to which Camillo has been trusted. He has advised on personal matters, been a counsellor in the bedchamber, a privy counsellor in the most literal sense, as well as the sort of counsellor of state that we later see him to be. He has exemplified what Bacon sets out in his essay 'Of Counsell':

> The greatest Trust, betweene Man and Man, is the Trust of *Giuing Counsell.* For in other Confidences, Men commit the parts of life;...But to such, as they make their *Counsellours,* they commit the whole: By how much the more, they are obliged to all Faith and integrity. The wisest Princes, need not thinke it any diminution to their Greatnesse, or derogation to their Sufficiency, to rely vpon *Counsell.*[17]

The primary meaning of 'Confidences'—though it might also imply things said in secret—is 'firm trust, reliance, faith',[18] from the *fides* in *confidentia.* This is why Bacon writes of 'all faith and integrity'. There is something almost religious in the role of such a counsellor. Camillo has 'cleansed' the king's 'bosom, I from thee departed | Thy penitent reformed'. Like the Curate who prepares to counsel Cardenio, and more extensively like Paulina in the last act of *The Winter's Tale*, acting as counsellor and spiritual guide to the assiduously penitent king (5.1.1–6), Camillo's conduct is 'priest-like'. His advice resembles the ghostly counsel given by Protestant ministers to remorseful sinners, or the prayers of Catholic priests in the sacrament of confession.

Contrary to Bacon's advice in what he came to call his *Counsels*,[19] Leontes overrules Camillo. Insisting that his wife 'deserves a name | As rank as any flax-wench that puts to | Before her troth-plight' (278–80), he whirls into paranoia, where the nothing that breeds the fantasy consumes a world of value and distinction:

> Is whispering nothing?
> Is leaning cheek to cheek? Is meeting noses?
> Kissing with inside lip?...
> Why then the world and all that's in't is nothing,
> The covering sky is nothing, Bohemia nothing,
> My wife is nothing, nor nothing have these nothings
> If this be nothing. (286–98)

Cordelia's insistent 'Nothings' obstructed the delusions of the love-trial. Leontes' more dynamic 'nothings'—obsessive, emphatic, epistrophic—turn everything inside out and become the engine of chaos. The irregular, driven syntax, shifting from abrupt, rhetorical questions to sweeping declarations, which make the world and sky witness as in an oath by Othello yet empty them of substance by making them not-nothings, leads straight into the vortex of 'if'. This could be an oath if we took it to be a curse that all the everythings in Leontes' life would be nothings if Hermione were not false, as they are now that he believes she is.

What is astonishing is not just the rapidity with which the nihilism gobbles up even what is said—into empty repetition—but the sudden shift in pace as Camillo and Leontes rebut each other. It is what should never happen between a counsellor and his king, a childish giving of the lie which in other contexts would lead to a fight:

> CAMILLO No, no, my lord.
> LEONTES It is. You lie, you lie.
> I say thou liest, Camillo, and I hate thee,... (301–2)

Language cannot secure what the characters want to have fixed. Both are looking to have the last word, the word that is final. In one of Shakespeare's early plays they would have sworn what Hebrews 6: 16 calls 'an othe for confirmation... an end of all strife', a speech act that claims to be irrefutable. We are far beyond, at this point, the nuts and bolts of the Act to Restrain Abuses, but the changed theatrical climate does work strongly on Shakespeare's imagination, and on how it is possible to insist. In a peculiarly post-1606 way, Camillo and Leontes are reduced to yea and nay (see p. 12).

Camillo does what he can, which is to temporize. By accepting the king's belief, he is able to exert some leverage. Leontes consequently agrees to follow his counsellor's advice, that is, to restore the queen to favour, though only because, he claims, it was already his idea ('Thou dost advise me | Even so as I mine own course have set down' (341–2)) and not to betray any resentment to Polixenes ('as thou hast advised me' (351)). Needless to say, the king is incapable of following the advice he accepts. Within moments Polixenes enters saying that his reception has altered. It is characteristic of Leontes' deluded self-regard to observe the forms of good kingship and breach them, as when he insists that he cannot be a tyrant because he is giving Hermione a trial (which ignores due process) or consults the oracle at Delphi then dismisses what it says.

Camillo finds himself in the position of Pisanio in *Cymbeline*, obliged by sworn obedience to murder on behalf of his master. In the British play, the loyal servant reflects,

How? That I should murder her,
Upon the love and truth and vows which I
Have made to thy command? (3.2.11–13)

He refuses to obey, despite his oath of service. In early modern terms, this is the right decision to take, though not an easy one. (Later, Posthumus laments, believing that Imogen is dead, 'O Pisanio, | Every good servant does not all commands, | No bond but to do just ones' (5.1.5–7)). It is a characteristic, late play predicament. In *Pericles*, the desire for reward overcomes scruples, and murderous servants excuse themselves by saying they are sworn (see p. 8). Camillo, however, is as exemplary as Pisanio—it is the situation that creates the drama—even though it means forswearing (breaking) his sworn obedience as well as forswearing (refusing) to do evil:

If I could find example
Of thousands that had struck anointed kings
And flourished after, I'd not do't. But since
Nor brass, nor stone, nor parchment bears not one,
Let villainy itself forswear't. (1.2.358–62)

The soliloquy is more about demonstrating the clarity of his judgement, and his counsellor-like decisiveness, than exploring a stretching dilemma. Even when counselling himself, Camillo is exact and true.

Counsel is in his nature. So when he goes to Polixenes, he imparts advice along with his warning:

> mark my counsel,
> Which must be e'en as swiftly followed as
> I mean to utter it; or both yourself and me
> Cry lost, and so good night!
> POLIXENES On, good Camillo.
> CAMILLO I am appointed him to murder you. (408–12)

This again is exemplary, hitching decisiveness to speed. As the author of *The Counsellor* puts it: 'we perswade not our Counsellor to trifle the time, but execute speedely. For celeritie tempered with wise counsell, is alwaies profitable.'[20] This, though, is a tragicomedy, not a pageant of the courtly virtues. Camillo can only protect Polixenes by commanding the keys of the posterns, but that means that he can only protect himself by flight, which is not just wrong in a counsellor but abandons Hermione to greater risk. 'Neither is it fit', it says in *The Counsellor*, 'that any Counsellor, should goe into forraine nations, vnlesse he be publiquely sent as Ambassadour, Gouernour, or Commaunder in warre, least by such absence the commonweale be damnified' (96). Camillo will do this again, after sixteen years in Bohemia, when he accompanies Florizel and Perdita back to Sicily. No doubt the gods are guiding him towards fulfilment of the oracle, but his conscious motives are mixed. He tells the audience that he facilitates the elopement, which means betraying Polixenes, because he has 'a woman's longing' to see Sicily again (4.4.650).

What persuades Polixenes to fly? The disfavour he detects in Leontes, the urgent warning from Camillo, but also what he is told about the king's deluded swearing. Something unmanageable wells up when Camillo tells Polixenes that the verity of Hermione's innocence hangs on Bohemia's word against Leontes', who 'thinks, nay . . . he swears . . . that you haue touched his queen | Forbiddenly' (1.2.414–17). Polixenes' appalled rebuttal, 'O, then my best blood turn | To an infected jelly' (417–18), resembles, in its post-1606, profanity-avoiding way, the conditional self-curse that was, as we have repeatedly seen, traditionally embedded in an oath. Denial is of no avail, however, because, as Camillo troublingly declares, to swear against Leontes' oath-bound thought—to invert his thought with an oath—reinforces what is resisted:

Swear his thought over
By each particular star in heaven, and
By all their influences, you may as well
Forbid the sea for to obey the moon
As or by oath remove or counsel shake
The fabric of his folly, whose foundation
Is piled upon his faith, and will continue
The standing of his body. (424–31)

Hermione had spoken of oaths seeking to 'unsphere the stars' (p. 446). Camillo imagines reinstalling what Leontes' oath about Polixenes has deranged. You could swear by every star—hang an oath from each of all the myriad points of light in the sky—and, to bring it down to earth, swear also by the astrological influence that these heavenly bodies have on human affairs. Yet the effort would be in vain. The power of a destructive oath strikes him as irreversible, itself like a force of nature. Nor would counsel be any more effective (Camillo speaks from experience). What exactly, in this exchange, does the rare phrase 'swear . . . over' mean? If it means swearing to overturn Leontes' thought (swearing against his delusion), it brings in train its contrary, to intensify by swearing over, or over and over (even against). That is how the phrase is used by Cesario/Viola in *Twelfth Night*:

And all those sayings will I overswear,
And all those swearings keep as true in soul
As doth that orbèd continent the fire
That severs day from night. (5.1.262–5)

The audience hears neither Leontes' oath nor Camillo's overswearing. Is the reference to an offstage, unheard scene? More likely, the acute asseverations ('No, no, my lord', 'You lie') are retrospectively counted as swearing. This is something that happens elsewhere in the oath-constrained late plays. At the end of *The Tempest*, for example, Gonzalo asks the Boatswain, 'Now, blasphemy, | That swear'st grace o'erboard: not an oath on shore?' (5.1.221–2); even at the height of the storm, the audience has heard the seaman say nothing stronger than 'A plague upon . . .' (1.1.32). Reliance on report enables at this point in *The Winter's Tale* a more analytical account of how Leontes' swearing rests on 'his faith'—a belief unsecured by evidence, that is itself halfway to utterance. We shall soon hear the king swear 'on my faith' that Hermione has a merely goodly appearance (2.1.72). What requires further attention is why 'oath' and 'counsel' *go together* in Camillo's perplexed advice to Polixenes.

On the way to that we need to ask another question. What does Diana mean in *All's Well* when she tells Bertram, ''Tis not the many oaths that makes the truth, | But the plain single vow that is vowed true' (4.2.22–3)? However 'makes' is taken, it must include 'constructs, creates'. *The Winter's Tale* combines a troubled awareness that truths can be sanctioned troths and beliefs that spring from faith with a scepticism about those people that (in Bacon's essay 'Of Truth') 'delight in Giddinesse; And count it a Bondage to fix a Beleefe'.[21] 'It is not onely,' Bacon goes on, 'the Difficultie, and Labour, which Men take in finding out of *Truth* ... that doth bring *Lies* in fauour: But a naturall, though corrupt Loue, of the *Lie* it selfe' (1–2). The giddy, paranoid ethos of Sicily springs from Leontes' jealousy, his suspicion, and experimental flair. But when oaths can make the truth, give substance to a lie, jealousy itself seems the product of deeper epistemological difficulty.

* * *

Compare Act 2 of *Cymbeline*, where another oath seals up belief in the infidelity of a wife. Of course, it can be asked in what sense Posthumus and Imogen are 'married'. That is the word used in the opening lines of the play (1.1.18), but it is less decisive than it seems. When Posthumus goes into exile, the tokens he exchanges with Imogen—the ring and the bracelet—are exactly of the kind given to secure, rather than complete, early modern spousals. Cloten roughly tells Imogen that 'The contract you pretend with that base wretch ... is no contract, none' (2.3.108–10). She takes this view seriously enough explicitly to reject his suit, lest her silence be cited as consent (90–1).[22] Later, we are told in the dream vision that Posthumus was married in Jupiter's temple, though how clandestinely (and therefore precariously) the god does not say (5.5.199–200). There is an obvious dramaturgical reason for the audience hearing this so late: uncertainty about the status of the marriage makes Posthumus' (and Imogen's) insecurities about having and holding more volatile and credible.

Iachimo sets out the 'circumstances' of his supposed seduction of Imogen. His account of the chamber is potent, however readily Posthumus resists it. We might be lurking behind the arras, like Cardenio, looking on at a scene of betrothed betrayal:

The roof o'th' chamber
With golden cherubins is fretted. Her andirons—
I had forgot them—were two winking Cupids

> Of silver, each on one foot standing, nicely
> Depending on their brands. (87–91)

The long, appreciative account that Iachimo gives of the chamber displays his credentials as a witness, while tantalizing Posthumus with anticipation and innuendo ('winking Cupids'). The passage chimes with Lorna Hutson's observation, 'We are inclined to forget how much is not actually staged in a Renaissance play, because [of] the *enargeia*, or vividness and presence, of various characters' narrations of events,'[23] except that the audience has witnessed the scene that Iachimo is describing—so near the truth, but so falsely—and we did not then 'see' on stage the things that are agreed by Posthumus to be true. We are put into Posthumus' position of 'seeing' what we are told to believe.

Iachimo next flashes, like a conjurer, the bracelet given to Imogen by Posthumus. Things are present now, but the airy glimpse of the token makes it the more susceptible to redefinition. Told of how Imogen 'stripped it' from her arm, in a devastatingly sexual gesture, Posthumus breaks out with the near-oath 'Jove' (98–101). The description works on him so powerfully that he gives Iachimo the ring that was his wife's token, to undo an exchange of faith that he is coming to regard as false:

> The vows of women
> Of no more bondage be to where they are made,
> Than they are to their virtues, which is nothing! (110–12)

Yet his language remains generalized, more imperative than indicative. His suspicion of Imogen can still be checked by Philario's advice. This old friend of his father becomes, in effect, his counsellor:

> Have patience, sir,
> And take your ring again; 'tis not yet won.
> It may be probable she lost it, or
> Who knows if one her woman, being corrupted,
> Hath stol'n it from her? (113–17)

This whole deceitful sequence had started with a reminder by Iachimo of his sworn 'covenant' with Posthumus (a rival bond to his contract with Imogen), to which he added a cunning show of post-1606 fastidiousness about swearing. He lets Posthumus know that, to require him to swear to the truth of his testimony, especially in a climate where swearing is no longer quite the thing, would be to cast doubt on his nobility

(p. 27) as well as his good faith, which a fellow-gentleman would surely not require:

> Sir, my circumstances,
> Being so near the truth as I will make them,
> Must first induce you to believe; whose strength
> I will confirm with oath, which I doubt not
> You'll give me leave to spare when you shall find
> You need it not. (61–6)

This is ingeniously evasive around the forcefield of the oath. Iachimo does not merely hope to avoid swearing to a lie (in practice, he will swear, when it helps him), but to stay close to the truth. What he tells Posthumus is indeed 'near the truth', given his penetration of Imogen's chamber and his enjoyment of her body when he eases the bracelet from her arm and drinks in the crimson birthmark under her breast.

After Philario has counselled him, Posthumus decides to doubt for a bit longer. The bracelet, he says, might have been stolen. At which point Iachimo swears his oath, the more charged for his supposed reluctance to come out with such an utterance, and, the more painfully for an audience, ironically effective for being in the narrowest sense true:

> IACHIMO By Jupiter, I had it from her arm.
> POSTHUMUS Hark you, he swears, by Jupiter he swears.
> 'Tis true, nay, keep the ring, 'tis true. I am sure
> She would not lose it. Her attendants are
> All sworn and honourable. (121–5)

Oaths of office or service concur with the oath of testimony, which now makes the truth for Posthumus. He is reduced to swearing 'by Jupiter' that Iachimo swears 'By Jupiter'. Even when he later regrets ordering Pisanio to murder his wife, he has faith in her infidelity. It is one of the many places in the late plays where oaths are dangerous. Philario continues to counsel him, urging patience and bringing perspective—'This is not strong enough to be believed' (131)—but the oath secures conviction. Posthumus, like Leontes, and like Florizel after him, rejects advice: 'Never talk on't' (132). When Iachimo tells him of the birthmark, it merely seals what is subscribed.

The pivotal importance of the oath is subtly reinforced by what Belarius tells the princes and the audience—a couple of scenes later, in another part of the play—about the circumstances of his exile. Once close to Cymbeline at court, he fled to Wales, taking with him the infant Guiderius and Arviragus, because he was falsely accused of treachery in a deception that was bound by oaths:

> in one night
> A storm or robbery, call it what you will,
> Shook down my mellow hangings, nay, my leaves,
> And left me bare to weather....
> My fault being nothing, as I have told you oft,
> But that two villains, whose false oaths prevailed
> Before my perfect honour, swore to Cymbeline
> I was confederate with the Romans. (3.3.61–8)

The parallel with Imogen is surely clear.[24] She too is betrayed in one night, and shaken of all her fruit. Iachimo's false oath is more believed than her honour, and she is taken to be confederate with a Roman.

* * *

Unwise or inept counsel is not hard to find in Shakespeare. Polonius is complacent and foolish, Kent provocative, Wolsey corrupt. *Cymbeline* gives a more extended, cautionary account of a badly counselled king. The Queen and Cloten encourage Cymbeline to exile the virtuous Posthumus and not to pay the tribute money promised and owed to Rome. When Augustus' army invades, he craves their advice: 'Now for the counsel of my son and queen! | I am amazed with matter' (4.3.27–8). This is all wrong in Renaissance terms. Cloten is a fool, disqualified by any measure. The Queen is clever enough, but ruled out by more than her vice. Counsel from your wife could not be dispassionate; the ideal counsellor was a greybeard.[25] Charles I was ridiculed for taking counsel from Henrietta Maria.[26] At the end of the play, when the natural kinship bond between father and lost princes, and the marriage vows of Imogen and Posthumus, are restored, so is the promise to pay 'our wonted tribute, from the which | We were dissuaded by our wicked queen' (5.6.462–3).

In *The Winter's Tale*, by contrast, Camillo and Paulina are good counsellors, both in line—except for gender, to which I shall return—with the early modern literature of and about advice. Those advising a king should give 'faithfull and good counsell' says Lipsius. They should not flatter but 'lay open the pure and simple troth'.[27] This emphasis recurs. In A.D.B.'s *The Court of the Most Illustrious and Most Magnificent James, the First* (1619), a passage about the importance of exercising freedom of speech (in order to tell the truth) leads into a discussion of the nature of truth itself. 'What truth is', it modestly says in the margin: Pilate's question answered (John 18: 38). 'Tis far better', A.D.B. states, 'and much more commendable, to suffer death it selfe, than either to oppresse or suppresse Truth or good councell.'[28] Faithful to the truth, the counsellor should also be faithful in the sense of being loyal. Lipsius again, citing ancient authorities, declares: '*I Call those Counsellers,* who being faithfull, and hauing experience, ... do geue good aduise, ... *I termed them faithfull, that is to say good men. For I hold* the best men, to be faithfullest' (G3r).

Good advice may spring from such attributes of the mind as experience and judgement, but it only becomes counsel in *utterance*. Add its linguistic weight to its grounding in truth and faith and there is an obvious affinity with oaths, vows, and the rest. In *The Counsellor*, we are told that a virtuous counsellor values justice, which means that he values *fides*, as recommended in the *De Officiis*:

> The foundation of [justice] is fidelitie, which (*Cicero* defineth it) to be a constant and true performing of word and promise.[29] A iust Counsellor therefore doth affirme things true, not doubtfull, obserueth his promises, standeth to compactes, restoreth what he boroweth, and to the performing his faith is not compelled by lawe, by witnesse, or oath, but by his owne willing consent· freewill and word, which he accounteth as a lawe. (101)

Moreover, counsel removes doubt and aims at finality, like the 'othe for confirmation' that is 'an end of all strife' (cf. p. 451). We might these days think of counsel as complicating, qualifying, open-ended. The early modern view was different; decisiveness was expected. In *The Picture of a Perfit Common Wealth* (1602), Thomas Floyd writes: 'Counsellours are necessarie to bee required, and thought expedient, to resolue al doubts, to decide debates, ... Counsailours are called by ... learned authours, The keyes of certaintie.'[30] Thirdly, a virtuous counsellor, like an oath, depends on and fosters trust—the quality for which Leontes used to value Camillo. The faithfulness and honesty of advice in the past make it natural to accept advice in the present.

Finally, a counsellor is 'bound' to be faithful not just because holding an office of trust requires and encourages 'fidelitie'[31] but because it is an office that men are typically sworn to. *The Counsellor* has no doubt that such an arrangement is desirable: 'Let the Counsellors speach therefore be ... graue, simple, holy, and true. And it is fit each man should speake sworne, to the ende God may be the witnes of his minde' (96). Privy counsellors were sworn in. The Jacobean oath of office was full of undertakings to be faithful and honest:

> You shall sweare, To be a true and faithfull Servant unto the *Kings Majestie*, ... you shall in all things to be moved, treated, and debated in Councell, faithfully and truly declare your minde and opinion according to your heart and conscience, ... You shall to your utmost beare faith and allegiance unto the *Kings Majestie*, his Heires, and lawfull Successors, ... you shal doe as a faithfull and true Servant and Subject ought to doe to his *Majesty*.[32]

Here then is a deep reason why Camillo says that neither oath nor counsel can remove or shake Leontes' folly. Any counsel given is underpinned by an oath. Such is the pressure of Leontes upon his counsellors to believe his lie, however, that they are drawn to swear to their counsel in a more immediate, even profane, way.

When, in 2.1, Hermione is brought before the king and his counsellors, the post-1606 substitution of saying for swearing does not work in her favour. Leontes declares ''tis Polixenes | Has made thee swell thus', and the queen replies:

> But I'd say he had not,
> And I'll be sworn you would believe my saying,
> Howe'er you lean to th' nayward. (63–6)

Taken aback, embarrassed, and sensing that she should not lend credibility to the accusation by countering it too strongly (swearing it over), which would leave the king no way back, Hermione is also too confident that her truth is self-evident. Like Desdemona, who is slow to swear her honesty, she does not yet understand how deluded her husband is. A Jacobean audience must have registered on some level that she is subjected to constraints that are an issue for the play as a whole. Limited by her sex, but also by the Act, she cannot call on Divine witness. The consequences of this are dire, especially because, in her reluctance, Hermione makes play with the constraints, and declares that she will not say, as she 'would', but will swear, which she hardly can. 'But I'd say he had not, | And I'll be sworn you would believe my saying.' The substitution of (not quite) saying for (not yet) swearing makes her sound evasive, too clever for the matter in hand, while her sophisticated phrasing awkwardly manages to imply, through its juggling of moods and tenses, that she will not swear to her truth but only to Leontes' willingness to believe her, i.e., from his point of view, to his credulity, all of which fans his mistrust.

Hermione is taken away guarded. The lords are not remotely persuaded of her guilt, so counsel and oath sound together. The first lord invokes heaven as witness of her purity (131–4). Antigonus swears 'By mine honour' that the queen is true, or, more coarsely,

Be she honour-flawed—
I have three daughters: the eldest is eleven;
The second and the third nine and some five;
If this prove true, they'll pay for't. By mine honour,
I'll geld 'em all. (145–9)

A Jacobean audience would find it extraordinary that Antigonus is put into this position, and prompted to such crudity. The counsellors have already sworn to the fidelity of their counsel. And in any case, as we have heard, 'A iust Counsellor...is not compelled by lawe, by witnesse, or oath, but by his owne...freewill and word.' So far from being swayed, Leontes' response is to ask why *he* is not believed: 'What? Lack I credit?' (159). Treatises agree that although a king should listen with judgement to counsel,[33] he should not stubbornly resist it. '*Let him auoide* Obstinacie', writes Lipsius, '*For this is a diuine saying of the Prince* Marcus. It is more decent and conuenient that I should follow the aduise, of so many, and such worthy friends, then that they should onely be ruled by my will' (G2v). Floyd agrees: 'let none contemne the counsel of their friends, nor reiect the aduice of the wise, preferring his wit before their wisedome, nor leane to wilfulnes, lest had I wist come too late' (80).

Leontes strikes the characteristic note of Stuart prerogative government: 'Our prerogative | Calls not your counsels...We need no more of your advice' (165–70). Significantly, however, the drama of counsel is not over. He has sent Cleomenes and Dion to Delphos: 'now from the oracle | They will bring all, whose spiritual counsel had...' (187–8). The idea of taking *counsel* from an oracle is not unprecedented,[34] but it is hardly standard usage. It reflects the play's preoccupation, as does the irruption into the action of 'true' and 'honest' Paulina, 'Your most obedient counsellor' (2.3.55). From the outset, she is in danger of being brushed off as a scold, not just because what she says is unwelcome to the king but because there is no early modern model for a woman as royal counsellor. (Queen Elizabeth and Queen Anne had their ladies in waiting, whose access and influence could be great, but counsel was a different matter.) The consequences are felt by her husband, whose failure to curb her leads him to be charged with disposing of Hermione's baby.

Counsellors have their dilemmas. In *The Winter's Tale* they must snatch what they can from Leontes' volatility. How Camillo temporizes, tacks, and breaks his oath to serve we have seen. Antigonus is unenviably pressured to swear an oath not 'for confirmation' but open-endedly to whatever the king may require. Such misuse of oaths was associated with tyranny:[35]

Swear by this sword
Thou wilt perform my bidding.
ANTIGONUS I will, my lord. (168–9)

Piling threat on top of abuse, Leontes says that, if Antigonus' oath on the sword, added to his oath of fealty, is not enough to bind him to effect something like infanticide, he and his wife, Paulina, will be executed.

We enjoin thee,
As thou art liegeman to us, that thou carry
This female bastard hence, and that thou bear it
To some remote and desert place, quite out
Of our dominions; and that there thou leave it,...
ANTIGONUS I swear to do this, though a present death
Had been more merciful. (173–85)

The oath is not forgotten in the horror and hope of his mission. Antigonus will say in Bohemia that Hermione appeared to him in a dream—whether as a ghost or, as the audience will come to feel, the projection of his guilt—and spoke of this oath (3.3.29). As he lays the baby down he says he is 'by oath enjoined to this' (52). It is questionable, of course, how obliged he is. It was a point of dispute how binding a coerced oath was (Antigonus must swear or be executed), and how extreme the threat had to be pre-emptively to invalidate such a bond.[36] Overarching this was the generally agreed principle (found most often in scripture, but transferable to classical Sicily and Bohemia) that an oath to perform a sin is not a valid oath. Antigonus might reasonably have taken the baby to a safe, warm home. But the gods do that in any case.

For there is a second, major oath in Sicily, sworn upon a sword, which gives an audience hope that the child will be preserved. When Cleomenes and Dion return from Delphos they are required to 'swear upon this sword of justice' that they are delivering the oracle from Apollo's priest, sealed and unread.

All this we swear.

LEONTES Break up the seals, and read.

OFFICER [*reads*] Hermione is chaste, Polixenes blameless, Camillo a true subject, Leontes a jealous tyrant, his innocent babe truly begotten, and the King shall live without an heir if that which is lost be not found. (3.2.129–34)

This is the counsel of the oracle. It also counts as testimony—in Cicero's *Topica* xx an oracle represents the strongest testimony. You could force a conjunction by noting that, in classical rhetoric, testimony and oaths belong together as inartificial proofs. But Shakespeare had long been conscious of a more radical link, tying together oath and oracle as confirmations of truth. As Julia says of Proteus, too trustingly in this case, 'His words are bonds, his oaths are oracles'.[37] The oracle in *The Winter's Tale* is the more truthful for being conditional about the future. The counsel of the oracle is both word and promise, both a binding assertion of Hermione's innocence and a prediction that 'the King shall live without an heir if that which is lost be not found'.

⋆ ⋆ ⋆

When Simon Forman saw *The Winter's Tale* in 1611, he was impressed by the oracle and made a note of what it said but he was even more struck by Autolycus, who offered both entertainment and the practical pleasure of drawing a moral:

> Remember also the Rog that cam in all tottered like coll pixci and howe he feyned him sicke & to have bin Robbed of all that he had and howe he cosened the por man of all his money, and after cam to the shep sher with a pedlers packe & ther cosened them Again of all their money And howe he changed apparrell with the kinge of Bomia his sonn, and then howe he turned Courtier &c. Beware of trustinge feined beggars or fawninge fellouss.[38]

The engaging shape-shifter is indeed not to be *trusted*. He is not merely, as in Ovid, a wily thief, but a rogue who, like Autolykos in the *Odyssey*, deceives through oaths.[39] In early modern terms he is the apogee of those 'huckesters, or chapmen of choyse, who retayling small wares, are not able to better their owne estate, but wyth falshode, lying and periurye, byndinge ofttymes the vtterance of their petye sales wyth an huge othe'.[40] From perjury to cutting purses is a small step and mere economy.

Autolycus' pack is full of stuff that shows the audience that the bonds of word and promise are not the monopoly of court society. The gloves, bracelets, and necklaces that he sings about as he enters, the 'Golden coifs, and stomachers | For my lads to give their dears' (4.4.214–25), quickly make the transition from thing to bond at the sheep-shearing feast. 'If I were not in love with Mopsa', the Clown tells him,

> thou shouldst take no money of me, but being enthralled as I am, it will also be the bondage of certain ribbons and gloves.
>
> MOPSA I was promised them against the feast, but they come not too late now.
>
> DORCAS He hath promised you more than that, or there be liars.
>
> MOPSA He hath paid you all he promised you. Maybe he has paid you more, which will shame you to give him again.
>
> CLOWN Is there no manners left among maids?...
>
> MOPSA I have done. Come, you promised me a tawdry-lace and a pair of sweet gloves. (226–42)

So much for promise, what of word? The ballads in the pack parody Leontes' faith in the power of oaths to verify an absurdity, such as the fish that soared forty thousand fathom above the sea and sang a song denouncing the hardness of maidens' hearts. 'Is it true too, think you?' asks Dorcas. 'Five justices' hands at it, and witnesses more than my pack will hold' (271–3). The witnesses would be sworn, as would the justices' subscriptions. Which does not make the ballad more true.

The song that Mopsa, Dorcas, and Autolycus (later, the Clown) sing also reflects back on the love-triangle of Leontes, Hermione, and Polixenes. The title that the pedlar gives it—'Two Maids Wooing a Man'—might be Shakespeare's invention, because it does not appear in the two surviving seventeenth-century manuscripts of the melody with words. If so, it cues us to notice how aptly the song harnesses the rivalry of Mopsa and Dorcas for the Clown. From the manuscripts we know that the tune, which Dorcas says they had a month before Autolycus' visit, was quite sophisticated, and its performance by three of the King's Men may have been the more so, because the manuscripts include 'vocal ornaments indicating that it was sung by a professional court and/or theatre singer'.[41] In execution as well as content it closes the gap between the court world of Sicily and that of the shepherds in Bohemia.

The content is worth scrutiny. 'It becomes thy oath full well', sings Mopsa, who is competing with Dorcas for the Clown, 'Thou to me thy secrets tell.' But no, replies Dorcas,

> Thou hast sworn my love to be.
> MOPSA Thou hast sworn it more to me.
> Then whither goest? Say, whither? (288–96)

This sets oath against oath, as in an early Shakespeare comedy. It might almost be *The Two Gentlemen of Verona*. The man has sworn his love to two women; perhaps he has espoused them both. In contrast to Leontes' court, however, which explodes in jealousy, the rough pastoral world of Bohemia manages to contain these rivalries, and does so in the harmony of song. In one of the extant manuscripts there are additional lines, which show that the man being wooed is about to leave entirely. Not to grange or mill (to do business for a farm) but who knows where.[42] It would probably over-interpret to apply this to the Clown, who will soon leave his rival wenches to go to Sicily and count himself a gentleman born after Perdita's fardel is opened. If Shakespeare knew this fuller version of the song, he has the Clown cut it off where he does ('We'll have this song out anon by ourselves' (297)), not just to stop Autolycus singing his prick-song with the girls but to limit the lyrics to the core situation of two suitors betrayed by a double troth.

Such a situation is not uncommon. It becomes the crux of the Cardenio story. Before seeking the hand of Luscinda, Don Ferdinand had seduced the lower-born Dorotea after a handfast in her chamber witnessed by her maid before a religious icon. Next day, the Don does not return, nor the day after that. From being the fortunate wife of a nobleman, Dorotea becomes an abandoned maid, who goes in pursuit of her lover disguised—in Shakespearean fashion—as a young man. In the end, she gets him back, reconciling him to their betrothal, which leaves Luscinda free to marry Cardenio.[43] But the circumstances of her loss are as powerful as this resolution. They are part of what attracted the author of *A Lover's Complaint* to this stretch of *Don Quixote*. The potential for a similar tale of exploitation and abandonment is marked out strongly in *Pandosto* and residually in *The Winter's Tale*. I have in mind the courtship and betrothal of Florizel and Perdita.

In *Pandosto* the old shepherd who has brought up Fawnia knows that Dorastus is a prince, and he worries that his girl will be seduced and abandoned: 'faire wordes and sweete promises are two great enemies to a maydens honestie' (E4v). The dangers are compounded by the secrecy of their betrothal. Though Dorastus assures his mistress that 'I loue thee . . . not to misuse thee as a Concubine, but to vse thee as my wife: I can promise no more,' his 'solemne protestation' must be taken (for ill or good) as an act of faith. When they 'plight their troath each to other' there are no witnesses to seal the deal. We might justly remember Imogen: 'Men's vows are women's traitors' (3.4.53). Perdita is more circumspect. Already betrothed to Florizel (who speaks of 'that nuptial which | We two have sworn shall come'

(4.4.50–1)), she enters the play full of doubts about the inequality of their relationship, and his possible change of purpose (4.4.35–40). Florizel moves to reassure her with a more public espousal. As the Clown, Mopsa, and Dorcas sing offstage, somewhere beyond the action, the couple take their vows before the Old Shepherd and Polixenes and Camillo in disguise. Forman noted how 'the kinge of Bohemia his sonn maried that wentch & howe they fled into Cicillia to Leontes'.[44]

This is importantly not quite right—though it shows how fluid the process of espousal and marriage could be, especially in the eyes of a looker-on—for when the couple, fleeing Polixenes' disapproval, get to Sicilia, Leontes asks Florizel whether 'You are married?' and he has to admit, 'We are not, sir, nor are we like to be' (5.1.203–4). But the handfasting is highly structured and secured by binding language. From 'I take thy hand' (4.4.348), the whiteness and softness of which he praises, Florizel quickly shifts into what Polixenes calls his 'protestation':

Let me hear
What you profess.
FLORIZEL Do, and be witness to't.
POLIXENES And this my neighbour too?
FLORIZEL And he, and more
Than he; and men, the earth, the heavens, and all,
That were I crowned the most imperial monarch,
Thereof most worthy, were I the fairest youth
That ever made eye swerve, had force and knowledge
More than was ever man's, I would not prize them
Without her love; for her employ them all,
Commend them and condemn them to her service
Or to their own perdition. (354–64)

Perdita herself, eschewing this rhetoric of elated commitment and implicit imprecation—the parameters of oath-swearing—matches her lover in sentiment, and the Old Shepherd moves to a contract. Not for the first or last time in the play, there is an emotionally loaded, apparently binding handclasp: 'Take hands, a bargain' (369). 'Come on', Florizel urges,

Contract us fore these witnesses.
OLD SHEPHERD Come, your hand;
And, daughter, yours.
POLIXENES Soft, swain, a while, beseech you.
Have you a father? (375–8)

It is a measure of the consistency of the play that Polixenes should couch his warning as a matter of *counsel*. 'By my white beard', he swears—on one of his qualifications for counselling—'The father . . . should hold some counsel | In such a business' (392–8).

The tense and difficult handfasting shows Florizel to be a serious swearer who nonetheless avoids profanity with his cleanly invocation of 'the heavens, and all' as witness to his intentions. The spousal is wrenched off its path by Polixenes' rage, which has been compared to that of Leontes in its suddenness and excess. Once the king has stormed off stage, another oath completes the vow. In fear of the contract failing, this is an exaggerated utterance:

FLORIZEL It cannot fail but by
The violation of my faith, and then
Let nature crush the sides o'th' earth together
And mar the seeds within. Lift up thy looks.
From my succession wipe me, father! I
Am heir to my affection. (464–9)

The threat to nature's germens if he breaks his faith to Perdita has overtones of Lear in the storm.[45] He does not say, like Leontes, 'Affection, thy intention stabs the centre' (1.2.140); his 'affection' is not so extravagantly destructive; but it is disorderly in denying Bohemia's natural succession. The intensity of the vow needs tempering with counsel. Hence Camillo's next line: 'Be advised.'

But Florizel will not be advised, or rather, he says that he already is, 'and by my *fancy*', which is borderline insanity (i.e. fantasy). He now erupts into a full-scale oath of immense reach:

CAMILLO This is desperate, sir.
FLORIZEL So call it. But it does fulfil my vow.
I needs must think it honesty. Camillo,
Not for Bohemia, nor the pomp that may
Be thereat gleaned; for all the sun sees, or
The close earth wombs, or the profound seas hides
In unknown fathoms, will I break my oath
To this my fair beloved. (473–80)

The grandly sweeping negations that swing out from his oath intoxicate Florizel's purpose; ears in the audience attuned to extremity will remember, if not Leontes' 'nothings', then the vast scale of what Camillo says would be needed to overswear the king's oath, founded on his faith. Save your advice for my father is Florizel's message: 'cast your good counsels | Upon his passion' (483–4).

In *Pandosto*, the lovers amass treasure once they have plighted their troth, recognizing that they will not be able to live together unless they go into exile. This is unattractive but sensible. By staging the formal handfast Shakespeare creates a crisis which prevents this sort of calculation. Yet the moral picture is blurred because Florizel, disobeying his father, now begins a career as a deceiver[46] which does not sit well with his oaths. Changing clothes with Autolycus, he takes on some of his mendacity, telling Leontes, when he arrives in Sicily, that he comes with friendly greetings from his father, and that Perdita is the daughter of the King of Libya (5.1.137–67). So much for the conventional wisdom that gentlemen and princes are truth-tellers (see p. 27).

If not in palaces, where is verity in Bohemia? It would be sentimental as well as patronizing to go along with Autolycus' judgement of the rustics as naively truthful, sworn into affiliation with trust: 'Ha, ha! What a fool honesty is, and trust—his sworn brother—a very simple gentleman!' (4.4.584–5). Though the pedlar has no difficulty in convincing the inexperienced Old Shepherd and Clown, when they encounter him in Florizel's costume, that he is an influential courtier, they are not so simple as to miss the opportunity to bribe him. According to report, when they fall into the hands of the irate Polixenes they 'Forswear themselves as often as they speak' in order to save their skins (5.1.199). As the play's obsession with honesty and trust—with truth, one might say, and faith—works its way into Act 5, the Clown is quick to assume the lying prerogatives of a gentleman. (Such is the convenience of the honour code, that a gentleman should not be expected to swear when giving his word yet he freely asserts his status by oaths that demand belief.[47]) Meeting the pedlar again, after becoming a member of the Sicilian royal family, he promises to 'swear to the Prince' that Autolycus is 'as honest a true fellow as any is in Bohemia'. The Old Shepherd, as though familiar with the Act to Restrain Abuses, observes, 'You may say it, but not swear it', but the Clown knows his rights: 'Not swear it now I am a gentleman? Let boors and franklins say it; I'll swear it' (5.2.140–4). This recalls the satirical exchange in *Cymbeline* where the base gentleman Cloten boasts about his oafish, offstage swearing—a distinctively post-1606 topic, the abuse and vulgarity of oaths, which, in a post-1606 play, we are also not allowed to hear (2.1.1–11). What makes the Clown's lines more significantly involving and integral to *The Winter's Tale* is the Old Shepherd's persistent worry 'How if it be false, son?' and the Clown's recklessness with truth (think of Leontes on the queen's adultery): 'If it be ne'er so false, a true gentleman may swear it' (145–6).

* * *

We have seen that, in Act 2, Paulina becomes the king's 'counsellor'. This is most unusual. Early modern treatises do not write about female counsel; if anything, they say that a courtier-counsellor should avoid 'womanish altercation, or chiding'.[48] The Queen in *Cymbeline* is not an attractive precedent, but in the final act of *The Winter's Tale* Paulina is firmly in charge. Her chiding has been reined in, but she still counsels Leontes over the 'counsel' of his lords not to remarry, despite Sicilia's lack of an heir (5.1.44). After he praises her proven wisdom ('O, that ever I | Had squared me to thy counsel!' (51–2)), she demands:

Will you swear
Never to marry but by my free leave?
LEONTES Never, Paulina, so be blest my spirit.
PAULINA Then, good my lords, bear witness to his oath.
CLEOMENES You tempt him over-much. (69–73)

This is about keeping the king for Hermione and fulfilling the oracle. But it is also a remarkable reversal of the opening acts, where Leontes gets others to swear, including Paulina's husband Antigonus. This points to a subtler parallel. Leontes and Paulina are so conjoined that they might almost be married to one another in the absence of their spouses. For sixteen years, until the Old Shepherd and the Clown testify to Antigonus' death, Paulina does not know whether her spouse is dead, though she assumes and swears that he is so ('on my life' (5.1.43)). Leontes does not know that Hermione is alive, because he believes he has seen her dead, incited, the audience might conclude, given that oaths can make the truth, by Paulina's twist to saying/swearing after Leontes hears of Mamillius' death: 'I say she's dead. I'll swear't. If word nor oath | Prevail not, go and see' (3.2.201–2).

There is matter in this swearing all the way down to the language used when the statue of Hermione comes to life: 'Would you not deem it breathed, and that those veins | Did *verily* bear blood?', wonders Leontes, to which Paulina adds, 'It is required | You do awake your *faith*' (5.3.64–5, 94–5). The faith that must be awakened is not just belief in Paulina's powers nor a crypto-religious credulity about statues coming to life nor even (though this is part of it) the active, substantiating faith that an oath can make the truth. It is the fidelity that makes it possible for the miraculous to occur—the miraculous not being that a statue is shown to be a woman (which is little more than a theatrical coup) but the trust and truth in Leontes and Hermione that allows them, after sixteen years of loss, to reinvest their faith and recapitulate their betrothal when the queen steps down and takes the king's hand. 'Nay, present your hand', Paulina urges him: 'When she was young, you wooed her. Now, in age, | Is she become the suitor?' (107–9). This is a gesture we have seen before, between Polixenes and the queen—then so hideously misconstrued by Leontes, now returned to marriage and hope.

It would be wrong to stop at this point, for there are three parallel endings to the play, though critics only notice two. First there is the discovery of Perdita's royal identity, which allows her in the play's last speech to be acknowledged as 'troth-plight' to Florizel (5.3.152). This is the ending that attracted Forman, who wrote nothing about the statue scene, which concludes the second handfasting plot. Third, there is a marriage between the play's two principal counsellors. Leontes suddenly reveals that his oath to marry only with Paulina's consent was reciprocated ('a match... made between's by vows' (138–9)). Now he knows where to find her

> An honourable husband. Come, Camillo,
> And take her by the hand, whose worth and honesty
> Is richly noted, and here justified
> By us, a pair of kings. (144–7)

Whether Paulina accepts Camillo is up to the actor and director. It should, however, be clear how purposefully Shakespeare ends the play by bringing together hands that have done so much to guide the action through disaster with good, faithful counsel.

18
Epilogue

It is tempting to end this book, as other books on Shakespeare have ended, with the epilogue to *The Tempest*. The average worn-out scholar would like nothing better than to be Prospero, bidding farewell to the reader as the magus/dramatist does to the theatre audience and his so potent art. Even if one resists a full-blown version of this conceit, there is plenty in Prospero's speech that would facilitate synthesis and resolution. His epilogue elides bonds as spells with the bonds of service—as in *Macbeth* and *All's Well*—and it encourages metadramatic reflection on how a play's relationship with an audience is contractual. This is a point that Ben Jonson makes in explicit, derisive detail in the induction to *Bartholomew Fair* (1614), but it is latent in the bonds between actor and audience in every Shakespeare play:

> Now my charms are all o'erthrown,
> And what strength I have's mine own,
> Which is most faint. Now 'tis true
> I must be here confined by you
> Or sent to Naples. Let me not,
> Since I have my dukedom got,
> And pardoned the deceiver, dwell
> In this bare island by your spell;
> But release me from my bands
> With the help of your good hands.... (1–10)

From the bound to the loose, from servitude to freedom, from a winding sheet to new life. Prospero's plea for applause is a request for the help of hands that—without much extrapolation—evokes the benign handshakes and tearing up of legal bonds that we have heard about quite often over the last seventeen chapters. There is even, as befits a late play, a judiciously unprofane asseveration: 'Now 'tis true...'. What more could be needed for a grand conclusion to this book? Unfortunately, this is by no means the last speech that Shakespeare wrote. We know that *Henry VIII* and *Cardenio*—discussed in Chapters 15 and 17—were composed in about 1612–13, a year or two after *The Tempest*, and that they were followed by *The Two Noble Kinsmen* (1613–14). That all three plays were written in collaboration with John Fletcher makes a perfect cadence even harder to achieve. The earliest play discussed in any detail in this study—*2 Henry VI* (*c.*1591)—is also a collaboration. When it comes to untidy teleology, Shakespeare's end is much like his beginning.

One thing that can be said with confidence is that, to the end of his known output, Shakespeare dealt in binding language. In *The Two Noble Kinsmen*, Palamon and Arcite are imprisoned by Theseus for fighting against him with their uncle, Creon. Arcite, released at the intercession of a relative, is sworn (offstage) 'Upon his oath and life' to leave Athens (2.2.250). That he breaks this oath is one precursor of his death at the end of the play, when he loses the hand of Emilia. His rival, Palamon, escaped from prison but still in chains, swears, in a scene attributed to Shakespeare, that he would fight Arcite over Emilia if he were able to do so (3.1.34). The formula that he uses, 'By all oaths in one', obeys the Act of 1606 while contriving to be forceful. A harmless subplot episode involving a schoolmaster, five countrymen, five wenches, and a taborer counterpoints these situations. The Second Countryman, disappointed of an encounter with Cicely the seamstress's daughter, says that 'She swore by wine and bread she would not break' (3.5.48). The two kinsmen are more committed. Arcite releases Palamon from his shackles, and, tied by a given 'faith' (3.6.1), they meet and fight, only to be interrupted by Theseus and his court. 'By Castor', Theseus cries, 'both shall die.'

In a stylized, strong sequence that was scripted by Fletcher but which owes a great deal to Shakespearean dramaturgy, those on stage around Theseus come out with a dozen oath-like 'conjurings' to urge him not to execute the miscreants: 'by our tie of marriage' (Hippolyta), 'By your own spotless honour' (Emilia), 'by your most noble soul' (Pirithous), and so on (195–208). What ensues is almost a re-run of the scene in *Troilus and Cressida* with which this book began. Hippolyta plays the part of Andromache, urging her husband not to be bound by his oath. Emilia, like Cassandra, adds, 'O my noble brother, | That oath was rashly made' (226–7). In any case, Emilia announces, she has 'another oath 'gainst yours' (230), namely Theseus' prior oath that he 'would ne'er deny me anything | Fit for my modest suit and your free granting. | I tie you to your word now' (234–6). Caught between oaths, like Achilles in the earlier play, Theseus shows some relief at being given a way out, but since this involves (at Emilia's behest) Palamon and Arcite swearing to depart from Athens and not contend over her, and since they refuse to swear, the bonds are not so much released as pulled into a tangle that can only be cut through by trial by combat after all. As in Chapter 8, the testing of oaths and bonds must come through physical force.

For the reader who has come this far, it will not be astonishing to learn that yet another play is articulated by such knots of language. This book has shown beyond doubt that Shakespeare had extensive recourse to oaths, vows, promises, contracts, penal bonds, covenants, and the like. He gravitated to sources in which binding language was represented, but he also introduced or supplemented it when adapting situations. In early modern England, relationships of many kinds were mediated and secured by utterances and subscriptions that had a more or less sacred charge. Shakespeare seized upon this social fact not with the passivity of a tepid observer but as a man implicated in credit, trust, and the ambiguities of performative language by his upbringing, involvement in legal cases, and experience as an actor.

The plays were caught up in debates about the acceptability and binding power of oaths, vows, and the rest. They do not passively reflect the positions taken up by lawyers, divines, or even poets, but draw on everyday discourse, and how attitudes, which were always plural, were worked out in the saying of what people felt able to say (e.g. how profane they could be, how firmly they would have to asseverate to be believed). We noted in the Introduction that the major variable in Shakespeare's use of binding language is genre. The matrix of social practice—who swore or engaged, and by what—within which the plays were formed was by comparison relatively stable. Yet circumstances could combine to change the climate, and, looking back over the output, it is possible to detect a shape, or shading. There were new opportunities and constraints during the early years of the reign of King James, turning on slander, equivocation, conspiracy, blasphemy, and allegiance. These fed back sharply into the theatre after the passing into law of the Act to Restrain Abuses (1606), but the Act needs itself to be regarded as a textual contribution—albeit a potent one—to an ongoing argument about profanity in which the playhouse had things to say, not merely cuts to make. By the same token it is worth underscoring what this book has repeatedly shown, that plays do not address such issues in the same way as tracts and polemics. Working with status, motive, and interaction, Shakespeare was far more interested than the treatise-writers in how oaths and vows are used to persuade, and are means not just of assurance but of deception and self-deception. He knew that words can bind individuals in affective and trust-enlarging ways that go beyond the content of an utterance, but also that oaths can be edged with violence in assertion as well as promise and may attack while binding.

This is a book about drama, but it seems important, at this late stage, to turn back to the Sonnets—as promised more than once—because they reinforce the conviction that has grown during the writing of this work that Shakespeare was not just drawn to oaths, vows, sealed bonds, and the like because of what they brought into performance, but was more substantially and deeply preoccupied with what they tell us about the make-up of truth. In the sonnets to the so-called dark lady, we find the poet swearing ('*by heaven*, I think my love as rare...') but also reporting 'deep oaths' too blasphemous or shaming to be put on paper.[1] At first he merely asserts that the mistress is fair though black. The claim needs bolstering with oaths once she proves unfaithful, or, if you doubt the poet, once he calls her false to blacken and coerce her.[2] The poet has sworn her fairness as though seeking to confirm the truth that should sustain his oaths. Swearing and forswearing bond where no trust exists. Perjury connects, thanks to knowing self-deception: 'When my love swears that she is made of truth | I do believe her though I know she lies' (138.1–2).

Like such earlier collections as Daniel's *Delia*,[3] *Shake-speares Sonnets* as published in 1609 had a tripartite structure: 152 poems to the youth and dark lady, then 2 anacreontic-style sonnets, followed by the longer *A Lover's Complaint*, in which a young woman seduced and abandoned by an attractive youth laments her betrayal but confesses that she is still infatuated.[4] In my edition of the *Sonnets* (1986) and in *Motives of Woe* (1991),[5] I looked for linguistic, situational, and thematic connections between the parts of the 1609 quarto. Writing the present book has helped me see that oaths, vows, and other articulate bonds are integral to the design. They are not just richly represented because love plots bring in declarations of truth and faith, though that is one reason, no doubt, why the sonnet provided a natural arena for Shakespeare to explore how binding language can be.

The most cursory reading of *A Lover's Complaint* shows the prominence and perversity of binding. When we first see the abandoned maid she is breaking the posied rings and discarding the jewels and favours that were given as pledges of love—even as tokens of betrothal—in the early modern period. The young man's seduction of the plainant was advanced by vows and a 'strong-bonded oath' that were known by the maid to be false though they were reportedly said by him never to have been sworn by him before, and by the flattering declaration that he has bedded a sacred nun, 'All vows and consecrations giving place' (279, 263). Should we compare this nun with those in *Measure for Measure*, whom Isabella aspires to join (Chapter 11)? Indirectly, perhaps, but much closer are the usually neglected 'anacreontic' sonnets, 153–4. These describe how Cupid lay asleep beside a well, 'Whilst many nymphs that vowed chaste life to keep | Came tripping by' (154.3–4). The neoclassical nuns are quickly caught up in an off-colour conceit. When the 'fairest votary' mock-sexually dunks Cupid's blazing arrow in the well (154.5), the effect is like boiling a kettle, more ardent than cooling. Vows of chastity and restraint cannot quell desire. 'Love's fire heats water, water cools not love' (154.14). To recognize the importance of oaths and vows is to see why 153–4 round off the sequence.

That the Sonnets often overlap with the plays is not a sign that they are off-scourings but that Shakespeare felt impelled to pursue the make-up of truth-telling outside as well as in the theatre. Put it another way: that the Sonnets are in a different medium from the plays confirms the significance to him of binding language in a way no further accumulation of dramatic examples could. This is not to imply an exclusive, intentionalist base. We certainly do not need to make autobiographical assumptions about the Sonnets to grasp this exploratory drive, especially as the sequence rises to a climax of self-excoriating other-blame in the last of the dark lady poems, number 152.

In loving thee thou know'st I am forsworn,
But thou art twice forsworn to me love swearing:
In act thy bed-vow broke, and new faith torn
In vowing new hate after new love bearing.
But why of two oaths' breach do I accuse thee
When I break twenty? I am perjured most,
For all my vows are oaths but to misuse thee,
And all my honest faith in thee is lost.
For I have sworn deep oaths of thy deep kindness,
Oaths of thy love, thy truth, thy constancy,
And to enlighten thee gave eyes to blindness,
Or made them swear against the thing they see.
    For I have sworn thee fair—more perjured eye
    To swear against the truth so foul a lie.

Vows and oaths are charged here with a violent energy and absoluteness that is as integral to their status as speech acts as their claims to moral assertion. Yet this is reflected back upon, in that queasy, less deceived state which often follows a binding utterance. It is a fine thing to prepare to swear, to bring everything to the point where hope and credit calls itself truth, and belief is manufactured, quite otherwise to inhabit the compromised aftermath. In the sonnet, vows and oaths are entangled, and the search for clarity requires the poet to identify a general truth (which is at least ostensibly false) that all his vows are oaths to abuse. Swearing is internalized and sight-transforming—as we noticed in the case of Leontes (Chapter 17)—until the poet becomes a version of the blind-seeing Cupid that will figure in the anacreontic sonnets. Love is grounded on broken vows. The poet is bound by their looseness.

The end of any worthwhile book ought to be the start of others. Despite the length of *Shakespeare's Binding Language*, there is plenty left to say about such plays as *Much Ado About Nothing*, *As You Like It*, or *1* and *2 Henry IV.* More largely, although I engage with, among others, *King Johan*, *The Jew of Malta*, *Antonio's Revenge*, *Hoffman*, *The Puritan Widow*, *Catiline*, *The Witch*, and *'Tis Pity She's a Whore*, I have not comprehensively investigated early modern drama. That several of the plays discussed are collaborations with Fletcher or Middleton, or contain additions or substitutions from Middleton, is sufficient reason to wish that we had close, comparative analyses. Attribution studies have identified Middleton's characteristic oaths and expletives ('*a my troth*, *beshrew...heart*, *cuds*, *cuds me*, *la you/why la*, *life*, *my life for yours*,...*pox*, *puh*, *push*, and *'slife*')[6] but more work is needed to explore and explain their incidence. The field is full of plays, from Marlowe to Massinger and Shirley, from *The Alchemist* to *The Broken Heart*, that would reward attention in their own right along the lines advanced by this book.

What is less clear is whether our understanding would develop more rapidly from a piecemeal output of essays or from a systematic language-based approach drawing on the electronic databases that now cover so much of the canon. We can get some sense of the likely benefits and drawbacks of the latter by consulting an archive 'designed to contain all passages in Greek texts, both literary and inscriptional, composed between the introduction of alphabetic writing and the year 322 BC that contain, report, or refer to oaths or acts of swearing'.[7] The 'Oath in Archaic and Classical Greece' database (2004–7) gives results that are much richer than those that can be generated from the existing electronic corpus of English literary and historical texts because the citations carry with them often illuminating commentary. Yet the database has not, by itself, greatly influenced classical studies. What it has done is lay foundations for essays and books. Research undertaken for it informs Judith Fletcher's admirable *Performing Oaths in Classical Greek Drama* (2012) and it has since provided raw material for full-length explorations of *Oath and State in Ancient Greece* (2013) and *Oaths and Swearing in Ancient Greece* (2014).[8] Systematic findings are valuable, but they are most useful when sifted and interpreted—especially when it comes to drama—by those who have an eye for the exception as well as the rule.

Shakespeare's Binding Language was not written, however, to encourage others to look at oaths, vows, and profanities across the field of early modern drama. The modest but still far-reaching intention was to highlight and bring into focus particular kinds of verbal and performative behaviour in Shakespeare. To excavate and map anything that is conceptually difficult and socially complex, it is desirable to get to its edges, to arrive at the parameters which delimit and animate practice. For that reason, this book has ranged across a lot of historical, religious, and philosophical material, while remaining open at its core to the variousness of utterance and circumstance in which Shakespeare's plays took shape.

Notes

CHAPTER I INTRODUCTION

1. A text often cited is Hebrews 6: 16: 'For men verely sweare by him that is greater *then them selues*, and an othe for confirmation is among them an end of all strife.'
2. *Troilus and Cressida*, ed. David Bevington, Arden Shakespeare, 3rd series (Walton-on-Thames: Nelson, 1998), 328, quoting here uncut from *The Plays of William Shakespeare*, ed. Samuel Johnson, 8 vols (1765), VII, 532.
3. For Johnson, oaths, and casuistry, see Jonathan Clark, 'Religion and Political Identity: Samuel Johnson as a Nonjuror', in Jonathan Clark and Howard Erskine-Hill, eds, *Samuel Johnson in Historical Context* (London: Palgrave, 2002), 79–145, Adrian Lashmore-Davies, '"The Casuistical Question": Oaths and Hypocrisy in the Writings of Johnson and Bolingbroke', in Jonathan Clark and Howard Erskine-Hill, eds, *The Interpretation of Samuel Johnson* (Basingstoke: Palgrave Macmillan, 2012), 84–119.
4. *Certayne Sermons, Or Homilies Appoynted by the Kynges Maiestie* (1547), L3v–M3v.
5. Christopher White, *Of Oathes: Their Obiect, Forme, and Bond* (1627), 23.
6. *Oedipus*, lines 353–70; *Aeneid*, e.g. III.118–20, V.72–103, VI.236–63. *Iliad*, II.400–30; see George Chapman, *Seaven Bookes of the Iliades of Homere, Prince of Poets* (1598), 32–3.
7. William Perkins, *A Discourse of Conscience* (1596), 75; cf. Perkins, *The Whole Treatise of the Cases of Conscience* (1606), 395.
8. 'Against Swearyng', *Certayne Sermons*, M3r.
9. Robert Sanderson, *De Juramento: Seven Lectures Concerning the Obligation of Promissory Oathes* (1655), 56.
10. In Dryden's adaptation of the play (1679), Priam persuades Hector to stay until Troilus rouses him to rebel.
11. *A Midsummer Night's Dream*, 3.2.93. For con-found as mutually securing see *OED*, found, *v.*[2]; *OED*, confound, *v.*, adds to 1–2 ('To defeat utterly, … overthrow') a reminder that 'confound' could be used imperatively in curses (i.e. swearing) to mean 'bring to perdition'. I am grateful to Niamh Kerrigan-Plaisted for discussion of this passage.
12. *2 Henry VI*, 5.1.180–1; *3 Henry VI*, 5.1.92–4.
13. Jean le Breton (?), *Britton* (late twelfth century), tr. Francis Morgan Nichols (1865; Washington, DC: Byrne, 1901), on the oath of fealty to the king taken by

males of 'twelve years old and upwards' admitted to a tithing (152) and on fealty sworn with a hand or hands on the Holy Gospels (366).

14. Henry de Bracton, *De Legibus et Consuetudinibus Angliae* (mid-thirteenth century); *Bracton on the Laws and Customs of England*, ed. George Woodbine and tr. Samuel E. Thorne, 4 vols (Cambridge, Mass.: Belknap/Harvard University Press, 1968–77), II, 228–33.
15. e.g. *A Midsummer Night's Dream*, 1.2.242–5, 3.2.124–35, 246–54.
16. *The Taming of the Shrew*, 4.1.66–7, 4.2.165, and 4.3.10; 5.1.80–8.
17. See esp. *King John*, 3.1.189–223. On confessional differences, similarities, and controversy see e.g. Johann P. Sommerville, 'The "New Art of Lying": Equivocation, Mental Reservation, and Casuistry', in Edmund Leites, ed., *Conscience and Casuistry in Early Modern Europe* (Cambridge: Cambridge University Press, 1988), 159–86.
18. *2 Henry IV*, 4.1.278–349.
19. Robert Boyle, *A Free Discourse against Customary Swearing* (1695), 110–11. The publisher's preface dates this posthumously printed work to the late 1640s/early 1650s.
20. 3 James I, c. 21, quoted from Hugh Gazzard, 'An Act to Restrain Abuses of Players (1606)', *Review of English Studies*, 61 (2010), 495–528, p. 495.
21. See, most ambitiously, Gary Taylor, ''Swounds Revisited: Theatrical, Editorial, and Literary Expurgation', in Taylor and John Jowett, *Shakespeare Reshaped 1606–1623* (Oxford: Clarendon Press, 1993), 51–106.
22. Barbara Mowat, 'Q2 *Othello* and the 1606 "Act to Restraine Abuses of Players" ', in Christa Jansohn and Bodo Plachta, eds, *Varienten—Variants—Variantes* (Tübingen: Max Niemeyer Verlag, 2005), 91–106, Ian Donaldson, *Ben Jonson: A Life* (Oxford: Oxford University Press, 2011), 235–6.
23. *Cymbeline*, 4.3.18.
24. White, *Of Oathes*, 14.
25. See *OED*, bind, *v.*, 15a, 'To tie (a person, oneself) up in respect to action; to oblige by a covenant, oath, promise or vow.'
26. *De Juramento*, 94, 227–9.
27. John Downame, *Four Treatises* (1608), 2. The analysis goes back to Augustine; see Richard Cosin on such oaths, in his *Apologie for Svndrie Proceedings by Iurisdiction Ecclesiasticall* (1593), Pt III, 36.
28. See e.g. Herbert H. Clark, *Using Language* (Cambridge: Cambridge University Press, 1996), 136–41.
29. John Milward, *Iacobs Great Day of Trouble, and Deliuerance: A Sermon Preached at Pauls Crosse, the Fifth of August 1607* (1610), A4r.
30. *OED*, religion, *n.*, etymology.
31. *A Godly and Learned Exposition of Christs Sermon in the Mount* (1608), 153.
32. See e.g. the Benedictus, recited after the second lesson, in the Elizabethan and Jacobean 'Order for Morning Praier Daily Throughout the Yeare': 'To perfourme thy mercy promysed to our forefathers: and to remember his holy couenaunt. | To performe the othe whiche he sware to oure forefather Abraham', *The Booke of Common Praier* (1559), A4v–5r.

33. Craig Muldrew, *The Economy of Obligation: The Culture of Credit and Social Relations in Early Modern England* (Basingstoke: Macmillan, 1998), 141.
34. '...id est dictorum conventorumque constantia et veritas', *De Officiis*, I.xxii [7] (ed. Walter Miller, Loeb Classical Library (London: Heinemann, 1913)); translation from *The First Book of Tullies Offices Translated Grammatically* (1616), ch. 9.
35. The original passage reads, entire: 'Eius autem vinculum est ratio et oratio, quae docendo, discendo, communicando, disceptando, iudicando conciliat inter se homines coniungitque naturali quadam societate' (*De Officiis*, Loeb, I.xvi [50]).
36. Thomas Wilson, *The Arte of Rhetorique* (1553), preface.
37. Montaigne, *The Essayes: Or, Morall, Politike and Millitarie Discourses*, tr. John Florio (1603), 16.
38. *Essays*, tr. John Florio (1613), 16.
39. John Marston, *The Wonder of Women: Or, The Tragedie of Sophonisba* (1606), C2v.
40. *The Boke Named the Gouernour* (1531), fol. 184v.
41. *A Swoord Agaynst Swearyng* (1579), fol. 3r. What perjury was, in religious, never mind legal, terms, how many varieties there were, and how it should be punished, turned out to be more complicated than the denunciation it invited; see e.g. Downame, *Four Treatises*, 47–76.
42. *A Collection of Emblemes, Ancient and Moderne* (1635), Bk II, illustr. xxii.
43. *OED*, oath, *n.*, 'Cognate with Old Frisian *ēth* , *ēd* (West Frisian *eed*), Middle Dutch *eet*, (in compounds) *eed-* (Dutch *eed*), Old Saxon *ēð*... further etymology uncertain'. The *OED* also records Celtic usage (Early Irish, Old Welsh), though not as a channel into early modern English.
44. For the self-curse in the Old Testament see 'Oath' (esp. 'Definition and Form') in *Encyclopaedia Judaica*, 2nd edn, ed. Fred Skolnik et al., 26 vols (Detroit: Thomson Gale, 2007); for awareness of this during Shakespeare's lifetime see e.g. Perkins, *Whole Treatise of the Cases of Conscience*, 382–3, 'in every Oath there be foure distinct things. First, an Asseueration of the truth;... Secondly, a confession of the omnipotent presence, wisedome, iustice and truth of God;... Thirdly, Prayer and Inuocation,... Fourthly, Imprecation, in which a man acknowledging God the the iust reuenger of a lie, bindes himselfe to punishment, if he shall sweare falsely, or speake an vntrueth wittingly or willingly.'
45. Kyriaki Konstantinidou, 'Oath and Curse', ch. 2 of Alan H. Sommerstein and Isabelle C. Torrance, with others, *Oaths and Swearing in Ancient Greece* (Berlin: Walter de Gruyter, 2014); cf. Alan H. Sommerstein and Andrew J. Bayliss, with others, *Oath and State in Ancient Greece* (Berlin: Walter de Gruyter, 2013), esp. 4, 153–4.
46. *OED*, vow, *n.* and *v.*, derives the word from Latin *vōtum* and *vōvēre* ('to promise solemnly, to pledge, dedicate, etc.') through Anglo-Norman *vu(u, vou, vo* and Old French *vo, vou, vowe, veu.*
47. *OED*, vow, *n.*, 3, citing *A Midsummer Night's Dream*, 1.1.175–6. For an earlier instance see e.g. the Elizabethan marriage service, where there is no vow *to* God, and the plighting of troth between bride and groom is called 'the vow and couenaunte betwixt them made' (*The Booke of Common Praier* (1559), O6r–v).

48. See e.g. Alain Boreau, *Le Désir dicté: Histoire du vœu religieux dans l'Occident médiéval* (Paris: Les Belles Lettres, 2014).
49. Electronic searching confirms their late sixteenth-century emergence.
50. *OED* 5, citing *2 Henry VI*, 3.2.158–9 ('A dreadful oath, sworn with a solemn tongue! | What instance gives Lord Warwick for his vow?').
51. Both spellings are current in e.g. Henry Swinburne, *A Treatise of Spousals, or Matrimonial Contracts*, composed in about 1600 (1686).
52. *The Tempest*, 4.1.52 (he then calls Ferdinand's oath a 'vow' (55)), *Henry V*, 2.3.42; cf. Herbert Alexander Ellis, *Shakespeare's Lusty Punning in 'Love's Labour's Lost': With Contemporary Analogues* (The Hague: Mouton, 1973), 167–8.
53. e.g. *Hamlet*, 2.2.508.
54. *OED*, protest, 6.
55. *OED*, protest, *v.*, 2, 3a–c.
56. *All's Well That Ends Well*, 4.2.28–30.
57. *Vouch* stems from Latin *vocare* ('to call') again through Old French and Anglo-Norman (*OED*, vouch, *v.*).
58. Once by Bolingbroke in *Richard II*, twice by Iachimo in *Cymbeline* (who draws on the word's legal associations). For an account of incidence generally, influenced by the use of *covenant* to translate Hebrew *berit* in English bibles ('bond', 'bond of peace', 'testament', 'league' were also used), see Naomi Tadmor, 'People of the Covenant and the English Bible', *Transactions of the Royal Historical Society*, 22 (2012), 95–110.
59. *OED*, defy, *v.* 1a.
60. *OED*, adjure, *v.*, 1, 'To bind under oath; to command or appeal to (a person) to do something in the name of God or a god, or under penalty of some punishment or curse.'
61. John Bale (or Miles Coverdale), *A Christen Exhortacion vnto Customable Swearers* (1543), fol. 11r.
62. *De Juramento*, 173. For 'obtestation' as an exclamation, a 'taking God and the world to witnes' that might fall just this side of an oath, see George Puttenham, *The Arte of English Poesie* (1589), 157.
63. e.g. Jeremy Taylor, *Ductor Dubitantium: Or, The Rule of Conscience in All her Generall Measures*, 2 vols (1660), II, 514–15.
64. e.g. George Chapman, *The Reuenge of Bussy D'Ambois* (1613), G2r.
65. e.g. George Sandys, *A Relation of the State of Religion* (1605), E1r.
66. Taylor, *Ductor Dubitantium*, II, 94.
67. *A Briefe Treatise of Oathes Exacted by Ordinaries and Ecclesiasticall Iudges* (1590), 56.
68. 57. 'By inspection of the Gospels and not by touching.'
69. From Latin *corpus*, body, via Old French *corporal* (twelfth century). See *OED*, corporal, *adj. and n.*[3], 5a: 'corporal oath [Medieval Latin *corporale juramentum*;...]: an oath ratified by corporally touching a sacred object, *esp.* the gospels, but sometimes the consecrated host, or relics of saints, and in heathen times the altar, etc., of an idol, as distinguished from a merely verbal oath, to which the body was, as it were, not a party.'

70. Part III, ch. 4. For context see Ethan H. Shagan, 'The English Inquisition: Constitutional Conflict and Ecclesiastical Law in the 1590s', *Historical Journal*, 47 (2004), 531–65.
71. Thomas Randolph, *Aristippus: Or, The Ioviall Philosopher* (1630), 10. 'Virtual touch will not do, it must be actual and non-intellective (beyond understanding).'
72. 2.2.122–35. Cf. Andrew Gurr, 'Stephano's Leather Bottle', *Notes and Queries*, 59:4 (2012), 549–50.
73. John Earle, *Micro-cosmographie: Or, A Peece of the World Discovered in Essayes and Characters* (1628), H5v–8v, at H6r.
74. *A Godly and Learned Exposition of Christs Sermon in the Mount*, 171.
75. *Sir Thomas Ouerburie his Wife with New Elegies . . . Whereunto are Annexed, New Newes and Characters* (1616), G8v–H1v, at H1r.
76. The profanities of Abiezer Coppe, for instance, became notorious, and not just thanks to his enemies. Citing Revelation 10: 6, he declares in *A Second Fiery Flying Roule* (1649): 'It's meat and drink to an Angel [who knows none evill, no sin] to sweare a full mouth'd oath.'
77. William Vaughan, *The Arraignment of Slander Periury Blasphemy, and Other Malicious Sinnes* (1630), 123–4.
78. 2.1.50 and 3.2.347, 2.2.408 and 3.2.120, 4.5.57 ('Gis' is 'Jesus').
79. For examples see Jonathan Michael Gray, *Oaths and the English Reformation* (Cambridge: Cambridge University Press, 2013), 28–30.
80. Robert Parsons, *A Christian Directorie Guiding Men to their Saluation* (1585), 736.
81. Gillian Woods, *Shakespeare's Unreformed Fictions* (Oxford: Oxford University Press, 2013), 1–4.
82. Henry Fitzsimon, *The Iustification and Exposition of the Diuine Sacrifice of the Masse* (1611), 130–1.
83. *A Royalist's Notebook: The Commonplace Book of Sir John Oglander* (London: Constable, 1936), 196, 197.
84. *Antony and Cleopatra*, 1.3.82 (a 'target' is a shield); Robert Greene, *The Honorable Historie of Frier Bacon, and Frier Bongay* (*c.*1589, pub. 1630), C2r; *As You Like It*, 3.2.355; *Every Man in his Humour* (F), 1.5.89, in *The Cambridge Edition of the Works of Ben Jonson*, gen. eds David Bevington, Martin Butler, and Ian Donaldson, 7 vols (Cambridge: Cambridge University Press, 2012), IV; *Cymbeline*, 4.2.295 (meaning, 'By God's pity, by the merest pity of God'); *The White Devil*, 5.3.203, in *The Works of John Webster*, ed. David Gunby et al., 3 vols (Cambridge: Cambridge University Press, 1995–2007), I; *The Puritan Widow*, 1.4.9, ed. Donna B. Hamilton, in *Thomas Middleton: The Collected Works*, gen. eds Gary Taylor and John Lavagnino (Oxford: Clarendon Press, 2007).
85. Boyle, *A Free Discourse*, 32, citing Galatians 6: 7 and 1 Corinthians 3: 19. By the mid-seventeenth century, and probably during Shakespeare's lifetime, euphemistic oaths were routinely known as 'minced'. As the *OED* shows, the adjective derives from *mince* meaning 'cut up', 'diminish' (overlapping with *minish*), and thus 'extenuate' (1533), 'palliate' (1591) and 'use a euphemistic substitution'

(as when Henry V, wooing the Princess of France, declares, 'I know no ways to mince it in love, but directly to say, "I love you"' (5.2.125–6), and Antony tells a messenger: 'Mince not the general tongue. | Name Cleopatra as she is called in Rome' (1.2.94–5)). From 1549, *mince* could mean 'To utter in an affectedly refined or precise manner'.

86. Cf. David Schalkwyk, *Speech and Performance in Shakespeare's Sonnets and Plays* (Cambridge: Cambridge University Press, 2002), 70–1.
87. On misarticulation disclosing falsehood, see Chapter 8 (p. 235).
88. *Boke Named the Gouernour*, fol. 184r.
89. *The First Folio of Shakespeare: A Transcript of Contemporary Marginalia*, ed. Akihiro Yamada (Tokyo: Yushodo Press, 1998), 290 (*Cymbeline*, 3.4.53), 64 (*As You Like It*, 3.4.14–40).
90. The paradigmatic instance was Jacob covenanting with Laban, as related by Shylock. See p. 157.
91. Judith Fletcher, *Performing Oaths in Classical Greek Drama* (Cambridge: Cambridge University Press, 2012), 14.
92. See e.g. Alison Weir, *Elizabeth the Queen* (1998; London: Vintage, 2008), 166, 427.
93. *As You Like It*, 4.1.161–2; *Twelfth Night*, 3.1.148.
94. Steven Shapin, *A Social History of Truth: Civility and Science in Seventeenth-Century England* (Chicago: University of Chicago Press, 1994), 69, quoting Henry Peacham, *The Compleat Gentleman* (1622) and Curtis Brown Watson, *Shakespeare and the Renaissance Concept of Honor* (Princeton: Princeton University Press, 1960).
95. Shapin, *Social History of Truth*, 92, quoting [Brydges?], *Horae Subseciuae* (1620).
96. e.g. Pisanio instructed to murder Imogen by Posthumus (*Cymbeline*, 3.2.11–20).
97. Shapin, *Social History of Truth*, 88, quoting Aristotle, *History of Animals*.
98. A.P., *Natural and Morall Questions and Answeres* (1598), D5r–v.
99. T.G., *The Rich Cabinet Furnished with Varietie of Excellent Discriptions, Exquisite Charracters, Witty Discourses, and Delightfull Histories* (1616), fol. 110r.
100. *Timon of Athens*, 4.3.135–6.
101. See the spread of their lines in *2 Henry IV*, 2.4, *Henry V*, 2.1.
102. This is the contention of David Womersley, *Divinity and State* (Oxford: Oxford University Press, 2010), 329–30.
103. 'Causa, tempus, locus, occasio, instrumentum, modus': Quintilian, *Institutio Oratoria*, ed. and tr. Harold Edgeworth Butler, Loeb Classical Library, 4 vols (London: Heinemann, 1920–1), 5.10.23. Cf. Lorna Hutson, *Circumstantial Shakespeare* (Oxford: Oxford University Press, 2015), esp. ch. 1.
104. Holger Schott Syme, *Theatre and Testimony in Shakespeare's England: A Culture of Mediation* (Cambridge: Cambridge University Press, 2012), esp. introd. and ch. 1.
105. Syme, *Theatre and Testimony*, 46–58.

106. Laura Gowing, *Domestic Dangers: Women, Words, and Sex in Early Modern London* (Oxford: Clarendon Press, 1998), 50–1.
107. *The Winter's Tale*, 1.2.51–2.
108. *Much Ado About Nothing*, 4.1.268–76.
109. *Purchas his Pilgrimage: Or, Relations of the World and the Religions Obserued in All Ages and Places Discouered, from the Creation vnto this Present* (1613), 211. Cf. Colchos, in Asia Minor, 'Swearing they hold an excellent qualitie, and to be a fashion-monger in oathes, glorious' (292).
110. *Purchas his Pilgrimage*, 577 (cf. 581); see Chapter 8.
111. Richard Hakluyt, *The Principal Nauigations*, 3 vols (1599–1600), II, Ggg5r.
112. Leo Africanus says that the Arabs of Barbary, by contrast, 'keepe their couenant most faithfully; ... they had rather die then breake promise' (*A Geographical Historie of Africa* (1600), D2v). On the Amerindians, see e.g. Hakluyt, *Principal Nauigations*, III, X2r, III, Y4r.
113. See George Sandys, *A Relation of a Iourney begun An Dom: 1610* (1615), H3r–v.
114. Robert Dallington, *The View of Fraunce* (1604), Y1v–2r.
115. Jean Hotman, *The Ambassador* (1603), E4v–5r.
116. *Julius Caesar*, 2.1.271, 279, 298–300.
117. Frances A. Shirley, *Swearing and Perjury in Shakespeare's Plays* (London: George Allen and Unwin, 1979), 90.
118. See e.g. Ann Jennalie Cook, *Making a Match: Courtship in Shakespeare and his Society* (Princeton: Princeton University Press, 1991), chs 7–8, B. J. Sokol and Mary Sokol, *Shakespeare, Law, and Marriage* (Cambridge: Cambridge University Press, 2003), chs 1, 5–6, Subha Mukherji, *Law and Representation in Early Modern Drama* (Cambridge: Cambridge University Press, 2006), ch. 1.
119. A good, brief example is set by William O. Scott, '"A Woman's Thought Runs Before her Actions": Vows as Speech Acts in *As You Like It*', *Philosophy and Literature*, 30 (2006), 528–39.
120. e.g. Lorna Hutson, *The Usurer's Daughter: Male Friendship and Fictions of Women in Sixteenth-Century England* (London: Routledge, 1994) and her *The Invention of Suspicion: Law and Mimesis in Shakespeare and Renaissance Drama* (Oxford: Oxford University Press, 2007); Luke Wilson, *Theaters of Intention: Drama and the Law in Early Modern England* (Stanford, Calif.: Stanford University Press, 2000); Paul Raffield, *Images and Cultures of Law in Early Modern England: Justice and Political Power, 1558–1660* (Cambridge: Cambridge University Press, 2004) and his *Shakespeare's Imaginary Constitution: Late Elizabethan Politics and the Theatre of Law* (Oxford: Hart, 2010); Bradin Cormack, *A Power to do Justice: Jurisdiction, English Literature, and the Rise of Common Law, 1509–1625* (Chicago: University of Chicago Press, 2007); Paul Raffield and Gary Watt, eds, *Shakespeare and the Law* (Oxford: Hart, 2008); Andrew Zurcher, *Shakespeare and Law* (London: Arden Shakespeare, 2010); Bradin Cormack, Martha Nussbaum, and Richard Strier, eds, *Shakespeare and the Law: A Conversation among Disciplines and Professions* (Chicago: Chicago University Press, 2013).

121. Lorna Hutson, 'Not the King's Two Bodies: Reading the "Body Politic" in Shakespeare's *Henry IV*, Parts I and II', David Harris Sacks, 'The Promise and the Contract in Early Modern England: Slade's Case in Perspective', in Hutson and Victoria Kahn, eds, *Rhetoric and Law in Early Modern Europe* (New Haven: Yale University Press, 2001), 166–98, 28–53.
122. Latin, 'he has taken upon himself'; *OED*, assumpsit, *n.*, a 'A promise or contract, oral or in writing not sealed, founded upon a consideration', b 'An action to recover damages for breach or non-performance of such contract.'
123. See esp. the classic essays by J. H. Baker, 'New Light on *Slade's Case*', Pts 1 and 2, *Cambridge Law Journal*, 29 (1971), 51–67, 213–36, David Ibbetson, 'Sixteenth Century Contract Law: *Slade's Case* in Context', *Oxford Journal of Legal Studies*, 4 (1985), 295–317, and R. H. Helmholz, 'Assumpsit and *Fidei Laesio*', *Law Quarterly Review*, 91 (1975), 406–32.
124. Cf. Hutson, *The Usurer's Daughter*, esp. 139–48, *Invention of Suspicion*, esp. 15–17, 56–7, 296–302.
125. The majority view, that *Troilus* was written for performance at the Inns of Court, was first set out by Peter Alexander, '*Troilus and Cressida*, 1609', *The Library*, 4th ser. 9 (1928–9), 267–86. For doubts, see *Troilus and Cressida*, ed. Bevington, 88–9.
126. Hobbes, *Leviathan* (1651), ch. 14; P. S. Atiyah, *Promises, Morals, and Law* (Oxford: Clarendon Press, 1981).
127. *Shakespeare's Promises* (Baltimore: Johns Hopkins University Press, 1999), 90–1, 198–206.
128. 'Swearing in Public: More and Shakespeare', *English Literary Renaissance*, 27 (1997), 197–232. See now his *Mortal Thoughts: Religion, Secularity, and Identity in Shakespeare and Early Modern Culture* (Oxford: Oxford University Press, 2013), ch. 4.
129. *Shakespeare and the Grammar of Forgiveness* (Ithaca, NY: Cornell University Press, 2011), 4–5.
130. For résumés of the field see *Études épistémè*, 24 (2013), *Aspects du serment en Angleterre (XVIe–XVIIIe siècles).*
131. Christopher Hill, *Society and Puritanism in Pre-Revolutionary England* (London: Secker and Warburg, 1964), ch. 11.
132. Defoe, *An Essay upon Projects* (1697), 227–51, pp. 249–50.
133. See Melissa Mohr, 'Defining Dirt: Three Early Modern Views of Obscenity', *Textual Practice*, 17 (2003), 253–75, also her *Holy Shit: A Brief History of Swearing* (New York: Oxford University Press, 2013), chs. 4–5; Tony McEnery, *Swearing in English: Bad Language, Purity and Power from 1586 to the Present* (London: Routledge, 2006), chs 3–4. For the shifting contours of obscenity see e.g. Geoffrey Hughes, *Swearing: A Social History of Foul Language, Oaths and Profanity in English*, 2nd edn (London: Penguin, 1998), *An Encyclopedia of Swearing: The Social History of Oaths, Profanity, Foul Language, and Ethnic Slurs in the English-Speaking World* (Armonk, NY: M. E. Sharpe, 2006).
134. David Martin Jones, *Conscience and Allegiance in Seventeenth Century England: The Political Significance of Oaths and Engagements* (Rochester, NY: University of

Rochester Press, 1999), Edward Vallance, *Revolutionary England and the National Covenant: State Oaths, Protestantism, and the Political Nation, 1553–1682* (Woodbridge: Boydell, 2005).

135. See his *Argument and Authority in Early Modern England: The Presupposition of Oaths and Offices* (Cambridge: Cambridge University Press, 2006). For a compendium see Richard Garnet (?), comp., *The Book of Oaths* (1649).
136. 'In 1585-6 the Chamberlain paid for the printing of 500 copies of the constables' oaths "with additions";... By 1585–6 Hugh Singleton, the City printer, produced 2,800' copies of *The Oath of Every Freeman*, 'a printed reiteration of the freeman's oral ritual of admission to the commonality'. Mark Jenner, 'London', in Joad Raymond, ed., *The History of Popular Print Culture*, Vol. I, *Cheap Print in Britain and Ireland to 1660* (Oxford: Oxford University Press, 2011), 294–307, pp. 305–6.
137. See her *Domestic Dangers*.
138. Victoria Kahn, *Wayward Contracts: The Crisis of Political Obligation in England, 1640–1674* (Princeton: Princeton University Press, 2004), 36.
139. John Spurr, 'Perjury, Profanity and Politics', *Seventeenth Century*, 8 (1993), 29–50, 'A Profane History of Early Modern Oaths', *Transactions of the Royal Historical Society*, 6th ser. 11 (2001), 37–63, '"The Strongest Bond of Conscience": Oaths and the Limits of Tolerance in Early Modern England', in Harald E. Braun and Edward Vallance, eds, *Contexts of Conscience in Early Modern Europe, 1500–1700* (Basingstoke: Palgrave Macmillan, 2004), 151–65.
140. Some, more recent philosophers would agree with Cassandra that the purpose makes strong the vow. See e.g. Michael H. Robins, *Promising, Intending, and Moral Autonomy* (Cambridge: Cambridge University Press, 1984); Michael E. Bratman, *Intention, Plans, and Practical Reason* (Cambridge, Mass.: Harvard University Press, 1987), *Faces of Intention: Selected Essays on Intention and Agency* (Cambridge: Cambridge University Press, 1999).
141. e.g. *De Juramento*, 64, J. L. Austin, *How to Do Things with Words*, 2nd edn, ed. J. O. Urmson and Marina Sbisà (Oxford: Oxford University Press, 1975), 10–11. In both, more intentionally couched formulations can be found.
142. Andrew Gurr, *The Shakespearean Stage, 1574–1642*, 4th edn (Cambridge: Cambridge University Press, 2009), 96. 'Under favour' means 'saying this by your leave, protected by your gracious permission.'
143. For early steps see W. B. Worthen, *Shakespeare and the Force of Modern Performance* (Cambridge: Cambridge University Press, 2003), esp. introd.; more recently and philosophically, James Loxley and Mark Robson, *Shakespeare, Jonson, and the Claims of the Performative* (Abingdon: Routledge, 2013).
144. *How to Do Things with Words*, 22.
145. Jacques Derrida, *Limited Inc* (Evanston, Ill.: Northwestern University Press, 1988), 16–19, 67–72, 88–107—cf. Stanley Cavell, *A Pitch of Philosophy: Autobiographical Exercises* (Cambridge, Mass.: Harvard University Press, 1994), ch. 2—Judith Butler, *Excitable Speech: A Politics of the Performative* (New York: Routledge, 1997), Andrew Parker and Eve Kosofsky Sedgwick, 'Introduction',

in Parker and Sedgwick, eds, *Performativity and Performance* (New York: Routledge, 1995), 1–18.

146. The Belott–Mountjoy papers, accessible as an appendix to Charles Nicholl's absorbing study *The Lodger: Shakespeare on Silver Street* (2007; London: Allen Lane, 2008), show Shakespeare telling Daniel Nicholas that Charles Mountjoy promised 'about the some of ffyftye poundes' to his daughter and Stephen Belott on their marriage, but in court, under oath, he deposed 'what certayne porcion he Rememberithe not. / nor when to be payed' (289, cf. 293; 290).
147. Aristotle, *Rhetoric*, I.xv; Quintilian, *Institutio Oratoria*, V.vi.
148. For origins see Aristotle, *Rhetoric*, I.xv, where oaths are categorized, in forensic oratory, with laws, witnesses, contracts, and torture. Cf. Kathy Eden, *Poetic and Legal Fiction in the Aristotelian Tradition* (Princeton: Princeton University Press, 1986), esp. ch. 1.
149. Henry Peacham, *The Garden of Eloquence*, rev. edn (1593), 67–8, 75–6.
150. *Boke Named the Gouernour*, fol. 193r.
151. See e.g. William Prynne, *Histrio-Mastix: The Players Scourge, or, Actors Tragaedie* (1633), **3v, 81–8, 520 (citing Gosson), 930.
152. Phillip Stubbes, *Anatomie of Abuses* (1583), L8v.
153. *Micro-cosmographie*, E3r–4v, at E3v–4r.
154. John Taylor, 'To my Approued Good Friend M. Thomas Heywood', one of the prefatory poems in Thomas Heywood, *Apology for Actors* (1612).
155. *The Famous Victories of Henry the Fifth* (1598), G2r; *Pierce Penilesse* (1592), in *The Works of Thomas Nashe*, ed. Ronald B. McKerrow, 5 vols, rev. F. P. Wilson (Oxford: Blackwell, 1958), I, 213. For further discussion see p. 254.
156. White, *Of Oathes*, 2–3, 14–15, John Bulwer, *Chirologia: Or, The Natural Language of the Hand* (1644), 50–4, 102–5, Sanderson, *De Juramento*, 161–2, 179–82. As John Spurr has pointed out: 'In many languages verbs for swearing are derived from roots meaning "to grasp" or "to hold". Taking an oath often involves holding or touching inanmimate objects' ('Profane History', 45).
157. See e.g. Richard Firth Green, *A Crisis of Truth: Literature and Law in Ricardian England* (Philadelphia: University of Pennsylvania Press, 1999), ch. 2.
158. On the physicality of voice-production, drawing on Pliny and the Bible, see the dedication to William Gearing, *A Bridle for the Tongue: Or, A Treatise of Ten Sins of the Tongue* (1663), Aa3r–4r. For thoughts about oaths and the voice in *King John*, which are capable of wider application, see Gina Bloom, *Voice in Motion: Staging Gender, Shaping Sound in Early Modern England* (Philadelphia: University of Pennsylvania Press, 2007), ch. 2.
159. e.g. Saxony, reaching out to Austria, in a play that owes much to *Hamlet*, 'Thus doe I plight thee troth, and promise peace,' to which the latter replies: 'Nay, but thy eyes agree not with thy heart; | In vowes of combination, ther's a grace | That shewes the intention in the outward face' (Henry Chettle, *The Tragedy of Hoffman: Or, A Reuenge for a Father* (1602–3; pub. 1631), D1r).

160. *Measure for Measure*, 5.1.37–46, 198–9; *All's Well*, 5.3.171–6, 292–301.
161. e.g. Sanderson, *De Juramento*, 150–1.
162. 1.5.151; cf. Beatrice on Benedick's eating his s/word (p. 30), and Pistol in *Henry V*: 'Sword is an oath, and oaths must have their course' (2.1.91).
163. See the evidence from rhyming and homophone lists in E. J. Dobson, *English Pronunciation 1500–1700*, 2nd edn (Oxford: Clarendon Press, 1968), Fausto Cercignani, *Shakespeare's Works and Elizabethan Pronunciation* (Oxford: Clarendon Press, 1981).
164. See e.g. Thomas Becon, *An Inuectyue Agenst the Moost Wicked [and] Detestable Vyce of Swearing, Newly Co[m]piled by Theodore Basille* (1543), seven times.
165. *Excitable Speech*, 155. Behind Butler's thought here is Shoshana Felman, *The Literary Speech Act: Don Juan with J. L. Austin, or Seduction in Two Languages*, tr. Catherine Porter (Ithaca, NY: Cornell University Press, 1983).
166. Condren, *Argument and Authority*, 249–50.
167. William Burton catches the dilemma, in another key, in his *Caueat for Suerties* (1593): 'Men think that fraud doth so ouerflow, that they cannot vse too many words in their bonds, and bargaines. And on the contrarie side they thinke that fraud lyeth and lurketh in multitude of words: and that they be fit matter for wrangling heads to worke vppon. And yet as men do sweare much because one man wil not trust another, so in bargaining men do vse manie words, because one man doth vse to deceaue another' (62–3).
168. Richard Stephens, John Atkins, and Andrew Kingston, 'Swearing as a Response to Pain', *NeuroReport*, 20:12 (5 August 2009), 1056–60.
169. For some highly provisional findings in cognitive psychology and neuroscience see: Timothy Jay, *Why We Curse: A Neuro-Psycho-Social Theory of Speech* (Philadelphia: John Benjamins, 2000), Timothy Jay and Kristin Janschewitz, 'The Pragmatics of Swearing', *Journal of Politeness Research*, 4 (2008), 267–88; Steven Pinker, *The Stuff of Thought: Language as a Window into Human Nature* (London: Penguin, 2007), 325–38; Mohr, *Holy Shit*, 250–1.
170. Herbert J. Schlesinger, *Promises, Oaths, and Vows: On the Psychology of Promising* (New York: Analytic Press, 2008), 20–2, 50–8, 83–8.
171. Sonnet 115.
172. On 'the promise of future action' as 'an interrupted act', see Schlesinger, *Promises, Oaths, and Vows*, 41–6, 89.
173. Adam Phillips, *Missing Out* (London: Hamish Hamilton, 2012), xiii.
174. Cf. William Vitek, *Promising* (Philadelphia: Temple University Press, 1993), 2.
175. Francis Bacon, 'Of Custome and Education', in *The Essayes or Counsels, Civill and Morall*, rev. edn (1625), 231–4, p. 232.
176. *The Merchant of Venice*, 5.1.154–5.
177. Thomas Wright, *The Passions of the Minde in Generall* (1604), 125–6, Robert Burton, *The Anatomy of Melancholy* (1621), 160.
178. S. T. Coleridge, *Shakespearean Criticism*, ed. Thomas Middleton Raysor, 2nd edn, 2 vols (London: Everyman, 1960), I, 199.

CHAPTER 2 EARLY REVENGE

1. On medieval oaths of fealty see p. 6. The oath sworn to Henry VI by thirty-two secular peers at the 1459 Parliament has been a particular focus for historians.
2. *2 Henry VI*, 5.1.180–1. Cf. the excuse given by Clarence, in *3 Henry VI*, for reverting to the Yorkists: 'Perhaps thou wilt object my holy oath. | To keep that oath were more impiety | Than Jephthah, when he sacrificed his daughter' (5.1.92–4).
3. *3 Henry VI*, 1.2.22–7.
4. Hugh Craig, 'The Three Parts of *Henry VI*', in Craig and Arthur F. Kinney, eds, *Shakespeare, Computers, and the Mystery of Authorship* (Cambridge: Cambridge University Press, 2012), 40–77, pp. 69–72.
5. John Kerrigan, *Revenge Tragedy: Aeschylus to Armageddon* (Oxford: Clarendon Press, 1996), 12–18.
6. Kerrigan, *Revenge Tragedy*, 4–5.
7. Cf. Michael Goldman's reflections on 'the promise of action' in his *Acting and Action in Shakespearean Tragedy* (Princeton: Princeton University Press, 1985), 9.
8. Though it is taken from Ovid's *Heroides*, 2.66, a school text not a pious source: 'The gods grant that this may be the height of your glory' (tr. *Norton Shakespeare*).
9. Line 138. Cf. Robert Greene (or Henry Chettle) abusing Shakespeare as 'an vpstart Crow, beautified with our feathers, that with his *Tygers hart wrapt in a Players hyde,* supposes he is as well able to bombast out a blanke verse as the best of you: and beeing an absolute *Iohannes fac totum,* is in his owne conceit the onely Shake-scene in a countrey' (*Greenes, Groats-worth of Witte* (1592), F1v).
10. Romans 12: 19; cf. Deuteronomy 32: 35.
11. This tragedy of unknown authorship is mentioned by Nashe in 1589 and Lodge in 1596; there is a reference to a performance of what is probably the same play in Henslowe's *Diary* for 1594.
12. *Antonio's Revenge*, ed. Reavley Gair, Revels Plays (Manchester: Manchester University Press, 1978), 3.1.36–7.
13. *Hamlet*, 1.5.31; cf. p. 15.
14. *Thyestes*, lines 520–1, in Seneca, *Tragedies*, ed. and tr. Frank Justus Miller, Loeb Classical Library, 2 vols (London: Heinemann, 1917), II.
15. *The Seconde Tragedie of Seneca Entituled Thyestes*, tr. Jasper Heywood (1560), C2r.
16. *Thyestes*, ed. R. J. Tarrant (Atlanta: Scholars Press, 1985), n. to line 544 on p. 168.
17. The likelihood of Shakespeare reading *Orbecche*—a celebrated tragedy during his lifetime—strikes me as high. He could certainly have read the story on which the tragedy is based in Cinthio's *Hecatommithi* (1565), 2.2, a book which provided in Italian the major source for *Othello*.
18. *Thyestes*, ed. Tarrant, 200.
19. Robert Parker, *Miasma: Pollution and Purification in Early Greek Religion* (Oxford: Clarendon Press, 1983), 186–7. Cf. *The Oxford Classical Dictionary*, 4th edn, ed. Simon Hornblower et al. (Oxford: Oxford University Press, 2012), 'Oaths', 'The

punishment for perjury... often called for "the complete destruction of the perjuror and his family"' (references to Andocides and Pliny the Younger).

20. '... solidamque pacis alliget certae fidem' (lines 970–3).
21. Line 1024; *Seconde Tragedie of Seneca Entituled Thyestes*, D8v.
22. Walter Burkert, *Homo Necans: The Anthropology of Ancient Greek Sacrificial Ritual and Myth*, tr. Peter Bing (Berkeley: University of California Press, 1983), 35–8; cf. Burkert's *Greek Religion: Archaic and Classical*, tr. John Raffan (Oxford: Blackwell, 1985), 250–2, and, more recently, Alan H. Sommerstein and Isabelle C. Torrance, with others, *Oaths and Swearing in Ancient Greece* (Berlin: Walter de Gruyter, 2014), esp. 138–42.
23. Burkert, *Homo Necans*, 36–7, *Greek Religion*, 251.
24. Livy, *The Romane Historie*, tr. Philemon Holland (1600), 17.
25. Cf. Burkert, *Homo Necans*, 35.
26. Further back, in ancient Greece, oath and sacrifice were so closely associated that the same word *horkos, horkia* could refer to both.
27. This account draws on the obvious sources, including Jörg Rüpke, *Religion of the Romans*, tr. and ed. Richard Gordon (Cambridge: Polity, 2007), esp. chs 6–7, John Scheid, 'Sacrifices for Gods and Ancestors', in Rüpke, ed., *A Companion to Roman Religion* (Chichester: Blackwell/Wiley, 2011), 263–71.
28. *Homo Necans*, 36–7.
29. Lactantius says that he made it illegal, *Divinarum Institutionum*, 1.21.
30. *Iliad*, XXIII.166–78, *Aeneid*, X.517–20.
31. *Greek Historical Inscriptions: 404–323 BC*, ed. with introduction, translations, and commentaries by P. J. Rhodes and Robin Osborne (Oxford: Oxford University Press, 2003), 88. For contexts see Paul Cartledge, *After Thermopylae: The Oath of Plataea and the End of the Graeco-Persian Wars* (Oxford: Oxford University Press, 2013), esp. chs 2–3.
32. *Seven Against Thebes*, lines 42–8, in *Aeschylus*, ed. and tr. Alan H. Sommerstein, Loeb Classical Library, 3 vols (Cambridge, Mass.: Harvard University Press, 2008), I.
33. See e.g. Pat Southern, *The Roman Army: A Social and Institutional History* (2006; Oxford: Oxford University Press, 2007), 134.
34. *Historie*, tr. Holland, 41.
35. Plutarch, *The Lives of the Noble Grecians and Romanes*, tr. Thomas North (1579), 108.
36. *Lives*, tr. North, 109.
37. *Catiline his Conspiracy*, 1.1.482–7, ed. Inga-Stina Ewbank, in *The Cambridge Edition of the Works of Ben Jonson*, gen. eds David Bevington, Martin Butler, and Ian Donaldson, 7 vols (Cambridge: Cambridge University Press, 2012), IV.
38. *On the Genealogy of Morality*, ed. Keith Ansell-Pearson, tr. Carol Diethe, rev. edn (Cambridge: Cambridge University Press, 2007), 2.3, at p. 38.
39. *The Tragedy of Hoffman: Or, A Reuenge for a Father* (1631), I4r–v.
40. George Puttenham, *The Arte of English Poesie* (1589), 72–4.

41. 'To the shades of our brothers'.
42. The text, which survives in a mid-eighteenth-century edition, but which probably dates from the middle of the sixteenth century, is most easily consulted in modernized form, as *The Tragical History of Titus Andronicus*, in Geoffrey Bullough, ed., *Narrative and Dramatic Sources of Shakespeare*, 8 vols (London: Routledge, 1957–75), VI, 34–44.
43. See the capable discussion in Robert S. Miola, *Shakespeare and Classical Tragedy: The Influence of Seneca* (Oxford: Clarendon Press, 1992), 18–22.
44. *Troades*, line 767, in Seneca, *Tragedies*, ed. and tr. Miller.
45. See Marcus' incitement of Lucius' son, young Lucius, to an oath after Chiron and Demetrius are exposed as the rapists of Lavinia: 'Lavinia, kneel; | And kneel, sweet boy, the Roman Hector's hope' (4.1.86–7). Arthur's precipitation of himself from the battlements in *King John* (4.3.1–10) would have behind it for educated members of the Elizabethan audience Astyanax's death-leap from Troy's one remaining high tower.
46. 'To the readers', in *The Sixt Tragedie of the Most Graue and Prudent Author Lucius, Anneus, Seneca, Entituled Troas with Diuers and Sundrye Addicions to the Same* (1559).
47. 'And shall hys sprightes haue no rewarde | their angers to appayse?', *Troas*, C1r.
48. See *The Lamentable and Tragical History of Titus Andronicus, with the Fall of his Sons in the War of the Goths, with the Manner of the Ravishment of his Daughter Lavinia, by the Empress's Two Sons*, in Bullough, ed., *Narrative and Dramatic Sources of Shakespeare*, VI, 44–8.
49. *Ein sehr klägliche Tragaedia von Tito Andronico und der hoffertigen Käyserin*, in *Engelische Comedien und Tragedien* (1620).
50. Jan Vos, *Aran en Titus: Of, Wraak en Weerwraak. Treurspel* (1641), B3r–C1v. Several printings of Vos's play survive from the 1640s.
51. Edward Ravenscroft, *Titus Andronicus: Or, The Rape of Lavinia* (1687), 4.
52. See the informative account in Michael D. Friedman with Alan Dessen, *Titus Andronicus*, Shakespeare in Performance, 2nd edn (Manchester: Manchester University Press, 2013), 204.
53. For the former sense see many uses of 'rape' in Acts 2, 4, and 5; for the latter see 1.1.401–2 ('"Rape" call you it, my lord, to seize my own').
54. The interpretation is familiar, and given the details of the script, unavoidable: see e.g. David Willbern, 'Rape and Revenge in *Titus Andronicus*', *English Literary Renaissance*, 8 (1978), 159–82, p. 168, Kerrigan, *Revenge Tragedy*, 196–7.
55. Cf. pp. 25, 157.
56. Cf. Katherine A. Rowe, 'Dismembering and Forgetting in *Titus Andronicus*', *Shakespeare Quarterly*, 45 (1994), 279–303, p. 293.
57. Thomas P. Anderson, '"What is Written Shall be Executed": "Nude Contracts" and "Lively Warrants" in *Titus Andronicus*', *Criticism*, 45 (2003), 301–21, p. 302.
58. For other elements derived from *Thyestes*, see e.g. Miola, *Shakespeare and Classical Tragedy*, 23–4.
59. 'Bind' and 'bound' occur five times in ten lines, 'stop their mouths' and 'Stop close their mouths' three times in seven (5.2.156–66). Cf. *Thyestes*, line 685.

60. For fuller discussion see Kerrigan, *Revenge Tragedy*, 196–9.
61. e.g. *Love's Labour's Lost*, 2.1.189.

CHAPTER 3 SWEARING IN JEST

1. *Gesta Grayorum: Or, The History of the High and Mighty Prince, Henry Prince of Purpoole... who Reigned and Died, a.d. 1594* (1688), 1.
2. Excerpted in REED, *Inns of Court*, ed. Alan H. Nelson and John R. Elliott, Jr, 3 vols (Cambridge: D. S. Brewer, 2010), 366–79.
3. The title page of the 1598 quarto reads '... As it was presented before her Highnes [Elizabeth I] this last Christmas'; a revival was proposed, and probably performed, for Queen Anne at the end of the Christmas season, 1604–5.
4. Gray's Inn, located in the Parish of Portpool.
5. A number of these routines, including bills 'subscribed' by the Prince's ten followers, plans for 'ye entertaynment of forraine Princes & Embassadours', lists of officers, and of 'Decrees, and Statutes', a 'proclamation' to bring about order, and a projected 'holding of a Court Leet and Baron for ye Prince', are paralleled in the Oxford revels, 'St John's College Christmas Prince', 1607–8, in REED, *Oxford* (London: British Library, 2004), ed. John R. Elliott and Alan H. Nelson (University), Alexandra F. Johnston and Diana Wyatt (City), 2 vols, 340–81.
6. *Gesta Grayorum*, 22.
7. The charge that 'a Sorcerer or Conjurer' (a member of Gray's Inn imagined as resembling Dr Pinch, in Shakespeare's play?) brought in 'a Company of base and common Fellows, to make up our Disorders with a Play of Errors' falls into a parody of legal procedures, and should be read in the same satirical spirit as what follows: 'When we were wearied with mocking thus at our own Follies' (23–4). My view of this diverges from that of Lynne Magnusson, in her pioneering essay, 'Scoff Power in *Love's Labour's Lost* and the Inns of Court: Language in Context', *Shakespeare Survey*, 57 (2004), 196–208, p. 203.
8. So named because the Prince of Purpoole in 1594–5 was Henry Helmes of Norfolk.
9. *Gesta Grayorum*, 27–30. *The French Academie* is by Pierre de La Primaudaye, *Galiatto* is probably Lyly's *Gallathea* and *Guizo*, Stefano Guazzo's *Ciuile Conuersation*, tr. George Pettie (1581); 'the Neoterical writers' are Theocritus, Catullus, and the like.
10. REED, *Inns of Court*, 378–9.
11. Sir Benjamin Rudyerd, *Le Prince d'Amour: Or, The Prince of Love* (1660), 42.
12. 'Gray's Inn Christmas Revels', REED, *Inns of Court*, 488–99, p. 489.
13. 'Middle Temple Parliament Book', 5 February 1590, 'Lord*es* of Misrule p*ro*hibited': '... that no outcries in the night should be made, nor chambers broken open by anie gentlemen of this house (as by lord of Candlemas night or such like misord*er*)', REED, *Inns of Court*, 118. Cf. 'Inner Temple Parliament Book', 10 February 1611, against Christmas revels 'Neither shall there bee any Lorde or breaking vpp of any mans Chamber', REED, *Inns of Court*, 145.

14. For the resentments and plots of the lawyer-poet John Davies (nicknamed Stradilax) against Richard Martin, Christmas Prince at the Middle Temple, 1597–8, see *Le Prince d'Amour*, 78–9, 82, 87–8. A week after the Prince ended his reign, Davies walked into the Temple hall during dinner and beat Martin on the head with a stick until it broke (he was expelled for three years). At the St John's Christmas Revels, 1607–8, there was a stabbing (REED, *Oxford*, 368).
15. *2 Henry IV*, 3.2.11–21.
16. Edmond Bicknoll, *A Swoord Agaynst Swearyng* (1579), fol. 38v.
17. Natalie Zemon Davis, 'The Reasons of Misrule', in her *Society and Culture in Early Modern France* (Cambridge: Polity Press, 1987), 97–123, p. 100.
18. For an example, from Lincoln's Inn, dating back to 1439, see Sir William Dugdale, *Origines Juridiciales* (1666), 242.
19. Dugdale, *Origines*, 286.
20. Wilfred R. Prest, *The Inns of Court under Elizabeth I and the Early Stuarts 1590–1640* (London: Longman, 1972), 121.
21. G. R. M. Ward, completed by James Heywood, *Oxford University Statutes*, 2 vols (London: Pickering, 1845–51), II, xx.
22. Closest to the point are R. S. White, *Natural Law in English Renaissance Literature* (Cambridge: Cambridge University Press, 1996), 150–1 and Claire Asquith's bizarre attempt to read the play as a Roman Catholic *drame à clef*, 'Oxford University and *Love's Labour's Lost*', in Dennis Taylor and David N. Beauregard, *Shakespeare and the Culture of Christianity in Early Modern England* (New York: Fordham University Press, 2003), 80–102, pp. 82–3. In performance, Ian Judge's 1993 RSC *Love's Labour's Lost* was set in an Edwardian Oxbridge, while Kenneth Branagh's half-musical film version (2000) has a campus setting.
23. *Gesta Grayorum*, 36.
24. *Gesta Grayorum*, 40–1.
25. See James McConica, 'Elizabethan Oxford: The Collegiate Society', in *The History of the University of Oxford*, Vol. III, *The Collegiate University*, ed. James McConica (Oxford: Clarendon Press, 1986), 645–732, pp. 645–66; Victor Morgan, *A History of the University of Cambridge*, Vol. II, *1546–1750* (Cambridge: Cambridge University Press, 2004), esp. 111, 116–21, 131–46, 252–3, 318–19.
26. 'Injunctions Prescribed by Queen Elizabeth's Visitors', in *Collection of Statutes for the University and Colleges of Cambridge*, [ed. James Heywood] (London: William Clowes, 1840), 315–25, pp. 315, 321.
27. 'Peck's Book', 1594–6, REED, *Cambridge*, ed. Alan H. Nelson, 2 vols (Toronto: Toronto University Press, 1989), 357.
28. 'Letter from the Privy Council to the University', REED, *Cambridge*, 348–9, p. 348 ('the like le*ttr*e to . . . Oxenforde', p. 349).
29. See e.g. 'Letter from Andrew Perne VC to Lord Burghley, Chancellor' 1580–1, REED *Cambridge*, 297. 'Warrant to the Constables of Chesterton', REED, *Cambridge*, 1589–90, 325–6, 'Warrant to the Constables of Chesterton', REED, *Cambridge*, 1591–2, 339–40. The exclusion was restated by James I shortly after his accession, REED, *Cambridge*, 395–7.

30. Frederick S. Boas, *University Drama in the Tudor Age* (Oxford: Clarendon Press, 1914), 226.
31. REED, *Cambridge*, 725.
32. See Roslyn Richek, 'Thomas Randolph's *Salting* (1627), its Text, and John Milton's Sixth Prolusion as Another Salting', *English Literary Renaissance*, 12 (1982), 103–31, Alan Nelson, 'A Salting at St John's', *The Eagle*, 69, no. 291 (Easter, 1983), 23–30, Elizabeth Ann Perryman Freidberg, 'Certain Small Festivities: The Texts and Contexts of Thomas Randolph's Poems and Cambridge Entertainments', University of Cambridge Ph.D. dissertation, 2 vols (1994), I, 19–141, REED, *Cambridge*, 996–1001.
33. *The Life and Times of Anthony Wood, Antiquary, of Oxford, 1632–1695, Described by Himself*, ed. Andrew Clark, 5 vols (Oxford: Oxford Historical Society, 1891–1900), I, 139. 'Penniless Bench', notes Wood in MS, 'is a seat joyning to St Martin's Church apud Quadrivium where butter women and hucksters use to sit.'
34. Frances Yates, *The French Academies of the Sixteenth Century* (London: Warburg Institute, 1947).
35. Geoffrey Bullough, ed., *Narrative and Dramatic Sources of Shakespeare*, 8 vols (London: Routledge, 1957–75), I, 427–8, 434–5.
36. 'Letter from Robert Some VC and Heads to the Privy Council', REED, *Cambridge*, 1591–2, 341–3, p. 342. Cf. 'Letter from Robert Some VC and Heads to Lord Burghley, Chancellor', 340–1; 'Letter from the Privy Council to the University', 348–9. The plague had long been a reason for excluding plays and players from both universities; see the evidence from 1575–93 gathered by Frederick S. Boas, *University Drama in the Tudor Age* (Oxford: Clarendon Press, 1914), 220–7.
37. 2.1.38. The fellows of Oxbridge colleges were for the most part young men, waiting to leave the university for a church living and marriage.
38. Edward Jones, writing from Stepney on 12 September 1592, to an unknown recipient, quoted in *John Nichols's The Progresses and Public Processions of Queen Elizabeth: A New Edition of the Early Modern Sources*, gen. eds Elizabeth Goldring et al., 5 vols (Oxford: Oxford University Press, 2014), III, 601.
39. Paul Slack, *The Impact of Plague in Tudor and Stuart England* (London: Routledge, 1985), 32. Cf. Morgan, *History of the University of Cambridge*, II, 222, *History of the University of Oxford*, III, ed. McConica, 649.
40. 'Injunctions Prescribed by Queen Elizabeth's Visitors', *Collection of Statutes . . . Cambridge*, [ed. Heywood], 320.
41. For a text with commentary see Rebecca Totaro, ed., *The Plague in Print: Essential Elizabethan Sources, 1558–1603* (Pittsburgh: Duquesne University Press, 2010), ch. 2.
42. See e.g. *Love's Labour's Lost*, ed. John Kerrigan, New Penguin Shakespeare (Harmondsworth: Penguin, 1982), 150.
43. Christopher Ricks, '*Doctor Faustus* and Hell on Earth', *Essays in Criticism*, 35 (1985), 101–20, rpt in his *Essays in Appreciation* (Oxford: Oxford University Press, 1996), 1–18. For more recent critical scholarship on early modern writing and

the plague see esp. Margaret Healy, *Fictions of Disease in Early Modern England: Bodies, Plagues and Politics* (Basingstoke: Palgrave, 2001), chs. 2–3, Rebecca Totaro, *Suffering in Paradise: The Bubonic Plague in English Literature from More to Milton* (Pittsburgh: Duquesne University Press, 2005), Ernest B. Gilman, *Plague Writing in Early Modern England* (Chicago: University of Chicago Press, 2009).

44. Cf. *Love's Labour's Lost*, ed. H. R. Woudhuysen, Arden Shakespeare, 3rd series (London: Nelson, 1998), 64, Magnusson, 'Scoff Power', 204.
45. '*Doctor Faustus* and Hell on Earth', 4.
46. Ricks cites evidence (of which there is much) from F. P. Wilson, *The Plague in Shakespeare's London* (London: Oxford University Press, 1927), 50–3. Cf. J. Leeds Barroll, *Politics, Plague, and Shakespeare's Theater: The Stuart Years* (Ithaca, NY: Cornell University Press, 1991).
47. Slack, *Impact of Plague*, 26.
48. Bicknoll, *A Swoord Agaynst Swearyng*, fol. 27r. Cf. John Downame, 'A Treatise of Swearing', in his *Four Treatises* (1608), 33–4, where the plague brought down by God to punish vain swearing infects the language used to describe the contagion of blasphemy that is spread by swearers.
49. For a summary of changes see *Love's Labour's Lost*, ed. Woudhuysen, 331–2.
50. Steve Rappaport, *Worlds within Worlds: Structures of Life in Sixteenth-Century London* (Cambridge: Cambridge University Press, 1989), 298.
51. Rappaport, *Worlds within Worlds*, 298.
52. Timothy Raylor, *Cavaliers, Clubs, and Literary Culture: Sir John Mennes, James Smith, and the Order of the Fancy* (Newark, Del.: University of Delaware Press, 1994), 72–83, Michelle O'Callaghan, *The English Wits: Literature and Sociability in Early Modern England* (Cambridge: Cambridge University Press, 2007), esp. chs 1, 3, 7.
53. The fair was held about a mile out of town. See the 'Petition to VC concerning the Lord of Taps', 12 September 1607, in REED, *Cambridge*, 412. For the naming ritual of this 'ancient functionary "arm'd all over with spiggots and fossets"', see Christopher Wordsworth, *Social Life at the English Universities in the Eighteenth Century* (Cambridge: Deighton Bell, 1874), 187.
54. Thomas Randolph, *Aristippus: Or, The Ioviall Philosopher* (1630), 10–11, p. 10. See this volume, pp. 19–20.
55. For contexts see Gina Bloom, 'Manly Drunkenness: Binge Drinking as Disciplined Play' (on wager cups), Laurie Ellinghausen, 'University of Vice: Drink, Gentility, and Masculinity in Oxford, Cambridge, and London', and Adam Zucker, 'The Social Stakes of Gambling in Early Modern London', in Amanda Bailey and Roze Hentschell, *Masculinity and the Metropolis of Vice, 1550–1650* (Basingstoke: Palgrave, 2010), 21–44, 45–65, 67–86.
56. *OED*, protestation, *n.*, 3; *OED* dates sense 5, 'A declaration of objection or dissent', from 1638, but it must have been emergent.
57. Christopher White, *Of Oathes: Their Obiect, Forme, and Bond* (1627), 19–20. Cf. less strenuously Jeremy Taylor, *Ductor Dubitantium: Or, The Rule of Conscience in all her Generall Measures*, 2 vols (1660), II, 290.

58. William Perkins, *The Whole Treatise of the Cases of Conscience* (1606), 398–9. Cf. his *Godly and Learned Exposition of Christs Sermon in the Mount* (1608), 151.
59. Robert Sanderson, *De Juramento: Seven Lectures Concerning the Obligation of Promissory Oathes* (1655), 99–100.
60. *OED*, pretermit, *v.*, 1, 'To neglect or omit (an action, duty, etc.); to leave undone or unused.'
61. George Puttenham, *The Arte of English Poesie* (1589), 72–4; John Milton, 'The Verse', *Paradise Lost*, 2nd edn (1674), A4v.
62. Cf. White, *Natural Law*, 148–58, esp. p. 155.
63. Johan Huizinga, *Homo Ludens: A Study of the Play-Element in Culture* (London: Routledge, 1949), 10.
64. *Homo Ludens*, 38–40.
65. Diary for 1 January 1668, quoted in A. Wigfall Green, *The Inns of Court and Early English Drama* (New Haven: Yale University Press, 1931), 92.
66. Cf. Biron, 'I'll lay my head to any good man's hat | These oaths and laws will prove an idle scorn' (1.2.286–7).
67. Cf. Huizinga, *Homo Ludens*, 11–12.
68. Cf. Huizinga, *Homo Ludens*, 12.
69. On Navarrus and his influence see e.g. Perez Zagorin, *Ways of Lying: Dissimulation, Persecution, and Conformity in Early Modern Europe* (Cambridge, Mass.: Harvard University Press, 1990), ch. 8.
70. Richard Cosin, *An Apologie for Svndrie Proceedings by Iurisdiction Ecclesiasticall* (1593), Pt III, 14.
71. John Bale (or Miles Coverdale), *A Christen Exhortacion vnto Customable Swearers* (1543), fol. 8v.
72. See Sir Edward Coke's account 'Of Perjury' in *The Third Part of the Institutes of the Laws of England* (1644): an oath is 'sacred, and . . . deeply concerneth the consciences of Christian men, . . . By the ancient law of England in all Oathes Equivocation is utterly condemned; . . . And this is grounded upon the law of God. . . . If equivocation should be permitted tending to the subversion of truth, it would shake the foundation of Justice' (165–6).
73. REED, *Inns of Court*, 651–9, p. 653.
74. Quoting Barnabe Barnes, *The Diuils Charter* (1607), B3v.
75. Bale (or Coverdale), *Christen Exhortacion*, fol. 7v.
76. See e.g. Constance at *King John*, 2.2.7–10.
77. See *Il principe*, ch. 18.
78. Pierre de La Primaudaye, *The French Academie*, tr. T.B. (1586), 416–17. Cf. Taylor, *Ductor Dubitantium*, II, 96.
79. Cosin, *An Apologie for Svndrie Proceedings*, Pt III, 21–2.
80. Sanderson, *De Juramento*, 232.
81. Cosin, *An Apologie for Svndrie Proceedings*, 22.
82. Perkins, *Whole Treatise*, 396.
83. *An Apologie for Svndrie Proceedings*, 22.

84. As noted several times in this book, esp. in Chapter 12, knots are a routine early modern image of the ties of sworn obligation.
85. No one could admonish Shakespeare, as Sir Rees ap Vaughan does Horace (Ben Jonson) in Dekker's *Satiro-mastix* (1602), 'You shall sweare not to bumbast out a new Play, with the olde lynings of Iestes, stolne from the Temples Reuels' (M1r). The relationship between *Love's Labour's Lost* and the Inns of Court revels is one of shared rather than stolen jokes.
86. *Ductor Dubitantium*, I, 456.
87. Quoting a revealing passage in the anonymous *A Plaine Description of the Auncient Petigree of Dame Slaunder* (1573), E4v.
88. *OED*, statute, *n.*[1], 4(as in 'a bond or recognizance by which the creditor had the power of holding the debtor's lands in case of default').
89. On the possible origins of the latter in Roman law and 'the civilian maxim, *quod principi placuit habet vigorem legis* ("what pleases the prince has the force of law")', see Paul Raffield, *Images and Cultures of Law in Early Modern England: Justice and Political Power, 1558–1660* (Cambridge: Cambridge University Press, 2004), 115–16. The style of government could be at issue: see the installation of the Christmas Prince in the hall at St John's College, Oxford, 1607–8, where 'many speaches were made..., some com*m*endinge a monarchicall state of Gouernmente, and ye sometimes suddayne necessitye of Dictators, others discom*m*endinge both' (REED, *Oxford*, 342).
90. Taylor, *Ductor Dubitantium*, II, 431–2.
91. *Ductor Dubitantium*, II, 431.
92. See e.g. Martin Ingram, 'Reformation of Manners in Early Modern England', in Paul Griffiths, Adam Fox, and Steve Hindle, eds, *The Experience of Authority in Early Modern England* (Basingstoke: Macmillan, 1996), 47–88.
93. See e.g. 'Letter from Robert Some VC ...', REED, *Cambridge*, 1591–2, 341–3 against travelling players, bull- and bear-baiting, and other 'vaine games', and the Privy Council's reply (340–1, p. 341): 'there may no Plaies or Interludes of com*m*on Plaiers be vsed or sett forthe either in the vniversity or in any other place within the compasse of ffiue miles... nor any shewes of vnlawfull games that are forbidden by the Statutes of this Realme.'
94. Slack, *Impact of Plague*, 49.
95. For further discussion see p. 292.
96. *De Juramento*, 23–5.
97. Alfred Harbage, '*Love's Labor's Lost* and the Early Shakespeare', *Philological Quarterly*, 41 (1962), 18–36, p. 27.
98. Mary Ellen Lamb, 'The Nature of Topicality', *Shakespeare Survey*, 38 (1985), 49–59, pp. 56–7; Gillian Woods, 'Catholicism and Conversion in *Love's Labour's Lost*', in Laurie Maguire, ed., *How to do Things with Shakespeare: New Approaches, New Essays* (Oxford: Blackwell, 2008), 101–30, p. 106; enlarged in ch. 2 of her *Shakespeare's Unreformed Fictions* (Oxford: Oxford University Press, 2013), 72.
99. For differing views see Hugh M. Richmond, 'Shakespeare's Navarre', *Huntington Library Quarterly*, 42 (1978–9), 193–216; Albert H. Tricomi, 'The Witty

Idealization of the French Court in *Love's Labour's Lost*', *Shakespeare Studies*, 12 (1979), 25–33. Cf. the judicious assessment in the New Cambridge Shakespeare, *Love's Labour's Lost*, ed. William C. Carroll (Cambridge: Cambridge University Press, 2009), 27–8.

100. Translation of 'Bereblock's Commentary' on the queen's visit, in REED, *Oxford*, 979–83, p. 980.
101. 'Miles Windsor's Narrative', in REED, *Oxford*, 126–35, p. 129; cf. Anthony Wood's account of the visit, and his 'Life of Richard Edwards', from *Athenae Oxonienses*, quoted by REED, *Oxford*, 875–9, p. 877, 879–81, p. 880.
102. REED, *Inns of Court*, 371–2.
103. *Gesta Grayorum*, 21.
104. *Prince d'Amour*, 88–9.
105. REED, *Oxford*, 380 (cf. 345).
106. Sir George Buck, *The Third Universitie of England: Or, A Treatise of the Foundations of all the Colledges, Auncient Schooles of Priviledge, and of Houses of Learning, and Liberall Arts, within and about . . . London* (1615), ch. 47. According to Buck this Art 'requireth knowledge in Grammar, Rhetorike, Philosophie, Historie, Musick, Mathematikes, and in other Arts' and its heraldry consisted of 'Gules a cross Argent, and in the first corner of the scutcheon, a *Mercuries Petasus* Argent, and a Lyon Gules in Cheefe Or'.
107. Garrett Mattingly, *Renaissance Diplomacy* (1955; Penguin: Baltimore, 1964), 182–3.
108. *Gesta Grayorum*, 5; *Prince d'Amour*, 89.
109. Sir Thomas Elyot, *The Boke Named the Gouernour* (1531), Bk III, ch. 6; 'Against Swearyng and Periury', *Certayne Sermons, Or Homilies Appoynted by the Kynges Maiestie* (London, 1547), L3v–M3v, M2r; White, *Of Oathes*, which starts from Joshua 9: 19, 'Wee haue sworne vnto them by the Lord God of Israel: now therefore we may not touch them'; Robert Sanderson, *De Juramento: Seven Lectures Concerning the Obligation of Promissory Oathes* (1655), 132–4.
110. See e.g. 'Styx, *or Leagues*', in Sir Francis Bacon, *The Wisedome of the Ancients*, tr. Sir Arthur Gorges (1619), 14–18.
111. Mattingly, *Renaissance Diplomacy*, 19.
112. See Anna Riehl Bertolet, 'The Tsar and the Queen: "You Speak a Language that I Understand Not"', in Charles Beem, ed., *The Foreign Relations of Elizabeth I* (Basingstoke: Palgrave, 2011), 101–23, pp. 108–11. The tsar wanted their secret league to be secured with an oath and the kissing of a cross; the queen thought it sufficient to subscribe her pledge in her own hand 'by the word of a Christian Prince'.
113. Mattingly, *Renaissance Diplomacy*, 35.
114. William Perkins, *A Discourse of Conscience* (1596), 71. There were, in practice, scholastic complications, since some Roman Catholics believed that the Pope could dispense with vows to God but not the oaths that bound individuals together; see e.g. Thomas Preston, *A Theologicall Disputation Concerning the Oath of Allegiance* (1613), 105–6, citing Domingo de Soto and others.

115. Sanderson, *De Juramento*, 233; cf. Cosin, *An Apologie for Svndrie Proceedings*, Pt III, 17.
116. Jean Hotman, *The Ambassador* (1603), E4r–6v.
117. Alberico Gentili, *De Legationibus Libri Tres*, ed. and tr. Gordon J. Laing, 2 vols (New York: Oxford University Press, 1924), II, 74. He cites Appian, *Roman History*, which Shakespeare apparently knew in the 1578 tr. by William Barker (?).
118. Either fighting in 'his [i.e. France's] wars' or 'his [i.e. Navarre's] wars, that were in France's interests and so refundable'.
119. The Duke of Sully estimated that Henry IV owed 296 million *livres* in 1596, about half to bankers and foreign powers, and the balance owed on *rentes*, alienated royal revenues, and demesne (Navarre had already mortgaged most of his own patrimony). Cf. Richard Bonney, *The King's Debts: Finance and Politics in France, 1589–1661* (Oxford: Clarendon Press, 1981), 54–6, 319.
120. On Elizabeth's complaints about the 4 million *livres* owed to her, see Mark Greengrass, *France in the Age of Henri IV: The Struggle for Stability*, 2nd edn (1995; London: Routledge, 2013), 138.
121. See the haberdasher Hobson's dialogue with the queen in Thomas Heywood, *If You Know Not Me You Know Nobody, Part II*, ed. Madeleine Doran, Malone Society (Oxford: Oxford University Press, 1935), 2,088–94, capably discussed by Theodore B. Leinwand, *Theatre, Finance and Society in Early Modern England* (Cambridge: Cambridge University Press, 1999), 27–8.
122. Greengrass, *France in the Age of Henri IV*, 138.
123. Greengrass, *France in the Age of Henry IV*, 139.
124. Cf. Lorna Hutson, *The Invention of Suspicion: Law and Mimesis in Shakespeare and Renaissance Drama* (Oxford: Oxford University Press, 2007), 17, 298–9.
125. Raphael Holinshed, *Chronicles*, 6 vols (1587), VI, 158, quoting text at The Holinshed Project, <http://www.cems.ox.ac.uk/holinshed/>, accessed 1 December 2011.
126. John Cowell, *The Interpreter* (1607), A4v, entry for *Acquittance*.
127. *OED*, specialty, *n.*, 7.
128. *OED*, number, *n.*, 1–2, 14, 17.
129. Matthew 7: 3–5.
130. Recorded by the *OED* in Scottish sources from 1619 and *c.*1650.
131. See e.g. *The Romane Historie Written by T. Livius of Padua*, tr. Philemon Holland (1600), where Brutus 'reciteth the oth of the people, That they should suffer none to be king, . . . from whence might arise any danger to their libertie. This moth is the thing (quoth hee) that with all diligence, and by all meanes possible is to be maintained' (45). In Elizabethan pronunciation, *moth/mot/mote* would sound like *m-oath*, all with a firm final consonant.
132. See *OED*, moot, *n.*[1], 2–4.
133. On the gypsy's knot see *Love's Labour's Lost*, ed. Woudhuysen, 139.
134. More obscurely, but consistently with the erudite wit of the play, 'salve in the mail' is not just the lotion in a bag that Costard says he does not need, because the folk remedy of a plantain will ease his broken shin, but the salutation of a letter coming in the sort of bag that was typically used for mail (in the modern sense), the sort of diplomatic packet or bag in which the specialities of 2.1.163

are bound. See Holofernes on Berowne's letter, at p. 100, and *OED*, mail, *n.*[2], 1 and 2.

135. Prolusion VI, sect. 3, John Milton, *Latin Writings: A Selection*, ed. and tr. John K. Hale (Assen: Van Gorcum, 1998), 82–3 and n.
136. *OED*, salve, *n.*[4] (now obsolete).
137. *Homo Ludens*, 110.
138. Cf. 2.1.100–2, where the Princess plays with the thought that the King could be saved from his oath by 'ignorance' of it.
139. Cf. the analysis by Patricia Parker, 'Preposterous Reversals: *Love's Labor's Lost*', *Modern Language Quarterly*, 54 (1993), 435–82, pp. 447–53.
140. See e.g. 'Where I was woont to seeke the honny Bee...', 'Seest how bragge yond bullocke beares...', *The Lawiers Logike* (1588), fols 15v–16r, [23]r.
141. 'Gray's Inn Christmas Revels', REED, *Inns of Court*, 493.
142. For the scale of charges and overview of the procedure see Martin Ingram, *Church Courts, Sex and Marriage in England, 1570–1640* (Cambridge: Cambridge University Press, 1987), 56, 331–2.
143. Cowell, *Interpreter*, Ggg2r, entry for *Purgation*.
144. Cf. Matthew 18: 18.
145. Taylor, *Ductor Dubitantium*, I, 444. *OED*, correption, *n.*, 1, 'Reprehension, reproof. *Obs.*'
146. See e.g. White, *Of Oathes*, 52.

CHAPTER 4 A WORLD-WITHOUT-END BARGAIN

1. R. M. Hare, 'The Promising Game', *Revue internationale de philosophie*, 70 (1964), 398–412, rpt in Philippa Foot, ed., *Theories of Ethics* (Oxford: Oxford University Press, 1967), 115–27.
2. John R. Searle, 'How to Derive "Ought" from "Is"', *Philosophical Review*, 73 (1964), 43–58, rpt in Foot, ed., *Theories of Ethics*, 101–14. The arguments can be found in revised form in his *Speech Acts: An Essay in the Philosophy of Language* (Cambridge: Cambridge University Press, 1969).
3. Johan Huizinga, *Homo Ludens: A Study of the Play-Element in Culture* (London: Routledge, 1949), 50–1, cf. 63.
4. *Homo Ludens*, 46.
5. *Homo Ludens*, 47.
6. H. R. Woudhuysen pertinently cites *OED*, dispatch, *n.*, 2, 'Official dismissal or leave to go, given to an ambassador after completion of his errand', in his edn of *Love's Labour's Lost*, Arden Shakespeare, 3rd series (London: Nelson, 1998). Cf. 5 a, 'The getting (of business, etc.) out of hand; ... (prompt or speedy) execution.' In *Renaissance Diplomacy* (1955; Penguin: Baltimore, 1964), Garrett Mattingly writes, 'Having concluded negotiations, embassies were expected to go home promptly' (38).
7. See the articles by Michael Gordon, 'The Invention of a Common Law Crime: Perjury and the Elizabethan Courts', *American Journal of Legal History*, 24

(1980), 145–70, 'The Perjury Statute of 1563: A Case History of Confusion', *Proceedings of the American Philosophical Society*, 124 (1980), 438–54.

8. In Adrian Streete, ed., *Early Modern Drama and the Bible: Contexts and Readings, 1570–1625* (Basingstoke: Palgrave, 2012), 118–35.
9. 'The Promising Game', in Foot, ed., *Theories of Ethics*, 124.
10. On branding on the forehead as an old punishment for blasphemous oaths, see e.g. Pierre de La Primaudaye, *The French Academie*, tr. T.B. (1586), 121.
11. *French Academie*, 418.
12. Robert Sanderson, *De Juramento: Seven Lectures Concerning the Obligation of Promissory Oathes* (1655), 101.
13. 'An Act for the Punishment of Such as Shall Procure or Commit any Wilful Perjury' (5 Elizabeth c. 9), para 5.
14. 3.1.61–116; see pp. 93–5.
15. *OED*, salve, *n.*[4]. *Pace* Armado at 3.1.71–2, and as Mote implies at 70, this would make a 'salve' an '*envoi*' after all, the solution of a riddle, a resolving epilogue.
16. *OED*, salve, *n.*[1], 2a.
17. *OED*, forswear, *v.*, 1.
18. *OED*, forswear, *v.*, 3.
19. Christopher White, *Of Oathes: Their Obiect, Forme, and Bond* (1627), 24–5; John Mabb, *The Afflicted Mans Vow* (1609), 25.
20. Sanderson, *De Juramento*, 242–3.
21. *De Juramento*, 244.
22. *Summa Theologica*, II.ii, q. 89 art. 8. See e.g. Robert Bellarmine, *Tractatus de Potestate Summi Pontificis in Rebus Temporalibus, Adversus Gulielmum Barclay* (1610), ch. xxvii, citing this passage and discussions of Peter Lombard, *Sententiae*, dist. 39.
23. *De Juramento*, 100, 249.
24. *Homo Ludens*, 13.
25. As early as 1510, Russian masquing costumes are recorded at the court of Henry VIII. See Daryl W. Palmer, *Writing Russia in the Age of Shakespeare* (Aldershot: Ashgate, 2004), 1–2. Palmer places the Shakespeare episode in a broad, cultural context at 89–92.
26. 'As for the truth of his word, the Russe for the most part maketh small regard of it, so he may gaine by a lie and breeche of his promise', notes the queen's ambassador, Giles Fletcher, in his book *Of the Russe Common Wealth* (1591), 152, quoted in Geoffrey Bullough, ed., *Narrative and Dramatic Sources of Shakespeare*, 8 vols (London: Routledge, 1957–75), I, 433.
27. Robert Tofte, *Alba* (1598), G5r.
28. 5.2.1–58, 123–35; see *OED*, favour, *n.*, 7. Against accepting gifts when engaged in diplomacy see Jean Hotman, *The Ambassador* (1603), D7v–D8r; Alberico Gentili is more tolerant of selective acceptance, *De Legationibus Libri Tres*, ed. and tr. Gordon J. Laing, 2 vols (New York: Oxford University Press, 1924), II, 131, 189.
29. *OED*, favour, *n.*, 9a 'appearance, aspect' and 9b, 'the countenance, face'.

30. *OED*, vouch, *v.*, 1a. Cf. John Cowell, *The Interpreter* (1607), Zzz2v, entry for *Voucher* ('*Aduocatio* . . . a calling in of one into the Court at the petition of a party that hopeth to be helped thereby').
31. See e.g. James Balmford, *A Short and Plaine Dialogue Concerning the Vnlawfulnes of Playing at Cards or Tables, or Any Other Game Consisting in Chance* (1593), A4v–6v and Thomas Gataker's response, *Of the Nature and Vse of Lots: A Treatise Historicall and Theologicall* (1619), 148–73 (referring back to the Old Testament, Jerome, and Augustine). Balmford sent back *A Modest Reply to Certaine Answeres, which Mr Gataker B.D. in his Treatise of the Nature, and Vse of Lotts, Giveth to Arguments in a Dialogue* (1623), 55–6, 103–4, 108–11, 124–7, which prompted Gataker to publish *A Iust Defence of Certaine Passages in a Former Treatise Concerning the Nature and Vse of Lots* (1623), 197–242.
32. *De Juramento*, 224.
33. *A Treatise of Spousals, or Matrimonial Contracts*, composed *c.*1600 (1686), 62–3. Ch. 10 is entitled 'By what Form of Words Spousals *de futuro* are contracted.'
34. *A Midsummer Night's Dream*, 3.2.122–35.
35. *OED*, favour, *n.*, here 8–9, 'comeliness, beauty . . . appearance'.
36. *De Juramento*, 251.
37. Irene G. Dash, 'Oath-Taking', ch. 2 of her *Wooing, Wedding, and Power: Women in Shakespeare's Plays* (New York: Columbia University Press, 1981), 9–30, pp. 9–10. R. S. White views the men more generously in 'Oaths and the Anticomic Spirit in *Love's Labour's Lost*', in Alan Brissenden, ed., *Shakespeare and Some Others: Essays on Shakespeare and Some of his Contemporaries* (Adelaide: Dept of English, University of Adelaide, 1976), 11–29.
38. 5:37. See Biron's droll play on this verse at 1.1.54 (p. 75).
39. Cowell, *Interpreter*, Gg3v, entry on *Forfeiture* begins: '*(forisfactura)* commeth of the French word *(forfaict.* i. *scelus)* but signifieth in our language, rather the effect of transgressing a penall lawe, then the transgression it selfe: as forfeiture of Escheates.'
40. On the role of tokens, favours, and gifts in the cementing of betrothals see e.g. Diana O'Hara, *Courtship and Constraint: Rethinking the Making of Marriage in Tudor England* (Manchester: Manchester University Press, 2000), ch. 2.
41. Perf. 1597–8; Sir Benjamin Rudyerd, *Le Prince d'Amour: Or, The Prince of Love* (1660), 23.
42. Incompetence in acting was almost as much an expectation as heckling was a convention in academic entertainments and Christmas Revels. See e.g. the Oxford 'St John's College Christmas Prince', 1607–8, *REED Oxford*, 354–5, 357, 373–9 (where 'Detraction' is a character placed among the spectators).
43. Robert Parsons, *A Christian Directorie Guiding Men to their Saluation* (1585), 721, and this volume, p. 21; cf. William Perkins, *A Direction for the Government of the Tongue according to Gods Word* (1593).
44. *Homo Ludens*, 40–1, 90–5.
45. In the 1594–5 *Gesta Grayorum* (1688), the Prince of Purpoole's champion came into the hall in full armour, on horseback, and, riding round the fire, stayed and

declared that if anyone denied the sovereignty of his Prince, 'I do challenge, in Combat, to fight with him, . . . And in token hereof, I gage my Gauntlet' (9). Cf. *Le Prince d'Amour*, 9, 'Gray's Inn Christmas Revels' 1617–18, in REED, *Inns of Court*, 488–99, p. 489.

46. Thomas Nashe, *Summers Last Will and Testament* (1600), in *The Works of Thomas Nashe*, ed. Ronald B. McKerrow, 5 vols, rev. F. P. Wilson (Oxford: Blackwell, 1958), III, 292 (lines 1872, 1885). This entertainment was probably written in the autumn of 1592, for performance at Archbishop Whitgift's house on his estate in Croydon, in retreat from the plague in London.
47. REED, *Oxford*, 372.
48. 1.1.1–7, 136; 5.2.13–15, 647.
49. *OED*, life, *n.*, 7a.
50. See e.g. Dash's account, cited in n. 37.
51. Paul Griffiths, *Youth and Authority: Formative Experiences in England 1560–1640* (Oxford: Clarendon Press, 1996), 55.
52. John Michael Gray, *Oaths and the English Reformation* (Cambridge: Cambridge University Press, 2013), 41.
53. Griffiths, *Youth and Authority*, 263–4.
54. For long delays, see Swinburne, *Treatise of Spousals*, 110–14.
55. Martin Ingram, *Church Courts, Sex and Marriage in England, 1570–1640* (Cambridge: Cambridge University Press, 1987), 132–3; on the persistence of spousals see e.g. Laura Gowing, *Domestic Dangers: Women, Words, and Sex in Early Modern London* (Oxford: Clarendon Press, 1996), 178.
56. 1.2.179–80 See e.g. Roland Mushat Frye, *The Renaissance 'Hamlet': Issues and Responses in 1600* (Princeton: Princeton University Press, 1984), 82–92.
57. 'Punishing Perjury in *Love's Labour's Lost*', 134.
58. Searle, 'How to Derive "Ought" from "Is"'. For a suggestive critique of Hare's approach, drawing on Huizinga's *Homo Ludens*, see Mary Midgley, 'The Game Game', *Philosophy*, 49 (1974), 132–53.
59. *Promising, Intending, and Moral Autonomy* (Cambridge: Cambridge University Press, 1984), 2.
60. Slack, *Impact of Plague*, 19.
61. Slack, *Impact of Plague*, 42–3.
62. See the discussion of this apparently lost play in the *Norton Shakespeare*, 803.
63. REED, *Oxford*, 354.
64. Performed on Twelfth Night, 1614, at Whitehall.
65. *OED*, maintain, *n.*, 3a.
66. *Homo Ludens*, ch. 4.
67. *OED*, rook, *n.*[1], 2 a–c, 'disreputable, greedy, garrulous, or slovenly person. . . . cheat, swindler, . . . foolish person, a gull'; *daw*, *v*, 2a, c 'silly fellow, simpleton . . . untidy woman, slut'.
68. W. H. Auden and Chester Kallman, *Love's Labour's Lost: Operatic Pastoral*, in *Libretti and Other Dramatic Writings by W. H. Auden, 1939–1973*, ed. Edward Mendelson (Princeton: Princeton University Press, 1993), 326.

69. Cf. Dorothea Kehler, 'Jaquenetta's Baby's Father: Recovering Paternity in *Love's Labor's Lost*', *Renaissance Papers 1990*, 45–54.
70. Heneage Finch, 'Arithmetic Lecture' (Inner Temple, *c.*1605). REED, *Inns of Court*, 651–9, p. 653.

CHAPTER 5 GROUP REVENGE

1. Livy, *Ab Urbe Condita Libri* (*The History of Rome*), I.59.1; quoting *Titi Livi ab Urbe Condita Libri*, Pt I, Bks I–X, ed. Wilhelm Weissenborn and H. J. Müller (Leipzig: Teubner, 1898).
2. On the etymology of 'religion' see the Introduction, p. 11.
3. Geoffrey Bullough, ed., *Narrative and Dramatic Sources of Shakespeare*, 8 vols (London: Routledge, 1957–75), IV, 18.
4. Sir William Cornwallis, *Essayes* (1600–1), Nn6r–v.
5. Cf. 'Shakespeare as Reviser' (1987), in my *On Shakespeare and Early Modern Literature: Essays* (Oxford: Oxford University Press, 2001), 3–22, pp. 11–16.
6. On 'marble heaven' as a Senecan trace, from John Studley's trans. of the pseudo-Senecan *Hercules Oetaeus*, see Gordon Braden, *Renaissance Tragedy and the Senecan Tradition: Anger's Privilege* (New Haven: Yale University Press, 1985), 176.
7. The drawing attributed to Henry Peacham, dated 1594, has been reproduced many times. See e.g. Andrew Gurr, *The Shakespearean Stage 1574–1642*, 4th edn (Cambridge: Cambridge University Press, 2009), 243.
8. Cf. the circling of Lorrique by the counter-plotters when they swear revenge, discussed on p. 54 (Henry Chettle, *The Tragedy of Hoffman: Or, A Reuenge for a Father*, *c.*1602 (1631), K1r).
9. 275–82, following Q1 at line 281 rather than the unacceptable, Norton reading 'between thine arms'.
10. *Titus Andronicus*, ed. Jonathan Bate, Arden Shakespeare, 3rd series (London: Routledge, 1995), 204.
11. On the eloquence and violence of hands in the play, see Michael Neill, '"Amphitheatres in the Body": Playing with Hands on the Shakespearean Stage', in his *Putting History to the Question: Power, Politics, and Society in English Renaissance Drama* (New York: Columbia University Press, 2000), 167–203, pp. 189–93.
12. *Ein sehr klägliche Tragaedia von Tito Andronico und der hoffertigen Käyserin*, in *Engelische Comedien und Tragedien* (1620), quoting the text and tr. given in Albert Cohn, *Shakespeare in Germany in the Sixteenth and Seventeenth Centuries* (London: Asher and Co., 1865), 199–200.
13. *Spieltexte der Wanderbühne*, ed. Manfred Brauneck and Alfred Noe, 6 vols in 7 (Berlin: Walter de Gruyter, 1970–2007), I, 494–5. I am grateful to George Oppitz-Trotman for discussion.
14. Cf. Chapter 16 (pp. 422, 438).
15. *De Juramento: Seven Lectures Concerning the Obligation of Promissory Oathes* (1655), 150.
16. See the Introduction, pp. 19–20, 23.

17. For a text see *The Forme and Maner of Making and Consecrating Bishops, Priests, and Deacons* (1596), A7r–B4r; 'othe concerning the Queenes Supremacie' (B1v), promises (B2v–3r).
18. Richard Firth Green, *A Crisis of Truth: Literature and Law in Ricardian England* (Philadelphia: University of Pennsylvania Press, 1999).
19. For context and qualification see Andy Wood, 'Custom and the Social Organisation of Writing in Early Modern England', *Transactions of the Royal Historical Society*, 9 (1999), 257–69.
20. *The Bond of Association, 1584*, ed. Ian W. Archer and F. Douglas Price (2011), in *English Historical Documents* Online, V(A), *1558–1603*, London: Routledge.
21. See e.g. Anne Barton, introd. to New Penguin *Hamlet*, ed. T. J. B. Spencer (Harmondsworth: Penguin, 1980), 10–11. The sworn revenge was, in practice, constrained. The bond was drawn up by the Privy Council, and signing of it was meant to be restricted.
22. For discussion, see David Cressy, 'Binding the Nation: The Bonds of Association, 1584 and 1696', in DeLloyd J. Guth and John W. McKenna, eds, *Tudor Rule and Revolution* (Cambridge: Cambridge University Press, 1982), 217–34.
23. The story of Hamlet is first recorded in the twelfth-century *Gesta Danorum* by Saxo Grammaticus. This work had some distribution, in various forms, in the sixteenth century (see Julie Maxwell, 'Counter-Reformation Versions of Saxo: A New Source for *Hamlet*', *Renaissance Quarterly*, 57 (2004), 518–60), but it is agreed that Shakespeare's play derives from the version of events given in the fifth volume of François de Belleforest's *Les Histoires tragiques*, published several times in France from 1570. An English translation appeared, apparently encouraged by the success of Shakespeare's play, in 1608; *The Hystorie of Hamblet* is edited with a commentary in Geoffrey Bullough, ed., *Narrative and Dramatic Sources of Shakespeare*, 8 vols (London: Routledge, 1957–75), VII, 81–124.
24. pp. 49, 53.
25. Quentin Skinner, *Forensic Shakespeare* (Oxford: Oxford University Press, 2014), ch. 6.
26. *Antony and Cleopatra* (5.2.339).
27. At *2 Henry VI*, 3.2.256–71, in a passage which anticipates *Hamlet*, Salisbury asks Henry VI to imagine that a venomous serpent, who might kill him, is sliding towards him when he is asleep, but this is another allegorical snake-as-usurper, rather than a piece of natural history, the serpent being 'false Suffolk'.
28. See e.g. William Perkins, *A Discourse of Conscience* (1596), 46.
29. Exodus 20: 13; Perkins, *Discourse of Conscience*, 46.
30. Cf. John Kerrigan, 'Hieronimo, Hamlet and Remembrance', *Essays in Criticism*, 31 (1981), 105–26, largely incorporated into my *Revenge Tragedy: Aeschylus to Armageddon* (Oxford: Clarendon Press, 1996), ch. 7.
31. William Ian Miller, *Eye for an Eye* (Cambridge: Cambridge University Press, 2006), ch. 7.
32. William Gearing, *A Bridle for the Tongue: Or, A Treatise of Ten Sins of the Tongue* (1663), 72.

33. *OED*, oath, *n.*
34. Derek Parfit, *On What Matters*, 2 vols (Oxford: Oxford University Press, 2011), I, 184.
35. '*Enter the ghost in his night gowne*' is the stage direction in the First Quarto (1603), reflecting theatre practice.
36. As others have pointed out, Pedringano takes an oath of secrecy on Lorenzo's sword in Act 2 of *The Spanish Tragedy*.
37. *The Revenger's Tragedy*, ed. MacDonald P. Jackson, in *Thomas Middleton: The Collected Works*, gen. eds Gary Taylor and John Lavagnino (Oxford: Clarendon Press, 2007), 1.4.56–64.
38. Julia Reinhard Lupton, *Thinking with Shakespeare* (Chicago: University of Chicago Press, 2013), 81.

CHAPTER 6 TIME AND MONEY

1. See e.g. Craig Muldrew, *The Economy of Obligation: The Culture of Credit and Social Relations in Early Modern England* (Basingstoke: Macmillan, 1998), 174–8.
2. *The Casebooks Project: A Digital Edition of Simon Forman and Richard Napier's Medical Records 1596–1634*, <http://www.magicandmedicine.hps.cam.ac.uk/>, accessed 3 March 2014, shows the stress induced by surety; for a bad dream about inherited debt see Muldrew, *Economy of Obligation*, 183.
3. See the celebrated exchange between Michel Serres and Bruno Latour, *Conversations on Science, Culture, and Time*, tr. Roxanne Lapidus (Ann Arbor: University of Michigan Press, 1995), 57–61.
4. Matthew D. Wagner, *Shakespeare, Theatre, and Time* (Abingdon: Routledge, 2012), 45.
5. See e.g. Paul Glennie and Nigel Thrift, *Shaping the Day: A History of Timekeeping in England and Wales 1300–1800* (Oxford: Oxford University Press, 2009), 175.
6. Glennie and Thrift, *Shaping the Day*, 409.
7. Compare e.g. *Michaelmas Term*, 3.3.22–34, where Easy comes to St Paul's to meet Blastfield at two o'clock. 'Two has struck,' he tells the Boy, who answers, 'No, sir, they are now a-striking,' as Shortyard and Falselight, disguised as a Sergeant and a Yeoman, clamp their hands on his shoulders and arrest him for debt. Ed. Theodore B. Leinwand, in *Thomas Middleton: The Collected Works*, gen. eds Gary Taylor and John Lavagnino (Oxford: Clarendon Press, 2007).
8. *The Art of Thriving: Or, The Plaine Path-way to Preferment. Together with The Mysterie and Misery of Lending and Borrowing* (1636), A2v–3r.
9. Quoting the comprehensive 1599 edition, marginal gloss.
10. *The Debt Book: Or, A Treatise Vpon Romans 13. ver. 8* (1625), A2v.
11. Joan Ozark Holmer, '"When Jacob Graz'd His Uncle Laban's Sheep": A New Source for *The Merchant of Venice*', *Shakespeare Quarterly*, 36 (1985), 64–5.
12. Miles Mosse, *The Arraignment and Conuiction of Vsurie* (1595), 57. There is a marginal note to '*Plutarch. lib. de non foenerando*', which points, via Latin translation, to his *Moralia*: 'And like as king *Darius* sent against the citie of *Athens* his

lieutenants generall *Datis* and *Artaphernes,* with chaines, cordes and halters in their hands, therewith to binde the prisoners which they should take; semblablie these usurers bring into *Greece* with them their boxes and caskets full of schedules, bils, handwritings, and contracts obligatorie, which be as good as so many irons and fetters to hang upon their poore debters' (*The Philosophie, Commonlie Called, the Morals Written by the Learned Philosopher Plutarch of Chaeronea*, tr. Philemon Holland (1603), 284). For more about Shakespeare and Plutarch on usury, see Chapter 13.

13. *OED*, damnify, *v.*, 1, 'To cause injury, loss, or inconvience to'.
14. Linda Woodbridge, *English Revenge Drama: Money, Resistance, Equality* (Cambridge: Cambridge University Press, 2010), esp. chs 3–4.
15. These facts, which can be found in the standard biographies, are drawn into conjunction with the play by W. Nicholas Knight, 'Equity, *The Merchant of Venice* and William Lambarde', *Shakespeare Survey*, 27 (1974), 93–104.
16. *A General Discourse Against the Damnable Sect of Vsurers* (1578), fols 20v–21r.
17. On interpretations and appropriations of this verse see e.g. Benjamin Nelson, *The Idea of Usury: From Tribal Brotherhood to Universal Otherhood*, 2nd edn (Chicago: University of Chicago Press, 1969).
18. *A Treatise of Vsurie* (1611), 99.
19. Cf. Mosse, *Arraignment and Conuiction of Vsurie*, 27.
20. Cf. the career of Harry Dampit, 'trampler of time', who started as a petty laywer, trampling around London and its courts, but who now makes time work for him as a usurer. Thomas Middleton, *A Trick to Catch the Old One*, 1.4, ed. Valerie Wayne, in *Middleton: Collected Works*, gen. eds Taylor and Lavagnino.
21. See John T. Noonan, *The Scholastic Analysis of Usury* (Cambridge, Mass.: Harvard University Press, 1957), esp. 43–4, e.g. William of Auxerre ('It is proper to the usurers to sell time').
22. Thomas Wilson, *A Discourse Vppon Vsurye by Waye of Dialogue and Oracion* (1572), 85.
23. 4.3.3–7; cf. among many examples Quomodo, Easy, and Shortyard in *Michaelmas Term*, 2.3, ed. Leinwand, in *Middleton: Collected Works*, gen. eds Taylor and Lavagnino.
24. *The Examination of Vsury, in Two Sermons* (1591), 20. Cf. Mosse, 'herein (no question) I commit *vsurie*. For I sell the time, and make a gaine of lending' (*Arraignment and Conuiction of Vsurie*, 62).
25. e.g. Fenton, *Treatise of Vsurie*: 'To sell wares for time, and in respect of time to sell dearer, may be free from vsurie: Either in respect of the rising of the commoditie so sold, if by the ordinarie course of seasons, it will be worth more at the day of paiment of the money, then it was at the time of sale and deliuerie. Or in case a man can neither vent his commoditie for present money; nor keep it longer without corruption or detriment to the ware' (20–1).
26. *Consuetudo, vel Lex Mercatoria: Or, The Ancient Law-Merchant* (1622), 14–15.
27. Fenton, *Treatise of Vsurie*, 23.

28. Francis Bacon, 'Of Vsurie', in *The Essayes or Counsels, Civill and Morall*, rev. edn (1625), 239–46, p. 242.
29. Caesar, *General Discourse*, fol. 8v, quoted above; Fenton, *Treatise of Vsury*, 26–8.
30. See e.g. John Bale (or Miles Coverdale), *A Christen Exhortacion vnto Customable Swearers* (1543): 'Lawful it is also for the magistrates / whan they put enye manne in offyce / to take an othe of hym / that he shal be trewe / diligent / and feythfull therin / as Iacob / for the commodite and profytt of his posterite / toke an othe of Laban the idolatrer' (fol. 7r).
31. William Perkins, *A Discourse of Conscience* (1596), 71. Cf. e.g. Richard Cosin, *An Apologie for Svndrie Proceedings by Iurisdiction Ecclesiasticall* (1593), Pt III, 23.
32. See George Carleton, *Tithes Examined and Proued to bee Due to the Clergie* (1606), fol. 9r.
33. Park Honan, *Shakespeare: A Life* (Oxford: Oxford University Press, 1998), 292–3.
34. See e.g. the discussion of Raymond of Pennaforte (fl. 1234) in Nelson, *Idea of Usury*, 17–18. For an echo of this see Wilson, *Discourse Vppon Vsurye*, 64.
35. Aristotle, *Politics*, 1258b, tr. H. Rackham, Loeb Classical Library (London: Heinemann, 1944).
36. Gerard Malynes, *Consuetudo*, 326: '*Aristotle* in his Politickes... monsters, from time to time.'
37. Wilson continues, with another allusion to time: 'Likewyse *Suydas* vpon *Aristophanes* in *nubibus* sayeth, that such money which bringeth forth money is a swelling monster, waxing euerye moneth bigger one then an other, and so horrible swelleth from time to time, as no man by wordes is able to vtter.' *Suidas* (from *souda*, 'the fortress') is a tenth-century classical encyclopedia, thought in the early modern period to be the name of a commentator, here glossing *The Clouds*.
38. *3 Henry VI*, 2.5.35–6.
39. Fenton, *Treatise of Vsurie*, 13; quoting and translating Cicero, *De Senectute*, xv.51.
40. Samuel Schoenbaum, *William Shakespeare: A Compact Documentary Life*, rev. edn (Oxford: Oxford University Press, 1987), 322.
41. Alan Stewart, *Shakespeare's Letters* (Oxford: Oxford University Press, 2008), ch. 4.
42. Schoenbaum, *William Shakespeare: A Compact Documentary Life*, 240–1.
43. Norton has 'for barren metal', following the Quarto; Folio 'of' strikes me as the better reading.
44. Sly-hock? Getting into *hock* probably goes back to hock-day and hock-tide, 'an important term-day' (*OED*, 'Hock-day', *n.*) when rents were paid, debts due, etc.
45. As a late, clarifying example, see Thomas Goodwin, *Christ Set Forth in his Death* (1642), 'Yea Christ thus trusted God, upon his single Bond; but we for our assurance, have both Christ and God bound to us, even God with his surety, Christ, (for he is Gods Surety as well as ours.) A double Bond from two such Persons, whom would it not secure?' (6). There are earlier, informative uses in Thomas

Lodge, *An Alarum against Vsurers* (1584), 12, Thomas Dekker and John Webster, *West-ward Hoe* (1607), F1v, and Sir John Harington, *Epigrams* (1618), M5v.

46. See Blackstone's *Commentaries on the Laws of England*, 4 vols (1765–9), II, 340, quoted in *The Merchant of Venice*, ed. John Drakakis, Arden Shakespeare, 3rd series (London: Arden, 2010), in the note to 'single bond': 'whereby the obligor obliges himself, his heirs, executors, and administrators, to pay a certain sum of money to another at a day appointed. If this be all, the bond is called a single one, *simplex obligatio.*'
47. Cf. *Michaelmas Term*, ed. Leinwand, in *Middleton: Collected Works*, gen. eds Taylor and Lavagnino: 'we'll try his honesty, and take his single bond, of body, goods, and lands' (3.4.240–1).
48. Cf. Caesar's contention that usury is forbidden because 'inequalitie in bargainyng is against nature' (*Discourse*, fol. 11r).
49. *Treatise of Vsurie*, 63. Girolamo Zanchi, 1516–90, was an Italian Protestant divine.
50. Both parties should also, in theory, be secured by the notary's professional oath not to draw up improper bonds. Presumably—if the audience thinks this far—Antonio's notary takes the proposed forfeit to be minatory and symbolic rather than to be exacted.
51. *OED*, shy, *adj.*, 2a, 'of persons . . . suspicious, distrustful'.
52. *The Autobiography of a Seventeenth-Century Rabbi: Leon Modena's 'Life of Judah'*, tr. and ed. Mark R. Cohen (Princeton: Princeton University Press, 1988), 155–7. It was not the first such vow; see 130.
53. 'Of Vsurie', 245.
54. *Consuetudo*, 30–1.
55. *Arraignment and Conuiction of Vsurie*, 55.
56. Cf. Ian MacInnes, '"Ill luck? Ill luck?": Risk and Hazard in *The Merchant of Venice*', in Barbara Sebek and Stephen Deng, eds, *Global Traffic: Discourses and Practices of Trade in English Literature and Culture from 1550–1700* (Basingstoke: Palgrave Macmillan, 2008), 39–55.
57. Norman Jones, *God and the Money Lenders: Usury and the Law in Early Modern England* (Oxford: Blackwell, 1989), 11, Giovanni Ceccarelli, 'Risky Business: Theological and Canonical Thought on Insurance from the Thirteenth to the Seventeenth Century', *Journal of Medieval and Early Modern Studies*, 31 (2001), 607–58, Laurence Fontaine, *The Moral Economy: Poverty, Credit, and Trust in Early Modern Europe* (New York: Cambridge University Press, 2014), 186.
58. David Ibbetson, 'Early Modern Lawyers and Literary Texts', Inaugural Lecture, Centre for Mediaeval and Early Modern Law and Literature, University of St Andrews, 3 October 2012.
59. *Treatise of Vsurie*, 95.
60. See e.g. Craig Muldrew, '"Hard Food for Midas": Cash and its Social Value in Early Modern England', *Past and Present*, 170 (2001), 78–120, pp. 102–4.
61. 'The Theme of the Three Caskets', in *The Standard Edition of the Complete Psychological Works of Sigmund Freud*, ed. James Strachey et al., 24 vols (London: Hogarth Press, 1953–74), XII, 291–301.

62. Extract from *Gesta Grayorum*, ed. Sir F. Madden, in Geoffrey Bullough, ed., *Narrative and Dramatic Sources of Shakespeare*, 8 vols (London: Routledge, 1957–75), I, 511–14, p. 514.
63. Schoenbaum, *William Shakespeare: A Compact Documentary Life*, 39–40.
64. *Trade and Usury* (1524), in *Luther's Works*, Vol. XLV, ed. Walther I. Brandt (Philadelphia: Mulhenberg Press, 1962), 245–310, pp. 252–6.
65. See the quotation from Henry Estienne, *A World of Wonders*, tr. Richard Carew (1607), 128—admittedly a French source—in David Hawkes, *The Culture of Usury in Renaissance England* (Basingstoke: Palgrave Macmillan, 2010), 130.
66. William Burton, *A Caueat for Suerties: Two Sermons of Suertiship* (1593), B4v.
67. Cf. Jean E. Howard, *Theater of a City: The Places of London Comedy, 1598–1642* (Philadelphia: University of Pennsylvania Press, 2007), ch. 2, and Amanda Bailey, *Of Bondage: Debt, Property, and Personhood in Early Modern England* (Philadelphia: University of Pennsylvania Press, 2013), esp. introd. and ch. 5.
68. Cf. Pierre Bourdieu, *Outline of a Theory of Practice*, tr. Richard Nice (Cambridge: Cambridge University Press, 1977), 8.
69. Quoted by John Gross, *Shylock: A Legend and its Legacy* (1992; New York: Touchstone, 1994), 157.
70. Cf. David Schalkwyk, 'The Impossible Gift of Love in *The Merchant of Venice* and the Sonnets', *Shakespeare*, 7 (2011), 142–55, pp. 145–7.
71. It is also used once by Morocco (2.7.24).
72. John Cowell, *The Interpreter* (1607), X4v; cf. *OED*, deed, *n.*, 4.
73. *Dr Faustus*, A-Text, 2.1.60, 88–114 (also B-Text), in *Christopher Marlowe: 'Dr Faustus' and Other Plays*, ed. David Bevington and Eric Rasmussen (Oxford: Clarendon Press, 1995).
74. *Discourse Vppon Vsurye*, 98.
75. 'Although that the last time of paiment of the monies by force of the Condition, is a convenient time, in which the money may be numbred before Sun set', some flexibility in arrangements was permissible. See Wade's Case, Trin. 43 Eliz. Rot. 406, in the Common Pleas, in Sir Edward Coke, *The Reports* (1658), 478–9.

CHAPTER 7 SHYLOCK AND WEDLOCK

1. *'Tis Pity She's a Whore*, ed. Derek Roper (Manchester: Manchester University Press, 1975), 5.6.11–12.
2. Cf. the Hippolyta/Soranzo and Vasques intrigue, and the tangential plot in which Philotis is vowed to the inept Bergetto then takes the 'chaste vows' (4.2.30) of convent life.
3. The medieval legend that Jews practised ritual murder and cannibalism has often been related to Shylock's imagery at 1.3.42 and 2.5.14–15 (see e.g. James Shapiro, *Shakespeare and the Jews* (New York: Columbia University Press, 1996), esp. 109–11), but a further connection might run between his contracting to have a pound of flesh without a jot of blood and the widely understood point that Jews 'may not

eat the Blood of any Beast of the Earth' (quoting Leone da Modena, *The History of the Rites, Customes, and Manner of Life, of the Present Jews, throughout the World* (1637; 1650), 92). Cf. Menasseh ben Israel's letter *To His Highnesse the Lord Protector of the Common-wealth of England, Scotland, and Ireland* (1655), 24.

4. *Payback: Debt and the Shadow Side of Wealth* (London: Bloomsbury, 2008), 152.
5. e.g. Aquinas, *Summa Theologica*, II.ii, q. 154 art. 12; Dante, *Inferno*, XI.46–51.
6. Henry Swinburne, *A Treatise of Spousals, or Matrimonial Contracts*, composed *c.*1600 (1686), 56.
7. Genesis 27. The episode is comically recalled in *The Merchant* when blind Old Gobbo does not recognize his own son when he puts his hand on his hairy head and takes it to be his face (2.2.80–8).
8. *The Jew of Malta*, 2.3.48, in *Christopher Marlowe: 'Dr Faustus' and Other Plays*, ed. David Bevington and Eric Rasmussen (Oxford: Clarendon Press, 1995).
9. John Foxe, *A Sermon Preached at the Christening of a Certaine Iew at London* (1578), C2v.
10. 'Ye haue heard that it hathe bene said, An eye for an eye, and a tooth for a tooth. But I say vnto you, Resist not euil: but whosoeuer shal smite thee on thy right cheke, turne to him the other also' (Matthew 5: 38–9).
11. See e.g. Benjamin Ravid, '*Contra Iudaeos* in Seventeenth Century Italy: Two Responses to the *Discorso* of Simone Luzzatto by Melchiore Palontrotti and Giulio Morosini', *AJS Review*, 7 (1982), 301–51, pp. 319–20.
12. On the presence of *conversos*, more or less converted Jews, in Elizabethan England see Janet Adelman, *Blood Relations: Christian and Jew in 'The Merchant of Venice'* (Chicago: University of Chicago Press, 2008), 5–7.
13. Marochitanus Samuel, *The Blessed Jew of Marocco: Or, A Blackmoor Made Whit*, tr. Thomas Calvert (1648), 18.
14. *The Vnfortunate Traveller*, in *The Works of Thomas Nashe*, ed. Ronald B. McKerrow, 5 vols, rev. F. P. Wilson (Oxford: Blackwell, 1958), II, 304–6.
15. *A Compendious and Most Marueilous History of the Latter Tymes of the Iewes Commune Weale*, tr. Peter Morwen (1558), M3r–v.
16. *The Famous and Memorable Workes of Iosephus*, tr. Thomas Lodge (1602), 787.
17. Menasseh ben Israel, *Vindiciae Judaeorum: Or, A Letter in Answer to Certain Questions Propounded by a Noble and Learned Gentleman, Touching the Reproaches Cast on the Nation of the Jewes* (1656), 13–14.
18. Naomi Tadmor, 'People of the Covenant and the English Bible', *Transactions of the Royal Historical Society*, 22 (2012), 95–110, p. 101.
19. See e.g. Peter Martyr Vermigli, *The Common Places*, tr. Anthonie Marten (1583), comparing *kerith* (later *berith*) with Latin *foedus* (i.e. league) from 'the verbe *Ferire*, To strike; bicause the ambassadors of each partie killed a hog' (Pt II, 582, 587)—cf., as with *corban* (this volume, p. 177), the classical oath-sacrifices discussed in Chapter 2 (esp. pp. 49–54); Jean Calvin, *Aphorismes of Christian Religion: Or, a Verie Compendious Abridgement of M. I. Calvins Institutions... by M. I. Piscator* (1596), 39–40; Andrew Willet, *An Harmonie Vpon the First Booke of Samuel* (1607), 218–19.

20. From the initial proposal for the bond, that a pound of 'flesh...be cut off' (1.3.145), to Portia's insistence that Shylock 'prepare... to cut off the flesh.... nor cut thou less nor more | But a just pound of flesh' (4.1.319–21). Cf. William Ian Miller, *Eye for an Eye* (Cambridge: Cambridge University Press, 2006), 44–5, 80.
21. *On the Genealogy of Morality*, ed. Keith Ansell-Pearson, tr. Carol Diethe, rev. edn (Cambridge: Cambridge University Press, 2007), 2.6, pp. 40–1.
22. *A History of the Common Law of Contract: The Rise of the Action of Assumpsit* (Oxford: Clarendon Press, 1975), 124.
23. Cf. William O. Scott, 'Conditional Bonds, Forfeitures, and Vows in *The Merchant of Venice*', *English Literary Renaissance*, 34 (2004), 286–305, esp. pp. 286–99.
24. See Tim Stretton, 'Contract, Debt Litigation and Shakespeare's *The Merchant of Venice*', *Adelaide Law Review*, 31 (2010), 111–25, p. 119. Stretton refers to Anon, *An Introduction to the Knowlege and Vnderstandyng aswel to Make as also to Perceyue the Tenour and Forme of Indentures Obligations* (1550), fols xxi–xxii.
25. Babylonian Talmud, *Shevu'ot* 22a. For Rav Hai ben Sherira Gaon, *Mishpetei Shevu'ot*, printed in Venice during Shakespeare's lifetime (1602), see Marvin J. Heller, *The Seventeenth Century Hebrew Book: An Abridged Thesaurus*, 2 vols (Leiden: Brill, 2011), II, 86–8.
26. Kenneth Charlton, *Education in Renaissance England* (1965; Abingdon: Routledge, 2007), 118–19.
27. On his Hebrew learning see Max Engammare, 'Humanism, Hebraism and Scriptural Hermeneutics', in Torrance Kirby, Emidio Campi, and Frank A. James III, eds, *A Companion to Peter Martyr Vermigli* (Leiden: Brill, 2009), 161–74.
28. Vermigli, *Common Places*, Pt II, 368.
29. Jean Calvin, *Commentaries on the Four Last Books of Moses, Arranged in the Form of a Harmony*, ed. and tr. Charles William Bingham, 4 vols (Edinburgh: Calvin Translation Society, 1852–5), II, 409. Calvin probably drew on *compendia* rather than directly on rabbinical commentary.
30. *Common Places*, Pt II, 371. Though Vermigli is focused on Exodus 20: 16 (cf. Deuteronomy 5: 20), against bearing false witness, 'abuse his name' prompts a reference in the margin to Exodus 20: 7 (cf. Deuteronomy 5: 11), against taking God's name in vain, where the Hebrew for 'He will not hold him guiltlesse' is *lo yenakeh*. In his transliteration, Vermigli vocalizes the final syllable of the verb, but not the middle one. I am grateful to Theodor Dunkelgrün for elucidating the Hebrew, and for his advice on the diffusion of Talmudic lore in early modern England.
31. See Numbers 6.
32. *Common Places*, Pt III, 182.
33. *Common Places*, Pt III, 182; cf. 187 for Vermigli's objections to Kimhi's account of the Hebrew.
34. *The Whole Treatise of the Cases of Conscience* (1606), 409.
35. *Pseudo-martyr* (1610), 114–15.

36. See e.g. Robert Parsons, *The Seconde Parte of the Booke of Christian Exercise* (1590), on 'Howe Christ was fore-tolde to Iewe and Gentile', where he cites 'Rabbi Ionathan, Rabbi Selomoth, Aben Ezar, and others' (183).
37. *Ductor Dubitantium: Or, The Rule of Conscience*, 2 vols (1660), II, 208.
38. Ben Jonson, *The Alchemist*, 4.5.25–32, in *The Cambridge Edition of the Works of Ben Jonson*, gen. eds David Bevington, Martin Butler, and Ian Donaldson, 7 vols (Cambridge: Cambridge University Press, 2012), III.
39. See Jason P. Rosenblatt, *Renaissance England's Chief Rabbi: John Selden* (Oxford: Oxford University Press, 2006), 60, which argues that Jonson got the emendation from Selden: 'Martial has accused a Jewish poet of violating his boy and refuses to believe his oath of innocence: "There, you deny it, and swear to me by the Thunderer's temple. I don't believe you: swear, circumcised one, by Anchialus [*Anchialum*]." Selden's emendation [*iura, verpe, iperan chi olam*] relies on an ancient and very well-known Rabbinic formula that he cites frequently and in detail, the *mi shepara*.'
40. *Purchas his Pilgrimage: Or, Relations of the World and the Religions Obserued in All Ages and Places Discouered, from the Creation vnto this Present* (1613), 121.
41. See 'Oath' (esp. 'Definition and Form') in *Encyclopaedia Judaica*, 2nd edn, ed. Fred Skolnik et al., 26 vols (Detroit: Thomson Gale, 2007).
42. The Geneva Bible protests too much by twice telling its readers in the margin that Jacob is not being dishonest when he does his deal with Laban: 'Iaakob herein vsed no deceit: for it was Gods commandement . . . ', 'This declareth that the thing, which Iaakob did before, was by Gods commandement, and not through deceite' (Genesis 30: 37, 31: 9). Cf. the fascinating, full discussion, to much the same effect, in *A Commentarie of Iohn Caluin, Vpon the First Booke of Moses Called Genesis*, tr. Thomas Tymme (1578), on Genesis 30: 37.
43. *Common Places*, Pt II, 537.
44. *On the Jews and their Lies*, in *Luther's Works*, Vol. XLVII, ed. Franklin Sherman (Philadelphia: Fortress Press, 1971), 137–306, pp. 226–7.
45. Cf. Alexander Ross, *Pansebeia: Or, A View of All Religions in the World* (1655), 39.
46. This treatise was translated out of Italian and published in 1637 as *The History of the Rites, Customes, and Manner of Life, of the Present Jews, Throughout the World*; quoting here the 1650 edn, 74.
47. *Vindiciae Judaeorum*, 35.
48. *Vindiciae Judaeorum*, 35.
49. Stuart Weinberg Gershon, *Kol Nidrei: Its Origin, Development, and Significance* (Northvale, NJ: Aronson, 1994), 29.
50. See Gershon, *Kol Nidrei*, ch. 9. Cf. the still-useful entry in the *Jewish Encyclopedia* (1901–6) online, at <http://www.jewishencyclopedia.com/>, accessed 21 May 2014, and the authoritative summary in *Encyclopaedia Judaica*, ed. Skolnik et al.
51. Paul Hyams, 'Faith, Fealty and Jewish "Infideles" in Twelfth-Century England', in Sarah Rees Jones and Sethina Watson, eds, *Christians and Jews in Angevin England: The York Massacre of 1190, Narratives and Contexts* (Woodbridge: Boydell, 2013), 125–47, pp. 141–2.

52. Gershon, *Kol Nidrei*, 34.
53. Gershon, *Kol Nidrei*, 35.
54. Gershon, *Kol Nidrei*, 103.
55. Yaacov Deutsch lists five accounts in nine discussions of Yom Kippur published between 1508 and 1624, in his *Judaism in Christian Eyes: Early Modern Description of Jews and Judaism* (New York: Oxford University Press, 2012), table 2.1.
56. Cf. Purchas's debt to Buxtorf on circumcision, noted by Eva Johanna Holmberg, *Jews in the Early Modern English Imagination: A Scattered Nation* (Farnham: Ashgate, 2011), 84.
57. *The Jewish Synagogue: Or, An Historical Narration of the State of the Jewes at this Day Dispersed over the Face of the Whole Earth* (1657), 234. In a reply to Menasseh ben Israel's arguments for readmitting the Jews to England, William Prynne made the same objection to the *Shemoneh Esrei*, which include a call to God to forgive sinners, that it made the Jews no better than Catholics, relying on papal pardons; see his *Case of the Jewes Stated: Or, The Jewes Synagogue Opened* (1656), 4.
58. Gershon, *Kol Nidrei*, 97, of the medieval period. Cf. the *Jewish Encyclopedia*, 'Kol Nidre': 'It cannot be denied that, according to the usual wording of the formula, an unscrupulous man might think that it offers a means of escape from the obligations and promises which he had assumed and made in regard to others.'
59. See 'Jewish opposition' in the *Jewish Enclopedia*, 'Kol Nidre'.
60. See Mark R. Cohen, 'Leone da Modena's Riti: A Seventeenth-Century Plea for Social Toleration of Jews', *Jewish Social Studies*, 34 (1972), 287–321 n. 4 and p. 293.
61. *History of the Rites*, 72–3.
62. Quoted in Asa Kasher and Shlomo Biderman, 'Why was Baruch de Spinoza Excommunicated?', in David S. Katz and Jonathan I. Israel, *Sceptics, Millenarians and Jews* (Leiden: Brill, 1990), 98–141, pp. 128–9.
63. See e.g. Jacob Marcus, *The Jew in the Medieval World: A Sourcebook, 315–1791* (New York: JPS, 1938), 49–50.
64. 'Kol Nidre', in his *Ritual Psycho-Analytic Studies* (London: Hogarth Press, 1931), 167–219, p. 172; his source is Frankel, *Die Eidesleistung der Juden* (1840). 'Sabaot' is Hebrew for 'hosts', as in the Old Testament description of God as 'the Lord of Hosts'. For Dathan and Abiram see Numbers 16.
65. Moses Avigdor Shulvass, *The Jews in the World of the Renaissance* (Leiden: E. J. Brill, 1973), 213.
66. *The Autobiography of a Seventeenth-Century Venetian Rabbi: Leon Modena's 'Life of Judah'*, tr. and ed. Mark C. Cohen (Princeton: Princeton University Press, 1988), 136.
67. Hitler's accusations about Jewish lying, invoking Schopenhauer in support, recur through *Mein Kampf*.
68. *Shakespeare's Maidens and Women*, in *The Works of Heinrich Heine*, ed. C. G. Leland et al., 12 vols (London: Heinemann, 1892–1905), I, 241–441, p. 399.
69. Those wanting to argue that usury is so immoral that it was only permitted temporarily to the Israelites (a view which goes back to Aquinas and beyond), could appeal to rabbinical sources. See Miles Mosse, *The Arraignment and*

Conuiction of Vsurie (1595), '*Galatinus* reporteth out of their *Talmud*, that it was the iudgement of the Iewish *Rabbines*, that in that place of the *Psalme* [15.5], *He that hath not giuen his money to vsurie,* God did not onely forbid it towardes the Iewes: but *etiam ad vsuram Goi*, euen toward him, which was a *Gentile*' (125).

70. *The Philosophie, Commonlie Called, the Morals Written by the Learned Philosopher Plutarch of Chaeronea*, tr. Philemon Holland (1603), 285.
71. e.g. Thomas Wilson, *A Discourse Vppon Vsurye by Waye of Dialogue and Oracion* (1572), 171.
72. Mosse, *Arraignment and Conuiction of Vsurie*, 8. Wolfgang Musculus (Müslin or Mauslein), 1497–1563, was a Reformation theologian, born in Duss, Moselle.
73. Francis Bacon, *The Essayes or Counsels, Civill and Morall*, rev. edn (1625), 239–46, p. 239; Mosse, *Arraignment and Conuiction of Vsurie*, 159. Cf. e.g. Wilson, *Discourse Vppon Vsurye*, 93, Fenton, *Treatise of Vsurie*, 52, Gerard Malynes, *Consuetudo, vel Lex Mercatoria: Or, The Ancient Law-Merchant* (1622), 328.
74. Philipp Caesar, *A General Discourse Against the Damnable Sect of Vsurers* (1578), M3r.
75. See e.g. the exchange between Witgood and three creditors in Middleton's *A Trick to Catch the Old One*, 4.3, who admit to a 'secret delight' in keeping a man in prison and getting his 'carcass'; ed. Valerie Wayne, in *Thomas Middleton: The Collected Works*, gen. eds Gary Taylor and John Lavagnino (Oxford: Clarendon Press, 2007).
76. Wilson, *Discourse Vppon Vsurye*, 47. Cf. e.g. Edward Knight, *The Triall of Truth Wherein are Discouered Three Greate Enemies vnto Mankinde, as Pride, Priuate Grudge, and Priuate Gaine* (1580), C1r.
77. *Common Places*, Pt II, 369.
78. John Gross, *Shylock: A Legend and its Legacy* (1992; New York: Touchstone, 1994), 74.
79. *Nedarim* 64b, tr. H. Freedman, in *The Babylonian Talmud*, tr. Salis Daiches et al., gen. ed. Isidore Epstein, 35 vols (London: Soncino, 1935–52).
80. Joan Ozark Holmer, *'The Merchant of Venice': Choice, Hazard and Consequence* (Basingstoke: Macmillan, 1995), 49, 52.
81. e.g. Foxe, *A Sermon Preached at the Christening of a Certaine Iew*, B3r.
82. Alexander Ross, *Pansebeia: Or, A View of all Religions in the World with the Severall Church-governments from the Creation, to These Times* (1655), 37.
83. Anthony Hecht, '*The Merchant of Venice*: A Venture in Hermeneutics', in his *Obbligati: Essays in Criticism* (New York: Athenaeum, 1986), 140–229, pp. 157–8. My thanks to Jonathan Post for alerting me to this discussion.
84. Matthew 5: 33: 'it was said to them of olde time, Thou shalt not forsweare thy self, but shalt performe thine othes to the Lord …'
85. *Common Places*, Pt II, 369–70.
86. Jacques Derrida, 'What is a "Relevant" Translation?', *Critical Inquiry*, 27 (Winter 2001), 174–200, p. 185.
87. The rabbis debate whether breaking more than one oath about some matter is worse than breaking a single oath about it; e.g. Babylonian Talmud, *Shev'uot* 3b–4a.

88. Magdalene College, Cambridge, Pepys Ballad 1.144-5. See the English Broadside Ballad Archive at <http://ebba.english.ucsb.edu/ballad/20063/image> (accessed 6 November 2014).
89. Quoted by Simpson, *History of the Common Law of Contract*, 110.
90. This slice of Selden's table talk, which resonates so strongly with Shylock's lines ('Let him look to his bond', 'I stay here on my bond' (3.1.42, 4.1.237)), is quoted by Rosenblatt, who notes: 'In both *De Successionibus ad Leges Ebraeorum in Bona Defunctorum* and *De Jure Naturali et Gentium juxta Disciplinam Ebraeorum*, Selden devotes much space to the fierce Talmudic formula (Babylonian Talmud, tractate *Bava Metzia*, 48a), quoted in full in the original Hebrew, designed to ensure that one keep one's contract.' Here is a translation of the formula: 'He who punished the generations of the flood and of the dispersion [of languages at Babel] and of the inhabitants of Sodom and Gemorrah, and the Egyptians who were washed away in the sea, will exact vengeance of him who does not stand by his word [who does not keep his contract].' See Rosenblatt, *Renaissance England's Chief Rabbi*, 60.
91. Swinburne, *Treatise of Spousals*, 8.
92. For a different interpretation see Alan W. Powers, '"What He Wills": Early Modern Rings and Vows in *Twelfth Night*', in James Schiffer, *'Twelfth Night': New Critical Essays* (Abingdon: Routledge, 2011), 217–28, p. 219.
93. On the oath as *sacramentum* see pp. 53, 292, 376; on 'inartificial proof' in rhetorical (originally Aristotelian) thought, see p. 148.
94. Malynes, *Consuetudo*, 97.
95. e.g. Wilson, *Discourse Vppon Vsurye*, 85. Cf. Mosse, *Arraignment and Conuiction of Vsurie*, 7.
96. 3.1.98–101. If the Frankfurt 'diamond', squandered by the runaways (71–2), is set in a ring, as might be expected, then they sell or barter two rings, in parallel with the other lovers.
97. *John Selden on Jewish Marriage Law: The Uxor Hebraica*, tr. with commentary by Jonathan Ziskind (Leiden: Brill, 1991).
98. The best account remains Colin Burrow, 'Shakespeare and Humanistic Culture', in Charles Martindale and A. B. Taylor, eds, *Shakespeare and the Classics* (Cambridge: Cambridge University Press, 2004), 9–27, pp. 22–4.
99. Mosse, *Arraignment and Conuiction of Vsurie*, 167–8.
100. Park Honan, *Shakespeare: A Life* (Oxford: Oxford University Press, 1998), 391–8.

CHAPTER 8 MIGHTY OPPOSITES

1. 'A kind of wine', supposedly named from a village near Lisbon. *OED*, charneco, *n.*
2. e.g. the combat between Bernier and Gautier in *Raoul de Cambrai*, discussed in my *Revenge Tragedy: Aeschylus to Armageddon* (Oxford: Clarendon Press, 1996), 153–4.

3. See George Neilson, *Trial by Combat* (Glasgow: William Hodge, 1890), 162–4, on fourteenth-century French provisions.
4. 'English books of ritual of the later Middle Ages contain a formula for the blessing of the shield and the sword for use in judicial duel', *Catholic Encyclopedia*, 'Ordeals', <http://www.newadvent.org/cathen/11276b.htm>, accessed 1 November 2013.
5. Cf. pp. 53, 292, 376, 389.
6. Cf. Sister Mary Bonaventure Mroz, *Divine Vengeance: A Study in the Philosophical Backrounds of the Revenge Motif... in Shakespeare's Chronicle History Plays* (1941; New York: Haskell House, 1971), esp. 40–3.
7. Neilson, *Trial by Combat*, 158–60, 205–6.
8. See Markku Peltonen, *The Duel in Early Modern England* (Cambridge: Cambridge University Press, 2003), e.g. 12.
9. *Vincentio Saviolo his Practise* (1595), S3v.
10. Richard Jones, *The Booke of Honor and Armes* (1590). That 'The duel of honour ultimately derived from various medieval forms of single combat—most importantly from the judicial duel' remains the view of modern scholars, see Peltonen, *Duel*, 3, and more largely Mervyn James, 'English Politics and the Concept of Honour, 1485–1642', rpt in his *Society, Politics and Culture: Studies in Early Modern England* (Cambridge: Cambridge University Press, 1986), 308–415, though such pamphlets as *The Charge of Sir Francis Bacon Knight... Touching Duells* (1614) advance the view that the *duello* was an innovation not connected with judicial combat because it was un-Christian and it cut out the authority of the monarch (Peltonen, *Duel*, e.g. 13–14).
11. Andrew Zurcher, *Shakespeare and Law* (London: Arden Shakespeare, 2010), 132–5. For the text of medieval oaths of fealty go to Britton and Bracton, noted in the Introduction, nn. 13 and 14.
12. Raphael Holinshed et al., *Chronicles*, 6 vols (1587), VI, 493.
13. *Shakespeare's Promises* (Baltimore: Johns Hopkins University Press, 1999), 43.
14. *OED*, deraign, *v.*[1], 1 '*Law*. To prove, justify, vindicate; *esp.* to maintain or vindicate (a right, claim, etc.), by wager of battle'.
15. *Bracton on the Laws and Customs of England*, tr. George Woodbine, ed. Samuel E. Thorne, 4 vols (Cambridge, Mass.: Belknap/Harvard University Press, 1968–77), II, 399.
16. The Marshal causes 'his Clarke to bring foorth the booke, wherevpon the Combatters were solemnelie sworne', first, that the appeal and its rebuttal are true, then, in a second oath, that no 'engen, instrument, herbe, charme, or inchantment' has been brought into the lists to interfere with a fair fight and the judgement of God, and finally, in a third oath, that each would use his 'vttermost endeuour and force to proue thine affirmation, either by death or deniall of thine aduersarie'; *The Booke of Honor and Armes* (1590), 78–9.
17. *Booke of Honor*, 79.
18. Holinshed, *Chronicles* (1587), VI, 494; cf. *Richard II*, 1.3.42–5.
19. *OED*, oath, *n.*

20. e.g. (italics added), 'the Lies which are giuen vppon certeine and apparant words, are they which in truth do *bind* the partie belied vnto proofe' (7), 'To this manner of Lie no man is *bound* to make answere' (8), 'such lies doo not *bind* the aduerse partie' (9), 'I stand *bound* to repulse and make answere vnto such outragious words, and consequentlie am forced to answere, *He lieth*, whereby I am disburthened, and lay the burthen on him, by which meane I become discharged of mine obligation, and binde him vnto the proofe' (19).
21. See e.g. Monsieur insulting Clermont: *The Reuenge of Bussy D'Ambois: A Tragedie* (1613), B4v.
22. See p. 504 n. 23.
23. Quoting the English translation, *The Hystorie of Hamblet* (1608), in Geoffrey Bullough, ed., *Narrative and Dramatic Sources of Shakespeare*, 8 vols (London: Routledge, 1957–75), VII, 81–124, p. 86.
24. *Edmund Ironside*, ed. Eric Sams (London: Fourth Estate, 1985), 5.2; lines 1938–40.
25. There were plenty of pirates in the late sixteenth century who could have given Chettle the idea of writing a play about revenge for a father executed for piracy, but *Hoffman* (discussed in Chapter 2) may have the starting-point it does because it is indebted to the lost *Hamlet*.
26. For earlier accounts, with an entirely different bent from my own, see William Lawrence, 'Hamlet's Sea-Voyage', *PMLA*, 59 (1944), 45–70, Karl P. Wentersdorf, 'Hamlet's Encounter with the Pirates', *Shakespeare Quarterly*, 34 (1983), 434–40, and Mary Floyd-Wilson, 'Hamlet, the Pirate's Son', *Early Modern Literary Studies*, 19 (2009), 12.1–11.
27. *De Officiis*, III.xxix [107]; *Marcus Tullius Ciceroes Thre Bokes of Duties*, tr. Nicholas Grimald (1556), fols 151v–52r.
28. Jean Bodin, *Les Six livres de la République* (1576); *The Six Bookes of a Commonweale*, tr. Richard Knolles (1606), 1–3, 630. Bodin argues that although, ideally, one should not make agreements with pirates, it might be necessary, as it was for Pompey, who treated with the Mediterranean pirates (see *Antony and Cleopatra*, 2.6).
29. Jeremy Taylor, *Ductor Dubitantium: Or, The Rule of Conscience in All her Generall Measures*, 2 vols (1660), II, 515.
30. For a conclusion that will strike the modern reader as more reasonable, and that indicates levels of debate, see William Perkins, *The Whole Treatise of the Cases of Conscience* (1606), 394: 'Some Diuines are of opinion, that the oath is to be kept, and some say no: but generally it is answered, that it must be kept,... for my part, I leaue it in suspense.'
31. Howard Eiland, 'Heidegger's Etymological Web', *Boundary 2*, 10 (1982), 3–58, p. 49; quoted by William Ian Miller, *Eye for an Eye* (Cambridge: Cambridge University Press, 2006), 95.
32. Cf. Bassanio in *The Merchant of Venice*, 'great debts... Hath left me gaged' (1.1.130).

33. John Cowell, *The Interpreter* (1607), Ii1v.
34. Richard Firth Green, *A Crisis of Truth: Literature and Law in Ricardian England* (Philadelphia: University of Pennsylvania Press, 1999), 51.
35. Holinshed, *Chronicles* (1587), VI, 493.
36. Quoting the subtitle of *The Eighth Liberal Science: Or, A New-Found-Art and Order of Drinking* (1650), which draws in many of the old jokes. For earlier material see the widely read pamphlet, German by origin, *Disputatio Inauguralis Theoreticopractica, Jus Potandi*, tr. Richard Brathwaite as *A Solemne Ioviall Disputation, Theoreticke and Practicke; Briefely Shadowing the Law of Drinking Together* (1617).
37. Gina Bloom, 'Manly Drunkenness: Binge Drinking as Disciplined Play', in Amanda Bailey and Roze Hentschell, eds, *Masculinity and the Metropolis of Vice, 1550–1650* (Basingstoke: Palgrave Macmillan, 2010), 22–44, p. 31.
38. See Rebecca Lemon, 'Compulsory Conviviality in Early Modern England', *English Literary Renaissance*, 99 (2013), 381–414.
39. John Selden, *The Duello: Or, Single Combat* (1610), 23.
40. *Richard II*, 1.1.62.
41. J. L. Austin, *How to Do Things with Words*, 2nd edn, ed. J. O. Urmson and Marina Sbisà (Oxford: Oxford University Press, 1975), 5, and frequently thereafter.
42. Austin's classification of 'I bet' as contractual rather than declaratory is as a result questionable: *How to Do Things with Words*, 7. See *OED*, bet, *n.*, 1a.
43. On these groups see François Billacois, *The Duel: Its Rise and Fall in Early Modern France*, ed. and tr. Trista Selous (New Haven: Yale University Press, 1990), 44.
44. *The Essayes: Or, Morall, Politike and Millitarie Discourses*, tr. John Florio (1603), 609.
45. See e.g. the measuring of lances, before the combat between Hereford and Mowbray in Holinshed (*Chronicles* (1587), VI, 494), *Booke of Honor*, 77 ('Launces and other weapons'), 82 (swords).
46. *As You Like It*, 5.4.78–9.
47. George Gascoigne, *A Delicate Diet, for Daintiemouthde Droonkardes* (1576), A4r, B3r. His source is an 'Epystle' attributed to Augustine, though more probably a sermon by Caesar of Arles; see Charles T. Prouty, *George Gascoigne: Elizabethan Courtier, Soldier, and Poet* (New York: Columbia University Press, 1942), 247.
48. *Bacchus and Civic Order: The Culture of Drink in Early Modern Germany* (Charlottesville, Va: University of Virginia Press, 2001), 104.
49. Billacois, *Duel*, 197.
50. Bullough, ed., *Narrative and Dramatic Sources*, VII, 109–10.
51. George Hale, *The Priuate Schoole of Defence* (1614), induction.
52. Inserting 'ill' and adopting 'all's', as is usual, rather than reproducing Norton edn.
53. Brian Cummings, *Mortal Thoughts: Religion, Secularity, and Identity in Shakespeare and Early Modern Culture* (Oxford: Oxford University Press, 2013), 214. Cf. more diffusely Michael Witmore, *Culture of Accidents: Unexpected Knowledges in Early Modern England* (Stanford, Calif.: Stanford University Press, 2001), 87–8.
54. 'How if I answer no?', he asks Osric, when invited to fight (5.2.126).

55. The verse reads 'In manibus tuis sortes meae' in the Clementine Vulgate (*Biblia Sacra Vulgatae Editionis* (1592)) 'My lottes are in thy handes' in the Douai version (*The Holie Bible: Faithfully Translated into English, Out of the Authentical Latin* (1609–10)). The Geneva Bible reads, 'My times are in thine hand' (Psalm 31: 15), and characteristically glosses it, 'Whatsoeuer changes come, thou gouernest them by thy prouidence.'
56. *Summa Theologica*, II.ii.95.8, quoting <http://www.newadvent.org/summa>, accessed 14 November 2013.
57. *Basilikon Doron* (1599), 68. At the same time, James disagreed with the authors and divines who opposed games of chance 'vpon a mistaken ground, which is, that the playing at Cards or Dice is a kinde of casting of lot, and therefore vnlawful... a sorte of Prophecie'; though disapproving of wasted time and money, he was not in principle against a man betting 'vpon the hazard of the running of the Cardes or Dice, aswel as he would do vpon the speed of a horse or a Dogge' or any such 'gageours vpon vncertenties' (146–8).
58. *Anti-Duello: The Anatomie of Duells, with the Symptomes Thereof* (1632), 6, 33.
59. *A Short and Plaine Dialogue Concerning the Vnlawfulnes of Playing at Cards or Tables, or Any Other Game Consisting in Chance* (1593), A5r.
60. See e.g. Thomas Gataker, *Of the Nature and Vse of Lots: A Treatise Historicall and Theologicall* (1619), 200. Further rounds of Balmford and Gataker's dispute are recorded in n. 31 of Chapter 4.
61. Billacois, *Duel*, 12.
62. Billacois, *Duel*, 201.
63. *Historiae Danicae*, tr. Oliver Elton (1894), in Bullough, ed., *Narrative and Dramatic Sources*, VII, 60–79, p. 61; *Hystorie of Hamblet*, 86.
64. Cf. the numerous uses of 'aduantage' in *Vincentio Sauiolo his Practise*, or Iachimo on his 'vantage' in the wager with Posthumus (*Cymbeline*, 5.6.198). The tennis score, 'Advantage', recorded in the eighteenth century, flows from this.

CHAPTER 9 OATHS, THREATS, AND *HENRY V*

1. *The Half-Pay Officers* (1720), 10–11.
2. William Hazlitt, *Characters of Shakespear's Plays* (London: R. Hunter, 1817), 203–14; on his Irish family background, and childhood years in Co. Cork, see the *Oxford Dictionary of National Biography* and Tom Paulin, *The Day-Star of Liberty: William Hazlitt's Radical Style* (London: Faber, 1998), 2–6. For Edward Dowden's account of Henry as an energetic Victorian see his *Shakspere: A Critical Study of his Mind and Art*, 15th edn (London: Kegan Paul, Trench, Trübner, 1875), 209–21; W. B. Yeats's more negative view can be found in 'At Stratford-on-Avon' (1901), in his *Essays and Introductions* (London: Macmillan, 1961), 96–110.
3. *Archipelagic English: Literature, History, and Politics 1603–1707* (Oxford: Oxford University Press, 2008).
4. Three ways into this debate: Philip Edwards, *Threshold of a Nation: A Study in English and Irish Drama* (Cambridge: Cambridge University Press, 1979), 75–6;

David J. Baker, *Between Nations: Shakespeare, Spenser, Marvell, and the Question of Britain* (Stanford, Calif.: Stanford University Press, 1997), 16–65; Willy Maley, 'The Irish Text and Subtext of Shakespeare's English Histories', in Richard Dutton and Jean Howard, eds, *A Companion to Shakespeare's Works*, 4 vols (Oxford: Blackwell, 2003), Vol. II, *The Histories*, 94–124, pp. 105–15.

5. See Introduction, p. 8. For evidence of expurgation in *Henry V*, see Andrew Gurr's New Cambridge edn (Cambridge: Cambridge University Press, 1992), 213.
6. *Lawes and Orders of Warre Established for the Good Conduct of the Seruice in Ireland* (1599), para. 3. Such rules were standard; see e.g. William Garrard, *The Arte of Warre* (1591), para. 10, which adds, at para. 30: 'there shal no souldiers or other men, procure or stir vp any quarrell with any stranger, that is of any other nation and such as serue vnder one head and Lord with them, neither in their gaming or otherwise, vpon paine of the losse of his life.'
7. J. O. Bartley, *Teague, Shenkin and Sawney: Being an Historical Study of the Earliest Irish, Welsh and Scottish Characters in English Plays* (Cork: Cork University Press, 1954), 123.
8. William Camden, 'Ireland', 145, in his *Britain* (1610).
9. Camden adds, immediately, that the Irish are often '*forsworne*' and do not fear '*damnation for perjury*'. On swearing allegiance to the crown see e.g. Barnabe Rich, *New Description of Ireland* (1610), 31, *A Catholicke Conference* (1612), 2, *A True and a Kinde Excuse* (1612), 11.
10. *Captaine Thomas Stukeley* (1605), D3v; *The Irish Masque* (1613), lines 36, 73, 101–3, ed. David Lindley, in *The Cambridge Edition of the Works of Ben Jonson*, gen. eds David Bevington, Martin Butler, and Ian Donaldson, 7 vols (Cambridge: Cambridge University Press, 2012), IV.
11. Edmund Spenser, *A View of the Present State of Ireland* (1596?), ed. W. L. Renwick (Oxford: Clarendon Press, 1970), 59, 'and so do the Irish use now to swear by their lord's hand, and to forswear it, hold it more criminal than to swear by God'; H.C., *Dialogue of Silvynne and Peregrynne* (MS 1599) 'the Irish (whose comon oathe is, either by theire lordes, or Christian gossips hande)' (quoting *CELT: Corpus of Electronic Texts*, <http://www.ucc.ie/celt/>, accessed 19 July 2010); Rich, *New Description*, 'inioyned to sweare by their Land-lordes hand' (29). Cf. John Bulwer, *Chirologia* (1644): 'The wilde Irish doe ordinarily use to sweare by this seat of faith and minister of virtue, the Right Hand' (103).
12. Katherine Simms, Bardic Poetry Database, School of Advanced Studies Dublin, <http://bardic.celt.dias.ie/main.html>, accessed 19 July 2010 (seven entries).
13. 'By Cheshu', *Half-Pay Officers*, 12, 14, 45; in *Henry V*, and 'by Jeshu', repeatedly. 'God's plud' (and 'God's plood'), 'God's will', 3.2.19, 4.8.2, 9.
14. 3.3.43, 54–8.
15. 4.3.116, 23–4, 30–1.
16. *As You Like It*, 2.7.148–50. Near the end of *Henry V*, Burgundy laments that living 'as soldiers' has reduced the French 'To swearing and stern looks' (5.2.59–61).

17. On beheading in Ireland, see Patricia Palmer, *The Severed Head and the Grafted Tongue: Literature, Translation and Violence in Early Modern Ireland* (Cambridge: Cambridge University Press, 2014).
18. Legally, this sort of menacing language could itself constitute *assault* (*OED*, *n.*, 3). See e.g. John Cowell, *The Interpreter* (1607), E2v, citing William Lambarde, *Eirenarcha*. See *Eirenarcha* (1579), I.vii, at pp. 135–6, or, among the later, rev. edns, to which Cowell refers, the one closest in date to the play (1599), II.iii, at pp. 129–31.
19. Bartley, *Teague*, 41.
20. *As You Like It*, 5.4.84.
21. John Norden, *The Mirror of Honor* (1597), 48–9. Compare e.g. Richard Crompton, *The Mansion of Magnanimitie* (1599), D1r–v, F1r–v. Both dedicated to Essex, the latter seems to be a background source for *Henry V*.
22. Relevant material is gathered in *Sources of Four Plays Ascribed to Shakespeare*, ed. G. Harold Metz (Columbia, Mo.: University of Missouri Press, 1989).
23. On the attribution of 'at least Act 2' to Shakespeare, see *King Edward III*, ed. Giorgio Melchiori, New Cambridge Shakespeare (Cambridge: Cambridge University Press, 1998), 15–17.
24. For the Countess of Salisbury scenes, Froissart was supplemented by the 46th novel in William Painter, *The Palace of Pleasure* (1566). See *Edward III*, ed. Melchiori, 'Appendix: The Use of Sources', 178–216.
25. *Richard II*, 2.3.147–50, 3.3.34–47, 102–19; *1 Henry IV*, 4.3.62–7, 103, 5.1.42–71, 5.2.36–8.
26. Prince Harry, at *1 Henry IV*, 5.4.42, endorsed by Tom McAlindon, 'Swearing and Forswearing in Shakespeare's Histories: The Playwright as Contra-Machiavel', *Review of English Studies*, 51 (2000), 208–29, p. 228; cf. Joseph M. Lenz, 'The Politics of Honor: The Oath in *Henry V*', *Journal of English and Germanic Philology*, 80 (1981), 1–12, esp. pp. 1–2, and Conal Condren's better-informed 'Understanding Shakespeare's Perfect Prince: Henry V, the Ethics of Office and the French Prisoners', *Shakespearean International Yearbook*, 9 (2009), 195–213, p. 201.
27. See *OED*, assure, *v.*, 7–11, for legal associations and overlaps with oath-taking.
28. *1 Henry IV*, 1.3.187–8; 2.5.467; *2 Henry IV*, 4.3.266–311.
29. e.g. 'Against Swearyng and Periury', *Certayne Sermons, Or Homilies Appoynted by the Kynges Maiestie* (1547), L3v–M3v, at M2v; William Perkins, *A Discourse of Conscience* (1596), 75, and *The Whole Treatise of the Cases of Conscience* (1606), 395; Christopher White, *Of Oathes: Their Obiect, Forme, and Bond* (1627), 24–8; Robert Sanderson, *De Juramento: Seven Lectures Concerning the Obligation of Promissory Oathes* (1655), 61–3, 74–6.
30. *The Cronicle History of Henry the Fift* (1600), E2r. Cf. T.P., *Of the Knowledge and Conducte of Warres* (1578), 11, on the 'stronge bande and league of frendshyp' that should hold between a general and his soldiers.
31. Sir John Smythe, *Certen Instructions, Observations and Orders Militarie* (1594), 73–4. Cf. Garrard, *Arte of Warre* (1587), para. 11. On ancient military oaths, see e.g.

Barnabe Rich, *A Path-Way to Military Practise* (1587), G3v–4r and William Segar, *Honor Military, and Ciuill* (1602), 6–8, though the topic was widely discussed.

32. Norton edn (line 26) follows Q. F is muted to 'By this hand'.
33. Compare Marlowe's hero at Damascus (discussed e.g. by Robert Egan, 'A Muse of Fire: *Henry V* in the Light of *Tamburlaine*', *Modern Language Quarterly*, 29 (1968), 15–28, p. 24), committed by his oath to slaughter; *Tamburlaine the Great* (1590), D5v, E2v–3r. The logic of a binding threat goes beyond self-exculpation: you have been warned in Damascus or Harfleur (or Eastcheap), and I must keep my word, especially as a soldier, so the fault is yours if the blow descends.
34. See *OED*, defy, *v.*, 1a.
35. *OED*, forfeit, *n.*, 2–4; *v.*, 1b and 2; forfeitable, *adj.*
36. Cf. e.g. Sanderson, *De Juramento*, 175–7.
37. Norton's correction of Pistol's French—here quoted from the Folio (Q has 'ma foy')—to '*par ma foi*' (4.4.33) is too zealous.
38. See Craig Muldrew, *The Economy of Obligation: The Culture of Credit and Social Relations in Early Modern England* (Basingstoke: Macmillan, 1998).
39. *OED*, gage, *n.*[1], 1.
40. Cf. *King Henry V*, ed. Emma Smith, Shakespeare in Production (Cambridge: Cambridge University Press, 2002), 15.
41. See the stage history in *Henry V*, ed. Gurr, 44–5.
42. Cf. Willy Maley, '"Let a Welsh Correction Teach You a Good English Condition": Shakespeare, Wales and the Critics', in Maley and Philip Schwyzer, eds, *Shakespeare and Wales: From the Marches to the Assembly* (Farnham: Ashgate, 2010), 177–89, p. 178.
43. 3.2.19 (Norton follows Q; not in F).
44. Cf. Peter Stallybrass and Ann Rosalind Jones, 'Fetishizing the Glove in Renaissance Europe', *Critical Inquiry*, 28 (2001), 114–32, esp. pp. 125–31, and David Pascoe on the pseudo-Shakespearean verses 'Upon a pair of gloves', in 'Shakespeare's Williams', *Essays in Criticism*, 60 (2010), 197–219, pp. 206–7.
45. Cf. Henry's declaration before Agincourt 'That he which hath no stomach to this fight' will have 'crowns for convoy put into his purse' (4.3.35–7), another gesture in which noble bounty is a form of dismissal.
46. 4.8.20–52. In the 1975 RSC production, directed by the aptly named Terry Hands, one actor doubled Scrope and Williams; see *King Henry V*, ed. Smith, 123.
47. Rémy Ambühl, 'A Fair Share of the Profits? The Ransoms of Agincourt (1415)', *Nottingham Medieval Studies*, 50 (2006), 129–50, p. 129.
48. K. B. McFarlane, 'The Investment of Sir John Fastolf's Profits of War', *Transactions of the Royal Historical Society*, 5th ser. 7 (1957), 91–116.
49. *Caveto*, 'beware'.
50. Over-corrected to '*Coup' la gorge*' in Norton.
51. Cf. *Henry V*, ed. Gurr, 23–8.
52. Lines 36–7. Norton takes the oath from Q; F's 'I say, I will make him eate …' looks like patchy expurgation.

53. In the sequence modelled on this, in *Sir Iohn Old-castle* (1600), Harpoole makes a summoner eat the scroll and seal which he has brought against Sir John at the behest of the Bishop of Rochester (C2r–3v). He is forced to eat his own binding words. Behind both, parodically, is Ezekiel 2–3, where the prophet eats a scroll or roll of a book which turns to honey for sweetness in his mouth.
54. Cf. Henry to Williams, 'Give me thy glove, soldier. | Look, here is the fellow of it' (4.8.36–7).
55. On small coins including groats used to bind agreements ('earnest money', 'God's penny') see e.g. David J. Ibbetson, 'Sale of Goods in the Fourteenth Century', *Law Quarterly Review*, 107 (1991), 480–99 and Richard Firth Green, *A Crisis of Truth: Literature and Law in Ricardian England* (Philadelphia, 1999), 51. For later instances, into the nineteenth century, see the *OED* on *God's-penny*.
56. Raphael Holinshed, *The Third Volume of Chronicles* (1586), 553–4. Cf. Sir Roger Williams (sometimes regarded as the original of Fluellen) who, in his *Briefe Discourse of Warre* (1590), categorizes Henry's victory with that of Alexander over Darius, Caesar over Pompey, and other instances of 'olde trained Legions' and 'a few experimented Souldiers' defeating much larger, untried forces (4).
57. 4.8.74–106. With a choice between English losses of 'not aboue fiue and twentie' and the 'aboue fiue or six hundred persons' that 'other writers of greater credit affirme', Shakespeare opted for the former (*Third Volume of Chronicles*, 555).
58. *Selections from Johnson on Shakespeare*, ed. Bertrand H. Bronson with Jean M. O'Meara (New Haven: Yale University Press, 1986), 206.
59. Note the Old French and Anglo-Norman origins (*feid, onor, onour*) of even their English oaths.
60. When idle, the French compete with oaths that mock their own triviality, as in Bourbon's boasts about his horse. 'By the white hand of my lady,' says Orléans, 'he's a gallant prince.' 'Swear by her foot,' replies the Constable, 'that she may tread out the oath' (3.7.86–7).
61. For Mountjoy, see Richard Dutton, '"Methinks the Truth Should Live from Age to Age": The Dating and Contexts of *Henry V*', *Huntington Library Quarterly*, 68 (2005), 173–204, pp. 197–201.
62. 5.0.29–34, 5.2.12 (using the F reading silently, and wrongly, emended in Norton) and 222–3.
63. e.g John Derricke, *The Image of Irelande with a Discouerie of Woodkarne* (1581), where the rebels 'sweare that all the Princ's freends, through bloudie sworde shall die. [★ They vowe, the Englishe hostes destruction]' (F4v) and Rory Óg O'More declares, 'Sir Henry now, who gouernes Irishe soyle, | Hath made an othe, to breuiate my daies' (H4r).
64. Henry Sidney, *Memoir*, in *A Viceroy's Vindication? Sir Henry Sidney's Memoir of Service in Ireland 1556–1578*, ed. Ciaran Brady (Cork: Cork University Press, 2002), sworn e.g. 47, 50, 51, 52, 54, 61, 70, 72, 74, 75, 100; unreliable, disloyal, and broken, 61, 72, 74, 75, 89, 90, 97. The topic recurs in Rory Rapple, *Martial Power and Elizabethan Political Culture: Military Men in England and Ireland, 1558–1594* (Cambridge:

Cambridge University Press, 2009); for *clú*, *glóir*, and *eineach* (as against *onóir*) in the breaking of your word, see also Brendan Kane, *The Politics and Culture of Honour in Britain and Ireland, 1541–1641* (Cambridge: Cambridge University Press, 2010), 129–31.

65. *A Viceroy's Vindication?*, 87.
66. See e.g. *Calendar of State Papers, Ireland, 1509–1573*, 412 ('The chieftains of this rebellion are James M'Maurice…and McCarthy More') and 497 (his submission), *Calendar of State Papers, Ireland, 1574–1585*, 178–9 (further rebellion), 182 ('brought to his end'); also Anthony M. McCormack, 'Fitzgerald, James fitz Maurice', *Dictionary of Irish Biography*. Patricia Palmer explores his motives (articulated in Latin, Irish, and English) to bring out the limitations of Shakespeare's MacMorris in 'Missing Bodies, Absent Bards: Spenser, Shakespeare and a Crisis in Criticism', *English Literary Renaissance*, 36 (2006), 376–95, pp. 385–6. References to this MacMorris are widespread; Palmer notes Thomas Churchyard's *The Moste True Reporte of Iames Fitz Morrice Death* (1579), while Willy Maley draws my attention to Edward Hake, *Newes out of Powles Churchyarde* (1579), F3v, Richard Becon, *Solon his Follie* (1594), 83.
67. Terry Clavin, 'Fitzmaurice, Patrick (d. 1600)', 'Fitzmaurice, Thomas (d. 1590)', *Dictionary of Irish Biography*; on Padraigín and his cultural world, see Palmer, 'Missing Bodies', 387–9.
68. *Calendar of State Papers, Ireland, 1603–1606*, 22 (cf. Sir D. Plunket Barton, *Links Between Ireland and Shakespeare* (Dublin: Maunsel, 1919), 127, and, for a sweep of MacMorrises, 114–36); J. J. N. McGurk, 'Fitzmaurice, Thomas,… (1574–1630)', *Oxford Dictionary of National Biography*, Judy Barry, 'FitzMaurice, Thomas (1574–1630)', *Dictionary of Irish Biography*.
69. See the notorious ch. 18 of *Il principe* which argues that a prince need not keep his word.
70. 'Styx, *or Leagues*', in Sir Francis Bacon, *The Wisedome of the Ancients*, tr. Sir Arthur Gorges (1619), 14–18, pp. 15–16.
71. If, as is occasionally argued, Nashe is remembering this action not from *The Famous Victories* but another play, now lost, which includes the same oath, Shakespeare's omission becomes even more striking.
72. Cf. *Henry V*, ed. Gurr, 23.
73. See p. 218; *Richard II*, 1.3.172–85.
74. 5.2.342–3. This oath was well known; Holinshed makes much of it (*Third Volume of Chronicles*, 572–3) and it is reproduced in *The Book of Oaths* (1649), comp. Richard Garnet (?), rpt several times into the eighteenth century.

CHAPTER 10 TROILUS, CRESSIDA, AND CONSTANCY

1. 'The Preface to the Play', *Troilus and Cressida*, in *The Works of John Dryden*, ed. H. T. Swedenberg, Jr et al., 20 vols (Berkeley: University of California Press, 1956–2000), XIII, 225–48, pp. 225–6.
2. 'Preface', 236 (cf. 247). Maximillian E. Novak's commentary in the California edn supplies the Loeb tr. of *Ars Poetica*, lines 126–7 (noting one minor diver-

gence in Dryden's Latin): 'Have it kept to the end even as it came forth at the first, and have it self-consistent.'

3. William Hazlitt, *Characters of Shakespear's Plays* (London: R. Hunter, 1817), 90–1.
4. See e.g. Katherine Rowe, 'Inconstancy: Changeable Affections in Stuart Dramas of Contract', in Mary Floyd-Wilson and Garrett A. Sullivan, eds, *Environment and Embodiment in Early Modern England* (Basingstoke: Palgrave, 2007), 90–102, pp. 90–2.
5. Thomas Wilson, *The Arte of Rhetorique* (1553), B3v. On Shakespeare's use of 'An Epistle to perswade a young ientleman to Mariage', translated from Erasmus by Wilson, at F1v–I2v, see e.g. T.W. Baldwin, *On the Literary Genetics of Shakespere's Poems and Sonnets* (Urbana, Ill.: University of Illinois Press, 1950), 183–5. This passage, which is representative of its period in imputing 'fikilnesse' to women merely on constitutional grounds, can be taken as one source or analogue for the description of the 'fickle maid full pale' at the start of *A Lover's Complaint.*
6. Raoul Lefevre, *The Recuyell of the Historyes of Troye*, tr. William Caxton (*c.*1474); John Lydgate, *The Hystorye Sege and Dystruccyon of Troye* (1513). See the extracts and commentary in Geoffrey Bullough, ed., *Narrative and Dramatic Sources of Shakespeare*, 8 vols (London: Routledge, 1957–75), VI.
7. Lipsius' *De Constantia Libri Duo* (1584) was translated by John Stradling. See the essays 'Of Constancie', in *The Essayes: Or, Morall, Politike and Millitarie Discourses*, tr. John Florio (1603), 21–2, 'Of Repenting', 483–92, with its celebrated third sentence, '*Constancie it selfe is nothing but a languishing and wauering dance*', and 'Of Diverting and Diversions', 499–505.
8. *Julius Caesar*, 2.1.226, 3.1.60, 2.1.298–301. For a lucid discussion, see Geoffrey Miles, *Shakespeare and the Constant Romans* (Oxford: Clarendon Press, 1996), ch. 7.
9. *Seaven Bookes of the Iliades of Homere*, tr. George Chapman (1598), L2v. This is not the language of the same passage in the Latin tr. by Andreas Divus (in Jean de Sponde's Greek/Latin parallel-text Homer) which was Chapman's major source.
10. See e.g. Lipsius, arguing that adversity 'trieth or prooueth vs; it maketh vs mirrours of patience ... It doth strengthen vs, for that the same is (as it were) our school-house wherein God traineth vp his seruantes in Constancy and vertue'; *Two Bookes of Constancie*, tr. Stradling (1595), 77–8.
11. *De Officiis*, I.xxiii [7].
12. *The First Book of Tullies Offices Translated Grammatically* (London, 1616), ch. 9.
13. *Marcus Tullius Ciceroes Thre Bokes of Duties*, tr. Nicholas Grimald (1556), B1v.
14. 'I constantly do think— | Or rather, call my thought a certain knowledge', Paris at 4.1.41–2; *OED*, constancy, *n.*, 5.
15. Craig Muldrew, *The Economy of Obligation: The Culture of Credit and Social Relations in Early Modern England* (Basingstoke: Macmillan, 1998), esp. chs 5–6.
16. *Tragedy of King Lear*, 1.1.99–100 (1.1.100–1 in the Norton conflated text).
17. See e.g. *Tusculan Disputations*, IV.xxxv.
18. For an account that brings Hobbes (along with Seneca and Bodin) to bear on faith and trust in the play, see William O. Scott, 'Risk, Distrust, and Ingratitude in Shakespeare's *Troilus and Cressida*', *Studies in English Literature*, 52 (2012), 345–62.

19. e.g. Lipsius, *Two Bookes of Constancie*, esp. I.iv–vi, Sir William Cornwallis, 'Of Opinion', in his *Essayes* (1600), K3r–5v.
20. *OED*, plight, *n.*[1], 1.
21. *OED*, plight, *n.*[2], 1a.
22. *OED*, plight, *n.*[1], 3.
23. Because it can edge into overconfidence; see esp. Hector at 2.2.13–14, 'The wound of peace is surety, | Surety secure.'
24. *The Iron Age, Part I* (1632), D4r.
25. See e.g. Ann Jennalie Cook, *Making a Match: Courtship in Shakespeare and his Society* (Princeton: Princeton University Press, 1991), ch. 5, and Diana O'Hara, *Courtship and Constraint: Rethinking the Making of Marriage in Tudor England* (Manchester: Manchester University Press, 2000), ch. 3.
26. Note to 3.2.56–7 in his edn of *Troilus and Cressida*, Arden Shakespeare, 3rd series (Walton-on-Thames: Nelson, 1998). See further Emily Ross, '"Words, Vows, Gifts, Tears and Love's Full Sacrifice": An Assessment of the Status of Troilus and Cressida's Relationship According to Customary Elizabethan Marriage Procedures', *Shakespeare*, 4 (2008), 413–37.
27. 1.2.6, 1.3.267.
28. Heather James, *Shakespeare's Troy: Drama, Politics, and the Translation of Empire* (Cambridge: Cambridge University Press, 1997), 106–12.
29. 2.2.96–111, 4.7.100–4, 5.3.7–93.
30. Most thoughtfully, Colin Burrow, introd. to *Troilus and Cressida*, ed. R.A. Foakes, rev. edn (London: Penguin, 2006), xxi–lxxiv, pp. xli–xliv.
31. *OED*, amen, *int. and n.*, 2–3 and 4, 'Truly, verily'.
32. *Troilus and Criseyde*, III.1296–1302, citing, for convenience, *The Riverside Chaucer*, 3rd edn, gen. ed. Larry D. Benson (New York: Houghton Mifflin, 1987).
33. III.1499–652, esp. 1541–54.
34. After the parting, similarly, the truths vowed by the lovers are put into diminishing perspective. Aeneas says that Hector, off to his combat with Ajax, 'must think me tardy and remiss, | That swore to ride before him to the field' (4.5.141–2). A broken oath already, so early in the day, yet the harm is only to be thought remiss.
35. He does rush offstage, leaving Pandarus to break the bad news to Cressida, but only to 'go meet' Paris and Deiphobus, who are bringing Antenor from the Greek camp (4.2.72, 4.4).
36. O'Hara, *Courtship and Constraint*, 59–60, 88–90. Cf. Catherine Richardson, '"A Very Fit Hat": Personal Objects and Early Modern Affection', in Tara Hamling and Catherine Richardson, eds, *Everyday Objects: Medieval and Early Modern Material Culture and its Meanings* (Farnham: Ashgate, 2010), 289–98.
37. *Recuyell*, in Bullough, ed., *Narrative and Dramatic Sources*, VI, 203.
38. 'No, but' follows Q and F, but see the layout in Bevington's Arden edn, and the New Cambridge *Troilus and Cressida*, ed. Anthony B. Dawson (Cambridge: Cambridge University Press, 2003), where 'No' is given a line to itself, encouraging an actor to pause before 'But something ...'.

39. V.1038–43. *Ek*, 'moreover, likewise'; *yaf*, 'gave'; *bet*, 'better, more satisfactorily'; *pencel*, 'small pennon, streamer'.
40. V.1660–81. 'Who will now believe in any more oaths'?
41. *Iron Age, Part I*, F3r–v.
42. *Iron Age, Part II* (1632), C1r–C2r, E3r–v. Henryson's poem appeared in sixteenth-century edns of Chaucer from Thynne's *The Workes of Geffrey Chaucer* (1532).
43. Robert Sanderson, *De Juramento: Seven Lectures Concerning the Obligation of Promissory Oathes* (1655), 226; cf. Christopher White, *Of Oathes: Their Obiect, Forme, and Bond* (1627), 52. For the view that a promise, but not a promissory oath, could be released by this means, see William Perkins, *The Whole Treatise of the Cases of Conscience* (1606), 393, John Downame, *Foure Treatises* (1608), 66.
44. On these threats see e.g. Laurie E. Maguire, 'Performing Anger: The Anatomy of Abuse(s) in *Troilus and Cressida*', *Renaissance Drama*, ns 31 (2002), 153–83.
45. Cf., among many analogues, 'the true mother of Constancie is PATIENCE', in Lipsius, *Two Bookes of Constancie*, 9.
46. It is used chiefly by female characters, such as Mistress Quickly in *2 Henry IV*, Valeria in *Coriolanus*, and Ophelia in *Hamlet*, though MacMorris has an Irish version, 'law', when at his most insistent (see p. 238).
47. Norton's allocation of 'As I kiss thee' to Diomedes is one of the less satisfactory of several solutions to a textual crux in Q and F.
48. Peter Stallybrass, 'Worn Worlds: Clothes and Identity on the Renaissance Stage', in Margreta de Grazia, Maureen Quilligan, and Peter Stallybrass, eds, *Subject and Object in Renaissance Culture* (Cambridge: Cambridge University Press, 1996), 289–320, p. 313.
49. On gage as pledge see John Cowell, *The Interpreter* (1607), Ii1v–2r, cited in Chapter 8 (p. 224). Cf. Troilus' would-be convinced declaration before the parting, 'I will throw my glove to Death himself | That there's no maculation in thy heart' (4.5.62–3).
50. III.1254–74, 1744–71 ('Canticus Troili'). Cf. Ann Thompson, *Shakespeare and Chaucer: A Study in Literary Origins* (Liverpool: Liverpool University Press, 1978), 144.
51. O'Hara, *Courtship and Constraint*, 71.
52. 'Let Paris bleed, 'tis but a scar to scorn: | Paris is gored with Menelaus' horn' (1.1.107–8).
53. e.g. Gary Taylor, '*Troilus and Cressida*: Bibliography, Performance, and Interpretation', *Shakespeare Studies*, 15 (1982), 99–136.
54. Norton's 'like' has no textual basis and is presumably a misprint.
55. National Theatre, 1999; Edinburgh Festival, 2006. For a scholarly account, see Roger Apfelbaum, *Shakespeare's 'Troilus and Cressida': Textual Problems and Performance Solutions* (Cranbury, NJ: Associated University Presses, 2004), ch. 8.
56. *Love's Labour's Lost*, 5.2.394; for medieval precedents see Ralph Hexter, *Equivocal Oaths and Ordeals in Medieval Literature* (Cambridge, Mass.: Harvard University Press, 1975), 34–6.

57. See the informative note on *tokens* as plague spots in Cotgrave, Dekker, Shakespeare, and elsewhere, in *Love's Labour's Lost*, ed. H. R. Woudhuysen, Arden Shakespeare, 3rd series (Walton-on-Thames: Nelson, 1998), 5.2.423.
58. This is Luther, *De Captivitate Babylonica* (1520), ch. 2, my translation, though the claim is widely found. See *OED*, testament, *n.*, II, noting the fusion created when 'Greek *diathēkē*, "disposition, arrangement", was applied to both a covenant (*pactum, foedus*) between parties, and to a testament or will (*testamentum*)'.

CHAPTER 11 BINDING LANGUAGE IN *MEASURE FOR MEASURE*

1. e.g. Jean Calvin, *The Institution of Christian Religion* (1561), Bk 2, ch. 8 (on 'The third Commaundement'), and William Perkins, *The Whole Treatise of the Cases of Conscience Distinguished into Three Bookes* (1606), 382–3. On prayer, cf. Thomas Gataker, *Of the Nature and Vse of Lots* (1619), 151, citing Cicero, Augustine, Aquinas, Calvin, Melanchthon.
2. For 'votarist' as one who prays, see *Timon of Athens*, 4.3.27.
3. e.g. Jean Calvin, *The Sermons of M. Iohn Caluin vpon the Fifth Booke of Moses Called Deuteronomie*, tr. Arthur Golding (1583), 831–2. For the received view of this see Perkins, *Whole Treatise*, 400–11; for Protestant sympathy with vow-taking, John Mabb, *The Afflicted Mans Vow* (1609), 23–38.
4. See e.g. Martin Luther, *De Votis Monasticis* [*On Monastic Vows*] (1521), Jean Calvin, *Institution*, Bk 4, ch. 13, Peter Martyr Vermigli, *The Common Places*, tr. Anthonie Marten (1583), Pt III, 175–92. For recapitulation see (among many) Perkins, *Whole Treatise*, 411–22.
5. Théodore de Bèze, *The Pope's Canons*, tr. T.S. (1587), C8v–D1r.
6. 4.2.156. Cf. 2.3.3–5, 'Bound by my charity and my blest order, | I come to visit the afflicted spirits | Here in the prison.'
7. 4.3.136. *OED*, combind, *v.*, *obs.*, 'bind together' ('A form arising from confusion of *combine* and *bind*'), though see also combine, *v.*, 1 b, 'conjoin, band together, associate'.
8. 1.3.19. For a legal parallelism in their binding see John Cowell's glossary of law terms, *The Interpreter* (1607), Zz1r, which defines *Nunne* as 'a woman that hath by vowe bound her selfe to a single and chast life' and says of *Arrest*: 'a certaine restraint of a mans person,... binding it to become obedient to the will of the lawe.'
9. George Flinton, *A Manual of Prayers*, rev. edn (1604), 116.
10. As reported by Gracious Menewe, *A Plaine Subuersyon or Turnyng Vp Syde Down of All the Argumentes, that the Popecatholykes Can Make for the Maintenaunce of Auricular Confession* (1555), E8v–F1v and William Vaughan, *The Spirit of Detraction, Coniured and Convicted* (1611), 127.
11. See e.g. Vincent Bruno, *A Short Treatise of the Sacrament of Penance* (1597), 21–5, on searching the conscience and numbering sins. For the Protestant view, see 'An Homilee of Repentaunce, and of True Reconciliation vnto God', in John

Jewel, *The Second Tome of Homilees* (1571), 508–43, p. 531: 'it is agaynst the true Christian libertie, that any man shoulde be bound to the numbryng of his synnes.'

12. See esp. pp. 376–7.
13. For discussion in a Shakespearean context see e.g. Sarah Beckwith, *Shakespeare and the Grammar of Forgiveness* (Ithaca, NY: Cornell University Press, 2011), 42.
14. 4.3.147; Jeremy Taylor, *Ductor Dubitantium: Or, The Rule of Conscience in All her Generall Measures*, 2 vols (1660), II, 41.
15. For the general, Protestant mentality, and paradoxical laxity of a bound law, see again Taylor, *Ductor Dubitantium*, II, 14, echoing another Pauline source (Romans 7): 'However the laws were established, yet according as they goe off, or goe less, or fall into desuetude or disobligation, so the band of conscience grows less, till it be quite eas'd by abrogation; the law binding by its establishment, and the conscience being bound by the life of the law, as the law dies the conscience is at ease.'
16. *Forasmuch as his Maiestie vnderstandeth, that there be diuers ancient and other good and necessary lawes and statutes of this his kingdome of England which do inflict . . . punishments . . . vpon such as vnlawfully hunt or enter into any forest* (16 May 1603).
17. Cf. Marc Shell, *The End of Kinship: 'Measure for Measure', Incest, and the Ideal of Universal Siblinghood* (Stanford, Calif.: Stanford University Press, 1988), 51.
18. John 8: 44.
19. Cf. Graham Bradshaw, *Shakespeare's Scepticism* (Brighton: Harvester, 1987), 212.
20. See Cowell, *Interpreter*, H2r, under *Bayle*: 'The reason why it is called *Bayle*, is, because by this meanes the party restrained, is deliuered into the hands of those that bind themselues for his forth-comming.'
21. e.g. Vaughan, *Spirit of Detraction*, 'To the Reader', A1r–2v.
22. William Perkins, 'To the Reader', in his *A Direction for the Government of the Tongue According to Gods Word* (1593), A2r.
23. e.g. Robert Parsons, *A Christian Directorie Guiding Men to their Saluation* (1585), 'Who can remoue . . . without great difficultie, a longe custome of dronkennes, of swearing, . . . ?' (821) and *A Treatise Tending to Mitigation Towardes Catholike-subiectes in England* (1607), 'the man that accustometh to sweare rashly putteth himselfe in manifest danger to sweare also falsely, and therby sinneth mortally' (302); Bruno, *Short Treatise*, 'If hee haue sworne without reuerence or trueth, or necessitye: . . . made any VOWE which he hath not obserued . . . murmured, or detracted the good name of others, or . . . reuealed their secret sinnes' (88–90); Flinton, *Manual*, 'I haue spoken many vaine wordes [and] not spoken of my neighbour, with that charity, wherewith I would others should speake of me . . . I have sworne by Faith and Troth without necessitie and I *cry God mercie for it*' (113–15).
24. See e.g. Edmond Bicknoll, *A Swoord Agaynst Swearyng* (1579), 21–2, William Perkins, *A Godly and Learned Exposition of Christs Sermon in the Mount* (1608), 151: 'where is much swearing vsually, there cannot but be much periurie.'
25. James VI and I, *Basilikon Doron: Or, His Maiesties Instructions to his Dearest Sonne, Henry the Prince*, London edn (1603), 14.

26. *Spirit of Detraction*, 144. Vaughan's interest goes back to his thoughts about lies, swearing, perjury, cursers and blasphemers, deceit, and sworn promises in *The Golden-groue Moralized in Three Bookes* (1600), chs 17–22.
27. Perkins, *Direction*, 53.
28. *Thomas Middleton: The Collected Works*, gen. eds Gary Taylor and John Lavagnino (Oxford: Clarendon Press, 2007), 1575.
29. For conventional post-Reformation explication see e.g. John Carter, *A Plaine and Compendious Exposition of Christs Sermon in the Mount* (1627), which begins its gloss on '*With what measure you mete, it shall bee measured to you againe*' with the comment: 'So that if wee desire to haue and hold a good name in the world, it lyeth vs in hand to be charie of other folkes good name' (100).
30. See e.g. Perkins, *Christs Sermon in the Mount*, 187.
31. Jean Calvin, *A Harmonie Vpon the Three Euangelists, Matthew, Mark and Luke with the Commentarie of M. Iohn Caluin*, tr. E.P. (1584), 209, Perkins, *Christs Sermon in the Mount*, 414–16.
32. *Direction*, 51.
33. *De Sermone Domini in Monte Secundum Matthaeum*, Bk 1, ch. 16 [sect. 50]. See the tr. from John J. Jepson, *St Augustine: The Lord's Sermon on the Mount* (Westminster, Md: Newman Press, 1948), in Geoffrey Bullough, ed., *Narrative and Dramatic Sources of Shakespeare*, 8 vols (London: Routledge, 1957–75), II, 418–19.
34. There are many analyses of judging and judgement in the play. On slander in *Measure* see M. Lindsay Kaplan, *The Culture of Slander in Early Modern England* (Cambridge: Cambridge University Press, 1997), ch. 4, and Kenneth Gross, *Shakespeare's Noise* (Chicago: Chicago University Press, 2001), ch. 3. Cf. Ina Habermann, *Staging Slander and Gender in Early Modern England* (Aldershot: Ashgate, 2003).
35. See p. 8.
36. 'Oath/s' four times, usually in legal contexts, 'vow/s' and 'vowed' six times, in settings that are religious or to do with betrothal and marriage.
37. See the text of Whetstone's play in Bullough, ed., *Narrative and Dramatic Sources*, II, 442–513, p. 477.
38. See Gary Taylor, ''Swounds Revisited: Theatrical, Editorial, and Literary Expurgation', in Gary Taylor and John Jowett, *Shakespeare Reshaped 1606–1623* (Oxford, 1993), 51–106, pp. 103–5.
39. Quoting the text in J. P. Kenyon, ed., *The Stuart Constitution 1603–1688*, 2nd edn (Cambridge: Cambridge University Press, 1986), 36–7.
40. See David Colclough, *Freedom of Speech in Early Modern England* (Cambridge: Cambridge University Press, 2005), 77–92.
41. Colclough, *Freedom of Speech*, 214. Cf. David Cressy, *Dangerous Talk: Scandalous, Seditious, and Treasonable Speech in Pre-Modern England* (Oxford: Oxford University Press, 2010), 101–7.
42. John Jowett and Gary Taylor, '"With New Additions": Theatrical Interpolation in *Measure for Measure*', in their *Shakespeare Reshaped*, 107–236, pp. 151–86, John

Jowett, introd. to *'Measure for Measure*: A Genetic Text', in *Middleton: Collected Works*, ed. Taylor and Lavagnino, 1542–6.

43. Laura Gowing, *Domestic Dangers: Women, Words, and Sex in Early Modern London* (Oxford: Clarendon Press, 1996), 111.
44. See e.g. Perkins, *Direction*, 11, citing the homilies of St John Chrysostom: 'The tongue is placed in the middle of the mouth, and it is compassed in with lippes and teeth as with a double trench, to shewe us, howe we are to use heede and preconsideration before we speake.'
45. *Spirit of Detraction*, 235.
46. *Spirit of Detraction*, 236.
47. Anon, *A Plaine Description of the Auncient Petigree of Dame Slaunder* (1573), B5v, quoting Moses in Exodus. Cf. Cressy, *Dangerous Talk*, 6–10.
48. *Sermons on Job*, tr. Arthur Golding (1574), 556. Cf. Gross, *Shakespeare's Noise*, 48.
49. Roland Mushat Frye, *Shakespeare and Christian Doctrine* (Princeton: Princeton University Press, 1963), 291. For the view that *Measure* is relatively sympathetic to clerical Catholicism and auricular confession see David N. Beauregard, 'Shakespeare on Monastic Life: Nuns and Friars in *Measure for Measure*', in Dennis Taylor and David N. Beauregard, eds, *Shakespeare and the Culture of Christianity in Early Modern England* (New York: Fordham University Press, 2003), 311–35.
50. *Spirit of Detraction*, 'Epistle Dedicatorie', *2r.
51. For a history, see R. H. Helmholz, *The Oxford History of the Laws of England*, Vol. I, *The Canon Law and Ecclesiastical Jurisdiction from 597 to the 1640s* (Oxford: Oxford University Press, 2004), ch. 11. On the diversity of courts involved, including Star Chamber, see Martin Ingram, 'Law, Litigants and the Construction of "Honour": Slander Suits in Early Modern England', in Peter Coss, ed., *The Moral World of the Law* (Cambridge: Cambridge University Press, 2000), 134–60, pp. 140–3.
52. Ralph Houlbrooke, *Church Courts, Sex and Marriage in England, 1570–1640* (Cambridge: Cambridge University Press, 1987), 292–3, Gowing, *Domestic Dangers*, 32.
53. Gowing, *Domestic Dangers*, 263, Ingram, 'Law, Litigants', 146. On the legal practice of interpreting slanderous words *in mitiori sensu* ('in the milder sense'), to avoid such escalation, see J. H. Baker, *An Introduction to English Legal History*, 4th edn (London: Butterworths, 2002), 441–2.
54. 1 and 2 Philip and Mary c. 13 and 2 and 3 Philip and Mary c. 10. See John H. Langbein, *Prosecuting Crime in the Renaissance: England, Germany, France* (Cambridge, Mass.: Harvard University Press, 1974), chs 2 and 4, Holger Schott Syme, *Theatre and Testimony in Shakespeare's England: A Culture of Mediation* (Cambridge: Cambridge University Press, 2012), ch. 1.
55. See e.g. the soliloquy 'No might nor greatness in mortality' (3.1.416–19).
56. For royal sensitivity before James see e.g. the warning against slandering Elizabeth, in *A Proclamation Conteyning her Maiesties Pleasure, How Those Shalbe Dealt Withall, Which Haue Falsly Slandered her Maiesties Proceedings and her Ministers* (1600).

57. Ferdinando Pulton, *De Pace Regis et Regni* (1609), B1r–v. For the closeness of slander to battery see the apt malapropism and gloss at 2.1.160–3.
58. A number of editors have taken 'to her by oath' from F2—though this invites, unhelpfully, the further correction 'affianced to *him* by oath'.
59. Gowing, *Domestic Dangers*, 167–8.
60. *OED*, grange, *n.*, 2b.
61. Bernard Capp, *When Gossips Meet: Women, Family, and Neighbourhood in Early Modern England* (Oxford: Oxford University Press, 2003), 215–16.
62. A fuller, two-stanza version appears in Fletcher's *Rollo, Duke of Normandy* (1617–20). See Jowett, introd. to *'Measure for Measure*: A Genetic Text', in *Middleton: Collected Works*, ed. Taylor and Lavagnino, 1542, and n. on p. 1570.
63. *OED*, seal, *n.*[2], 1 b–c, e, i.
64. *OED*, seal, *n.*[2], 2 a–b.
65. Cf. Pisanio at *Cymbeline*, 3.4.32–8: 'Kings, queens, and states, | Maids, matrons, nay, the secrets of the grave | This viperous slander enters.'
66. A 'medlar' is a flat, open-bottomed pear, eaten when over-ripe; common term for 'prostitute'.
67. *Promos and Cassandra*, 468–9.
68. *Promos and Cassandra*, 497–8. On knights of the post see e.g. William Bullein, *A Dialogue bothe Pleasaunte and Pietifull* (1564), fol. 17v, Edward Knight, *The Triall of Truth* (1580), fol. 39v; it is often said that Shakespeare had read E.S., *The Discoverie of the Knights of the Poste* (1597).
69. See e.g. Barbara J. Shapiro, *'Beyond Reasonable Doubt' and 'Probable Cause': Historical Perspectives on the Anglo-American Law of Evidence* (Berkeley: University of California Press, 1991), *A Culture of Fact: England, 1550–1720* (Ithaca, NY: Cornell, 2000), esp. ch. 1.
70. Thomas Lupton, *The Second Part and Knitting Vp of the Boke Entituled Too Good to Be True* (1581), O1v; cf. Bullough, ed., *Narrative and Dramatic Sources*, II, 514–24, p. 522.
71. 4.1.25–33. On domestic privacy and revelation in cases of scandal/slander see Gowing, *Domestic Dangers*, 71.
72. Lorna Hutson, *The Invention of Suspicion: Law and Mimesis in Shakespeare and Renaissance Drama* (Oxford: Oxford University Press, 2007), 289.
73. See esp. Richard Moran, 'Getting Told and Being Believed', *Philosophers Imprint*, 5:5 (August 2005).
74. See the extract from *Hecatommithi*, in Bullough, ed., *Narrative and Dramatic Sources*, II, 420–30, p. 425, and the material from *Epitia*, 430–42, pp. 438–9. Also, e.g., Taylor, *Ductor Dubitantium*, II, 102.
75. Putting himself on oath, James continues: 'I protest before the great God, and since I am here as vpon my Testament, it is no place for me to lye in, that ye shall neuer finde with any Hieland or bordor theeues ... moe lyes and vile periuries, then with these phanaticke spirits'; *Basilikon Doron*, 34. On Angelo's 'sins of aversion (greed, oath-breaking and slander)', and the play's anti-puritan bent, see Peter Lake with Michael Questier, *The Antichrist's Lewd Hat: Protestants,*

Papists and Players in Post-Reformation England (New Haven: Yale University Press, 2002), ch. 15, quoting p. 652.

76. See e.g. Cowell, *Interpreter*, Nnn2v, under *Scandalum Magnatum*; Sir Edward Coke, on *De Libellis Famosis* (1605, Easter Term, 3 James I, Court of Star Chamber), in *Quinta Pars Relationum Edwardi Coke Equitis Aurati ... The Fift Part of the Reports of Sr. Edward Coke Knight* (1605), fols 125r–6r; Pulton, *De Pace Regis et Regni*, B1v. On the operation of the law, see Cressy, *Dangerous Talk*, 29–33.
77. *Spirit of Detraction*, 'Epistle Dedicatorie', *2r.
78. See his discussion with the Duke/Friar, 4.2.167–73.
79. 'And I absolve you from every bond'—using the same Latin word that is also used for the bond of an oath (Tridentine Rite of Confession).
80. Bruno, *Short Treatise*, 2.
81. See e.g. Menewe, *Plaine Subuersyon*, E3v.
82. 'Lazarus', *The Towneley Plays*, ed. Martin Stevens and A. C. Cawley, 2 vols (Oxford: Oxford University Press for the Early English Text Society), I, 425–31, lines 97–101. For 'sudary' see the Electronic *Middle English Dictionary*, 2 (a): 'A piece of linen used in Biblical times to wrap the head of a corpse before burial'. Cf. 'All his bondys, losyth hem asundyr ...', in 'The Raising of Lazarus', *The N-Town Play: Cotton MS Vespasian D.8*, ed. Stephen Spector, 2 vols (Oxford: Oxford University Press for the Early English Text Society, 1991), I, 230–45, lines 429–33. The medieval association between the unbinding of Lazarus and the loosing of the bonds of sin through absolution is documented in Thomas Rendall, 'Liberation from Bondage in the Corpus Christi Plays', *Neuphilologische Mitteilungen*, 71 (1970), 659–73, pp. 666–7.
83. See the commonplace cited by Tim Stretton, *Women Waging Law in Elizabethan England* (Cambridge: Cambridge University Press, 1998), 16: 'in *foro conscientie* [forum of conscience] there is never any doubt or question concerning the fact being truly and sincerely discovered by the voluntary confession of the partie but in *foro contentiese* [forum of contest] the judge dothe often erre and is deceaved by presumpcion and probabilities.'
84. See e.g. Hutson, *Invention*, 21–2.
85. On which see Stretton, *Women Waging Law*, ch. 4.
86. *Promos and Cassandra*, 497.
87. For contrasting accounts of the confessional element see Huston Diehl, '"Infinite Space": Representation and Reformation in *Measure for Measure*', *Shakespeare Quarterly*, 49 (1998), 393–410, pp. 408–10, which finds a Calvinist outlook, and Claire Griffiths-Osborne, '"The Terms for Common Justice": Performing and Reforming Confession in *Measure for Measure*', *Shakespeare*, 5 (2009), 36–51, which tacks in a Catholic direction.
88. See, most dismissively, Debora Shuger, *Censorship and Cultural Sensibility: The Regulation of Language in Tudor-Stuart England* (Philadelphia: University of Pennsylvania Press, 2006), 223.
89. Augustine, *De Mendacio*, sect. 2.
90. See e.g. Perkins, *Direction*, 64.

91. See Houlbrooke, *Church Courts*, 261, Eleanor Hubbard, *City Women: Money, Sex, and the Social Order in Early Modern London* (Oxford: Oxford University Press, 2012), 80.
92. Cf. Shuger, *Censorship and Cultural Sensibility*, 110–12.
93. Gowing, *Domestic Dangers*, 68. Cf. Timon's outburst, 'Maid, to thy master's bed! | Thy mistress is o'th' brothel' (*Timon of Athens*, 4.1.12–13).

CHAPTER 12 KNOTS, CHARMS, RIDDLES

1. Laurie Maguire and Emma Smith, 'Many Hands: A New Shakespeare Collaboration?', *Times Literary Supplement*, 20 April 2012.
2. Quoting the edn of *The Witch*, ed. Marion O'Connor, in *Thomas Middleton: The Collected Works*, gen. eds Gary Taylor and John Lavagnino (Oxford: Clarendon Press, 2007).
3. Among earlier instances see e.g. G.B., *A Most Wicked Worke of a Wretched Witch* (1592), A2v.
4. e.g. James Carmichael, *Newes from Scotland* (1592), A3v, where the witches 'kisse [Satan's] Buttockes, in signe of duetye to him [and] he receiued their oathes for their good and true seruice towards him'; James VI, *Daemonologie* (1597), esp. ch. 6, 'The Deuilles contract with the *Magicians*'.
5. William Perkins, *A Discourse of the Damned Art of Witchcraft* (1608), 173–4. Cf. Thomas Cooper, *The Mystery of Witch-craft* (1617), 207.
6. For contexts see Mariangela Tempera, 'The Knots in the Text: Thomas Middleton's *The Witch*', in Carmela Nocera, Persico Gemma, and Rosario Portale, eds, *Rites of Passage: Rational/Irrational, Natural/Supernatural, Local/Global* (Soveria Mannelli, Catanzaro: Rubbettino, 2003), 137–44, pp. 140–2.
7. e.g., Perkins, *Discourse of Witchcraft*, 132–3.
8. See e.g. Scott Cunningham's many-times reprinted *Earth Power: Techniques of Natural Magic* (St Paul, Minn.: Llewellyn, 1983), ch. 12.
9. John Cotta, *The Triall of Witchcraft* (1616), 90. For knots tied to ease pain and heal sickness see P. G. Maxwell-Stewart, *Satan's Conspiracy: Magic and Witchcraft in Sixteenth-Century Scotland* (East Linton: Tuckwell, 2001), 61, 100.
10. 1.3.10–16. See e.g. the sorcerer giving winds tied in a rope with three magical knots to mariners, illustrating Olaus Magnus, *Historia de Gentibus Septentrionalibus* (1555), Bk III, ch. xv.
11. Fertility could be secured by untying the 'knot of Hercules' in a bride's girdle. See Ben Jonson, *Hymenaei* (1606), A4v, esp. the poet's marginal note; *Hymenaei*, ed. David Lindley, lines 42–3 and n. 20 on p. 704, in *The Cambridge Edition of the Works of Ben Jonson*, gen. eds David Bevington, Martin Butler, and Ian Donaldson, 7 vols (Cambridge: Cambridge University Press, 2012), II.
12. *De la démonomanie des sorciers* (1580), 58r–59v. The 1587 edn refers back to the Roman belief.
13. The discussion comes in the added Bk II of 'A Discourse vpon Diuels and Spirits', which follows the main text of the *Discouerie*: '*This knot or ligament is*

become so notorious... that the Laws of several Nations have prohibited the performance thereof; neither is it fit to be openly described in this place' ('Discourse', 71).

14. See O'Connor's note in her edn of *The Witch*, in *Thomas Middleton*, gen. eds Taylor and Lavagnino.
15. See Henry N. Paul, *The Royal Play of Macbeth* (New York: Macmillan, 1950), 58–9, on Le Loyer and Shakespeare on the 'phantosmes and imaginations' of usurping tyrants.
16. Pierre Le Loyer, *A Treatise of Specters or Straunge Sights* (1605), 137–45, p. 138.
17. 4.1.30–1. Cf. the boiled, 'unbaptizèd brat' and 'barley soaked in infants' blood', at *The Witch*, 1.2.15–16, 5.2.45.
18. See Christopher A. Faraone, *Ancient Greek Love Magic* (Cambridge, Mass.: Harvard University Press, 1999), 101–3.
19. *OED*, knot, *n.*[1], 12, *obs.*
20. e.g. Stephen Gardiner, *De Vera Obedientia... 1536... Translated into English* (1553), H1r–v.
21. e.g. 'rehearse the bonds of words; and in the end of euerie bond, saie oftentimes; Remember thine oth and promise. And bind him stronglie to thee,' in Reginald Scot, *Discouerie of Witchcraft* (1584), Bk XV, ch. 17 (424). The association was probably reinforced by the long-running and for Protestants heretical claim of the Catholic Church to use the power of the keys (Matthew 16: 19) to 'bind' by cursing or banning.
22. e.g. '*these very Characters, Sigils, Lamins, &c. are Compacts themselves, which the Devils did at first cunningly disguise with strange Repetitions in uncouth Language*', in Bk II, ch. 7 of the 'Discourse', in Scot, *Discouerie* (1665 edn), 69.
23. As repeatedly in Scot, *Discouerie*, Bk XV.
24. 'Charms and Riddles', in Northrop Frye, *Spiritus Mundi: Essays on Literature, Myth, and Society* (Bloomington, Ind.: Indiana University Press, 1976), 123–47, p. 137.
25. *OED*, conjuration, *n.*, II (2–6) but also I. Cf. conjuring, *n.*, 1.
26. *OED*, knot, *n.*[1], 18; *Julius Caesar*, 3.1.118, *The Merry Wives of Windsor*, 4.2.102–3.
27. Barnabe Barnes, *The Diuils Charter* (1607), Prologus.
28. p. 53. For a judicious account of the relationship between *Catiline* and early seventeenth-century plots see Ian Donaldson, *Ben Jonson: A Life* (Oxford: Oxford University Press, 2011), 281–4.
29. pp. 57 and 77, citing George Puttenham, *The Arte of English Poesie* (1589). The witches' 'Double, double'—explicit in 4.1—can almost be heard in what Puttenham says of rhymes in the sestina, 'enterweauing one with another by knots, or as it were by band,... all as the maker will double or redouble' (72).
30. 1.3.116–18; cf. Lady Macbeth at 1.5.13–14 ('thou...shalt be | What thou art promised'), Banquo at 3.1.1–2 ('Thou hast it now: King, Cawdor, Glamis, all | As the weird women promised').
31. Keith Thomas, *Religion and the Decline of Magic* (1971; Harmondsworth: Peregrine, 1978), 211–12. On the late medieval overlap between charms and spells see

Eamon Duffy, *The Stripping of the Altars: Traditional Religion in England 1400–1580*, 2nd edn (New Haven: Yale University Press, 2005), 266–87.

32. The element of blasphemous rite has an anti-Catholic aspect. Cf. King James's apocalyptic account of the amphibious, amphibolent agents of the Pope as Antichrist—Jesuits, in effect—'sent forth by this three-fold authoritie for the defence of their Triple-crowned Monarch', who use 'Gunpowder' against king and state, in the *Premonition* to his rpt *Apologie for the Oath of Allegiance* (1609), n2r–v.
33. *Basilikon Doron* (1603), 45–6.
34. 1 Samuel 28. Catholic interpreters thought it probable that the apparition was the spirit of Samuel; Protestants tended to the view that it was an evil spirit or devilish illusion. See e.g. the notes in the Geneva, Bishops', and Douai–Rheims Bibles.
35. Daniel Tiffany, *Infidel Poetics: Riddles, Nightlife, Substance* (Chicago: University of Chicago Press, 2009), 138.
36. *Infidel Poetics*, 8.
37. Cf. J. L. Austin, *How to Do Things with Words*, 2nd edn, ed. J. O. Urmson and Marina Sbisà (Oxford: Oxford University Press, 1975).
38. *Metamorphoses*, VII.192–209 (cf. Seneca, *Medea*, 750–69). See Scot, *Discouerie*, Bk XII, ch. 7 (225–6); Middleton, *The Witch*, 5.2.20–32 (mostly in Latin).
39. Henry Holland, *A Treatise Against Witchcraft* (1590), F3v. In the *Discouerie*, Scot notes that, for demonologists such as Bodin, witches 'curse, blaspheme, and prouoke God', Bk II, ch. 9 (32); his own sceptical conclusion admitted the blasphemy: 'Witchcraft is in truth a cousening art, wherin the name of God is abused, prophaned and blasphemed', Bk XVI, ch. 2 (472). Cf. 'the horrible and greuous blasphemies, thei commit in their conjurations', in Francis Coxe, *A Short Treatise Declaringe the Detestable Wickednesse, of Magicall Sciences as Necromancie, Coniurations of Spirites, Curiouse Astrologie and such Lyke* (1561), B1r; 'all the attemptes, proceedinges and conclusions of Sorcerers, Witches, and the rest of that hellishe liuerie, are meere blasphemers', in W.W., *A True and Iust Recorde, of the Information, Examination and Confession of all the Witches, Taken at S. Ofes in the Countie of Essex* (1582), A3v. For 'conjurationes' that raise 'apparitions' as a means by which the Devil tempts men to 'the euerlasting perdition of their soul and body', see James VI, *Daemonologie*, 14.
40. *Discourse of Witchcraft*, e.g. *3r–v, *6r ('explicite in manner and forme, or implicite by degrees of superstitious proceeding'), 41–55 ('As God therefore hath made a couenant with his people, so Satan ioynes in league with the world, labouring to bind some men vnto him' (46)).
41. Cf. Gary Wills, *Witches and Jesuits: Shakespeare's 'Macbeth'* (New York: Oxford University Press, 1995), 60–1. For 'great bond' used of election and salvation see e.g. Luis de Granada, *The Sinners Guyde* (1598), 68.
42. See e.g. Thomas Wilson who cites oracles to exemplify what *ambiguitas* is, in *The Rule of Reason* (1551), Q2v–3r.

43. *OED*, tine/tyne, *v.*[2], 1, 'To lose; to suffer deprivation of; to cease to have or enjoy'.
44. *His Maiesties Speach in this Last Session of Parliament . . . Together with a discourse of the maner of the discouery of this late intended treason, ioyned with the examination of some of the prisoners* (1605), F3v.
45. e.g. by William Barlow, 'with one blast at one blow, . . . *darkenes* . . . had with this blowing vp, bin blown in and ouer this whole nation . . . when these lightes had bin extinguished. And blowne out should they haue bin, vnlesse *the father of lightes* had caused light to shine out of darkenesse by discouering and reuealing this worke of darkenesse', in *The Sermon Preached at Paules Crosse, the Tenth Day of Nouember being the Next Sunday after the Discouerie of this Late Horrible Treason* (1606), D1v–3r; and by Lancelot Andrewes, 'till the deadly *blow* had been given', 'A Sermon Preached before the King's Majestie, at White-Hall, on the V. of November. A.D. MDCVI', in *Lancelot Andrewes: Selected Sermons and Lectures*, ed. Peter McCullough (Oxford: Oxford University Press, 2005), 146–61, p. 151.
46. For Edward's 'heavenly gift of prophecy', see 4.3.158; Andrewes, 'A Sermon Preached . . . on the V. of November. A.D. MDCVI', 155.
47. Anon, *A True and Perfect Relation of the Whole Proceedings Against the Late Most Barbarous Traitors, Garnet a Iesuite, and his Confederats* (1606), H4v.
48. Cf. the supposedly possessed in Samuel Harsnett's *Declaration of Egregious Popish Impostures* (1603), a tract well known to Shakespeare, drawn on in *King Lear*, which describes '*how* Maho *did first sweare vpon the blessed sacrament, and kissed it, and then vppon the booke of exorcismes, and then kist that likewise*' (202).
49. *His Maiesties Speach*, E3v. Cf., among many texts, I.H., *The Diuell of the Vault: Or, The Vnmasking of Murther* (1606).
50. David Cressy, *Dangerous Talk: Scandalous, Seditious, and Treasonable Speech in Pre-Modern England* (Oxford: Oxford University Press, 2010), 6.
51. *Mischeefes Mysterie: Or, Treasons Master-peece* (1617), 17. Herring wrote in Latin, no doubt to reach continental audiences.
52. 'A Sermon Preached . . . on the V. of November. A.D. MDCVI', 153.
53. For one such seamless transition see *Mischeefes Mysterie*, 42.
54. B2v–3r, B4v.
55. *True and Perfect Relation*, H4v–I1r. Cf., among others, Robert Cecil, Earl of Salisbury, declaring that equivocation would 'teare in sunder all the bondes of humane conuersation' (*An Answere to Certaine Scandalous Papers, Scattered Abroad vnder Colour of a Catholicke Admonition* (1606), C3v). Though dwarfed by the massive, early modern corpus of writing about equivocation, the modern, scholarly literature is substantial. For ways into the field see Johann P. Sommerville, 'The "New Art of Lying": Equivocation, Mental Reservation, and Casuistry', in Edmund Leites, ed., *Conscience and Casuistry in Early Modern Europe* (Cambridge: Cambridge University Press, 1988), 159–84, Perez Zagorin, *Ways of Lying: Dissimulation, Persecution, and Conformity in Early Modern Europe* (Cambridge, Mass.: Harvard University Press, 1990).

56. Written *c.*1598, and circulated in manuscript. See e.g. A. E. Malloch, 'Father Henry Garnet's Treatise of Equivocation', *Recusant History*, 15 (1981), 387–95. For a recent, sympathetic account, see Robert Miola, 'Two Jesuit Shadows in Shakespeare: William Weston and Henry Garnet', in Ken Jackson and Arthur F. Marotti, eds, *Shakespeare and Religion: Early Modern and Postmodern Perspectives* (Notre Dame, Ind.: University of Notre Dame Press, 2011), 25–45.
57. An English Catholic reaction against equivocation pre-dated the Gunpowder Plot. See e.g. Christopher Bagshaw, *A Sparing Discouerie of our English Iesuits* (1601), 6–12, Anthony Copley, *An Answer to a Letter of a Iesuited Gentleman* (1601), 91–3 and *Another Letter of Mr. A. C. to his Dis-Iesuited Kinseman* (1602), 18, 61, 72.
58. Jeremy Taylor, *Ductor Dubitantium: Or, The Rule of Conscience in all her Generall Measures*, 2 vols (1660), II, 101, 106.
59. For the earlier periods see David Martin Jones, *Conscience and Allegiance in Seventeenth Century England: The Political Significance of Oaths and Engagements* (Rochester, NY: University of Rochester Press, 1999), 21, 31.
60. For a sceptical account of his motives see M. C. Questier, 'Loyalty, Religion and State Power in Early Modern England: English Romanism and the Jacobean Oath of Allegiance', *Historical Journal*, 40 (1997), 311–29.
61. G. W. Prothero, *Select Statutes and Constitutional Documents Illustrative of the Reigns of Elizabeth and James I* (Oxford: Clarendon Press, 1913), 7.
62. Park Honan, *Shakespeare: A Life* (Oxford: Oxford University Press, 1998), 354.
63. *Adages I i 1 to I v 100*, ed. R. A. B. Mynors, tr. Margaret Mann Phillips, *Collected Works of Erasmus*, 89 vols (Toronto: University of Toronto Press, 1974–), XXXI, 149–50. Cf. Maurice Palmer Tilley, *A Dictionary of the Proverbs in England in the Sixteenth and Seventeenth Centuries* (Ann Arbor: University of Michigan Press, 1950), P 289. I am grateful to Johann Sommerville for advice on this point.
64. Compare 'the knot of the question' (twice), 'the knot of the controuersie' in James VI and I, *A Remonstrance of the Most Gratious King Iames I... For the Right of Kings, and the Independance of their Crownes* (1616), 64 and 123, 121; for attempted untyings see 96, 167, 189.
65. *Triplici Nodo, Triplex Cuneus: An Apology for the Oath of Allegiance* (1607), 83.
66. John Donne, *Pseudo-martyr: Wherein out of Certaine Propositions and Gradations, this Conclusion is Euicted. That Those which are of the Romane Religion in this Kingdome, May and Ought to take the Oath of Allegiance* (1610), 150–1, 156 ('that Oath, which they take in the Colledge at Rome, by a Constitution of the Pope; *that they shall returne into England, to preach the Catholique faith*'); 178–9 (for the Ignatian knot of obedience); 143–4, 166, 191–2 (fourth vow, to the Pope).
67. Donne, *Pseudo-martyr*, 326. Even before the Oath was current, many on the king's side doubted that its knot would hold; see e.g. Thomas Morton, *An Exact Discoverie of Romish Doctrine in the Case of Conspiracie and Rebellion* (1605), 45: 'when the Pope shall send but his Bull of freeing of our English, the bond of their oath will prooue as strong as the knot of a bulrush.'
68. e.g. 'Against Swearyng and Periury', in *Certayne Sermons, Or Homilies Appoynted by the Kynges Maiestie* (1547), L3v–M3v; Edmond Bicknoll, *A Swoord Agaynst*

Swearyng (1579); William Vaughan, *The Golden-groue Moralized* (1600), chs 18–20.

69. A 'Bill for Offenders in Swearing, Drunkenness &c.' came to the Commons in 1566; another, 'agaynst blasphemous swareinge', sponsored by Sir Francis Hastings in 1601, was read, amended, and sent to the Lords. A similar bill 'For Reformation of the common Sin of Swearing and Blasphemy' was brought in 1604. See Paul, *Royal Play of Macbeth*, 306–8, Hugh Gazzard, 'An Act to Restrain Abuses of Players (1606)', *Review of English Studies*, 61 (2010), 495–528, pp. 517–18.
70. The 1604 bill, reintroduced, went through further committee stages, and led to a new or restyled bill entitled 'An Act for the Punishment of Profane, Blasphemous, and Irreligious Swearing', the immediate precursor of the 1606 Act. This prehistory makes it harder to accept the recently advanced claim in James Shapiro, *1606: William Shakespeare and the Year of 'Lear'* (London: Faber and Faber, 2015), 252, 396, that the Act was 'precipitated' by John Day's *The Ile of Guls* (1606), which, like Chapman, Jonson, and Marston's *Eastward Hoe* (1605), provoked the authorities by satirizing the Scots. That there was 'much speech in parliament' about the play (according to a letter by Sir Thomas Hoby) might have strengthened the hand of the expurgators, but it is not mentioned in relation to profanity and blasphemy and not all responses will have been negative. For Hoby, see Thomas Birch, ed., *The Court and Times of James the First*, 2 vols (London: Henry Colburn, 1848), I, 59–63, pp. 60–1.
71. 3 James I, c. 21 (quoted from Gazzard, 'Act', 495).
72. The statute begins 'For the preuenting and auoyding of the great abuse of the holy Name of God in Stage-playes, Interludes, Maygames, ...'.
73. e.g. Paul's detailed, overstretched attempt to show that the language of the second half of *Macbeth* became bolder once the Act passed into law and the restricted nature of its exclusions was clear: *Royal Play of Macbeth*, 304–16.
74. David Nash, *Blasphemy in the Christian World: A History* (New York: Oxford University Press, 2007), 107.
75. From the leading Catholic (the Archpriest) George Blackwell 'to the Catholic Clergy and Laity of England. Nov. *7, 1605*', in Hugh Tootell, *Dodd's Church History of England from the Commencement of the Sixteenth Century to the Revolution in 1688*, ed. M. A. Tierney, 5 vols (London: Charles Dolman, 1839–43), IV, cxi.
76. e.g. James, *Daemonologie*, 63–4.
77. Alain Cabantous, *Blasphemy: Impious Speech in the West from the Seventeenth to the Nineteenth Century*, tr. Eric Rauth (New York: Columbia University Press, 2002), 27.
78. Henry Goodcole, *The Wonderfull Discouerie of Elizabeth Sawyer a Witch Late of Edmonton* (1621), C1r–v.
79. *The Witch of Edmonton* (1658), H4r.
80. See Thomas, *Religion and the Decline of Magic*, 212. Even when James did perform the touching ceremony, as an adjunct of the royal prerogative, he refused to make a sign of the cross over diseased flesh with the gold angel. See Raymond Crawfurd, *The King's Evil* (Oxford: Clarendon Press, 1911), 88–9.

81. *A Right Frutefull and Approoued Treatise, for the Artificiall Cure of that Malady Called in Latin Struma, and in English, the Evill, Cured by Kinges and Queenes of England* (1602), D2r.
82. Cf. 'Cupid hoodwinked with a scarf', *Romeo and Juliet*, 1.4.4, or the four cupids 'hoodwinckt with Tiffiny scarfs' in Francis Beaumont, *The Masque of the Inner Temple and Grayes Inne* . . . *1612* (1613), C2r.
83. See e.g. the 'scarfs, ribons and laces' worn by members of 'The order of the Lord of misrule' in Phillip Stubbes, *The Anatomie of Abuses* (1583), M2r, or the 'Scarfs' purportedly, though not actually 'Made all of Ancients [ensigns, flags], taken from your foes' worn by the 'Counterfayte Captaine' in Samuel Rowlands, *Looke to It: For, Ile Stabbe Ye* (1604), C1r.
84. Cf. G. K. Hunter's note in his Arden Shakespeare, 2nd series, *All's Well* (London: Methuen, 1959), 111: 'We learn in *The First Part of Jeronimo*, II.vi.15ff., that the "amorous knot" in the scarf was tied by the lady who gave the favour.' Also, Ellen Belton, '"To Make the 'Not' Eternal": Female Eloquence and Patriarchal Authority in *All's Well, That Ends Well*', in Gary Waller, ed., *All's Well, That Ends Well: New Critical Essays* (New York: Routledge, 2007), 125–39, p. 135.
85. Fausto Cercignani, *Shakespeare's Works and Elizabethan Pronunciation* (Oxford: Clarendon Press, 1981), 25.
86. When it comes to the question of chronology, it is easier to imagine this line written after *Macbeth* than before it.
87. The audience has already heard Mariana urging Diana to resist Bertram's 'promises, enticements, oaths, tokens', though at that point Paroles was presented as an agent of these 'suggestions' (3.5.15–18).
88. Jasper Mayne, *The Amorous Warre* (pub. 1648), 5.2.
89. *Othello*, 4.2.64. A group of toads is known as a 'knot'.
90. Cf. *Macbeth*, 5.10.19–20.
91. Despite the disapproval of Protestant reformers, vows of pilgrimage to Rome, Jerusalem, and Compostela were among those 'reserved' to the Holy See for dispensation or commutation. The orthodox view in England was that of Peter Martyr Vermigili, 'Vowes of sole life, and those whereby men bind themselues to go on pilgrimage, as it is in Poperie, are to be accounted vngodlie', *The Common Places*, tr. Anthonie Marten (1583), in *Propositions out of Genesis*, 154.
92. Henry Swinburne, *A Treatise of Spousals, or Matrimonial Contracts*, written *c.*1600 (1686), 117–18.
93. See Lady Macbeth at 1.6.15, behind her the witches (4.1.10–11, 20–1, 35–6).
94. *Macbeth*, 5.1.57–8.
95. Knot, *n.*[1], 10b.
96. Aristotle, *De Arte Poetica Liber*, ed. Rudolf Kassel (Oxford: Clarendon Press, 1965), 1455b. Translations from *Greek–English Lexicon*, comp. Henry George Liddell and Robert Scott, rev. others, 9th edn (Oxford: Clarendon Press, 1996).
97. 'Nodus erroris' in the frequently reprinted *scholia* on Terence attributed to Aelius Donatus (actually by Evanthius). For text, translation, and discussion see

Joel B. Altman, *The Tudor Play of Mind: Rhetorical Enquiry and the Development of Elizabethan Drama* (Berkeley: University of California Press, 1978), 132–3.

98. Galit Hasan-Rokem and David Shulman, 'Afterword', in their edited essay collection, *Untying the Knot: On Riddles and Other Enigmatic Modes* (New York: Oxford University Press, 1996), 316–20, p. 319.
99. 'Charms and Riddles', 138–9.
100. R. D. Laing, *Knots* (London: Tavistock, 1970), prefatory note.
101. Cf. the 'juggling fiends' in *Macbeth* (5.10.19–20).

CHAPTER 13 BENEFITS AND BONDS

1. Anon, *Timon*, ed. James C. Bulman and J. M. Nosworthy (Oxford: Malone Society, 1980), 6.
2. James C. Bulman, Jr, 'Shakespeare's Use of the "Timon" Comedy', *Shakespeare Survey*, 29 (1976), 103–16, pp. 106–7.
3. e.g. the essays by G. Wilson Knight, esp. 'The Pilgrimage of Hate: An Essay on *Timon of Athens*', in his *The Wheel of Fire* (Oxford: Oxford University Press, 1930).
4. The prevailing attribution of scenes and speeches to Middleton is summarized by John Jowett in the Canon and Chronology section of Gary Taylor and John Lavagnino, eds, *Thomas Middleton and Early Modern Textual Culture: A Companion to the Collected Works* (Oxford: Clarendon Press, 2007), 356–7. In this chapter I indicate Middleton's likely involvement when most pertinent to discussion.
5. Thomas Lodge, *Wits Miserie, and the Worlds Madnesse Discouering the Deuils Incarnat of this Age* (1596), 30. Cf. Roger Fenton, *A Treatise of Vsurie Diuided into Three Bookes* (1611), 67.
6. *The Philosophie, Commonlie Called, the Morals Written by the Learned Philosopher Plutarch of Chaeronea*, tr. Philemon Holland (1603), 283.
7. *Tragedy of King Lear*, 2.2.430 [2.4.259], 4.1.61 [67]. Quotations are from the Folio-based *Tragedy* in the *Norton Shakespeare*, except where the material is Quarto-only, in which case the Norton *History of King Lear* is cited. References to the conflated text in the same edn are given, as economically as possible, in square brackets.
8. See *timē*, in the *Greek–English Lexicon*, comp. Henry George Liddell and Robert Scott, rev. others, 9th edn (Oxford: Clarendon Press, 1996).
9. For the quibble see the quotation from *The Wasp* (late 1630s) in *Timon of Athens*, ed. John Jowett (Oxford: Oxford University Press, 2004), 24: 'Your Timonist, or, as well call 'em, Time-ist, is your only man, for he is allowed, or at least takes allowance, to rail at authority . . . ' For some thoughts about Timon and time see Angus Fletcher, *Time, Space, and Motion in the Age of Shakespeare* (Cambridge, Mass.: Harvard University Press, 2007), 72–6.
10. Cf. *Tragedy*, 1.1.88 [89].
11. Ilana Krausman Ben-Amos, *The Culture of Giving: Informal Support and Gift-Exchange in Early Modern England* (Cambridge: Cambridge University Press, 2008), 208.

12. John M. Wallace, '*Timon of Athens* and the Three Graces: Shakespeare's Senecan Study', *Modern Philology*, 83 (1986), 349–63. Cf. Felicity Heal, *The Power of Gifts: Gift-Exchange in Early Modern England* (Oxford: Oxford University Press, 2014), 19–20.
13. *The Woorke of the Excellent Philosopher Lucius Annaeus Seneca Concerning Benefyting*, tr. Arthur Golding (1578), Gg4v.
14. e.g. Sir Thomas Elyot, *The Boke Named the Gouernour* (1531), S1v, Henry Peacham, *The Compleat Gentleman* (1622), 193.
15. *Culture of Giving*, 261 (with one change to punctuation).
16. Ben Jonson, *The Alchemist*, 2.2.41–94, ed. William Sherman (with Peter Holland), in *The Cambridge Edition of the Works of Ben Jonson*, gen. eds David Bevington, Martin Butler, and Ian Donaldson, 7 vols (Cambridge: Cambridge University Press, 2012), III.
17. 'Non potest beneficium manu tangi; res animo geritur'; 'A benefit cannot possibly be touched by the hand; its province is the mind.' *De Beneficiis*, I.v.2, in Seneca, *Moral Essays*, tr. John W. Basore, Loeb Classical Library, 3 vols (London: Heinemann, 1928–35), III.
18. *Nicomachean Ethics*, IV.iii.24–5.
19. Cicero, *Letters to Atticus*, XIII.12, which quotes Hesiod, was often cited. For Aquinas see *Summa Theologica,* II.ii.106, Article 6. There is a brief but full discussion in Erasmus, *Adages*, I.i.36, 'Eadem mensura' ('By the same measure'). See *Adages I i 1 to I v 100*, ed. R. A. B. Mynors, tr. Margaret Mann Phillips, *Collected Works of Erasmus*, 89 vols (Toronto: University of Toronto Press, 1974–), XXXI, 85.
20. *Imagines*, xii.
21. *Summa Theologica*, II.ii.106, 6.
22. Ben-Amos, *Culture of Giving*, 260.
23. 3.7.102–4; see also 3.4.20–8.
24. Ben-Amos, *Culture of Giving*, 206; Heal finds money less problematic, *Power of Gifts*, 55–6, but writes extensively about 'Bribes and Benefits' (ch. 7).
25. *OED* notes the word's Native American origin (from 1844 in English): 'Chinook Jargon *pátlač* to give, a gift, a giving-away ceremony.'
26. A. D. Nuttall, *Timon of Athens* (Hemel Hempstead: Harvester, 1989), 17.
27. Jacques Derrida, *Given Time. 1, Counterfeit Money*, tr. Peggy Kamuf (Chicago: Chicago University Press, 1992), 26–7.
28. e.g. III.x.1–2.
29. For the claim see Nuttall, *Timon of Athens*, 46.
30. On the risks and damaging effects of surety see pp. 147, 150, 167–8. The problems are there in Plutarch; see *Philosophie*, 288.
31. Cf. 'Food as Gift' in Heal, *The Power of Gifts*, 35–43.
32. Ben-Amos, *Culture of Giving*, 198–201.
33. III.xv.1–4 ('. . . sine sponsore', 'without a surety').
34. *Essay on the Gift*, tr. W. D. Halls (1990; London: Routledge, 2002), 17.
35. Georges Davy, *La Foi jurée: étude sociologique du problème du contrat, la formation du lien contractuel* (Paris: Alcan, 1922).

36. See e.g. Alain Testart, 'Uncertainties of the "Obligation to Reciprocate": A Critique of Mauss', in Wendy James and N. J. Allen, *Marcel Mauss: A Centenary Tribute* (New York: Berghahn, 1998), 97–110, pp. 101–3.
37. Lewis Hyde, *The Gift: How the Creative Spirit Transforms the World* (1979; Edinburgh: Canongate, 2007), 31.
38. See *Essay on the Gift*, 62, and, for objections, Testart, 'Uncertainties', 105–6.
39. In Shakespeare's source, *The True Chronicle Historie of King Leir and his Three Daughters* (perf. 1594, pub. 1605), the absence of a male heir is brought out. 'My gracious Lord,' a nobleman says, 'I hartily do wish, | That God had lent you an heyre indubitate, | Which might have set upon your royall throne,... | By whose succession all this doubt might cease'; see Geoffrey Bullough, ed., *Narrative and Dramatic Sources of Shakespeare*, 8 vols (London: Routledge, 1957–75), VII, 337–402, lines 43–7.
40. Ben-Amos, *Culture of Giving*, 23, 34.
41. Quoted by William O. Scott in his 'Contracts of Love and Affection: Lear, Old Age, and Kingship', *Shakespeare Survey*, 55 (2002), 36–42, p. 36.
42. For recently argued Senecan contexts see Colin Burrow, *Shakespeare and Classical Antiquity* (Oxford: Oxford University Press, 2013), 196–9, Kathy Eden, 'Liquid Fortification and the Law in *King Lear*', in Bradin Cormack, Martha Nussbaum, and Richard Strier, eds, *Shakespeare and the Law: A Conversation among Disciplines and Professions* (Chicago: Chicago University Press, 2013), 203–20, pp. 203–7.
43. Scott, 'Contracts of Love and Affection', 36 n. 2.
44. *Antony and Cleopatra*, 5.2.85–91.
45. Eight uses, out of forty-three in all of Shakespeare; closest is Antony with four.
46. Andrew Zurcher, 'Gift and Condition in *King Lear*', Kingston Shakespeare Seminars, 13 March 2014, at <http://backdoorbroadcasting.net/>, accessed 3 October 2014. See earlier William Flesch, *Generosity and the Limits of Authority: Shakespeare, Herbert and Milton* (Ithaca, NY: Cornell University Press, 1992), ch. 2, Curtis Perry, *The Making of Jacobean Culture: James I and the Renegotiation of Elizabethan Literary Practice* (Cambridge: Cambridge University Press, 1997), 115–37, Alison V. Scott, *Selfish Gifts: The Politics of Exchange and English Courtly Literature, 1580–1628* (Madison: Fairleigh Dickinson University Press, 2006), 27–39.
47. Ben-Amos, *Culture of Giving*, 19.
48. *OED*, profess, *v.*, 1 a–c, 3 ('To make profession of, to lay claim to (often with implication of insincerity)').
49. E. Catherine Dunn, *The Concept of Ingratitude in Renaissance English Moral Philosophy* (Washington, DC: Catholic University of America Press, 1946), 58 (cf. 48–50).
50. I am grateful to George Garnett for advice on this point.
51. *OED*, subscribe, *v.*, 3 b. *intr.* 'To give or acknowledge allegiance *to* a person; to make one's submission *to*; (more generally) to submit, yield, give in. *Obs.*' At lines 2509–13 of *Leir*, the Gallian King says, 'Feare not, my friends, you shall receyve no hurt, | If you'l subscribe unto your lawfull King, | And quite revoke

your fealty from *Cambria,* | And from aspiring *Cornwall* too, whose wives | Have practisde treason 'gainst their fathers life.'

52. See the astute discussion in Michael Pennington, *Sweet William: A User's Guide to Shakespeare* (London: Nick Hern Books, 2012), 203–6.
53. *King Leir,* line 709.
54. As when she leans over the ailing Lear and says 'restoration hang | Thy medicine on my lips' (4.6.23–4 [4.7.26–7]).
55. For a tangential, possible echo of French *cordelier*, 'tier of knots', see Philippa Berry, *Shakespeare's Feminine Endings: Disfiguring Death in the Tragedies* (London: Routledge, 1999), 155.
56. *OED*, according, *adj.* and *adv.*, 2.
57. *OED*, 3.
58. *OED*, cord, *v.*[2], 1.
59. *OED*, cord, *n.*[1], 1 b, citing *Othello*, 3.3.393–4 ('If there be cords, or knives, | Poison, or fire').
60. Ben-Amos, *The Culture of Giving*, 18.
61. e.g. Cristina Léon Alfar, *Fantasies of Female Evil: The Dynamics of Gender and Power in Shakespearean Tragedy* (Plainsboro, NJ: Associated University Presses, 2003), 94, Alexander Leggatt, *Shakespeare's Tragedies: Violation and Identity* (Cambridge: Cambridge University Press, 2005), 145.
62. 'KENT I say yea. LEAR By Jupiter, I swear no. | KENT By Juno, I swear ay' (2.2.191–2 [2.4.19–21]).
63. John Bale (or Miles Coverdale), *A Christen Exhortacion vnto Customable Swearers* (1543), fol. 7v.
64. e.g. James Cleland, *Heropaideia: Or, The Institution of a Young Noble Man* (1607), 199: 'Wherefore wee saie that the simple word of a Prince is as good as a subiects oath.' Cf. Anna Riehl Bertolet, 'The Tsar and the Queen: "You Speak a Language that I Understand Not"', in Charles Beem, ed., *The Foreign Relations of Elizabeth I* (Basingstoke: Palgrave Macmillan, 2011), 101–23, pp. 110–11.
65. *History*, 1.1.152, *Tragedy*, 1.1.161 [165].
66. *OED*, ban, *v.*, I and II.
67. *OED*, ban, *v.*, 4.
68. e.g. Edmond Bicknoll, *A Swoord Agaynst Swearyng* (1579), where the title page announces 'Examples of Gods Iuste and visible punishment vpon blasphemers, periurers, and suche as haue procured Gods wrath by cursing and bannyng, which we cal execration'.
69. *The Tempest*, ed. David Lindley, New Cambridge Shakespeare (Cambridge: Cambridge University Press, 2002), commentary.
70. Dunn, *Concept of Ingratitude*, 30.
71. Quoted by Dunn from his *Politeuphuia, Concept of Ingratitude*, 78.
72. *Tragedy*, 1.4.237–43 [252–8], giving 'Nature' the capital it has in Folio.
73. *Shakespeare's Curse: The Aporias of Ritual Exclusion in Early Modern Royal Drama* (Abingdon: Routledge, 2014), 4.

74. Mark 11: 12–14, 20–5; Matthew 21: 18–22.
75. *The Boke of Common Praier* (1552), fol. 125r.
76. Henry Peacham, *The Garden of Eloquence*, rev. edn (1593), K4v.
77. 1.5.35 [33], 3.6.13 [13], 4.5.174–7 [4.6.178–81].
78. *OED*, imperative, *adj. and n.*, from Latin 'imperare', 'to command'.
79. *Greek–English Lexicon*, comp. Liddell and Scott.
80. George Puttenham, *The Arte of English Poesie* (1589), 46.
81. For a searching account of the legal basis see D. Fox, 'The Structures of Monetary Nominalism in the Pre-Modern Common Law', *Journal of Legal History*, 34 (2013), 139–71.
82. Karl Marx, *Capital: Critique of Political Economy*, Vol. I, tr. Ben Fowkes (1976; Harmondsworth: Penguin, 1990), 227–8.
83. 4.3.71–5. I follow the Folio in 'If thou wilt not promise... If thou dost perform' where some editions (including Norton) read 'If thou wilt promise' and 'If thou dost not perform'. The emendation is weak but it is a measure of Timon's misanthropy that reversing the declaration still makes sense.
84. e.g. II.iii.3–vi.1.
85. pp. 73–4, 113–15, 188, 288.
86. Thomas Shadwell, *The History of Timon of Athens, The Man-Hater* (1678), 42–4.
87. *History of King Lear*, 13.14 [3.6.17].
88. *Tragedy*, 4.5.150–3 [4.6.154–7].
89. Karl Marx, *Early Writings*, tr. Rodney Livingstone and Gregor Benton, introd. Lucio Colletti (1974; Harmondsworth: Penguin, 1992), 376–7.
90. *Essayes* (1600–1), Mm1v.
91. Ben-Amos, *Culture of Giving*, 83–4, summarizes this historiography. For a valuable account in relation to drama, see William C. Carroll, *Fat King, Lean Beggar: Representations of Poverty in the Age of Shakespeare* (Ithaca, NY: Cornell University Press, 1996).
92. Ben-Amos, *Culture of Giving*, 261.
93. *2 Henry VI*, 4.1.137 ('banditto').
94. *OED* gives this etymology: 'Italian *bandito* "proclaimed, proscribed", in plural *banditi*, noun, "outlaws", past participle of *bandire* = medieval Latin *bannīre* to proclaim, proscribe'.
95. 1.2.130–1 [131–2]; *Timon of Athens*, 1.2.105.
96. Henry Wilkinson, *The Debt Book: Or, A Treatise Vpon Romans 13. ver. 8* (1625), 94.
97. Luke Wilson, *Theaters of Intention: Drama and the Law in Early Modern England* (Stanford, Calif.: Stanford University Press, 2000), 179–80.
98. On wooded common land, see e.g. Oliver Rackham, *Woodlands* (London: HarperCollins, 2006), 26, 56–7, 105; on the shore, see e.g. Hugo Grotius, *Mare Liberum* (1609), ed. and tr. Ralph van Deman Magoffin as *The Freedom of the Seas* (New York: Carnegie Endowment, 1916), 28–31, citing Cicero, Virgil, and Celsus.
99. 'The Life of Alcibiades', in Plutarch, *The Lives of the Noble Grecians and Romanes*, tr. Thomas North (1579), 210–36, p. 221.

100. See 'The Life of Marcus Antonius' in Plutarch, *Lives*, tr. North, 970–1010, p. 988.
101. Francis Bacon, 'Of Vsurie', in *The Essayes or Counsels, Civill and Morall*, rev. edn (1625), 239–46, p. 239.
102. Pierre Bourdieu, *Outline of a Theory of Practice*, tr. Richard Nice (Cambridge: Cambridge University Press, 1977), 12.
103. 4.5.254–5 [4.7.257], cf. 5.1.46 [5.2.55] and 5.3.202–3 [227–8].
104. *The Essayes: Or, Morall, Politike and Millitarie Discourses*, tr. John Florio (1603), 12–13, p. 12.
105. 'Life of Marcus Antonius', 1003–4.

CHAPTER 14 REFORMATION I

1. Paolo Prodi, *Il sacramento di potere: Il giuramento politico nella storia costituzionale dell'Occidente* (Bologna: Società editrice il Mulino, 1992), 403–17.
2. For summaries of the controversy see the introd. to *The Political Works of James I: Reprinted from the Edition of 1616*, ed. Charles Howard McIlwain (Cambridge, Mass.: Harvard University Press, 1918), xlix–lxxx; W. B. Patterson, *King James VI and I and the Reunion of Christendom* (Cambridge: Cambridge University Press, 1997), chs 3–5; Conal Condren, *Argument and Authority in Early Modern England: The Presupposition of Oaths and Offices* (Cambridge: Cambridge University Press, 2006), ch. 13; Stefania Tutino, *Law and Conscience: Catholicism in Early-Modern England, 1570–1625* (Aldershot: Ashgate, 2007), chs. 5–7; Bernard Bourdin, *The Theological-Political Origins of the Modern State: The Controversy between James I of England and Cardinal Bellarmine*, tr. Susan Pickford (Washington, DC: Catholic University of America Press, 2010), esp. ch. 6.
3. *The First Booke of the Christian Exercise Appertayning to Resolution* (1582). For contexts see Victor Houliston, *Catholic Resistance in Elizabethan England: Robert Persons's Jesuit Polemic* (Aldershot: Ashgate, 2007), ch. 2.
4. *The Reports of Sir Edward Coke* (1658), 583–613, p. 590.
5. Jonathan Michael Gray, *Oaths and the English Reformation* (Cambridge: Cambridge University Press, 2013), 1. Cf. Thea Cervone, *Sworn Bond in Tudor England: Oaths, Vows and Covenants in Civil Life and Literature* (Jefferson, NC: McFarland, 2011), chs. 1–5.
6. Edward Hall, *The Union of the Two Noble and Illustre Famelies of Lancastre [and] Yorke* [Hall's Chronicle] (1548), fol. CCvr.
7. Hall, *Union of the Two Noble and Illustre Famelies*, fol. CCvr–v; John Foxe, *Actes and Monuments*, rev. edn (1583), 1078. Cf. Gray, *Oaths and the English Reformation*, 86–7.
8. Preamble to the Act in Restraint of Appeals to Rome (1533), 24 Henry VIII, c. 12. Quoting the text in *Documents of the English Reformation*, ed. Gerald Bray, corr. rpt (Cambridge: James Clarke and Co., 2004), 78–83, p. 78.
9. Stephen Gardiner, *De Vera Obedientia . . . 1536. And now Translated into Englishe* (1553), G6r–v.

10. Gray, *Oaths and the English Reformation*, 174–83.
11. A 'Protestation of Allegiance' to Elizabeth was signed by thirteen Appellants (who had requested toleration from the queen in return for a declaration of loyalty and expulsion of the Jesuits) in January 1603. On the secular priest John Cecil's proposed oath, presented by the French Ambassador to King James in 1604, see John Bossy, 'Henry IV, the Appellants and the Jesuits', *Recusant History*, 8 (1965–6), 80–122, esp. pp. 94–100. Cf. Tutino, *Law and Conscience*, 132.
12. *OED*, misprision, *n.*[1], 1 b, 'In full *misprision of treason*', glossed from Coke: 'In legall understanding it signifieth, when one knoweth of any treason..., and concealeth it'.
13. *OED*, praemunire, *n.*, 'A writ charging a sheriff to summon a person accused of asserting or maintaining papal jurisdiction in England'.
14. See e.g. *A Theologicall Disputation Concerning the Oath of Allegiance Dedicated to the Most Holy Father Pope Paul the Fifth* (1613), *A Cleare, Sincere, and Modest Confutation of the Vnsound, Fraudulent, and Intemperate Reply of T.F. who is Knowne to be Mr. Thomas Fitzherbert now an English Iesuite* (1616), *Roger Widdringtons Last Reioynder to Mr. Thomas Fitz-Herberts Reply Concerning the Oath of Allegiance, and the Popes Power to Depose Princes* (1619). Preston is usefully situated by Stefania Tutino, 'Thomas Preston and English Catholic Loyalism: Elements of an International Affair', *Sixteenth Century Journal*, 41 (2010), 91–109.
15. Cf. M. C. Questier, 'Loyalty, Religion and State Power in Early Modern England: English Romanism and the Jacobean Oath of Allegiance', *Historical Journal*, 40 (1997), 311–29, and 'Catholic Loyalism in Early Stuart England', *English Historical Review*, 123 (2008), 1132–65, esp. pp. 1134–52, responding to arguments more sympathetic to James advanced by Johann Peter Sommerville in his 'Jacobean Political Thought and the Controversy of the Oath of Allegiance' (University of Cambridge, Ph.D. 1981) and 'Papalist Political Thought and the Controversy over the Jacobean Oath of Allegiance', in Ethan H. Shagan, ed., *Catholics and the 'Protestant Nation'* (Manchester: Manchester University Press, 2005), 162–84.
16. *Triplici Nodo, Triplex Cuneus: Or, An Apology for the Oath of Allegiance* (1607), 10–11.
17. *Triplici Nodo*, 12.
18. *Triplici Nodo*, 12–13.
19. Cf. Robert Sanderson, fifty years later, in his *De Juramento: Seven Lectures Concerning the Obligation of Promissory Oathes* (1655), 200.
20. e.g. Richard Mocket, *God and the King* (1615), 18.
21. Robert Parsons, *The Iudgment of a Catholicke English-man... Concerninge a Late Booke set Forth, and Entituled; Triplici Nodo, Triplex Cuneus, or, An Apologie for the Oath of Allegiance* (1608), 9, 19–20.
22. See e.g. Thomas Morton, *A Full Satisfaction Concerning a Double Romish Iniquitie; Hainous Rebellion, and More then Heathenish Aequiuocation* (1606), 53–4: 'the Popes Bull of obedience is so *strictly* commaunded, as alwaies limited within the crooked hookes of this Parenthesis (*Rebus sic stantibus*) or (*Donec vires habeant*) that is, (*Till there be oportunitie,*) or (*Pro hac vice,* for this time.)'

23. This was the second, major thrust of Parsons against the Oath in his *Iudgment*, 'that the matter may quickly be ended: for that I presume no Catholicke in *England*, will deny to sweare all cyuill obedience that he oweth to his Maiesty' (8).
24. Quoting from 'Pope Paulus the fifth, to the English Catholikes', in *Triplici Nodo*, 9–16, p. 13.
25. Mocket, *God and the King*, 66. For an adroit reply, from a Catholic point of view, see John Floyd, *God and the King: Or, A Dialogue Wherein is Treated of Allegiance due to our Most Gracious Lord, King Iames* (1620).
26. e.g. Morton, *Full Satisfaction*, 52.
27. I am grateful to Conal Condren for discussion on this point. See e.g. Quentin Skinner, 'Conquest and Consent: Thomas Hobbes and the Engagement Controversy', in G. E. Aylmer, ed., *The Interregnum: The Quest for Settlement, 1646–1660* (London: Macmillan, 1972), 79–93, Glenn Burgess, 'Usurpation, Obligation and Obedience in the Thought of the Engagement Controversy', *Historical Journal*, 29 (1986), 515–36, Edward Vallance, 'Oaths, Casuistry, and Equivocation: Anglican Responses to the Engagement Controversy', *Historical Journal*, 44 (2001), 59–77, Condren, *Argument and Authority*, ch. 14.
28. David M. Loades, *Politics and Nation: England, 1450–1660*, 5th edn (Oxford: Blackwell, 1999), 336.
29. See the classic essay by Richard Rex, 'The Crisis of Obedience: God's Word and Henry's Reformation', *Historical Journal*, 39 (1996), 863–94.
30. Among innumerable accounts, see e.g. Perkins, *A Discourse of Conscience* (1596), 47.
31. Those of an Erastian, Anglican bent argued that the king's laws should be obeyed unless they went against scripture. Others, of a more puritan outlook, were inclined to treat matters indifferent with indifference.
32. *A Discourse of Conscience*, 90.
33. Jean Calvin, *The Institution of Christian Religion* (1561), 98.
34. *Triplici Nodo*, 103–4. *The Institution of a Christen Man* (1537), composed by a committee of 46 divines and bishops, reflected the reformed doctrines of the Henrician Church; it was revised in a moderate, Catholic direction in 1543 and 1546. See *A Sermon of Cuthbert Bysshop of Duresme made vpon Palme Sondaye Laste Past, before the Maiestie of our Souerayne Lorde Kyng Henry the VIII. . . . in Erth Next vnder Christ Supreme Heed of the Churche of Englande* (1539).
35. 'An Homilee Agaynst Disobedience and Wylful Rebellion' (six parts), in *The Second Tome of Homilees of Such Matters as were Promised, and Intituled in the Former Part of Homilees*, edn of 1571, 544–616, pp. 608–11.
36. *The True Lawe of Free Monarchies: Or, The Reciprock and Mutuall Dutie Betwixt a Free King, and His Naturall Subiectes* (1598), C5r.
37. Quoted by Sommerville, 'Jacobean Political Thought and the Oath of Allegiance', 25.
38. His grandfather went into exile rather than conform; two of his uncles, Jasper and Ellis Heywood, were Jesuits who died abroad; his stepfather, Richard Rainsford, was put in prison 1611–13 for refusing to swear the Oath of Allegiance.

39. *Pseudo-martyr* (1610), 166, introducing ch. 6.
40. See e.g. Everett Fergusson, *Baptism in the Early Church: History, Theology, and Liturgy in the First Five Centuries* (Grand Rapids, Mich.: Erdmans, 2009), esp. 34, 370–1, 425.
41. See e.g. Claude Nicolet, *The World of the Citizen in Republican Rome*, tr. P. S. Falla (Berkeley: University of California Press, 1980), 102–5 on *sacramentum dicere* as against the more usual oaths in Rome, *conjuratio* and *jusjurandum*.
42. Peter Cramer, *Baptism and Change in the Early Middle Ages* (Cambridge: Cambridge University Press, 1993), 63.
43. Matthew Henry, *A Treatise on Baptism.... Abridged from the Original Manuscript, and Now First Published* (1783), 162. Cf. the commentary on Matthew 28: 19 in the same author's *An Exposition of all the Books of the Old and New Testament*, 3rd edn, 6 vols (1721–5), V, 219: 'Baptism is a Sacrament, that is, it is *an Oath*,... It is an Oath of *Abjuration*, by which we renounce the World and the Flesh,... And an Oath of *Allegiance*, by which we resign, and give up *our selves* to God.'
44. Calvin, *Institution*, 96.
45. Cited and rebutted by James at *Premonition*, †1v–2r.
46. For the more explicit view, that 'in issuing the [Oath of Allegiance] James was aiming to modify the boundaries between spiritual and temporal authority by giving to the sovereign a form of spiritual, and not just temporal, supremacy', see Stefania Tutino, *Empire of Souls: Robert Bellarmine and the Christian Commonwealth* (New York: Oxford University Press, 2010), 128.
47. *Oaths and the English Reformation*, 8.
48. Thomas Starkey, *A Preface to the Kynges Hyghnes* (1536), 5.
49. e.g. Coke, *Calvins Case*, in *Reports*, 583–613, p. 590: 'By this Law of Nature is the Faith, Ligeance, and Obedience of the Subject due to his Soveraign.'
50. David Martin Jones, *Conscience and Allegiance in Seventeenth Century England: The Political Significance of Oaths and Engagements* (Rochester, NY: University of Rochester Press, 1999), 61.
51. *Discourse of Conscience*, 1.
52. For a state-of-the-art overview see M. W. F. Stone, 'Conscience in Renaissance Moral Thought: A Concept in Transition?', *Renaissance Studies*, 23 (2009), 423–44; on the complexity of More's position see Brian Cummings, *Mortal Thoughts: Religion, Secularity and Identity in Shakespeare and Early Modern Culture* (Oxford: Oxford University Press, 2013), ch. 2.
53. 'Conscience inforceth to Obedience by vertue of... its act of Binding'; William Ames, *Conscience with the Power and Cases Thereof* (1639), 7.
54. *Conscience with the Power and Cases Thereof*, 60.
55. *Discourse of Conscience*, 11, 37.
56. *Discourse of Conscience*, 71–2.
57. See the cardinal's letter at *Triplici Nodo*, 38.
58. James said that 'our English Fugitiues'—émigré priests, including Parsons—had misled Bellarmine into regarding the Oath of Allegiance as a re-imposition of

the Oath of Supremacy (*Triplici Nodo*, 46). It is likely that Parsons did have some influence in this way, and certain that, like many other English Catholics, he believed that the Oath of Allegiance brought in train the supremacy (see *Iudgment*, 73–4, and the Stonyhurst MS quoted by Questier in 'Loyalty', 321).

59. *Triplici Nodo*, 47.

60. e.g. Martinus Becanus, *The Confutation of Tortura Torti: Or, Against the King of Englands Chaplaine* (1610), *The English Iarre or Disagreement amongst the Ministers of Great Brittaine, Concerning the Kinges Supremacy* (1612). Among treatises justifying the supremacy are: Sir John Hayward, *A Reporte of a Discourse Concerning Supreme Power in Affaires of Religion* (1606), James Cook, *Iuridica Trium Quaestionum* (1608); William Tooker, *Duellum siue singulare certamen cum Martino Becano Iesuita* (1611); Robert Burhill, *Pro Tortura Torti, contra Martinum Becanum Iesuitam* (1611), *Contra Martini Becani* (1613), *De Potestate Regia, et Vsurpatione Papali pro Tortura Torti* (1613), Samuel Collins, *Epphata* (1617). Still one of the best discussions is Sommerville, 'Jacobean Political Thought and the Oath of Allegiance', 239–43. See also his 'Papalist Political Thought', which now doubts—wrongly, I believe—'that the principles which underlay the oath led ... to the royal supremacy and Protestantism' (177).

61. Sommerville, 'Jacobean Political Thought and the Oath of Allegiance', 332.

62. *An Apologie for the Oath of Allegiance ... Together, with a Premonition of his Majesties to all Most Mightie Monarches, Kings, free Princes and States of Christendome* (1609), *Premonition*, 21–2.

63. *A Remonstrance of the Most Gratious King Iames I. King of Great Britaine, France, and Ireland, Defender of the Faith, &c.... Against an Oration of the Most Illustrious Card. of Perron* (1616), 125.

64. Cf. Mocket, *God and the King*, 71–80.

65. Catholic versions of the history, owing much to Matthew Paris and Polydore Vergil, continued to circulate and impinge on the Oath of Allegiance controversy. See e.g. Francisco Suárez, *Defensio Fidei Catholicae*, in *Selections from Three Works of Francisco Suárez, S.J.*, 2 vols (Oxford: Clarendon Press, 1944), II (tr. Gwladys L. Williams et al.), 696.

66. *Remonstrance*, 273–4.

67. The word 'obedience' occurs most often in *Henry VIII* (eight times, half of those in scenes attributed to Shakespeare), with several further uses of 'obey*' and 'obedient', then joint-second most often in *Sir Thomas More* (five times, the same as *King Lear*), with *King John* coming next at four uses.

68. William Tyndale, *The Obedience of a Christen Man* (1528), fol. lxxxvi recto, fol. clvii r–clviii r.

69. *King Johan*, lines 4–7, in *The Complete Plays of John Bale*, ed. Peter Happé, 2 vols (Cambridge: D. S. Brewer, 1985–6), I.

70. For the keys see Isaiah 22: 22; for bind and loose see Aramaic *asar* and *share* or Hebrew *asar* and *hitir*—which mean 'to forbid and/or to permit some act which is determined by the application of the *halakhah*' (Samuel Tobias Lachs, *A*

Rabbinic Commentary on the New Testament: The Gospels of Matthew, Mark, and Luke (Hoboken, NJ: Ktav, 1987), 256–7).

71. *The Obedience of a Christen Man*, fol. cxxxvi verso.
72. *Premonition*, s1v–2r.
73. Gray, *Oaths and the English Reformation*, 47.
74. *A Necessary Doctrine and Erudition for any Christen Man* (1543), Q3r.
75. *A Christen Exhortacion vnto Customable Swearers* (1543), fol. 22v.
76. Anthony Hugget, *A Diuine Enthymeme of True Obedience: Or, A Taske for a Christian. Preached at Pauls Crosse the Tenth of September, 1615* (1615).
77. *OED*, assoil, *v.*, 1a, 'To absolve from sin, grant absolution to'.
78. *Obedience of a Christen Man*, lxxvii r–lxxix r.
79. 'Anneus Seneca hath thys most provable sentence', Veritas says to Civil Order: 'The gentyll free hart goeth never from obedyence' (2279–80).
80. For a comparison with Bale see Cervone, *Sworn Bond in Tudor England*, ch. 6.
81. Anon, *The Troublesome Raigne of Iohn King of England* (1591), F2r.
82. See Peter Milward, *Religious Controversies of the Elizabethan Age: A Survey of Printed Sources* (London: Scolar, 1978).
83. See e.g. Alison Shell, *Catholicism, Controversy, and the English Literary Imagination, 1558–1660* (Cambridge: Cambridge University Press, 1999), ch. 1.
84. See e.g. Alexandra Walsham, *Catholic Reformation in Protestant Britain* (Farnham: Ashgate, 2014), chs 1–2.
85. *King John*, 2.1.237.
86. Cf. Alison Thorne, '"O, lawful let it be | That I have room ... to curse awhile": Voicing the Nation's Conscience in Female Complaint in *Richard III*, *King John*, and *Henry VIII*', in Willy Maley and Margaret Tudeau-Clayton, eds, *This England, That Shakespeare: New Angles on Englishness and the Bard* (Farnham: Ashgate, 2010), 105–24.
87. Folger copy (of the Folio) number 7, as described in the library catalogue: 'formerly the property of St Alban's College (the English College), Valladolid, Spain, bears (on t.p.) the certificate of a censor for the Inquisition'. Readable online via <http://shakespeare.folger.edu>.
88. *Obedience of a Christen Man*, Ciiii r.
89. *Obedience of a Christen Man*, Ciiii r.
90. For discussion see e.g. Björn Quiring, *Shakespeare's Curse: The Aporias of Ritual Exclusion in Early Modern Royal Drama* (Abingdon: Routledge, 2013), 152–3.
91. Cf. Kelly Hunter, 'Constance in *King John*' (discussing her own performance in Gregory Doran's 2001 production), in Robert Smallwood, ed., *Players of Shakespeare 6* (Cambridge: Cambridge University Press, 2004), 37–49, pp. 43–6.
92. 3.1.188–215. I have edited away the full stop in Norton's 'the truth. Thou art unsure'.
93. See e.g. Perez Zagorin, *Ways of Lying: Dissimulation, Persecution, and Conformity in Early Modern Europe* (Cambridge, Mass.: Harvard University Press, 1990).
94. Sarah Beckwith, *Shakespeare and the Grammar of Forgiveness* (Ithaca, NY: Cornell University Press, 2011), 20.

95. *Triplici Nodo*, 34.
96. R. Doleman [Robert Parsons], *A Conference about the Next Succession to the Crowne of Ingland* (1595), e.g. 18, 25. For some angles on this treatise, see Robert Lane, '"The Sequence of Posterity": Shakespeare's *King John* and the Succession Controversy', *Studies in Philology*, 92 (1995), 460–81.
97. *Henry V*, 1.2.35–95.
98. For the record, see the classic essay by H. G. Richardson, 'The English Coronation Oath', *Transactions of the Royal Historical Society*, 4th ser. 23 (1941), 129–58.
99. Complications are noted by Richard L. Greaves, 'Concepts of Political Obedience in Late Tudor England: Conflicting Perspectives', *Journal of British Studies*, 22 (1982), 23–34.
100. e.g. Henry de Bracton, *De Legibus et Consuetudinibus Angliae* (mid-thirteenth century), ed. George Woodbine and tr. Samuel E. Thorne (Cambridge, Mass.: Harvard University Press, 1968), 4 vols, which cites one recension of the coronation oath at II, 304. See e.g. Richard Firth Green, *A Crisis of Truth: Literature and Law in Ricardian England* (Pennsylvania: University of Pennsylvania Press, 1999), 234–5, on the citation in the parliamentary record of Richard II's deposition, and in Langland, Gower, and Hoccleve, of his failure to keep his coronation oath.
101. For a text of 'The Oath and Fealtie, made by King *Iohn.* to Pope Innocentius', widely cited in the early modern period, see e.g. Richard Garnet (?), comp., *The Book of Oaths* (1649), 306–7.
102. Cf. Sanderson, *De Juramento*: 'a voluntary oath is the more binding, for being voluntary; because there is no straighter obligation then that which we take willingly upon our selves' (133).
103. *Troublesome Raigne of Iohn*, F2v.
104. The name is in Holinshed, but Shakespeare would have known the word's association with falsely directed faith. See *OED*, bigot, *n. and adj.*, 1 (1598).
105. At almost every point in the verse the name Lewis is monosyllabic.

CHAPTER 15 REFORMATION II

1. *Sir Thomas More*, ed. John Jowett, Arden Shakespeare, 3rd series (London: A. and C. Black, 2011), 424–32, Hugh Craig, 'The Date of *Sir Thomas More*', *Shakespeare Survey*, 66 (2013), 38–54.
2. It is likely that Henry Chettle contributed to the original text. The revisers are usually identified as Chettle, Heywood, Shakespeare, and Dekker.
3. In favour of early revision see Peter W. M. Blayney, '*The Booke of Sir Thomas Moore* Re-examined', *Studies in Philology*, 69 (1972), 167–91, Bart van Es, *Shakespeare in Company* (Oxford: Oxford University Press, 2013), 278–84; for the current consensus on 1603–4 see Scott McMillin, '*The Book of Sir Thomas More*: The Dates and Acting Companies' and Gary Taylor, 'The Date and

Auspices of the Additions to *Sir Thomas More*', in T. H. Howard-Hill, ed., *Shakespeare and 'Sir Thomas More': Essays on the Play and its Shakespearian Interest* (Cambridge: Cambridge University Press, 1989), 55–76 and 101–29; *Sir Thomas More*, ed. Jowett, 7, 361, 429–30.

4. John Bossy, 'Henry IV, the Appellants and the Jesuits', *Recusant History*, 8 (1965–6), 80–122, esp. pp. 94–100; Stefania Tutino, *Law and Conscience: Catholicism in Early Modern England, 1570–1625* (Aldershot: Ashgate, 2007), 132.
5. Michael Questier, 'Catholicism, Kinship and the Public Memory of Sir Thomas More', *Historical Journal*, 53 (2002), 476–509, esp. 491–7, 503–6.
6. This was the view promulgated by Thomas Stapleton's early biography, in *Tres Thomae:... D. Thomae Mori Angliae quondam Cancellarii Vita*, published in Douai in 1588. Modern, revisionist biographies have focused rather on More's publication of the *Apology* and *Debellation of Salem and Bizance* after his ostensible retirement. His views about the succession and supremacy were evidently well known.
7. Cf. Hugh Trevor-Roper's account of More as a 'Catholic who appealed... to Protestants, who was indeed himself half-Protestant'—something of an exaggeration—in his *Catholics, Anglicans and Puritans: Seventeenth-Century Essays* (London: Secker and Warburg, 1987), 21.
8. John Guy, *Thomas More* (London: Arnold, 2000), 12.
9. Questier, 'Catholicism, Kinship', 488. On 489–90, Questier notes that More is mentioned in the official account of the Powder Plot, *A True and Perfect Relation* (1606), as a loyalist to be distinguished from the treachery of the plotters.
10. Questier, 'Catholicism, Kinship', 488.
11. *Sir Thomas More*, ed. Jowett, 95.
12. *Sir Thomas More*, ed. Jowett, repeatedly in Scene 1. All quotations from this edition. The unrest is based on the Ill May Day riots against the wealthy foreign merchants and bankers of Lombard Street.
13. 'An Exhortacion, Concernyng Good Ordre and Obedience, to Rulers and Magistrates', in *Certayne Sermons, or Homelies Appoynted by the Kynges Maiestie* (1547), R1r–S4r.
14. *Troilus and Cressida*, 1.3.74–137, making trouble for Achilles.
15. *Triplici Nodo, Triplex Cuneus: Or, An Apologie for the Oath of Allegiance* (1607), 104.
16. For a romance analogue see Pericles' vow, 'by bright *Diana*... Vnsisserd shall this heyre of mine remayne' until Marina is married; *Pericles* (1609), E4v.
17. Peter Martyr Vermigli, *The Common Places*, tr. Anthonie Marten (1583), 178, 180.
18. John Foxe, *Actes and Monuments*, rev. edn (1583), 1188.
19. Cf. *Sir Thomas More*, ed. Jowett, 80–4.
20. Nicholas Harpsfield, *The Life and Death of Sir Thomas More, Knight*, in William Roper and Harpsfield, *Lives of Saint Thomas More*, ed. E. E. Reynolds (London: Dent, 1963), 51–175, p. 62.
21. Original Text 2b, line 7, in *Sir Thomas More*, ed. Jowett.
22. Most of it ended up with the Augustinian Canonesses at Newton Abbott, though a portion was given to the Dominican Convent at Stone, and other pieces went further afield, including one to Rome in connection with More's canonization.

23. I am grateful to Richard Rex for discussion of this point.
24. Original Text 2b, lines 18–21: 'I will commit ye prisoner unto Newgate, | Except meantime your conscience give you leave | To dispense with the long vow that you have made.'
25. Original Text 2b, line 22.
26. Robert Bellarmine, *Tractatus de Potestate Summi Pontificis in Rebus Temporalibus, Adversus Gulielmum Barclay* (1610), ch. xxvii.
27. See e.g. Perkins, *Discourse of Conscience*, 80.
28. Jonathan Michael Gray, *Oaths and the English Reformation* (Cambridge: Cambridge University Press, 2013), 49.
29. Francis Meres, *Palladis Tamia* (1598), quoted in *Sir Thomas More*, ed. Jowett, 11.
30. On what plotting meant, see Tiffany Stern, *Documents of Performance in Early Modern England* (Cambridge: Cambridge University Press, 2009), ch. 1, esp. the account of Munday and Jonson on pp. 27–8.
31. See Bellarmine's letter, in *Triplici Nodo*, at 37 and 43–4; James's replies are concentrated at 57–8, 100–4, 110–11. For Blackwell's own response to Bellarmine on this point see his *A Large Examination taken at Lambeth*...*of M. G. Blakwell* (1609), F3v.
32. *Triplici Nodo*, 102–3.
33. Cf. *Sir Thomas More*, ed. Jowett, 56.
34. Noting this, Alison Shell nevertheless argues, in her *Catholicism, Controversy and the English Literary Imagination 1558–1660* (Cambridge: Cambridge University Press, 2004), that Tilney's 'objection must have been to the Oath being addressed at all' (219), a proposition that feeds into Jowett's edn.
35. See *Sir Thomas More*, ed. Jowett, 115, on such added lines as 'It is necessary that we here do swear | Allegiance to King Henry's new made Queen.'
36. Gray, *Oaths and the English Reformation*, 119, 139, 167. Cf. Thea Cervone, *Sworn Bond in Tudor England: Oaths, Vows and Covenants in Civil Life and Literature* (Jefferson, NC: McFarland, 2011), ch. 3.
37. Guy, *Thomas More*, 167.
38. Rpt in Gray, *Oaths and the English Reformation*, 227.
39. *Life*, 147.
40. To Margaret Roper, *c.* 17 April 1534, in *The Correspondence of Sir Thomas More*, ed. Elizabeth Frances Rogers (Princeton: Princeton University Press, 1947), 501–7, p. 505.
41. Ch. 8 of Donne's treatise argues that 'if any Man haue receiued a scruple against this Oath, which he cannot depose and cast off, the Rules of their own Casuists, as this case stands, incline, and warrant them, to the taking thereof' (*Pseudo-martyr* (1610), 222).
42. See e.g. the letter of Margaret Roper to Alice Alington, in *Correspondence of More*, 514–32.
43. David Martin Jones, *Conscience and Allegiance in Seventeenth Century England: The Political Significance of Oaths and Engagements* (Rochester, NY: University of Rochester Press, 1999), 35.

44. The play is on *OED*, headless, *adj.*, 3, 'Brainless, foolish'.
45. See 'More's Discussion of Perjury', in *The Complete Works of St Thomas More*, Vol. VI, in 2 pts (New Haven: Yale University Press, 1981), 763–9, esp. 768–9.
46. John Davies, *Poems*, ed. Robert Krueger (Oxford: Clarendon Press, 1975), 13.
47. *Thomas Morus*, ed. and tr. Dana F. Sutton, 1.3 (lines 104–25). All quotations and translations are from this edition, at <http://www.philological.bham.ac.uk/more/>, accessed 31 July 2013.
48. For the motif of obedience see e.g. the short scene, 3.7, where royal servants come in to arrest More: 'Obedisse nostrum munus est. Thomas Morus | Auratus eques et quicquid est aliud levi | Attactu ictu munus agnoscat grave | Regii ministri' (lines 1233–6) ('Our bounden duty is to have obeyed. By our light touch let Thomas More, knight and whatever else he is, acknowledge the dutifulness of a royal servant').
49. Thomas More, great-grandson of the protagonist of the play, was in Rome at the time, though as a supporter of the anti-Jesuit, Appellant tendency in English Catholicism. See Questier, 'Catholicism, Kinship', 491–7.
50. There are conciliatory notes even in the *Premonition*, prefixed to the rev. edn of *Triplici Nodo*, i.e. *An Apologie for the Oath of Allegiance . . . Together, with a Premonition of his Majesties to all Most Mightie Monarches, Kings, free Princes and States of Christendome* (1609), where the Pope is characterized as Antichrist. For an overview see W. B. Patterson, *King James VI and I and the Reunion of Christendom* (Cambridge: Cambridge University Press, 1997).
51. On plays recorded only in Henslowe's *Diary* (1598–1603), on *Thomas Lord Cromwell* (pub. 1602) and the two parts of Chettle's *Cardinal Wolsey* (perf. 1601), see *Sir Thomas More*, ed. Jowett, 426.
52. The sequence in which Gardiner and Bonner plot against Cranmer and the reformers' views anticipates the last act of Shakespeare and Fletcher's play. Henry's queen, Katherine Howard, rebukes the Catholic bishops for their divided loyalty: 'God himselfe commaunds | The King to rule, and people to obay. . . . But you that are sworne seruants vnto *Rome,* | How are ye faithfull subiects to the King, | When first ye serue the Pope then after him?' They know, she says, that 'Scripture binds yee to obey' the king, but if he told them to resist the Pope 'Your slight obedience all the world should know' (*When You See Me, You Know Me* (1605), H2v–3r).
53. See the order of the coronation in the stage direction following 4.1.36, where the Lord Chancellor is listed. The audience hears Cromwell telling Wolsey, in the previous scene, 'Sir Thomas More is chosen | Lord Chancellor in your place' (3.2.394–5). The Lord Chancellor involved in the attempted discrediting of Cranmer (5.3) can hardly be assumed to be More.
54. Cf. Karen Sawyer Marsalek, 'Staging Allegiance, Re-membering Trials: *King Henry VIII* and the Blackfriars Theatre', in Kenneth J. E. Graham and Philip D. Collington, eds, *Shakespeare and Religious Change* (London: Palgrave, 2009), 133–50, pp. 135–7, 139–40.
55. The king's fears are widely recorded by his biographers. In relation to the Oath, see Johann Peter Sommerville, 'Jacobean Political Thought and the Controversy

of the Oath of Allegiance' (University of Cambridge, Ph.D. 1981), esp. 42–3, on the precautions taken against assassination after 1610, and the interrogation of the Catholic layman John Owen, who said, according to the Spanish Ambassador in 1615, that, if the Pope excommunicated the king, 'he would slay him if he could'.

56. *Premonition*, 6–8, in *An Apologie for the Oath of Allegiance.*
57. *A Remonstrance of the Most Gratious King Iames I. King of Great Britaine, France, and Ireland, Defender of the Faith, &c.... Against an Oration of the Most Illustrious Card. of Perron* (1616), 4–6. Cf. e.g. Pierre Coton, *The Hellish and Horribble Councell, Practised and Vsed by the Iesuites, (in their Priuate Consulations) When they Would Haue a Man to Murther a King* (1610).
58. James, *Premonition*, 121–7; cf. Richard Mocket, *God and the King* (1615), 84–8.
59. Raphael Holinshed et al., *Chronicles*, 6 vols (1587), VI, 864.
60. Harpsfield, *Life*, 158–61; cf. Guy, *Thomas More*, 188–95.
61. *De Vera Obedientia... 1536. And now Translated into Englishe* (1553), H2v.
62. 2.1.158; 2.2.87; 2.4.147, 4.1.31; 2.4.167–8.
63. William Ames, *Conscience with the Power and Cases Thereof* (1639), 19.
64. *Triplici Nodo*, 8.
65. 'Love is too young to know what conscience is...'
66. William Perkins *A Discourse of Conscience* (1596), 60.
67. *A Discourse of Conscience*, 60–1.
68. e.g. 3.1.121.
69. Holinshed, *Chronicles*, VI, 858.
70. The inventory of More's property in *Sir Thomas More* would, he says, amount to little, showing the restraint of an honest servant (16.60–1).
71. The whole scene, up to Henry's exit, leaving Wolsey to soliloquy and arrest, is held to be by Shakespeare.
72. For medieval and sixteenth-century concerns about equivocation and dissimulation, shading into perjury, see Gray, *Oaths and the English Reformation*, 36–8, 130–41.
73. Cited in *Miscellaneous Writings and Letters of Thomas Cranmer*, ed. John Edmund Cox, Parker Society 16 (Cambridge: Cambridge University Press, 1846), 538.
74. Attrib. Andrew Chertsey, *The Ordynarye of Crystyanyte or of Crysten Men* (1502), A4v.
75. For the reformers see the materials in J. D. C. Fisher, *Christian Initiation: The Reformation Period. Some Early Reformed Rites of Baptism and Confirmation and other Contemporary Documents*, Alcuin Club Collections 51 (London: SPCK, 1970).
76. See Bryan D. Spinks, *Reformation and Modern Rituals and Theologies of Baptism: From Luther to Contemporary Practices* (Aldershot: Ashgate, 1988), esp. 32–3.
77. Tyndale, *The Exposition of the Fyrste Epistle of Seynt Jhon with a Prologge before It* (1531), A6v.
78. *Obedience of a Christen Man*, lxxxix–xc.
79. See *Complete Works of More*, Vol. VIII, in 3 pts, ed. Louis A. Schuster et al. (New Haven: Yale University Press, 1973), 95–101, 213.

80. *Othello*, 2.3.317–18.
81. See Gordon P. Jeanes, *Signs of God's Promise: Thomas Cranmer's Sacramental Theology and the Book of Common Prayer* (London: Continuum, 2008), ch. 5.
82. 'The Ministration of Baptysme, to be Used in the Churche', *The Booke of Common Prayer, and Administracion of the Sacramentes, and other Rites and Ceremonies* (1559), R1v–8v, at R3v–4r.
83. *King Johan*, lines 2671–84, in *The Complete Plays of John Bale*, ed. Peter Happé, 2 vols (Cambridge: D. S. Brewer, 1985–6), I.
84. William Fulke, *A Briefe Confutation, of a Popish Discourse* (1583), 2.
85. The scene is in line with James's denial that 'infants... are by vertue of an oath taken in their Baptisme, bound to yeeld absolute obedience to Christs Vicar the Pope'; *Premonition*, t2r.
86. Holinshed, *Chronicles*, VI, 934.
87. Henry VIII, *Assertio Septem Sacramentorum: Or, Defence of the Seven Sacraments*, ed. Louis O'Donovan (New York: Benziger Brothers, 1908), 300–3.
88. *Responsio ad Lutherum*, in *Complete Works of More*, Vol. V, in 2 pts, ed. John M. Headley (New Haven: Yale University Press, 1969), 265. Cf. *A Dyaloge of Syr Thomas More Knyghte/A Dialogue Concerning Heresies*, in *Complete Works of More*, VI, 352.
89. Luther, *The Babylonian Captivity of the Church* (1520), tr. A. T. W. Steinhäuser, rev. Frederick C. Ahrens and Abdel Ross Wentz, in *Luther's Works*, Vol. XXVI, ed. Wentz (Philadelphia: Muhlenberg Press, 1959), 11–126, pp. 60–1.
90. *Obedience of a Christen Man*, Cxlv r.
91. Cf. 'An Homilee for Good Friday, Concerning the Death and Passion of our Sauiour Iesu Christ', in *The Second Tome of Homilees*, edn of 1571, 355–67, p. 359: 'In baptisme we promised to renounce the deuill and his suggestions, we promised to be (as obedient chyldren) alwayes following Gods will and pleasure.... If we be his children, let vs shew him our obedience, like as Christ openly declared his obedience to his father.'
92. Quoted here from the discussion of baptism in Richard Hooker, *Of the Lawes of Ecclesiastical Politie, Eight Bookes*, edn of 1611, 335.
93. See e.g. Hooker, *Lawes, Eight Bookes*, 338.

CHAPTER 16 CORIOLANUS FIDIUSSED

1. Anon, *A Myrrour for English Souldiers* (1595), B4r.
2. Cf. Thersites insulting Patroclus ('Thou idle immaterial skein of sleave-silk'—i.e. loop of silk thread) at *Troilus and Cressida*, 5.1.25–6, rather than *OED*, scarf, *n.*[1], 'A broad band of silk... worn (chiefly by soldiers or officials)', including Paroles in *All's Well* (see pp. 329–31).
3. *OED*, perfidious, *adj. (and n.)*.
4. For first steps with the names Volumnia, Virgilia, Aufidius, and Coriolanus see Kenneth Burke, '*Coriolanus*—and the Delights of Faction' (1966), rpt in *Kenneth Burke on Shakespeare*, ed. Scott L. Newstok (West Lafayette, Ind.: Parlor Press, 2007), 129–49, p. 147.

5. Plutarch, *The Lives of the Noble Grecians and Romanes*, tr. Thomas North (1579), 243.
6. Cf. Peter Holland, '*Coriolanus*: The Rhythms and Remains of Excess', in Leonard Barkan, Bradin Cormack, and Sean Keilen, eds, *The Forms of Renaissance Thought: New Essays in Literature and Culture* (London: Palgrave, 2009), 150–69, pp. 151–2.
7. See most fully Jonathan Goldberg, 'The Anus in *Coriolanus*', in his *Shakespeare's Hand* (Minneapolis: University of Minnesota Press, 2003), 176–85.
8. Holland, '*Coriolanus*', 151.
9. Cf. 5.1.18, Cominius, 'I minded him how royal 'twas to pardon'; Aufidius admits his 'sovereignty of nature' (4.7.35).
10. *The Romane Historie Written by T. Livius of Padua*, tr. Philemon Holland (1600), Bk II.
11. *Coriolanus*, ed. R. B. Parker, Oxford Shakespeare (Oxford: Clarendon Press, 1994), 212.
12. J. A. Crook, *Law and Life of Rome* (London: Thames and Hudson, 1967), 247.
13. See Sir Thomas Elyot, *The Dictionary* (1538), under '*Locuples fideiussor*, a sufficient suretie'; Richard Huloet, *Huloets Dictionarie Newelye Corrected* (1572), 'pledge, suretie, or warrant', under 'Borowe'; John Cowell, *The Interpreter* (1607), Ccc2r, under 'Pledge', Edward Phillips, *New World of English Words* (1658), 'a pledge, or surety', under '*Fidejussor*', Thomas Blount, *Glossographia* (1661), 'a Surety for another in a mony matter', under '*Fidejussor*'.
14. John Owen, *A Continuation of the Exposition of the Epistle of Paul the Apostle to the Hebrews* (1680), 159.
15. Definitions from Thomas Cooper, *Thesaurus Linguae Romanae et Britannicae* (1578), under *Fides*.
16. On this attribute of Jupiter see *Coriolanus*, 4.5.102–5.
17. See e.g. Arnaldo Momigliano, *On Pagans, Jews, and Christians* (Middletown, Conn.: Wesleyan University Press, 1987), 75–9.
18. *Historie*, tr. Holland, 15.
19. *The Oxford Classical Dictionary*, 4th edn, ed. Simon Hornblower et al. (Oxford: Oxford University Press, 2012), under '*Fides*'.
20. *Pericles* (1609), C4v, 'Thus is faith to be examined.'
21. 'How to Do Things with Austin and Searle: Speech-Act Theory and Literary Criticism', in Stanley Fish, *Is there a Text in This Class?* (Cambridge, Mass.: Harvard University Press, 1980), 197–245, esp. 200–20, quoting p. 200.
22. 'How to Do Things', 210–11.
23. 'How to Do Things', 205.
24. Cicero, *De Officiis*, I.vii [23]. Latin text quoted from the Loeb edn, ed. Walter Miller (London: Heinemann, 1913).
25. *Marcus Tullius Ciceroes Thre Bokes of Duties*, tr. Nicholas Grimald (1556), B1v.
26. Francis Bacon, *The Essayes or Counsels, Ciuill and Morall,* rev. edn (1625), 5.
27. *De Officiis*, III.xxvi–xxxii [99–115].

28. *Ciceroes Thre Bokes of Duties*, tr. Grimald, S8v, T1v; *De Officiis*, III.xxxi [111–12]. It is tempting to read 'auncesters' but *OED*, ancestor, *n.*, records 'ancytour, ansitor' among the forms of the word.
29. *Historie*, tr. Holland, 39–42; 20–1, p. 21.
30. *Historie*, tr. Holland, 102.
31. I.xiii. The *Discorsi sopra la prima deca di Tito Livio* (written *c.*1517) were available in Shakespeare's England, in Italian and in manuscript translation, though a translated text by E.D. was not printed until 1636. For their likely relevance to the play see Anne Barton, 'Livy, Machiavelli, and Shakespeare's *Coriolanus*', *Shakespeare Survey*, 38 (1985), 115–29.
32. Cf. Cathy Shrank, 'Civility and the City in *Coriolanus*', *Shakespeare Quarterly*, 54 (2003), 406–23, esp. pp. 406–12.
33. Hugh Oldcastle, augmented by John Mellis, *Briefe Instruction and Maner how to Keepe Bookes of Accompts* (1588), A6v. Cf. Craig Muldrew, *The Economy of Obligation: The Culture of Credit and Social Relations in Early Modern England* (Basingstoke: Macmillan, 1998), 128.
34. e.g. when Lycurgus makes the king, senators, and people of Sparta swear to keep his lawes and ordinances (*Lives*, tr. North, 63–4).
35. e.g. 'the oth of the people' against having kings; the soldiers, under the Dictatorship of Marcus Valerius, keeping 'sworne alleageance to the Consuls, supposing they were still bounde to warfare by vertue of that oath'; 'an ancient oath of the Commons' empowering the tribunes (*Historie*, tr. Holland, 44–5, 64, 125).
36. 1.10.89; 3.1.89, 110.
37. Giorgio Agamben, *The Sacrament of Language: An Archaeology of the Oath ('Homo Sacer' II, 3)*, tr. Adam Kotsko (Cambridge: Polity, 2010), 54.
38. *Lives*, tr. North, 215. Cf. among the list of surnames, 'And some Kings haue had surnames of ieast and mockery. As one of the *Antigones* that was called *Doson*, to saye, the Geuer: who was euer promising, and neuer geuing' (242).
39. Another of North's notes, 224.
40. *Ductor Dubitantium: Or, The Rule of Conscience in all her Generall Measures*, 2 vols (1660), II, 96.
41. 2.3.66–7, to which Coriolanus replies, 'Well then, I pray, your price o'th' consulship?' Plutarch says of Martius' election that 'offices of dignitie in the cittie were not then geuen by fauour or corruption. It was but of late time, and long after this, that buying and selling fell out in election of officers, and that the voyces of the electours were bought for money' (244). In Shakespeare's play, the decline has already begun.
42. *Coriolanus*, ed. Philip Brockbank, Arden Shakespeare, 2nd series (London: Methuen, 1976), 184.
43. *1 Henry IV*, 2.5.6.
44. Jacques Derrida, *The Politics of Friendship*, tr. George Collins (London: Verso, 1997), 99, 159, 237.
45. 2.3.102–7, following F's 'Wooluish' not Norton's 'womanish'.

46. *OED*, amen, *int. and n.*, 2–3 and 4, 'Truly, verily'. See p. 268.
47. Mark Kishlansky, *Parliamentary Selection: Social and Political Choice in Early Modern England* (Cambridge: Cambridge University Press, 1986), 10.
48. *OED,* vote, *n.* 'Vote' had something like its modern sense during Shakespeare's lifetime, but could also mean 'a vow; a solemn promise or undertaking' (1, *obs.*).
49. Kishlansky, *Parliamentary Selection*, 30.
50. David Schalkwyk, 'Text and Performance, Reiterated: A Reproof Valiant or Lie Direct?', *The Shakespearean International Yearbook*, 10 (2010), 47–75, p. 57.
51. *Hippolytus*, line 612; J. L. Austin, *How to Do Things with Words*, 2nd edn, ed. J. O. Urmson and Marina Sbisà (Oxford: Oxford University Press, 1975), 9–10.
52. *De Officiis*, III.xxix [107–8]; *Ciceroes Thre Bokes of Duties*, tr. Grimald, S7r.
53. See e.g. Robert Parsons, *A Quiet and Sober Reckoning* (1609), 460, Thomas Morton, *The Encounter against M. Parsons* (1610), 58.
54. See e.g. Sidney, *Astrophel and Stella* (1591), 20 (sonnet 47); Richard Brathwaite, *Natures Embassie* (1621), 40.
55. *1 Henry IV*, 3.1.242–52. In *Coriolanus*, 1.3.45–105, added to Plutarch, Valeria counterpoints the main action with 'in good faith', 'O' my word', 'I'll swear', 'O' my troth', 'I warrant', 'Indeed, la', 'Fie', 'In truth, la', 'Verily', 'In earnest, it's true', 'This is true, on mine honour', 'In truth'.
56. *Politics of Friendship*, tr. Collins, 123.
57. 4.5.67, 88, 100.
58. *OED* records 'service', *n.*[1], in this sense (4. a. 'The condition or employment of a public servant... chiefly of a soldier or sailor') from the late thirteenth century, 'the service' meaning the army or navy from 1707.
59. Walter Bourchier Devereux, *Lives and Letters of the Devereux, Earls of Essex... 1540–1646*, 2 vols (London: John Murray, 1853), II, 68.
60. See esp. Michael Neill, 'Servant Obedience and Master Sins: Shakespeare and the Bonds of Service', in his *Putting History to the Question: Power, Politics, and Society in English Renaissance Drama* (New York: Columbia University Press, 2000), 13–58, Judith Weill, *Service and Dependency in Shakespeare's Plays* (Cambridge: Cambridge University Press, 2005), 32–41, David Evett, *Discourses of Service in Shakespeare's England* (New York: Palgrave, 2005).
61. William Gouge, *Of Domesticall Duties* (1622), 622. The quotation is Titus 2: 10.
62. Nahum Tate, *The Ingratitude of a Common-wealth: Or, The Fall of Caius Martius Coriolanus* (1682), 39.
63. See e.g. Tullus and Martius' attempt in Plutarch's *Life of Coriolanus* to persuade the Volscians to 'break' their treaty with Rome (4.6.49), 'They aunswered them, they were ashamed to breake the league, considering that they were sworne to keepe peace for two yeres' (251), Livy on the oath-sacrifice made when the Romans and the Albans bind their 'covenant and composition' before the combat of the Horatii and the Curatii, the rites surrounding 'the solemne oth' of the ambassador Fecial, and the 'solemne oath and other ceremonies according to the auncient manner' required of the Veientians (*Historie*, tr. Holland, 17, 23–4, 159).

64. *Coriolanus*, ed. Brockbank, 279–80.
65. Plutarch, *Lives*, 253 (where they also seek the freedom of Rome, like the Latins); Dennis, *The Invader of his Country: Or, The Fatal Resentment* (1720), 71; Sheridan, *Coriolanus: Or, the Roman Matron* (1755), 75.
66. *De Officiis*, I.xvi [50]; *Ciceroes Thre Bokes of Duties*, tr. Grimald, C4v.
67. *De Officiis*, I.xvii [53–4]; *Ciceroes Thre Bokes of Duties*, tr. Grimald, C6r.
68. John King, *A Sermon Preached in Oxon: the 5. of November. 1607* (1607), 26. The Latin (translated by King) is based on Psalms 2: 3.
69. I have followed Folio 'thing' where Norton accepts Capell's emendation 'things' (to force an agreement with 'denials').
70. *OED*, for-, *prefix*[1].
71. 'Vsing', as one treatise notes, 'so manie great maximes of and for the state . . . as all the *Xenophons, Tacitusses, Machiauels*, yea, whatsoeuer Councellers to the Princes of Europe, may iustly learne example'; Alexandre de Pontaymeri, *A Womans Woorth, Defended against All the Men in the World* (1599), B6r.
72. Plutarch, *Lives*, 257; Loeb edn of *Plutarch's Lives*, tr. Bernadotte Perrin, 11 vols (London: Heinemann, 1914–26), IV (*Caius Martius Coriolanus*, xxxvi.4); cf. Momigliano, *On Pagans, Jews, and Christians*, 76.
73. On taking hands see e.g. Susan Treggiari, *Roman Marriage: Iusti Coniuges from the Time of Cicero to the Time of Ulpian* (Oxford: Clarendon Press, 1991), 149–51, B. J. Sokol and Mary Sokol, *Shakespeare, Law, and Marriage* (Cambridge: Cambridge University Press, 2003), 17–19, 95, 192.
74. Cf. Livy, where, in a famous passage, Latinus makes peace with Aeneas: 'whereupon, by giuing his right hand, he plight his troth, and faithfully promised them friendship and amitie. So the two generals made a league, and each host saluted other' (*Historie*, tr. Holland, 3).
75. Plutarch, *Lives*, 262.
76. See e.g. III.xxxiii [115]; *Ciceroes Thre Bokes of Duties*, tr. Grimald, T2v.
77. Tate, *Ingratitude of a Common-wealth*, 58; Sheridan, *Coriolanus*, 74.
78. *Ciceroes Thre Bokes of Duties*, tr. Grimald, S7v; *De Officiis*, III.xxix [108].
79. *De Officiis*, III.xxvi [99].
80. *Ciceroes Thre Bokes of Duties*, tr. Grimald, S5v–6r; *De Officiis*, III.xxix [104].
81. *De Officiis*, I.xvii [58]. For Cicero's disapproval of Coriolanus as an invader of his country see the *De Amicitia*, xi–xii.
82. 1.11.4–5, 3.1.9–11.
83. *Discourses upon the First Decade of T. Livius*, tr. E.D. (1636), II.xxxi.
84. Livy, *History*, tr. Holland, 65.
85. At 67–8, the Lords say, on the basis of Aufidius' negative story, that Coriolanus proposes to repay them only the cost of the campaign.
86. *Ingratitude of a Common-wealth*, 58.
87. By Menenius' count, the attack led by Coriolanus is the fourth breaking of a treaty by the Volscians during his lifetime (4.6.48–53).
88. Recalling Aufidius words, at 1.11.6–7. See p. 440.

89. In Plutarch, the second embassy to Coriolanus declares that 'The ROMAINES were no men that would euer yeld for feare' (254).
90. Machiavelli, *Discourses*, tr. E.D., III.xiii.
91. 'How to Do Things', 245.

CHAPTER 17 OATH AND COUNSEL

1. Quoting Miguel de Cervantes Saavedra, *The History of the Valorous and Wittie Knight-Errant, Don-Quixote of the Mancha*, tr. Thomas Shelton (1612), 222, 274–5.
2. On the probable debt of Theobald's play to *Cardenio* see e.g. *Double Falsehood: Or, The Distressed Lovers*, ed. Brean Hammond, Arden Shakespeare, 3rd series (London: Methuen 2010), 48–58, and, more extensively, David Carnegie and Gary Taylor, eds, *The Quest for 'Cardenio': Shakespeare, Fletcher, Cervantes, and the Lost Play* (Oxford: Oxford University Press, 2012).
3. For an exception see the paragraph on Leontes in Stuart M. Kurland, 'Shakespeare and James I: Personal Rule and Public Responsibility', in Andrew J. Power and Rory Loughnane, eds, *Late Shakespeare, 1608–1612* (Cambridge: Cambridge University Press, 2013), 209–24, pp. 220–1.
4. The best ways into the topic are: Judith Ferster, *Fictions of Advice: The Literature and Politics of Counsel in Late Medieval England* (Philadelphia: University of Pennsylvania Press, 1996); John Guy, 'The Rhetoric of Counsel in Early Modern England', in Dale Hoak, ed., *Tudor Political Culture* (Cambridge: Cambridge University Press, 1995), 292–310; and David Colclough, *Freedom of Speech in Early Stuart England* (Cambridge: Cambridge University Press, 2005), 62–76. Cf. Colclough's 'Talking to the Animals: Persuasion, Counsel and their Discontents in *Julius Caesar*', in David Armitage, Conal Condren, and Andrew Fitzmaurice, eds, *Shakespeare and Early Modern Political Thought* (Cambridge: Cambridge University Press, 2009), 217–33.
5. *Romeo and Juliet*, 2.1.154–60.
6. 'Verily' as an asseveration falls well short of 'oaths . . . not to stay'. Yet the family resemblance is there, as is noted by the homily 'Against Swearyng and Periury' which sought to discourage profanity while defending the legitimacy of oaths: 'Thus did oure sauior Christe sweare diuerse tymes, saiyng: verely verely' (Thomas Cranmer, *Certayne Sermons, or Homelies* (1547), L4v). Cf. Matthew 18: 3, John 5: 24.
7. Cf. David Schalkwyk, '"A Lady's 'Verily' Is as Potent as a Lord's": Women, Word and Witchcraft in *The Winter's Tale*', *English Literary Renaissance*, 22 (1992), 242–72, pp. 249–50.
8. 'Verily' has ten out of its thirteen Shakespearean uses after 1606, seven of them in *The Winter's Tale*, where 'sooth' comes four times, the joint-highest result in the output.
9. Homosexual interpretations go back to J. I. M. Stewart, *Character and Motive in Shakespeare: Some Recent Appraisals Examined* (London: Longmans, 1949), 30–9.

Behind Stewart's account is, of course, Freud's 1922 essay 'Some Neurotic Mechanisms in Jealousy, Paranoia, and Homosexuality'.

10. The classic account is by Stanley Cavell, 'Recounting Gains, Showing Losses: Reading *The Winter's Tale*', in his *Disowning Knowledge in Six Plays of Shakespeare* (Cambridge: Cambridge University Press, 1987), 193–221, esp. p. 199.
11. *OED*, friend, *n.* and *adj.*, 4, 'A lover or paramour, of either sex' (from 1490, and citing *Love's Labour's Lost*).
12. Anne Barton, '"Wrying but a Little": Marriage, Law and Sexuality in the Plays of Shakespeare', in her *Essays, Mainly Shakespearean* (Cambridge: Cambridge University Press, 1994), 3–30, p. 18.
13. Steven Shapin, *A Social History of Truth: Civility and Science in Seventeenth-Century England* (Chicago: University of Chicago Press, 1994), 75. Cf. the Introduction, pp. 27-8.
14. Sir William Cornwallis, *Essayes* (1600–1), D4v–5r.
15. *Pandosto: The Triumph of Time* (1588), A3r.
16. 'Of Counsaile', at Cc1r.
17. *The Essayes or Counsels, Ciuill and Morall* (1625), 115–24, p. 115.
18. *OED*, confidence, *n.*, 1.
19. The *Essayes*, first published—many of them—in 1597, became *The Essayes or Counsels* in 1625.
20. Wawrzyniec Goslicki [Laurentius Grimaldius Goslicius], *The Counsellor* (1598), 93.
21. *Essayes or Counsels*, 1–6, p. 1.
22. On the widely held, early modern belief, notably in relation to marriage, that 'to be silent is to consent', see Henry Swinburne, *A Treatise of Spousals, or Matrimonial Contracts*, written *c.*1600 (1686), 184; cf. 5, 132, 147, 183. Swinburne's own, more reasonable position was that 'To be silent, is not to consent' (184–5).
23. Lorna Hutson, *The Invention of Suspicion: Law and Mimesis in Shakespeare and Renaissance Drama* (Oxford: Oxford University Press, 2007), 127.
24. Cf. John Kerrigan, *Archipelagic English: Literature, History, and Politics 1603–1707* (Oxford: Oxford University Press, 2008), 136.
25. See e.g. Goslicki, *Counsellor*, 94.
26. Colclough, 'Talking to the Animals', 222.
27. Justus Lipsius, *Sixe Bookes of Politickes or Ciuil Doctrine*, tr. William Jones (1594), A5r.
28. *The Court of the Most Illustrious and Most Magnificent James, the First* (1619), 28–9.
29. Echoing Cicero, *De Officiis*, I.xxii [7]; see Introduction, p. 14. The original reads 'more and promise', which cannot be correct; *w* for *m* and *e* for *d* are explicable misreadings of manuscript copy.
30. *The Picture of a Perfit Common Wealth* (1602), 76–7.
31. Goslicki, *Counsellor*, 77.
32. 'The Oath of a Priue Counsellor, Framed Now in the Time of King James', in *The Book of Oaths*, comp. Richard Garnet (?) (1649), 143–5.
33. Lipsius, *Sixe Bookes*, G2v.

34. In the arguments to Books III and VI of *The Whole XII Bookes of the Aeneidos of Virgill*, tr. Thomas Phaer and Thomas Twyne (1573), for example, we read of the hero 'takyng counsell of the Oracle of *Apollo*' (F3r) and at Cumae 'he asketh counsel at the Oracle of *Apollo*' (P1v).
35. The tyrant, over-confident of his power to deliver, himself swears such oaths, as when Herod swears to give Salome whatever she requests and it turns out to be the head of St John the Baptist on a platter (see the homily 'Against Swearyng and Periury', M2v–3r). From the point of view of the subject, oaths imposed in the ecclesiastical courts and in cases taken to the Star Chamber—to open investigation, not settle points of doubt—were also denounced as 'tyrannical' (see e.g. James Morice, *A Briefe Treatise of Oathes Exacted by Ordinaries and Ecclesiasticall Iudges* (1590), 40, 52, 55–6).
36. For a digest and position see Jeremy Taylor, *Ductor Dubitantium: Or, The Rule of Conscience in All her Generall Measures*, 2 vols (1660), II, 514.
37. *The Two Gentlemen of Verona*, 2.7.75.
38. *Norton Shakespeare*, 3338, which glosses 'coll pixci' as 'Probably "colt-pixie," a mischievous sprite or fairy'.
39. *Metamorphoses*, XI.301–17; *Odyssey*, XIX.395.
40. Thomas Wilson, *A Discourse Vppon Vsurye* (1572), fol. 6r.
41. *The Winter's Tale*, ed. John Pitcher, Arden Shakespeare, 3rd series (London: Methuen, 2010), 390.
42. They are given in *The Winter's Tale*, ed. Pitcher, 392.
43. *Don Quixote*, 286–99, 399–410.
44. *Norton Shakespeare*, 3338.
45. *Tragedy of King Lear*, 3.2.6–9 (3.2.6–9 in the Norton conflated text); cf. *Macbeth*, 4.1.75.
46. For a trenchant discussion of the 'deceit, cheating and fraud' in Bohemia, and its contrast with Sicilia, see Holger Schott Syme, *Theatre and Testimony in Shakespeare's England: A Culture of Mediation* (Cambridge: Cambridge University Press, 2012), 230–1.
47. Cf. the Introduction, pp. 27, 41, and Iachimo, pp. 455–6.
48. A.D.B., *Court of King James*, 72.

CHAPTER 18 EPILOGUE

1. Sonnets 130.13, 152.9. For a supple, philosophically informed (Austinian) account of oaths in these poems, see David Schalkwyk, 'Shakespeare's Speech', *Journal of Medieval and Early Modern Studies*, 40 (2010), 373–400.
2. See esp. Ilona Bell, 'Rethinking Shakespeare's Dark Lady', in Michael Schoenfeldt, ed., *A Companion to Shakespeare's Sonnets* (Malden, Mass.: Blackwell, 2007), 293–313.
3. Samuel Daniel, *Delia. Containing Certaine Sonnets: With the Complaynt of Rosamond* (1592).

4. Katherine Duncan-Jones, 'Was the 1609 *Shake-speares Sonnets* Really Unauthorized?', *Review of English Studies*, 34 (1983), 151–71. For critique, and variations on this pattern in other verse books of the period, see Heather Dubrow, '"Dressing Old Words New"? Re-evaluating the "Delian Structure"', in Schoenfeldt, ed., *Companion to Shakespeare's Sonnets*, 90–103.
5. Shakespeare's *Sonnets and A Lover's Complaint*, New Penguin Shakespeare (Harmondsworth: Penguin, 1986); ed., *Motives of Woe: Shakespeare and 'Female Complaint'. A Critical Anthology* (Oxford: Clarendon Press, 1991).
6. MacDonald P. Jackson, 'Early Modern Authorship: Canons and Chronologies', in Gary Taylor and John Lavagnino, eds, *Thomas Middleton and Early Modern Textual Culture: A Companion to the Collected Works* (Oxford: Clarendon Press, 2007), 80–97, p. 84. Jackson's attention to this subject goes back to his *Studies in Attribution: Middleton and Shakespeare* (Salzburg: Universität Salzburg, 1979).
7. Quoting 'The Oath in Archaic and Classical Greece' website, directed by Alan H. Sommerstein: <http://www.nottingham.ac.uk/Classics/Research/projects/oaths/intro.aspx>, accessed 22 February 2015.
8. Judith Fletcher, *Performing Oaths in Classical Greek Drama* (Cambridge: Cambridge University Press, 2012), Alan H. Sommerstein and Andrew J. Bayliss, with others, *Oath and State in Ancient Greece* (Berlin: Walter de Gruyter, 2013), Alan H. Sommerstein and Isabelle C. Torrance, with others, *Oaths and Swearing in Ancient Greece* (Berlin: Walter de Gruyter, 2014).

Bibliography

SHAKESPEARE AND EARLY MODERN DRAMA

Bale, John, *The Complete Plays of John Bale*, ed. Peter Happé, 2 vols (Cambridge: D. S. Brewer, 1985–6).

Barnes, Barnabe, *The Diuils Charter* (1607).

Beaumont, Francis, *The Masque of the Inner Temple and Grayes Inne . . . 1612* (1613).

Captaine Thomas Stukeley (1605).

Chapman, George, *The Reuenge of Bussy D'Ambois* (1613).

Chapman, George, Ben Jonson, and John Marston, *Eastward Hoe* (1605).

Chettle, Henry, *The Tragedy of Hoffman: Or, A Reuenge for a Father* (1631).

Cinthio (Giambattista Cinzio Giraldi), *Orbecche* (1541).

Day, John, *The Ile of Guls* (1606).

Dekker, Thomas, *Satiro-mastix* (1602).

Dekker, Thomas, and John Webster, *West-ward Hoe* (1607).

Dennis, John, *The Invader of his Country: Or, The Fatal Resentment* (1720).

Dryden, John, *Troilus and Cressida* (1679), in *The Works of John Dryden*, ed. H. T. Swedenberg, Jr et al., 20 vols (Berkeley: University of California Press, 1956–2000), XIII, 225–48.

Edmund Ironside, ed. Eric Sams (London: Fourth Estate, 1985).

Ein sehr klägliche Tragaedia von Tito Andronico und der hoffertigen Käyserin, in *Engelische Comedien und Tragedien* (1620).

The Famous Victories of Henry the Fifth (1598).

Fletcher, John, *Rollo, Duke of Normandy*, in *The Dramatic Works in the Beaumont and Fletcher Canon*, gen. ed. Fredson Bowers, Vol. X (Cambridge: Cambridge University Press, 1996).

Ford, John, *'Tis Pity She's a Whore*, ed. Derek Roper (Manchester: Manchester University Press, 1975).

Ford, John, *The Broken Heart*, ed. T. J. B. Spencer, Revels Plays (Manchester: Manchester University Press, 1980).

Gesta Grayorum: Or, The History of the High and Mighty Prince, Henry Prince of Purpoole . . . who Reigned and Died, A.D. 1594 (1688).

Goffe, Thomas, *The Tragedy of Orestes* (1633).

Goldring, Elizabeth, et al., gen. eds, *John Nichols's The Progresses and Public Processions of Queen Elizabeth: A New Edition of the Early Modern Sources*, 5 vols (Oxford: Oxford University Press, 2014).

Greene, Robert, *The Honorable Historie of Frier Bacon, and Frier Bongay* (1630).

Heywood, Thomas, *If You Know Not Me You Know Nobody, Part II*, ed. Madeleine Doran, Malone Society (Oxford: Oxford University Press, 1935).

Heywood, Thomas, *The Iron Age, Parts I* and *II* (1632).

Jonson, Ben, *The Cambridge Edition of the Works of Ben Jonson*, gen. eds David Bevington, Martin Butler, and Ian Donaldson, 7 vols (Cambridge: Cambridge University Press, 2012).

Kyd, Thomas, *The Spanish Tragedy*, ed. Philip Edwards, Revels Plays (London: Methuen, 1959).

Marlowe, Christopher, *Tamburlaine the Great* (1590).

Marlowe, Christopher, *'Dr Faustus' and Other Plays*, ed. David Bevington and Eric Rasmussen (Oxford: Clarendon Press, 1995).

Marston, John, *Antonio's Revenge*, ed. Reavley Gair, Revels Plays (Manchester: Manchester University Press, 1978).

Marston, John, *The Wonder of Women: Or, The Tragedie of Sophonisba* (1606).

Mayne, Jasper, *The Amorous Warre* (1648).

Middleton, Thomas, *Thomas Middleton: The Collected Works*, gen. eds Gary Taylor and John Lavagnino (Oxford: Clarendon Press, 2007).

Molloy, Charles, *The Half-Pay Officers* (1720).

Munday, Anthony, and others, *The First Part of the True and Honorable Historie, of the Life of Sir Iohn Old-castle, the Good Lord Cobham* (1600).

Orrery, Roger Boyle, Earl of, *The History of Henry the Fifth* (1668).

Randolph, Samuel, *Aristippus: Or, The Ioviall Philosopher* (1630).

Ravenscroft, Edward, *Titus Andronicus: Or, The Rape of Lavinia* (1687).

Roffensis, ed. and tr. Dana F. Sutton, <http://www.philological.bham.ac.uk/roff/>

Rowley, Samuel, *When You See Me, You Know Me* (1605).

Rowley, William, Thomas Dekker, and John Ford, *The Witch of Edmonton* (1658).

Rudyerd, Sir Benjamin, *Le Prince d'Amour: Or, The Prince of Love* (1660).

Shadwell, Thomas, *The History of Timon of Athens, The Man-Hater* (1678).

Shakespeare, William, *The Plays of William Shakespeare*, ed. Samuel Johnson, 8 vols (1765).

Shakespeare, William, *All's Well That Ends Well*, ed. G. K. Hunter, Arden Shakespeare, 2nd series (London: Methuen, 1959).

Shakespeare, William, *The First Folio of Shakespeare*, prep. Charlton Hinman (New York: Norton, 1968).

Shakespeare, William, *Coriolanus*, ed. Philip Brockbank, Arden Shakespeare, 2nd series (London: Methuen, 1976).

Shakespeare, William, *Shakespeare's Plays in Quarto: A Facsimile Edition of Copies Primarily from the Henry E. Huntington Library*, ed. Michael J. B. Allen and Kenneth Muir (Berkeley: University of California Press, 1981).

Shakespeare, William, *Love's Labour's Lost*, ed. John Kerrigan, New Penguin Shakespeare (Harmondsworth: Penguin, 1982).

Shakespeare, William, *Henry V*, ed. Andrew Gurr, New Cambridge Shakespeare (Cambridge: Cambridge University Press, 1992).

Shakespeare, William, *Coriolanus*, ed. R. B. Parker, Oxford Shakespeare (Oxford: Clarendon Press, 1994).

Shakespeare, William, *Titus Andronicus*, ed. Jonathan Bate, Arden Shakespeare, 3rd series (London: Routledge, 1995).

Shakespeare, William, *The Norton Shakespeare*, gen. ed. Stephen Greenblatt, 1st edn (New York: Norton, 1997).

Shakespeare, William, *Love's Labour's Lost*, ed. H. R. Woudhuysen, Arden Shakespeare, 3rd series (London: Nelson, 1998).

Shakespeare, William, *Troilus and Cressida*, ed. David Bevington, Arden Shakespeare, 3rd series (Walton-on-Thames: Nelson, 1998).

Shakespeare, William, et al., *King Edward III*, ed. Giorgio Melchiori, New Cambridge Shakespeare (Cambridge: Cambridge University Press, 1998).

Shakespeare, William, *King Henry V*, ed. Emma Smith, Shakespeare in Production (Cambridge: Cambridge University Press, 2002).

Shakespeare, William, *The Tempest*, ed. David Lindley, New Cambridge Shakespeare (Cambridge: Cambridge University Press, 2002).

Shakespeare, William, *Troilus and Cressida*, ed. Anthony B. Dawson, New Cambridge Shakespeare (Cambridge: Cambridge University Press, 2003).

Shakespeare, William, *Timon of Athens*, ed. John Jowett, Oxford Shakespeare (Oxford: Oxford University Press, 2004).

Shakespeare, William, *Love's Labour's Lost*, ed. William C. Carroll, New Cambridge Shakespeare (Cambridge: Cambridge University Press, 2009).

Shakespeare, William, *The Merchant of Venice*, ed. John Drakakis, Arden Shakespeare, 3rd series (London: Arden, 2010).

Shakespeare, William, *The Winter's Tale*, ed. John Pitcher, Arden Shakespeare, 3rd series (London: Methuen, 2010).

Shakespeare, William, *Sir Thomas More*, ed. John Jowett, Arden Shakespeare, 3rd series (London: A. and C. Black, 2011).

Sheridan, Thomas, *Coriolanus: Or, the Roman Matron* (1755).

Spieltexte der Wanderbühne, ed. Manfred Brauneck, 2 vols (Berlin: Walter de Gruyter, 1970).

Tate, Nahum, *The Ingratitude of a Common-wealth: Or, The Fall of Caius Martius Coriolanus* (1682).

Theobald, Lewis (based on a script by William Shakespeare and John Fletcher?), *Double Falsehood: Or, The Distressed Lovers*, ed. Brean Hammond, Arden Shakespeare, 3rd series (London: Methuen 2010).

Thomas Morus, ed. and tr. Dana F. Sutton, <http://www.philological.bham.ac.uk/more/>

Timon, ed. James C. Bulman and J. M. Nosworthy (Oxford: Malone Society, 1980).

The Troublesome Raigne of Iohn King of England (1591).

The True Chronicle Historie of King Leir and his Three Daughters (1605), in Geoffrey Bullough, ed., *Narrative and Dramatic Sources of Shakespeare*, 8 vols (London: Routledge, 1957–75), VII, 337–402.

Vos, Jan, *Aran en Titus: Of, Wraak en Weerwraak. Treurspel* (1641).

Webster, John, *The Works of John Webster*, ed. David Gunby et al., 3 vols (Cambridge: Cambridge University Press, 1995–2007).

Whetstone, George, *Promos and Cassandra* (1578), in Geoffrey Bullough, ed., *Narrative and Dramatic Sources of Shakespeare*, 8 vols (London: Routledge, 1957–75), II, 442–513.

Wilkins, George, *The Miseries of Inforst Mariage* (1607).

OTHER PRIMARY SOURCES

Aeschylus, *Seven Against Thebes*, in *Aeschylus*, ed. and tr. Alan H. Sommerstein, Loeb Classical Library, 3 vols (Cambridge, Mass.: Harvard University Press, 2008), I.

Africanus, Leo, *A Geographical Historie of Africa* (1600).

Ames, William, *Conscience with the Power and Cases Thereof* (1639).

Andrewes, Lancelot, *Lancelot Andrewes: Selected Sermons and Lectures*, ed. Peter McCullough (Oxford: Oxford University Press, 2005).

Appian [Appianus of Alexandria], *An Auncient Historie and Exquisite Chronicle of the Romanes Warres, both Ciuile and Foren*, tr. William Barker (?) (1578).

Aquinas, St Thomas, *Summa Theologica*, <http://www.newadvent.org/summa>

Archer, Ian W., and F. Douglas Price, eds, *The Bond of Association, 1584*, in *English Historical Documents* Online, V(A), *1558–1603* (London: Routledge).

Aristotle, *Art of Rhetoric*, tr. J. H. Freese, Loeb Classical Library (London: Heinemann, 1926).

Aristotle, *Nicomachean Ethics*, tr. H. Rackham, rev. edn, Loeb Classical Library (London: Heinemann, 1934).

Aristotle, *Politics*, tr. H. Rackham, Loeb Classical Library (London: Heinemann, 1944).

Aristotle, *De Arte Poetica Liber*, ed. Rudolf Kassel (Oxford: Clarendon Press, 1965).

Ascham, Roger, *The Scholemaster* (1570).

Auden, W. H., and Chester Kallman, *Love's Labour's Lost: Operatic Pastoral*, in *Libretti and Other Dramatic Writings by W. H. Auden, 1939–1973*, ed. Edward Mendelson (Princeton: Princeton University Press, 1993).

Augustine of Hippo, *The Works of Aurelius Augustine, Bishop of Hippo*, tr. Marcus Dods, 15 vols (Edinburgh: T. and T. Clark, 1871–6).

Augustine of Hippo, *De Sermone Domini in Monte Secundum Matthaeum*, excerpt trans. (from John J. Jepson, *St Augustine: The Lord's Sermon on the Mount* (Westminster, Md: Newman Press, 1948)) in Geoffrey Bullough, ed., *Narrative and Dramatic Sources of Shakespeare*, 8 vols (London: Routledge, 1957–75), II, 418–19.

B., A. D., *The Court of the Most Illustrious and Most Magnificent James, the First* (1619).

B., G., *A Most Wicked Worke of a Wretched Witch* (1592).

The Babylonian Talmud, trans. Salis Daiches et al., gen. ed. Isidore Epstein, 35 vols (London: Soncino, 1935–52).

Bacon, Sir Francis, *The Charge of Sir Francis Bacon Knight . . . Touching Duells* (1614).

Bacon, Sir Francis, *The Wisedome of the Ancients*, tr. Sir Arthur Gorges (1619).

Bacon, Sir Francis, *The Essayes or Counsels, Civill and Morall*, rev. edn (1625).

Bagshawe, Christopher, *A Sparing Discouerie of our English Iesuits* (1601).

Bale, John (or Miles Coverdale), *A Christen Exhortacion vnto Customable Swearers* (1543).

Balmford, James, *A Short and Plaine Dialogue Concerning the Vnlawfulnes of Playing at Cards or Tables, or Any Other Game Consisting in Chance* (1593).

Balmford, James, *A Modest Reply to Certaine Answeres, which Mr. B.D. in his Treatise of the Nature, and Vse of Lotts, Giveth to Arguments in a Dialogue* (1623).

Barlow, William, *The Sermon Preached at Paules Crosse, the Tenth Day of Nouember being the Next Sunday after the Discouerie of this Late Horrible Treason* (1606).

Becanus, Martinus, *The Confutation of Tortura Torti: Or, Against the King of Englands Chaplaine* (1610).

Becanus, Martinus, *The English Iarre or Disagreement amongst the Ministers of Great Brittaine, Concerning the Kinges Supremacy* (1612).

Becon, Richard, *Solon his Follie* (1594).

Becon, Thomas, *An Inuectyue Agenst the Moost Wicked [and] Detestable Vyce of Swearing, Newly Co[m]piled by Theodore Basille* (1543).

Bellarmine, Robert, *Tractatus de Potestate Summi Pontificis in Rebus Temporalibus, Adversus Gulielmum Barclay* (1610).

Belleforest, François de, *Les Histoires tragiques*, Vol. 5 (1570).

Ben Israel, Menasseh, *To His Highnesse the Lord Protector of the Common-wealth of England, Scotland, and Ireland* (1655).

Ben Israel, Menasseh, *Vindiciae Judaeorum: Or, A Letter in Answer to Certain Questions Propounded by a Noble and Learned Gentleman, Touching the Reproaches Cast on the Nation of the Jewes* (1656).

Bèze, Théodore de, *The Pope's Canons*, tr. T.S. (1587).

Biblia Sacra Vulgatae Editionis [Clementine Vulgate] (1592).

Bicknoll, Edmond, *A Swoord agaynst Swearyng* (1579).

Blackwell, George, *A Large Examination taken at Lambeth . . . of M. G. Blakwell* (1609).

Blount, Thomas, *Glossographia* (1661).

Bodin, Jean, *Les Six livres de la République* (1576).

Bodin, Jean, *De la démonomanie des sorciers* (1580).

Bodin, Jean, *The Six Bookes of a Common-weale*, tr. Richard Knolles (1606).

Boyle, Robert, *A Free Discourse against Customary Swearing* (1695).

Bracton, Henry de, *Bracton on the Laws and Customs of England*, ed. George Woodbine and tr. Samuel E. Thorne, 4 vols (Cambridge, Mass.: Belknap/Harvard University Press, 1968–77).

Brathwaite, Richard, *A Solemne Ioviall Disputation, Theoreticke and Practicke; Briefely Shadowing the Law of Drinking Together* (1617).

Brathwaite, Richard, *Natures Embassie* (1621).

Bray, Gerald, ed., *Documents of the English Reformation*, corr. rpt (Cambridge: James Clarke and Co., 2004).

Breton, Jean Le (?), *Britton*, tr. Francis Morgan Nichols (1865; Washington, DC: Byrne, 1901).

Bruno, Vincent, *A Short Treatise of the Sacrament of Penance* (1597).

Buck, Sir George, *The Third Universitie of England: Or, A Treatise of the Foundations of all the Colledges, Auncient Schooles of Priviledge, and of Houses of Learning, and Liberall Arts, within and about . . . London* (1615).

Bullein, William, *A Dialogue bothe Pleasaunte and Pietifull* (1564).

Bullough, Geoffrey, ed., *Narrative and Dramatic Sources of Shakespeare*, 8 vols (London: Routledge, 1957–75).

Bulwer, John, *Chirologia: Or, The Natural Language of the Hand* (1644).

Burhill, Robert, *Pro Tortura Torti, contra Martinum Becanum Iesuitam* (1611).

Burhill, Robert, *Contra Martini Becani* (1613).

Burhill, Robert, *De Potestate Regia, et Vsurpatione Papali pro Tortura Torti* (1613).

Burton, Robert, *The Anatomy of Melancholy* (1621).

Burton, William, *A Caueat for Suerties: Two Sermons of Suertiship* (1593).

Buxtorf, Johann (the elder), *Synagoga Judaica* (1603).

Buxtorf, Johann (the elder), *The Jewish Synagogue: Or, An Historical Narration of the State of the Jewes at this Day Dispersed over the Face of the Whole Earth* (1657).

C., H., *Dialogue of Silvynne and Peregrynne* (MS 1599), in *CELT: Corpus of Electronic Texts*, <http://www.ucc.ie/celt/>.

Caesar, Philipp, *A General Discourse Against the Damnable Sect of Vsurers* (1578).

Calamy, Edmund, *A Practical Discourse Concerning Vows* (1697).

Calendar of State Papers, Ireland, 1509–1573, 1574–1585, 1603–1606, in *Calendar of State Papers Relating to Ireland [1509–1670]*, ed. Hans Claude Hamilton [et al.], electronic text (Burlington, Ontario: TannerRitchie, 2006–8).

Calvin, Jean, *The Institution of Christian Religion*, [tr. T.N.] (1561).

Calvin, Jean, *Sermons on Job*, tr. Arthur Golding (1574).

Calvin, Jean, *A Commentarie of Iohn Caluin, Vpon the First Booke of Moses Called Genesis*, tr. Thomas Tymme (1578).

Calvin, Jean, *The Sermons of M. Iohn Caluin vpon the Fifth Booke of Moses Called Deuteronomie*, tr. Arthur Golding (1583).

Calvin, Jean, *A Harmonie Vpon the Three Euangelists, Matthew, Mark and Luke with the Commentarie of M. Iohn Caluin*, tr. E.P. (1584).

Calvin, Jean, *Aphorismes of Christian Religion: Or, a Verie Compendious Abridgement of M. I. Calvins Institutions . . . by M. I. Piscator* (1596).

Calvin, Jean, *Commentaries on the Four Last Books of Moses, Arranged in the Form of a Harmony*, ed. and tr. Charles William Bingham, 4 vols (Edinburgh: Calvin Translation Society, 1852–5).

Camden, William, *Britain* (1610).

Carleton, George, *Tithes Examined and Proued to bee Due to the Clergie* (1606).

Carmichael, James, *Newes from Scotland* (1592).

Carter, John, *A Plaine and Compendious Exposition of Christs Sermon in the Mount* (1627).

The Casebooks Project, *A Digital Edition of Simon Forman and Richard Napier's Medical Records 1596–1634*, <http://www.magicandmedicine.hps.cam.ac.uk/>

Cervantes Saavedra, Miguel de, *The History of the Valorous and Wittie Knight-Errant, Don-Quixote of the Mancha*, tr. Thomas Shelton (1612).

Chaucer, Geoffrey, *Troilus and Criseyde*, in *The Riverside Chaucer*, 3rd edn, gen. ed. Larry D. Benson (New York: Houghton Mifflin, 1987).
Chertsey, Andrew, *The Ordynarye of Crystyanyte or of Crysten Men* (1502).
Church of England, *The Boke of Common Praier* (1552).
Church of England, *The Booke of Common Prayer, and Administracion of the Sacramentes, and Other Rites and Ceremonies* (1559).
Church of England, *The Forme and Maner of Making and Consecrating Bishops, Priests, and Deacons* (1596).
Churchyard, Thomas, *The Moste True Reporte of Iames Fitz Morrice Death* (1579).
Cicero, Marcus Tullius, *Marcus Tullius Ciceroes Thre Bokes of Duties*, tr. Nicholas Grimald (1556).
Cicero, Marcus Tullius, *The First Book of Tullies Offices Translated Grammatically* (1616).
Cicero, Marcus Tullius, *De Officiis*, ed. and tr. Walter Miller, Loeb Classical Library (London: Heinemann, 1913).
Cicero, Marcus Tullius, *Tusculan Disputations*, tr. J. E. King, Loeb Classical Library (London: Heinemann, 1927).
Cicero, Marcus Tullius, *Letters to Atticus*, tr. D. R. Shackleton Bailey, Loeb Classical Library, 4 vols (Cambridge, Mass.: Harvard University Press, 1999).
Cinthio (Giambattista Cinzio Giraldi), *Hecatommithi* (1565).
Cleland, James, *Heropaideia: Or, The Institution of a Young Noble Man* (1607).
Clowes, William, *A Right Frutefull and Approoued Treatise, for the Artificiall Cure of that Malady Called in Latin Struma, and in English, the Evill, Cured by Kinges and Queenes of England* (1602).
Coke, Sir Edward, *Quinta Pars Relationum Edwardi Coke Equitis Aurati . . . The Fift Part of the Reports of Sr. Edward Coke Knight* (1605).
Coke, Sir Edward, *The Third Part of the Institutes of the Laws of England* (1644).
Coke, Sir Edward, *The Reports of Sir Edward Coke* (1658).
Collins, Samuel, *Epphata* (1617).
Cook, James, *Iuridica Trium Quaestionum* (1608).
Cooper, Thomas, *Thesaurus Linguae Romanae et Britannicae* (1578).
Cooper, Thomas, *The Mystery of Witch-craft* (1617).
Copley, Anthony, *An Answer to a Letter of a Iesuited Gentleman* (1601).
Copley, Anthony, *Another Letter of Mr. A. C. to his Dis-Iesuited Kinseman* (1602).
Coppe, Abiezer, *A Second Fiery Flying Roule* (1649).
Cornwallis, Sir William, *Essayes* (1600–1).
Cosin, Richard, *Apologie for Svndrie Proceedings by Iurisdiction Ecclesiasticall* (1593).
Coton, Pierre, *The Hellish and Horribble Councell, Practised and Vsed by the Iesuites, (in their Priuate Consulations) When they Would Haue a Man to Murther a King* (1610).
Cotta, John, *The Triall of Witchcraft* (1616).
Cowell, John, *The Interpreter* (1607).
Coxe, Francis, *A Short Treatise Declaringe the Detestable Wickednesse, of Magicall Sciences as Necromancie, Coniurations of Spirites, Curiouse Astrologie and such Lyke* (1561).
Cranmer, Thomas, *Certayne Sermons, Or Homilies Appoynted by the Kynges Maiestie* (1547).

Cranmer, Thomas, *Miscellaneous Writings and Letters of Thomas Cranmer*, ed. John Edmund Cox, Parker Society 16 (Cambridge: Cambridge University Press, 1846).

Crompton, Richard, *The Mansion of Magnanimitie* (1599).

Dallington, Robert, *The View of Fraunce* (1604).

Daniel, Samuel, *Delia. Containing Certaine Sonnets: With the Complaynt of Rosamond* (1592).

Dante Alighieri, *La divina commedia*, ed. Giuseppe Vanelli, rev. edn (Milan: Hoepli, 1960).

Davies, Sir John, *Poems*, ed. Robert Krueger (Oxford: Clarendon Press, 1975).

Defoe, Daniel, *An Essay upon Projects* (1697).

De Granada, Luis, *The Sinners Guyde* (1598).

De Pontaymeri, Alexandre, *A Womans Woorth, Defended against All the Men in the World* (1599).

Derricke, John, *The Image of Irelande with a Discouerie of Woodkarne* (1581).

Despagne, John, *Anti-Duello: The Anatomie of Duells, with the Symptomes Thereof* (1632).

Donne, John, *Pseudo-martyr: Wherein out of Certaine Propositions and Gradations, this Conclusion is Euicted. That Those which are of the Romane Religion in this Kingdome, May and Ought to take the Oath of Allegiance* (1610).

Downame, John, *Four Treatises* (1608).

Dugdale, Sir William, *Origines Juridiciales* (1666).

Earle, John, *Micro-cosmographie: Or, A Peece of the World Discovered in Essayes and Characters* (1628).

The Eighth Liberal Science: Or, A New-Found-Art and Order of Drinking (1650).

Elizabeth I, *A Proclamation Conteyning her Maiesties Pleasure, How Those Shalbe Dealt Withall, Which Haue Falsly Slandered her Maiesties Proceedings and her Ministers* (1600).

Elyot, Sir Thomas, *The Boke Named the Gouernour* (1531).

Elyot, Sir Thomas, *The Dictionary* (1538).

Erasmus, Desiderius, *Adages I i 1 to I v 100*, ed. R. A. B. Mynors, tr. Margaret Mann Phillips, *Collected Works of Erasmus*, 89 vols (Toronto: University of Toronto Press, 1974–), XXXI.

Euripides, *Children of Heracles, Hippolytus, Andromache, Hecuba*, ed. and tr. David Kovacs, Loeb Classical Library (Cambridge, Mass.: Harvard University Press, 1995).

Euripides, *Trojan Women, Iphigeneia among the Taurians, Ion*, ed. and tr. David Kovacs, Loeb Classical Library (Cambridge, Mass.: Harvard University Press, 1999).

Fenton, Roger, *A Treatise of Vsurie* (1611).

Fitzsimon, Henry, *The Iustification and Exposition of the Diuine Sacrifice of the Masse* (1611).

Fletcher, Giles, *Of the Russe Common Wealth* (1591).

Flinton, George, *A Manual of Prayers*, rev. edn (1604).

Floyd, John, *The Picture of a Perfit Common Wealth* (1602).

Floyd, John, *God and the King: Or, A Dialogue Wherein is Treated of Allegiance due to our Most Gracious Lord, King Iames* (1620).

Foxe, John, *A Sermon Preached at the Christening of a Certaine Iew at London* (1578).

Foxe, John, *Actes and Monuments*, rev. edn (1583).

Fraunce, Abraham, *The Lawiers Logike* (1588).

Fulke, William, *A Briefe Confutation, of a Popish Discourse* (1583).

G., T., *The Rich Cabinet Furnished with Varietie of Excellent Discriptions, Exquisite Charracters, Witty Discourses, and Delightfull Histories* (1616).

Gardiner, Stephen, *De Vera Obedientia ... 1536 ... Translated into English* (1553).

Garnet, Richard (?), comp., *The Book of Oaths* (1649).

Garrard, William, *The Arte of Warre* (1591).

Gascoigne, George, *A Delicate Diet, for Daintiemouthde Droonkardes* (1576).

Gataker, Thomas, *A Iust Defence of Certaine Passages in a Former Treatise Concerning the Nature and Vse of Lots* (1623).

Gataker, Thomas, *Of the Nature and Vse of Lots: A Treatise Historicall and Theologicall* (1619).

Gearing, William, *A Bridle for the Tongue: Or, A Treatise of Ten Sins of the Tongue* (1663).

The Geneva Bible: A Facsimile of the 1560 Edition, introd. Lloyd E. Berry (Peabody, Mass.: Hendrickson, 2007).

Gentili, Alberico, *De Legationibus Libri Tres*, ed. and tr. Gordon J. Laing, 2 vols (New York: Oxford University Press, 1924).

Goodcole, Henry, *The Wonderfull Discouerie of Elizabeth Sawyer a Witch Late of Edmonton* (1621).

Goodwin, Thomas, *Christ Set Forth in his Death* (1642).

Goslicki, Wawrzyniec [Laurentius Grimaldius Goslicius], *The Counsellor* (1598).

Gouge, William, *Of Domesticall Duties* (1622).

Greene, Robert, *Pandosto: The Triumph of Time* (1588).

Greene, Robert (with Henry Chettle?), *Greenes, Groats-worth of Witte* (1592).

Grotius, Hugo, *Mare Liberum* (1609), ed. and tr. Ralph van Deman Magoffin as *The Freedom of the Seas* (New York: Carnegie Endowment, 1916).

H., I., *The Diuell of the Vault: Or, The Vnmasking of Murther* (1606).

Hake, Edward, *Newes out of Powles Churchyarde* (1579).

Hakluyt, Richard, *The Principal Nauigations*, 3 vols (1599–1600).

Hale, George, *The Priuate Schoole of Defence* (1614).

Hall, Edward, *The Union of the Two Noble and Illustre Famelies of Lancastre [and] Yorke* (1548).

Harington, Sir John, *Epigrams* (1616).

Harpsfield, Nicholas, *The Life and Death of Sir Thomas More, Knight*, in William Roper and Harpsfield, *Lives of Saint Thomas More*, ed. E. E. Reynolds (London: Dent, 1963), 51–175.

Harsnett, Samuel, *A Declaration of Egregious Popish Impostures* (1603).

Hayward, Sir John, *A Reporte of a Discourse Concerning Supreme Power in Affaires of Religion* (1606).

Heine, Heinrich, *Shakespeare's Maidens and Women*, in *The Works of Heinrich Heine*, ed. C. G. Leland et al., 12 vols (London: Heinemann, 1892–1905), I, 241–441.

Henry VIII, *A Necessary Doctrine and Erudition for any Christen Man* (1543).

Henry VIII, *Assertio Septem Sacramentorum: Or, Defence of the Seven Sacraments*, ed. Louis O'Donovan (New York: Benziger Brothers, 1908).

Henry, Matthew, *An Exposition of All the Books of the Old and New Testament*, 3rd edn, 6 vols (1721–5).

Henry, Matthew, *A Treatise on Baptism.... Abridged from the Original Manuscript, and Now First Published* (1783).

Henryson, Robert, *Testament of Cresseid*, in *The Workes of Geffrey Chaucer* (1532).

Henslowe, Philip, *Henslowe's Diary*, ed. R. A. Foakes and R. T. Rickert, 2nd edn (Cambridge: Cambridge University Press, 2002).

Herring, Francis, tr. and expanded by John Vicars, *Mischeefes Mysterie: Or, Treasons Master-peece* (1617).

His Maiesties Speach in this Last Session of Parliament... Together with a discourse of the maner of the discouery of this late intended treason, ioyned with the examination of some of the prisoners (1605).

Hitler, Adolf, *Mein Kampf*, tr. James Murphy, 2 vols in 1 (London: Hurst and Blackett, 1939).

Hobbes, Thomas, *Leviathan* (1651).

The Holie Bible: Faithfully Translated into English, Out of the Authentical Latin [Douai version] (1609–10).

Holinshed, Raphael, *The Third Volume of Chronicles* (1586).

Holinshed, Raphael, *Chronicles*, 6 vols (1587), at The Holinshed Project, <http://www.cems.ox.ac.uk/holinshed/>

Holland, Henry, *A Treatise Against Witchcraft* (1590).

Homer, *Seaven Bookes of the Iliades of Homere, Prince of Poets*, tr. George Chapman (1598).

Homer, *Odyssey*, tr. A. T. Murray, rev. George E. Dimock, Loeb Classical Library, 2 vols (Cambridge, Mass.: Harvard University Press, 1995).

Homer, *Iliad*, tr. A. T. Murray, rev. William F. Wyatt, Loeb Classical Library, 2 vols (Cambridge, Mass.: Harvard University Press, 1999).

Hooker, Richard, *Of the Lawes of Ecclesiastical Politie, Eight Bookes* (1611).

Hotman, Jean, *The Ambassador* (1603).

Hugget, Anthony, *A Diuine Enthymeme of True Obedience: Or, A Taske for a Christian. Preached at Pauls Crosse the Tenth of September, 1615* (1615).

Huloet, Richard, *Huloets Dictionarie Newelye Corrected* (1572).

The Institution of a Christen Man (1537).

James VI, *Daemonologie* (1597).

James VI, *The True Lawe of Free Monarchies: Or, The Reciprock and Mutuall Dutie Betwixt a Free King, and his Naturall Subiectes* (1598).

James VI, *Basilikon Doron* (1599).

James VI and I, *Basilikon Doron: Or, His Maiesties Instructions to his Dearest Sonne, Henry the Prince*, London edn (1603).

James VI and I, *Forasmuch as his Maiestie vnderstandeth, that there be diuers ancient and other good and necessary lawes and statutes of this his kingdome of England which do inflict...punishments...vpon such as vnlawfully hunt or enter into any forest* (16 May 1603).

James VI and I, *Triplici Nodo, Triplex Cuneus: An Apology for the Oath of Allegiance* (1607).

James VI and I, *An Apologie for the Oath of Allegiance... Together, with a Premonition of his Majesties to all Most Mightie Monarches, Kings, free Princes and States of Christendome* (1609).

James VI and I, with Pierre Du Moulin, *A Remonstrance of the Most Gratious King Iames I. King of Great Britaine, France, and Ireland, Defender of the Faith, &c.... Against an Oration of the Most Illustrious Card. of Perron* (1616).

Jewel, John, *The Second Tome of Homilees* (1571).

Johnson, Samuel, *Selections from Johnson on Shakespeare*, ed. Bertrand H. Bronson with Jean M. O'Meara (New Haven: Yale University Press, 1986).

Jones, Richard, *The Booke of Honor and Armes* (1590).

Jonson, Ben, *Hymenaei* (1606).

Josephus, Titus Flavius, *A Compendious and Most Marueilous History of the Latter Tymes of the Iewes Commune Weale*, tr. Peter Morwen (1558).

Josephus, Titus Flavius, *The Famous and Memorable Workes of Iosephus*, tr. Thomas Lodge (1602).

Kenyon, J. P., ed., *The Stuart Constitution 1603–1688*, 2nd edn (Cambridge: Cambridge University Press, 1986).

Kerrigan, John, ed., *Motives of Woe: Shakespeare and 'Female Complaint'. A Critical Anthology* (Oxford: Clarendon Press, 1991).

King, John, *A Sermon Preached in Oxon: the 5. of November. 1607* (1607).

Knight, Edward, *The Triall of Truth Wherein are Discouered Three Greate Enemies vnto Mankinde, as Pride, Priuate Grudge, and Priuate Gaine* (1580). Lactantius, *Divinarum Institutionum* (1541).

Lambarde, William, *Eirenarcha* (1579).

Lambarde, William, *Eirenarcha*, rev. edn (1599).

La Primaudaye, Pierre de, *The French Academie*, tr. T.B. (1586).

Lawes and Orders of Warre Established for the Good Conduct of the Seruice in Ireland (1599).

'Lazarus', *The Towneley Plays*, ed. Martin Stevens and A. C. Cawley, 2 vols (Oxford: Oxford University Press for the Early English Text Society, 1994), I, 425–31.

Lefevre, Raoul, *The Recuyell of the Historyes of Troye*, tr. William Caxton (*c.*1474).

Le Loyer, Pierre, *A Treatise of Specters or Straunge Sights* (1605).

Lipsius, Justus, *De Constantia Libri Duo* (1584).

Lipsius, Justus, *Sixe Bookes of Politickes or Ciuil Doctrine*, tr. William Jones (1594).

Lipsius, Justus, *Two Bookes of Constancie*, tr. John Stradling (1595).

Livy, *The Romane Historie*, tr. Philemon Holland (1600).

Livy, *Titi Livi ab Urbe Condita Libri*, Pt I, Bks I–X, ed. Wilhelm Weissenborn and H. J. Müller (Leipzig: Teubner, 1898).

Lodge, Thomas, *An Alarum against Vsurers* (1584).

Lodge, Thomas, *Wits Miserie, and the Worlds Madnesse Discouering the Deuils Incarnat of this Age* (1596).

Lucian, *Imagines* [*Essays in Portraiture*], in *Lucian*, Vol. IV, tr. A. M. Harmon, Loeb Classical Library (London: Heinemann, 1925).

Lupton, Thomas, *The Second Part and Knitting Vp of the Boke Entituled Too Good to Be True* (1581).

Luther, Martin, *De Captivitate Babylonica* (1520).

Luther, Martin, *De Votis Monasticis* (1521).

Luther, Martin, *The Babylonian Captivity of the Church* (1520), tr. A. T. W. Steinhäuser, rev. Frederick C. Ahrens and Abdel Ross Wentz, in *Luther's Works*, Vol. XXVI, ed. Wentz (Philadelphia: Muhlenberg Press, 1959), 11–126.

Luther, Martin, *Trade and Usury* (1524), in *Luther's Works*, Vol. XLV, ed. Walther I. Brandt (Philadelphia: Mulhenberg Press, 1962), 245–310.

Luther, Martin, *On the Jews and their Lies*, in *Luther's Works*, Vol. XLVII, ed. Franklin Sherman (Philadelphia: Fortress Press, 1971), 137–306.

Lydgate, John, *The Hystorye Sege and Dystruccyon of Troye* (1513).

Mabb, John, *The Afflicted Mans Vow* (1609).

Machiavelli, Niccolò, *Il principe* (1532).

Machiavelli, Niccolò, *Discourses upon the First Decade of T. Livius*, tr. E. D. (1636).

Magnus, Olaus, *Historia de Gentibus Septentrionalibus* (1555).

Malynes, Gerard, *Consuetudo, vel Lex Mercatoria: Or, The Ancient Law-Merchant* (1622).

Martial, *Epigrams*, tr. D. R. Shackleton Bailey, Loeb Classical Library, 3 vols (Cambridge, Mass.: Harvard University Press, 1993).

Menewe, Gracious, *A Plaine Subuersyon or Turnyng Vp Syde Down of All the Argumentes, that the Popecatholykes Can Make for the Maintenaunce of Auricular Confession* (1555).

Meres, Francis, *Palladis Tamia* (1598).

Metz, G. Harold, ed., *Sources of Four Plays Ascribed to Shakespeare* (Columbia, Mo.: University of Missouri Press, 1989).

Milton, John, 'The Verse', *Paradise Lost*, 2nd edn (1674).

Milton, John, *Latin Writings: A Selection*, ed. and tr. John K. Hale (Assen: Van Gorcum, 1998).

Milward, John, *Iacobs Great Day of Trouble, and Deliuerance: A Sermon Preached at Pauls Crosse, the Fifth of August 1607* (1610).

Mocket, Richard, *God and the King* (1615).

Modena, Leone Da, *The History of the Rites, Customes, and Manner of Life, of the Present Jews, throughout the World* (1637; 1650).

Modena, Leone Da, *The Autobiography of a Seventeenth-Century Rabbi: Leon Modena's 'Life of Judah'*, tr. and ed. Mark R. Cohen (Princeton: Princeton University Press, 1988).

Montaigne, Michel de, *The Essayes: Or, Morall, Politike and Millitarie Discourses*, tr. John Florio (1603).

Montaigne, Michel de, *Essays*, tr. John Florio (1613).

More, Thomas, *The Correspondence of Sir Thomas More*, ed. Elizabeth Frances Rogers (Princeton: Princeton University Press, 1947).

More, Thomas, *Yale Edition of the Complete Works of St Thomas More*, 15 vols (New Haven: Yale University Press, 1963–97).

Morice, James, *A Briefe Treatise of Oathes Exacted by Ordinaries and Ecclesiasticall Iudges* (1590).

Morton, Thomas, *An Exact Discoverie of Romish Doctrine in the Case of Conspiracie and Rebellion* (1605).

Morton, Thomas, *A Full Satisfaction Concerning a Double Romish Iniquitie; Hainous Rebellion, and More then Heathenish Aequiuocation* (1606).

Morton, Thomas, *The Encounter against M. Parsons* (1610).

Mosse, Miles, *The Arraignment and Conuiction of Vsurie* (1595).

A Myrrour for English Souldiers (1595).

Nashe, Thomas, *The Works of Thomas Nashe*, ed. Ronald B. McKerrow, 5 vols, rev. F. P. Wilson (Oxford: Blackwell, 1958).

A New Song, Shewing the Crueltie of Gernutus a Iew, who Lending to a Marchant a Hundred Crownes, Would Haue a Pound of his Flesh (*c.*1620), in the English Broadside Ballad Archive at <http://ebba.english.ucsb.edu/ballad/20063/image>

Norden, John, *The Mirror of Honor* (1597).

Oglander, Sir John, *A Royalist's Notebook: The Commonplace Book of Sir John Oglander* (London: Constable, 1936).

Oldcastle, Hugh, augmented by John Mellis, *Briefe Instruction and Maner how to Keepe Bookes of Accompts* (1588).

Overbury, Thomas, *Sir Thomas Ouerburie his Wife with New Elegies... Whereunto are Annexed, New Newes and Characters* (1616).

Ovid, *Metamorphoses*, ed. and tr. Frank Justus Miller, rev. P. G. Gould, Loeb Classical Library, 2 vols (Cambridge, Mass.: Harvard University Press, 1977–84).

Owen, John, *A Continuation of the Exposition of the Epistle of Paul the Apostle to the Hebrews* (1680).

P., A., *Natural and Morall Questions and Answeres* (1598).

P., T., *Of the Knowledge and Conducte of Warres* (1578).

Painter, William, *The Palace of Pleasure* (1566).

Parsons, Robert, *The First Booke of the Christian Exercise Appertayning to Resolution* (1582).

Parsons, Robert, *A Christian Directorie Guiding Men to their Saluation* (1585).

Parsons, Robert, *The Seconde Parte of the Booke of Christian Exercise* (1590).

Parsons, Robert [as R. Doleman], *A Conference about the Next Succession to the Crowne of Ingland* (1595).

Parsons, Robert, *The Iudgment of a Catholicke English-man... Concerninge a Late Booke set Forth, and Entituled; Triplici Nodo, Triplex Cuneus, or, An Apologie for the Oath of Allegiance* (1608).

Parsons, Robert, *A Quiet and Sober Reckoning* (1609).

Parsons, Robert, *A Treatise Tending to Mitigation Towardes Catholike-subiectes in England* (1607).

Peacham, Henry, *The Garden of Eloquence*, rev. edn (1593).
Peacham, Henry, *The Compleat Gentleman* (1622).
Perkins, William, *A Direction for the Government of the Tongue according to Gods Word* (1593).
Perkins, William, *A Discourse of Conscience* (1596).
Perkins, William, *The Whole Treatise of the Cases of Conscience* (1606).
Perkins, William, *A Discourse of the Damned Art of Witchcraft* (1608).
Perkins, William, *A Godly and Learned Exposition of Christs Sermon in the Mount* (1608).
Phillips, Edward, *New World of English Words* (1658).
A Plaine Description of the Auncient Petigree of Dame Slaunder (1573).
Plutarch, *The Lives of the Noble Grecians and Romanes*, tr. Thomas North (1579).
Plutarch, *The Philosophie, Commonlie Called, the Morals Written by the Learned Philosopher Plutarch of Chaeronea*, tr. Philemon Holland (1603).
Plutarch, *Plutarch's Lives*, tr. Bernadotte Perrin, Loeb Classical Library, 11 vols (London: Heinemann, 1914–26).
Powell, Thomas, *The Art of Thriving: Or, The Plaine Path-way to Preferment. Together with The Mysterie and Misery of Lending and Borrowing* (1636).
Preston, Thomas, *A Theologicall Disputation Concerning the Oath of Allegiance Dedicated to the Most Holy Father Pope Paul the Fifth* (1613).
Preston, Thomas, *A Cleare, Sincere, and Modest Confutation of the Vnsound, Fraudulent, and Intemperate Reply of T.F. who is Knowne to be Mr. Thomas Fitzherbert now an English Iesuite* (1616).
Preston, Thomas, *Roger Widdringtons Last Reioynder to Mr. Thomas Fitz-Herberts Reply Concerning the Oath of Allegiance, and the Popes Power to Depose Princes* (1619).
Prothero, G.W., *Select Statutes and Constitutional Documents Illustrative of the Reigns of Elizabeth and James I* (Oxford: Clarendon Press, 1913).
Prynne, William, *Histrio-Mastix: The Players Scourge, or, Actors Tragaedie* (1633).
Prynne, William, *The Case of the Jewes Stated: Or, The Jewes Synagogue Opened* (1656).
Pulton, Ferdinando, *De Pace Regis et Regni* (1609).
Purchas, Samuel, *Purchas his Pilgrimage: Or, Relations of the World and the Religions Obserued in All Ages and Places Discouered, from the Creation vnto this Present* (1613).
Puttenham, George, *The Arte of English Poesie* (1589).
Quintilian, *Institutio Oratoria*, ed. and tr. Harold Edgeworth Butler, Loeb Classical Library, 4 vols (London: Heinemann, 1920–1).
'The Raising of Lazarus', *The N-Town Play: Cotton MS Vespasian D.8*, ed. Stephen Spector, 2 vols (Oxford: Oxford University Press for the Early English Text Society, 1991), I, 230–45.
Rhodes, P. J., and Robin Osborne, eds, *Greek Historical Inscriptions: 404–323 BC* (Oxford: Oxford University Press, 2003).
Rich, Barnabe, *A Path-Way to Military Practise* (1587).
Rich, Barnabe, *A New Description of Ireland* (1610).
Rich, Barnabe, *A Catholicke Conference* (1612).
Rich, Barnabe, *A True and a Kinde Excuse* (1612).

Ross, Alexander, *Pansebeia: Or, A View of All Religions in the World with the Severall Church-governments from the Creation, to These Times* (1655).

Rowlands, Samuel, *Looke to It: For, Ile Stabbe Ye* (1604).

S., E., *The Discoverie of the Knights of the Poste* (1597).

Salisbury, Robert Cecil, Earl of, *An Answere to Certaine Scandalous Papers, Scattered Abroad vnder Colour of a Catholicke Admonition* (1606).

Samuel, Marochitanus, *The Blessed Jew of Marocco: Or, A Blackmoor Made Whit*, tr. Thomas Calvert (1648).

Sanderson, Robert, *De Juramento: Seven Lectures Concerning the Obligation of Promissory Oathes* (1655).

Sandys, George, *A Relation of the State of Religion* (1605).

Sandys, George, *A Relation of a Iourney begun An Dom: 1610* (1615).

Saviolo, Vincentio, *Vincentio Saviolo his Practise* (1595).

Scot, Reginald, *The Discouerie of Witchcraft* (1584).

Scot, Reginald, *The Discovery of Witchcraft*, enlarged edn (1665).

Segar, William, *Honor Military, and Ciuill* (1602).

Selden, John, *The Duello: Or, Single Combat* (1610).

Selden, John, *John Selden on Jewish Marriage Law: The Uxor Hebraica*, tr. with commentary by Jonathan Ziskind (Leiden: Brill, 1991).

Seneca, Lucius Annaeus, *The Sixt Tragedie of the Most Graue and Prudent Author Lucius, Anneus, Seneca, Entituled Troas with Diuers and Sundrye Addicions to the Same*, tr. Jasper Heywood (1559).

Seneca, Lucius Annaeus, *The Seconde Tragedie of Seneca Entituled Thyestes*, tr. Jasper Heywood (1560).

Seneca, Lucius Annaeus, *The Woorke of the Excellent Philosopher Lucius Annaeus Seneca Concerning Benefyting*, tr. Arthur Golding (1578).

Seneca, Lucius Annaeus, *Tragedies*, ed. and tr. Frank Justus Miller, 2 vols, Loeb Classical Library (London: Heinemann, 1917).

Seneca, Lucius Annaeus, *De Beneficiis*, in Seneca, *Moral Essays*, tr. John W. Basore, Loeb Classical Library, 3 vols (London: Heinemann, 1928–35), III.

Seneca, Lucius Annaeus, *Thyestes*, ed. R. J. Tarrant (Atlanta: Scholars Press, 1985).

Shakespeare, William, *The Sonnets and A Lover's Complaint*, ed. John Kerrigan (Harmondsworth: Penguin, 1986).

Sidney, Sir Henry, *A Viceroy's Vindication? Sir Henry Sidney's Memoir of Service in Ireland 1556–1578*, ed. Ciaran Brady (Cork: Cork University Press, 2002).

Sidney, Sir Philip, *Astrophel and Stella* (1591).

Simms, Katherine, Bardic Poetry Database, School of Advanced Studies Dublin, <http://bardic.celt.dias.ie/main.html>

Smith, Henry, *The Examination of Vsury, in Two Sermons* (1591).

Smythe, Sir John, *Certen Instructions, Observations and Orders Militarie* (1594).

Spenser, Edmund, *A View of the Present State of Ireland*, ed. W. L. Renwick (Oxford: Clarendon Press, 1970).

Stapleton, Thomas, *Tres Thomae:...D. Thomae Mori Angliae quondam Cancellarii Vita* (1588).

Starkey, Thomas, *A Preface to the Kynges Hyghnes* (1536).

Stubbes, Phillip, *Anatomie of Abuses* (1583).

Suárez, Francisco, *Defensio Fidei Catholicae*, in *Selections from Three Works of Francisco Suárez, S.J.*, 2 vols (Oxford: Clarendon Press, 1944), II (tr. Gwladys L. Williams et al.).

Swinburne, Henry, *A Treatise of Spousals, or Matrimonial Contracts* (1686).

Taylor, Jeremy, *Ductor Dubitantium: Or, The Rule of Conscience in All her Generall Measures*, 2 vols (1660).

Taylor, John, 'To my Approued Good Friend M. Thomas Heywood', in Thomas Heywood, *Apology for Actors* (1612).

Tofte, Robert, *Alba* (1598).

Tooker, William, *Duellum siue Singulare Certamen cum Martino Becano Iesuita* (1611).

Tootell, Hugh, *Dodd's Church History of England from the Commencement of the Sixteenth Century to the Revolution in 1688*, ed. M. A. Tierney, 5 vols (London: Charles Dolman, 1839–43).

Totaro, Rebecca, ed., *The Plague in Print: Essential Elizabethan Sources, 1558–1603* (Pittsburgh: Duquesne University Press, 2010).

A True and Perfect Relation of the Whole Proceedings Against the Late Most Barbarous Traitors, Garnet a Iesuite, and his Confederats (1606).

Tunstall, Cuthbert, *A Sermon of Cuthbert Bysshop of Duresme made vpon Palme Sondaye Laste Past, before the Maiestie of our Souerayne Lorde Kyng Henry the VIII. . . . in Erth Next vnder Christ Supreme Heed of the Churche of Englande* (1539).

Tyndale, William, *The Obedience of a Christen Man* (1528).

Tyndale, William, *The Exposition of the Fyrste Epistle of Seynt Jhon with a Prologge before It* (1531).

Vaughan, William, *The Golden-groue Moralized in Three Bookes* (1600).

Vaughan, William, *The Spirit of Detraction, Coniured and Convicted* (1611).

Vaughan, William, *The Arraignment of Slander Periury Blasphemy, and Other Malicious Sinnes* (1630).

Vermigli, Peter Martyr, *The Common Places*, tr. Anthonie Marten (1583).

Virgil, *The Whole XII Bookes of the Aeneidos of Virgill*, tr. Thomas Phaer and Thomas Twyne (1573).

Virgil, *Eclogues, Georgics, Aeneid I–VI*, tr. H. Rushton Fairclough, rev. G. P. Goold, Loeb Classical Library (Cambridge, Mass.: Harvard University Press, 1999).

Virgil, *Aeneid VII–XII, Appendix Vergiliana*, tr. H. Rushton Fairclough, rev. G. P. Goold, Loeb Classical Library (Cambridge, Mass.: Harvard University Press, 2000).

W., W., *A True and Iust Recorde, of the Information, Examination and Confession of all the Witches, Taken at S. Ofes in the Countie of Essex* (1582).

West, William, *Symboleography* (1590).

White, Christopher, *Of Oathes: Their Obiect, Forme, and Bond* (1627).

Wilkes, William, *Obedience: Or, Ecclesiastical Union* (1605).

Wilkinson, Henry, *The Debt Book: Or, A Treatise Vpon Romans 13. ver. 8* (1625).

Willet, Andrew, *An Harmonie Vpon the First Booke of Samuel* (1607).

Williams, Sir Roger, *Briefe Discourse of Warre* (1590).

Wilson, Thomas, *The Rule of Reason* (1551).

Wilson, Thomas, *The Arte of Rhetorique* (1553).
Wilson, Thomas, *A Discourse Vppon Vsurye by Waye of Dialogue and Oracion* (1572).
Wither, George, *A Collection of Emblemes, Ancient and Moderne* (1635).
Wright, Thomas, *The Passions of the Minde in Generall* (1604).

SELECT LIST OF SECONDARY SOURCES

Adelman, Janet, *Blood Relations: Christian and Jew in 'The Merchant of Venice'* (Chicago: University of Chicago Press, 2008).
Agamben, Giorgio, *The Sacrament of Language: An Archaeology of the Oath ('Homo Sacer' II, 3)*, tr. Adam Kotsko (Cambridge: Polity, 2010).
Altman, Joel B., *The Tudor Play of Mind: Rhetorical Enquiry and the Development of Elizabethan Drama* (Berkeley: University of California Press, 1978).
Anderson, Thomas P., '"What is Written Shall be Executed": "Nude Contracts" and "Lively Warrants" in *Titus Andronicus*', *Criticism*, 45 (2003), 301–21.
Atiyah, P. S., *Promises, Morals, and Law* (Oxford: Clarendon Press, 1981).
Atwood, Margaret, *Payback: Debt and the Shadow Side of Wealth* (London: Bloomsbury, 2008).
Austin, J. L., *How to Do Things with Words* [1962], 2nd edn, ed. J. O. Urmson and Marina Sbisà (Oxford: Oxford University Press, 1975).
Bailey, Amanda, *Of Bondage: Debt, Property, and Personhood in Early Modern England* (Philadelphia: University of Pennsylvania Press, 2013).
Baker, J. H., 'New Light on *Slade's Case*', Pts 1 and 2, *Cambridge Law Journal*, 29 (1971), 51–67, 213–36.
Baker, J. H., *An Introduction to English Legal History*, 4th edn (London: Butterworths, 2002).
Barton, Anne, 'Livy, Machiavelli, and Shakespeare's *Coriolanus*', *Shakespeare Survey*, 38 (1985), 115–29.
Barton, Anne, '"Wrying but a Little": Marriage, Law and Sexuality in the Plays of Shakespeare', in her *Essays, Mainly Shakespearean* (Cambridge: Cambridge University Press, 1994), 3–30.
Beckwith, Sarah, *Shakespeare and the Grammar of Forgiveness* (Ithaca, NY: Cornell University Press, 2011).
Ben-Amos, Ilana Krausman, *The Culture of Giving: Informal Support and Gift-Exchange in Early Modern England* (Cambridge: Cambridge University Press, 2008).
Berry, Philippa, *Shakespeare's Feminine Endings: Disfiguring Death in the Tragedies* (London: Routledge, 1999).
Bertolet, Anna Riehl, 'The Tsar and the Queen: "You Speak a Language that I Understand Not"', in Charles Beem, ed., *The Foreign Relations of Elizabeth I* (Basingstoke: Palgrave, 2011), 101–23.
Billacois, François, *The Duel: Its Rise and Fall in Early Modern France*, ed. and tr. Trista Selous (New Haven: Yale University Press, 1990).
Bloom, Gina, *Voice in Motion: Staging Gender, Shaping Sound in Early Modern England* (Philadelphia: University of Pennsylvania Press, 2007).

Bloom, Gina, 'Manly Drunkenness: Binge Drinking as Disciplined Play', in Amanda Bailey and Roze Hentschell, *Masculinity and the Metropolis of Vice, 1550–1650* (Basingstoke: Palgrave, 2010), 21–44.

Boas, Frederick S., *University Drama in the Tudor Age* (Oxford: Clarendon Press, 1914).

Boreau, Alain, *Le Désir dicté: Histoire du vœu religieux dans l'Occident médiéval* (Paris: Les Belles Lettres, 2014).

Bourdieu, Pierre, *Outline of a Theory of Practice*, tr. Richard Nice (Cambridge: Cambridge University Press, 1977).

Braden, Gordon, *Renaissance Tragedy and the Senecan Tradition: Anger's Privilege* (New Haven: Yale University Press, 1985).

Bradshaw, Graham, *Shakespeare's Scepticism* (Brighton: Harvester, 1987).

Bratman, Michael E., *Intention, Plans, and Practical Reason* (Cambridge, Mass.: Harvard University Press, 1987).

Bratman, Michael E., *Faces of Intention: Selected Essays on Intention and Agency* (Cambridge: Cambridge University Press, 1999).

Bulman, James C., Jr, 'Shakespeare's Use of the "Timon" Comedy', *Shakespeare Survey*, 29 (1976), 103–16.

Burgess, Glenn, 'Usurpation, Obligation and Obedience in the Thought of the Engagement Controversy', *Historical Journal*, 29 (1986), 515–36.

Burkert, Walter, *Homo Necans: The Anthropology of Ancient Greek Sacrificial Ritual and Myth*, tr. Peter Bing (Berkeley: University of California Press, 1983).

Burrow, Colin, *Shakespeare and Classical Antiquity* (Oxford: Oxford University Press, 2013).

Butler, Judith, *Excitable Speech: A Politics of the Performative* (New York: Routledge, 1997).

Cabantous, Alain, *Blasphemy: Impious Speech in the West from the Seventeenth to the Nineteenth Century*, tr. Eric Rauth (New York: Columbia University Press, 2002).

Capp, Bernard, *When Gossips Meet: Women, Family, and Neighbourhood in Early Modern England* (Oxford: Oxford University Press, 2003).

Cercignani, Fausto, *Shakespeare's Works and Elizabethan Pronunciation* (Oxford: Clarendon Press, 1981).

Cervone, Thea, *Sworn Bond in Tudor England: Oaths, Vows and Covenants in Civil Life and Literature* (Jefferson, NC: McFarland, 2011).

Clark, Herbert H., *Using Language* (Cambridge: Cambridge University Press, 1996).

Clark, Jonathan, 'Religion and Political Identity: Samuel Johnson as a Nonjuror', in Jonathan Clark and Howard Erskine-Hill, eds, *Samuel Johnson in Historical Context* (London: Palgrave, 2002), 79–145.

Cohn, Albert, *Shakespeare in Germany in the Sixteenth and Seventeenth Centuries* (London: Asher and Co., 1865).

Colclough, David, *Freedom of Speech in Early Modern England* (Cambridge: Cambridge University Press, 2005).

Colclough, David, 'Talking to the Animals: Persuasion, Counsel and their Discontents in *Julius Caesar*', in David Armitage, Conal Condren, and Andrew Fitzmaurice, eds, *Shakespeare and Early Modern Political Thought* (Cambridge: Cambridge University Press, 2009), 217–33.

Coleridge, S. T., *Shakespearean Criticism*, ed. Thomas Middleton Raysor, 2nd edn, 2 vols (London: Everyman, 1960).

Condren, Conal, *Argument and Authority in Early Modern England: The Presupposition of Oaths and Offices* (Cambridge: Cambridge University Press, 2006).

Condren, Conal, 'Understanding Shakespeare's Perfect Prince: Henry V, the Ethics of Office and the French Prisoners', *Shakespearean International Yearbook*, 9 (2009), 195–213.

Cook, Ann Jennalie, *Making a Match: Courtship in Shakespeare and his Society* (Princeton: Princeton University Press, 1991).

Cramer, Peter, *Baptism and Change in the Early Middle Ages* (Cambridge: Cambridge University Press, 1993).

Cressy, David, 'Binding the Nation: The Bonds of Association, 1584 and 1696', in DeLloyd J. Guth and John W. McKenna, eds, *Tudor Rule and Revolution* (Cambridge: Cambridge University Press, 1982), 217–34.

Cressy, David, *Treasonable Speech in Pre-Modern England* (Oxford: Oxford University Press, 2010).

Crook, J. A., *Law and Life of Rome* (London: Thames and Hudson, 1967).

Cummings, Brian, *Mortal Thoughts: Religion, Secularity, and Identity in Shakespeare and Early Modern Culture* (Oxford: Oxford University Press, 2013).

Dash, Irene G., *Wooing, Wedding, and Power: Women in Shakespeare's Plays* (New York: Columbia University Press, 1981).

Davy, Georges, *La Foi jurée: Étude sociologique du problème du contrat, la formation du lien contractuel* (Paris: Alcan, 1922).

Derrida, Jacques, *Limited Inc* (Evanston, Ill.: Northwestern University Press, 1988).

Derrida, Jacques, *Given Time. 1, Counterfeit Money*, tr. Peggy Kamuf (Chicago: Chicago University Press, 1992).

Derrida, Jacques, *The Politics of Friendship*, tr. George Collins (London: Verso, 1997).

Derrida, Jacques, 'What is a "Relevant" Translation?', *Critical Inquiry*, 27 (Winter 2001), 174–200.

Deutsch, Yaacov, *Judaism in Christian Eyes: Early Modern Description of Jews and Judaism* (New York: Oxford University Press, 2012).

Devereux, Walter Bourchier, *Lives and Letters of the Devereux, Earls of Essex . . . 1540–1646*, 2 vols (London: John Murray, 1853).

Dobson, E. J., *English Pronunciation 1500–1700*, 2nd edn (Oxford: Clarendon Press, 1968).

Donaldson, Ian, *Ben Jonson: A Life* (Oxford: Oxford University Press, 2011).

Duffy, Eamon, *The Stripping of the Altars: Traditional Religion in England 1400–1580*, 2nd edn (New Haven: Yale University Press, 2005).

Dunn, E. Catherine, *The Concept of Ingratitude in Renaissance English Moral Philosophy* (Washington, DC: Catholic University of America Press, 1946).

Eden, Kathy, *Poetic and Legal Fiction in the Aristotelian Tradition* (Princeton: Princeton University Press, 1986).

Ellis, Herbert Alexander, *Shakespeare's Lusty Punning in 'Love's Labour's Lost': With Contemporary Analogues* (The Hague: Mouton, 1973).

Études épistémè, 24 (2013), *Aspects du serment en Angleterre (XVIe–XVIIIe siècles)*.

Fish, Stanley, 'How to Do Things with Austin and Searle: Speech-Act Theory and Literary Criticism', in his *Is there a Text in This Class?* (Cambridge, Mass.: Harvard University Press, 1980), 197–245.

Fletcher, Angus, *Time, Space, and Motion in the Age of Shakespeare* (Cambridge, Mass.: Harvard University Press, 2007).

Fletcher, Judith, *Performing Oaths in Classical Greek Drama* (Cambridge: Cambridge University Press, 2012).

Fontaine, Laurence, *The Moral Economy: Poverty, Credit, and Trust in Early Modern Europe* (New York: Cambridge University Press, 2014).

Freud, Sigmund, *The Standard Edition of the Complete Psychological Works of Sigmund Freud*, ed. James Strachey et al., 24 vols (London: Hogarth Press, 1953–74).

Friedman, Michael D., with Alan Dessen, *Titus Andronicus*, Shakespeare in Performance, 2nd edn (Manchester: Manchester University Press, 2013).

Frye, Northrop, 'Charms and Riddles', in his *Spiritus Mundi: Essays on Literature, Myth, and Society* (Bloomington, Ind.: Indiana University Press, 1976), 123–47.

Gazzard, Hugh, 'An Act to Restrain Abuses of Players (1606)', *Review of English Studies*, 61 (2010), 495–528.

Gershon, Stuart Weinberg, *Kol Nidrei: Its Origin, Development, and Significance* (Northvale, NJ: Aronson, 1994).

Gilman, Ernest B., *Plague Writing in Early Modern England* (Chicago: University of Chicago Press, 2009).

Glennie, Paul, and Nigel Thrift, *Shaping the Day: A History of Timekeeping in England and Wales 1300–1800* (Oxford: Oxford University Press, 2009).

Goldman, Michael, *Acting and Action in Shakespearean Tragedy* (Princeton: Princeton University Press, 1985).

Gordon, Michael, 'The Invention of a Common Law Crime: Perjury and the Elizabethan Courts', *American Journal of Legal History*, 24 (1980), 145–70.

Gordon, Michael, 'The Perjury Statute of 1563: A Case History of Confusion', *Proceedings of the American Philosophical Society*, 124 (1980), 438–54.

Gowing, Laura, *Domestic Dangers: Women, Words, and Sex in Early Modern London* (Oxford: Clarendon Press, 1998).

Gray, Jonathan Michael, *Oaths and the English Reformation* (Cambridge: Cambridge University Press, 2013).

Greaves, Richard L., 'Concepts of Political Obedience in Late Tudor England: Conflicting Perspectives', *Journal of British Studies*, 22 (1982), 23–34.

Green, A. Wigfall, *The Inns of Court and Early English Drama* (New Haven: Yale University Press, 1931).

Green, Richard Firth, *A Crisis of Truth: Literature and Law in Ricardian England* (Philadelphia: University of Pennsylvania Press, 1999).

Griffiths, Paul, *Youth and Authority: Formative Experiences in England 1560–1640* (Oxford: Clarendon Press, 1996).

Gross, John, *Shylock: A Legend and its Legacy* (1992; New York: Touchstone, 1994).

Gross, Kenneth, *Shakespeare's Noise* (Chicago: Chicago University Press, 2001).

Gurr, Andrew, *The Shakespearean Stage, 1574–1642*, 4th edn (Cambridge: Cambridge University Press, 2009).

Gurr, Andrew, 'Stephano's Leather Bottle', *Notes and Queries*, 59:4 (2012), 549–50.

Guy, John, 'The Rhetoric of Counsel in Early Modern England', in Dale Hoak, ed., *Tudor Political Culture* (Cambridge: Cambridge University Press, 1995), 292–310.

Hare, R. M., 'The Promising Game', *Revue internationale de philosophie*, 70 (1964), 398–412, rpt in Philippa Foot, ed., *Theories of Ethics* (Oxford: Oxford University Press, 1967), 115–27.

Hasan-Rokem, Galit, and David Shulman, eds, *Untying the Knot: On Riddles and Other Enigmatic Modes* (New York: Oxford University Press, 1996).

Hawkes, David, *The Culture of Usury in Renaissance England* (Basingstoke: Palgrave Macmillan, 2010).

Hazlitt, William, *Characters of Shakespear's Plays* (London: R. Hunter, 1817).

Heal, Felicity, *The Power of Gifts: Gift-Exchange in Early Modern England* (Oxford: Oxford University Press, 2014).

Hecht, Anthony, '*The Merchant of Venice*: A Venture in Hermeneutics', in his *Obbligati: Essays in Criticism* (New York: Athenaeum, 1986), 140–229.

Helmholz, R. H., 'Assumpsit and *Fidei Laesio*', *Law Quarterly Review*, 91 (1975), 406–32.

Helmholz, R. H., *The Oxford History of the Laws of England*, Vol. I, *The Canon Law and Ecclesiastical Jurisdiction from 597 to the 1640s* (Oxford: Oxford University Press, 2004).

Hexter, Ralph, *Equivocal Oaths and Ordeals in Medieval Literature* (Cambridge, Mass.: Harvard University Press, 1975).

Hill, Christoper, *Society and Puritanism in Pre-Revolutionary England* (London: Secker and Warburg, 1964).

Holmberg, Eva Johanna, *Jews in the Early Modern English Imagination: A Scattered Nation* (Farnham: Ashgate, 2011).

Holmer, Joan Ozark, *'The Merchant of Venice': Choice, Hazard and Consequence* (Basingstoke: Macmillan, 1995).

Honan, Park, *Shakespeare: A Life* (Oxford: Oxford University Press, 1998).

Houlbrooke, Ralph, *Church Courts, Sex and Marriage in England, 1570–1640* (Cambridge: Cambridge University Press, 1987).

Howard, Jean E., *Theater of a City: The Places of London Comedy, 1598–1642* (Philadelphia: University of Pennsylvania Press, 2007).

Hubbard, Eleanor, *City Women: Money, Sex, and the Social Order in Early Modern London* (Oxford: Oxford University Press, 2012).

Hudson, Judith, 'Punishing Perjury in *Love's Labour's Lost*', in Adrian Streete, ed., *Early Modern Drama and the Bible: Contexts and Readings, 1570–1625* (Basingstoke: Palgrave, 2012), 118–35.

Huizinga, Johan, *Homo Ludens: A Study of the Play-Element in Culture* (London: Routledge, 1949).

Hutson, Lorna, *The Usurer's Daughter: Male Friendship and Fictions of Women in Sixteenth-Century England* (London: Routledge, 1994).

Hutson, Lorna, *The Invention of Suspicion: Law and Mimesis in Shakespeare and Renaissance Drama* (Oxford: Oxford University Press, 2007).

Hyde, Lewis, *The Gift: How the Creative Spirit Transforms the World* (1979; Edinburgh: Canongate, 2007).

Ibbetson, David, 'Sixteenth Century Contract Law: *Slade's Case* in Context', *Oxford Journal of Legal Studies*, 4 (1985), 295–317.

Ibbetson, David, 'Early Modern Lawyers and Literary Texts', unpublished inaugural lecture, Centre for Mediaeval and Early Modern Law and Literature', University of St Andrews, 3 October 2012.

Ingram, Martin, *Church Courts, Sex and Marriage in England, 1570–1640* (Cambridge: Cambridge University Press, 1987).

Ingram, Martin, 'Reformation of Manners in Early Modern England', in Paul Griffiths, Adam Fox, and Steve Hindle, eds, *The Experience of Authority in Early Modern England* (Basingstoke: Macmillan, 1996), 47–88.

Ingram, Martin, 'Law, Litigants and the Construction of "Honour": Slander Suits in Early Modern England', in Peter Coss, ed., *The Moral World of the Law* (Cambridge: Cambridge University Press, 2000), 134–60.

James, Heather, *Shakespeare's Troy: Drama, Politics, and the Translation of Empire* (Cambridge: Cambridge University Press, 1997).

James, Mervyn, 'English Politics and the Concept of Honour, 1485–1642', rpt in his *Society, Politics and Culture: Studies in Early Modern England* (Cambridge: Cambridge University Press, 1986), 308–415.

Jeanes, Gordon P., *Signs of God's Promise: Thomas Cranmer's Sacramental Theology and the Book of Common Prayer* (London: Continuum, 2008).

Jenner, Mark, 'London', in Joad Raymond, ed., *The History of Popular Print Culture*, Vol. I, *Cheap Print in Britain and Ireland to 1660* (Oxford: Oxford University Press, 2011), 294–307.

Jones, David Martin, *Conscience and Allegiance in Seventeenth Century England: The Political Significance of Oaths and Engagements* (Rochester, NY: University of Rochester Press, 1999).

Jones, Norman, *God and the Money Lenders: Usury and the Law in Early Modern England* (Oxford: Blackwell, 1989).

Kahn, Victoria, *Wayward Contracts: The Crisis of Political Obligation in England, 1640–1674* (Princeton: Princeton University Press, 2004).

Kaplan, M. Lindsay, *The Culture of Slander in Early Modern England* (Cambridge: Cambridge University Press, 1997).

Kasher, Asa, and Shlomo Biderman, 'Why was Baruch de Spinoza Excommunicated?', in David S. Katz and Jonathan I. Israel, *Sceptics, Millenarians and Jews* (Leiden: Brill, 1990), 98–141.

Kerrigan, John, *Revenge Tragedy: Aeschylus to Armageddon* (Oxford: Clarendon Press, 1996).

Kerrigan, John, 'Shakespeare as Reviser' (1987), rpt in Kerrigan, *On Shakespeare and Early Modern Literature: Essays* (Oxford: Oxford University Press, 2001), 3–22.

Kerrigan, William, *Shakespeare's Promises* (Baltimore: Johns Hopkins University Press, 1999).

Kishlansky, Mark, *Parliamentary Selection: Social and Political Choice in Early Modern England* (Cambridge: Cambridge University Press, 1986).

Knight, W. Nicholas, 'Equity, *The Merchant of Venice* and William Lambarde', *Shakespeare Survey*, 27 (1974), 93–104.

Lachs, Samuel Tobias, *A Rabbinic Commentary on the New Testament: The Gospels of Matthew, Mark, and Luke* (Hoboken, NJ: Ktav, 1987).

Laing, R. D., *Knots* (London: Tavistock, 1970).

Lake, Peter, with Michael Questier, *The Antichrist's Lewd Hat: Protestants, Papists and Players in Post-Reformation England* (New Haven: Yale University Press, 2002).

Langbein, John H., *Prosecuting Crime in the Renaissance: England, Germany, France* (Cambridge, Mass.: Harvard University Press, 1974).

Lashmore-Davies, Adrian, '"The Casuistical Question": Oaths and Hypocrisy in the Writings of Johnson and Bolingbroke', in Jonathan Clark and Howard Erskine-Hill, eds, *The Interpretation of Samuel Johnson* (Basingstoke: Palgrave Macmillan, 2012), 84–119.

Leinwand, Theodore B., *Theatre, Finance and Society in Early Modern England* (Cambridge: Cambridge University Press, 1999).

Lemon, Rebecca, 'Compulsory Conviviality in Early Modern England', *English Literary Renaissance*, 99 (2013), 381–414.

Lenz, Joseph M., 'The Politics of Honor: The Oath in *Henry V*', *Journal of English and Germanic Philology*, 80 (1981), 1–12.

Loades, David M., *Politics and Nation: England, 1450–1660*, 5th edn (Blackwell, 1999).

Lupton, Julia Reinhard, *Thinking with Shakespeare* (Chicago: University of Chicago Press, 2013).

McAlindon, Tom, 'Swearing and Forswearing in Shakespeare's Histories: The Playwright as Contra-Machiavel', *Review of English Studies*, 51 (2000), 208–29.

McConica, James, 'Elizabethan Oxford: The Collegiate Society', in *The History of the University of Oxford*, Vol. III, *The Collegiate University*, ed. James McConica (Oxford: Clarendon Press, 1986), 645–732.

McEnery, Tony, *Swearing in English: Bad Language, Purity and Power from 1586 to the Present* (London: Routledge, 2006).

McIlwain, Charles Howard, introd. to *The Political Works of James I: Reprinted from the Edition of 1616*, ed. McIlwain (Cambridge, Mass.: Harvard University Press, 1918).

Magnusson, Lynne, 'Scoff Power in *Love's Labour's Lost* and the Inns of Court: Language in Context', *Shakespeare Survey*, 57 (2004), 196–208.

Maguire, Laurie E., 'Performing Anger: The Anatomy of Abuse(s) in *Troilus and Cressida*', *Renaissance Drama*, ns 31 (2002), 153–83.

Maley, Willy, '"Let a Welsh Correction Teach You a Good English Condition": Shakespeare, Wales and the Critics', in Maley and Philip Schwyzer, eds, *Shakespeare and Wales: From the Marches to the Assembly* (Farnham: Ashgate, 2010), 177–89.

Malloch, A. E., 'Father Henry Garnet's Treatise of Equivocation', *Recusant History*, 15 (1981), 387–95.

Marcus, Jacob, *The Jew in the Medieval World: A Sourcebook, 315–1791* (New York: JPS, 1938).

Marx, Karl, *Capital: Critique of Political Economy*, Vol. I, tr. Ben Fowkes (1976; Harmondsworth: Penguin, 1990).

Marx, Karl, *Early Writings*, tr. Rodney Livingstone and Gregor Benton, introd. Lucio Colletti (1974; Harmondsworth: Penguin, 1992).

Mattingly, Garrett, *Renaissance Diplomacy* (1955; Penguin: Baltimore, 1964).

Mauss, Marcel, *Essay on the Gift*, tr. W. D. Halls (1990; London: Routledge, 2002).

Maxwell-Stewart, P. G., *Satan's Conspiracy: Magic and Witchcraft in Sixteenth-Century Scotland* (East Linton: Tuckwell, 2001).

Midgley, Mary, 'The Game Game', *Philosophy*, 49 (1974), 132–53.

Miles, Geoffrey, *Shakespeare and the Constant Romans* (Oxford: Clarendon Press, 1996).

Miller, William Ian, *Eye for an Eye* (Cambridge: Cambridge University Press, 2006).

Miola, Robert S., *Shakespeare and Classical Tragedy: The Influence of Seneca* (Oxford: Clarendon Press, 1992).

Mohr, Melissa, 'Defining Dirt: Three Early Modern Views of Obscenity', *Textual Practice*, 17 (2003), 253–75.

Mohr, Melissa, *Holy Shit: A Brief History of Swearing* (New York: Oxford University Press, 2013).

Momigliano, Arnaldo, *On Pagans, Jews, and Christians* (Middletown, Conn.: Wesleyan University Press, 1987).

Moran, Richard, 'Getting Told and Being Believed', *Philosophers Imprint*, 5:5 (August 2005).

Morgan, Victor, *A History of the University of Cambridge*, Vol. II, *1546–1750* (Cambridge: Cambridge University Press, 2004).

Mowat, Barbara, 'Q2 *Othello* and the 1606 "Act to Restraine Abuses of Players"', in Christa Jansohn and Bodo Plachta, eds, *Varienten—Variants—Variantes* (Tübingen: Max Niemeyer Verlag, 2005), 91–106.

Mukherji, Subha, *Law and Representation in Early Modern Drama* (Cambridge: Cambridge University Press, 2006).

Muldrew, Craig, *The Economy of Obligation: The Culture of Credit and Social Relations in Early Modern England* (Basingstoke: Macmillan, 1998).

Muldrew, Craig, '"Hard Food for Midas": Cash and its Social Value in Early Modern England', *Past and Present*, 170 (2001), 78–120.

Nash, David, *Blasphemy in the Christian World: A History* (New York: Oxford University Press, 2007).

Neill, Michael, *Putting History to the Question: Power, Politics, and Society in English Renaissance Drama* (New York: Columbia University Press, 2000).

Neilson, George, *Trial by Combat* (Glasgow: William Hodge, 1890).

Nelson, Alan H., ed., *Records of Early English Drama: Cambridge*, 2 vols (Toronto: Toronto University Press, 1989).

Nelson, Alan H., and John R. Elliott, Jr, eds, *Records of Early English Drama: Inns of Court*, 3 vols (Cambridge: D. S. Brewer, 2010).

Nelson, Alan H., John R. Elliott (University), Alexandra Johnston, and Diana Wyatt (City), eds, *Records of Early English Drama: Oxford*, 2 vols (London: British Library, 2004).

Nelson, Benjamin, *The Idea of Usury: From Tribal Brotherhood to Universal Otherhood*, 2nd edn (Chicago: University of Chicago Press, 1969).

Nicholl, Charles, *The Lodger: Shakespeare on Silver Street* (2007; London: Allen Lane, 2008).

Nietzsche, Friedrich, *On the Genealogy of Morality*, ed. Keith Ansell-Pearson, tr. Carol Diethe, rev. edn (Cambridge: Cambridge University Press, 2007).

Noonan, John T., *The Scholastic Analysis of Usury* (Cambridge, Mass.: Harvard University Press, 1957).

Nuttall, A. D., *Timon of Athens* (Hemel Hempstead: Harvester, 1989).

O'Hara, Diana, *Courtship and Constraint: Rethinking the Making of Marriage in Tudor England* (Manchester: Manchester University Press, 2000).

Parfit, Derek, *On What Matters*, 2 vols (Oxford: Oxford University Press, 2011).

Parker, Robert, *Miasma: Pollution and Purification in Early Greek Religion* (Oxford: Clarendon Press, 1983).

Pascoe, David, 'Shakespeare's Williams', *Essays in Criticism*, 60 (2010), 197–219.

Patterson, W. B., *King James VI and I and the Reunion of Christendom* (Cambridge: Cambridge University Press, 1997).

Paul, Henry N., *The Royal Play of Macbeth* (New York: Macmillan, 1950).

Peltonen, Markku, *The Duel in Early Modern England* (Cambridge: Cambridge University Press, 2003).

Pennington, Michael, *Sweet William: A User's Guide to Shakespeare* (London: Nick Hern Books, 2012).

Phillips, Adam, *Missing Out* (London: Hamish Hamilton, 2012).

Pinker, Steven, *The Stuff of Thought: Language as a Window into Human Nature* (London: Penguin, 2007).

Prest, Wilfred R., *The Inns of Court under Elizabeth I and the Early Stuarts 1590–1640* (London: Longman, 1972).

Prodi, Paolo, *Il sacramento di potere: Il giuramento politico nella storia costituzionale dell'Occidente* (Bologna: Società editrice il Mulino, 1992).

Questier, Michael, 'Loyalty, Religion and State Power in Early Modern England: English Romanism and the Jacobean Oath of Allegiance', *Historical Journal*, 40 (1997), 311–29.

Questier, Michael, 'Catholicism, Kinship and the Public Memory of Sir Thomas More', *Historical Journal*, 53 (2002), 476–509.

Questier, Michael, 'Catholic Loyalism in Early Stuart England', *English Historical Review*, 123 (2008), 1132–65.

Quiring, Björn, *Shakespeare's Curse: The Aporias of Ritual Exclusion in Early Modern Royal Drama* (Abingdon: Routledge, 2014).

Rappaport, Steve, *Worlds within Worlds: Structures of Life in Sixteenth-Century London* (Cambridge: Cambridge University Press, 1989).

Rapple, Rory, *Martial Power and Elizabethan Political Culture: Military Men in England and Ireland, 1558–1594* (Cambridge: Cambridge University Press, 2009).

Raylor, Timothy, *Cavaliers, Clubs, and Literary Culture: Sir John Mennes, James Smith, and the Order of the Fancy* (Newark, Del.: University of Delaware Press, 1994).

Reik, Theodor, 'Kol Nidre', in his *Ritual Psycho-Analytic Studies* (London: Hogarth Press, 1931), 167–219.

Rex, Richard, 'The Crisis of Obedience: God's Word and Henry's Reformation', *Historical Journal*, 39 (1996), 863–94.

Richardson, Catherine, '"A Very Fit Hat": Personal Objects and Early Modern Affection', in Tara Hamling and Catherine Richardson, eds, *Everyday Objects: Medieval and Early Modern Material Culture and its Meanings* (Farnham: Ashgate, 2010), 289–98.

Richardson, H. G., 'The English Coronation Oath', *Transactions of the Royal Historical Society*, 4th ser. 23 (1941), 129–58.

Richek, Roslyn, 'Thomas Randolph's *Salting* (1627), its Text, and John Milton's Sixth Prolusion as Another Salting', *English Literary Renaissance*, 12 (1982), 103–31.

Ricks, Christopher, '*Doctor Faustus* and Hell on Earth', *Essays in Criticism*, 35 (1985), 101–20, rpt in his *Essays in Appreciation* (Oxford: Oxford University Press, 1996), 1–18.

Robins, Michael H., *Promising, Intending, and Moral Autonomy* (Cambridge: Cambridge University Press, 1984).

Rosenblatt, Jason P., *Renaissance England's Chief Rabbi: John Selden* (Oxford: Oxford University Press, 2006).

Ross, Emily, '"Words, Vows, Gifts, Tears and Love's Full Sacrifice": An Assessment of the Status of Troilus and Cressida's Relationship According to Customary Elizabethan Marriage Procedures', *Shakespeare*, 4 (2008), 413–37.

Rowe, Katherine, 'Inconstancy: Changeable Affections in Stuart Dramas of Contract', in Mary Floyd-Wilson and Garrett A. Sullivan, eds, *Environment and Embodiment in Early Modern England* (Basingstoke: Palgrave, 2007), 90–102.

Rüpke, Jörg, *Religion of the Romans*, tr. and ed. Richard Gordon (Cambridge: Polity, 2007).

Sacks, David Harris, 'The Promise and the Contract in Early Modern England: Slade's Case in Perspective', in Lorna Hutson and Victoria Kahn, eds, *Rhetoric and Law in Early Modern Europe* (New Haven: Yale University Press, 2001), 28–53.

Schalkwyk, David, '"A Lady's 'Verily' Is as Potent as a Lord's": Women, Word and Witchcraft in *The Winter's Tale*', *English Literary Renaissance*, 22 (1992), 242–72.

Schalkwyk, David, *Speech and Performance in Shakespeare's Sonnets and Plays* (Cambridge: Cambridge University Press, 2002).

Schalkwyk, David, 'Shakespeare's Speech', *Journal of Medieval and Early Modern Studies*, 40 (2010), 373–400.

Schalkwyk, David, 'Text and Performance, Reiterated: A Reproof Valiant or Lie Direct?', *The Shakespearean International Yearbook*, 10 (2010), 47–75.

Scheid, John, 'Sacrifices for Gods and Ancestors', in Jörg Rüpke, ed., *A Companion to Roman Religion* (Chichester: Blackwell/Wiley, 2011), 263–71.

Schlesinger, Herbert J., *Promises, Oaths, and Vows: On the Psychology of Promising* (New York: Analytic Press, 2008).

Schoenbaum, Samuel, *William Shakespeare: A Compact Documentary Life*, rev. edn (Oxford: Oxford University Press, 1987).

Scott, William O., 'Contracts of Love and Affection: Lear, Old Age, and Kingship', *Shakespeare Survey*, 55 (2002), 36–42.

Scott, William O., 'Conditional Bonds, Forfeitures, and Vows in *The Merchant of Venice*', *English Literary Renaissance*, 34 (2004), 286–305.

Scott, William O., ' "A Woman's Thought Runs Before her Actions": Vows as Speech Acts in *As You Like It*', *Philosophy and Literature*, 30 (2006), 528–39.

Scott, William O., 'Risk, Distrust, and Ingratitude in Shakespeare's *Troilus and Cressida*', *Studies in English Literature*, 52 (2012), 345–62.

Searle, John R., 'How to Derive "Ought" from "Is" ', *Philosophical Review*, 73 (1964), 43–58, rpt in Philippa Foot, ed., *Theories of Ethics* (Oxford: Oxford University Press, 1967), 101–14.

Searle, John R., *Speech Acts: An Essay in the Philosophy of Language* (Cambridge: Cambridge University Press, 1969).

Serres, Michel, and Bruno Latour, *Conversations on Science, Culture, and Time*, tr. Roxanne Lapidus (Ann Arbor: University of Michigan Press, 1995).

Shagan, Ethan, 'The English Inquisition: Constitutional Conflict and Ecclesiastical Law in the 1590s', *Historical Journal*, 47 (2004), 531–65.

Shapin, Steven, *A Social History of Truth: Civility and Science in Seventeenth-Century England* (Chicago: University of Chicago Press, 1994).

Shapiro, Barbara J., *'Beyond Reasonable Doubt' and 'Probable Cause': Historical Perspectives on the Anglo-American Law of Evidence* (Berkeley: University of California Press, 1991).

Shapiro, Barbara J., *A Culture of Fact: England, 1550–1720* (Ithaca, NY: Cornell University Press, 2000).

Shapiro, James, *Shakespeare and the Jews* (New York: Columbia University Press, 1996).

Shapiro, James, *1606: William Shakespeare and the Year of 'Lear'* (London: Faber and Faber, 2015).

Shell, Alison, *Catholicism, Controversy, and the English Literary Imagination, 1558–1660* (Cambridge: Cambridge University Press, 1999).

Shirley, Frances A., *Swearing and Perjury in Shakespeare's Plays* (London: George Allen and Unwin, 1979).

Shrank, Cathy, 'Civility and the City in *Coriolanus*', *Shakespeare Quarterly*, 54 (2003), 406–23.

Simpson, A. W. B., *A History of the Common Law of Contract: The Rise of the Action of Assumpsit* (Oxford: Clarendon Press, 1975).

Skinner, Quentin, 'Conquest and Consent: Thomas Hobbes and the Engagement Controversy', in G. E. Aylmer, ed., *The Interregnum: The Quest for Settlement, 1646–1660* (London: Macmillan, 1972), 79–93.

Skinner, Quentin, *Forensic Shakespeare* (Oxford: Oxford University Press, 2014).

Slack, Paul, *The Impact of Plague in Tudor and Stuart England* (London: Routledge, 1985).

Sokol, B. J., and Mary Sokol, *Shakespeare, Law, and Marriage* (Cambridge: Cambridge University Press, 2003).

Sommerstein, Alan H., director, 'The Oath in Archaic and Classical Greece' (2004–7), <http://www.nottingham.ac.uk/Classics/Research/projects/oaths/intro.aspx>

Sommerstein, Alan H., and Andrew J. Bayliss, with others, *Oath and State in Ancient Greece* (Berlin: Walter de Gruyter, 2013).

Sommerstein, Alan H., and Isabelle C. Torrance, with others, *Oaths and Swearing in Ancient Greece* (Berlin: Walter de Gruyter, 2014).

Sommerville, Johann Peter, 'Jacobean Political Thought and the Controversy of the Oath of Allegiance' (University of Cambridge, Ph.D. 1981).

Sommerville, Johann P., 'The "New Art of Lying": Equivocation, Mental Reservation, and Casuistry', in Edmund Leites, ed., *Conscience and Casuistry in Early Modern Europe* (Cambridge: Cambridge University Press, 1988), 159–86.

Sommerville, Johann P., 'Papalist Political Thought and the Controversy over the Jacobean Oath of Allegiance', in Ethan H. Shagan, ed., *Catholics and the 'Protestant Nation'* (Manchester: Manchester University Press, 2005), 162–84.

Spurr, John, 'Perjury, Profanity and Politics', *The Seventeenth Century*, 8 (1993), 29–50.

Spurr, John, 'A Profane History of Early Modern Oaths', *Transactions of the Royal Historical Society*, 6th ser. 11 (2001), 37–63.

Spurr, John, '"The Strongest Bond of Conscience": Oaths and the Limits of Tolerance in Early Modern England', in Harald E. Braun and Edward Vallance, eds, *Contexts of Conscience in Early Modern Europe, 1500–1700* (Basingstoke: Palgrave Macmillan, 2004), 151–65.

Stallybrass, Peter, 'Worn Worlds: Clothes and Identity on the Renaissance Stage', in Margreta de Grazia, Maureen Quilligan, and Peter Stallybrass, eds, *Subject and Object in Renaissance Culture* (Cambridge: Cambridge University Press, 1996), 289–320.

Stallybrass, Peter, and Ann Rosalind Jones, 'Fetishizing the Glove in Renaissance Europe', *Critical Inquiry*, 28 (2001), 114–32.

Stern, Tiffany, *Documents of Performance in Early Modern England* (Cambridge: Cambridge University Press, 2009).

Stewart, Alan, *Shakespeare's Letters* (Oxford: Oxford University Press, 2008).

Stone, M. W. F., 'Conscience in Renaissance Moral Thought: A Concept in Transition?', *Renaissance Studies*, 23 (2009), 423–44.

Stretton, Tim, *Women Waging Law in Elizabethan England* (Cambridge: Cambridge University Press, 1998).

Stretton, Tim, 'Contract, Debt Litigation and Shakespeare's *The Merchant of Venice*', *Adelaide Law Review*, 31 (2010), 111–25.

Syme, Holger Schott, *Theatre and Testimony in Shakespeare's England: A Culture of Mediation* (Cambridge: Cambridge University Press, 2012).

Tadmor, Naomi, 'People of the Covenant and the English Bible', *Transactions of the Royal Historical Society*, 22 (2012), 95–110.

Taylor, Gary, ''Swounds Revisited: Theatrical, Editorial, and Literary Expurgation', in Taylor and John Jowett, *Shakespeare Reshaped 1606–1623* (Oxford: Clarendon Press, 1993), 51–106.

Taylor, Gary, and John Lavagnino, eds, *Thomas Middleton and Early Modern Textual Culture: A Companion to the Collected Works* (Oxford: Clarendon Press, 2007).

Testart, Alain, 'Uncertainties of the "Obligation to Reciprocate": A Critique of Mauss', in Wendy James and N. J. Allen, *Marcel Mauss: A Centenary Tribute* (New York: Berghahn, 1998), 97–110.

Thomas, Keith, *Religion and the Decline of Magic* (1971; Harmondsworth: Peregrine, 1978).

Tiffany, Daniel, *Infidel Poetics: Riddles, Nightlife, Substance* (Chicago: University of Chicago Press, 2009).

Tilley, Maurice Palmer, *A Dictionary of the Proverbs in England in the Sixteenth and Seventeenth Centuries* (Ann Arbor: University of Michigan Press, 1950).

Tlusty, B. Ann, *Bacchus and Civic Order: The Culture of Drink in Early Modern Germany* (Charlottesville, Va: University of Virginia Press, 2001).

Tutino, Stefania, *Law and Conscience: Catholicism in Early-Modern England, 1570–1625* (Aldershot: Ashgate, 2007).

Tutino, Stefania, *Empire of Souls: Robert Bellarmine and the Christian Commonwealth* (New York: Oxford University Press, 2010).

Vallance, Edward, 'Oaths, Casuistry, and Equivocation: Anglican Responses to the Engagement Controversy', *Historical Journal*, 44 (2001), 59–77.

Vallance, Edward, *Revolutionary England and the National Covenant: State Oaths, Protestantism, and the Political Nation, 1553–1682* (Woodbridge: Boydell, 2005).

Vitek, William, *Promising* (Philadelphia: Temple University Press, 1993).

Wagner, Matthew D., *Shakespeare, Theatre, and Time* (Abingdon: Routledge, 2012).

Wallace, John M., '*Timon of Athens* and the Three Graces: Shakespeare's Senecan Study', *Modern Philology*, 83 (1986), 349–63.

Walsham, Alexandra, *Catholic Reformation in Protestant Britain* (Farnham: Ashgate, 2014).

Ward, G. R. M., completed by James Heywood, *Oxford University Statutes*, 2 vols (London: Pickering, 1845–51).

White, R. S., 'Oaths and the Anticomic Spirit in *Love's Labour's Lost*', in Alan Brissenden, ed., *Shakespeare and Some Others: Essays on Shakespeare and Some of his Contemporaries* (Adelaide: Dept of English, University of Adelaide, 1976), 11–29.

White, R. S., *Natural Law in English Renaissance Literature* (Cambridge: Cambridge University Press, 1996).

Wills, Gary, *Witches and Jesuits: Shakespeare's 'Macbeth'* (New York: Oxford University Press, 1995).

Wilson, F. P., *The Plague in Shakespeare's London* (London: Oxford University Press, 1927).

Wilson, Luke, *Theaters of Intention: Drama and the Law in Early Modern England* (Stanford, Calif.: Stanford University Press, 2000).

Womersley, David, *Divinity and State* (Oxford: Oxford University Press, 2010).

Wood, Anthony, *The Life and Times of Anthony Wood, Antiquary, of Oxford, 1632–1695, Described by Himself*, ed. Andrew Clark, 5 vols (Oxford: Oxford Historical Society, 1891–1900).

Woodbridge, Linda, *English Revenge Drama: Money, Resistance, Equality* (Cambridge: Cambridge University Press, 2010).

Woods, Gillian, 'Catholicism and Conversion in *Love's Labour's Lost*', in Laurie Maguire, ed., *How to do Things with Shakespeare: New Approaches, New Essays* (Oxford: Blackwell, 2008), 101–30.

Woods, Gillian, *Shakespeare's Unreformed Fictions* (Oxford: Oxford University Press, 2013).

Yamada, Akihiro, ed., *The First Folio of Shakespeare: A Transcript of Contemporary Marginalia* (Tokyo: Yushodo Press, 1998).

Zagorin, Perez, *Ways of Lying: Dissimulation, Persecution, and Conformity in Early Modern Europe* (Cambridge, Mass.: Harvard University Press, 1990).

Zurcher, Andrew, *Shakespeare and Law* (London: Arden Shakespeare, 2010).

Zurcher, Andrew, 'Gift and Condition in *King Lear*', Kingston Shakespeare Seminars, 13 March 2014, at <http://backdoorbroadcasting.net/>

Index